MAKING SENSE OF THE GREAT WAR

The First World War was an unprecedented crisis, with communities and societies enduring the unimaginable hardships of a prolonged conflict on an industrial scale. In Belgium and France, the terrible capacity of modern weaponry destroyed the natural world and exposed previously held truths about military morale and tactics as falsehoods. Hundreds of thousands of soldiers suffered some of the worst conditions that combatants have ever faced. How did they survive? What did it mean to them? How did they perceive these events? Whilst the trenches of the Western Front have come to symbolise the futility and hopelessness of the Great War, Alex Mayhew shows that English infantrymen rarely interpreted their experiences in this way. They sought to survive, navigated the crises that confronted them, and crafted meaningful narratives about their service. *Making Sense of the Great War* reveals the mechanisms that allowed them to do so.

Alex Mayhew is Assistant Professor in Modern European History at the London School of Economics and Political Science.

Studies in the Social and Cultural History of Modern Warfare

General Editors
Robert Gerwarth, *University College Dublin*
Jay Winter, *Yale University*

Advisory Editors
Heather Jones, *University College London*
Rana Mitter, *University of Oxford*
Michelle Moyd, *Michigan State University*
Martin Thomas, *University of Exeter*

In recent years the field of modern history has been enriched by the exploration of two parallel histories. These are the social and cultural history of armed conflict, and the impact of military events on social and cultural history.

Studies in the Social and Cultural History of Modern Warfare presents the fruits of this growing area of research, reflecting both the colonization of military history by cultural historians and the reciprocal interest of military historians in social and cultural history, to the benefit of both. The series offers the latest scholarship in European and non-European events from the 1850s to the present day.

A full list of titles in the series can be found at: www.cambridge.org/modernwarfare

MAKING SENSE OF THE GREAT WAR

Crisis, Englishness, and Morale on the Western Front

ALEX MAYHEW
London School of Economics and Political Science

Shaftesbury Road, Cambridge CB2 8EA, United Kingdom

One Liberty Plaza, 20th Floor, New York, NY 10006, USA

477 Williamstown Road, Port Melbourne, VIC 3207, Australia

314–321, 3rd Floor, Plot 3, Splendor Forum, Jasola District Centre, New Delhi – 110025, India

103 Penang Road, #05–06/07, Visioncrest Commercial, Singapore 238467

Cambridge University Press is part of Cambridge University Press & Assessment, a department of the University of Cambridge.

We share the University's mission to contribute to society through the pursuit of education, learning and research at the highest international levels of excellence.

www.cambridge.org
Information on this title: www.cambridge.org/9781009168748

DOI: 10.1017/9781009168762

© Alex Mayhew 2024

This publication is in copyright. Subject to statutory exception and to the provisions of relevant collective licensing agreements, no reproduction of any part may take place without the written permission of Cambridge University Press & Assessment.

First published 2024
First paperback edition 2025

A catalogue record for this publication is available from the British Library

Library of Congress Cataloging-in-Publication data
Names: Mayhew, Alex, 1991- author.
Title: Making sense of the Great War : crisis, Englishness, and morale on the Western Front / Alex Mayhew, University of Birmingham.
Description: Cambridge ; New York, NY : Cambridge University Press, 2023. | Series: Studies in the social and cultural history of modern warfare | Includes bibliographical references.
Identifiers: LCCN 2023016278 (print) | LCCN 2023016279 (ebook) | ISBN 9781009168755 (hardback) | ISBN 9781009168748 (paperback) | ISBN 9781009168762 (epub)
Subjects: LCSH: World War, 1914-1918–Great Britain–Psychological aspects. | Military morale–Great Britain–History–20th century. | Great Britain. Army British Expeditionary Force–History. | Soldiers–Great Britain–Psychology. | Psychology, Military.
Classification: LCC D546 .M34 2023 (print) | LCC D546 (ebook) | DDC 940.3/41–dc23/eng/20230525
LC record available at https://lccn.loc.gov/2023016278
LC ebook record available at https://lccn.loc.gov/2023016279

ISBN 978-1-009-16875-5 Hardback
ISBN 978-1-009-16874-8 Paperback

Cambridge University Press & Assessment has no responsibility for the persistence or accuracy of URLs for external or third-party internet websites referred to in this publication and does not guarantee that any content on such websites is, or will remain, accurate or appropriate.

For
Kate Mayhew
(1978–2004)
and
Bo Treadwell
(1991–2014)

CONTENTS

List of Figures	*page* ix
List of Tables	xi
Acknowledgements	xiii
List of Abbreviations	xvii
Map of the Western Front	xix
Prologue	xxi
Introduction: Morale, Crisis, and Englishness	1

PART I The Environment

1 Familiarising the Western Front: Attachment to Belgium and France 35

2 Enduring the Western Front: Winter and Morale 80

PART II Social Groups

3 Defining Duty: Obligation and the Cultural Foundations of Morale 119

4 Imagining Home: Englishness in the Trenches 160

PART III Crisis and Morale

5 Hoping for Peace: Victory and the Future 197

6 Experiencing Crisis: Battle and Sensemaking, c. July 1917–June 1918 232

Conclusion 282

Appendix: Demographics of Six Regiments in the BEF 297
Bibliography 309
Index 345

LIST OF FIGURES

1.1	Ruins of the Cloth Hall in the City of Ypres, 1914	page 49
1.2	Battle of Menin Road Ridge, 20 September 1917	50
1.3	The destruction of 1916	52
1.4	The destruction of 1917	54
1.5	A burial party on the Western Front c. 1917	72
2.1	Members of the Middlesex Regiment seen returning from the trenches	88
2.2	An officer wading through a trench of half-frozen mud c. 1916	92
2.3	Soldiers crossing frozen stream in the snowy frontlines	95
2.4	British soldiers with their Christmas gift of a gramophone, France, 1914–1918	112
3.1	'The Jocks' entertainment troupe waiting to give a show	149
3.2	A crowd of soldiers at a British Army training school c. 1916.	151
4.1	Postcard: Take Me Back to Dear Old Blighty	187
4.2	Postcard: Little Grey Home in the West	189
6.1	Allied troops and German prisoners at the Menin Road, 1917	245
6.2	Postcard: British troops in Cambrai, 1917	251
6.3	A Mark IV female tank passing through Péronne, 23 March 1918	264
6.4	New recruits at Étaples, 1918	274

LIST OF TABLES

I.1	Factors affecting morale of troops	page 4
I.2	Factors promoting resilience	19
2.1	Percentage of days spent in various daily activities, 1914, 1916, 1917, and 1918 in 1st through 6th divisions, BEF	97
2.2	Frostbite and trench foot admissions/evacuations in 1916	105
2.3	Frostbite and trench foot admissions/evacuations in 1917/1918	105
6.1	Monthly rainfall in Ypres (mm), 1916–1918	241
6.2	Average monthly temperature (°C) in the British zone of operations 1915–1918	242
6.3	Average casualties (killed, wounded, gassed, and missing)	256
6.4	Average (mean) OR reinforcements, July 1917–June 1918	257
6.5	Average (mean) officer reinforcements, July 1917–June 1918	257
6.6	Origin of drafts arriving during the reorganisation of the BEF	259
6.7	Losses in five battalions in March 1918	267
6.8	Losses in five battalions in April 1918	268
6.9	Officer casualties in the 8th Bn. Border Regiment, 21–22 March 1918	269
6.10	Officer casualties in the 8th Bn. Border Regiment, 10–19 April 1918	269
6.11	Casualties in the 8th Bn. Border Regiment, 27–31 May 1918	270
6.12	Mean ages of soldiers who died on the Western Front	276
6.13	Modal age(s) of soldiers who died on the Western Front	277
6.14	Median age of soldiers who died on the Western Front	278
A.1	Home addresses of Border Regiment soldiers, 1914–1918	298
A.2	Home addresses of Devonshire Regiment soldiers, 1914–1918	299
A.3	Home addresses of Manchester Regiment soldiers, 1914–1918	300
A.4	Home addresses of Ox and Bucks LI soldiers, 1914–1918	301
A.5	Home addresses of Royal Fusiliers soldiers, 1914–1918	302
A.6	Home addresses of Royal Warwickshire Regiment soldiers, 1914–1918	303
A.7	Size of settlement: Homes of soldiers who died in 1914	304
A.8	Size of settlement: Homes of soldiers who died in 1916	304
A.9	Size of settlement: Homes of soldiers who died in 1917/1918	304

ACKNOWLEDGEMENTS

Writing does not come naturally to me, nor do the more isolating features of historical research. This might be why *Making Sense of the Great War* was nine years in the making. During this time, many people have helped me to reach the stage where it sits in print.

I suppose my first graduate job catalysed this chapter of my life. Had it not been for accepting a role in sales just out of my undergraduate degree, it is possible, or even likely, that I would have never decided to pursue a doctorate. As it was, the uncertainties of academia were (and still are) preferable to what I perceived to be the soullessness of selling flights.

Yet, it was not on a call centre floor but at the London School of Economics and Political Science (LSE) that this project was born. All the ideas found within this monograph crystallised and were refined during my time sitting, reading, talking, typing, and teaching in the LSE's increasingly sprawling campus next to Lincoln's Inn Fields. I owe a lot to the school, first for awarding me a four-year PhD scholarship, which supported my doctoral work, and then employing me several times as it was reshaped into its present form.

This is an expanded and revised version of my PhD and naturally bears a strong imprint of my doctoral supervisors. Their influence can be felt on almost every page. Without Heather Jones and David Stevenson, this monograph would not exist. Other peers and colleagues have helped me along the way. In the Department of International History, there was a community of historians that was a social as well as an intellectual outlet. I would particularly like to extend my thanks and comradeship towards Katherine Arnold, Bastiaan Bouwman, Alex Dab, Tanya Harmer, Anne Irfan, Judith Jacob, Paul Keenan, Will King, Tomasso Millani, Pete Millwood, Michael Rupp, Isaac Scarborough, Ian Stewart, and Max Skjönsberg.

At LSE100, the team (especially Chris Blunt, Rian Mulcahy, Jessica Templeton, and Jillian Terry) helped me to broaden my disciplinary horizons and to hone my skills as an educator. Our course office team (Fatima Jeetoo, Simon Jolly, and Christina Ogun) made it a uniquely welcoming place to work. Furthermore, my intimidatingly intelligent students have helped me to become a better scholar and to realise just how much I loved teaching. LSE LIFE, especially its director Claudine Provencher, gave me the space to complete the book alongside my work. It was a privilege to learn from a team that is so committed to improving our students' experiences, academic or otherwise.

During the 2022–2023 academic year, I was working at the University of Birmingham. This offered me the opportunity to teach the research contained here. I worked alongside new colleagues and rubbed shoulders with new students, especially on the MA in First World War Studies. I thoroughly enjoyed my time in the West Midlands primarily because of the History Department's unique collegiality. Amongst the sea of friendly faces, I am particularly thankful to have worked alongside Tom Ellis, Jonathan Boff, Ben Jackson, Sarah Kenny, Dan Whittingham, Matthew Francis, John Munro, Simon Jackson, and Glyn Prysor.

As I write this, I am about to return to the LSE and am eagerly anticipating teaching First World War studies in the Department of International History once again. However, I suspect each new generation of budding historians will probably encourage me to rethink many of the ideas in this book, but that is only a good thing.

Several other scholars have helped to shape my career. John Horne and Mark Connelly, who examined my doctoral thesis, provided the advice and encouragement necessary to turn my PhD into the text now sitting in your hands. Since then, John has kindly read much of my work and offered thoughtful and constructive advice at every opportunity. Elsewhere, Richard Grayson supervised the undergraduate thesis that contained the kernel of many ideas that laid the foundations for my doctoral work. Adrian Gregory, whom I first met as a bright-eyed secondary school student, has offered regular advice, and his work has inspired several ideas found in the chapters that follow.

Elsewhere, the Historial de la Grande Guerre has been a source of both financial and intellectual encouragement over the years. In 2016, I was lucky enough to attend a summer school (run by Franziska Heimburger, Tomás Irish, and Benoit Majerus), which was the origin of several themes that have fed into this and other projects. During this time, I met some inspiring early career researchers, including Jack Doyle, Jean-Phillipe Miller-Tremblay, Julie Powell, and Hanna Smyth, amongst many others. The scientific committee at the Historial (with financial support from the Gerda Henkel Institute) also awarded my doctoral work a scholarship in 2017. Elsewhere, membership of the International Society of First World War Studies (ISFWWS) had brought me into contact with a wide community of brilliant historians of the Great War. In fact, some of the ideas here, particularly those about hope and victorious peace, were first tested out in one of the ISFWWS' conference publications – *War Time: First World War Perspectives on Temporality* (pp. 194–219), published by Routledge. Conferences have also been a place to test out ideas and get some brilliant feedback – particularly those held by

ISFWWS; the First World War Network; and the War, Society, and Culture seminar at the Institute of Historical Research.

More practically, this book would not exist without the archives that hold the materials found within its pages. You can find their names littered throughout the footnotes, but I would like to extend my thanks to the archivists at each of these institutions for the help they extended to me over the years – some so long ago they are unlikely to remember me. I spent many days and weeks at British Library, Commonwealth War Graves Commission, Imperial War Museum, Keep Museum, Liddle Collection, National Archives, National Army Museum, National Meteorological Archive, and Soldiers of Oxfordshire Museum. I would encourage any scholar to visit the archives of the Manchester Regiment at the Tameside Local Studies Centre, which is staffed by some of the friendliest people I have ever met.

It was in these places that I was introduced to the soldiers whose letters, diaries, postcards, and journals helped me to craft this narrative. Their suffering and endurance are the engine of this book. With that in mind, I would like to thank their families, who donated their materials for historians such as myself to consult. Every effort has been made to trace copyright holders and to obtain their permission for the use of copyright material.

It is obvious to say, but Cambridge University Press' support has been essential, too. Michael Watson and his team have helped immensely with the process of preparing this book for publication. I also appreciate the faith shown in me by the editors of Studies in the Social and Cultural History of Modern Warfare, Robert Gerwarth and Jay Winter, as well as the advisory editors. Similarly, the thoughtful suggestions of the reviewers helped me to reshape parts of *Making Sense of the Great War*. I must also extend my gratitude to my indexer. Ruth Martin worked wonders; I doubt that I could have synthesised the ideas contained here better than her.

Significantly, I have also been immensely lucky to have a network of friends who have been a regular social outlet over the past decade. I am not sure they know how important they are to me. It would be difficult to name all of them here, and while most will never read this, I want to thank you: Ruby Brown, Jianfei Bu, George Burke, Hattie Burles, Ed Burrell, Joe Butchers, Tim Crombie, Tom Dwyer, Jacob Fisher, Laurie Gehardt, Johnnie Gray, Laurie Hart, Rachel Heeley, Luke Hester, Gus Hewlett, Will Lawn, Ken Mawhinney, Robbie O'Neill, Will Parry, Kealey Rigden, Danny Swift, Caroline Treadwell, and James Twomey. If by any chance you have reached the end of this list and not found your name here, I can only apologise. I promise it was laziness, not ingratitude.

My family, too, have been a source of great support. Unfortunately, my aunt, Doris, and grandmother, Beryl, did not live to see this in print. They were from a generation that was almost able to reach out and touch the Great War. My uncle Harry, however, is still going strong and is a willing conduit of stories that can bring a black-and-white past to life. My aunt Helen – *not* of that generation, I hasten to add – has always been an advocate and is amongst the most generous people I know. Cathy, my stepmother, encouraged me to tread this path and should also be thanked for putting up with my dad, Ken, who has still failed to retire. He tirelessly read every page of this book. However, since he left history to become an economist, I do wonder if this may have been an opportunity to live vicariously through me, making it more of a pleasure than a chore. My mum, Gillian, may not have the same intrinsic interest in the material here, but without her encouragement I doubt I would have pursued a doctorate. She has always believed in me more than I have myself.

Last, but by no means least, my most heartfelt thanks are for Emily, without whom I would have suffered far more from the isolation that often accompanies a historian's labour. Her patience, humour, and support mean more than I could ever say.

Ultimately, though, this monograph is dedicated to two people who have been of great significance in my life, even though they have not been with us for many years: my sister, Kate, and good friend, Bo. The drive to pursue this research and to do what I find interesting stems in large part from having known and lost them. Their graves sit close to each other, and while they might be gone, they are not forgotten.

ABBREVIATIONS

AOC	author's own collection
BEF	British Expeditionary Force
BHQ	Battalion Headquarters
BL	British Library Collections
Bn.	Battalion
CO	commanding officer
CoE	Church of England
Coy	Company
CWGC	Commonwealth War Graves Commission (Archive)
GHQ	General Headquarters
GRU	Graves Registration Unit
GWA	Great War Archive
IWM	Imperial War Museum Collection
LHCMA	Liddell Hart Centre for Military Archives
LIDDLE	Liddle Collection, University of Leeds
MR	Manchester Regiment Archives
NAM	National Army Museum Archive
NCO(s)	non-commissioned officer(s)
NMA	National Meteorological Archive
OR(s)	other rank(s)
POW(s)	prisoner(s) of war
RAMC	Royal Army Medical Corps
RFC	Royal Flying Corps
RFM	Royal Fusiliers Museum Archive
SOFO	Soldiers of Oxfordshire Museum Archive
TGA	Tate Archive
TKM	The Keep Museum Archive, Dorchester
TNA	The National Archives
YMCA	The Young Men's Christian Association

xviii ABBREVIATIONS

Regimental Ranks in the Infantry

Regimental Ranks in the Infantry

Pte.	Private	
L/Cpl.	Lance Corporal	
Cpl.	Corporal	
Sgt.*	Sergeant	
CQMS.**	Company Quartermaster Sergeant	
CSM/WOII	Company Sergeant Major/ Warrant Officer 2nd Class (1915)	*'Other Ranks'*
RQMS	Regimental Quartermaster Sergeant	* In 1914–18 it was sometimes Sjt., but has been modernised here.
RSM/WOI	Regimental Sergeant Major/ Warrant Officer 1st Class (1915)	** Sometimes Colour-Sergeant.
2nd Lt.	Second Lieutenant	
Lt.	Lieutenant	
Capt.	Captain	*Commissioned Officers*
Maj.	Major	
Lt.Col.	Lieutenant Colonel	

	Unit of command	Number of men under command (approx.)
Private	N/A	None
Corporal/Lance Corporal	Section	c. 7–12
Sergeant	Platoon second in command	N/A
Second Lieutenant/Lieutenant	Platoon	c. 50
Captain	Company	c. 200–250
Major	Battalion second in command	N/A
Lieutenant Colonel	Battalion commanding officer	c. 1,000

Senior Officers

Col.	Colonel	Command: N/A – Staff Officer Rank
Brig. Gen.	Brigadier General	Command: Brigade [c. 3,000–4,000 men]
Maj. Gen.	Major General	Command: Division [c. 16,000–18,000 men]
Lt. Gen.	Lieutenant General	Command: Corps [c. 50,000 men]
Gen.	General	Command: Army [c. 100,000 men]
Not abbreviated	Field Marshal	Command: Army Group [c. 1 million men]

MAP OF THE WESTERN FRONT

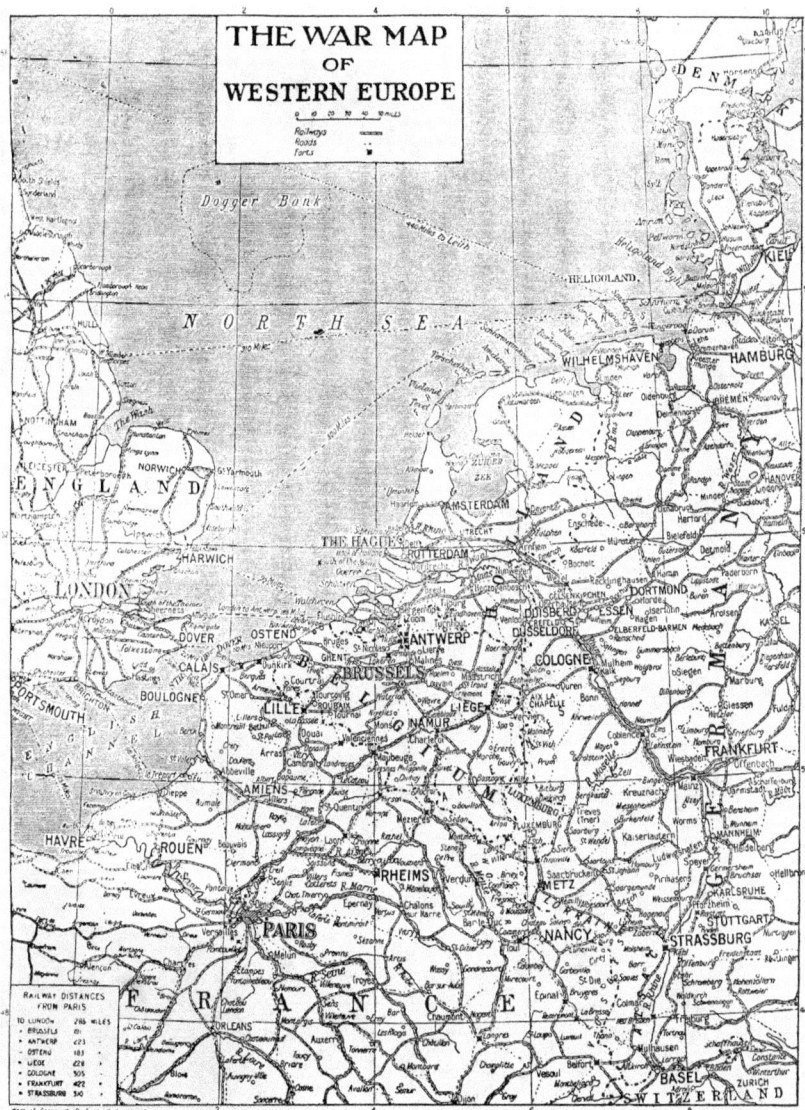

Map 1 The war map of Western Europe, *c.* 1915. Here the reader will find the locations of many of the places referenced in this book. Originally from J.A. Hammerton (ed.), *The War Illustrated Album De Luxe – Volume 1: The First Phase* (London, 1915).

Source: The Print Collector/Heritage Images via Getty Images.

PROLOGUE

It was 9 March 1918 and a soldier sat braced against the biting cold under a blanket in a small hut somewhere on the Western Front. The First World War had been raging for three and a half years, while France and Flanders had been in the grips of winter for several months. The cracked and – in places – empty windowpanes offered a glimpse of the surrounding countryside and his battalion's encampment but did little to preserve the feeble heat within his quarters. He was not the only combatant struggling to keep warm, and, frankly, he probably felt lucky to have a solid roof over his head.

The British Expeditionary Force (BEF) was still recovering from 1917's bitterly disappointing and painful campaign, which had seen men labouring and dying at Third Ypres. War weariness lay heavy in the air; even the new drafts had heard the stories of toil and terror. Since then, one in four battalions had been disbanded, and the British had shifted away from an offensive strategy in the west. The war seemed very far from being won. Worse still, the extension of the line had necessitated the construction of new defensive networks, which ensured that every man spent the winter months digging and shivering. There had been very limited time to integrate new men, let alone learn the intricacies of the new doctrine of 'defence in depth'. Worryingly, rumours were now spreading that the enemy was preparing a huge offensive, their goal being to smash the Entente before their new American allies could disembark on the French coast en masse.

Despite the numbness in his hands, this soldier (like most of his comrades) still found the energy to write to his loved ones. As he addressed the letter to 'Master Bentley Bridgewater, 12 Wellington Square, London', an image of his son and their family home would have been conjured in his mind's eye. This vision might have allowed him to briefly escape his present discomfort. He maintained regular contact with his wife, but on this occasion he wanted to personally congratulate his 'dearest old boy' on his reading, explain how he had been working at night because of German shellfire, and update his 'dear old chap' on his condition. In his letters, he also created a fictional account of his adventures in the trenches alongside a cast of recurring characters: Bobby, Bill, Mr Bird, and 'the cat'.

These tales were crafted by a man desperate to maintain his paternal link with home, but they were also an opportunity for him to consider his place and role in the war effort. The Bridgewaters' Chelsea home was a world away from Belgium and France. Yet the stories that Bentley's 'ever-loving Daddy' penned to him provided a window onto the conflict, although it was built with frosted glass. He made sense of the war through narratives and fantasy with his characters embarking on 'journeys' across Belgium and France. Able to find freedom and peace at will, they escaped the trenches, freely traversing the frontlines and returning to England's safety. At the same time, though, they were imbued with a deep sense of duty and returned to 'do their bit': engaging in raids, killing Germans, taking prisoners, and winning medals. These stories were written at a time when the enemy seemed to be in the ascendancy, yet Bridgewater remained confident that the arrival of peace was simply a question of time. However, this could not be *any* peace; the sacrifices demanded and necessitated a *victorious* end to war.[1]

Bridgewater's letters echo many of this book's themes. It explores how servicemen endured the Western Front during the Great War, what underpinned their morale, and how they perceived crises such as that which was brewing in late 1917 and early 1918. It will argue that their endurance and perception of crises were conditioned by their psychologies and their relationship with their surroundings. Bentley's father's perception of the war was influenced by his environment and social groups: namely by the Western Front, the military, his family, and his community at home. These gave meaning to his experiences and normalised them to the extent that they filtered into the fiction he crafted for his son. As narrator, he was able to generate agency. Such attempts to interpret the conflict were widespread. Narratives informed how individuals perceived and interpreted their lives. While these narratives might fail to capture reality, the desire to construct the world along such lines arguably lies at the heart of human intelligence and the subjective experiences of both past and present. Humans continually deploy narratives and attempt to draw meaning from them.[2] This can help

---

[1] NAM 1993-02-508: Letters sent to Bentley Bridgewater by his father in France, Letters 2 and 9 March and 2 May 1918.

[2] For the influence of the narrative on historiography, see H. White, 'The Value of Narrativity in the Representation of Reality', in W.J.T. Mitchell (ed.), *On Narrative* (Chicago, IL, 1981) and *Metahistory: The Historical Imagination in Nineteenth Century Europe* (Baltimore, MD, 1973). For broader themes in 'narrative psychology', see, for example, M. Bamberg and M. Andrews, *Consider Counter-Narratives: Narrating, Resisting, Making Sense* (Amsterdam, 2004) or J. László, *The Science of Stories: An Introduction to Narrative Psychology* (Abingdon, 2008). It is worth noting that 'narrative psychology' is sometimes used as a counterpoint to the 'rational actor model' and to dismiss logical decision making. That is not the purpose here; it is purely meant to point to the way in which humans inherently and instinctively create narratives.

people to 'safely and efficiently acquire information' and assist in adapting to and surviving habitats.³ Narratives can also reveal the 'intentions, goals, and values' of actors and communities.⁴ Those created by the soldiers of the Great War were no exception.

The First World War has come to be seen as a 'tragedy' and the Western Front as a lesson in futility.⁵ Yet, the men serving there rarely saw it as such. In this predominantly static war, stories, memories, and narratives helped soldiers to make sense of time. By drawing on and layering their 'past', 'present', and 'future', they made sense of their experiences.⁶ Lessons drawn from their lives before the war, as well as fantasies about the future, underpinned their perception of the conflict. However, infantrymen's lives and perceptions were framed and manipulated by their immediate physical environment and social setting. Sometimes, both crept in subtly; at others, they imposed themselves violently.

Soldiers' changing military, physical, social, and moral situation was emphasised in their embarkation leaflets before they left England. Men were told they were going 'abroad as a soldier of the King to help our French comrades against the invasion of a common Enemy'. This experience 'will need your courage, your energy, your patience', and each man was reminded 'that the honour of the British Army depends on your individual conduct'.⁷ Such ideas were internalised. Consequently, some of the men were able to simply conclude: 'We are in France now ... and we are not out for a picnic.'⁸ The war and the war zone constrained soldiers' outlook.

These narratives helped to sustain morale, which was at least partly a product of culture. According to Stuart Hall, culture 'depends on its participants interpreting meaningfully what is around them, and "making sense" of

---

³ M. Scalise Sugiyama, 'Food, Foragers, and Folklore: The Role of Narrative in Human Subsistence', *Evolution and Human Psychology*, Vol. 21 (2001), pp. 221–240.
⁴ J.P. Borgas, O. Vincze and J. László, 'Social Cognition and Communication: Background, Theories and Research', in J.P. Borgas, O. Vincze and J. László (eds.), *Social Cognition and Communication* (New York, 2014), p. 7.
⁵ M. Hough, S. Ballinger and S. Katwala, *A Centenary Shared: Tracking Public Attitudes to the First World War, 2013–16* (London, 2016).
⁶ For the importance of what is sometimes called 'phenomenological' time, see P. Ricoeur, *Time and Narrative: Volume 3* (Chicago, IL, 1988), esp. ch. 4. For temporality during the First World War, A. Luptak, H. Smyth and L. Halewood (eds.), *War Time: First World War Perspectives on Temporality* (Abingdon, 2018); J. Horne, 'The End of a Paradigm? The Cultural History of the Great War', *Past & Present*, Vol. 242, No. 1 (February 2019), pp. 178–179; N. Beaupré, 'La Guerre comme expérience du temps et le temps comme expérience de guerre: hypothèses pour une histoire du rapport au temps des soldats français de la grande guerre', *Vingtième Siècle Revue d'Histoire*, No. 117 (2013).
⁷ NAM 1998-12-111-2: Lt. Arthur Royce Bradbury, Printed Embarkation Leaflet.
⁸ IWM Documents.2554: W.J. Martin, Letter 31 December 1916.

the world, in broadly similar ways'.⁹ This is key to understanding how the infantrymen studied here endured the First World War and helps to explain how humans cope with trauma more generally. This book reveals the ways in which this process worked and how good morale cultivated resilience. It will do so by focusing on English infantrymen's perception and understanding of crisis. By demonstrating the ways in which soldiers coped with crisis, it underlines their ability to construe their experiences constructively. High morale was often, therefore, an internalised affair – one directed by perceptions and achieved through mechanisms such as hope. Hope, in such circumstances, was a cognitive process, rather than an emotion, and was subconsciously directed by soldiers' environments and interpretations of the war. Ultimately, this allowed the soldiers to develop clear goals, which focused on their subjective 'home' and victorious peace. Men's relationship with their surroundings inculcated a sense that the military, victory, and the Western Front provided their clearest pathway to their goals. This sensemaking was made possible by the narratives that they produced.

While such an approach is distinctive, numerous studies have explored morale and endurance in 1914–1918.¹⁰ Some scholars have been drawn to the British Army in particular.¹¹ Why, they ask, did the BEF not experience a

---

⁹ S. Hall, 'Introduction', in S. Hall (ed.), *Representation: Cultural Representations and Signifying Practices* (London, 1997, 2003), p. 2.

¹⁰ For a general introduction, A. Watson, 'Morale' in J. Winter (ed.), *The Cambridge History of the First World War Volume II: The State* (Cambridge, 2014). For the British Army, G. Sheffield, *Command and Morale: The British Army on the Western Front 1914–1918* (Barnsley, 2014). For the British and German Armies, A. Watson, *Enduring the Great War: Combat, Morale and Collapse in the German and British Armies* (Cambridge, 2008). For the British Army in the Middle East, J. Kitchen, *The British Imperial Army in the Middle East: Morale and Identity in the Sinai and Palestine Campaigns* (London, 2014). For the British Army in Italy, G. Oram, 'Pious Perjury: Discipline and Morale in the British Force in Italy, 1917–1918', *War in History*, Vol. 9 No. 4 (2002). For Irish Regiments in the British Army, T. Bowman, *The Irish Regiments in the Great War: Discipline and Morale* (Manchester, 2004). For Canadian soldiers, T. Cook, *The Secret History of Soldiers: How Canadians Survived the Great War* (London, 2018). For the Royal Navy, L. Rowe, *Morale and Discipline in the Royal Navy during the First World War* (Cambridge, 2018). For France, E. Saint-Fuscien, *À vos ordres? La relation d'autorité dans l'armée française de la Grande Guerre* (Paris, 2011) or L.V. Smith, *Between Mutiny and Obedience: The Case of the French Fifth Infantry Division during World War I* (Princeton, 1994). For Italy, V. Wilcox, *Morale and the Italian Army during the First World War* (Cambridge, 2016). For Russia, J.A. Sanborn, *Drafting the Russian Nation: Military Conscription, Total War and Mass Politics, 1905–1925* (DeKalb, 2002). For Austria-Hungary, M. Cornwall, 'Morale and Patriotism in the Austro-Hungarian Army, 1914–1918', in J. Horne (ed.), *State, Society and Mobilization in Europe during the First World War* (Cambridge, 1997), pp. 173–192.

¹¹ G. Sheffield, *Leadership in the Trenches: Officer–Man Relations, Morale and Discipline in the British Army in the Era of the First World War* (Basingstoke, 2000); J.G. Fuller, *Troop*

collapse or mutiny on the scale of other armies during the conflict?[12] While it never experienced a major breakdown, some suggest that the BEF did face several crises during which morale appeared particularly fragile. The retreat after the Battle of Mons in 1914 and the slow transformation of the war into one of static trench lines after the Battle of the Aisne was one such moment.[13] The failure of the Battle of the Somme in 1916 to bring about the war's end has also been highlighted as a time when morale was at a low ebb.[14] Lastly, many scholars point to late 1917 and early 1918 as the period when the British Army came closest to internal combustion.[15] The BEF's one wartime mutiny occurred in September 1917 at a major training camp at Étaples known as the 'Bull Ring'. The arrest of a New Zealander, followed by the shooting of a corporal in the Gordon Highlanders (as well as a French woman) by the military police, sparked several days of unrest.[16] Only a few months later, the army in Belgium and France faced its 'major crisis'.[17] On 21 March 1918, enemy storm troopers emerged from dense morning fog, and the BEF retreated rapidly in the face of the first wave of the German spring offensives. Some historians have suggested that this setback was, at least in part, a product of a fragile spirit amongst the men of the Fifth Army. Yet, even at its most stretched, the army did not disintegrate, and the threat was eventually overcome and reversed.[18] Using these three periods (late 1914, late 1916, and 1917–1918), this book probes the enduring stalemate that underpinned them, asking what promoted morale and deflected crisis.

Soldiers frequently failed to recognise the 'crises' that have been identified in scholarly studies of the war. Of course, those men involved in the combat on days such as 1 July 1916 or 21 March 1918 would have sensed a growing tactical crisis. Yet, outside combat, soldiers' failure – or unwillingness – to

---

Morale and Popular Culture in the British and Dominion Armies, 1914–1918 (Oxford, 1991).

[12] I.F.W. Beckett, T. Bowman and M. Connelly, *The British Army and the First World War* (Cambridge, 2017), pp. 153–154.

[13] Watson, *Enduring the Great War*, pp. 141–144.

[14] P. Fussell, *The Great War and Modern Memory* (Oxford, 1975, 2000), p. 14; A.J.P. Taylor, *The First World War: An Illustrated History* (London, 1963, 1969), p. 140.

[15] D. Englander, 'Discipline and Morale in the British Army, 1917–1918', in Horne, *State, Society and Mobilization*, p. 141.

[16] D. Gill, and G. Dallas, 'Mutiny and Etaples Base in 1917', *Past & Present*, No. 69 (November 1975), pp. 88–112.

[17] Beckett, Bowman and Connelly, *The British Army and the First World War*, p. 152.

[18] For Étaples, Gill and Dallas, 'Mutiny at Etaples Base in 1917', pp. 88–112. For the Spring Offensive, P. Hart, *1918: A Very British Victory* (London, 2008, 2009); D. Stevenson, *With Our Backs to the Wall: Victory and Defeat in 1918* (London, 2014), pp. 30–112; J. Boff, *Winning and Losing on the Western Front: The British Third Army and the Defeat of Germany in 1918* (Cambridge, 2012), pp. 1–2; N. Lloyd, *The Western Front: A History of the First World War* (London, 2021), esp. pp. 396–453.

perceive these moments as crises was fundamental to their understanding of the conflict. The troops studied here were, for the most part, more concerned with overcoming the daily stresses of life at war – such as those of exhaustion or comfort. They also thought obsessively about the past and future and filtered their experiences through these lenses. That men often failed to perceive crises may be a product of the divergence of historical time from local or individual time horizons. Both are informed by assumptions about the world and its processes.[19] In short, the war became their 'new normal'. Soldiers were able to overcome challenges by deploying a plethora of coping mechanisms drawn from their surroundings, both physical and social, as well as their own psychological resources. Habituation, projection, information aversion, and nostalgia coalesced with attitudes and ideas drawn from the men's cultural, institutional, social, and physical situation.

Narratives formed around these things. They overlapped and influenced the troops in myriad ways. This played a central role in their resilience and allowed men to adapt to, find meaning in, and even justify the conflict. Furthermore, these mechanisms encouraged the troops to develop a sense of agency, even in the face of a military that enforced discipline and uniformity. Soldiers carved out their own meaningful world, in which they maintained the semblance of control over their destinies. Morale was a much more complex phenomenon than a simple series of inputs and outputs. It was a process, as complex as it was multifaceted.

Alexander Watson has deepened the historical understanding of First World War morale, highlighting that most men coped with the conditions that confronted them at the front, accepted their service as a duty, and were 'hardwired' to believe in both victory and their survival. This book builds upon his comparative study of British and German soldiers.[20] It looks specifically at English infantrymen and provides deeper insights into their identity and patriotic instincts, something that underpinned their psyches and morale. It also broaches new issues – for example, the weather, rituals of burial, the impact of smell, the role of dreams, and the nature of duty. Furthermore, it investigates change over time by focusing on temporal case studies of crisis war phases and tracks change (and, potentially, breakdown) in soldiers' motivation at these stages of the war. A wider array of interdisciplinary theories are used to break new ground. It provides novel insights into infantrymen's sensemaking, rationality, and endurance by providing a forensic analysis

---

[19] J. Horne, 'Inventing the "Front": Cognition and Reality in the Great War', Lecture at King's College London, 1 November 2016. Also, J. Horne, 'The End of a Paradigm?', *Past & Present*, Vol. 242, No. 1 (February 2019). For discussions of the nature of historical time, see R. Koselleck, *Futures Past: On the Semantics of Historical Time*, trans. K. Tribe (New York, 1979, 2004).

[20] Watson, *Enduring the Great War*, pp. 141, 232–235.

of perceptions of crisis and war. Soldiers' responses (or lack thereof) to crises are used to understand how resilience functions or does not function, which in turn sheds light on soldiers' endurance. Here, then, is a new approach to morale and a novel methodology, which is relevant beyond First World War studies.

There are two overlapping but distinct questions in studies of morale: how do men endure war, and how do they overcome combat? The first five chapters take a 'history of mentalities' perspective on morale, drawing primarily on the record of individual soldiers, and concentrate on the first of these questions, though they throw light on the latter. The final chapter, however, focuses on battalion war diaries and unit histories and weaves battle back into the analysis by focusing on the events of 1917 and early 1918. The use of concepts drawn from anthropology, social psychology, and sociology allows this book to focus not only on what kept men in the trenches but also on what sustained them on arduous route marches, during trying working parties, or while plagued by crippling boredom in a dugout or billet.

To do so, it draws on new national and local archival material. However, the fragmentary nature of many, if not most, veterans' collections means that sources are often composed of incomplete narratives. To offset this, *Making Sense of the Great War* engages with a broad collection of source materials and seeks the unifying ideas and themes embedded in them. Unlike many previous histories, it will not present the same well-thumbed memoirs and novels as it builds its argument. This is a book that is concerned with how the soldiers perceived the war *at the time* and borrows heavily from Ross Wilson's 'ethnohistory' approach to the Great War.[21] This is why this book tends to exclude personal reflections on combat. Combat is hard, if not impossible, to historicise. There were moments of shock, despondency, and crisis amidst the chaos of battle. Yet these moments were relatively rare and are hard to trace with accuracy, as letters and diaries were often written in the days and weeks following the events.[22] Elsewhere, this book seeks to give voice to the rank and file by utilising documents and objects that were more readily produced and used by them.

To begin mapping soldiers' mentalities, over 250 servicemen's private collections (of varying sizes) were consulted. Some ninety of these men were

---

[21] R.J. Wilson, *Landscapes of the Western Front: Materiality during the Great War* (London, 2012) and R.J. Wilson, 'Strange Hells: A New Approach to the Western Front', *Historical Research*, Vol. 81, No. 211 (2008). For the history of mentalities during the Great, see especially S. Audoin-Rouzeau and A. Becker, *14–18: Understanding the Great War*, trans. C. Temerson (New York, 2002) and S. Audoin-Rouzeau, *Men at War 1914–1918: National Sentiment and Trench Journalism in France during the First World War*, trans. H. McPhail (Oxford, 1992, 1995).

[22] For the problems of writing a history of battle, see J. Keegan, *The Face of Battle: A Study of Agincourt, Waterloo and the Somme* (Harmondsworth, 1983), esp. pp. 16–17.

officers, rose from the ranks, or were military chaplains. The overrepresentation of commissioned men plagues any study of this sort. However, while their accommodation and conditions were better, officers deployed similar strategies to their men as they endured chronic crises. Where differences existed, such as in their perceptions of duty or England, these are explored. The size of some soldiers' files means that certain men – such as H.T. Madders, A.P. Burke, or Lt. J.H. Johnson – are referenced more frequently than others. Furthermore, some famous characters, such as Charles Carrington, appear alongside little-known soldiers. However, the analysis is generally restricted to personal material produced during the war, and the individuals were all chosen at random from six regiments from across England: two from the North West (the Border and Manchester Regiments) and one each from the West Midlands (the Royal Warwickshires), the South East (the Ox and Bucks Light Infantry), the South West (the Devonshires), and London (the Royal Fusiliers). This will help to build a picture of how local identity underpinned men's patriotism, as well as accounting for regional and urban/rural variation.

The use of these letters and diaries is not without its difficulties. Some scholars have questioned how much men were willing to divulge.[23] Others, however, believe that they conveyed their lives in surprising detail.[24] While 'proximity to events does not mean the sentiments expressed in letters or diaries were transparent', there is much they can teach us.[25] Michael Roper has argued that 'the real value of letters as psychological sources becomes evident once we accept that emotional states are not wholly conscious, and take into account what is hinted at, unspoken, or unspeakable'.[26] Censorship and self-censorship certainly played a role, so to unpick men's 'emotional states' this study uses a wide array of contemporary letters, postcards, diaries, soldiers' newspapers (published by units across the BEF), poems, war souvenirs, and cartoons. Each of these sources has its own limitations, depending on the medium or audience, but by seeking correlations general themes can be explored. The contemporary documents are supported, where necessary, by memoirs and supplemented by a plethora of institutional documents, including POW interviews, battalion war diaries, meteorological reports, and training manuals. These are triangulated to build as complete a picture of

---

[23] I.R. Bet-El, *Conscripts: Forgotten Men of the Great War* (Stroud, 2009), pp. 135, 137.

[24] M. Hanna, 'A Republic of Letters: The Epistolary Tradition in France during World War I', *American Historical Review*, Vol. 108, No. 5 (2003), pp. 23–24 and K. Hunter, 'More than an Archive of War: Intimacy and Manliness in the Letters of a Great War Soldier to the Woman He Loved, 1915–1919', *Gender & History*, Vol. 25, No. 2 (August 2013), p. 339.

[25] M. Roper, *The Secret Battle: Emotional Survival in the Great War* (Manchester, 2009), pp. 20–21.

[26] Ibid., p. 21.

soldiers' mentalities as possible, and the chapters that follow reflect the ideas that emerged from the historical record with the greatest salience.

While this is naturally an interpretive task, it has allowed the study to make informed generalisations. Furthermore, these findings are, in the final section, used to complement a 'top-down' analysis of the British Army in late 1917 and early 1918, which questions why it was at this stage that soldiers' morale faltered and how the BEF responded to the German spring offensives. By studying the words and thoughts of soldiers, this book looks at how men made sense of Belgium and France and were in turn moulded by service there. It focuses on the infantry because it was their experience that was, arguably, the most consistently demoralising. To concentrate on English soldiers is not to suggest their British or Imperial identities were unimportant, but their sense of local and regional Englishness did play the most prominent role in their perception of the war. Soldiers recognised themselves as English, and their very parochial sense of Englishness subsumed their Britishness and visions of the Empire.[27] Some men even referred to the BEF as the 'English Army'.[28]

The soldiers studied here have mainly been drawn from the six regiments and, where possible, their museums' collections. The geographical spread aims to give as representative a picture as possible and has informed the choice of material. This was based on regiment and periodisation (whether the sources relate to the three crisis moments under examination) and not on the size of the file or a preliminary review of its contents. This reduces the risk of any selectivity or bias when utilising the soldiers' files. It also focuses on the Western Front because the source material originating there is of a greater breadth and depth and this book seeks to understand how the physical environment influenced soldiers' morale. Given the number of men who fought in 1914–1918, it is inappropriate to project any single narrative onto their war experiences, especially for those combatants and auxiliary troops of colour who came to Europe from across the globe.[29] Nevertheless, as Vanda Wilcox has suggested, historians can provide valuable 'snapshots ... of officers and men' that help to build a broader picture.[30]

This book offers just such a 'snapshot'. The introduction will explain its concepts and methods. First, it explores what is meant by 'morale'. It then

---

[27] T.J. Kealy, 'A Blight on "Blighty"', *The Sussex Patrol*, Vol. 1, No. 11 (1 April 1917), p. 4.
[28] IWM Documents.8631: Diary of an Unidentified Soldier in the Border Regiment, 25 December 1914; Capt. G.K. Rose, *The Story of the 2/4th Oxfordshire and Buckinghamshire Light Infantry* (Oxford, 1920), p. 132.
[29] For these histories see, for instance, S. Das, *India, Empire and First World War Culture: Writings, Images, and Songs* (Cambridge, 2018); A. Maguire, *Contact Zones of the First World War: Cultural Encounters Across the British Empire* (Cambridge, 2021); D. Olusoga, *The World's War: Forgotten Soldiers of Empire* (London, 2014).
[30] Wilcox, *Morale in the Italian Army*, p. 17.

describes the relationship between morale, the physical environment, and social groups (including the importance of the 'regiment' in the British Army), and then outlines the psychological processes that influenced men's reactions to war. It also clarifies *Making Sense of the Great War*'s conceptualisation of crisis. Lastly, the rationale behind the focus on English infantrymen is justified more thoroughly.

Introduction
Morale, Crisis, and Englishness

As a phenomenon, morale is as illusory as it is fundamental. Several 'key terms' are associated with it. 'Consent and coercion' describe how men either willingly fought and continued to accept war or reacted to a variety of 'sticks'.[1] Niall Ferguson sees morale as a product of both. Coercion through discipline and punishment worked alongside tactics to build consent, such as food, leave, rest, and religion.[2] Vanda Wilcox has underlined 'compliance' as 'the most common response of men across Europe'.[3] The definitions and determinants of morale are interrelated, and the diversity of the scholarly interpretations of morale rests, in part, on the different ways in which academics and military thinkers have classified it. Generally, though, 'it is seen as the foundation of proper management, which aims at increasing the collective capacity of a defined group', be it 'immediate' or 'imagined'.[4] It often accompanies analyses of 'discipline', which is sometimes framed as a response to external stimuli, and seen as the force that 'determined whether, in the heat of battle, officers could be sure of the obedience of their men'.[5] On the other hand, morale 'is a force that comes from within' and 'determined whether [...] men] would willingly enter the fray in the first instance'.[6]

During the Great War morale was associated with good 'character' and 'moral discipline'.[7] The military believed that high morale was a natural by-product of soldiers strong in morals and patriotic spirit. Later in the twentieth century, this moral understanding of morale gave way to a more collective and democratic interpretation of the phenomenon.[8] In 1914–1918, however, the

---

[1] A. Kramer, 'Recent Historiography of the First World War – Part I' and 'Recent Historiography of the First World War – Part II', *Journal of Modern European History*, Vol. 12 (2014), pp. 5–27 and 155–174.
[2] N. Ferguson, *The Pity of War: Explaining World War I* (London, 1998), ch. 12.
[3] V. Wilcox, *Morale and the Italian Army* (Cambridge, 2016), p. 16.
[4] D. Ussishkin, *Morale: A Modern British History* (Oxford, 2017), p. 1.
[5] T. Bowman, *Irish Regiments in the Great War* (Manchester, 2004), p. 10; L. Rowe, *Morale and Discipline in the Royal Navy* (Cambridge, 2018), p. 56.
[6] Rowe, *Morale and Discipline*, p. 56.
[7] Ussishkin, *Morale*, p. 49.
[8] Ibid., pp. 73–103.

British Army saw it as part of the same matrix as *élan* (or 'spirit') and *esprit de corps*. *Infantry Training* (1914) argued that this would 'help the soldier bear fatigue, privation, and danger cheerfully' and '[i]mbue him with a sense of honour'. A variety of indicators were highlighted, including confidence in superiors and comrades, initiative, self-confidence, self-restraint, obedience, regimental pride, courage, disregard for self, and combat effectiveness.

Morale was closely associated with the concept of the 'offensive spirit' that was pervasive in military thinking at the time.[9] J.F.C. Fuller believed that 'morale' was a 'truly magical word' that conjured 'all the apparitions of victory without endowing them with any tangible form'.[10] The war itself underlined the importance of unit cohesion. A platoon training manual published in 1918 defined morale as a soldier's 'pride in his unit which makes a man unwilling to bring discredit on it and ready at need to sacrifice himself for his success'.[11] Such ideas were clearly drawn from the cultural assumptions of the period. As such, morale was encouraged by the development of appropriate officer – man relations, welfare, and discipline, as well as training regimes, cultural pursuits, and team games.[12]

This understanding of morale helps to explain how it was interpreted at the time but lacks the analytical weight necessary to explain how and why men endured (or endure) war. In fact, as the conflict dragged on, it became apparent that every combatant had their breaking point. Censorship reports began to explore the nexus of men's endurance. In the German Army, there were even studies conducted that focused on soldiers' combat motivation.[13] However, it was the pressures of the next global conflagration (and the lessons of 1914–1918) that encouraged a more academic analysis of the components of morale.

The Second World War focused military attention on morale. The complexity of morale was evident in S.L.A. Marshall's *Men Against Fire*. Marshall, who had served on the Western Front during 1918, conducted hundreds of interviews with American servicemen. He concluded that 'morale is the thinking of an army'.[14] This definition reveals morale's layers. More interested in attitude, Samuel Stouffer led a social scientific investigation into American soldiers' adjustment to the military after 1941 and provided a framework for the analysis of the individual at war. Amongst its many insights were several

---

[9] General Staff (War Office), *Infantry Training (4 – Company Organisation)* (1914), p. 2.
[10] J.F.C. Fuller, *Training Soldiers for War* (London, 1914), p. 1.
[11] IWM LBY EPH 62: War Office, *Platoon Training 1918* (1918), p. 20.
[12] Ussishkin, *Morale*, esp. chapters 1 and 2.
[13] A. Watson, *Enduring the Great War: Combat, Morale and Collapse in the German and British Armies* (Cambridge, 2008), p. 9.
[14] S.L.A. Marshall, *Men against Fire. The Problem of Battle Command in Future War* (New York, 1966), p. 158.

ideas that influenced this book. First, the project warned against top-down understandings of morale.[15] It also outlined the unique problems of infantry morale – especially their proximity to combat, exposure to fire, and deficiencies in basic training. Infantrymen often wanted to switch to other branches of the military perceived as less dangerous, since they believed that they would remain under enemy fire until injury, death, or peace. The authors also introduced the concept of 'relative deprivation'. Soldiers rationalised their service by comparing their situation, comfort, and danger to other members of the armed forces, or civilians in the war zone.[16] The British were also more diligent in charting military morale during 1939–1945. Daily censorship summaries and reports on morale were sent to General Headquarters (GHQ) and used to assess 'the personal concern of troops, their broad social and political perspectives, and their willingness to fight'.[17] Confronted with mass democracy (and aware that every combatant was vulnerable to breakdown), the military no longer saw their men as automatons. Morale was increasingly viewed as a complex of causation.

Since then, there have been a wealth of historical analyses of morale. The definitions tend to be more practical. Alexander Watson defined it 'as the readiness of a soldier or a group of soldiers to carry out the commands issued by military leadership'.[18] Vanda Wilcox approached it more systematically. Seeing it as the interaction between men and the military, she borrowed Jonathan Fennell's definition: 'the willingness of an individual or group to prepare for and to engage in an action required by an authority or institution'.[19] This study embraces this encapsulation of morale. Yet, military morale involves competing emotions; both positive and negative appreciations of individual and institutional actions and policies are at play and change over time. Wilcox argued that studies of morale must also 'differentiate between troops' sentiment before, during, and after combat'.[20] Fennell successfully synthesised the issues that can affect morale (see Table 1). These include endogenous (internal) and exogenous (external) factors that cannot really be disentangled.[21]

---

[15] S.A. Stouffer, E.A. Suchman, L.C. DeVinney, S.A. Star, and R.M. Williams Jr, *The American Soldier: Adjustment during Army Life: Volume 1* (New York, 1949), p. 84.
[16] Ibid., pp. 120, 330.
[17] J. Fennell, *Fighting the People's War: The British and Commonwealth Armies and the Second World War* (Cambridge, 2019), pp. 10–11.
[18] A. Watson, 'Morale', in J. Winter (ed.), *Cambridge History of the First World War*, Vol. II (Cambridge, 2014), p. 176.
[19] Wilcox, *Morale and the Italian Army*, p. 4; J. Fennell, *Combat and Morale in the North African Campaign* (Cambridge, 2011), p. 9.
[20] Wilcox, *Morale and the Italian Army*, p. 4.
[21] Fennell, 'In Search of the "X" Factor', p. 809.

Table I.1 *Factors affecting morale of troops, commanders and army*

Endogenous factors			Exogenous factors			
Institutional	Social	Individual	Economic	Cultural	Environmental	Situational
Command	Leadership	Disposition	Technology	Law	Terrain	Information
Discipline	Cohesion	Background	Output	Values/Ethics	Climate	Rumour
Selection	Esprit de corps	Coping strategies		View of enemy		Friction
Doctrine		Relationship with home				Antecedents
Welfare/Education		Fear/Confidence				
Ethos/Duty		Experience				
Training		Fatigue/Rest				
Organisation						
Supply						

Source: Adapted from J. Fennell, 'In Search of the "X" Factor: Morale and the Study of Strategy', *Journal of Strategic Studies*, Vol. 37, No. 6–7 (2014), p. 809.

However, morale is a process as well as an end-state. This monograph is generally concerned with the former but will also investigate the latter. It will consider the influence of the environment, social groups, and internal psychologies while exploring a variety of morale's stimuli (both internal and external). It probes individuals' perceptions of institutional factors such as duty or training, social factors such as leadership or home, and exogenous factors including the government's war aims, the enemy, weather, or the terrain. It also focuses on individuals and how they made sense of and rationalised the conflict. Morale is, therefore, also considered to be a process through which servicemen, positively or negatively, rationalised their role as soldiers and constructive members of the military. This underpinned their willingness 'to prepare for or engage in an action'.

Could soldiers rationalise their place in the army? Did they exercise such agency? Studies into military discipline suggest otherwise.[22] The use of 'rationality' stems from a psychological approach to morale. It was about persevering through hardships and making sense of one's service. Morale is influenced by an array of issues dependent on circumstance and is the product of a plethora of reactions to different stimuli, situations, and environments. It was maintained and (potentially) destroyed at the intersection of soldiers' physical environment, social groups (both immediate and imagined), and their psychological world.

The Environment and Morale

The Western Front was the stage on which men's lives played out. As an environment, it was hybrid, 'at once natural and social'.[23] This book pursues a history in which 'humans and the environment' are embedded 'within one narrative, a co-history made of multiple interrelations'.[24] In many historical

---

[22] C. Jahr, *Gewöhnliche Soldaten: Desertion und Deserteure im deutschen und britischen Heer 1914–1918* (Göttingen, 1998).

[23] For 'environmental history', see P. Sutter, 'The World with Us: The State of American Environmental History', *Journal of American History*, Vol. 100, No. 1 (June 2013), pp. 94–119. This has influenced a number of the more interdisciplinary scholars of the Great War. See P. Cornish and N.J. Saunders, *Bodies in Conflict: Corporeality, Materiality, and Transformation* (London, 2009); R. Osgood and M. Brown, *Digging up Plugstreet: The Archaeology of a Great War Battlefield* (Sparkford, 2009); J.A. Wearn, A. Philip Budden, S.C. Veniard and D. Richardson, 'The Flora of the Somme Battlefield: A Botanical Perspective on a Post-Conflict Landscape', *First World War Studies*, Vol. 8, No. 1 (2017), pp. 63–77; R.P. Tucker, T. Keller, J.R. McNeill and M. Schmid (eds.), *Environmental Histories of the First World War* (Cambridge, 2018); S. Daly, M. Salvante and V. Wilcox (eds.), *Landscapes of the First World War* (Cham, 2018).

[24] F. Locher and G. Quenet, 'Environmental History: The Origins, Stakes, and Perspectives of a New Site for Research', trans. W. Bishop, *Revue d'histoire moderne et contemporaine*, Vol. 4, No. 56 (2009), pp. 11–12.

'environmental studies', grand narratives chart changes in the natural world.[25] Yet, others focus on the environment's role in shaping identities and ideas.[26] Individuals are influenced, both consciously and unconsciously, by what surrounds them, and they often mentally reconstruct their surroundings, drawing lessons from the natural world, and imbuing it with emotion and meaning. It can even be 'nationalized'.[27] Linda Nash has argued 'that agency is something that emerges from humans' relationship with their physical settings'.[28] Spatial analyses have similarly revealed the ways in which social relations are constructed and undertaken at the local level; landscapes can become the focus of cultural conflict, while spaces can distort perceptions of time and patterns of life.[29]

Such ideas help to explain soldiers' morale. The environment provided the setting for the narratives men weaved. It clouded decision making but also provided some tools for survival. One military censor explained that studying their morale involved 'peering into vast depths where one "sees the wheels go round"'. He found that the 'intricacy of men's minds' was in synchronicity with 'the complex machinery of war'. The censor went on: 'so far as the spirit of the men is concerned, there seems little that can clog or hitch the mechanism'.[30] Men adapted to and began to mirror the patterns of the war: the systems of rotation, the 'morning hate', and other dimensions of army life in Belgium and France became predictable and routine. Indeed, battle was a punctuation mark. The Western Front – its trenches, towns, and landscapes – occupied a central role in the soldiers' perceptions of their war experience.

Soldiers' diaries were littered with references to carrying on 'as normal'. This sense of normality was constructed against the physical environment.[31] A process of cognitive habituation took place, which saw men adapt to their new world. They found meaning in it and through minor acts (such as naming

---

[25] P. Brimblecombe, *The Big Smoke: A History of Air Pollution in London Since Medieval Times* (Cambridge, 1987).

[26] See esp., F. Braudel, *The Mediterranean and the Mediterranean World in the Age of Philip II Vol: I–II*, trans. S. Reynolds (London, 1949, 1972–1973, 1995). Also R. Nash, *Wilderness and the American Mind* (New Haven, 1967, 1982) or H.M. MacKenzie, *The Empire of Nature: Hunting, Conservation and British Imperialism* (Manchester, 1988).

[27] R. White, 'The Nationalization of Nature', *Journal of American History*, Vol. 86, No. 3 (December 1999), pp. 976–989.

[28] L. Nash, 'Furthering the Environmental Turn', *The Journal of American History*, Vol. 100, No. 1 (June 2013), p. 132.

[29] A. Torre, 'A "Spatial Turn" in History? Landscapes, Visions, Resources', *Annales: Histoire, Sciences Sociales*, Vol. 63, No. 5 (2008), pp. 1127–1144. Also P. Stock, 'History and the Uses of Space', in P. Stock (ed.), *The Uses of Space in Early Modern History* (Basingstoke, 2015), p. 7.

[30] IWM Documents. 4041: Capt. M. Hardie, 'Report on III Army Morale, January 1917', p. 1.

[31] LIDDLE/WW1/GS/0137: Pte. O.G. Billingham, Diary 1917–1918.

trenches or tending to gardens and allotments) were able to mask their loss of agency.[32] Of course, men were not socialised by the Western Front alone; they continued to be encumbered by their previous life experiences, although some were so young that the conflict may have been central to their development. Human beings are quick to adapt, and this new environment influenced and constrained the ways in which they were able to make sense of the war.

The environment limited soldiers' perspectives. It not only constrained their vision in the trenches; it affected them in subtler ways.[33] It provided chances for escapism and opportunities to justify or come to terms with their experiences. The Sinai and Palestine front is at the forefront of Edward Woodfin's analysis of morale.[34] The flora, fauna, geography, and climate of the Western Front were just as important for combatants in Western Europe.[35] Ross Wilson has highlighted the importance of 'understanding the soldiers' "sense of place" within the war landscape'. It was 'this perception of "place" [that] enabled troops to attribute meaning to the violent, unpredictable, and alien scenes they witnessed and inhabited'.[36] Men's relationship with the 'material landscape' influenced their perceptions of agency and action.[37]

However, the Western Front's landscapes could become soldiers' greatest foe.[38] In fact, winter provided a 'common enemy' against which the energies of both sides were directed.[39] Weather appears to have impeded men's willingness to follow orders, and disciplinary issues were most evident during

---

[32] R. Wilson, '"Tommifying" the Western Front, 1914-1918', *Journal of Historical Geography*, Vol. 37, No. 3 (2011).

[33] A. Becker, 'Le front militaire et les occupations de la Grande Guerre comme laboratoires de destruction de la nature et de la culture', in P. Bonin and T. Pozzo, *Nature ou Culture: Les colloques de l'institut universitaire de France* (Saint-Etienne, 2015), pp. 193-204. For the Italian Front, see T. Keller, 'The Mountains Roar: The Alps during the Great War', *Environmental History*, Vol. 14, No. 2 (2009).

[34] E. Woodfin, *Camp and Combat on the Sinai and Palestine Front* (London, 2012).

[35] J. Lewis-Stempel, *Where Poppies Blow: The British Soldier, Nature, the Great War* (London, 2016).

[36] R. Wilson, *Landscapes of the Western Front: Materiality during the Great War* (London, 2012), p. 1.

[37] Ibid., pp. 7-8. See also D. Harraway, *Simians, Cyborgs, and Women: The Reinvention of Nature* (London, 1991); B. Latour, 'The Powers of Association', in J. Law (ed.), *Power, Action and Belief: A New Sociology of Knowledge?* (London, 1987), pp. 264-280; E. Hirsch and M.O. O'Hanlon (eds.), *The Anthropology of Landscape: Perspective on Space and Place* (Oxford, 1995); C. Tilley, *A Phenomenology of Landscape: Paths, Places and Monuments* (Oxford, 1994).

[38] A. Fletcher, *Life, Death and Growing Up on the Western Front* (Cambridge, MA, 2013), p. 143. See also M.I. Gurfein and M. Janowitz, 'Trends in Wehrmacht Morale', *The Public Opinion Quarterly*, Vol. 10, No. 1 (Spring 1946), p. 83.

[39] T. Ashworth, *Trench Warfare, 1914-1918: The Live and Let Live System* (London, 1980, 2000), p. 26.

winter.⁴⁰ Unsurprisingly, then, Dan Todman has argued that 'mud' is 'used to evoke a broader myth of the horror of the First World War'.⁴¹ Santanu Das has demonstrated the suffering (both physical and psychological) was engendered by these 'slimescapes'.⁴² The physical environment was capable of sapping men's strength and ate at their resilience. Nonetheless, Tony Ashworth argued that 'soldiers strove with success for control over their environment and thereby radically changed the nature of their war experience'.⁴³ There were active and quiet parts of the frontline. 'Cushy' sectors were 'tolerable, even comfortable' and provided a 'profound' contrast to active sectors. The environment often influenced local truces.⁴⁴

W.H.R. Rivers contended that men had found it hard to adapt.⁴⁵ The Western Front was frequently a violent world, where there were persistent reminders of their mortality. The destruction was at once disgusting, perverse, and unnerving.⁴⁶ It was 'the notion of uncontrollability, which was the primary cause of stress'.⁴⁷ Yet, despite the difficulties of frontline life, the 'moral' universe there might have been preferable to that of rear zones since military discipline was generally more relaxed in the trenches.⁴⁸ Indeed, Stéphane Audoin-Rouzeau found that a 'brotherhood' emerged amongst the French soldiers who had suffered on the frontlines. The death of comrades did not remove them from this group and led to the formation of a 'cult of the dead'.⁴⁹

In this way, the environment formed a part of the emotional and mystical world of soldiers. Infantrymen generated agency by personalising their surroundings. British soldiers asserted ideas of ownership over their areas of operations.⁵⁰ The physical landscape fused with identity and the Anglicisation of the forward zones was a key part of the men's psychological recalibration. Some areas became infamous. The men internalised an alternative map of northern France and Belgium, which was at once familiar, evocative, 'enchanted and mythical'.⁵¹ These names were 'expressive of cultural identity'.⁵² The existence

---

[40] Bowman, *Irish Regiments in the Great War*, pp. 50–51.
[41] D. Todman, *The Great War: Myth and Memory* (London, 2005), p. 20.
[42] S. Das, *Touch and Intimacy in First World War Literature* (Cambridge, 2005), pp. 35–72.
[43] Ashworth, *Trench Warfare*, pp. 14–15.
[44] Ibid., p. 176.
[45] E. Jones, 'The Psychology of Killing: The Combat Experience of British Soldiers during the First World War', *Journal of Contemporary History*, vol. 41, no. 2 (2006), pp. 229–231.
[46] Wilson, *Landscapes of the Western Front*, pp. 80–86.
[47] Watson, *Enduring the Great War*, p. 34.
[48] Jones, 'The Psychology of Killing', 229–231.
[49] S. Audoin-Rouzeau, *Men at War 1914–1918: National Sentiment and Trench Journalism in France during the First World War*, trans. H. McPhail (Oxford, 1992, 1995), pp. 83–85.
[50] C. Ward, *Living on the Western Front: Annals and Stories, 1914–1919* (London, 2013), pp. 95–98, 204.
[51] P. Chasseaud, *Rats Alley: Trench Names of the Western Front, 1914–1918* (Stroud, 2006), p. 47.
[52] Ward, *Living on the Western Front*, p. 92.

of 'front-line gardening' demonstrates such assertions of identity in microcosm.⁵³ Similarly, archaeological evidence – in the form of food, drink, alcohol, and personal comforts – reflected 'small expressions of personality in the midst of the ranks'.⁵⁴

Social Groups and Morale

Soldiers' immediate and imagined social groups also influenced their morale. This theme is knitted throughout *Making Sense of the Great War*. Men's social groups were layered. At war, they revolved around the 'regiment', battalion, company, platoon, or section. However, they also included imagined social groups, which encompassed family, friends, and colleagues in England. Many men continued to see themselves as part of their community back home. These social groups could provide comfort, solace, and resolve, but they could also coerce, explicitly and implicitly.

Morris Janowitz and Edward A. Shils argued that 'primary group' cohesion allowed German soldiers to endure the strain of combat and continue fighting towards the end of the Second World War.⁵⁵ 'Primary group theory' has influenced much of the literature on morale, including John Baynes' study of regimental *esprit de corps* in the Second Battalion Scottish Rifles at Neuve Chapelle in 1915.⁵⁶ Beyond the immediate group, military culture can also be powerful. It informs 'habitual practices, default programs, hidden assumptions, and unreflected cognitive frames'.⁵⁷ In fact, some scholars argue it exerts more influence on soldiers than ideology or doctrine; it creates an organisational identity and provides a framework for appropriate action.⁵⁸ It can inform soldiers' ideas and assumptions through military acculturation.⁵⁹ Military culture is 'a particular variant of organizational culture' and focuses 'on [the] patterns of cognition and practice [within these] organizations'. These are built 'from the past' and embedded 'in methods of operation, routines, expectations, and basic assumptions'.⁶⁰

---

[53] Watson, *Enduring the Great War*, p. 24.
[54] Osgood and Brown, *Digging up Plugstreet*, p. 104.
[55] E.A. Shils and M. Janowitz, 'Cohesion and Disintegration in the Wehrmacht in World War II', *Public Opinion Quarterly*, Vol. 12 (1948), pp. 280–315.
[56] J. Baynes, *Morale: A Study of Men and Courage. The Second Scottish Rifles at the Battle of Neuve Chapelle 1915* (London, 1987).
[57] I.V. Hull, *Absolute Destruction: Military Culture and the Practices of War in Imperial Germany* (Cornell, 2005), p. 2.
[58] P.R Mansoor and W. Murray, 'Introduction', in P.R. Mansoor and W. Murray (eds.), *The Culture of Military Organizations* (Cambridge, 2019), pp. 2–4.
[59] Hull, *Absolute Destruction*, pp. 1–23, 95–99.
[60] Ibid., p. 92.

The British Army's 'ethos focused on a preference for amateurism, a distaste for prescription, and an emphasis on the character of the individual'.[61] Such ideas were emphasised in training. The army's regimental system also played a significant role. Most infantry regiments were affiliated with a county or counties and nominally recruited from these areas. Some units could trace their histories back centuries. This system created a social space through its traditions and power of assimilation, which was fundamental to overcoming the impact of heavy casualties.[62] Units drew upon their local allegiances (to a city, county, or region) and celebrated their personal histories. While the pre-war military reforms of Secretaries of State for War Cardwell (1868–1874) and Haldane (1905–1912) were designed to increase military efficiency and preparedness, they had also embedded units within their local settings. In many cases, local patriotism encouraged men to enlist in a particular regiment in 1914. Training, drill, commemorations, and publications ensured that soldiers remained aware of their unit's local allegiances and traditions.[63] This bred an allegiance to an imagined place of origin and bound 'men to a sense of a shared past'.[64] Many New Army battalions were integrated into these umbrella structures. Volunteers and later conscripts were aware of their unit's 'ancestry' and often wanted to add to their regiment's battle honours.[65]

Samuel Stouffer and S.L.A. Marshall highlighted the power of the military social group during the Second World War.[66] Marshall emphasised the benefits of training.[67] Successful systems of military indoctrination and instruction facilitate military efficiency. However, mutinies and indiscipline suggest that other forces are also at play. More recent scholarship contends that the British Army was aware of a need to channel and control culture. During the latter stages of the war, the BEF organised political and social instruction, though

---

[61] A. Fox, *Learning to Fight: Military Innovation and Change in the British Army, 1914–1918* (Cambridge, 2018), p. 21.

[62] Bowman, *Irish Regiments in the Great War*, pp. 10–31.

[63] A.F.M. Ferryman, *Regimental War Tales, 1741–1914: Told for the Soldiers of the Oxfordshire and Buckinghamshire Light Infantry. The Old 43rd and 52nd* (Oxford, 1915). Also Sir H. Newbolt, *The Story of the Oxfordshire and Buckinghamshire Light Infantry: The Old 43rd and 52nd* (London, 1915).

[64] M. Connelly, *Steady the Buffs! A Regiment, a Region, and the Great War* (Oxford, 2006), p. 7; A. Allport, *Browned Off and Bloody-Minded: The British Soldier Goes to War* (New Haven, 2015), pp. 22–25.

[65] 'To the East Yorkshire Regiment', *The 'Snapper'*, Vol. XIII, No. 2 (February 1918), p. 1; 'The Battle Honours of the Gloucestershire Regiment', *The Fifth Glo'ster Gazette* (1 December 1916), p. 16; 'What the Shropshires Did on the Ypres-Langemarck Road', *The Dud*, Vol. 1, No. 2 (1 July 1916), p. 10.

[66] Stouffer, et al., *The American Soldier* and Marshall, *Men against Fire*.

[67] Marshall, *Men against Fire*, p. 22.

the impact was limited.[68] All armies were forced to begin harnessing and developing their soldiers' loyalties to hearth, home, and nation.[69] Yet the military could also manipulate men through training. Several scholars maintain 'that the policy of constant aggression mandated by the command structure prevailed in the end'.[70] Hew Strachan has described the other impacts of training on morale: it counters boredom, generates professional pride, creates unit cohesion, develops new tactical thinking, and helps soldiers get to grips with new technology.[71] It can teach and empower.

The BEF put a lot of faith in their training regimes, yet there was a shift in the focus of military instruction. In 1914 it had focused on the battalion or company, but by 1918 the platoon had become the key building block.[72] Men also received more specialist training as the war went on and commentators believed that this benefited soldiers' 'initiative and self-reliance' and increased morale.[73] Nonetheless, drill still took centre stage. It was used to develop 'soldierly spirit', 'unhesitating obedience', and *esprit de corps*.[74] J.F.C. Fuller believed that it created 'a mass of men dominated by a spirit which is produced by the thoughts of each individual being concentrated on one image or idea'.[75]

Of course, the military could be coercive. John Keegan highlighted the power of crowd psychology and the benefits of junior leadership and small-unit cohesion.[76] In contrast, Eric Leed has suggested that military coercion was alienating and left soldiers incapable of engaging with events.[77] Denis Winter also believed that combatants became increasingly passive but suggested that

---

[68] MacKenzie, 'Morale and the Cause: The Campaign to Shape the Outlook of Soldiers in the British Expeditionary Force, 1914-1918', *Canadian Journal of History/Annales Canadiennes d'Histoire*, Vol. XXV (August 1990), pp. 215-232.

[69] Watson, *The Cambridge History of the First World War*, p. 195.

[70] L.V. Smith, *Between Mutiny and Obedience: The Case of the French Fifth Infantry Division during World War I* (Princeton, 1994) and A. Watson, 'Culture and Combat in the Western World, 1900-1945', *The Historical Journal*, Vol. 51, No. 2 (June 2008), p. 530.

[71] H. Strachan, 'Training, Morale and Modern War', *Journal of Contemporary History*, Vol. 41, No. 2 (2006). Also V. Wilcox, 'Training, Morale and Battlefield Performance in the Italian Army, 1914-1917', in J. Krause (ed.), *The Greater War: Other Combatants and Other Fronts, 1914-1918* (Basingstoke, 2014).

[72] General Staff (War Office), *Infantry Training (4 Company Organisation)* (London, 1914); SS 143, *Instructions for the Training of Platoons for Offensive Action, 1917* [this was followed in 1918 by *The Training and Employment of Platoons*]; G.M. Harper, *Notes on Infantry Tactics & Training* (London, 1919), p. 26.

[73] B.H.L. Hart, *New Methods in Infantry Training* (Cambridge, 1918), p. 3.

[74] Ibid., pp. 3-4.

[75] Fuller, *Training Soldiers for War*, pp. 14-15.

[76] J. Keegan, *The Face of Battle: A Study of Agincourt, Waterloo and the Somme* (Harmondsworth, 1983), pp. 204-280.

[77] E.J. Leed, *No Man's Land: Combat and Identity in World War I* (Cambridge, 1979, 1981).

they were able to 'find a satisfactory home within the army'.[78] According to some, military justice left no space for complaint and subdued insurrection.[79] Yet, Tony Ashworth argued that the frontlines' 'live-and-let-live system' rested on German and British soldiers' perception of their General Staffs as the enemy of the frontline soldier.[80] Men could think and act outside the confines of military discipline and official culture. Even here, though, coercion and military structures remained dominant forces.[81] The British Army's disciplinary system was relatively harsh, but as the war went on the BEF also embraced an increasingly civilian identity, which produced a degree of flexibility that helped it survive the conflict.[82]

Civilian culture – and links to the civilian world – played an important part in morale.[83] Peter Simkins has suggested 'that the nature of British society in 1914–1918 provided a bedrock of social cohesion which prevented the BEF from total collapse'.[84] Jay Winter highlighted Britain's 'highly disciplined labour force' and its contribution to the 'BEF's obedience and robustness'.[85] Gary Sheffield has similarly argued that inter-rank relations were built upon Britain's pre-war class relations. The paradigm of deference–paternalism between the upper-class (or upper-middle-class) officers and working-class other ranks sustained men.[86] Yet, this was more revealing of men's desire to fulfil a particular role than an investment in this social dynamic. It has also been suggested that men's pre-war life (particularly those of the urban working classes) might have engendered a resilience to hardship.[87] Coping mechanisms developed in peace (especially those of impassivity and solidarity) also appear to have supported many working-class men in the trenches.[88] Peter

[78] D. Winter, *Death's Men: Soldiers of the Great War* (London, 1978), p. 140.
[79] B. Ziemann, *War Experiences in Rural Germany* (Oxford, 2011).
[80] Ashworth, *Trench Warfare*.
[81] For a more explicit statement of this, M. Van Creveld, *Fighting Power: German and US Army Performance: 1939–1945* (London, 1983). For a discussion of how the French Army actively adapted its disciplinary policy during the war, allowing it to become less severe, see Saint-Fuscien, *À vos orders?*
[82] Jahr, *Gewöhnliche Soldaten*.
[83] J. Meyer, *Men of War: Masculinity and the First World War in Britain* (Basingstoke, 2009); Roper, *The Secret Battle*; A. Fox, '"I Have Never Felt More Utterly Yours": Presence, Intimacy, and Long-Distance Marriages in the First World War', *Journal of British Studies*, Vol. 61, No. 3 (2022), pp. 676–701.
[84] P. Simkins, 'Everyman at War: Recent Interpretations of the Front Line Experience', in B. Bond (ed.), *The First World War and British Military History* (Oxford, 1991), p. 301.
[85] J. Winter, *The Experience of World War I* (London, 1988, 2000), p. 159.
[86] G. Sheffield, *Leadership in the Trenches: Officer–Man Relations, Morale and Discipline in the British Army in the Era of the First World War* (Basingstoke, 2000), pp. 72–73.
[87] A. Gregory, *The Last Great War: British Society and the First World War* (Cambridge, 2008), p. 278.
[88] J. Bourne, 'The British Working Man in Arms', in H. Cecil and P. Liddle (eds.), *Facing Armageddon: The First World War Experienced* (London, 1996, 2003), pp. 342–350.

Hodgkinson has recently echoed many of these arguments but focused instead on the 'Victorian' attributes of manliness and stoicism.[89] Yet, the most significant of these pre-war cultures have generally been ignored by historians: the powerful influence of respectability and men's political passivity.

The historian J.G. Fuller was the first to reveal how the army continued to embrace popular culture. Leisure activities behind the lines imbued men with the 'humour and sceptical stoicism' to persevere through adverse frontline experiences.[90] There is evidence of soldiers' coping mechanisms in the oral and literary culture of the army. Songs, trench journals, and theatre nurtured courage and became an outlet for sarcasm and veiled criticism.[91] The civilian identity of some units also appears to have been a crucial aspect of their endurance.[92] Leonard Smith has investigated the ways in which the traditions of democratic and republican France interacted and interrelated with discipline.[93] Similarly, Joshua Sanborn has discussed the importance of patriotism and collective identity in the Imperial Russian Army.[94] The patriotic instincts of the BEF's soldiers were equally significant.

Craig Gibson has looked closely at relationships that developed outside the boundaries of the military. Despite tensions, the interactions between British soldiers and local civilians reminded British troops of the home for which they were fighting.[95] Sexual relationships between men and civilian women behind the lines were also significant.[96] All of these factors informed and manipulated soldiers' frames of reference and influenced their perceptions of the conflict in ways that need to be explored further. Social groups were also imagined. The link between combatants and home remained deep and sustaining. Letters,

---

[89] P. Hodgkinson, *Glum Heroes: Hardship, Fear and Death – Resilience and Coping in the British Army on the Western Front, 1914-1919* (Exeter, 2016), pp. 93-105.

[90] J.G. Fuller, *Troop Morale and Popular Culture in the British and Dominion Armies, 1914-1918* (Oxford, 1991), pp. 175-8.

[91] E. Hanna, '"Say It with Music": Combat, Courage and Identity in the Songs of the RFC/RAF, 1914-1918', *British Journal for Military History*, Vol. 4, No. 2 (2018), pp. 91-120.

[92] H. McCartney, *Citizen Soldiers: The Liverpool Territorials in the First World War* (Cambridge, 2011).

[93] Smith, *Between Mutiny and Obedience*, pp. 175-214.

[94] A. Sanborn, *Drafting the Russian Nation: Military Conscription, Total War and Mass Politics 1905-1925* (DeKalb, 2002), p. 12.

[95] C. Gibson, *Behind the Front: British Soldiers and French Civilians 1914-1918* (Cambridge, 2014) and 'Sex and Soldiering in France and Flanders: The British Expeditionary Force along the Western Front, 1914-1919', *International History Review*, Vol. 23 (2001), pp. 539-579.

[96] B. Cherry, *They Didn't Want to Die Virgins: Sex and Morale in the British Army on the Western Front* (Wolverhampton, 2016); S. Grayzel, 'Mothers, Marraines, and Prostitutes: Morale and Morality in First World War France', *International History Review*, Vol. 19 (1997), pp. 66-82; J. Bourke, *Dismembering the Male: Men's Bodies, Britain and the Great War* (London, 1996), pp. 155-156.

postcards, and parcels provided a tangible link with home, which was a source of emotional sustenance and influenced men's sensemaking. Michael Roper has highlighted how common emotional reactions to the conflict coexisted with cultural attitudes drawn from men's particular 'class cultures and idioms of expression'.[97]

The majority of the BEF's soldiers (whatever their background might have been) were young men, frequently unmarried, and too young (or too poor) to have taken part in mass politics. Seventy per cent of them were below the age of thirty, while 40 per cent were under twenty-four.[98] In fact, by 1916 the largest demographic groups were twenty-one and under.[99] This affected their reactions to the war and meant that their relationship with England was most frequently filtered through personal relationships rather than the state. It was the image of a subjective and personalised imagined social (and physical) world that fed men's patriotism, but this proved to be a justification for their suffering and a source of sustenance.

Religion was a pillar of some imagined social worlds. It provided both solace and support. Edward Madigan and Patrick Houlihan have argued that military clergy played an important role in maintaining fighting men's spirit.[100] Adrian Gregory has pointed to the existence of an internalised religiosity at this time.[101] Religion and other cultural phenomena were interwoven with men's immediate and imagined social groups and played a role in the way that they made sense of war and service. This book will focus on the ways in which the military social context and the imagined social worlds at home influenced soldiers' perceptions of duty and helped them to cope with war.

Individual Psychologies and Morale

Soldiers' psychologies were not an exogenous variable. Yet, as men internalised and processed what they encountered, they re-projected an adulterated picture. John Keegan believed that 'some exploration of the combatant's emotions ... is essential to the truthful writing of military history'.[102] Their frames of reference and instinctive cognitive impulses distorted the world around them, often imbuing their social and physical surroundings with

---

[97] Roper, The Secret Battle, pp. 13, 31.
[98] Ibid., p. 5. Also J. Winter, The Great War and the British People (Basingstoke, 2003), p. 72.
[99] See Chapter 6.
[100] E. Madigan, Faith under Fire: Anglican Army Chaplains and the Great War (Basingstoke, 2011) and P.J. Houlihan, Clergy in the Trenches: Catholic Military Chaplains of Germany and Austria Hungary (Chicago, 2011).
[101] Gregory, The Last Great War, pp. 152–186.
[102] Keegan, The Face of Battle, p. 17.

meaning and significance. The English infantrymen's *Weltanschauung* – literally 'world perception', the internal conditions that influence actors' very understanding of their surroundings – are the third feature of morale explored in this book.[103] V. G. Liulevicius described this as a 'mindscape ... the mental landscape conjured up by looking out over an area: ways of organizing the perception of territory, its characteristic features, and landmarks'.[104] The external world was inseparable from the soldiers' internal domain.[105]

Features of morale have been revealed in *histoire des mentalités* approaches to 1914–1918.[106] By mapping soldiers' thinking, they have provided a complex picture of soldiers' feelings and motivations.[107] As well as exploring cultural belief systems, these studies have underlined the changing nature of violence during these years and the psychological impact of wounds and suffering. Some of these scholars have suggested that a process of brutalisation took place during conflict.[108] After all, the war was as much a psychological as a physical experience. Many years ago, Arthur Marwick argued that twentieth-century conflict had forced individuals to undergo 'colossal psychological change'.[109] Furthermore, soldiers cognitive processes helped them to come to terms with war. Yet, psychology remains underused in historical studies of morale. Several scholars have begun to tackle the subject with the support of literature from this discipline, and Alexander Watson's work is an example of the effective application of this interdisciplinary approach.[110]

---

[103] For *Weltanschauung* and soldiers, see O. Bartov, *Hitler's Army: Soldiers, Nazis, and War in the Third Reich* (Oxford, 1992), esp. pp. 134, 148.

[104] V.G. Liulevicius, *War Land on the Eastern Front: Culture, National Identity and German Occupation in World War I* (Cambridge, 2009), p. 151.

[105] For discussions of 'worldviews', see P.G. Hiebert, *Transforming Worldviews: An Anthropological Understanding of How People Change* (Grand Rapids, 2008). For *Weltanschauung*, S. Freud, 'Lecture XXXV: A Philosophy of Life', *New Introductory Lectures on Psycho-Analysis*, trans. W.J.H. Sprott (New York, 1933) or H.-G. Gadamer, *Truth and Method* (London, 1975).

[106] S. Audoin-Rouzeau and A. Becker, *14–18: Understanding the Great War*, trans. C. Temerson (New York, 2002), p. 18.

[107] Audoin-Rouzeau, *Men at War*, pp. 36–184.

[108] Ibid., pp. 25–27, 35. For the brutalisation thesis, see G.L. Mosse, *Fallen Soldiers: Reshaping the Memory of the World Wars* (Oxford, 1990). For discussions of violence and destruction, see R. Gerwarth and J. Horne, 'Vectors of Violence: Paramilitarism in Europe after the Great War, 1917–1923', *The Journal of Modern History*, Vol. 83, No. 3 (September 2011); R. Gerwarth, *The Vanquished: Why the First World War Failed to End, 1917–1923* (London, 2016); A. Kramer, *Dynamic of Destruction: Culture and Mass Killing in the First World War* (Oxford, 2007), p. 68.

[109] A. Marwick, *War and Social Change in the Twentieth Century* (London, 1974), pp. 11–14.

[110] Watson, *Enduring the Great War*, p. 5. See also Hodgkinson, *Glum Heroes*, pp. vi–xvii and S. Linden, *The Called It Shell Shock: Combat Stress in the First World War* (Exeter, 2016). Also N. Dixon, *On the Psychology of Military Incompetence* (London, 1976, 1994).

There have been several other psychological approaches to the study of the war.[111] Strikingly, the belief that endurance might be linked to a primaeval instinct (and desire) to fight and kill can be found in several historical investigations. It certainly seems that some men enjoyed and even gloried in fighting.[112] This begs an important question: are humans programmed to accept war? Douglas Fry provides the most nuanced answer to this question. There is an innate human capacity for aggression, but the pervasiveness of peaceful social groups in prehistory indicates that there is also a solid foundation for the pursuit of peace.[113] Fry's more encouraging message about human psychology holds true for these First World War soldiers. Varied attempts were made to construe the conflict constructively rather than antagonistically. Static warfare also offered fewer opportunities for individuals to display their martial prowess. Furthermore, as Benjamin Ziemann has explained, killing can only be understood as 'the product of a complex military organization' that 'provides the technology, personnel and institutional resources for the perpetration of violence'.[114]

Men were capable of attributing sense to the conflict, and this played a central role in their endurance. Cultural geographer Tim Edensor has argued that as humans 'we may be able to "see" that an environment is unfamiliar, but it is the processes conducted by the rest of the senses that enable us to navigate strange places without harm. We can temporarily renegotiate our sensorial arrangement with everyday life in order to protect ourselves, as we instinctively know whether we are in an "understood" environment or one that is alien to us'.[115] Conscious and unconscious mechanisms of normalisation, familiarisation, and personalisation helped infantrymen to understand the world around them. It quickly became routine: 'one remembers various

---

Watson uses E. Becker's discussion of fear and death, P.L. Bernstein's notions of risk, S.E. Taylor and J.D. Brown's theories of positivity, and S. Milgram's model of obedience.

[111] Jones, 'The Psychology of Killing', p. 236; S. Wessely, 'Twentieth-Century Theories of Combat Motivation and Breakdown', *Journal of Contemporary History*, Vol. 41. No. 2 (April 2006), pp. 269–286.

[112] J. Bourke, *An Intimate History of Killing: Face-to-Face Killing in Twentieth Century Warfare* (London, 1999), p. 13; Ferguson, *The Pity of War*, p. 357. See also J. Glenn Gray, *The Warriors: Reflections on Men in Battle* (New York, 1959, 1970).

[113] D.P. Fry, *The Human Potential for Peace: An Anthropological Challenge to Assumptions about War and Violence* (Oxford, 2005).

[114] B. Ziemann, *Violence and the German Soldier in the Great War: Killing, Dying, Surviving*, trans. A. Evans (London, 2017), p. 5.

[115] T. Edensor, 'Sensing the Ruin', *The Senses and Society*, Vol. 2, No. 2 (2007), pp. 217–232 referenced by M. Leonard, 'A Senseless War', *World War I Centenary: Continuations and Beginnings*, ww1centenary.oucs.ox.ac.uk/body-and-mind/a-senseless-war/, accessed 19 June 2016.

incidents, but most days were very similar to each other'.[116] Men attempted to re-calibrate their experience, often using their environment and social group as a point of reference.

However, too many scholarly studies assume that agency and action are conscious, but much of our past, like our present, is fuelled by the unconscious. 'Dual-process theory' describes how humans process information in two different ways. In system one (intuition or impulse), reasoning is automatic and fast. Driven by habit and emotion, it requires little or no thought. In system two, decisions are often reflective or underwritten by reasoning. Slower and more volatile, this system is informed by conscious judgements and attitudes, drawing on knowledge and information.[117] It is, therefore, important to understand how instinctive and unconscious cognitive mechanisms (as well as slower and more considered reactions) impacted morale and men's perception of and reaction to crisis.

Alexander Watson has argued that 'human faith, hope and optimism, no less than cultural traits, discipline, primary groups and patriotism, explain why and how men were willing and able to fight in the horrendous conditions of the Western Front'.[118] Self-deception and an inflated sense of their own chances of survival also helped men to navigate the horrors.[119] Soldiers' 'hope' should be added to this list. Ultimately, combatants wanted to survive and for peace to come. Hope is a cognitive function, one that is influenced by emotions but is ultimately goal-orientated. It is 'goal-directed thinking in which people perceive that they can produce routes to desired goals (pathways thinking) and the requisite motivation to use those routes (agency thinking)'.[120] Positivity and optimism (and their antitheses) operate within the boundaries of hope, which can be affected by emotional reactions – such as anger, despondency, disappointment, or confidence – to obstacles that arise in the pursuit of objectives. Tellingly, the war was perceived as a 'route march' at the end of which was peace.[121] Peace became a sustaining point of reference.

---

[116] RFM.ARC.2012.264: Sgt. Osborn, Diary 23 and 25 September 1914; IWM Documents.4761: Cpl. R.G. Plint, Memoir of 1916, p. 11.

[117] D. Kahneman, 'A Perspective on Judgement and Choice', *The American Psychologist*, Vol. 59, No. 9 (2003) and *Thinking, Fast and Slow* (London, 2012); F. Strack and R. Deutsch, 'Reflective and Impulsive Determinants of Social Behaviour', *Personality and Social Psychology Review*, Vol. 8, No. 3 (2004).

[118] Watson, *Enduring the Great War*, p. 107.

[119] Ibid., esp. pp. 85–107.

[120] S.J. Lopez, C.R. Snyder, and J.T. Pedrotti, 'Hope: Many Definitions, Many Measures', in S.J. Lopez and C.R. Snyder (eds.), *Positive Psychological Assessment: A Handbook of Models and Measures* (London, 2003), p. 94.

[121] IWM Documents.4041: Capt. M. Hardie, '3rd Section Report on Complaints, Moral, Etc. (1916)'. See also NAM 2005-02-6: Capt. M. Asprey, Letter Mother 27 September 1914; IWM Documents.12339: Brig. Gen, G.A. Stevens, Letter to Mother, 11 November 1916; IWM Documents.7035: Lt. J.H. Johnson, Diary 28 and 31 December 1916; NAM 7403-

As infantryman William Anderson noted in his diary: 'we hear odd bits of peace talk ... our most fervent hopes are that these straws show which way the wind blows, and that very soon we may be retracing our steps towards our dear homeland, looking forward to happier times'.[122] Soldiers' interpretation of the war as a long road to *victorious* peace bred resilience.[123]

Psychological resilience was another key dimension of soldiers' morale. Resilience refers 'to the process of coping with or overcoming exposure to adversity or stress'.[124] Modern militaries have developed programmes to inculcate psychological resilience in service members. Even these have an unknown effect, and one hundred years ago no such institutional procedures existed. Nonetheless, many of the ingredients of psychological resilience outlined in modern studies can be found in the First World War infantrymen studied here (see Table 2). The factors influencing resilience highlight how the individual, the group, and the physical environment coalesce.

The environment, as well as the military and the war, was normalised, understood, and overcome through habituation and familiarisation. Habituation sees organisms cease or decrease their reaction to stimuli, helping explain how humans adapt to war. Reduced reactions could, for example, have influenced perceptions of shellfire or helped to normalise the restrictive discipline of the military. Normal reactions can return if the stimuli are reduced or removed, which might explain men's more pronounced reactions to war after leave.[125] 'Habituation training' can help to clarify how men adjusted and readjusted to the frontlines. In some cases, however, stronger stimuli yield little habituation.[126] Habituation is both multidimensional and specific. Men could normalise certain aspects of war, while still finding new or

---

29-486-144: Sgt. H. Hopwood, Letter 12 October 1917; IWM Documents.11289: H.T. Madders, Diary 14 October 1918; IWM Documents.12339: Brig. Gen. G.A. Stevens, Letters October through December 1916.

[122] IWM Documents.5092: Pte. W.M. Anderson, Diary 11 November 1916.

[123] A. Mayhew, 'Hoping for Victorious Peace: Morale and the Future on the Western Front', in A. Luptak, H. Smyth, and L. Halewood (eds.), *War Time: First World War Perspectives on Temporality* (Abingdon, 2018).

[124] L.S. Meredith et al., 'Promoting Psychological Resilience in the U.S. Military', *Rand Health Quarterly*, Vol. 1, No. 2 (Summer 2011); www.ncbi.nlm.nih.gov/pmc/articles/PMC4945176/, accessed 9 August 2017. See also R. McGarry, S. Walklate, and G. Mythen, 'A Sociological Analysis of Military Resilience: Opening Up the Debate', *Armed Forces & Society*, Vol. 41, No. 2 (2015), pp. 199–220.

[125] IWM Documents.16345: 2nd Lt. D. Henrick Jones, Letter to his Wife 25 December 1916; RFM.ARC.2495.5: Sgt. S. Gill, Diary 30 October 1916; IWM Documents.11289: H.T. Madders, Diary 2 March 1918.

[126] C.H. Rankin et al., 'Habituation Revisited: An Updated and Revised Description of Behavioural Habituation', *Neurobiology of Learning and Memory*, Vol. 92 (2009), pp. 136–137.

Table I.2 *Factors promoting resilience*

Individual-level factors	Unit-level factors	Community-level factors
Positive coping (managing circumstances)	Command climate (pride, support and leadership)	Belongingness (integration, friendship, etc.)
Spiritual coping (faith-based beliefs and support)	Teamwork (co-ordination and flexibility)	Cohesion (bonds with community/shared values)
Positive affect (deploying positive emotions)	Cohesion (combined actions, bonding and commitment)	Connectedness (quality and number of connections with people or place)
Positive thinking (enthusiasm, reframing, hope)		Collective efficacy (perception of group's ability to work together)
Realism (realistic expectations and perceived agency)		
Behavioural control (self-regulation, self-management, self-enchantment)		
Physical fitness		
Altruism (selfless concern for others' welfare)		

Source: Adapted from L.S. Meredith et al., 'Promoting Psychological Resilience in the U.S. Military', *Rand Health Quarterly*, Vol. 1, No. 2 (Summer 2011), pp. xiv–xv.

shocking experiences terrifying. What is more, dishabituation can occur when strong stimuli reduce reductive responses which helps to explain occasions when men entered a period of having the 'wind-up'.

Habituation varied in effectiveness between individuals, and some men never adjusted while others broke down.[127] Shell shock and war neurosis, or more recently Post-Traumatic Stress Disorder (PTSD), demonstrated how fear, stress, and trauma can undermine endurance. Every individual had a breaking point. Either a single disruptive event or prolonged exposure to trauma damages psychological defence mechanisms.[128] Approximately 36 per cent of British

---

[127] RFM.ARC.2012.958: E.T. Marler, Diary October – December 1916.
[128] For shell shock and PTSD, see B. Shephard, *A War of Nerves: Solders and Psychiatrists, 1914–1994* (London, 2002); P. Leese, *Shell Shock: Traumatic Neurosis and the British*

post-war pensions were awarded to men with war neurosis. However, it is estimated that there were '325,000 psychiatric casualties during the war, 143,000 of them cases of shell shock [... and that] this represents only 5.7 per cent of the army's military manpower'.[129] Some cases were undoubtedly unreported.[130] Yet, most men did adjust to war, perhaps because of long-term habituation.[131]

Soldiers' psychological responses to the war were underpinned by their 'frames of reference' and constrained by 'bounded rationality'. These concepts help to explain how decisions are influenced by the environment, culture, and available information. Human rationality and choice are contingent on perceived opportunities and influenced by perspective and supposition. A 'frame of reference' is 'the context, view-point, or set of presuppositions or of evaluative criteria within which a person's perception and thinking seem always to occur, and which constrains selectively the course and outcome of these activities'.[132] Decisions and perceptions are produced by subjective readings of situations. Importantly, these are 'malleable'.[133] Sönke Neitzel and Harold Welzer have shown the significance of frames of reference in their analysis of German soldiers' experiences in 1939–1945. 'The ability', they argued, 'to interpret and decide presupposes orientation and knowledge of what one is dealing with and what consequences a decision can have. And a frame of reference is what provides orientation'. A member of a specific group is unable 'to interpret what he sees outside references not of his own choice or making'. These frames 'guarantee economy of action so that most of what happens can be sorted within a familiar matrix'. Frames of reference include:

1. Those that 'comprise of socio-historical space that, in most respects, can be clearly delimited' – such as the duration of a dictatorial regime.
2. Those that 'consist of a concrete constellation of sociohistorical events' – such as a war.

Soldiers of the First World War (Basingstoke, 2002); E. Jones and S. Wessely, *Shell Shock to PTSD: Military Psychiatry from 1900 to the Gulf War* (Hove, 2005); E. Jones, 'War Neuroses', *Journal of the History of Medicine and Allied Sciences*, Vol. 67, No. 3 (2012), pp. 345–373; F. Reid, *Broken Men: Shell Shock, Treatment and Recovery in Britain, 1914–1930* (London, 2011); J. Bourke, *Fear: A Cultural History* (London, 2005), ch. 7.

[129] Beckett, Bowman and Connelly, *The British Army*, p. 158.
[130] Leese, *Shell Shock*, p. 9.
[131] Rankin, 'Habituation Revisited', pp. 136–137.
[132] 'Frame of Reference', in A. Bullock, and O. Stallybrass (eds.), *The Fontana Dictionary of Modern Thought* (Bungay, 1977), p. 243.
[133] N.S. Newcombe, D.H. Uttal, and M. Sauter, 'Spatial Development', in P.D. Zelazo (ed.), *The Oxford Handbook of Development Psychology: Volume I Body and Mind* (Oxford, 2013), p. 576.

3. Those that are 'the special characteristics, modes of perception, interpretative paradigms, and perceived responsibilities that an individual brings to a specific situation'.[134]

Theories of 'bounded' rationality also underline the importance of frames of reference (as well as their fragility and fluidity). Rational action rests on the brain's ability to process information, which depends on one's environment and how long one has to process situations.[135] Bounded rationality has been used (particularly in behavioural economics) to explain why actors fail to adhere to the 'rational agent model'. Such work refutes the idea that actors make the best or even most logical decisions and seeks to explain why humans do not always pursue their optimal benefit or satisfaction.

Bounded rationality posits that 'the central characteristic of agents is not that they reason poorly but that they often act intuitively and based on imperfect information. And the behaviour of these agents is not guided by what they are able to compute, but by what they happen to see at a given moment'.[136] Even then, what a person sees is often highly subjective. Information aversion (or avoidance) and bias mean that individuals regularly process information that supports or substantiates previously held beliefs.[137] Soldiers' confidence that the war was being won rested, at least in part, on such psychological apparatus. Rationality is not predetermined; it is influenced by expectation, imagination, socialisation, and one's physical surroundings.

The physical environments and social groups studied here overlapped with and were filtered by the troops' psychologies. The interaction between them helped men to adapt to war and informed the narratives they created to make sense of their experiences. They influenced soldiers' rationalisation of the conflict and their place within it, helping troops to develop a sense of agency. Infantrymen perceived the war as personally significant. However, how did this relate to crisis?

CRISIS

There are two overlapping variants of crisis: chronic and acute. The former confronted soldiers every day. Lacking immediate 'solutions', these were

---

[134] S. Neitzel and H. Welzer, *On Fighting, Killing and Dying: The Secret Second World War Tapes of German POWs* (New York, 2012), p. 8.

[135] G. Gigerenzer and D.G. Goldstein, 'Reasoning the Fast and Frugal War: Models of Bounded Rationality', in *Psychological Review*, Vol. 103, No. 4. (1996), pp. 650–669.

[136] D. Kahneman, 'Maps of Bounded Rationality: Psychology for Behavioral Economics', *The American Economic Review*, Vol. 93, No. 5 (December 2003), pp. 1449–1475, esp. 1469.

[137] R. Golman, D. Hagmann, and G. Loewenstein, 'Information Avoidance', *Journal of Economic Literature*, Vol. 55, No. 1 (March 2017), pp. 96–135.

'unlikely to abate in the short to medium turn'.[138] Significantly, chronic crises demonstrate that 'crisis is not [necessarily] a one-off or exogenous occurrence but rather a routine condition that poses a particular set of challenges to those living within it'.[139] Intellectual historian Reinhart Koselleck argued that 'chronic' crises can be understood as 'a state of greater or lesser permanence, as in a longer or shorter transition towards something better or worse or towards something altogether different'. In contrast, an acute crisis is a 'moment' that requires a 'decision' or response.[140]

The persistent crises that confronted soldiers (such as the discomfort caused by military life and the weather or their dislocation from home) were chronic. These were a feature of infantrymen's new environments and had to be borne or were situations beyond their capacity to change. Overcoming them involved developing coping strategies. Sometimes these arose organically, drawing on innate skills of adaptability and endurance, or were built around men's social group, the army, or their environment. In contrast, acute crises (often accompanying a particular event such as a bombardment or combat) required a more immediate response. Soldiers needed to be provided with adequate tools (both conceptual and practical) to make the best or most desirable decision in these circumstances. As such, the quality of soldiers' training and their leadership were amongst the most influential factors in responding in moments of acute crisis. Morale was sustained by men's ability to endure chronic crises and to overcome (or even fail to register) acute crises.

Five chronic crises are charted in this book: the destruction and sameness of the war zone, the exhaustion caused by the physical environment, the pressures of military authority and service, separation from home, and the length of the war. These sapped morale. Yet, soldiers' ability to endure these everyday, overlapping, low-level stresses underpinned their endurance; this influenced (or contextualised) how they reacted to moments of heightened acute crisis, such as retreat or action with the enemy. It was only at the point that crises demanded, encouraged, or required action (such as calls for a negotiated peace, collective disobedience, mutiny, or a self-inflicted wound) that morale faltered. This could be caused by the cumulative effect of the war's chronic crises or in reaction to the acute crises that men encountered, especially amidst

---

[138] J.D. Sachs, 'Resolving the Debt Crisis of Low-Income Countries', *Brookings Papers on Economic* Activity, Vol. 2002, No. 1 (2002), pp. 257–286; G. Conway, 'Presidential Address: Geographical Crises of the Twenty-First Century', *The Geographical Journal*, Vol. 175, No. 3 (September 2009), p. 221; M. O'Keefe, 'Chronic Crises in the Arc of Insecurity: A Case Study of Karamoja', *Third World Quarterly*, Vol. 31, No. 8 (2010), p. 1271.

[139] C.J. Gerry, 'Review: *Crisis and the Everyday in Postsocialist Moscow* by Shevchenko, Olga', *The Slavonic and East European Review*, Vol. 89, No. 1 (2011), p. 184.

[140] R. Koselleck (trans. W. Richter), 'Crisis', *Journal of the History of Ideas*, Vol. 67, No. 2 (April 2006), pp. 358, 382.

battle. In either case, men's ability to endure was undermined. The first four chapters chart the mechanisms by which men overcame chronic crisis. The fifth and sixth chapters then explore the ways in which a chronic crisis became corrosive to morale and the impact of acute crisis during the German spring offensives in 1918.

Making Sense of the Great War shifts the perspective away from the crises facing military commanders. However, it uses such moments – as defined in the secondary literature as mutiny or the threat of major morale collapse – to frame its investigation. During battle and combat tactical emergencies would have been palpable to the men involved. Yet, this book examines how men survived the stalemate that was the subtext of the conflict, even at these moments. It sheds new light on key events by first investigating the reactions of ordinary soldiers during such moments. This will also facilitate an analysis that can be contextualised in terms of an army that was evolving demographically: from a predominantly regular force to one composed of volunteers and then conscripts.

In 1914 and 1916, soldiers generally ended the year confident, optimistic, and resilient. However, in late 1917 and 1918, chronic crises (compounded by the bitter disappointments of 1917) began to eat away at the resilience of infantrymen. This offers the clearest example of a trough in morale. By focusing on the perpetual stalemate on the Western Front, the chapters unpick these 'crisis moments' and how they were perceived by the soldiers at the time.

Crisis Moment One: Morale in 1914

There were a variety of acute crises in the BEF during the campaigns of 1914. The German invasion of Belgium and France pushed the BEF to its limits and by the beginning of November 1914 'the fighting in Flanders [was] reaching crisis point'.[141] While the professional BEF's morale is understudied, it can be viewed as an extension of debates regarding its quality and effectiveness. James Edmonds, the author of many of the volumes of the official *History of the Great War*, described the BEF of 1914 as the 'best trained, best organised, and best equipped ... army that ever went forth to war', thus laying the foundations for the myth of the pre-eminence of the 'Old Contemptibles'.[142]

---

[141] N. Lloyd, *The Western Front: A History of the First World War* (London, 2021), pp. 40, 58, 78.

[142] J.E. Edmonds, *History of the Great War Based on Official Documents. Military Operations. France and Belgium 1914. Mons, The Retreat to the Seine, the Marne and the Aisne August–October 1914* (London, 1925), pp. 10–11.

This appeared to be confirmed by the Southborough Commission (or the Royal Commission on Shell Shock), which concluded that there had been little or no instance of psychological breakdown amongst regulars.[143] Such conclusions later informed John Baynes' analysis of Neuve Chapelle and the importance of *esprit de corps*.[144]

However, such conclusions have been revised. The battles of Mons and Le Cateau are now seen in a more negative light.[145] According to Gary Sheffield, the BEF was 'the right army for a different sort of war than the one it actually came to fight'.[146] Significantly, large numbers of Reservists brought nominally regular units up to strength.[147] There was very little time to reintegrate these men and reacquaint them with military procedures, which undermined their confidence.[148] Institutional problems degraded this further. Paddy Griffith, Dan Todman, and others have criticised the quality of generalship, tactics, and procedures of command and control in 1914.[149] Britain's serious deficiencies in manpower and materiel have also been highlighted.[150] Alexander Watson has revealed the prevalence of self-inflicted wounds, the large numbers of men surrendering, and high incidence of psychological collapse during this period.[151] In his view, 1914 represented the BEF's major crisis in morale. This demoralisation stemmed from men's shock at the unexpected length and nature of the war, and from poor preliminary training. Furthermore, it has been suggested that the army's resilience might have been undermined by the fact that its ranks were filled by 'society's most disadvantaged men'.[152] Yet, did these men understand this period of the war as a crisis, and how did environmental factors help to shape their perceptions of the conflict.

---

[143] Jones, 'The Psychology of Killing', p. 231.
[144] Baynes, *Morale*.
[145] A. Gilbert, *Challenge of Battle: The Real Story of the British Army in 1914* (Oxford, 2014), pp. 63-153.
[146] G. Sheffield, *Forgotten Victory: The First World War: Myths and Realities* (London, 2002), p. 117.
[147] R. Grayson, *Belfast Boys: How Unionists and Nationalists Fought and Died Together in the First World War* (London, 2009), p. 26.
[148] Watson, *Enduring the Great War*, p. 145.
[149] Todman, *The Great War*, 79; G. Sheffield and D. Todman, 'Command and Control in the British Army on the Western Front', in G. Sheffield and D. Todman (eds.), *Command and Control on the Western Front: The British Army's Experience 1914-18* (Chalford, 2007), pp. 1-11; P. Griffith, 'The Extent of Tactical Reform in the British Army', in P. Griffith (ed.), *British Fighting Methods in the Great War* (London, 1996), pp. 5-6.
[150] G. Corrigan, *Mud, Blood and Poppycock* (London, 2003, 2004), p. 48; Todman, *The Great War*, p. 78.
[151] Watson, *Enduring the Great War*, pp. 141-44.
[152] Ibid., pp. 146-50.

Crisis Moment Two: Morale in 1916

The experience of Britain's New Army volunteers has been covered more extensively, as has the Somme campaign. However, the soldiers' perceptions of crisis have not. The narrative of morale has often followed that of tactical developments.

The difficulties of training large numbers of volunteers and the problems of supply and logistics meant that units were trained with inadequate arms and were directed by officers with little experience.[153] It appears that the arrival of the Kitchener Armies on the Western Front correlated with increased rates of shell shock. John Keegan's description of the combatants on 1 July as 'bands of uniformed innocents' paints a similar picture.[154] Yet, the highest numbers of volunteers joined the army in 1914 as news of the bloody battles filtered back to Britain. Even if they did not comprehend the experience of war, these soldiers understood that it caused large numbers of casualties.[155] Those who went into battle on 1 July 1916 may not have been overwhelmed by unmatched expectations. However, Tim Travers has found evidence of an increasingly fragile spirit towards the end of July.[156] The horrors of mass death and acute crises caused by tactical failures could dampen spirits. As such, Paul Fussell believed that 'a terrible gloom overcame everyone at the end of 1916'.[157]

Yet, volunteers' training has been cast in a more positive light in recent years. At least it encouraged *esprit de corps*.[158] Gary Sheffield has argued that men ended the Somme campaign with increased confidence in their own military capabilities. It appears that British morale remained high at the end of 1916.[159] In fact, it had been bolstered by successful tactical innovations, evidence of Allied material superiority, and the sight of German prisoners.[160] Whilst fatigue was setting in towards the end of September, this (alongside the Tommies' humour) engendered resilience. Nonetheless, historian William Philpott has suggested that 'even if allied soldiers believed they were winning, their wish for peace remained strong, and their reasons for fighting on were

---

[153] Winter, *Death's Men*, p. 39; P. Simkins, *Kitchener's Army: The Raising of the New Armies* (Barnsley, 1988, 2007), pp. 212-320.
[154] Watson, *Enduring the Great War*, p. 147; Keegan, *The Face of Battle*, p. 226.
[155] Gregory, *The Last Great War*, pp. 44-5, 49; C. Pennell, *A Kingdom United: Popular Responses to the Outbreak of the First World War in Britain and Ireland* (Oxford, 2012), esp. pp. 144-146. Also P. Liddle, *The Soldier's War 1914-18* (London, 1988), pp. 18-19.
[156] T. Travers, *The Killing Ground: The British Army, the Western Front & the Emergence of Modern War* (Barnsley, 2009), p. 113.
[157] P. Fussell, *The Great War and Modern Memory* (Oxford, 1975, 2000), p. 14; A.J.P. Taylor, *The First World War: An Illustrated History* (London, 1963,1969), p. 140.
[158] M. Samuels, *Command or Control? Command, Training and Tactics in the British and German Armies, 1888-1918* (London, 1995, 2003), p. 120; I.F.W. Beckett and K. Simpson (eds.), *A Nation in Arms* (Barnsley, 1985, 2014), p. 235.
[159] Sheffield, *Forgotten Victory*, p. 186.
[160] Watson, *Enduring the Great War*, pp. 150-53.

shifting'.[161] The idea of a 'shift' in morale needs to be studied further. How were the men who survived the Somme Campaign coming to terms with war, and how did the environment, social groups, and soldiers' psychologies influence this process?

Crisis Moment Three: Morale in Winter 1917 to Spring 1918

The resilience of conscripts has been a matter of much debate, yet there have been few comprehensive study of the morale of these soldiers. If morale was low in winter 1917/1918, how did it recover during the period of retreat the following spring? Attempts to explain the collapse of the British front after 21 March 1918 (in the Fifth Army sector in particular) were made in its aftermath. James Edmonds noted that 'while there were instances of panic and disordered retreat ... the spirit of the troops remained strong'.[162] The distinction between chronic and acute crisis helps to explain this since Edmonds did concede that a lack of training had left the BEF unprepared for defensive warfare.[163]

However, historians have disagreed with this assessment.[164] Morale and spirit were crucial issues on 21 March 1918. Alexander Watson concluded that 'the Third Ypres had left the BEF despondent and lacking manpower'.[165] Both Martin Middlebrook and John Keegan believed this contributed to a collapse in the Fifth Army. While accepting difficulties were exacerbated by the heavy fog, Middlebrook suggested that as many as nine-tenths of the British units withdrew without strongly engaging the enemy.[166] While some battalions 'gave their all', Keegan pointed to high casualty rates amongst commanding officers as evidence of disorganisation and poor combat performance. These studies concluded that the reverses were caused by low morale and physical issues, such as exhaustion.[167]

In contrast, Lyn Macdonald underlined the success of German infiltration tactics and argued that units surrendered only when already overwhelmed.[168] Similarly, Peter Hart has put the fog, the inadequacy of British 'defence in depth', and German tactics at the heart of his analysis and emphasised the

---

[161] W. Philpott, *Bloody Victory: The Sacrifice on the Somme* (London, 2010), pp. 403, 410–11.
[162] J. Edmonds in A. Green, *Writing the Great War: Sir James Edmonds and the Official Histories 1915-1948* (London, 2003), p. 147.
[163] Green, *Writing the Great War*, pp. 145–159.
[164] Travers, *The Killing Ground*, p. 239.
[165] Watson, *Enduring the Great War*, p. 184. For the most up-to-date analysis of Third Ypres, see N. Lloyd, *Passchendaele: A New History* (London, 2017).
[166] M. Middlebrook, *The Kaiser's Battle* (Barnsley, 1978, 2009).
[167] J. Keegan, *The First World War* (London, 1998, 1999), p. 438. Also R. Holmes, *The Western Front* (London, 1999), p. 218.
[168] L. Macdonald, *To the Last Man: Spring 1918* (London, 1998).

resilience of the troops.[169] Jonathan Boff has argued that surrendering during this period was rational and based on an assessment of the tactical situation. In fact, statistics indicate that morale might have been more fragile during the Hundred Days Offensive.[170] Indeed, Alexander Watson has suggested that morale was in a process of rehabilitation during the autumn and winter of 1917 and that British soldiers retained a belief in ultimate victory.[171] Yet, David Stevenson has reorientated this debate, claiming that morale had not been entirely restored by 21 March, 'the real change came *after*'.[172] The German offensives might have 'galvanised the British'.[173] In fact, David Englander believed the spring battles might have *forestalled* a major mutiny.[174] If this is the case, then how and why did acute crisis forestall a collapse in morale? To resolve these questions, *Making Sense of the Great War* focuses on English infantrymen's mentalities and reaction to the war during these three case study moments.

ENGLISHNESS AND THE BRITISH ARMY

The focus on one of the four 'home nations' allows for a detailed analysis of national and local identity or patriotism in morale. Although Englishness and Britishness were closely intertwined in this period, men were driven by a 'defensive patriotism' that was frequently constructed around their specific 'English' identity.[175] Soldiers' patriotism was rhetorical and performative and did not focus on abstract notions of the state. Infantrymen drew primarily on visions of their homelands and specific peoples and places. 'Englishness' has

---

[169] P. Hart, *1918: A Very British Victory* (London, 2008, 2009), pp. 64-106.
[170] J. Boff, *Winning and Losing on the Western Front: The British Third Army and the Defeat of Germany in 1918* (Cambridge, 2012), pp. 92-122.
[171] Watson, *Enduring the Great War*, pp. 154-155.
[172] D. Stevenson, *With Our Backs to the Wall: Victory and Defeat in 1918* (London, 2014), pp. 267-268.
[173] Ibid.
[174] D. Englander, 'Discipline and Morale in the British Army, 1917-1918', in J. Horne (ed.), *State, Society and Mobilization in Europe during the First World War* (Cambridge, 1997), p. 141.
[175] For patriotism during the First World War, see N. Wouters and L. van Ypersele (eds.), *Nations, Identities and the First World War: Shifting Loyalties to the Fatherland* (London, 2018). For Britain specifically, W.J. Reader, *'At Duty's Call': A Study in Obsolete Patriotism* (Manchester, 1988); K. Robert, 'Gender, Class, and Patriotism: Women's Paramilitary Units in First World War Britain', *The International History Review*, Vol. 19, No. 1 (1997); S.R. Grayzel, '"The Outward Sign and Visible Sign of Her Patriotism": Women, Uniforms, and National Service during the First World War', *Twentieth Century British History*, Vol. 8, No. 2 (1997); P. Ward, '"Women of Britain Say Go": Women's Patriotism in the First World War', *Twentieth Century British History*, Vol. 12, No. 1 (2001); D. Monger, *Patriotism and Propaganda in First World War Britain: The National War Aims Committee and Civilian Morale* (Liverpool, 2012).

traditionally been seen as quintessentially rural and southern, but recent scholarship has highlighted that the local – be it rural or urban, northern or southern – was the bedrock of English national identity.[176] Men's powerful sense of duty was often fed by a desire to protect their communities and the landscapes of home. It helped them to justify their service and provided a coping mechanism as they retreated into the imagined homelands that gave substance to their visions of England.

Britain and its empire occupied the thoughts of some Britons in this era.[177] Jay Winter has suggested that imperial sentiment percolated through the classes, pointing to 'sentiments about nation and empire' being behind 'mass enlistment in the [mining] industry'.[178] Yet, identity is complex and life in early twentieth-century Britain existed 'at the intersection of many other identities as well: regional, class, occupational, religious and ethnic'.[179] It was their sense of Englishness that lay at the heart of these soldiers' sense of self and day-to-day it was the region, town, or village that plucked at their heartstrings.[180]

Men acknowledged that their local patriotism formed an important part of a patchwork of Britishness.[181] Regimental magazines and the soldiers (both officers and men) often used 'England' as a proxy for Britain.[182] They shared

---

[176] See especially, P. Mandler, 'Against "Englishness": English Culture and the Limits to Rural Nostalgia, 1850-1940', *Transactions of the Royal Historical Society*, Vol. 7 (December 1997), esp. p. 170. For the power of the local, T. Hulme, '"A Nation of Town Criers": Civic Publicity and Historical Pageantry in Inter-War Britain', *Urban History*, Vol. 44, No. 2 (May 2017), pp. 270-292. For parish identities, K.D.M. Snell, *Parish and Belonging: Community, Identity and Welfare in England and Wales, 1750-1950* (Cambridge, 2006).

[177] A. Marwick, *The Deluge: British Society and the First World War* (London, 1989), p. 309; I.F.W. Beckett, 'The Nation in Arms, 1914-18', in I.F.W. Beckett and K. Simpson (eds.), *A Nation in Arms: A Social Study of the British Army in the First World War* (Manchester, 1985), p. 5.

[178] Winter, *The Great War and the British People*, p. 35.

[179] Originally discussing women in Britain, see Gregory, *The Last Great War*, p. 291.

[180] P. Readman, *Storied Ground: Landscapes and the Shaping of English National Identity* (Cambridge, 2018) and 'The Place of the Past in English Culture c. 1890-1914', *Past & Present*, No. 186 (February 2005), pp. 147-199; R. Colls, *Identity of England* (Oxford, 2002), pp. 225-228; J. Winter, 'British National Identity and the First World War', in S. Green and C. Whiting (eds.), *The Boundaries of the State in Modern Britain* (Cambridge, 1996); J. Winter, 'Popular Culture in Wartime Britain', in A. Roshwald and R. Stites (eds.), *European Culture in the Great War; The Arts, Entertainment and Propaganda, 1914-1918* (Cambridge, 1999), p. 330.

[181] A. Mayhew, 'English Patriotism and the Implicit Nation: Homelands and Soldiers' National Identity during the Great War', *English Historical Review*, Forthcoming.

[182] For unit journals, see 'From the *Daily Dispatch*', *The Manchester Regiment Gazette*, Vol. 1, No. 7 (1 November 1914); 'The Brand of Cain', *The Gasper*, No. 21 (30 September 1916). For soldiers, see IWM Documents.11445: Brig. Gen. H.E. Trevor, HET/1 – Letter to Mother 2 September 1914; IWM Documents.10933: Capt. G.B. Donaldson, Letters to his Mother 8, 9, 16, 28 June and 4, 9 and 10 July 1916; IWM Documents.20933: Capt. R.E.M. Young, Letter to Constance 9 December 1916; IWM

some characteristics with other groups in the British Isles, and across the British Empire, but expressions of Britishness or imperialism were generally focused on a conscious 'othering' of the enemy, different groups, and different ethnicities.[183] Furthermore, the infrequency with which the Empire is actually mentioned in letters and diaries offers some support to Bernard Porter's argument that Britain was less self-consciously imperialist (at least amongst the working classes) than is often assumed.[184] Soldiers' journals demonstrated an ambivalent attitude towards events such as Empire Day and suggested that it was mainly senior officers that vocalised imperial patriotism.[185] Of course, Englishness was also outwardly projected, and drew on 'othering', but it was built upon a foundation of more intimate, inward-facing, tangible relationships with home and locality. The war may have even strengthened these ties in contrast to 'an imagined German stereotype, and the British army's entrenchment in France'.[186]

These were *subject* not *citizen* soldiers. Unlike its continental counterparts, the British Army did not play a foundational part in the definition of the state and citizenship, yet, in many ways it *was* a mirror for society and reflected the significance of the local. This played an important role in *esprit de corps* and in 1914 most infantry regiments continued to be affiliated with a city, county, or counties.[187] Despite the formation of a centralised Army Council and General Staff following the Esher Report in 1904, the British Army remained 'a collection of individual regiments and corps, each fiercely independent, with its own traditions and customs'.[188]

Throughout the eighteenth and nineteenth centuries, regiments had numerical signifiers denoting their place in the British Army's order of battle (an 'unofficial "league table" of exclusivity').[189] For example, in 1781 the 52nd Regiment of Foot received its Oxfordshire designation. Later, in 1803, they were renamed the 52nd Oxfordshire Light Infantry. The reforms of Secretary of State for War Edward Cardwell (1868–1874) and Hugh Childers (1881) saw

---

Documents.20211: F. Hubard, Letter to Mr and Mrs Underhill 8 December 1917; IWM Documents.20770: A.L. Collis, Diary 3 January 1918; IWM Documents.17029: Capt. A.J. Lord, Letter to his Father 26 April 1918.

[183] This does not mean the bond is not strong. See E. Hobsbawm, *Nations and Nationalism since 1780* (Cambridge, 1990), p. 91.

[184] B. Porter, *The Absent-Minded Imperialists: Empire, Society, and Culture in Britain* (Oxford, 2004).

[185] 'The Meaning of Empire', *The Broad Arrow*, Vol. 95 (26 November 1915), p. 603; 'Half an-Hour with the C.O.', *The Gasper*, Vol. 14 (15 March 1916), p. 6.

[186] S. Malvern, 'War Tourisms: "Englishness", Art and the First World War', *Oxford Art Journal*, Vol. 24, No. 1 (2001), p. 47.

[187] Ussishkin, *Morale*, pp. 68–69.

[188] Sheffield, *Leadership in the Trenches*, p. 3.

[189] Ibid.

further attempts to tie units to their local community.[190] In 1881, the 52nd merged with the 43rd (Monmouthshire) Regiment to become the Oxfordshire and Buckinghamshire Light Infantry. However, the two battalions fostered distinct identities. The 1st Bn. Ox and Bucks, who were captured after the Siege of Kut in 1916, self-identified as the 43rd and the 2nd Bn., who served on the Western Front, still proudly referred to themselves as the 52nd. Nevertheless, the regimental umbrella offered a sense of collective identity and eventually allowed New Army units to share in pre-existing regimental traditions and histories.

In 1914, the six regiments focused on in this book retained a strong imprint of their assumed place of origin and celebrated their institutional past. The Border Regiment nominally recruited from sparsely populated Cumberland and Westmoreland; the Devonshire Regiment's depots lay across this predominantly rural county in the South West; the Manchester Regiment drew many of its men from the bustling conurbation of Southern Lancashire; the Oxfordshire and Buckinghamshire Light Infantry raised its units in the old cities and agricultural areas of these counties in the South East; the Royal Fusiliers were based in London; and the Royal Warwickshire Regiment contained men from across the Midland county's cities and countryside. Tellingly, these units identified themselves as English (as opposed to Irish, Scottish, or Welsh), and rarely as British.[191]

During the early months of the war 'local patriotism ... played an important role in drawing men to join Territorial and New Army units'.[192] Territorial divisions were generally regionally affiliated, and most New Army battalions were incorporated into existing regiments. Pals' battalions were purposefully built around the foci of community, factory, sports team, or class group.[193] Social divisions were significant; it was often 'less about who you served with, but much more obviously about who you didn't serve with'.[194]

Larger military units were also sometimes built around particular regions. Most famously, the 16th (Irish) and 36th (Ulster) Divisions were politically and geographically affiliated, and soldiers might have felt as great an allegiance to their division as they did to their battalion and regiment. There were also

---

[190] D. French, *Military Identities: The Regimental System, the British Army and the British People* (Oxford, 2005); D. Chandler and I. Beckett (eds.), *The Oxford Illustrated History of the British Army* (Oxford, 1994).

[191] TNA WO 95/2339/1: War Diary 16th Battalion Manchester Regiment, 'Address by the CO to the officers, NCOs and men of the 19th Bn. Manchester Regt. Feb. 1918' . Also Lt. Col. C. Wheeler (ed.), *Memorial Record of the Seventh (Service) Battalion The Oxfordshire and Buckinghamshire Light Infantry* (Oxford, 1921), p. 5; G.K. Rose, *The Story of the 2/4th Oxfordshire and Buckinghamshire Light Infantry* (Oxford, 1920), p. 74.

[192] McCartney, *Citizen Soldiers*, p. 57.

[193] Ussishkin, *Morale*, p. 97.

[194] Gregory, *Last Great War*, p. 78.

Scottish and Welsh divisions, while the 18th (Eastern) and 50th (Northumbrian) Divisions point to regional structures in predominantly English divisions, too. The 56th (London) Division fostered a particularly strong sense of common identity and produced its own soldiers' newspaper, *The Dagger or "London in the Line"*. This particular identity was by its infantry brigades, which were populated by Territorial soldiers from the London Regiment. Yet, brigade transfers between divisions, not to mention the reality of daily life, meant that it was towards smaller military structures – sections, platoons, companies, battalions, and regiments – that men felt their strongest and most enduring bonds.

The increasing need for new drafts and conscription did not entirely undermine units' regional and local identities.[195] Historian Helen McCartney revised conclusions about the 'nationalisation' of recruitment during the war.[196] Manpower demands necessitated centralised recruitment and a new 'strand-feed' system was introduced after 1916. It saw the United Kingdom divided into six command districts. However, the administrative structures of these districts allowed many units to retain some demographic homogeneity and men of similar regional backgrounds. Furthermore, regiments based in larger cities could rely on their own pool of men, though regiments from smaller urban areas or rural counties had to incorporate drafts from elsewhere. After November 1917, recruiting powers were 'passed from the Army Council to the Ministry of National Service'. Recruiting areas were 'redrawn, utilizing regional boundaries' and created 'more cohesive sets' of county recruiting pools. Telllingly, Mark Connelly's study of the East Kent Regiment found that 'a core of East Kent men ... was retained throughout the war' and locals continued to think of the regiment as their 'boys'. Even 'as conscripts began to flow in, the majority came from the south-east, which at least allowed a rough geographical unity to survive'.[197] The same was generally true of the six regiments studied here.[198]

****

How did soldiers perceive the world around them? How did they make sense of war? They created meaningful narratives. The book tackles this process thematically through three sections: 'The Environment', 'Social Groups', and 'Crisis and Morale'. The first of these focuses on the physical world. The second looks at men's perceptions of duty and explains how this was informed by their relationship with both civilian and military social groups. The men's

---

[195] See Appendix I.
[196] McCartney, *Citizen Soldiers*, pp. 62–66; I.R. Bet-El, *Conscripts: Forgotten Men of the Great War* (Stroud, 2009), p. 41.
[197] Connelly, *Steady the Buffs!*, p. 233.
[198] See Appendix.

psychologies are interwoven throughout this book, but the third section foregrounds these processes by exploring the role of hope and men's sensemaking. If any moment can be viewed as true crisis for morale, it was late 1917 and early 1918, which is the focus of the final chapter. For a short time, men feared that the war was unwinnable as battle lost its meaning. However, this was overcome, and the German spring offensives changed men's sensemaking.

Throughout the war, the interrelationship between men's physical environment, social groups, and their own psychologies allowed them to deflect crisis, construe their experiences as meaningful or constructive, and endure the war. Chapter 1 explores the ways in which men familiarised the physical environment of the Western Front, normalised it, and found meaning in their surroundings. Chapter 2 analyses the impact of weather on morale, arguing that this subsumed other concerns and changed men's perspectives on war during other seasons. The next two chapters outline the interaction of social groups and soldiers' frames of reference. Chapter 3 investigates how concepts of duty influenced soldiers' actions and interpretation of the conflict, while Chapter 4 reveals how men's perceptions and dreams of England became a coping mechanism. Next, Chapter 5 shows how visions of peace were sustaining and inextricably linked to victory. It suggests that the soldiers' morale hinged on their perceptions of victorious peace and battle. Finally, Chapter 6 explores battle's fading fortunes and how 'acute' crises (namely the German offensives) were experienced differently to 'chronic' ones. It uses institutional documents to analyse the period stretching from Passchendaele to the German spring offensives.

While morale was at a low ebb, the reverses in March 1918 rested on the paucity of training during the winter of 1917–1918 and units' limited understanding of 'defence in depth'. They did not have the tools to respond to the German attacks. Yet, this acute crisis also restored battle's meaning as semi-mobile warfare returned and battalions won small (but personally significant) victories as they withdrew. Ultimately, this book underlines the importance of human adaptability and argues that the ability to construe events constructively, to have goals, and see clear pathways to these goals, helped English infantrymen to endure the Western Front in 1914–1918. They were able to deflect crisis for as long as victorious peace seemed certain and worthwhile.

PART I

The Environment

1

Familiarising the Western Front
Attachment to Belgium and France

The alien, repetitive, and shocking sights and sounds in Belgium and France contributed to infantrymen's sense of chronic crisis. Shellfire scarred the world around them; human and natural history were destroyed, sometimes in front of their very eyes. Nevertheless, soldiers – even if appalled – were able to familiarise, normalise, and become attached to what confronted them.

The Dagger, a soldiers' newspaper published by the 56th (London) Division, published an article in late 1918 playing on the often unconscious processes by which men internalised the war zone.[1] The author imagined that he had just arrived home on leave. As he alighted at Victoria Station, 'he suddenly lost his memory, or rather that part of it which covered his pre-war experience. He remembered only the life and surroundings of the line'. He had disembarked in a 'large town called London' (a name he had had last heard in Arras) and surveyed his surroundings with a professional eye: 'The trenches, strong points, dug-outs, wire and so on ... are maintained and organised to a point of excellence' and 'discipline too becomes a reality here'.[2] The line began with a string of outposts along the river, which had 'a breastwork of solid granite' and were a 'comfortable height to fire over'. Worryingly, the defenders seemed 'idle'.[3] As he moved towards the rear, he found himself in the support line. This weaved its way down 'PICCADILLY TRENCH', before turning onto 'FLEET SUPPORT'. 'OXFORD TRENCH and HOLBORN TRENCH' formed the reserve line. Tube stations provided 'admirably equipped ... dug-outs', while 'lorry-jumping is here officially recognised'. Food of unusually high quality was available in 'CARLTON in HAYMARKET Communication Trench' and he found 'plentiful' water at a 'gigantic' water-point in 'TRAFALGAR SQUARE' and a smaller bronze one in 'PICCADILLY CIRCUS'. Moving further back, he encountered 'BRITISH MUSEUM', which was one of largest of the salvage dumps he had ever seen. Apparently 'scrounging parties are detailed to clear areas literally thousands of miles away'. Pleasantly surprised, he noted that 'evidently the line here is very, very

---

[1] Cinq Neuf, 'On the London Front', *The Dagger* (1 November 1918), p. 26.
[2] Ibid.
[3] Ibid., p. 27.

quiet' yet suspected that this had 'lulled the troops hereabouts into a false sense of security'. Consequently, he decided to 'patrol rather a nasty wood called BATTERSEA PARK'.[4]

The Western Front had become so familiar that this officer's mental map of the frontlines was transposed onto London with this satirical story pointing to the relationship that had developed between many men and their environment. This chapter describes how this came to be, and how these processes influenced soldiers' morale and sensemaking. It focuses on three central features of men's cognition: familiarisation, habituation, and attachment.

Their immediate physical surroundings dominated soldiers' present. George Mosse believed that service encouraged 'a heightened awareness of nature' and that imagined landscapes masked 'the reality of war'.[5] Men's experiences generally encouraged familiarisation with the world around them, which in turn cultivated meaning, created attachment, deflected crisis, and fostered endurance. This did not leave men ignorant of Belgium and France's horrors, but it made them more bearable, something that was aided by psychological habituation and normalisation. Men even developed an attachment to the places they inhabited. They were not passive inhabitants of the war zone. Instead, they explored it as tourists; traversed it by foot, road, and rail; invested it with personal and collective memories; became habituated to its more menacing characteristics; and spent time considering what their physical environment *meant*.

The environment has formed an increasingly important part of studies of modern war.[6] Even in twentieth-century conflicts, nature continued to play a central role and landscapes became actors of sorts. Tait Keller has revealed the ways in which the mountains conferred heroic stature onto soldiers serving in the Alps during the Great War.[7] British soldiers also developed a relationship with the physical world.[8] Combatants were revolted by the violation of the natural and human world, but trench warfare also saw the earth become a kind of home. Landscapes also provided a protective veil through which men interpreted the war.[9] An intimacy emerged from men's physical contact with their comrades and their surroundings.[10] The systems, processes, and patterns

---

[4] Ibid.
[5] Mosse, *Fallen Soldiers*, p. 107.
[6] C. Pearson, *Mobilizing Nature: The Environmental History of War and Militarization in Modern France* (Manchester, 2012).
[7] T. Keller, *Apostles of the Alps: Mountaineering and Nation Building in Germany and Austria* (Chapel Hill, 2016); Keller, 'The Mountains Roar', pp. 253–274.
[8] Ashworth, *Trench Warfare*, pp. 14–15; Jones, 'The Psychology of Killing', pp. 229–231. See also P.H. Hoffenberg, 'Landscape, Memory and the Australian War Experience, 1915-18', *Journal of Contemporary History*, Vol. 36 No. 1 (January 2001), pp. 111–131.
[9] Leed, *No Man's Land*, esp. pp. 37, 72, 105.
[10] Das, *Touch and Intimacy*, esp. ch. 2.

of soldiers' lives behind the lines helped men to develop relationships with the physical world and the civilians who shared these spaces.[11] Tommy's sense of place within the landscapes of Belgium and France was a key aspect of his 'endurance' and helps to explain 'why soldiers [chose to] fight'. By imbuing the Western Front with deep meaning, soldiers were able to adapt, accept, and find agency in their war experience. 'It was', Ross Wilson has argued, 'through the association with the landscapes which had been created by war, and the weapons and equipment of the conflict, that individuals took on and largely accepted their role within the army'.[12]

As the war transformed the natural world, another, less visible, process was taking place. Belgium and France were reconceptualised as trench lines were dug, and the BEF became a semi-permanent presence. The Western Front was anglicised. As many as 10,500 new trench names emerged as the war took on the character of a siege. These helped men to internalise an alternative map of northern France and Belgium. It became at once familiar, evocative, 'enchanted and mythical'.[13] Historian Chris Ward believes that these were 'a means by which immigrants asserted their presence'.[14] While these men never saw themselves as migrants, the towns and countryside were re-cast by the BEF's soldiers.[15] This could also occur in subtler forms, such as through the cultivation of allotments.[16] Tommy's material culture offers further evidence of his agency and character.[17]

This chapter explores the relationships that formed between infantrymen's morale and the Western Front. Individual and collective familiarisation took place. Men's engagement with the world was fed by psychological processes such as attachment.[18] Attachment theory explores the development of 'emotional

---

[11] Gibson, *Behind the Front*, pp. 53, 155. For other discussions of the area of British administration, A. Dowdall, 'Civilians in the Combat Zone: Allied and German Evacuation Policies at the Western Front, 1914-1918', *First World War Studies*, Vol. 6, No. 3 (2015), pp. 239-255. For sexual relationships, Gibson, 'Sex and Soldiering', 539-579; C. Makepeace, 'Male Heterosexuality and Prostitution during the Great War: British Soldiers' Encounters with *Maisons Tolérées*', *Cultural and Social History*, Vol. 9, No. 1 (2012), pp. 65-83; Grayzel, 'Mothers, Marraines, and Prostitutes', pp. 66-82; Bourke, *Dismembering the Male*, pp. 155-156.
[12] Wilson, *Landscapes of the Western Front*, p. 218.
[13] Chasseaud, *Rats Alley*, p. 47.
[14] Ward, *Living on the Western Front*, p. 92.
[15] Gibson, *Behind the Front*, esp. pp. 188-221.
[16] Watson, *Enduring the Great War*, p. 24.
[17] P. Cornish and N.J. Saunders, *Bodies in Conflict* and *Modern Conflict and the Senses: Killer Instincts?* (London, 2016); Becker, 'Le front militaire et les occupations de la Grande Guerre', pp. 193-204.
[18] J. Bowlby, 'The Nature of the Child's Tie to His Mother', *International Journal of Psycho-Analysis*, Vol. 39 (1958), pp. 350-373 and *Attachment and Loss. Vol. 1: Attachment* (New York, 1973).

and functional connections between place and people'.[19] The bond between infantrymen and their environment was central to his sensemaking and helped individuals to cope with an array of the chronic crises they encountered.

****

Most English infantrymen adjusted to the Western Front. This was an organic process aided by predictable patterns of rotation in and out of the trenches as well as movement across Belgium and France. These changes of scene alleviated some of the pressures of service and allowed soldiers to begin familiarising their environment. This continued throughout the war, and many English infantrymen felt that they were occupying a recognisable world. Except in the most churned battlefields, they inhabited a landscape that was identifiable. The troops chose to explore, repurpose, and reconceptualise it.

Their lives were not limited to trenches. During the war, the 123 battalions that served in I through IV Division between 1914 and 1918 spent approximately 46 per cent of their time in the frontlines and 20 per cent of days fighting.[20] This does not mean that they were engaged in combat of the sort witnessed on the Somme or at Passchendaele so regularly. The remainder of their time was spent in camps and billets. Even at the front, units could expect to spend between a quarter and half of their time in reserve or rest billets several miles behind the trenches.[21] Processes of rotation helped soldiers cope with the pressures of service and nurtured familiarisation. Servicemen often returned to the same places. They sometimes spent months in a particular area of Belgium or France, be it along the coastline stretching from Dunkirk to Le Havre, in Belgian and French Flanders, Artois, or Picardy.

Journeys on the Western Front: Familiarisation, Exposure, and Exploration

The British line was not unchanging. During the war, it grew and crept southwards from the channel ports. Battalions were tied to areas depending on that year's military strategy, and each sector was known for its 'nuances and

---

[19] H. Hashemnezhad, A.A. Heidari and P.M. Hoseini, '"Sense of Place" and "Place Attachment": A Comparative Study', *International Journal of Architecture and Urban Development*, Vol. 3, No. 1 (2013), p. 5.

[20] R. Grayson, 'A Life in the Trenches? The Use of *Operation War Diary* and Crowdsourcing Methods to Provide an Understanding of the British Army's Day-To-Day Life on the Western Front', *British Journal of Military History*, Vol. 2, No. 2 (2016), esp. p. 174.

[21] P. Simkins, 'Soldiers and Civilians: Billeting in Britain and France', in Beckett and Simpson, *A Nation in Arms*, p. 178.

specificities'.[22] In 1914, after the war became static, the BEF's line stretched only twenty-four miles from the north-east of Kemmel to east of Festubert – with French or Belgian troops plugging a few holes here and there. On the eve of the Battle of the Somme, it had grown to over eighty miles long and extended in a 'continuous [line] from north to south'. It started at Boesinghe (just north of Ypres) and ended at Maricourt on the banks of the river Somme. By 20 March 1918, it was 123 miles long. Beginning at the south-west corner of Houthulst Forest in Belgium, it passed through Barisis in Picardy to the St. Gobain Railway on the Aisne. Following the spring offensives, the line contracted and expanded alongside patterns of retreat and advance.[23]

Some parts of the line were renowned for being 'quieter' and less dangerous than others.[24] A few areas (such as the Ypres Salient) were occupied by the British for most of the war and bore a strong imprint of the BEF. Behind the frontlines, there was an 'immense infrastructure' comprising of 'hospitals, barracks, training camps, ammunition dumps, artillery parks, and telephone networks, as well as military roads and canals, but pre-eminently it meant railways'.[25] Some men arrived in these places while they still retained traces of their original form. Witnessing their conversion into 'industrial wastelands' was a traumatic experience.[26] It is no surprise, then, that peace saw an international movement to 'repair ruined lands' and to 'mask the death and destruction' with 'lush lands' that represented 'innocence, peace, and return to normalcy'.[27]

While this was a relatively limited front (especially compared to the vast expanses in the East), local geography varied and influenced the character of the warfare. Landscapes and geology could also inform soldiers' perceptions of the conflict more generally. The environments soldiers encountered sometimes acted as a foil for their emotions. In Flanders, for example, the water table necessitated the building of breastworks above the ground while, in the south, where the line extended through Picardy, men were forced to dig down into the soil itself. Loos' old coal mines and slag heaps were evidence of an industry that, in peace, helped to feed the French economy but now offered defenders an excellent strong-point and made battle an even more unpleasant experience for the attacker.[28] Around Arras, historic quarrying provided

---

[22] S. Audoin-Rouzeau, 'Combat and Tactics', in J. Winter (ed.), *Cambridge History of The First World War: Volume II: The State* (Cambridge, 2014), p. 161.

[23] 'Part XXII: The British Line in France', in HM Stationery Office, *Statistics of the Military Effort of the British Empire* (London, 1922), p. 639.

[24] Ashworth, *Trench Warfare, 1914–1918*, p. 15.

[25] D. Stevenson, *1914–1918: The History of the First World War* (London, 2004), p. 182.

[26] T. Keller, 'Mobilizing Nature for the First World War: An Introduction', in Tucker et al., *Environmental Histories*, p. 5.

[27] Ibid., p. 14.

[28] 'Battle of Loos', *Highland Light Infantry Chronicle*, Vol. XVI, No. 1 (1 January 1916), pp. 21–25.

soldiers with cavernous protection within the limestone itself. A subterranean life might have been safer, but it held its own traumas. In 1917, those units that were posted to the Yser Front served around Nieuport and spent much of their time staring out into the North Sea or surveying the river for an enemy crossing.[29] Some regions offered protection; others (particularly around Ypres) provided little to help servicemen survive. The red-brown mud found around the city also seemed to take on the quality of blood. In poor conditions, the heavily manured soil was also the perfect habitat for infectious organisms like *Clostridium*, which caused gas gangrene. Yet, mud was not omnipresent. Behind the lines (especially in better weather), there were opportunities to retreat into relatively unscarred countryside and settlements.

The war was a journey, and this fed an organic process of familiarisation. Most men's perceptions of Belgium and France were filtered through personal experience. It was what they saw, heard, and smelt that mattered as they built a picture of the Western Front. Their first trip across the Channel was dominated by anticipation and imagination; for those returning from leave or recuperation, it was tainted by trepidation. For many, this was their first international journey, but even the well-travelled sensed that this was a new passage in their lives.[30] Regular soldiers were accustomed to overseas service, but the cross-Channel voyage was a symbol of change.[31] Men glimpsed their sister service as Royal Navy destroyers accompanied traffic and were made aware that they were entering another nation's territory as their ships were inspected by French vessels, which provided them with their first opportunity to cheer their allies.[32]

Charles Dwyer spent several days at sea. When his boat hove to off Saint Nazaire, he and his comrades spent time staring at the novel building frontages.[33] Their first sight of land was met with 'a thrill of genuine excitement'.[34] Other men had less comfortable crossings and complained about the lack of refreshment or food. Many became nervous in bad weather.[35] Frederick William Child's trip from Southampton to Le Havre was a prolonged affair. The rough seas were compounded by embarkation delays in England and a long wait before being allowed to alight in France.[36] Child became very seasick in the cramped hold of the transport ship. However, when the

---

[29] TNA WO 95/3144/6: War Diary 2/5th Manchester Regt. July–September 1917.
[30] 'The 48th Regiment in the Great European War. A Brief Survey of the Operations in Which the Regiment Was Engaged', *The Talavera Magazine*, Vol. 1 No. 1 (1 January 1920), p. 3.
[31] J. Lewis-Stempel, *Six Weeks: The Short and Gallant Life of the British Officer in the First World War* (London, 2010), pp. 72–73.
[32] MR 1/17/34: Letter from Lt. Col. F.H. Dorling to his Wife 24 August 1914.
[33] IWM Documents.16676: C. Dwyer, Diary 3–5 September 1914.
[34] 'In Foreign Parts', *The Red Feather*, Vol. I, No. 4 (1 June 1915), p. 69.
[35] IWM Documents.14710: R.D. Sheffield, Letter to Father 9 November 1914.
[36] SOFO Box 16 Item 42: F.W. Child, Diary 18–20 November 1916.

opportunity arose, he walked and 'watched the ships go by + the hills + fires in the distance ... The scenery was lovely'.[37]

Soldiers' first steps on French soil were often in one of the ports facing the English Channel. The cobbled streets offered an uneven surface on which to regain their 'land legs', but this was a relatively peaceful introduction to the war. These bases maintained a near-constant British presence throughout the conflict – though sites such as Le Havre were briefly evacuated during the German advances of 1914. Familiarity was bred by the strong imprint Britain left on these places, some of which almost became BEF settlements. Some individuals felt they were remarkably 'English'.[38] However, in August 1914, the crowds of civilians welcoming the soldiers also underlined the 'foreignness' of the country.[39] Nevertheless, even in 1914, the majority of people that R.D. Sheffield encountered were from England.[40] One soldier had already come to consider Calais in the same breath as England and 'Hyde Park'.[41] A near-constant flow of soldiers passed through Boulogne, Calais, Le Havre and Rouen.[42] They quickly became semi-permanent centres of army logistics, and thousands of soldiers were based and billeted there.[43] So well-trodden were these routes that Lt. Frederic Anstruther formulated a code through which he could inform his father in which of these ports he had arrived.[44] In Le Havre, the British Army became a central feature of civic life. 1st Base HQ was established at Quai Transatlantique, while other headquarters, directorships, services, and supply depots requisitioned other buildings throughout the town. It became hard to believe that one was not in the United Kingdom. The same was true elsewhere. A post-war soldiers' travel guide noted that:

> During the war Boulogne became practically an English city; that is to say, a very large proportion of its inhabitants were British. There were huge rest camps for troops going on leave and returning from leave, situated near the harbour; hospitals sprang up in every direction, and were

---

[37] Ibid., Diary 19 November 1916.
[38] A. Mayhew, 'British Expeditionary Force Vegetable Shows, Allotment Culture, and Life Behind the Lines during the Great War', *Historical Journal*, Vol. 64, No. 5 (Dec. 2021), esp. pp. 1360–1361.
[39] IWM Con Shelf: Postcard Signed by 'The Mademoiselle from Armentieres', Extract from local paper, perhaps the *Bucks Advertiser*, regarding the experience of Pte J.T. Greenwood, Oxfordshire and Buckinghamshire Light Infantry, published 24 October 1914.
[40] IWM Documents.14710: R.D. Sheffield, Letter to Father 9 November 1914.
[41] IWM Documents.8631: Diary of an Unidentified Soldier of the [2nd Battalion] Border Regiment, 25 December 1914.
[42] IWM Documents.20770: A.L. Collis, Diary 3 and 19 January 1918.
[43] IWM Documents.8674: Pocket Diary 1914, August–September 1914; SOFO Box 16 Item 42: F.W. Child, Diary 19 November 1916.
[44] IWM Documents.9364: Lt. Frederic Anstruther, Letter to his Father 25 February 1915.

perpetually full of wounded soldiers; thousands of officers and clerks were employed upon the duties connected with a huge base.[45]

In 1916, R.E.P. Stevens reported that '[one] cannot realise we have arrived in another country everything seems so English'. Stevens found that he was 'only reminded the place was a French port by the names on the shops'. The surrounding countryside even looked like England.[46] These were pleasant places to pass some time while not on duty. M.F. Gower reported,

> Havre is quite a decent town with its gay shops and cafes, shady avenues of trees, gardens and squares and is quite lively especially after 6 p.m. when the cafes are open to British troops. It is very pleasant sitting in the latter sipping harmless beer, the only drawback are the number of beggars who come in and sing horrible songs thro' their noses.[47]

Men also consumed less 'harmless' alcohol and embraced the opportunity to satiate their carnal desires.[48]

Parts of the coast were within easy reach and offered the chance for a brief holiday. Paris Plage was particularly popular. R.E.P. Stevens noted that it was 'picturesque and brought to my mind a picture I once saw of the Pied Piper of Hamelin'.[49] It was in these Channel Ports that soldiers also felt closest to home as they stared across the breaking surf towards Blighty and consumed up-to-date newspapers from England.[50] By 1918, these hives of activity also reflected the war's international character. The sight of a large contingent of 'Chinese and Black men' in Le Havre (alongside the cafés) reminded H.T. Madders that he was no longer in England.[51]

The towns also became familiar through repeated exposure and activity. Soldiers spent long periods of time resting, training, or recuperating from injuries in these places.[52] In fact, their suburbs and surrounding countryside were transformed by the war. Sprawling networks of British rest and depot camps, hospitals, prisons, Prisoner of War (POW) camps, and administrative offices grew outside many of these settlements. Between them were allotment

---

[45] Lt. Col. T.A. Lowe, *The Western Battlefields: A Guide to the British Line* (London, 1920), p. 6.
[46] IWM Documents.12521: R.E.P. Stevens, Diary 2, 6 and 12 November 1916.
[47] IWM Documents.255: M.F. Gower, Letter to Flo 26 June 1917.
[48] IWM Documents.7453: Col. L.H.M. Westropp, Memoir, p. 61.
[49] IWM Documents.12521: R.E.P. Stevens, Diary 13 November 1916.
[50] IWM Documents.7953: Pte. F.G. Senyard, Letter to Wife 14 December 1916.
[51] IWM Documents.11289: H.T. Madders, Diary 29 March 1918. See Wilson, *Landscapes of the Western Front*, p. 92; X. Guoqi, *Strangers on the Western Front: Chinese Workers in the Great War* (London, 2011).
[52] IWM Documents.20770: A.L. Collis, Diary 18 December 1916–1 January 1917; SOFO Box 16 Item 30 3/4/J3/9: Lt. C.T. O'Neill, Diary 1–25 January 1918.

gardens built and maintained by soldiers.[53] There were church tents and a wide array of different trades – carpenters, tailors, shipwrights, coopers, and bakers, and an array of other 'support troops'.[54] Peculiarly British cultural pursuits also took place here. Sports and theatrical activities were common to nearly every part of the rear zone.[55] Nevertheless, the units posted to these bases permanently were blessed with theatre and music hall troupes that had more time to practice and buildings permanently set aside as theatres. The Royal Garrison Artillery Base Depot at Le Havre even maintained a complement of talented professional footballers.[56] More uniquely, in 1917 and 1918, the depot commander of Le Havre sought to improve yields in the soldiers' allotments by holding a vegetable competition and show in the city's Jardin St. Roche.[57]

Familiarity was not necessarily always positive. Training camps were rarely the location of soldiers' happiest memories. The most famous of these was the 'Bull Ring' at Étaples, where men were confined to a site on the outskirts of the town.[58] It began life in 1914 when new drafts were billeted there for the final stage of their training.[59] By 1916, it had grown exponentially with some 3,000 men training there each day.[60] 'Bull-ring' drill was strenuous but also became more specialised as the war went on.[61] The facilities diversified: there were shooting ranges, mock trenches and battlefields, live-fire exercises, gas simulations, and lectures that sought to teach men 'how to behave and what to avoid in France [and, presumably, Belgium]'.[62] It might have offered a first taste of warfare, but this experience fuelled common grievances. P.R. Hall recalled that the instructors were particularly hostile; the treatment of the men was a 'disgrace to the army and to GHQ'. Hall was left with the impression of a 'dirty and uncared for' place.[63] R.E.P. Stevens felt that the training indicated that 'they [GHQ] don't know what to do with us'.[64] It is unsurprising this was

---

[53] 'A Modest Beginning', *The Spud*, No. 1 (2 March 1918), 1 and 'Play for Your Side', *Sport & Spuds*, '20th Course' (27 August 1918), p. 1.
[54] 'Extract from "Le Havre" March 25th A.D. 2015', *The Hanger Herald*, No. 7 (1 April 1915), pp. 1–2.
[55] Fuller, *Troop Morale*, pp. 72–133.
[56] BL Tab.11748.aa.4.65: Charity Football Match Programme 25 November 1917.
[57] BL Tab.11748.aa.4.1-122: First World War, Misc. Leaflets, Programmes, Documents 90–113.
[58] IWM Documents.15268: E. Grindley, Memoir, p. 4; LIDDLE/WW1/GS/0313: Pte. C. Clark, Memoir, p. 25.
[59] IWM Documents.11442: Lt. Col. K.F.B. Tower, Memoir, p. 5.
[60] IWM Documents.1708: Lt. W.B. Medlicott, Diary – Book 2, p. 7.
[61] 'S.O.S. Lights', *24th Battalion Journal*, No. 1 (16 September 1916), p. 9.
[62] IWM Documents.2619: L. Wilson, Memoir, p. 18. Institutional documents quite frequently only refer to 'France' when discussing the Western Front.
[63] IWM Documents.1690: P.R. Hall, Memoir, p. 30.
[64] IWM Documents.12521: R.E.P. Stevens, Diary 13–18 November 1916.

the location of the BEF's worst wartime mutiny in September 1917.⁶⁵ Despite this, though, in 1918 young conscripts were still arriving at Étaples and other camps for 'toughening up' that men reported was 'general fooling' that 'nearly broke our hearts'.⁶⁶

However, Étaples was not universally despised. 2nd Lt. W.J. Lidsey had a better experience in November 1916. Detailed for specialist training alongside the Royal Flying Corps, he stayed in billets that were much better than those of the infantry. The experience was improved further by a happy carriage ride to training alongside a young French woman.⁶⁷ It was not only one long drilling exercise. The camp, like others in Belgium and France, also catered for other pastimes. There were 'hospitals – stores – main roads constructed cobbled – goods station – recreation huts in large numbers, YMCA, Scottish churches, church army & huts by private people – canteens Cinema – concerts in YMCA & Other huts'.⁶⁸ Despite these diversions, conversation was often directed towards 'events ... "up the line"'.⁶⁹ Unpleasant though they may have been, these experiences were a tentative introduction to the Western Front and kick-started an institutionally driven process of familiarisation and normalisation.⁷⁰

Men moved up the line from these camps. Much of the movement necessitated route marches, which offered offered a tiring but intimate introduction to Belgium and France. Some men enjoyed the exercise, and others found the experience of 'passing through so many villages and towns' diverting. The sights (materiel, places, and people) helped them to make sense of the war's progress beyond their unit.⁷¹ The experience of marching could also help to solidify *esprit de corps*. Men sang as they marched and used the lyrics to express a common identity and to 'grouse'.

However, journeys were often arduous. In 1914, nearly all travel was done on foot. This could prove problematic for morale. The 4th Bn. Royal Fusiliers reported that during a 'freezing' night march on 20 November, the men's discipline had been 'very bad'.⁷² They faced a similar problem on 30 November when many men fell out during a march to

---

⁶⁵ LIDDLE/WW1/GS/0313: Pte. C. Clark, Memoir, p. 25.
⁶⁶ LIDDLE/WW1/ADD/104: Pte. A.G. Old, Diary 2–6 April 1918; IWM Documents.16824: R.C.A. Frost, Memoir, p. 1.
⁶⁷ IWM Documents.16504: 2nd Lt. W.J. Lidsey, Diary 23 November 1916.
⁶⁸ RFM.ARC.3032: L/Cpl. C. White, Diary 4 January 1917.
⁶⁹ Ibid.
⁷⁰ Strachan, 'Training, Morale and Modern War', p. 216.
⁷¹ IWM Documents.16676: C. Dwyer, Diary 4–11 October 1914; IWM Documents.12819: Maj. J.S. Knyvett, Diary 24 October 1914; MR 2/17/57: 2nd Lt. Frederick Thomas Kearsley Woodworth, Extract from F.T.K. Woodworth's Diary. 1914–1918 – 25 March 1918; LIDDLE/WW1/GS/0583: 2nd Lt. Sydney Frankenburg, Diary 27 October 1918.
⁷² TNA WO 95/1431/1: War Diary 4th Bn. Royal Fusiliers, 20 November 1914.

Westoure.[73] Between 24 August and 5 September 1914, the 2nd Bn. Ox and Bucks marched 178 miles with only one day's rest.[74] By 1916, units were still spending between eleven and twelve days on the move between October and December.[75] Marching remained a central feature of the infantrymen's experience. In 1917, a unit shifting from Neuve Chapelle to Arras could still expect several days of tiring travel. Furthermore, during the chaos of the British retreat after 21 March 1918, battalions spent over a week retreating (and fighting) on foot.[76] Nevertheless, marching helped soldiers to become personally acquainted with the Western Front.

In later years, soldiers benefited from the BEF's more sophisticated logistical apparatus. Lorries, boats, and trains transported servicemen and offered them a different vision of Belgium and France. Some men journeyed on 'enormous barges' along the canals that connected towns and camps.[77] Travel in the ubiquitous 'cattle trucks' was less enjoyable. These train journeys, which sometimes lasted all night, left men tired, hungry, and thirsty. Some soldiers feared that they were more vulnerable to shellfire in these slow-moving locomotives.[78] There was also a 'sinister suggestion of equivalence' in the painted legend 'Hommes 40; Chevaux 8'.[79] However, W. Vernon concluded that while 'we don't have a very pleasant ride on the train [it is ...] still it is better than marching with a full pack'.[80] Many individuals focused on the scenery that passed them by (if travelling in daylight hours). Squatting on the floor of the cramped carriages, men peered through 'the [carriage's] grill'.[81] The slow pace of movement allowed them to observe the landscapes passing by, which sometimes provided views of unscarred countryside – a welcome vision of peace for men returning from the trenches.[82]

The patterns of rotation meant that divisional or brigade rest camps became familiar waypoints. Yet, rest was rare amidst the fatigues, working parties, and training programmes that took place in such places. When given the opportunity, though, soldiers would walk to explore and unwind. The chance to wander

---

[73] Ibid., 30 November 1914.
[74] TNA WO 95/1348: War Diary 2nd Bn. Oxfordshire and Buckinghamshire Light Infantry, Extract from the Diary of Lt. Col. H.R. Davies, Commanding 52nd Light Infantry.
[75] October through December 1916 in War Diaries of TNA WO 95/1655/1: 2nd Bn. Border Regiment [16 days]; WO 95/1565/1: 1st Bn. Devonshire Regiment [13 days]; WO 95/1564/2: 2nd Bn. Manchester Regiment [8 days]; 2nd Bn. Oxfordshire and Buckinghamshire Light Infantry [13 days]; WO 95/1431: 4th Bn. Royal Fusiliers [8 days]; WO 95/1484/1: 1st Bn. Royal Warwickshire Regiment [12 days].
[76] Ibid. War Diary March–April 1918.
[77] IWM Documents.20329: H.E. Baker, Memoir, Part 6, p. 2.
[78] IWM Documents.11289: H.T. Madders, Diary 3 April 1918.
[79] C.S.W., *The Outpost*, Vol. III (1 July 1916), p. 118.
[80] IWM Documents.12771: W. Vernon, Letter marked 22 July 1918 – addressed to Miss L Vernon.
[81] C.S.W., *The Outpost*, Vol. III (1 July 1916), p. 118.
[82] Ibid. Also IWM Documents.15040: A.E. Heywood, Diary 15 November 1917.

upright in comparative safety was a welcome one.[83] In 1914, even the area surrounding Ypres retained traces of the pre-war world. Houses, civilians, and evidence of once peaceful communities remained, and Charles Dwyer visited a café barely a hundred metres behind the frontline.[84] Capt. Maurice Asprey was able to purchase fresh meat, eggs, and sweets from the farms around his rest camp.[85] Postcards collected and produced during this time show that towns still retained much of their original form.[86]

The extension of the line in 1916 offered men a new opportunity to explore Picardy. It was still relatively unscarred by the war, which improved men's morale.

> The neighbourhood of Amiens, prior to the great attack of July 1st [was] a very delightful country [...with] beautiful woods, full of shady trees; cold rivers, pleasant to bathe in; happy, smiling villages, inhabited by simple and hospitable villagers; and, last, but not least, the lovely city of Amiens, with its open-air cafes and tempting shop-windows brim full of life and interest.[87]

Yet, the Somme region fell victim to the conflict, becoming a 'dreary ... joke'.[88] However, orchards and valleys in rear areas continued to offer some distractions. Even in late 1917 and early 1918, it was still possible to find entertainment in a few locations close to the line.[89] A.E. Haywood spent many evenings drinking in the towns near his camp. On 11 November he 'went into the village ... and got pretty well oiled up on Vin Rouge and Benedictine and Vin Blanc with beer for a change'.[90] Conversing with locals in stuttering pidgin French was absorbing, and combatants embraced any opportunity to speak to somebody not wearing khaki.[91] Even in 1918, J. Grimston still enjoyed Arras (despite the intense fighting that had taken place there in 1917) for its limited shopping and theatre.[92] However, such diversions were often inaccessible to

---

[83] IWM Documents.16676: C. Dwyer, Diary 27 September 1914; IWM Documents.12027: S. Judd, 30 December 1914; IWM Documents.12521: R.E.P. Stevens, Diary 21 November 1916; LIDDLE/WW1/GS/0583: 2nd Lt. S. Frankenburg, Letter 19 December 1917; IWM Documents.14517: Capt. P. Ingleson, Letter to Miss Fulton 6 February 1918.
[84] IWM Documents.16676: C. Dwyer, Diary 24 October 1914.
[85] NAM 2005-02-6: Capt. M. Asprey, Letters to Mother 25 and 30 November and 4 December 1914 and Letters to Father 29 November and 20 December 1914.
[86] LIDDLE/WW1/GS/0946: D.G. Le May, Postcard 132. La Grande Guerre 1914–15: 'Ruines de VERMELLES (Pas-de-Calais), – Cette ville réoccupée par nos troupes après une lutte héroïque qui dura plusieurs semaines A.R. vis Paris 132.'
[87] Lowe, *The Western Battlefields*, p. 16.
[88] LIDDLE/WW1/GS/0273: Capt. C. Carrington, Incomplete Letters to Mother 1916 [No. 89-105].
[89] NAM 7403-29-486-144: Sgt. H. Hopwood, Letter to Mother & All 15 December 1917.
[90] IWM Documents.15040: A.E. Heywood, Diary 11 November 1917.
[91] W. Louis Ruhl, 'A Prize Packet', *The Castronical*, Vol. I, No. 3 (1 May 1916), p. 6.
[92] IWM Documents.14752: J. Grimston, Diary 24 February 1918.

poorer men in the rank and file who frequently complained about the cost of living and price of entertainment.⁹³

The relative comfort of rear zones encouraged a more constructive relationship with the environment. The *BEF Times* characterised 'Pop' [Poperinghe] as 'our holiday resort ... horrible ... as it was ... It provided a break of sorts from the eternal mud and shells', though it had 'somehow fallen into disrepute'. It was vulnerable to shellfire but remained a relative haven compared to nearby Ypres. These places were prized for their *comparative* security. Another man recalled that 'Pop':

> stood for everything that meant civilization to the British Army. The road from Poperinghe to Ypres was known to every soldier: to march eastwards on this road meant work, trenches, mud – everything unpleasant; to march westwards meant rest, a 'comfy' dinner in the town, and possibly an evening at the club.⁹⁴

Soldiers explored Belgium and France as soldier-tourists when they could, seeking out novel sights and experiences.⁹⁵ An article in one soldiers' journal, written after the Germans had been driven away from Arras, produced a short history of the city so that soldiers could recognise places of significance (where shellfire had not reduced them to rubble).⁹⁶ It was, perhaps, such an interest that led S.R. Hudson to collect spoons as mementoes of his time there as well as in Amiens, Boulogne-sur-Mer, and Doullens.⁹⁷ Men developed more intimate memories and diversified their routines; they saw new things and met new people.⁹⁸ Activities ranged from the mundane to the intimate. While 'cleaning equipment' behind the lines, soldiers were 'unofficially' 'frying eggs, drinking *café-au-lait* – the more fortunate ones, *café-au* something else, or teaching English to some ambitious demoselle [sic]'.⁹⁹ Henry Lawson only wished that he had a camera to 'show [his mother that] we are happy and do have amusing times'.¹⁰⁰ These places and regions were a tonic for the frontlines'

---

⁹³ LIDDLE/WW1/GS/0144: A&C Black and Company, Employees of A.C. Black Publishers, Letters 1917–1918 from E.G. Gilscott; IWM Documents.7953: Pte. F.G. Senyard, Letter 14 December 1916.
⁹⁴ Lowe, *The Western Battlefields*, p. 11.
⁹⁵ A. Mayhew, 'A War Imagined: Postcards and the Maintenance of Long-Distance Relationships during the Great War', *War in History*, Vol. 28, No. 2 (April 2021), pp. 12–17.
⁹⁶ 'Arras', *The Dagger*, No. 1 (1 November 1918).
⁹⁷ IWM Documents.13760: Maj. S.R. Hudson, Images of Memento Spoons from the Western Front.
⁹⁸ K. Cowman, 'Touring Behind the Lines: British Soldiers in French Towns and Cities during the Great War', *Urban History*, Vol. 41, No. 1 (February 2014), pp. 105–123.
⁹⁹ J.T.S., 'Chez la Coiffeuse', *The Outpost*, Vol. III, No. 3 (1 June 1916), p. 3.
¹⁰⁰ LIDDLE/WW1/GS/0933: H. Lawson, Letter to his Mother 16 September 1917.

destruction.[101] As such, F.L. Clark wrote to Lt. J.H. Johnson on 12 December 1916: 'Plugstreet must seem even as the abode of the blessed to you' after 'the hell's delight of the Somme'.[102]

Familiarising and Coping with the Frontlines

It was harder (and more dangerous) to familiarise the firing line. The destruction could be overwhelming, and soldiers sometimes felt that this was a world bereft of life.[103] The frontlines also contained constant reminders of combatants own mortality. In late 1914, shellfire had already shattered the landscape. J.E. Mawer explained that 'it is a sight to see the Villages we go through with most of the houses blown down by the shell[s]'.[104]

By 1915, Ypres was a 'dead city', 'its glories ... gone for ever'.[105] A soldier walking through its ruins was confronted by 'the broken walls of the Cloth Hall overshadowed by a fantastic fragment of the great church of St Martin, the crumbling belfry sliced by a gigantic shell'.[106] It created an 'impression of sadness and utter desolation' and left some soldiers 'overwhelmed by the tragedy of it all'.[107] However, it was still possible to interact with the city's rich history. Many buildings surrounding the marketplace were 'ruins', but a roofless café remained on Rue Jules Capron. On Rue d'Elverdinghe, there were also some 'modest shops and cafés' with flagstaffs 'tilted over the freshly swept roadway'. These became a symbol of resistance. Gardens, still bright with flowers, could also be explored even if the houses behind them had been reduced to a 'single red brick wall'.[108] 'Picturesque Ypres still stood, though torn and maimed, a shadow of her former self.'[109] The cellars, which also operated as shelters (and occasionally tombs), were places of discovery.[110] St Martin's sacristy had escaped the worst of the destruction and works 'by old Flemish masters still hung on the wall'. By 1916, though, there was little left except ruins, 'gigantic holes', and 'the rugged spikes of the ruined cathedral'.[111] Even so, Ypres' piles of ancient masonry, 'mighty

---

[101] IWM Documents.15040: A.E. Heywood, Diary 14 November 1917; IWM Documents.17029: Capt. A.J. Lord, Letter to Father 29 December 1917.
[102] IWM Documents.7035: Lt. J.H. Johnson, Letter from F.L. Clark 12 December 1916.
[103] IWM Documents.16020: Capt. E. Lycette, Memoir, p. 55; NAM 1998-08-31: Pte. A. J. Symonds, Diary 26–29 July 1916.
[104] SOFO Box 16 Item 35 3/4/C/2: Pte. J.E. Mawer, Letter to Wife c. Christmas 1914, Doc.29.
[105] For the pre-war origins of these kinds of description see M. Connelly and S. Goebel, *Ypres* (Oxford, 2018).
[106] 'The Dead City of Ypres', *The "Snapper*, Vol. X, No. 6 (June 1915), p. 103.
[107] Ibid.
[108] Ibid., pp. 103–104.
[109] 'Ypres. April/May,1915', *Cambridgeshire Territorial Gazette*, No. 4 (1 October 1916), p. 73.
[110] Ibid., p. 77.
[111] 'Reflections on Being Lost in Ypres at 3 a.m.', *The Wipers Times*, Vol. 1, No. 1 (12 February 1916).

Figure 1.1   Ruins of the Cloth Hall in the City of Ypres, 1914.

Source: Photo12/Universal Images Group via Getty Images.

rampart caverns', and the 'many cellars of her mansions' became a sort of 'home' for the British soldier and retained a strange beauty.[112]

The destruction became more pronounced as the years passed. Along the line, there was 'the same complete annihilation of the treasures of centuries'.[113] As he made his way to the trenches, Pte. F.G. Senyard felt that he was leaving any trace of 'civilisation' behind him.[114] Dilapidated villages and inanimate trench lines made the journey a 'horror'.[115] Forward zones felt 'unearthly'.[116] The 'terrible sights' of 'trees like stumps and every inch of the hill sides churned up with shell fire' resembled 'hell'.[117] It was the evidence of personal loss that was most depressing. Lt. W.B. Medlicott noted that artillery fire had 'scattered all the belongings right and left – there is nothing more depressing. School books etc. ... all in a sodden mush on the floor'.[118] By the winter of

---

[112] Ibid. Also 'By a Visitor', *The Wipers Times*, Vol. 1, No. 2 (26 February 1916).
[113] 'The Dead City of Ypres', p. 104.
[114] IWM Documents.7953: Pte. F.G. Senyard, Diary 14 and 17 December 1916; IWM Documents.1665: A.P. Burke, 26 November 1916.
[115] IWM Documents.7035: Lt. J.H. Johnson, Diary 22 November 1916; IWM Documents.12521: R.E.P. Stevens, Diary 21 November 1916.
[116] IWM Documents.12521: R.E.P. Stevens, Diary 25 December 1916; LIDDLE/WW1/GS/0266: Pte. E.A. Cannon, Diary 14 September 1916.
[117] RFM.ARC.2012.958: E.T. Marler, Diary 18 and 24 November and 8 December 1916.
[118] IWM Documents.1708: Lt. W.B. Medlicott, Diary – Book 2 [p. 10].

Figure 1.2 Battle of Menin Road Ridge. German prisoners being marched through the Cathedral Square, Ypres, 20 September 1917.

Source: Lt. Ernest Brooks/Imperial War Museums via Getty Images.

1916, Picardy was also a 'beastly' vista.[119] It had become a landscape of 'desolated villages' in which 'no trace remains to mark the site of the many peaceful homes … Save for a few shattered trees, and the countless wooden crosses'. It resembled 'a South African veldt'.[120] The battlefield had been reduced to little more than shapeless forms of rubble and mud.[121] In 1917 and 1918, much of the fighting occurred in areas that had already been the scene of combat. This sometimes imbued the fighting with the aura of futility. Men were shocked by the 'hideous' panoramas produced by both Third Ypres and the Spring Offensives.[122] Lt. J.H. Johnson was confronted by 'debris, graves and [the] loneliness of desolation'.[123] By April 1918, 2nd Lt D. Henrick Jones was desperate to escape this 'beastly country'.[124]

---

[119] B.M. 'Tommy Atkins', *The Mudlark or the Bedfordshire Gazette*, Vol. 3 (1 June 1916), p. 6; IWM Documents.16504: 2nd Lt. W.J. Lidsey, Diary 2, 4 and 18 November 1916.

[120] 'Our Christmas Greeting', *The "Snapper"*, Vol. XII, No. 12 (1916), p. 126.

[121] RFM Box 2014.9: Officers Photographs taken on the Front in France, Photograph D 309 – The roads of Flers.

[122] IWM Documents.16060: Rev. C.H. Bell, Letter to Herbert c. January 1918; IWM Documents.7233: Col. F. Hardman, Letter 3 April 1918; IWM Documents.14752: J. Grimston, Diary 24 April 1918.

[123] IWM Documents.7035: Lt. J.H. Johnson, Diary 18 February 1918.

[124] IWM Documents.16345: 2nd Lt. D. Henrick Jones, Letter to Wife 2 April 1918.

Despite inducing such reactions, the frontlines did have their own character. David Isaac Griffiths thought the trenches around the Scarpe River resembled 'a "prehistoric home"'.[125] The landscape was transformed at dawn and dusk.[126] Paul Nash explained that nightfall saw 'the monstrous lands take on a changing aspect [and the] landscape is so distorted from its own gentle forms'. The 'works of men' and light meant that 'nothing seems to bear the imprint of God's hand'. It could have been 'a terrific creation of some malign fiend working a crooked will on the innocent countryside'.[127] In such circumstances, the natural world could become an antagonist. The scarred slope facing Siegfried Sassoon in his poem *Attack* was 'menacing' and the sun 'glow'ring'.[128] G.A. Stevens found that he preferred the line around St Quentin (battered as it was) to 'beastly old Flanders which one hates now'.[129]

No Man's Land created its own anxieties. It was a space that eventually needed to be crossed and contained all kinds of horrors. There was always the chance that an enemy raiding party might emerge from the darkness without warning. Scouting parties forced men to confront their fears. These patrols, which left during the night, risked contact with the enemy and oblivion. The impenetrable darkness and the featureless landscapes meant it was easy to get lost and men sometimes vanished. On 21 November 1916, for example, a lance corporal of the 9th Royal Fusiliers disappeared without a trace after being left injured in a shell hole.[130]

Many felt that the frontlines were 'dead'.[131] Lt. J.H. Johnson described Arras as a 'city of ruins' and the area between there and Bapaume was a 'land of desolation – ruined and dead'.[132] Spiritually minded soldiers suspected these spaces were haunted or contained some paranormal force. Several individuals reported seeing crosses in the sky, being visited by angels, or witnessing heavenly signs.[133] On 27 December 1916, Charles Carrington recorded 'ghosts – ghost stories' in his diary.[134] The lack of context makes this entry difficult to unpick, but the dead appear to have been playing on his mind. The landscape's emptiness certainly created a ghostly visage. Those who had seen

---

[125] D.I. Griffiths, Letter to 'Batchie' 9 April 1917, *Europeana 1914–1918*, www.europeana1914-1918.eu/en/contributions/20788#prettyPhoto, accessed 15 November 2016.
[126] 'Aftermath' in S. Sassoon, *The War Poems of Siegfried Sassoon* (London, 1919), p. 91.
[127] TGA 8313: P. Nash, Letter to Margaret 6 April 1917.
[128] 'Attack' in Sassoon, *The War Poems*.
[129] IWM Documents.12339: Brig. Gen. G.A. Stevens, Letter to Mother 4 March 1918.
[130] TNA WO 95/1857/2: War Diary 9/ Royal Fusiliers, 21 November 1916.
[131] IWM Documents.7953: Pte. F.G. Senyard, Letter to Wife 17 December 1916.
[132] IWM Documents.7035: Lt. J.H. Johnson, Diary 8 December 1917.
[133] O. Davies, *A Supernatural War: Magic, Divination, and Faith during the First World War* (Oxford, 2019). See also L. Ruickbie, *Angels in the Trenches: Spiritualism, Superstition and the Supernatural during the First World War* (London, 2018).
[134] LIDDLE/WW1/GS/0273: Capt. C. Carrington, 27 December 1916.

Figure 1.3 The destruction of 1916. British troops at the Battle of Morval (Somme), September 1916. During the Somme battles, Picardy's once-attractive countryside became a lunar landscape pockmarked by shell holes, while villages were reduced to rubble. Note the chalky soil.

Source: Photo12/Universal Images Group via Getty Image.

these places before they were disfigured by shellfire were able to layer what confronted them with memories of a more peaceful time. Possibly reflecting this, Cecil White believed that the Somme had become a place of 'phantom' woods.[135] After the fighting at Cambrai in November 1917, J. Grimston noted that while 'not so smashed as Arras' it was now 'a city of the dead'. 'Not a soul [was] to be seen' along the 'rotten bumpy road' leading through its ruins.[136]

However, the frontlines could be fascinating, and some men were drawn to the destruction. They were a muse for Capt. G.K. Rose in his drawings of the Western Front. His pictures charted the sights he encountered: quaint and peaceful villages, barbed-wired trench lines, and the devastation. His drawings of the Baroque town square in Arras were reminiscent of the sketches of an amateur artist on his Grand Tour.[137] The ruination seemed senseless, but sites (at least where there were still discernible features) remained interesting.

---

[135] RFM.ARC.3032: L/Cpl. C. White, Diary 26 January 1918.
[136] IWM Documents.14752: J. Grimston, Diary 14 October 1918.
[137] Capt. G.K. Rose, *The Story of the 2/4th Oxfordshire and Buckinghamshire Light Infantry*. See also IWM Art 4905: G.K. Rose, 'Arras, Grande Place, September 29 1917' and IWM Art 4900: G.K. Rose, 'Hebuterne Church, September 1917'.

Lt. J.H. Johnson believed that 'many people' would be drawn to the 'waste land ... long after Death passed over it'. Yet, there would be 'worlds of difference' compared to 'those who saw it killed and just after'.[138]

Mutilated landscapes could also be familiarised. Veterans returning to Belgium and France after 1918 were sometimes angered by the battle zone's restoration.[139] During the war, when the frontlines had shifted (such as after the German withdrawals in early 1917), some men grasped the opportunity to explore the old frontlines. J.M. Humphries enjoyed the 'novelty' of searching for souvenirs.[140] John Masefield found that the old Somme battlefield evoked pathos but also believed that they were symbolic of the BEF's advance to victory.[141] The destruction could similarly be normalised. Stylised images of trenches were used on dinner menus, conference programmes, and Christmas cards produced by units. These included depictions of scarred frontline landscapes littered with barbed wire, shattered tree stumps, and shell-damaged towns.[142]

There was some strange beauty in destruction.[143] Paul Nash believed that any artist would find their muse amidst the devastation. He became obsessed with 'those wonderful trenches at ... dawn and sundown' and the 'wide ..., flat and scantly wooded' landscapes 'pitted' with shell holes and littered with the 'refuge of war'.[144] V.G. Bell was not so skilful an artist as Nash, but he was also struck by the resilience of nature. His drawings depicted 'hooded crows', owls, or the stray dogs that he encountered in the trenches.[145] He made sense of the sights through his art and recorded nearly everything: landscapes, animals, military activities, the trenches, and his billets. The rubbish, the shell holes, the destruction, and the rats were catalogued and internalised.[146]

Even if soldiers failed to see this beauty, the experience of the frontlines could inculcate a sense of authority, confidence, and power. This was revealed in the common phrase 'Before You Come Up', which was sometimes sometimes

---

[138] IWM Documents.7035: Lt. J.H. Johnson, Diary 10 January 1918.
[139] F. Ueköller, 'Memories in Mud: The Environmental Legacy of the Great War', in Tucker et al., *Environmental Histories*, p. 282.
[140] NAM 1998-02-232: J.M. Humphries, Letter to "Mater" 13 September 1916.
[141] J. Masefield, *The Old Front Line* (New York, 1918).
[142] RFM.2013.9: Miscellaneous Documents, Card: 'Christmas Greetings from 17th Infantry Brigade, 'Xmas 16'.
[143] IWM Documents.12339: Brig. Gen. G.A. Stevens, Letter to Mother 6 November 1916; IWM Documents.12521: R.E.P. Stevens, Diary 10 November 1916; LIDDLE/WW1/GS/0583: 2nd Lt. Sydney Frankenburg, Letter 21 December 1917; IWM Documents.7035: Lt. J.H. Johnson, Diary 25 December 1917; IWM Documents.17029: Capt. A.J. Lord, Letter to Father 16 January 1918.
[144] TGA 8313: P. Nash, Letter to Margaret 6 April 1917.
[145] BL RP9518: V.G. Bell, Sketches: 'The Wastage of War', Men in a Trench in the 'Duck's Bill' at Night 7/11/15, and 'Pumping a Flooded Traffic Trench'.
[146] Ibid. Sketch Albums – Western Front 1915–16, Egypt & Palestine, 1917–1920.

Figure 1.4 The destruction of 1917. Soldiers in the trenches during the Battle of Passchendaele on November 1, 1917. By 1917, there were few discernible features left. Note the evidence of the high water table and much darker soil.

Source: Fotosearch/Getty Images.

rephrased as 'before your (regimental) number was dry', 'before you was breeched', 'before you nipped' or 'before your ballocks [sic] dropped'. These were 'crushing retort[s]' that meant:

> I was in the front line before you arrived from the base, I know more than you are capable of knowing, I've suffered more than you, I've done more than you, I'm a better solider than you and a better man. And I refuse to believe a word you say.[147]

Habituation helps to explain how combatants endured the war's chronic crises and the horrors of the frontlines. In her study of the Italian Army, Vanda Wilcox argued that 'a process of habituation, and a greater tolerance of the familiar, meant that passive acceptance often increased with exposure to life in the trenches'.[148] It can mitigate even the most bewildering of experiences and was a multifaceted process, exemplified in men's relationship with the novel smells and

---

[147] J. Brophy and E. Partridge, *The Long Trail: Soldiers' Songs and Slang 1914–18* (Aylesbury, 1965, 1969), p. 83.
[148] Wilcox, *Morale and the Italian Army*, p. 137.

sounds in the frontlines. Olfactory and auditory habituation occur organically outside more conventional and purposeful forms of habituation training.[149]

The Trenches' Stenches

The experience of the frontlines was multisensory, and the smells that met men in the trenches were sometimes shocking. The frontlines were littered with rubbish, shell fragments, barbed wire and 'everywhere the dead. / Only the dead were always present – present / As a vile sickly smell of rottenness'.[150] In some sectors the smell of corpses was ubiquitous; it was 'infecting the earth'.[151]

Awful smells coalesced to produce a particular aroma in the frontlines. 2nd Lt. Guy Chapman described it as 'a sickly stench. The mixed smell of exploded ... gas, blood, putrefying corpses and broken bricks'.[152] This smell-scape re-emphasised war's capacity for carnage. In active sectors, the scent of the dead was omnipresent. After combat, the smell of decomposing flesh was common to trenches or shell holes, which seemed to preserve the flavour of death.[153] The stench of corpses wafted across No Man's Land and the unsanitary conditions contributed to the undertone of faecal matter.[154] When possible, the dead were removed for burial, though shellfire – or trench work – sometimes disinterred rotten remains of old comrades and enemies. H.T. Madders had to live with the smell of some 'poor old transport horses'. Having 'rolled them' into a hole they continued to attract 'flies like bees' and to 'stink for days'.[155] Elsewhere, 'the nauseating smell of high explosive' struck men forcefully. It reminded troops approaching the frontlines of the dangers that awaited them there. One man noted that it left 'our hands ... numb'.[156]

---

[149] R. Pellegrino, C. Sinding, R.A. de Wijk and T. Hummel, 'Habituation and Adaptation to Odors in Humans', *Physiology & Behavior*, Vol. 177 (August 2017), pp. 13–19; I. Croy, W. Maboshe, and T. Hummel, 'Habituation Effects of Pleasant and Unpleasant Odors', *International Journal of Psychophysiology*, Vol. 88, No. 1 (April 2013), pp. 104–108; T. Rosburg and P. Sörös, 'The Response Decrease of Auditory Evoked Potentials by Repeated Stimulation – Is There Evidence for an Interplay between Habituation and Sensitization?' *Clinical Neurophysiology*, Vol. 127, No. 1 (January 2016), pp. 397–408.
[150] A.G. West, *The Diaries of a Dead Officer: Being the Posthumous Papers of A.G. West*, ed. C.J.M. West (London, 1918), pp. 81–83.
[151] TKM Item 90/50/2: C.J. Richards, Diary 16 September 1916; E. Spiers, 'The Scottish Soldier at War', in H. Cecil and P. Liddle (eds.), *Facing Armageddon. The First World War Experienced* (London, 1996, 2003), p. 318.
[152] LIDDLE/WW1/GS/0292: 2nd Lt. G. Chapman, Diary 16 November 1916.
[153] 'The Mermaid', *The Fifth Glo'ster Gazette*, No. 18 (1 April 1917), p. 19.
[154] A Commanding Officer, 'Notes on a Recent Visit to the Trenches', *The Red Feather*, Vol. 1, No. 3 (1 March 1915), p. 42.
[155] IWM Documents.11289: H.T. Madders, Diary 24 September 1918.
[156] 'Memories on Revisiting and Old Sector', *The Outpost*, Vol. V, No. 5 (1 September 1917), p. 168.

Pte. E.A. Cannon practised verse in the back pages of his diary. His unsophisticated poems reflected his visceral reaction to the smells he encountered: 'The stench here t'was / simply vile', so much so that he 'wondered if again I / should ever smile'.[157]

'Stench' and 'trench' were frequently rhymed in soldiers' newspapers.[158] The dead's presence was evident in the air as a constant reminder of the war's toll. This put a huge strain on frontline servicemen.[159] Other scents, such as that of an open wound, were also shocking. 'Rotten iron' produced its own aroma as rusting wire overwhelmed natural odours.[160] The poor sanitation led some men to report that the smell of 'shit' *was* 'the smell of Passchendaele [and] of the [Ypres] Salient'.[161] Rain had its own perfume, and some found that the hum of unwashed bodies was too much in the cramped conditions.[162] The reek of other men left some soldiers 'sad'.[163] The war had specific sensory facets, many of which reappeared in later memory processes. Smell can induce memory recall and Pte. Bert Fearns explained that 'smells are one of the big things'. 'I can often still smell gas today, and that manly dampness of men and mud at Yeepree [sic]'.[164] Sudden recollections, even of smell, are indicative of the place of traumatic memories within post-traumatic stress, both chronic and temporary.[165] However, they can also be positive. The whiff of 'HP Sauce' or 'hot tea outside on a cold day' took Fearns back to happier moments.[166]

Processes of habituation helped men to cope. The fact that they did not constantly bemoan the smell-scape suggests that they were able to ignore or adjust to it. A satirical sketch in *The B.E.F. Times* pointed to this process. On entering a frontline dugout, a senior officer exclaimed: 'Gawd! How this filthy place stinks.' He asked the men: 'what's this dreadful stench?' The

---

[157] LIDDLE/WW1/GS/0266: Pte. E.A. Cannon, Diary [Draft Poem from June 1918].
[158] G.H.P.S., 'The Yule Log', *The Fifth Glo'ster Gazette*, No. 17 (1 February 1917), p. 10; W.O.W., 'Pioneering Platitudes', *The Outpost*, Vol. VII, No. 1 (1 June 1918), p. 3.
[159] Watson, *Enduring the Great War*, p. 20.
[160] A. Bamji, 'Facial Surgery: The Patient's Experience', in H. Cecil and P. Liddle, *Facing Armageddon*, p. 494; Fussell, *The Great War and Modern Memory*, p. 69.
[161] Fussell, *The Great War and Modern Memory*, p. 331.
[162] IWM Documents.16020: Capt. E. Lycette, Memoir, p. 9.
[163] S. Audoin-Rouzeau, 'The French Soldier in the Trenches', in Cecil and Liddle, *Facing Armageddon*, p. 224.
[164] Pte. Bert Fearns in Osgood and Brown, *Digging up Plugstreet*, p. 105.
[165] M.P. Koss, A.J. Figueredo, I. Bell, M. Tharan and S. Tromp, 'Traumatic Memory Characteristics: A Cross-Validated Mediational Model of Response to Rape among Employed Women', *Journal of Abnormal Psychology*, Vol. 105, No. 3 (1996), pp. 421–432.
[166] Osgood and Brown, *Digging up Plugstreet*, p. 105.

frontline officer replied: 'It's no good worrying about that, it's peculiar to the tunnel.'[167] Soldiers grew familiar to scents and could become accustomed to the unpleasant sensory features of the frontlines. In fact, the smell held 'a grim fascination' for some men.[168]

The Sounds of War

The Western Front's soundscape was immersive. It too could be overcome, internalised, and normalised through habituation. For instance, many men were confident that they could predict the fall of shells by analysing the sound they made.[169] Charles Quinnell remembered that this was one of the first lessons a soldier learned in the trenches. 'You could tell by sound if a shell was going over you or was meant for you ... And if that shell was coming for [you,] you would lie right down, and believe you me, a man lying down takes a lot of hitting.'[170] Familiarity with the sounds of war contributed to morale and even helped men respond to acute crises such as bombardments.

Nonetheless, artillery fire was shocking. One soldier felt that 'modern warfare seems to me to be a series of stupendous efforts on the part of each opponent to outclass the other in creating an appalling noise or a ghastly mess'.[171] The sound of a bombardment could be stressful (even if it fell on enemy trenches). The *Manchester Weekly Times* described one attack as 'a confusion of lights of various colours ... and a tornado of sound, in which machine guns and trench mortars played their part'.[172] The orchestra of battle could be overwhelming. Even outside of combat, an incoming barrage was terrifying. On one occasion, H.T. Madders was suddenly woken up 'by the sound of his [Jerry's] shell coming towards us, [we] could only nestle closer to mother earth, it seemed as if he was going to blow us to smithereens, at last it dropped about 40 yds up the trench'.[173] His sudden awakening left him unable to gauge the shell's direction, and his sense of helplessness bred panic. Such incidences exposed men's vulnerabilities.

It could feel as if shells surrounded the men as batteries fired from their front and rear.[174] The 'roar' of their own shells passing overhead made 'a far more terrifying noise ... than the German shells bursting'.[175] Not only this,

---

[167] 'More Mud Than Glory', *The B.E.F. Times*, Vol. 2, No. 1 (15 August 1917), p. 12.
[168] IWM Documents.17029: Capt. A.J. Lord, Letter to Father 13 September 1918.
[169] Watson, *Enduring the Great War*, p. 106.
[170] IWM Sound 554: C. Quinnell, Interview Reel 10.
[171] S.M., 'High Explosives', *The Outpost*, Vol. III, No. 1 (1 March 1916), p. 20.
[172] IWM Documents.11585: 2nd Lt. C.W. Gray, Extract from *The Manchester Weekly Times* (Saturday, 28 October 1916).
[173] IWM Documents.11289: H.T. Madders, Diary 31 August 1918.
[174] IWM Documents.16504: 2nd Lt. W.J. Lidsey, Sunday, 12 November 1916.
[175] IWM Documents.10933: Capt. G.B. Donaldson, Letter to Mother 31 May 1916.

but when following a creeping barrage (or when in one's own trenches) a misplaced British shell was just a deadly as those of the 'Boche'. The cacophony was an enemy of sleep and anybody within earshot of active frontline areas would find their nights interrupted – if not ruined – by 'deafening' artillery fire. Tiredness left men depressed and anxious.[176] Even the quietest zones were interspersed with gunfire. Men sometimes sat 'at ease and think it fine' amongst 'a peaceful evening scene' when a 'Crump!' signalled the 'burst of a 5.9 / In your best fly-proof latrine'.[177] Sudden gunfire or explosions could induce greater shock than regular artillery fire and provided an unwanted reminder of reality.

Other men found that the clamour of munitions could break the tedium of trench life. It reminded them where they were.[178] The strike of a bullet could drag daydreaming soldiers violently back into the present: 'Smack that one buried itself in the back wall of the trench. I start instinctively with the guilty feeling that my man has fired and I have forgotten to signal the shock.'[179] The familiar sound of the 'occasional whizzbang which passes one's ear of a night lends colour to the probability that such a person [as the enemy] exists'.[180]

Some men became accustomed to the constant noise of guns and perceived periods of silence unnerving; it seemed unnatural, and lulls were met with suspicion. These played upon their imagination, particularly at night. Christmas 1914 was eerie because of the stillness in the frontlines. K.M. Gaunt reported that 'not a sound could be heard anywhere'.[181] W. Tapp claimed that he missed 'the sound of the shots flying over it is like a clock which has stopped ticking'.[182] The soldiers' time horizons became inextricably intertwined with the noises of modern warfare. A.L. Collis felt a similar unease in March 1918. There was an uncommon 'quietness' in the frontlines on the eve of the German offensive, which left his unit fearful.[183] Silence could be a precursor to greater violence and seemed less predictable.

Sound was a source of information, which helped soldiers gauge events beyond their immediate line of vision. For instance, 10 October 1914 was memorable for Maj. J.S. Knyvett as 'our first day within the sound of firing'.[184] The percussion and reverberations of distant artillery offered insights into events elsewhere.[185] More experienced soldiers found that the 'rumble' of the

---

[176] IWM Documents.16676: C. Dwyer, Diary 8 November 1914; IWM Documents.12339: Brig. Gen. G.A. Stevens, Letter to Biddy (his Wife) 17 November 1916.
[177] 'A Perfect Nightmare', *The Fifth Glo'ster Gazette*, No. 21 (1 November 1917), p. 5.
[178] A.G. West, *The Diary of a Dead Officer*, pp. 79-81.
[179] C.S.W., *The Outpost*, Vol. III (1 July 1916), p. 119.
[180] Ibid.
[181] IWM Documents.7490: L/Cpl. K.M. Gaunt, Letter 25 December 1914.
[182] IWM Documents.18524: Pte. W. Tapp, Diary 27 December 1914.
[183] IWM Documents.20770: A.L. Collis, Diary 1 March 1918.
[184] IWM Documents.12819: Maj. J.S. Knyvett, Diary 10 October 1914.
[185] Ibid.

guns was a reminder of what waited up the line. The near-constant background noise could create an atmosphere of foreboding. This was true for those support troops moving up to bolster the British defences during the German offensives after 21 March 1918.[186]

Men tended not to sing en route to the trenches; it was against orders Yet, when returning from a tour of duty and as the noise of the frontlines faded away, they began to sing marching songs anew. The changing soundscape confirmed that they had left the killing zone.[187] Songs were a mechanism to combat fear and historian Emma Hanna has suggested that singing also helped to bolster identities (both civil and military), vocalise patriotism, poke fun at the military, and reject victimhood.[188]

Camps had their own, more pleasant, soundscape. The 'noisy rattling' of guy ropes and tent flaps straining against the wind were accompanied, in later years, by the mechanical noises of trucks and engines alongside the sharp 'warning blast[s]' of slow-moving trains' whistles. The shouted orders of non-commissioned officers (NCOs) and officers, the 'rush' of mess tins, and the 'clamours of men' all contributed to a more peaceful auditory experience.[189] There were echoes of the civilian world: music, football and rugby crowds, theatre, and laughter. These provided an imperfect but comforting reminder of home.[190] Sometimes these noises induced feelings of nostalgia, but this was not necessarily a bad thing.[191] The sounds of comrades enjoying themselves helped A.P. Burke to relax. One evening he reported that 'noise that's going on in the different huts' was like a 'carnival night'. It was 'lovely' and made the sight and sound of a distant German 'straffing [sic]' less oppressive.[192]

Familiarity with the sounds of war could become a coping mechanism. Self-deception helped many soldiers to diminish the danger by reconceptualising weaponry. An article in *The Wipers Times* was entitled 'to Minnie' and dedicated to the 'P.B.I [poor bloody infantry]'. In it, the author personified enemy weaponry. The German *Minenwerfer*'s 'voice' was heard 'with dread'.

---

[186] 'N.M., 'Somewhere-', *The Outpost*, Vol. VI, No. 6 (1 April 1918), p. 199.
[187] Brophy and Partridge, *The Long Trail*, p. 25.
[188] E. Hanna, *Sounds of War: Music and the British Armed Forces during the Great War* (Cambridge, 2020).
[189] W.S.C., 'Back to the Line', *The Outpost*, Vol. IV (1 October 1916), p. 26.
[190] IWM Documents.5092: Pte. W.M. Anderson, Letter 15 November 1916; IWM Documents.15743: J.M. Nichols, Diary 17, 18 and 19 December 1916; IWM Documents.12521: R.E.P. Stevens, Diary 25 November 1916; IWM Documents.14752: J. Grimston, Diary 12 October 1918; IWM Documents.11289: H.T. Madders, Diary 2 and 5 January 1918; IWM Documents.7233: Col. F. Hardman, Letter to Parents 5 February 1918; IWM Documents.7035: Lt. J.H. Johnson, 1 January 1918. Also Fuller, *Troop Morale*, pp. 85–87.
[191] IWM Documents.2619: L. Wilson, Memoir, p. 45.
[192] IWM Documents.1665: A.P. Burke, Letter to Reg 2 November 1916.

It was a 'fickle jade' and 'traitorous minx'. The mortar had a 'raucous screech', which was particularly unpleasant when *she* 'force[d]' *her* 'blatant presence' and intruded 'uninvited'. His gendering of this weapon was taken further: 'once most loved of all your sex' Minnie was 'now hated with a loathing'. This feminisation became an aggressive psychological tool and the piece ended with the lines: 'when next my harassed soul you vex / You'll get some back at any rate'.[193] Whether this resentment of women was a product of personal slight (or bitterness at men's lot) is unclear. Weapons and military paraphernalia were often offered female form. It made retribution easier to imagine and may have been a reassertion of power.

Elsewhere, machine sounded like typewriters, while gas could be identified by its tell-tale 'flutter, flutter, crump'. This contrasted with the 'Whoo-Whoo-Whoo-WHOO-CRASH' of high-velocity shells.[194] Another soldier was able to distinguish between the noises of various 'High Explosives'. Mining caused 'a satisfying amount of noise and debris'. Upon detonation 'the earth rocks and rumbles with the concussion' causing 'a huge lump of the hitherto inoffensive landscape' to become 'violently aggressive'. In these moments the landscape became a weapon.[195] The experience of a mine's detonation was relatively rare and too unpredictable to be normalised. Other tools in the German arsenal were more familiar. Some frontline combatants learned to prepare for the 'concussion' of a high explosive shell, which felt like being 'hit ... over the head with something about as heavy as a cheese'. Of course, the effect was far more destructive and traumatic near the impact zone, especially if men were buried by a collapsing trench wall. The 'light shell or whizz bang' had 'a loud noise' but 'its destructive qualities' were 'small'. Shrapnel shells on the other hand had 'a weird sound, a loud explosion, and a tremendous clatter of falling pieces of ... shrapnel'. This sounded something like 'a Ford' whose owner had '"let her go all out"'. The 'hand bomb and the rifle grenade' were apparently about as effective as the 'whizz-bang'.[196]

Vanda Wilcox has argued that allusions to the sounds of conflict in Italian soldiers' songs allowed for the 'traumatic and alien soundscape of the war' to be 'rhetorically controlled'.[197] Refrains in the BEF such as *Hush! Here Comes a Whizz-Bang*, *The Bells of Hell*, or *We Are the Boys Who Fear No Noise* suggest that song played a similar role amongst British troops.[198] It is not clear to what extent familiarity genuinely offered protection, but even placebos can

---

[193] 'To Minnie (Dedicated to the P.B.I.)', *The Wipers Times*, Vol. 1, No.1 (31 July 1916), p. 1.
[194] J. Walker, *Words and the First World War: Language, Memory and Vocabulary* (London, 2017), p. 127.
[195] S.M., 'High Explosives', Ibid., p. 20.
[196] Ibid.
[197] Wilcox, *Morale and the Italian Army*, p. 119.
[198] Brophy and Partridge, *The Long Trail*, pp. 47–49.

bolster resilience. This heightened awareness also helped men to infuse the environment with meaning and to combat their own fear.

The 'alien' smell and soundscapes of the Western Front reveal how men's immediate environment became the focus of their attention. By diminishing and controlling their reactions, soldiers were able to overcome the chronic (and sometimes acute) crises accompanying service in the frontlines. Habituation and familiarisation were conscious and unconscious processes and stemmed from soldiers' familiarity with the world around them. Yet, any re-conceptualisation of their surroundings required that they controlled their fear and revulsion.

Familiarising the Western Front

Other tools helped soldiers to see beyond 'the great sameness' of the frontlines.[199] Places and settlements had forms and names long after they were reduced to rubble.[200] Maps (alongside signs recording the name of trenches, villages, and towns) encouraged men to recognise places as 'familiar' and to imagine that even the most shell-damaged parts of the Western Front were more orderly.[201]

Soldiers renamed the places they encountered. In 1914, official communiqués asked units to avoid using local names to avoid revealing troop movements and unit locations.[202] This catalysed a reimagining of Belgium and France. In September 1914, the *Illustrated London News* published images of handmade signs from the Ypres sector, including Somerset House, Hotel de Lockhart, and Plugstreet Hall. According to this article, these revealed the soldiers 'love of home and his capacity for making himself comfortable in the

---

[199] NAM 1992-04-57-16-5: Lt. Col. J.E Smart, Hand Sketched Maps 'M4 18 Rifles' and 'M5 20 Rifles'. Wilson, *Landscapes of the Western Front*, p. 101.
[200] For trench maps, see TNA WO 153 and WO 207. IWM Documents.13760: Maj. S.R. Hudson, Map of area around Toilly [1916].
[201] NAM 2000-10-304: Notes on the Area of Ablainzevile, France, from General Staff, 5th Army; TNA WO 223: Wt. W. 15534-9497. Spl. 4000. 2/17. F. & Q. (H.C.) Ltd. P. 17: Notes on the Area of the Ablainzeveille, Achiet-le-Grand, Achiet-le-Petit, Bihucourt, Bucquoy, Gomiecourt and Logeast Wood: Prepared by General Staff, Fifth Army; NAM 1980-01-4: Field Message Book (Army Form 153), 21 (Service) Bn Manchester Regiment, Situation Report 27 January 1918; LIDDLE/WW1/GS/0837: Capt. J. Isherwood, 1:20.000 map of Montbrehain, Edition 1.A; MR 2/17/67: Sgt. J. Palin, Maps [1/20,000 map of the Northern France; Also Hand Drawn Maps, including Mametz 1 July 1916]; IWM Documents.18455: Lt. Col. D.R. Turnbull, Letter to Sylvia 26 December 1916; MR 2/17/57: 2nd Lt. F.T.K. Woodworth, Diary 26 March 1918.
[202] TNA WO 95/1565/1: War Diary 1st Battalion the Devonshire Regiment: 'Appendix K. 10: Instructions for the Inspector-General of Communications [A1770]' [1914].

most adverse circumstances'.²⁰³ This rechristening continued throughout the war. Many places became infamous: Devil's Wood, Lousy Woods, and Wipers (or Ips). Frequently, this was a bottom-up process. Some names were references to precise geographical features; others were linguistic efforts to control a hostile environment or evidence of humour and irony. Many were nostalgic references to home or the product of personal, regimental, or group associations (including the commemoration of lost comrades).²⁰⁴ The power of local identity also revealed itself. Units from London named areas around Ploegsteert Wood after places in the United Kingdom's capital.²⁰⁵ Elsewhere, at Foncquevillers, a battalion of Brummies used the names of Birmingham's streets to christen their trenches.²⁰⁶

This fulfilled secondary cultural and psychological functions. It allowed men to document 'precise locations' in the morass and played a role in 'evoking events, memories, and associations. All this is a kind of referencing. The name becomes the key to open the databank, the password to enter the archive'.²⁰⁷ Peter Chasseaud has drawn a parallel between this and émigrés' use of familiar names when settling in new countries, concluding: 'the process undoubtedly staked a claim, but also established continuity with the past, and a sense of familiarity and security'.²⁰⁸

Many men embraced service on the Western Front as an opportunity for travel and discovery.²⁰⁹ English–French dictionaries and stand-alone translation texts suggest men hoped to engage with their new environment and its population.²¹⁰ The sights and sounds were things of interest, while the destruction was something to be experienced and recorded. Maj. G.H. Greenwell wrote home: 'Should I ever have seen Arras and Ypres, Albert and Péronne under such interesting conditions if there had been no war?'²¹¹ There were historic sites to visit. Lt. D. Henrick Jones hoped to see Rouen's 'cathedral and other famous places'.²¹²

After cameras were banned in 1914, a few intrepid men continued to photograph the frontlines. Charting their experiences, they focused on the

---

²⁰³ Chasseaud, *Rats Alley*, p. 23. See also IWM Documents.13260: Sgt. W. Summers, Diary of 1916, p. 12.
²⁰⁴ Chasseaud, *Rats Alley*, pp. 26, 47–56.
²⁰⁵ Ibid., pp. 22–23.
²⁰⁶ Lt. C.E. Carrington, *The War Record of the 1/5th Battalion The Royal Warwickshire Regiment* (Birmingham, 1922), p. 16.
²⁰⁷ Chasseaud, *Rats Alley*, p. 26.
²⁰⁸ Ibid., pp. 24–25.
²⁰⁹ Mayhew, 'A War Imagined', pp. 12–17.
²¹⁰ NAM 1998-10-306, *The Soldier's Word + Phrase Book French and German: Compiled by a Committee of Well-Known Teachers from Actual Experience of Soldiers' Needs* (George G. Harrap & Company [Undated]).
²¹¹ IWM Documents.11006: G.H. Greenwell, Letter 17 November 1917.
²¹² IWM Documents.16345: 2nd Lt. D. Henrick Jones, Letter to Wife 14 October 1914.

destruction.[213] Postcards also played an important role in recording the sights that soldiers encountered.[214] H.O. Hendry wrote on one such card: 'This is another building close by the church dear, I think it has been a school.'[215] He wanted to share what he saw. Yet, he was disappointed and 'could not get any decent cards love, this is a poor village, I wanted to get some ruins.'[216] Sydney Gill sent his wife a similar postcard of a 'typical country road + village, such as can be seen all over France'.[217] Men were sometimes granted on leave outside the zone of military operations. W. Vernon described one such trip 'we went through Paris, when we went up there I saw the big Tower called Eiffel Tower. It is a fine country all round there. I didn't think there was such nice scenery in France'.[218] Paris was always appreciated as a *real* escape. On one trip, Sgt. Henry Selly visited the Museé du Luxembourg and collected pictures of the sculptures he saw there.[219]

Soldiers' familiarity with the Western Front worked its way into their lingua franca.[220] French 'borrow words' entered their lexicon. 'Alleyman', 'Boche' and '*Pomme Fritz*' became synonyms for the Germans.[221] Other words hinted at their relationships with civilians. Most terms suggest these were quite basic interactions: verbs, nouns, and adjectives that facilitated understanding were most common. 'Alley' was used in place of 'run away', 'avec' indicated that the soldier desired spirits with his beverage, while 'bon', 'pas bon' or 'no bon' all indicated quality. Many phrases were bastardisations of their original form: *comme ça* was anglicised to 'comsah'; *fâché* became 'fashy' (anger); *pain* transformed into 'Japan' (bread); *manger* was converted to 'Mongey' (food); while 'bongo boosh' meant 'tasty

---

[213] LIDLLE/WW1/GS/0758: Capt. E.L. Higgins, Photographs of Shelled Farmhouse, Barbed Wire Defences, Men Digging Trenches, Ruined Villages, and Dug-Outs.
[214] Ibid. Postcards: Doullens – Vue sur l'Authie; No. 1–3 Guerre 1914-15-16. Doullens (Somme); Guerre 1914-16. Doullens (Somme); No. 81. La Grande Guerre 1914–15 – Albain St Nazaire (P.-de-C.) ['What Remains of the Town-Hall after the battle']; LIDDLE/WW1/GS/0699: J.L. Hampson, Postcards of 'Grande Boucherie Tournaisienne – Spécialité de Moutons' and 'Bailleul (Nord) – Rue de Cassel – Cassel Street'.
[215] LIDDLE/WW1/GS/0746: H.O. Hendry, Postcard 'Mazingarbe (P.-de-C) – Ecole Communale de Garcons'.
[216] Ibid.
[217] RFM.ARC.2495.5: Sgt. S. Gill, YMCA Postcard.
[218] IWM Documents.12771: W. Vernon, Letter to Miss. L. Vernon 22 July 1918.
[219] NAM 2000-09-153-51: Sgt. Henry Selley, Various Postcards of Venus from the Museé du Luxembourg [9–13]. NAM 7403-29-486-144: Sgt. H. Hopwood, Letter to Mother & All 1 July 1918.
[220] SOFO Box 16 Item 30: Lt. C.T. O'Neill, Diary 15 February 1918; IWM Documents.1665: A.P. Burke, Letter to Reg 26 October 1916.
[221] Brophy and Partridge, *The Long Trail*, pp. 64, 74.

morsel' and bore only a passing resemblance to *bonne bouche*.[222] The term 'Napoo' – meaning 'finished; empty; gone; non-existent' – was 'corrupted from the French *Il n'y en a plus*'.[223] Flemish (and Flanders' landscape) also crept into daily usage. 'Bund' described the region's many banks and dams.[224] Some terms were used exclusively by officers – such as 'embusqué' for shirker.

Soldiers' slang extended beyond *Franglais*. Towns and settlements were renamed. 'Bert' became Albert's *nom de guerre*.[225] Euphemisms humanised and diminished the dreadfulness. Death was known colloquially as 'hanging on the old barbed wire'.[226] Heavy guns were known as 'big boys' or 'Billy Wells' (a famous boxer of the period), while high-calibre shells were referred to as 'Black Marias' or, after 1916, 'Coal Boxes'.[227] Trench Mortars were simply 'footballs'.[228] Shelling was referred to as 'hate' or more comically as 'bonking'.[229] Reality only crept into the mundane: an empty bottle of beer was known as a 'dead soldier'.[230]

Men's repeated exposure to the Western Front fuelled familiarisation. Men reinterpreted the environment and the war. Far from passive observers, they were able to see the Western Front as more than just the canvas for their suffering; it became a place of personal significance. As Yi-Fu Tuan has argued, perceptions of landscapes are 'fleeting unless one's eyes are kept to it for some other reason, either the recall of historical events that hallowed the scene or the recall of its underlying reality in geology and structure'.[231] Tellingly, each part of the Western Front could be viewed with a familiar eye. Even the trenches could be 'traversed until its every feature was imprinted on the memory', while 'every part of the landscape' and 'almost every hole was intensely familiar'.[232]

---

[222] Ibid. pp. 75, 98, 111, 122.
[223] Ibid., p. 123. See also RFM.ARC.2012.146.1: Albert Victor Arthur, Diary 20 September 1917.
[224] Brophy and Partridge, *The Long Trail*, p. 78.
[225] Ibid., p. 71. Also NAM 1999-09-74: Pte. Sidney Platt and Pte. Vincent Platt, Notes on the Pronunciation of Loos, Hulloch, Ypres, Rheims, Béthune, Chocques, and Lille.
[226] Brophy and Partridge, *The Long Trail*, p. 78.
[227] Ibid., pp. 71–72.
[228] Ibid., p. 101.
[229] Ibid., pp. 75, 107.
[230] Ibid., p. 90.
[231] Y. Tuan, *Topophilia: A Study of Environmental Perception, Attitudes, and Values* (Englewood Cliffs, NJ, 1974), pp. 93–94.
[232] 'Memories on Revisiting an Old Sector', *The Outpost*, Vol. V., No. 5 (1 September 1917), p. 169.

Personalising the Western Front

Familiarity allowed soldiers to internalise the environment.[233] Landscapes were imbued with meaning and resonated with soldiers. The battlefields, frontlines, and rear areas were layered with memories, both personal and collective. These formed around specific experiences and moments, fusing with the physical world and making the Western Front a patchwork of sites of memory. Pierre Nora describes a '*lieu de mémoire*' as 'any significant entity, whether material or non-material in nature which ... has become a symbolic element of the memorial heritage of any community'.[234] Belgium and France became a symbolic space for both units and individuals and provided conceptual reference points that helped combatants make sense of the war.

The histories conjured by these sites did not have to be positive; even unhappy events were meaningful. Different sectors were characterised by commonly held impressions. One article in the *BEF Times* described the different characteristics of the line stretching from 'Wipers' to 'Vilecholle'.[235] Ypres was at once unpleasant and poignant. It was hard to 'cultivate a love for the salient' but it had come to embody 'Kultur and its effect'.[236] Tellingly, the author had actively 'cut out' memories of Passchendaele. Saying that, the Somme had been 'anything but an enjoyable experience, and we were all heartily glad when our turn came to go out to "rest"'. Shattered landscapes were still significant. 'War ruins' symbolised the desecration of France and the enemy's barbarity.[237] Albert's church steeple and Ypres' cloth hall were particularly popular symbols amongst the troops of the BEF. Smaller towns such as Arras, Bailleul, or Doullens also resonated strongly with servicemen.[238] S. Smith collected

---

[233] Masefield, *The Old Front Line*.
[234] P. Nora (ed.), *Realms of Memory: The Construction of the French Past. Vol. 1: Conflicts and Divisions*, trans. A. Goldhammer (New York, 1996), p. xvii.
[235] F.J.R., 'For Future Historians of the War', *The B.E.F. Times: A Facsimile Reprint of the Trench Magazine* (15 August 1917 [believed misprint of 1918]), p. xi.
[236] Ibid.
[237] E. Danchin, *Le temps des ruines 1914-1921* (Rennes, 2015) and 'Destruction du patrimoine et figure du soldat allemande dans les cartes postales de la Grande Guerre', *Amnis*, Vol. 10 (2011), http://journals.openedition.org/amnis/1371, accessed 8 February 2018.
[238] NAM 2005-02-6: Capt. M. Asprey: Postcards of Albert 'avant et après' the German Bombardments; H.T. Madders, Postcard Collection to Arthur; IWM Documents.7076: S.A. Newman, Postcards of Arras; LIDLLE/WW1/GS/0758: J.L. Hampson, Postcards of 'Grande Boucherie Tournaisienne – Spécialité de Moutons' and 'Bailleul (Nord) – Rue de Cassel – Cassel Street'; LIDLLE/WW1/GS/0758: Capt E.L. Higgins, Postcards of Doullens ['Vue sur l'Authie', 'No. 1, No. 2 and No. 3 Guerre 1914-1915-1916' and 'Guerre 1914-1916']; IWM Documents.11289: H.T. Madders, Postcard Collection to Arthur; LIDDLE/WW1/GS/0746: H.O. Hendry, Postcard: 'La Grande Guerre 1914-1915. Aspect de FESTUBERT (P.-de-C.), après le combats héroïques et victorieux qu'y soutinrent les alliés'.

postcards depicting the damaged basilica of Albert. These showed the old building in ruins with its famous 'Leaning Virgin' hanging precariously from its roof.[239] As a religious site, it became a striking indication of Germanic brutality. In such ways, the environment could symbolise the justice of the Allies' cause.

Memories of happier times played a pivotal role in helping individuals to personalise the Western Front. *The BEF Times*' author fondly remembered the 'comparative peace and comfort' of Neuve Eglise and Hill 63 during a quieter period of the war.[240] Yet, enemy advances during spring 1918 meant that 'the Hun inhabits, for the moment, all our old haunts'. As a consequence, this soldier was bitter and wanted vengeance.[241] Cheerful memories of football matches and dinner parties motivated him to protect what remained of the sector.[242] Another recalled Loos, not for the fighting that took place there in 1915 but for the camaraderie during an 'enjoyable Xmas day'. A church service under 'Tower Bridge' had included a heartfelt rendition of *God Save the King* 'within 300 yards of the Hun Lines'. This was followed by a lavish dinner 'in the old brewery cellars'.[243] Amiens had been 'one of the most comfortable sectors that we have ever struck' as a consequence of to its functioning canteens and dances. 'The whole back area soon rivalled London's night clubs' with the 'exception [of . . .] the rustle of petticoats'.[244] Significant, the city's buildings escaped relatively unscathed until the Germans approached the town in April 1918 so it provided many men with their first sight 'houses and civilians' for many weeks.[245] There were shops and markets and soldiers were able to visit the theatre or cinema.[246] For others, Amiens' heritage and history provided a welcome distraction.[247] G.A. Stevens felt that 'nothing can hide the beauty' of the city.[248] Those men with enough disposable income could withdraw money here to cover a nice lunch or purchase luxuries otherwise difficult to obtain such as Martini cocktails, lobster, fresh chicken, or other 'extras' needed to supplement dinners in the Officers' Mess.[249]

---

[239] MR 3/17/145: Pte S. Smith, Postcards 3 (Albert) Somme and Guerre 1914–1916 No. 80 Albert (Somme).
[240] Ibid.
[241] F.J.R., 'For Future Historians of the War', p. xv.
[242] Ibid.
[243] Ibid., p. xv.
[244] Ibid. pp. xxii–xxiii.
[245] IWM Documents.7035: Lt. J.H. Johnson, Diary 9 January 1918.
[246] Ibid.
[247] NAM 1998-08-31: Pte. A.J. Symonds, Diary 15 August 1916. Symonds also enjoyed visiting Couin.
[248] IWM Documents.12339: Brig. Gen. G.A. Stevens, Letter to Mother 6 November 1916. See also Michelin's Illustrated Guides to the Battle-Fields (1914–1918), *Amiens: Before and during the War* (Michelin & Cie, 1919).
[249] IWM Documents.16504: 2nd Lt. W.J. Lidsey, Diary 14 and 16 November 1916.

For many, it was the relationships that they built with locals (often when billeted in their homes or farms) that were most consequential.[250] Despite warnings from the authorities, in many areas locals remained 'willing to take all risks'. Even in 1917, one soldiers' newspaper noted that '[m]any still continue to till their shell-stricken fields. Others seek to obtain a livelihood by catering for the wants of the most fastidious individual – the British "Tommy"'. Their small canteens and estaminets were places where soldiers could briefly forget the war (even if they felt that the food was overpriced).[251] For J.L. Hampson, these human connections fused with the environment. His diaries were filled with the names and postal addresses of people he met, both soldiers and civilians.[252] Sgt. Harry Hopwood remembered the kindnesses of the locals he encountered.[253] It made the sight of ruined villages and towns all the more dispiriting and one man noted that 'we never knew how much they meant until we lost them. "Pop" [Poperinghe] became a skeleton of its former self, from which the inhabitants were forced to flee; Bailleul is now a heap of ruins; Béthune is unrecognizable; Doullens and Amiens are sadly changed'.[254] Individuals relationship with the people, places, and spaces of Belgium and France nurtured a determination to defend it. Furthermore, the destruction convinced many soldiers that they must ensure it could 'never happen again'.[255]

Men's comradeship was also transposed onto the physical world. Capt. W.S. Ferrie, Pte. William Harrop, and Pte. H.S. Innes kept photographic postcards frozen in location and time. They were mementoes of friendships and locations.[256] Ferrie included biographical details in the photographic postcards he sent home: his captain was 'good', however one NCO was 'a Cambridge Mathematical Scholar and was proving to be a very poor sergeant'.[257] Another soldier, J.L. Hampson, had companions sign the back of their photographs.[258]

---

[250] LIDDLE/WW1/GS/0699: J.L. Hampson, Photograph Postcard of 'Mlle Elisa Audenaert'; MR 2/17/53: Patrick Joseph Kennedy, Postcards from Marie Souise; F.J.R., 'For Future Historians of the War', p. xv.
[251] J.T.S, 'The French Peasantry in the War Zone', *The Outpost*, Vol. 4, No. 3 (January 1917), p. 84.
[252] LIDDLE/WW1/GS/0699: J.L. Hampson, Names and Addresses in 'Telephone Days', 'At Home Days', and 'Memorandum' in Diary '1917 in Belgium and France' and Blank Pages of Letts Pocket Diary 1918.
[253] NAM 7403-29-486-144: Sgt. H. Hopwood, Letter to Mother & All 26 December 1917.
[254] Lowe, *The Western Battlefields*, pp. 11–12.
[255] IWM Documents.1708: Lt. W.B. Medlicott, Diary, Book 2, 3 October 1916, p. 11; IWM Documents.12339: Brig. Gen. G.A. Stevens, Letter to Mother 27 January 1918.
[256] LIDDLE/WW1/GS/0833: Pte. H.S. Innes, Photographic Postcards of Sergeants and of Group of Soldiers in Camp.
[257] IWM Documents.12643: Capt. W.S. Ferrie, Photographic Postcards, File 6.
[258] LIDDLE/WW1/GS/0699: J.L. Hampson, Photograph Postcards, 1: Joe Diamond, R.S.M., L/Cpl Anderson, Sgt Ferrar, American. and J.L. Hampson, 2: Joe Diamond and J.L. Hampson, Box 2.

For similar reasons, Pte. A. Joy's autograph book became a relic of sorts; it contained notes from family members but also the signatures of comrades and the locations where they met. These were often accompanied by words of encouragement, cartoons, or bawdy poems.[259] In his notebook, Guy Chapman recorded each of his men's military identification number, rank, name, height/size, religion, the outcome of his service (wounded, hospital, promotions), and previous occupation.[260] Some NCOs followed a similar practice. C.H. Insom kept a list of his comrades and details about their lives.[261] These were a physical manifestation of the 'bond' between individuals that served in the frontlines.[262]

The interweaving of memory, human connection, and the environment was evident in the pilgrimage texts written by veterans after 1918.[263] The roads were a central feature of H. Williamson's post-war journey across France and Flanders. The highway 'from Poperinghe to Ypres' was familiar to hundreds of thousands of men. Its straight roadway, crumbling houses, scarred elms, grassy edges, surrounding cropland, unmarked graves, heavy traffic, and the feel of the paved road underfoot were seared into Williamson's memory.[264] Lt. Col. T.A. Lowe's 1920 guide for the Western Front was written to enable old soldiers to rediscover such places. He hoped his reader 'will find himself able to roam at will over the ground and visit the spots which for various reasons may be sacred to him'. Such sites might have been the location of 'working parties and reliefs' or 'the scene of some patrol incident ... or the attack on a wood or village'.[265] These all formed a part of men's mental maps, which both supplanted and incorporated the destruction.

Death and Commemoration

The commemoration of the dead played a pivotal role in the process of familiarisation. The network of graves and monuments charted the war's ebb

---

[259] NAM 1992-09-139: Pte. A. Joy, Autograph Book: G.L. Gowing; W.L. Shipton; A.L. Wood; W.J. Hunt; T.H. Potter; G.A. Richardson; Pte. W.H. Gibbs; Pte G. Williams; G.L. Gowing; J. Baker; L/Cpl. James Hall; Pte John J. Miller; Pte. Moon.

[260] LIDDLE/WW1/GS/0292: 2nd Lt. Guy Chapman, Diary 1/1: List of men under his command, 1916.

[261] IWM Documents.16336: C.H. Isom, List of soldiers in his unit, 1918.

[262] IWM Documents.8059: Maj. S.O.B. Richardson, Letter to Mother and Sister 1916 [No. 4].

[263] J.O. Coop, *A Short Guide to the Battlefields* (Liverpool, 1920); Anon., *A Pilgrim's Guide to the Ypres Salient* (London, 1920); *The Illustrated Michelin Guide to the Battlefields: Ypres and the Battles of Ypres* (Clermont-Ferrand, 1919). Although some of these were produced for a wider audience than just veterans.

[264] H. Williamson, *The Wet Flanders Plain* (Norwich, 1929, 1987), pp. 46–48.

[265] Lowe, *The Western Battlefields*, p. 1.

and flow.²⁶⁶ An important feature of the physical world, they provided both concrete and conceptual reference points. These memorials ensured that even the newest arrivals were aware of the sacrifices of their forebears. Individuals were encouraged to acknowledge their place in a community of soldiers – living and fallen – and ensured that *esprit de corps* extended beyond the living. Collective memories (and sacrifice) were embedded in the environment, offering a further justification for soldiers' continued suffering.

Infantrymen were unable to ignore the dead.²⁶⁷ In a spare moment, V.G. Bell sketched a picture of another soldier sitting on a fire-step staring at a cross reading: 'Pte. A. Jones XII Middlesex. TP E JT. RIP'.²⁶⁸ Bell described the scene: 'in a British first line trench. One of many who have died at their posts, now buried below the actual fire-step.'²⁶⁹ This grim reality could be hugely detrimental to morale and resilience. On the night of 9/10 July 1916, the 11th Bn. Border Regiment occupied trenches that were plagued by death. Officers were unable to collect more than twenty men to undertake a bombing mission. Many others reported sick. The medical officer informed a court of enquiry that these infantrymen had been 'digging out the dead in the trenches and carrying them down as well as living in the atmosphere of decomposed bodies'. The impact of heavy casualties on 1 July, physical exhaustion, sorting through deceased comrades' kits, incessant shellfire, and exposure in an open trench undermined their endurance. Kirkwood concluded that 'few, if any, are not suffering from some degree of shell shock'.²⁷⁰ Chronic crises – namely the omnipresence of death and destruction – became harder to endure amidst the acute crises of combat or a bombardment. In fact, they undermined soldiers' ability to respond to these.

Men's letters offered glimpses of this horror. A few soldiers acknowledged the existence of German dead and even revelled in their presence as evidence of success.²⁷¹ Yet, descriptions of deceased comrades tended to be

---

[266] Wilson, *Landscapes of the Western Front*, esp. pp. 35–36, 128–170. See also N. Silk, '"Some Corner of a Foreign Field That Is Forever England": The Western Front as the British Soldiers' Sacred Land', in A. Beyerchen and E. Sencer (eds.), *Expeditionary Forces in the First World War* (London, 2019), pp. 289–311.

[267] IWM Documents.16676: C. Dwyer, Diary 22 September, 12–13 and 30 October 1914; IWM Documents.12819: Maj. J.S. Knyvett, Diary 19 October 1914, p. 19; IWM Documents.17029: Capt. A.J. Lord, Letter to Father 21 April 1918; IWM Documents.11289: H.T. Madders, Diary 24 and 28 August 1918.

[268] BL RP9518: V.G. Bell, 'A British Front Line Trench 3/3/16'.

[269] Ibid.

[270] RAMC 446/18: 'Extracts from the proceedings of a court of enquiry re failure on the part of the 11th Border Regiment, 97th Infantry Brigade, to carry out an attack'.

[271] IWM Documents.11445: Brig. Gen. H.E. Trevor, Letter to Mother 3 October 1914; IWM Documents.18524: Pte. W. Tapp, Diary 26 November 1914; IWM Documents.1665: A.P.

fragmentary.²⁷² One letter reported 'of course we came across one or two poor Tommies but the boys have buried them'.²⁷³ The loss of friends was a shock, but the events were generally left undescribed.²⁷⁴ However, there was no lack of detail in the correspondence of Reginald Neville. He was remarkably honest with his father, perhaps because he was a veteran of the Boer War. In one graphic account, he explained how 'one poor devil [... was] coughing and spitting his very soul out' and a sergeant had his 'leg blown off' by a shell.²⁷⁵ On another occasion, he described how another shell had killed several members of his unit. 'As soon as it got dark we collected some bits of men, put them in a sandbag, carried out the recognisable bodies over the top and dumped them in a shell hole'.²⁷⁶ Such incidents were not rare. Three privates in the 16th Bn. Manchester Regiment went missing during a bombardment on the night of 14/16 June 1917. When a rescue party reached their trench all they could find were 'the remains of 3 bodies ... but no identification was obtainable'.²⁷⁷ Archaeological evidence points to the damage that artillery wrought on the human body. Skeletal remains reveal that multiple fractures, lost limbs, gaping wounds, and fractured skulls were common.²⁷⁸ Sometimes the dead were left unburied.²⁷⁹ Bodies littered battlefields and during warmer weather they were infested with flies, while rigor mortis meant that their limbs were often outstretched at odd and unnatural angles.²⁸⁰

Men had to cope with this. Practical strategies such as quick burials, disinfection, and the cleaning of trenches accompanied a variety of psychological mechanisms. Alexander Watson suggests soldiers sought to diminish the impact of death. Self-deception helped to combat their sense of mortality.

Burke, Letter to Reg 25–27 November 1916; IWM Documents.20211: F. Hubard, Letter to Mr and Mrs Underhill 8 December 1917.

²⁷² IWM Documents.16676: C. Dwyer, Diary 14 and 19 September and 16 October 1914; IWM Documents.18524: Pte. W. Tapp, Diary 26 November 1914; IWM Documents.20211: F. Hubard, Letter to Mr and Mrs Underhill, 8 December 1917; IWM Documents.11976: Lt Col. A.H. Cope, Diary 26 March 1918, p. 13.

²⁷³ IWM Documents.1665: A.P. Burke, Letter to Reg 7 July and 25–27 November 1916.

²⁷⁴ IWM Documents.11289: H.T. Madders, Diary 24 August 1918.

²⁷⁵ SOFO Box 16 3/4/N/2: Lt. Reginald N. Neville, Letters to Father 13 July and 19 September 1917.

²⁷⁶ Ibid. Letter to Father 11 December 1917.

²⁷⁷ TNA WO 95/2339/1: 16th Bn. Manchester Regiment, Appendix II, Casualties June 1917.

²⁷⁸ Wilson, *Landscapes of the Western Front*, pp. 36–37; P.Y. Desfossés, A. Jacques and G. Prilaux, 'Arras "Actiparc" les oubliés du "Point du Jour"', *Sucellus*, Vol. 54 (2003), p. 90; P. Bura, 'Étude anthropologique de la sépulture multiple', *Sucellus*, Vol. 54 (2003), p. 93.

²⁷⁹ IWM Documents.11173: Reverend E.N. Mellish, Letter in *St Paul's, Deptford, Parish Church Magazine* 18 April 1918.

²⁸⁰ IWM Documents.11289: H.T. Madders, Diary 28 and 29 August 1918; MR 2/17/53: Patrick Joseph Kennedy, German Postcards [Nos. 126, 138, 164, 282, 283, 284, 294 and 440]; IWM PC 1784: Maj. Frederick Hardman, Photographic Postcards of Various Dead British Soldiers.

Frontline soldiers also learned to normalise the dead and, as already described, mocked the enemy's instruments of destruction. Positive illusions (such as Charles Quinnell's confidence that he could trace a shell's trajectory) and a religious belief in the afterlife were also important.[281] Capt. A.J. Lord tried to ignore the bodies. He told his father that 'the dead, no matter in what shape or form, no longer cause the slightest concern', although he continued to find the groans of the wounded haunting.[282]

The internment of comrades and friends was never pleasant.[283] Yet, it offered the opportunity for a last display of intimacy and burial could prove cathartic. Where possible, soldiers spent time burying their dead and marking the locations with crosses, shell fragments, or rifle butts.[284] Significantly, memorial rites emphasised resurrection and life after death.[285] Where time allowed, soldiers would hold a brief service and even hasty internments were completed 'reverently'.[286] The very act of commemoration could provide some solace. Charles Dwyer felt that he generated some agency as he carved crosses for the graves of deceased comrades.[287]

Heavy casualties created a network of cemeteries and isolated white crosses.[288] The presence of so many graves on the battlefield is evidenced in the numbers that were damaged by shellfire.[289] These were locations invested with meaning and reminders of the survivors' cause: to fight on in memory of the dead.[290] The landscape was littered with temporary crosses or bottles containing the details of a casualty and charted previous years' fighting.[291] One soldier retraced his steps across the battlefields after 1918 and found that '[t]he sight that touches me up most is the number of little crosses, denoting the graves of our lads who were killed in the advance'.[292] In 1914, civilians often shared the same dangers as combatants and the death of a

---

[281] Watson, *Enduring the Great War*, pp. 88–102.
[282] IWM Documents.17029: Capt. A.J. Lord, Letter to his Father 28 August 1918.
[283] IWM Documents.14707: F. Worrall, Memoir, p. 4.
[284] IWM Documents.16676: C. Dwyer, Diary 21 September, 16 and 22 October 1914; IWM Documents.4772: Canon E.C. Crosse, Diary 4 July 1916.
[285] MR 3/17/91: Memorial Service Programme.
[286] MR 2/17/57: 2nd Lt. Frederick Thomas Kearsley Woodworth, Diary 29 March 1918 'Thorpe's Death'.
[287] IWM Documents.16676: C. Dwyer, Diary 21 September 1914.
[288] CWGC/1/1/10/C/WG 1406.2: Memorial Crosses and Unit Memorials – Lists: Plotted Map of N.E. France & Part of Belgium.
[289] CWGC/1/1/10/C/WG 1406: Memorial Crosses and Unit Memorials – General File, Temporary Memorials 25B and 'List of Temporary Memorials' esp. 20th Battalion Royal Fusiliers at Ceguel British Cemetery. Also, Acquisition of Land – France – DGRE Files, L1.15.3 'Very Valuable Report' O.C. G.R. Units: Somme 6.5.17.
[290] IWM Documents.12819: Maj. J.S. Knyvett, Diary 17 February 1918.
[291] IWM Documents.10933: Capt. G.B. Donaldson, Letter to Mother 29 June 1916.
[292] IWM Documents.15040: A.E. Heywood, Diary 14 November 1918.

Figure 1.5 A burial party on the Western Front *c*. 1917.

Source: Popperfoto via Getty Images/Getty Images.

soldier could become part of the fabric of local memory.[293] In an interview with a member of the Graves Registration Unit (GRU), one French civilian recounted how two British soldiers had been killed around his home. One had been shot through the brain as he picked an apple from his orchard, while the other knelt on his doorstep and returned fire until he too had been shot dead by the enemy.[294] Of course, this was more common in the war's early days when civilians occupied the battle zone in greater numbers.

Bonds of comradeship existed between the living and dead. Burials were moments for collective remembrance that acknowledged the dead's sacrifice.

---

[293] Dowdall, 'Civilians in the Combat Zone', 240, 243.
[294] CWGC/1/1/1/MU 3 Catalogue No. 3 Box 2029: Early Letters about Graves: Report to The Hon. Arthur Stanley C.V.O., M.P. 10 May 1915.

Men even attended other units' services (especially if there was music), perhaps because the ceremony offered some comfort.[295] Illustratively, on a cold day in December 1914, a GRU officer was struggling to erect a cross over the grave of a soldier 'in some out of the way turnip field'. Some passing soldiers noticed and 'obtained leave to fall out and help'. After burying the body, 'without a word they all sprang as one man to attention and solemnly saluted the grave of their dead comrade-in-arms. It was a most impressive and touching sight'.[296] This spontaneous reaction reflected the connection many felt with those killed in service. Furthermore, it mirrored the Edwardian culture of reverence and respect for the dead. Funeral practices were therapeutic and drew on values of respectability.[297] New Army servicemen displayed similar intimacy. After 1 July 1916, survivors in the 8th and 9th Bns. Devonshire Regiment buried thirteen officers and 148 comrades in two trenches in the old frontline at Mansel Copse. Filling in the trenches, they levelled the ground and then enclosed them with barbed wire and subverted its martial purpose. They were 'anxious that grass seed should be sown this year and specially Devonshire plants'.[298] The 8th and 9th Devons attempted to re-nationalise the frontlines and used Devon as their muse. Such measures could boost morale and *esprit de corps*. The flora of south-west England were a proud regimental symbol and reminder of home; they honoured the dead and comforted the living by helping men inhabiting a line otherwise bereft of life.

In the 'sameness' of shattered landscapes, cemeteries became oases for reflection. One Horticultural Department report evaluated the 'value' of sowing annuals in these cemeteries. It noted that the plants helped 'to brighten places often very barren and desolate'. While annuals need to be replanted each spring, they are bright and vibrant, tend to bloom all season long, are cheaper, and require less attention. The authorities believed that 'they cheer our men'.[299] Soldiers were 'constant visitors to our cemeteries' and 'frequently pass ... when on the march'. Cemeteries offered 'relief and interest' for servicemen who would

---

[295] SOFO Box 23A Box 2E: Rev. K.C. Jackson, Diary 27 and 28 August 1916; SOFO Box 23A: Capt. J.H. Early, Daily Routine 12 December 1916 – 4.00 pm Burials; RFM.ARC.2495.5: Sgt. S. Gill, Diary 10 October 1916.

[296] CWGC/1/1/1/MU 1 Catalogue 1 Box 2029: Narrative Letters and Reports, Report from R.A.L. Broadley 6 December 1914.

[297] J. Walvin, 'Dust to Dust: Celebrations of Death in Victorian England', *Historical Reflections/Réflexions Historiques*, Vol. 9, No. 3 (Fall 1982), pp. 353-371; J.-M. Strange, '"She Cried a Very Little": Death, Grief and Mourning in Working-Class Culture, c. 1880-1914', *Social History*, Vol. 27, No. 2 (2002), pp. 143-161 and *Death, Grief and Poverty in Britain, 1870-1914* (Cambridge, 2005), pp. 1-26.

[298] CWGC/1/1/1/WG 549.1: Acquisition of Land – France – DGRE Files: 21-15. 3 D.G.R.& E 'Somme' Report 1 August 1916.

[299] Ibid.

'adorn' graves with 'plants and shrubs found in derelict gardens'.[300] In fact, the maintenance of cemeteries apparently became a 'point of pride' for men billeted nearby.[301] These sites were a testimony to the Edwardian love of gardening and became a means of resistance against the war's destruction.[302]

Men's connection with the dead was also maintained through institutional and regimental memory. Histories of the Imperial (now Commonwealth) War Graves Commission have demonstrated that the preservation of British (and British Empire) graves was driven by an ethos of 'uniformity regardless of rank, race or creed'. The locations, size, and structure of cemeteries were informed by common standards.[303] However, large-scale grave concentration only took place after hostilities ended. During the war, memorials to sacrifices and exploits emerged from personal or unit-directed memorialisation.[304] In fact, the Directorate of Graves Registration and Directories was sometimes willing to establish memorials at the behest of individual battalions.[305] Many of these were in areas that were of special significance to the units. By 1918, there were approximately ninety-five 'battle exploit' memorials on the Western Front, while the number of unit and personal memorials was incalculable.[306]

At Dantzig Alley, a five-foot cross was erected in memory of the officers and men of the 20th Bn. Manchester Regiment and placed next to that of fifty-seven British soldiers of an unidentified unit.[307] Memorials were sometimes crafted from local stone and maintained by the local populace.[308] At Verneuil Chateau, one had been carved from local limestone and inscribed in French: 'R.I.P. Compagne 1914.15.16.17 Le 57e Rmt. d'Infie Francais aux Camarades

---

[300] CWGC/1/1/1/SDC 72: A.W. Hill's Reports on Horticulture, Report 1: Reports on Thirty Seven Cemeteries Visited between March 15th and 31st 1916.

[301] A.W. Hill's Reports on Horticulture, The Care of British Graves in France and the Work of the Horticultural Department: Report by Lieutenant A.W. Hill on his visit to France March 18th–April 8th, 1917.

[302] D. Ottewill, *The Edwardian Garden* (New Haven, CT, 1989). Also J. Kay, '"No Time for Recreations Till the Vote Is Won"? Suffrage Activists and Leisure in Edwardian Britain', *Women's History Review*, Vol. 16, No. 4 (2007), pp. 540–542.

[303] J. Summers, *Remembered: The History of the Commonwealth War Graves Commission* (London, 2007), pp. 14–17; P. Longworth, *The Unending Vigil: The History of the Commonwealth War Graves Commission* (Barnsley, 1967, 2003), p. 86.

[304] CWGC/1/1/10/C/WG 1406: Memorial Crosses and Unit Memorials – General File.

[305] CWGC/1/1/10/C/WG 14061 PT.1: Memorial Crosses and Unit Memorials – Divisions; Brigades; Regiments; Etc. – General File, 4/C32/330/V Letter 4 March 1932 to Adjutant, The Rifle Brigade.

[306] Ibid. AB/NH. Unit Battle Exploit Memorials 13 July 1926.

[307] Ibid. Temporary Unit Memorials [1406] No. 5 Area IWGC Albert 23.7.24.

[308] CWGC/1/1/1/MU 1: Narrative Letters and Reports, Report from R.A.L. Broadley 6 December 1914; The Mobile Unit & The Graves Registration Commission to The Hon. Arthur Stanley, C.V.O. M.P. 13 April 1915 and Early Letters about Graves, Report to The Hon. Arthur Stanley C.V.O., M.P. 10 May 1915.

Anglais tombés au champ d'honneur dans le Secteur de Verneuil.' It was a monument to shared loss and 'honour'.[309] Regiments celebrated past exploits and built bridges between new drafts and their predecessors. Having served in Belgium and France since August 1914, the 2nd Bn. Ox and Bucks Light Infantry had several memorials preserving the unit's collective memory of loss and heroism. In October 1917, the battalion unveiled a memorial near Langemarck and Gheluvelt. The service was led by the battalion's old commanding officer and dedicated to the 'memory of 5 officers and 70 NCOs and Men, 52nd Light Infantry, killed in action 21–23 Oct 1914 some of whom are buried near this spot'.[310] Static war meant that these were often part of the battlefield. Passing soldiers would have been aware that they were traversing or relinquishing hallowed ground, which explains why one report on morale claimed that this 'loss of ground [... had] acted as a powerful tonic on the moral [sic] of the army' after March 1918.[311]

Memorialisation nurtured a sense of ownership.[312] Ypres became a 'sacred monument' for the British.[313] Historian Mark Connelly has argued that a 'consensus around the meaning of Ypres was constructed' producing an 'imagined landscape' that 'linked veterans, the bereaved, and the town's native inhabitants'.[314] This process began during the conflict.[315] The city was a kind of tomb.[316] Graves and battle-scarred landscapes were physical reminders of a

---

[309] CWGC/1/1/10/C/WG 1406: Memorial Crosses and Unit Memorials – Lists, Temporary Memorials 25A.

[310] TNA WO 95/1348: War Diary 2nd Battalion Oxfordshire and Buckinghamshire Light Infantry, 11 October 1917. See also Memorial Crosses and Unit Memorials – General File, Lists of Temporary Memorials, Temporary Memorials 22a.

[311] TNA WO 256/33: Report on BEF Morale 12 July 1918, p. 1.

[312] Ward, *Living on the Western Front*, pp. 92–97.

[313] CWGC/1/1/9/B/WG 360 PT.1: Ypres – General File: Draft [1] of Letter from H.M. Ambassador in Brussels to the Belgian Minister for Foreign Affairs [Report of Anglo-Belgian Conference at Ypres 14 July 1919]. See also M. Connelly, 'The Ypres League and the Commemoration of the Ypres Salient, 1914–1940', *War in History*, Vol 16, No. 1 (2009), pp. 51–76. See also J.M. Winter, *Sites of Memory Sites of Mourning: The Great War in European Cultural History* (Cambridge, 1995, 2003), pp. 52–53; S. Goebel, *The Great War and Medieval Memory: War, Remembrance and Medievalism in Britain and Germany, 1914–1940* (Cambridge, 2007), pp. 29–30, 175–176. For 'sacred places' in the Anzac context see K.S. Inglis, *Sacred Places: War Memorials in the Australian Landscape* (Melbourne, 1998, 2008).

[314] Connelly, 'The Ypres League', p. 53.

[315] D. Lauwers, 'Le Saillant d'Ypres entre reconstruction et construction d'un lieu de mémoire: un long processus de négociations mémorielles de 1914 à nos jours', unpublished Ph.D. thesis, European University Institute (2014); Connelly, 'The Ypres League', pp. 54–55.

[316] CWGC/1/1/9/B/WG 360 PT.1: Ypres – General File, Extract from *Illustrated Sunday Herald* 15 February 1920 – Julius. M. Price (the well-known War Correspondent & Artist), 'Picnics at Ypres: The Desecration of Britain's Holy Ground'; Cutting from the

debt owed to the fallen. One Scottish trench journal explained that the BEF's survivors 'lived to mourn' the fallen, who would 'never fade from our memories'. Their 'sacrifice will be as an incentive to others'.[317] This sentiment was evident on monuments' dedications, which often included phrases lifted from the bible such as 'BETTER [usually worded greater] LOVE HATH NO MAN THAN THIS – THAT A MAN LAY DOWN HIS LIFE FOR HIS FRIENDS.' Elsewhere, they included descriptions of 'GALLANT DEFENCE' or simple pleas to remember the dead.[318]

National history nurtured other connections between the landscape and the dead of other wars. History held broad appeal (across all classes) during this period.[319] One man found himself thinking about Napoleon.[320] Others were confident that the battles of 1914–1918 would take their rightful place in this historical record.[321] Moments from English, British, and regimental history had taken place in northern France and Belgium. Calais was England's last possession on the continent, while Agincourt, Crécy, and Waterloo were sites of historical significance. J.W. Fortescue (the British Army's official historian) published *The British Soldier's Guide to Northern France and Flanders*. In this affordable pamphlet, Fortescue explained that 'the Low Countries and Northern France are the oldest and most familiar of the British Army's campaigning grounds ... This ... is an attempt to enable Regiments to form some idea of the time and circumstances of their former visits to this area'.[322] Connections were drawn to the campaigns of William III and the Duke of Wellington. Each regiment's exploits were described, as were the historic battles and events that had occurred throughout the British zone of operations.[323] Even further back in history 'Englishmen [had] fought and died for Merrie England' during the campaigns of Edward III and Henry V.[324] One

---

Daily Chronicle of 15th January, 1920; 17.3.28.3 'A Memorial in Ypres' Letter to the Editor of *The Times* from R.C. Padre.

[317] Uncle Bob, 'Letter', *The Outpost*, Vol. IV, No. 2 (1 December 1916), p. 55.

[318] CWGC/1/1/10/C/WG 1406: Memorial Crosses and Unit Memorials – Lists, Temporary Memorial Sketches of Unit Memorials, esp. Wieille Chapelle New C.C. – Stone Memorial to King Edward's Horse and Memorial to 6th Seaforth Highlanders in Mont du Hem Cemetery. Also List of Temporary Memorials in Cemeteries No. 1 Area P.R. 1723/AS.

[319] Readman, 'The Place of the Past', pp. 147–199.

[320] IWM Documents.11289: H.T. Madders, Diary 1 November 1918.

[321] SOFO Box 16 Item 36: W.J. Cheshire, Diary 14 September 1914; IWM Documents.12339: Brig. Gen. G.A. Stevens, Letter to Mother 2 November 1916; SOFO Box 16 Item 12: Capt. L.W.E.O. Fullbrook-Leggatt, Regimental Orders Saturday 8 December 1917 [describing action on 30 November].

[322] J.W. Fortescue, *The British Soldier's Guide to Northern France and Flanders*, (London: *The Times*, Undated), p. 1.

[323] Ibid.

[324] Viking, 'Historical Coincidences', *The Outpost*, Vol. V (1 March 1918), p. 166.

popular song's lyrics were 'literally true'. It went '[h]ere we are, here we are, here we are again!' In this regard, the Great War represented continuity. Nonetheless, Fortescue concluded: 'in every case France was the enemy, and the general front of the British was towards the West and South. Now, with that most gallant nation for our friend, we face in the opposite direction'.[325]

****

Ross Wilson has observed that 'whereas the battlefields were the scenes of destruction and death, ruined buildings and scenes of brutality, the ways in which soldiers responded to these conditions acted to alter and shift the meanings of the landscape'.[326] This provided 'a different context in which to consider their lives at the front'.[327] English infantrymen developed an attachment to the physical world. They familiarised the Western Front through exposure and exploration, which helped them to normalise and overcome what confronted them. It was possible for soldiers to become habituated to the Western Front's more distressing sights, sounds, and scents. They also nurtured meaning and developed deep bonds with their surroundings. Geographer D.W. Meinig has argued that landscapes are 'defined by our vision and interpreted by our minds' and are 'composed not of what lies before our eyes but what lies within our heads'.[328] France and Flanders became a meaningful space, but it never threatened to become home. Men remained keen to escape, and individuals from other parts of the world had very different responses to the Englishmen studied here.

'Place attachment' (a concept borrowed from environmental psychology and sociology) helps to explain this. It does not necessitate a preferential perception of a landscape but rests on a person's experiential relationship with their surroundings. Psychologists Leila Scannell and Robert Gifford have described this process as 'the bonding that occurs between individuals and their meaningful environments'. 'Attachment is an effective, proximity-maintaining bond that can be expressed without an underlying purpose of control.'[329] Though frequently an individual phenomenon, it can also take place collectively. Personal connections are built upon memories, connections,

---

[325] Fortescue, *British Soldier's Guide to Northern France and Flanders*, p. 1.
[326] Wilson, *Landscapes of the Western Front*, p. 162.
[327] Ibid., p. 143.
[328] D.W. Meinig (ed.), *The Interpretation of Ordinary Landscapes* (Oxford, 1979), pp. 3, 33–34. Referenced and discussed in P. Readman, '"The Cliffs Are Not Cliffs": The Cliffs of Dover and National Identities in Britain, c.1750–c.1950', *History: The Journal of the Historical Association*, Vol. 99 No. 335 (April 2014), esp. pp. 244–245.
[329] L. Scannell and R. Gifford, 'Defining Place Attachment: A Tripartite Organizing Framework', *Journal of Environmental Psychology*, Vol. 30 (2010), pp. 1–2, 4.

and feelings of growth, whereas shared attachment stems from symbolic cultural meanings or communal historical experiences, values, and symbols. Personal memories of places, people, and events; the collective memorialisation of dead comrades; and institutional and historical memory helped to cultivate a connection with the Western Front.

Various processes feed place attachment. It can be driven by affect and some researchers point to topophilia (a very positive perception of an environment).[330] Others suggest that attachment stems from an emotional investment in, or pride about, a space. Significance can be bred by fear, hatred, or ambivalence. Yet, it is generally more positive emotions that are most significant. Displays of human kindness, feelings of comradeship, or moments of relaxation and discovery nurtured soldiers' relationships with particular locations. Cognition is also influential as 'memories, beliefs, meaning and knowledge' can become fused with places and spaces.[331]

Familiarity is a central pillar of cognitive place attachment. The Western Front was intensely familiar. Exposure and exploration allowed men to acquire beliefs tied to their experiences in Belgium and France, to seek meaning in the world around them, and to develop knowledge particular to the landscapes there. This became intertwined with soldiers' self-perception: their sense of duty, their role as combatants, and their membership of a community were all informed by this physical frame. Attachment was demonstrated behaviourally.[332] Soldiers renamed the frontlines, incorporated French into their vernacular, collected images of the sights they encountered, and eventually returned on pilgrimages after the war. Religious pilgrimage and reconstruction (physical or conceptual) are indicators of place attachment.[333]

This also served psychological functions. Place attachment provides actors with the perception of security and wellbeing.[334] It also gave meaning and structure to the conflict, which was invaluable to morale. Place attachment nurtures feelings of continuity. Memories are projected onto the physical environment, which can become part of personal histories and shared cultural

---

[330] Tuan, *Topophilia*.
[331] Scannell and Gifford, 'Defining Place Attachment', p. 3.
[332] Ibid., p. 4.
[333] For reconstruction, W. Michelson, *Man and His Urban Environment: A Sociological Approach, with Revisions* (Reading, MA, 1976). For pilgrimage, S.M. Low, 'Symbolic Ties That Bind', in I. Altman and S.M. Low (eds.), *Place Attachment* (New York, 1992) and S. Mazumdar and S. Mazumdar, 'Religion and Place Attachment: A Study of Sacred Place', *Journal of Environmental Psychology*, Vol. 24 (2004), pp. 385–397.
[334] Bowlby, *Attachment and Loss*, esp. pp. 70, 204, 373. Also S. Chatterjee, 'Children's Friendship with Place: A Conceptual Inquiry', *Children, Youth and Environments*, Vol. 15 (2005), pp. 1–26.

events.[335] The Western Front became the stage for the pursuit of victorious peace and bonds are sometimes produced by the expectation or success of goal pursuit.[336] Scannell and Gifford have argued that this can 'lead to place dependence, a type of attachment in which individuals value a place for the specific activities that it supports or facilitates'.[337]

Men's relationship with the Western Front helped to combat chronic crisis and deflect acute crisis. By layering memories upon the environment, infantrymen were able to see beyond the destruction. Their attachment to Belgium and France offered a sense of security, the perception of order, and familiarity in a world that was frequently confusing. Yet, as the next chapter will show, the environment still sapped their energy and resilience.

---

[335] C.L. Twigger-Ross and D.L. Uzzell, 'Place and Identity Processes', *Journal of Environmental Psychology*, Vol. 16 (1996), pp. 205–220 and S.M. Low, 'Cross-Cultural Place Attachment: A Preliminary Typology', in Y. Yoshitake, R.B. Bechtel, T. Takahashi and M. Asai (eds.), *Current Issues in Environment-Behavior Research* (Tokyo, 1990).

[336] Scannell and Gifford, 'Defining Place Attachment', p. 6; G.T. Kyle, A.J. Mowen and M. Tarrant, 'Linking Place Preferences with Place Meaning: An Examination of the Relationship between Place Motivation and Place Attachment', *Journal of Environmental Psychology*, Vol. 24 (2004), pp. 439–454.

[337] Scannell and Gifford, 'Defining Place Attachment', p. 6.

2

Enduring the Western Front
Winter and Morale

The environment was a foil for several of the war's chronic crises. In 1914, Canon H.R. Bate recalled that 'the chief trials were the winter and the weather'.[1] Sgt. Thomas Eldridge confessed that 'the only thing Dad [that I] don't like [about the war ...] is thinking of being in the trenches in the winter'.[2] Infantrymen were preoccupied with the difficulties of daily life at war. The bulk of this book's source material comes from autumn and winter. During these months, the weather and military routines dominated men's lives and could become overwhelming and were always a distraction. Daily challenges of warmth, food, and sleep were often soldiers' most pressing concerns. Combatants' relationship with winter (and the environment) helps to explain their resilience and how they dealt with periods of psychological stress. It also reveals the flexible nature of their frames of reference. Other seasons lost their relevance as winter came to encompass the worst of the Western Front and induced different reactions to warfare during warmer months.

Cold weather can be debilitating for military personnel.[3] During the Great War, these were generally described as 'quiet periods' since fewer men were wounded or killed in action.[4] However, at this time trench life became a fight against the elements, which encouraged local truces with the enemy and damaged discipline.[5] Mud became a common theme in soldiers' memories of the conflict.[6] The cold, rain, and snow also recur through combatants'

---

[1] IWM Documents.10782: Canon H.R. Bate, Memoir, p. 3.
[2] NAM 7804-65: Sgt. Thomas Eldridge, Undated Letter to Children.
[3] B.C. Nindl et al., 'Perspectives on Resilience for Military Readiness and Preparedness: Report of an International Military Physiology Roundtable', *Journal of Science and Medicine in Sport*, Vol. 21, No. 11 (November 2018), pp. 1116–1124.
[4] Maj. T.J. Mitchell and G.M. Smith, *History of the Great War Based on Official Documents: Medical Services, Casualties and Medical Statistics of the Great War* (London, 1931), p. 46.
[5] Fletcher, *Life, Death and Growing Up*, p. 143; Ashworth, *Trench Warfare*, p. 26; Bowman, *Irish Regiments in the Great War*, pp. 50–51.
[6] Das, *Touch and Intimacy*, ch. 1. Also F. Uekötter, 'Memories in Mud: The Environmental Legacy of the Great War' in Tucker et al., *Environmental Histories*, pp. 278–295.

descriptions of winter at war.[7] Other issues also defined these periods: the darkness, men's tiredness, the inadequacy of quarters, the occasional paucity of food, and the incessant working parties.[8] These sapped men's strength, leaving men exhausted, and chipped away at their morale. This had the capacity to leave soldiers 'timid or apathetic', more likely to 'shirk' their duties, and less resilient to combat and violence.[9] Individuals experienced physical and psychological 'burnout'.[10] Modern studies indicate that this leads to sub-optimal physical and cognitive performance, which is evidenced in sluggishness, lethargy, and distractedness.[11] In fact, it seems that shell shock was often the product of exhaustion.[12] At the very least, men were more likely to be frustrated and angry during the winter period.[13]

The relationship between histories of conflict and wintertime was evident at other times in the past.[14] During the Napoleonic Wars, 'General Winter' personified these months. Indeed, the elements helped to destroy Napoleon's Army when it invaded Russia in 1812. Later, Primo Levi provided a vivid account of how winter could impact the human experience. Levi was incarcerated at Auschwitz between 1944 and 1945, and his memoir revealed the torment engendered by winter: 'We fought with all our strength to prevent the arrival of winter. We clung to the warm hours ... but it was all in vain.'[15] Winter meant death or suffering 'minute by minute, all day, every day'.[16] Levi felt that conventional language could not do justice to the awfulness. '[I]t was the very discomfort ... that kept us aloft in the void of bottomless despair.'[17]

Winter's chronic crises diverted soldiers' attention away from the bigger picture. For some, it was the harshest part of their war experience.

---

[7] G. Corrigan, *Mud, Blood and Poppycock: Britain and the First World War* (London, 2003, 2004), p. 299; Todman, *The Great War*, pp. 2, 9.
[8] For billets, see Gibson, *Behind the Front*, pp. 109-146. For working parties see Fuller, *Troop Morale*, pp. 62, 92-93. For food see R. Duffett, *The Stomach for Fighting: Food and the Soldiers of the Great War* (Manchester, 2012), ch. 6.
[9] Watson, *Enduring the Great War*, pp. 38-39, 200-215.
[10] D. Zohar, 'Predicting Burnout with a Hassle-Based Measure of Role Demands', *Journal of Organizational Behaviour*, Vol. 18, No. 2 (1997), pp. 101-115.
[11] L.S. Aaronson et al., 'Defining and Measuring Fatigue', *Journal of Nursing Scholarship*, Vol. 31, No. 1 (March 1999), pp. 45-50; S.M. Marcora, W. Staiano, and V. Manning, 'Mental Fatigue Impairs Physical Performance in Humans', *Journal of Applied Physiology*, Vol. 106, No. 3 (January 2009), pp. 857-864.
[12] Leese, *Shell Shock*, pp. 25-26, 39, 91.
[13] Wilson, *Landscapes of the Western Front*, pp. 91, 115, 144.
[14] O. Beattie and J. Geiger, *Frozen in Time: The Fate of the Franklin Expedition* (London, 1987, 2004); M. Zuckoff, *Frozen in Time: An Epic Story of Survival and a Modern Quest for Lost Heroes of World War II* (London, 2013).
[15] P. Levi, *If This Is a Man: The Truce*, trans. S. Woolf (London, 1987), p. 129.
[16] Ibid., p. 130.
[17] Ibid., p. 23.

Infantrymen suffered under the combined effects of exposure, over-exertion, and high levels of stress.[18] Chronic crises, especially exhaustion, were made worse by winter. However, the misery became sustaining; it reorientated men's frames of reference and became the focus of their discontent. Surviving winter helped to reshape their perceptions of war once the season retreated. The emotional relationship that men formed with winter was one that went beyond that of discomfort. This chapter reveals the features of the season and their impact on the infantrymen who endured it. It will assess the ways in which they coped and reveal winter's ability to distort men's frames of reference.[19]

****

Winter in Belgium and northern France could be severe.[20] The trenches, tents, corrugated iron huts, and billets sometimes provided less protection than England's worst urban slums and dilapidated rural dwellings. As such, infantrymen often believed that winter *at war* was incomparable to winter *at home*. The weather in 1916 was particularly harsh, but it was not perceived as the worst winter of the war. In 1917–1918, the weather coalesced with ineffective military campaigning and left combatants less resilient. A variety of issues coalesced to make winter a time of persistent chronic crises.

The Cold

The cold was a key feature of soldiers' lives during wintertime. A word frequency analysis of the letters and diaries used in this book shows that 'cold' was mentioned as frequently as one in every 100 words.[21] It even appeared frequently in Douglas Haig's diary.[22]

In 1914, the nights had been cold during the otherwise warm period before and after the retreat from Mons, which made the regular night marches trying.[23] C. Dwyer first recorded a 'very cold' night's sleep on 19 September,

---

[18] T.A. Wright and R. Cropanzano, 'Emotional Exhaustion as Predictor of Job Performance and Voluntary Turnover', *Journal of Applied Psychology*, Vol. 83, No. 3 (June 1998), pp. 486–493.

[19] The focus of this book is on early winter in 1914 and 1916. In contrast, the analysis of 1917–1918 extends from the beginning of winter through to spring.

[20] See p. 164.

[21] This analysis was run using NVivo. This percentage refers to the regularity of a word's usage in the soldiers' documents – letters, diaries, and memoirs – that were used in this study. In this instance, 'cold' was used with a frequency of 1.3 words out of every 100. This only included words more than three letters in length.

[22] TNA WO 256/25-28: Field Marshal D. Haig's Diary, November–December 1916; December 1917; January–February 1918; March 1918.

[23] RFM.ARC.2012.264: Sgt. Osborn, Diary 24 August 1914.

and thereafter they occurred regularly.[24] John Edwin Mawer found September's weather to be variable. The cold nights contrasted with the 'very hot' days.[25] W.J. Cheshire and his unit were 'all shivers'.[26] Between 17 and 20 September, another man 'endured the most perished [cold]' during the hours of darkness. By late November, it was 'bitter' all day, and he struggled to keep warm in the trenches.[27] On 3 October, H.E. Trevor confessed that the 'worst' part of the war was the 'cold' of the early mornings.[28] One Border Regiment soldier's daily diary entries became less detailed until they simply read, 'very cold'.[29] S. Judd's diary also began to focus exclusively on the temperature.[30] Once the weather turned, many men became dejected. L/Cpl. K.M. Gaunt believed that the weather was 'indescribable', while T.A. Silver remembered that the freezing temperatures left him and others 'weary'.[31] However, stoicism characterised men's responses and when there were activities to divert their attention the cold became less oppressive. Gaunt still described Christmas as a 'magnificent day'.[32]

In 1916, infantrymen continued to write obsessively about the temperature.[33] The cold became as important as the fighting in Lt. Guy Chapman's narrative of the final days of the Somme Campaign.[34] It became 'too cold'.[35] Men were more willing to admit that it dampened their spirit and made them sick.[36] Sgt. G. Skelton remembered that the tail end of the campaign was plagued by 'constant' cold weather.[37] A.P. Burke was scornful of his brother's complaints about a cold spell in Manchester. It could never compare to France where it always seemed to be 'cold and miserable'.[38] G.A. Stevens told his

[24] IWM Documents.16676: C. Dwyer, Diary 19 September 1914.
[25] SOFO Box 16 Item 35: Pte. J.E. Mawer [Doc. 14] Letter 23 September 1914 and [Doc. 16] Letter 2 October 1914; IWM Documents.12819: Maj. J.S. Knyvett, Journal 22 October 1914; S. Judd, Diary 6 October 1914.
[26] SOFO Box 16 Item 36: W.J. Cheshire, Diary 14 September 1914.
[27] SOFO Box 16 Item 35: Pte. J.E. Mawer, [Doc. 24] Letter to Wife Undated [c. 17 November 1914].
[28] IWM Documents.11445: Brig. Gen. H.E. Trevor, Letter to Mother 3 October 1914.
[29] IWM Documents.8674: Pocket Diary 1914, 1–31 December.
[30] IWM Documents.12027: S. Judd, Diary November–December 1914.
[31] IWM Documents.7490: L/Cpl. K.M. Gaunt, Letter 9 January 1915; IWM Documents.7715: T.A. Silver, Memoir 1914.
[32] IWM Documents.7490: L/Cpl. K.M. Gaunt, Letter 25 December 1914.
[33] IWM Documents.1422: Lt. Col. A.V. Spencer, Diary 15 November 1916; IWM Documents.20770: A.L. Collis, Diary 19–25 December 1916; J.M. Nichols, 19 December 1916.
[34] LIDDLE/WW1/GS/0292: 2nd Lt. G. Chapman, Diary 13 and 15 November 1916.
[35] RFM.ARC.2012.958: E.T. Marler, Diary 22 October 1916.
[36] RFM.ARC.2495.5: Sgt. S. Gill, Diary, Book 7, 6 October 1916.
[37] IWM Documents.13966: Sgt. G. Skelton, Memoir, pp. 62–63.
[38] IWM Documents.1665: A.P. Burke, Letter to Reg 21 November and 15 December 1916 and Letter to Tot 26 November 1916.

parents that the 'desperate cold' in late October meant his unit was having a 'rotten time'. November was no less 'horrible'.[39] It left 2nd Lt. W.J. Lidsey's company 'positively beaten'.[40] Frederick Child feared the weather had turned again in early December. Freezing winds and fog affected his sleep and made marching difficult.[41] The frost and ice were no longer thawing.[42] R.E.P. Stevens was 'colder than ever' and felt 'miserable' and 'like an icicle'.[43] The cold sometimes created bitterness towards the 'authorities'. At a time when he was scrounging for firewood, Capt. R.E.M. Young found his superiors' orders 'unreasonable'.[44] Pte. William Anderson told his wife that the cold was making it difficult for some of his comrades to imagine their lives after the war. Frozen in time, it was the cold (not the violence) that convinced him that 'war is absolutely the maddest thing the World knows'.[45] The reaction of the men in 1916 was more negative than those of 1914, though this may have been due to the severity of the weather itself. Furthermore, these soldiers (many of whom middle-class volunteers) were, perhaps, more susceptible to the cold or were more willing to admit its impact upon them than their regular forebears. However, resilience still typified the responses of most of these men.[46]

The winter of 1917–1918 saw the cold sap men's physical and psychological strength to an extent that temperature alone cannot explain. The 'hard extreme cold' was felt strongly.[47] It also appeared as though winter had come much earlier. Reverend E.N. Mellish noted that it was already getting cold in October. The trenches became a 'painful experience'.[48] '[B]itter' temperatures left 2nd Lt. Sydney Frankenburg feeling 'miserable'. He began to 'suffer' from

---

[39] IWM Documents.12339: Brig. Gen. G.A. Stevens, Letter to Father 20 October 1916 and to his Mother 17 and 29 November 1916; IWM Documents.11006: G.H. Greenwell, Diary 10 November 1916.
[40] IWM Documents.16504: 2nd Lt. W.J. Lidsey, Diary 21 November 1916.
[41] SOFO Box 16 Item 42: F.W. Child, Diary 30 November and 2 and 18–20 December 1916; IWM Documents.1708: Lt. W.B. Medlicott, Diary 20 October 1916. Also for cold troubling sleep, see IWM Documents.14441: Lt. L.W. Cubbitt-Ireland, Letter to 'My Dear B' 16 December 1916. For fog, IWM Documents.12105: Reverend M.A. Bere, Diary 28 November 1916; RFM.ARC.2012.958: E.T. Marler, Diary 22 October 1916.
[42] IWM Documents.7953: Pte. F.G. Senyard, Letter to Wife 28 December 1916.
[43] IWM Documents.12521: R.E.P. Stevens, Diary 21, 27, 28, and 29 November 1916.
[44] IWM Documents.20933: Capt. R.E.M. Young, Letter to Constance 9 December 1916.
[45] IWM Documents.5092: Pte. W.M. Anderson, Letters to Wife 1 and 6 December 1916.
[46] IWM Documents.1665: A.P. Burke, Letter to Reg 15 December 1916; IWM Documents.12339: Brig. Gen. G.A. Stevens, Letter to Mother and Father 28 October 1916; IWM Documents.16504: 2nd Lt. W.J. Lidsey, Diary 8 November 1916; IWM Documents.11006: G.H. Greenwell, Letter 10 November 1916.
[47] IWM Documents.11289: H.T. Madders, Diary 9, 14, 16, 19, 22, and 31 January 1918; IWM Documents.1690: P.R. Hall, Memoir, p. 19.
[48] IWM Documents.11173: Reverend E.N. Mellish, Letter in October 1917 edition of *St Paul's, Deptford, Parish Church Magazine*.

cold fingers and wrists and was upset that nobody could warm them.[49] The 'awful' cold weather continued over Christmas and New Year with 'no signs of change'. January was 'colder than ever and [there was a] bitter wind'.[50] C.T. O'Neill and Pte. C.E. Wild arrived in France for the first time in January 1918 and were struck by the low temperatures: 'the conditions [are] awful to one from home'.[51] Veterans, too, were adversely affected. Capt. A.J. Lord complained it was 'too cold to fight'.[52] As in previous years, it also made sleep very difficult.[53]

In early March, the unremitting 'icy cold' returned, and Col. Hardman reported that his unit was 'getting a taste of some real winter weather'.[54] The 'cold' continued after 21 March, and many infantrymen were fixated on it.[55] Pte. C.E. Wild dedicated more of his diary to the temperature than combat.[56] For Capt. Arthur Agius, the cold was as important a feature of the spring withdrawals as the loss of equipment and his fear of a German victory.[57] Lt. Col. Arthur Stockdale Cope believed the cold weather was as demoralising as the enemy's successes. The cold made sleep nearly impossible during the brief moments of rest.[58] By April, the daytime weather was 'wonderful', but the cold nights were still very 'trying'.[59]

The Rain

Rain was inescapable. Men's clothes became sodden as they worked (sometimes submerged up to their thighs) in poorly drained trenches. They were more vulnerable to the cold when wet, and it was frequently the cause of ill health. Severe flooding also undermined the structural integrity of defences, which added to men's physical labour, discomfort, and exhaustion. Another word frequency analysis reveals that references to rain occupied around 0.78 per cent of men's diaries and letters at this time of year. When combined with terms such as wet (0.47 per cent) and water (0.42 per cent), 1.67 out of every

---

[49] LIDDLE/WW1/GS/0583: 2nd Lt. Sydney Frankenburg, Letters 21 and 30 December 1917.
[50] IWM Documents.7035: Lt. J.H. Johnson, Diary 23 December 1917 and 6 January 1918.
[51] SOFO Box 16 Item 30: C.T. O'Neill, Diary 6, 9–15, 26–27 January 1918, 16, 20–21, 25–26 February 1918, 1–4, 8, 11, and 25 March 1918; MR 4/17/388/1: Pte. C.E. Wild, Diary 12–13, 16–18, and 25 February 1918.
[52] IWM Documents.17029: Capt. A.J. Lord, Letter to Dad 29 December 1917.
[53] Ibid., Letter to Dad 30 December 1917; IWM Documents.11976: Lt. Col. A.H. Cope, Diary 26 March 1918.
[54] IWM Documents.7233: Col. F. Hardman, Letter 1 March 1918.
[55] SOFO Box 16 Item 29: Lt. J.E.H. Neville, Diary 22 March 1918.
[56] MR 4/17/388/1: Pte. C.E. Wild, Diary 22 March–11 April 1918.
[57] IWM Documents.8589: Capt. A.J.J.P. Agius, Extract from a Letter received from France 28 March 1918.
[58] IWM Documents.11976: Lt. Col. A.H. Cope, Diary 26 and 29 March 1918.
[59] IWM Documents.12339: Brig. Gen. G.A. Stevens, Letter to Mother Easter Monday 1918.

100 words written by soldiers were in some way related to rain. It was a dominant feature of wintertime.[60]

Heavy rainfall created engineering and psychological challenges in 1914 and made movement very trying.[61] H.E. Trevor reported wet weather on 22 September. He told his mother that it was worst at night.[62] He was, however, struck by the remarkable resilience of his men and noted that sickness was uncommon. By 13 November, he had changed his opinion, noting sarcastically that 'the conditions are very far from luxurious'. It was 'foul' since 'it rains most days and nights'.[63] Prolonged exposure to the elements made it harder to cope. K.F.B. Tower remembered that being 'soaking wet' left his unit 'thoroughly miserable'.[64] Pte. W. Tapp recorded that the trenches were 'knee deep and in some places waist deep in water'. He had a 'rotten bad' time.[65] S. Judd noted that the heavy rain lasted 'nearly all day' on nineteen occasions between 11 November and 31 December.[66] As a result, he became irritable and depressed. Charles Dwyer explained that some men were left unwell by the 'soakings'.[67] The climactic conditions influenced one soldier's perception of combat, and he explained that 'we were going down like raindrops'.[68] Yet, many men were unwilling to admit that they were suffering.[69]

Rain dominated late 1916. The trenches' drainage had improved little. Heavy rain left 'water ... lapping the step' of Cpl. R.G. Plint's dugout.[70] The forward areas were treacherous and difficult to navigate. As R.E.P. Stevens moved up the line, the pounding rain left his unit's 'hopes dashed to despair' and made the vision of destruction all the more depressing.[71] After another month of wet and 'miserable' weather, he was downcast and pessimistic: 'everything is wet with the recent rains and how I shall settle I cannot say'.

---

[60] 'Rain' also reflects the usage of 'rains', 'rained', and 'raining'. 'Wet' also includes 'wetting'.
[61] RFM.ARC.2012.264: Sgt. Osborn, Diary 26–27 August and 12 September 1914.
[62] IWM Documents.11445: Brig. Gen. H.E. Trevor, Postcard to Evelyn Parker 22 September 1914 and Letter to his Mother 3 October 1914.
[63] Ibid., Letter 13 November 1914.
[64] IWM Documents.11442: Lt. Col. K.F.B. Tower, Memoir, p. 5.
[65] IWM Documents.18524: Pte. W. Tapp, Diary 8 December 1914, pp. 7–8.
[66] IWM Documents.12027: S. Judd, Diary 11 November–31 December 1914.
[67] IWM Documents.16676: C. Dwyer, Diary 1 October and 6 November 1914; IWM Documents.7371: Postcard Signed by 'The Mademoiselle from Armentieres', Extract from local paper.
[68] IWM Documents.8631: Diary of an Unidentified Soldier in the 2nd Bn. Border Regiment, 18 December 1914. Also IWM Documents.18524: Pte. W. Tapp, Diary 27 December 1914; NAM 1992-04-159, Anon account of Battle of Mons, pp. 20, 28–29.
[69] NAM 1997-02-11: Reminiscences of Unknown Guardsman 13 August to 3 November 1914, Diary 8–13 September 1914.
[70] IWM Documents.4761: Cpl. R.G. Plint, Memoir, p. 12.
[71] IWM Documents.12521: R.E.P. Stevens, Diary 6, 9, 11, 18, 20, 21 November 1916.

The rain became a metaphor for enemy artillery bombardments.[72] 2nd Lt. W.J. Lidsey seems to have sensed this, too: 'we were not worried by shell fire, but the mud and rain was very trying'.[73] Even when not raining, frontline areas remained flooded.[74] W.J. Lidsey found one road to the trenches (already pockmarked by shell holes) submerged under six inches of water.[75] The area around A.P. Burke's billet was like a 'pond', and he complained that his blankets were 'wet through'. The water went 'over the shoe tops everywhere you go'. It was the 'most miserable village we have ever struck in France', and it was 'a job to put ones [sic] troubles in his old kit bag ... by gad this game is getting washed out'.[76] Soldiers became soaked to the skin on route marches. One officer 'could feel water running down the inside of my leggings and filling my boots ... I had not a dry rag on me'.[77]

The apparent ceaselessness of the rain was particularly wearisome.[78] It also disrupted leisure activities. R.E.P. Stevens kept to his tent during the evenings and wore a groundsheet 'for shelter' when outside. After six days of incessant rain, his syntax and handwriting began to reflect his emotional and physical state: 'generally tired'.[79] Rain made time stand still as normal routines were suspended. Sgt. S. Gill's diary, on 8 November, simply read: 'Rain – Rain – RAIN... Rain... Back to Billet – nothing doing'.[80] It was physically punishing. On 20 November, Gill was caught in a violent rain and hailstorm, which 'seemed to cut lumps out of our faces'.[81]

In 1917–1918, the rain became more depressing. Passchendaele was plagued by heavy rainfall and men believed it had undermined operations.[82] P.R. Hall asserted that the 'torrents of rain' had led to the failures at Third Ypres.[83] Soldiers endured days, weeks, and then months of rain.[84] C.T. O'Neill's experiences were dominated by rain, which fell day and night.[85] Days of 'little

---

[72] Ibid., 25 and 26 December 1916.
[73] IWM Documents.16504: 2nd Lt. W.J. Lidsey, Diary 7 November 1916.
[74] RFM.ARC.2012.958: E.T. Marler, Diary 23 October 1916.
[75] IWM Documents.16504: 2nd Lt. W.J. Lidsey, Diary 2 November 1916.
[76] IWM Documents.1665: A.P. Burke, Letter 26 November 1916.
[77] IWM Documents.7233: Col. F. Hardman, Letter 29 October 1916. Also IWM Documents.1422: Lt. Col. A.V. Spencer, Diary 14 November 1916.
[78] IWM Documents.7233: Col. F. Hardman, Letter 29 October 1916.
[79] IWM Documents.12521: R.E.P. Stevens, Diary 11 November 1916.
[80] RFM.ARC.2495.5: Sgt. S. Gill, Diary 8–9, 18, and 25 November and 5 December 1916.
[81] Ibid., 11 November.
[82] See p. 157.
[83] IWM Documents.1690: P.R. Hall, Memoir, p. 19.
[84] RFM.ARC.2012.146.1: Albert Victor Arthur, Diary 4–9 October 1917; IWM Documents.15433: S.B. Smith, 8–10 and 21 October 1917.
[85] SOFO Box 16 Item: C.T. O'Neill, Diary 11, 15–17, and 20–23 January and 7–8, 13, and 24 February, and 3–5, 19, and 29–30 March 1918.

Figure 2.1 Members of the Middlesex Regiment are seen returning from the trenches in the pouring rain during the Somme campaign.

Source: Daily Mirror/Mirrorpix via Getty Images.

rain' were so rare that they became noteworthy.[86] H.T. Madders' diary entries became short and resentful and on 16 January 1918 he was 'wet through and cold'. Three days later it was 'still awful weather, raining and thawing miserably'.[87] The trenches were correspondingly 'awful', and dugouts collapsed regularly.[88] Some men were unable to escape the wet weather in rear zones. Maj. J.S. Knyvett's billets were 'badly flooded', and 'some of the roads in the area [...were] as much as 1 ½ feet under water for continuous lengths of 200 yards or more'.[89] Rain began to be seen as an insurmountable obstacle crippling the chances of victory for the British Expeditionary Force and an impediment to military campaigning.[90] After 21 March, it continued to be significant. In April, J. Grimston was thankful it had not rained despite his camp being shelled.[91] During the fighting, Pte. C.E. Wild was just as concerned

---

[86] Ibid. 11 February 1918.
[87] IWM Documents.11289: H.T. Madders, Diary 16, 19 and 27 January 1918.
[88] IWM Documents.7035: Lt. J.H. Johnson, Diary 15 January 1918.
[89] IWM Documents.12819: Maj. J.S. Knyvett, Journal 17 January 1918.
[90] IWM Documents.4160: Lt. Col. J.D. Wyatt, Diary 3 February 1918; IWM Documents.14752: J. Grimston, Diary 4 and 19 March 1918.
[91] IWM Documents.14752: J. Grimston, Diary 19 and 30 March, 8 and 27 April 1918.

about the heavy rain as the casualties.⁹² During this period, J.E.H. Neville began to use the rain as a metaphor for unfounded rumours or unpleasant news.⁹³ It was a central feature (and cause) of the general depression of 1917–1918.

Rain sapped men's morale to a greater extent than the cold. Bruce Bairnsfather summed up frontline soldiers' experiences in his cartoon *The Communication Trench*. A dejected soldier stood in the pouring rain up to his ankles in water. He looked on with a cigarette, sodden and unlit, and pondered a problem – was it better to brave 'the top and risk it' or subject himself to 'another mile of this'.⁹⁴ Sometimes the danger was preferable to the challenges of incessant rain and flooding. It was difficult to escape and became even more disheartening when it undermined military efficiency.

Mud

Mud (also referred to as shit) was a constant during wintertime. References to mud represent 0.63 per cent of the soldiers' words in letters and diaries. It became a central feature of the desolate landscape and the war's horror. The clinging sludge could be several feet deep; it made movement and supply immensely tiring. Lt. Gen. E.L.M. Burns remembered that it had inflicted the most 'misery and hardship on the soldier'.⁹⁵

Mud became a pressing issue during the transition to trench warfare in 1914, especially in areas prone to heavy rain and flooding. A lack of duckboards made traversing the lines difficult. In some places, mud extended up each side of the trench; it was impossible to escape the mire. In October, the Border Regiment were 'up to our knees in mud and water'.⁹⁶ S. Judd was still 'knee deep in water and mud' a month later.⁹⁷ Mud dominated soldiers' daily routine. J. Shaddick's Christmas day was 'miserable ... on the whole'. His 'glorious feed for dinner' consisted of a biscuit, a piece of cheese, and 'plenty of mud'.⁹⁸ It got everywhere and when Pte. A.E. Hutchinson was captured on 21 December he was 'well caked up in mud, blood and water'.⁹⁹ The mud prompted Pte. W. Tapp to feel some affinity with the Germans during the

---

⁹² MR 4/17/388/1: Pte. C.E. Wild, Diary 27 March and 7 April 1918.
⁹³ SOFO Box 16 Item 29: Lt. J.E.H. Neville, Diary 27 March 1918.
⁹⁴ B. Bairnsfather, *The Communication Trench*, https://blackersletters.com/2016/02/16/wednesday-february-16th/bairnsfather-fragments-from-france/, accessed 29 August 2017.
⁹⁵ Lt. Gen. E.L.M. Burns in C.E. Wood, *Mud: A Military History* (Washington, DC, 2006, 2007), p. 77.
⁹⁶ IWM Documents.8631: Diary of an Unidentified Soldier in the 2nd Bn. Border Regiment, 18 November 1914.
⁹⁷ IWM Documents.12027: S. Judd, Diary 12 November 1914.
⁹⁸ IWM Documents.17180: J. Shaddick, Memoir, p. 11.
⁹⁹ NAM 1982-12-70: Pte. A.E. Hutchinson, Journal: 'The True Story of My First Day of Captivity in the Hands of the Huns'.

Christmas Truce: 'a lot can talk English they all say it is a pity to fire while were [sic] all up to our knees in mud'.[100] He was, however, happy to note that their trenches were in a worse condition than his own. C.E. Wood believed that men's inability to remain clean was especially depressing and frustrating. Soldiers were trained to uphold cleanliness and in the late Edwardian period dirt was synonymous with contagion and disease; it was symbolic of the underprivileged lives of the working classes.[101] Despite this, soldiers complained surprisingly little.

Social stigma (not to mention discomfort) accompanied dirtiness, and in later years this affected soldiers' self-perception and morale.[102] In late 1916, the mud on the Somme became an antagonist. The conditions were 'simply awful'.[103] Some injured men were even tied to posts so that they did not drown.[104] G.H. Greenwell wrote, '[W]e think mud, Dream mud and eat mud' and complained that 'last winter I thought was bad, but this winter in the Battle Area is quite unimaginable'.[105] Any movement was difficult. G.A. Stevens reported that 'many of the men were up to the knees in mud and I had cases of officers and men being stuck for "hours" in the mud'.[106] Men returned from the line 'unwashed' and 'unshaven' with 'eyes swollen' and 'features drawn'.[107] They looked forward to the opportunity to 'clean up' in the rear zone, but the mud there often made this impossible. 2nd Lt. W.J. Lidsey's 'filthy' camp was also 'knee-deep in mud'. On one occasion, when moving back up the line, he fell up to his armpits in a shell hole full of 'liquid' mud that 'plastered [him] head to foot'. He felt 'beastly' and 'beaten'.[108] Frederick William Child encountered 'roads ... deep with mud'.[109] A.P. Burke explained that the mud was 'everywhere', while Canon E.C. Crosse described the Western Front as 'all' mud.[110] Lt. Ireland lamented that the mud and wet

---

[100] IWM Documents.18524: Pte. W Tapp, Diary 24/25 December 1914.
[101] V. Kelly, *Soap and Water: Cleanliness, Dirt and the Working Classes in Victorian and Edwardian Britain* (London, 2010).
[102] Wood, *Mud*, p. 79.
[103] IWM Documents.20211: F. Hubard, Letter to Mr and Mrs Underhill, 25 October 1916; RFM.ARC.2495.5: Sgt. S. Gill, 8 October and 18 and 28 November 1916; IWM Documents.1422: Lt. Col. A.V. Spencer, Diary 14 November 1916; IWM Documents.18455: Lt. Col. D.R. Turnbull, Letter to Sylvia 11 December 1916.
[104] IWM Documents.12105: Reverend M.A. Bere, Diary 19 November 1916.
[105] IWM Documents.11006: G.H. Greenwell, Letter 4 November 1916.
[106] IWM Documents.12339: Brig. Gen. G.A. Stevens, Letter to Mother 29 November 1916.
[107] Ibid.
[108] IWM Documents.16504: 2nd Lt. W.J. Lidsey, Diary 1–2, 4, 6–7, and 21 November 1916.
[109] SOFO Box 16 Item 42: F.W. Child, Diary 8 December 1916.
[110] IWM Documents.1665: A.P. Burke, Letter to Tot 26 November 1916; IWM Documents.4772: Canon E.C. Crosse, Diary 5 September 1916; IWM Documents.15743: J.M. Nichols, Diary 22–23 December 1916.

weather 'were a frightful hindrance to everything'.[111] Ernest Marler believed the Western Front was a great 'puddle of mud'. The 'rivers of mud' encrusted his clothes, equipment, and food and relegated him to a species of subhuman. He also pitied the horses that he had seen stuck fast in muddy fields.[112] The conditions worried commanders and memoranda noted how fatigued men became while traversing the mud-caked lines.[113] The landscape became mud, which took on the geological features of the 'chalky' bedrock and created a 'desolate outlook' so appalling that 'one could go mad'.[114]

At times during 1917, the mud was an impediment to any movement at Third Ypres.[115] Many saw it as *the* enemy.[116] The mud had arrived earlier than in previous years. H.E. Baker remembered that the 'few men' remaining in 9th Bn. Devonshire Regiment 'after the terrible Ypres 3 battle' were little interested in the enemy but 'had a lot to say about the appalling conditions under which they had to fight'. These servicemen believed that 'many more deaths' had been caused by men drowning in mud than by enemy action.[117] Official records offer little to corroborate these claims, and there are few descriptions of such deaths in official diaries written at the time. However, the fear of drowning was ever-present.[118] It was, perhaps, such sentiment that led Maj. Gen. V.G. Toft to conclude that Passchendaele had been 'a muddy and bloody shambles'.[119] Similar attitudes were evident amongst Belfast's soldiers.[120] The mud led many men (even veterans of previous campaigns) to conclude that it had been the 'worst experience of modern warfare' they had 'yet struck'.[121] P.R. Hall thought that the 'clinging mud' had sent men mad with 'battle fatigue'.[122] After the battle, mud continued to chip away at men's resilience. In January 1918, 2nd Lt. Sydney Frankenburg became distressed when he was unable to clean the filth off himself.[123] H.T. Madders was regularly 'plastered

---

[111] IWM Documents.14441: Lt. L.W. Cubbitt-Ireland, Letter 21 December 1916.
[112] RFM.ARC.2012.958: E.T. Marler, Diary 4 and 25-26 October; 2, 9, 14 and 17-19 November; and 8-12 and 15-16 December 1916.
[113] SOFO Box 23A Item 1: Capt. J.H. Early, Report to Battalion HQ 7:30am 25 November 1916.
[114] IWM Documents.12521: R.E.P. Stevens, Diary 26 and 28 December 1916.
[115] RFM.ARC.2012.146.1: Albert Victor Arthur, Diary 7 October 1917.
[116] IWM Documents.15433: S.B. Smith, Letters 21 and 29 October 1917.
[117] IWM Documents.20329: H.E. Baker, Memoir: Part 6, p 4.
[118] Discussions of drowning tend to occur in post-war memoirs. J. Curran, '"Bonjoor Paree!" The First AIF in Paris, 1916-1918', *Journal of Australian Studies*, Vol. 23 (1999), p. 20; Das, *Touch and Intimacy*, p. 36. Others claim that these descriptions 'are mostly fiction'. See Corrigan, *Mud, Blood, and Poppycock*, pp. 354-355.
[119] IWM Documents.14169: Maj. Gen. V.G. Tofts, Memoir, p. 11.
[120] Grayson, *Belfast Boys*, pp. 119-130.
[121] IWM Documents.11006: G.H. Greenwell, Letter 29 August 1917.
[122] IWM Documents.1690: P.R. Hall, Memoir, p. 19.
[123] LIDDLE/WW1/GS/0583: 2nd Lt. Sydney Frankenburg, Letters 15 and 16 January 1918.

Figure 2.2 An officer wading through a trench of half-frozen mud *c.* 1916.
Source: Culture Club/Getty Images.

with mud' in rear zones that were otherwise 'all mud'.[124] Lt. J.H. Johnson found that 'keeping the post clear ... heart breaking and spirit crushing: like he who had to fill a bucket with holes in it'.[125] During the fighting in March and April 1918, mud continued to play an important role. The 1/7th Bn. Manchester Regiment were sent into support on 22 March, but their progress was hampered when their transport buses became 'stuck in the mud'.[126] Even as Pte. C.E. Wild's battalion retired, his diary remained most concerned with the 'mud and water'.[127] At one point in April, Capt. P. Ingleson had to dig both his platoon sergeant and his dinner out of the gluttonous muck.[128] H.T. Madders regularly found himself up to his knees or thighs in mud when fighting. In such circumstances, battle could become a footnote to the weather.[129]

Snow and Frost

The snow and frost also made regular appearances in soldiers' letters and diaries. Snow was referenced nearly once in every 200 words, while 0.30 per cent of the words were devoted to the frost.[130] Though harsh and unpleasant, these were easier for soldiers to bear than the cold, rain, and mud. Neither was a constant. Snow and frost occurred occasionally and even helped to combat the mud by solidifying the quagmire. Both could be beautiful or ethereal, covering the scars of war and brightening evenings as moonlight reflected off carpeted landscapes. Nonetheless, they contributed to winter's chronic crises.

In 1914, the snow and frost played a secondary role to the other features of winter. W.J. Cheshire recorded several nights of 'white frost' in October.[131] Pte. W. Tapp noted that a seven-day tour of the line during November had witnessed 'all kinds of weather', including 'snow and sharp frosts'.[132] S. Judd first logged snowfall on 19 November. It fell 'fast' and was accompanied by 'thick frost'. He documented the snow in a more neutral tone than the rain, perhaps because it combated the mud as it became more compact. He was so aggrieved by one thaw that it was the most important part of his diary entry, despite his unit suffering five casualties.[133] Snow might have been less oppressive than rainfall, but it still formed a part of the matrix of winter weather.

---

[124] IWM Documents.11289: H.T. Madders, Diary 15 and 18 January 1918.
[125] IWM Documents.7035: Lt. J.H. Johnson, Diary 15 January 1918.
[126] MR 2/17/57: 2nd Lt. F.T.K. Woodworth, Diary 22 March 1918.
[127] MR 4/17/388/1: Pte. C.E. Wild, Diary 23 March–7 April 1918.
[128] IWM Documents.14517: Capt. P. Ingleson, Letter to Gwen c. April 1918.
[129] IWM Documents.11289: H.T. Madders, Diary 6–7 April 1918.
[130] Snow also includes 'snowed', 'snowing' and 'snows.' Frost incorporates 'frosts'.
[131] SOFO Box 16 Item 36: W.J. Cheshire, Diary 8 and 12 October 1914.
[132] IWM Documents.18524: W. Tapp, Diary 22 November 1914. Also RFM.ARC.2012.264: Sgt. Osborn, Diary 1 October 1914.
[133] IWM Documents.12027: S. Judd, Diary 18 and 23 November 1914.

It prompted Judd to retreat into himself. On 21 December, the only thing he wrote in his diary was 'Little snow and rain – cold'.[134]

In 1916, soldiers appear to have perceived the snow and frost more negatively. It was a more severe winter after all. A.P. Burke told his sister on 21 November that the snow and frost had made marching more difficult. He was exhausted, and the snow and frost made the 'bleak moors' he traversed all the bleaker.[135] 2nd Lt. W.J. Lidsey felt the frost 'painfully'. It was almost as if he was becoming a part of the frozen landscape. Frosts sometimes lasted all day and were particularly oppressive when accompanied by 'pea soup fog'.[136] Even behind the lines Pte. Percy Thompson noted that the snow was not 'too pleasant'.[137] Yet, unlike the rain, frost and snow did not preclude recreation, which offered a diversion (albeit a cold one). J.M. Nichols described the snow in a matter-of-fact manner during a period of training. The weather was less bothersome than having to 'always ... wear [a] Gas Helmet'.[138] The snow was also symbolic. Reverend M.A. Bere reported that the end of the 1916 campaign was marked by a 'raging blizzard' on 18 November.[139] Perhaps because the fighting had ceased, some soldiers found that it rendered the devastated country 'picturesque'.[140] The first frosts also provided a welcome relief from the morass created by the wet weather. R.E.P. Stevens was happy when he awoke 'to see everything crisp and white with frost which had not been felt or noticed in the darkness'. However, the inevitable thaw meant this was a temporary relief. Stevens became downhearted as the sticking mud returned later in the day.[141] W.J. Lidsey believed these thaws only exacerbated the impact of rain, combining to produce 'one beastly quagmire'.[142]

The experience of 1917 appears to have amplified soldiers' negative reactions. P.R. Hall remembered the 'periods of heavy snow' as an important part of 'that terrible winter'.[143] The snow became yet another antagonist after the Battle of Cambrai. John Nash's painting of the Artists' Rifles attacking Welsh Ridge on 30 December 1917 illustrated this. In *Over the Top*, the snow plays a

---

[134] Ibid. 21 December 1914.
[135] IWM Documents.1665: A.P. Burke, Letters to Tot and Reg 21 November 1916.
[136] IWM Documents.16504: 2nd Lt. W.J. Lidsey, Diary 16–18 and 29 November 1916; RFM.ARC.2012.958: E.T. Marler, Diary 21 October and 17 November 1916.
[137] SOFO Box 29 Item 4: Pte. Percy Thompson, Letter to Adelaide [undated] from Rouen c. September/October 1916.
[138] IWM Documents.15743: J.M. Nichols, Diary 19 December 1916.
[139] IWM Documents.12105: Reverend M.A. Bere, Letter to Family 18 November 1916.
[140] RFM.ARC.3032: L/Cpl. C. White, Diary 30 January 1917.
[141] IWM Documents.12521: R.E.P. Stevens, Diary 21 November 1916.
[142] IWM Documents.16504: 2nd Lt. W.J. Lidsey, Diary 18 November 1916; IWM Documents.14441: Lt. L.W. Cubbitt-Ireland, Letter 21 December 1916; IWM Documents.7953: Pte. F.G. Senyard, Letter 28 December 1916.
[143] IWM Documents.1690: P.R. Hall, Memoir, p. 19.

Figure 2.3 Soldiers crossing frozen stream in the snowy frontlines.

Source: Pen and Sword Books/Universal Images Group via Getty Images.

more prominent role than the shell bursts in the distance. The cordite smoke could easily be mistaken for the dark clouds that plagued France and Flanders in wintertime. Snow dominates the landscape. One man, killed by enemy fire, lies face down, the lack of a visible wound giving the impression he was overcome by the whiteness below. Nash intended the painting to convey war's futility.[144] Come December Capt. A.J. Lord was describing the frozen snow in despairing tones. The 'ground [was] frozen to a depth of several inches', and the trenches were being raked by a 'bitter wind'.[145] His thirst drove him to 'drink snow-water'. January 1918 was cold. 2nd Lt. Sydney Frankenburg considered the frost and snow to be 'the heaviest ... we have had as yet'.[146] Lt. J.H. Johnson believed the hard frosts had caused illness amongst his men.[147] Behind the lines, Reverend M.A. Bere labelled the snow as 'savage'

---

[144] P. Gough, *A Terrible Beauty: British Artists in the First World War* (Bristol, 2010), p. 21; J.P. Stout, *Coming Out of War: Poetry, Grieving, and the Culture of the World Wars* (Tuscaloosa, 2005, 2016), p. 35.
[145] IWM Documents.17029: Capt. A.J. Lord, Letter to Father 29 December 1917.
[146] LIDDLE/WW1/GS/0583: 2nd Lt. Sydney Frankenburg, Letter 8 January 1918.
[147] IWM Documents.7035: Lt. J.H. Johnson, Diary 16 January 1918.

and grumbled that his chamber pot had frozen. He looked forward to the snow melting, though he accepted this was a sentiment unlikely to be shared by frontline soldiers: 'in spite of the pain I think they prefer the cold dry frost'.[148] The snow plagued H.T. Madders' life. On 16 January, there had been 'about a 1ft of snow', which left him 'wet through and cold'.[149] Snow helped to create the unhappy world that J. Grimston inhabited in early March.[150] Frosts continued during the March battles and made combat even more gruelling. Of course, they posed less of a problem than either the rain or mud.[151] In some sectors, the snow still lay as late as 19 April.[152]

Exhaustion and Supplies

Often, men could see no further than their exhaustion. John Brophy and Eric Partridge recalled that 'one basic fact about the War on the Western Front is that it was fought by men who were almost always tired, because they got little and disturbed sleep in the line, and because they were, day in and day out, weighed down by appalling physical burdens'.[153] 'Sleep' and 'rest' form relatively small percentages of soldiers' overall word usage, possibly because they were so rare. Yet, exhaustion was implicit in their letters and diaries, especially during winter.[154]

Time out of the line was frequently referred to as *so-called* 'rest'. Good health, nice food, rest and amenities, and clean, dry clothing all boosted soldiers' spirits.[155] Yet winter impeded movement, interrupted sleep, eroded trenches, and undermined the structural integrity of billets. Units were also deployed on working parties, and these long nights meant that these were particularly arduous. The winter months were a busy time (see Table 2.1).[156] While men in the BEF were generally well catered for, winter compounded

---

[148] IWM Documents.12105: Reverend M.A. Bere, Letters 3, 5, 6, 8 and 9 January 1918.
[149] IWM Documents.11289: H.T. Madders, 16 January 1918.
[150] IWM Documents.14752: J. Grimston, Diary 2 March 1918.
[151] SOFO Box 16 Item 29 Lt. J.E.H. Neville, Diary 22–24 March 1918.
[152] IWM Documents.14752: J. Grimston, Diary 19 April 1918.
[153] Brophy and Partridge, *The Long Trail*, p. 129.
[154] An NVivo word frequency analysis shows that 'sleep' (inclusive of 'sleeping') occurs with a weighted percentage of 0.29 per cent and 'rest' (as well as 'rested' and 'resting') at 0.26 per cent.
[155] F.M. Richardson, *Fighting Spirit: A Study of Psychological Factors in War* (New York 1978), p. 171. Also Fennell, *Combat and Morale*, p. 10.
[156] R. Grayson, 'A Life in the Trenches? The Use of *Operation War Diary* and Crowdsourcing Methods to Provide an Understanding of the British Army's Day-to-Day Life on the Western Front', *British Journal for Military History*, Vol. 2 No. 2 (2016). See also www.operationwardiary.org/.

Table 2.1 Percentage of days spent in various daily activities, 1914, 1916, 1917, and 1918 in 1st through 6th divisions, BEF

	Fighting	Frontlines (no fighting)	Movement	Training	Resting	Reserve	Support	Domestic	Residue
Oct.–Dec. 1914	31%	25%	20%	2%	5%	1%	0%	5%	9%
Oct.–Dec. 1916	11%	23%	13%	17%	4%	1%	1%	8%	21%
Oct.–Dec. 1917	15%	20%	13%	18%	3%	1%	1%	9%	19%
Jan.–March 1918	11%	31%	7%	16%	2%	1%	2%	8%	22%
1914–1918	**20%**	**27%**	**13%**	**10%**	**5%**	**2%**	**1%**	**7%**	**16%**

Source: Operation War Diary. I would like to thank Operation War Diary (and Richard Grayson) for allowing me to use this data.

supply problems and soldiers' provisions were frequently inferior to the claims of the *Official History*.[157]

The winter of 1914 saw more fighting than in later years. Twenty-five per cent of units' time was spent in the frontlines at the mercy of the elements. In 1916 and 1917/1918, the men remained in trenches between 34 and 43 per cent of the time but were less likely to be fighting. This might have improved their chances of survival, but they still had to cope with the boredom and faced winter without any hope of a break in the deadlock. However, units spent less time in 'movement' so the pressures of long route marches appear to have reduced over time. Nonetheless, units spent marginally less time 'resting'. Importantly, too, it appears that training increased in volume and soldiers' routines became more diverse. Domestic activities – such sport and leisure, parades, or church activities – also became more common. At the same time, the more tiring 'residue activities' (including laborious and dangerous working parties, depressing burials, and back-breaking construction work) doubled in frequency after 1914.

In 1914 the logistical organisation of the British Army was still in flux. The strains of a static war coalesced with the difficulty of supplying troops for winter. William Robertson, then the Quartermaster-General of the BEF, reported on 1 September 1914 that even where food was available its distribution remained imperfect. This problem was heightened as the ground behind the lines became more difficult to traverse.[158] Robertson reported that the 'roads about here are now very bad indeed' and cast doubt on the effectiveness of horse-drawn transport in such conditions.[159] The gap between supply and demand left men hungry and inadequately protected from the weather. It was only in November that the BEF ordered fur coats, coat liners, warm long coats, and macintoshes for its men. Many of these did not reach France until the first week of December.[160]

Poorly equipped for winter, men faced relentless work just to maintain the trench lines. J. Shaddick wrote:

> What a miserable time we had on the whole … When we were out [of the trenches] we had to go up nighttimes [sic] digging reserve trenches or else

---

[157] Duffett, *The Stomach for Fighting*. In the absence of Army Service Corps sources, this study, like Duffett's, rests on the personal records of soldiers as evidence of soldiers' provisions.

[158] LHCMA Robertson 7/1/1: Letter from General William Robertson to Major Clive Wigram, 1 September 1914.

[159] LHCMA Robertson 2/2/2: Letter from Robertson to Sir John Cowans, 12 November 1914.

[160] LHCMA Robertson 2/2/6: Copy of Telegram 'Position as Regards Supply Warm Clothing' Q/CR/1300, 19 November 1914; LHCMA Robertson 2/2/9: Letter from Robertson to Cowans, 20 November 1914.

carrying up stores for those in the trenches and when in the trenches we had to work hard building up the trenches with sandbags.[161]

Trench service was equally tiring. S. Judd got no sleep because heavy rain and flooding forced him to stand up throughout the night.[162] On 24 November, the supplies in his unit were so low that they resorted to breaking ice ponds and boiling the water they collected from these.[163] Life at the front became very trying; water, food, and warm clothing were frequently hard to come by. This might help to explain the Home Front's rush to knit clothes for soldiers. Balaclavas, socks, and other garments were symbolic of civilians' dedication to the cause *and* a response to the soldiers' urgent need for supplies.[164]

By 1916, the BEF's logistical capabilities had improved. However, the unrelenting battle against the elements was tiring and could be deeply frustrating, and 'it was [still] not unusual for all manner of supplies to fail to reach the men at the front'.[165] Soldiers complained that their food and clothing were inadequate. Reverend E.N. Mellish informed his congregation in England that 'the officers and men [in his battalion] have been very hard worked, and the weather has made these last months harder still'.[166] Men were still detailed for 'carrying parties' and subjected to strenuous retraining as the winter lull was used to integrate new drafts, restructure units, and introduce new tactical doctrine.[167] It could be a draining experience just finding the trenches. W.J. Lidsey explained that each man had to closely follow the soldier in front of him. The concentration required left his men 'tired out' and some nearly passed out through exhaustion.[168] Keeping warm was also a trial. Lighting a fire, where permissible, gave only limited relief as the sodden earth did all it could to combat the warmth provided by the flames. In the line, men had to fix collapsing defences, which required near-constant maintenance.[169]

---

[161] IWM Documents.17180: J. Shaddick, Memoir, p. 14.
[162] IWM Documents.12027: S. Judd, Diary 11 December 1914.
[163] IWM Documents.18524: W. Tapp, Diary 1914, p. 3.
[164] R. van Emden and S. Humphries, *All Quiet on the Home Front: An Oral History of Life in Britain during the First World War* (Barnsley, 2003, 2017), p. 17.
[165] Duffett, *The Stomach for Fighting*, p. 160.
[166] IWM Documents.11173: Reverend E.N. Mellish, Letter in March 1917 *St Paul's, Deptford, Parish Magazine*.
[167] TNA WO 95/1348: War Diary 2nd Bn. Oxfordshire and Buckinghamshire Light Infantry; TNA WO 95/1857: War Diary 9th Bn. Royal Fusiliers; TNA WO 95/2403/1: War Diary 11th Bn. Border Regiment.
[168] IWM Documents.16504: 2nd Lt. W.J. Lidsey, Diary 2 and 21 November 1916; IWM Documents.12521: R.E.P. Stevens, Diary 14 December 1916.
[169] IWM Documents.12521: R.E.P. Stevens, Diary 27 December 1916. It possible that this was done using water pumps. However, these involved strenuous effort and were laborious.

Yet, one 1916 censor noted an 'unexpected' absence of grousing about food and kit in soldiers' letters home.[170] Nevertheless, many men did complain. Pte. F.G. Senyard was disappointed with his 'drab ration of stewed mutton (no salt), no bread or biscuits, and a piece of cheese'.[171] On 17 December, he informed his wife that his unit had 'no blankets until today'.[172] It was presumably for similar reasons that R.E.P. Stevens' section had been forced to sleep 'in our overcoats'.[173] Men's glee and surprise at the welcome provision of food and cigarettes during their Christmas celebrations probably reflects how drab their food usually was. Outside of festivities, men were more likely to have a 'poor dinner'.[174] Some infantrymen also reported an inadequate supply of arms.[175] Such problems were more pronounced during wintertime service when men were more reliant on these supplies. Capt. R.E.M. Young was bitter that his alternative sources of food and fuel were unavailable. He was restricted to 'Government rations'.[176] Despite these complaints, the soldiers of the BEF were *relatively* well catered for throughout the war.

In 1917–1918, the situation became more complex. Troops' exhaustion and the perceived paucity of provisions intersected with the aftershocks of Passchendaele, the German counterattack at Cambrai, and the German spring offensives. Many men felt that supplies remained inadequate and this seemed to reflect wider setbacks. The enemy's submarine campaign was causing shortages on the Home Front, which may have been felt by the fighting men, too. Reverend E.N. Mellish beseeched his old congregation in London to send items (including socks) to his battalion.[177] In mid-December, Lt. J.H. Johnson complained that there was a 'scarcity of bread and rather poor rations'. He only had '2 biscuits and half a slice of bread to dig on'.[178] Similar grievances continued well into the new year.[179] Limited water supplies again forced some men to melt snow.[180] A.J. Lord lamented the struggles of 'poor Tommy'. In a letter to his father, he explained that rum was their only sleeping aid. It provided a 'few hours, sound, saving' slumber before the 'cold and wet' made sleep impossible.[181] H. Milner remembered how each

---

[170] IWM Documents.4041: Capt. M. Hardie, '3rd Section Report on Complaints, Moral, Etc (1916)'.
[171] IWM Documents.7953: Pte. F.G. Senyard, Letter to Wife 14 December 1916.
[172] Ibid. Letter to Wife 17 December 1916.
[173] IWM Documents.12521: R.E.P. Stevens, Diary 21 November 1916.
[174] IWM Documents.15743: M. Nichols, Diary 24 December 1916.
[175] IWM Documents.16020: Capt. E. Lycette, Memoir, p. 56.
[176] IWM Documents.20933: Capt. R.E.M. Young, Letter to Constance 9 December 1916.
[177] IWM Documents.11173: Rev. E.N. Mellish, Letter in *St Paul's, Deptford, Parish Church Magazine*, October 1917.
[178] IWM Documents.7035: Lt. J.H. Johnson, Diary 14 December 1917.
[179] LIDDLE/WW1/GS/0137: Pte. O. Billingham, Diary 8 February 1918.
[180] IWM Documents.17029: Capt. A.J. Lord, Letter to his Father 29 December 1917.
[181] Ibid. Letter 30 December 1917.

tablespoonful was stored religiously in soldiers' mugs and 'sipped as we worked ... I think it really was a lifesaver under those conditions: it used to warm us'.[182]

The amount of work required to transform the British lines once the BEF shifted to a strategy of 'defence in depth' led Col. F. Hardman to conclude that 'rest is unknown in France'. His unit's daily routine consisted of 'rising before the lark each morning, groaning all day under loads of barbed wire ... marching miles and miles and even the major is not undisturbed'. 'Rest' simply meant 'rest from the line', but the frontlines offered a '"rest" from "fatigue"'.[183]

The problem of exhaustion came to a head during the *Kaiserschlacht*. After 21 March, men were forced to survive on little or no sleep. Many lost their kit and were left with nothing to protect them from the elements.[184] The combined pressure of the weather and combat was an incredible strain. By Easter, the 4th Bn. Royal Fusiliers had 'been in the trenches for weeks on end'. The unit had endured poor weather, German attacks, and inadequate defensive positions. The barbed wire needed constant improvement (usually during the hours of darkness).[185] Standing to each morning in a waterlogged trench led A.J. Lord to conclude that 'I've had enough of "Dawn" to last me a lifetime'.[186] The increased mobility of the fighting also created logistical chaos. Lt. Col Arthur Stockdale Cope's troops were left hungry as battle stopped any supplies from reaching them. They had little more than their weapons and ammunition. Even coats were a rarity. When food and water did arrive, they were 'very short rations' and had to be shared sparingly.[187] Suffering similar hardships on 21 and 22 March, Pte. O. Billingham wrote erratically in his diary 'NO FOOD ALL DAY. NO FOOD ALL DAY'.[188] Outside of combat, many men focused on these chronic crises rather than the acute military crisis unfolding before them. Battle appeared less frequently in their diaries than their most immediate concerns: food, sleep, and the weather.

Billets and Sleep

Poor food, provisions, and overwork contributed to men's exhaustion and sapped morale. Yet for the working-class infantrymen, these were common

---

[182] IWM Documents.20755: H. Milner, Memoir, p. 18.
[183] IWM Documents.7233: Col. F. Hardman, Letter to Parents 1 March 1918.
[184] IWM Documents.8589: Capt. A.J.J.P. Agius, Extracts from a Letter Received from France 28 March 1918; IWM Documents.11976: Lt. Col. A.H. Cope, Diary 25, 26, 27, 28, and 29 March 1918.
[185] IWM Documents.11173: Reverend E.N. Mellish, Writing in Easter 1918 edition of *St Paul's, Deptford, Parish Church Magazine*.
[186] IWM Documents.17029: Capt. A.J. Lord, Letters to Father 1 and 21 April 1918.
[187] IWM Documents.11976: Lt. Col. A.H. Cope, Diary 25 and 26 March 1918.
[188] LIDDLE/WW1/GS/0137: Pte. O. Billingham, Diary 21 and 22 March 1918.

currency.[189] Perhaps surprisingly, the pitiable state of their sleep quarters was more aggrieving. Complaints became a muted protest, and infantrymen sometimes viewed their poor quarters as evidence of an uncaring and ineffective military institution.

In 1914, men were often forced to sleep in waterlogged ditches. C. Dwyer and his comrades dug holes in the side of their trench 'to put our heads in'. Even his commanding officer had to settle for a newly dug hole in the garden of a cottage.[190] H.E. Trevor informed his wife that 'the cold and damp at nights is the worst and sleeping under ground near a river doesn't make matters better'.[191] Even the billets behind the lines were 'far from luxurious'.[192] Withdrawal from the line often 'meant going back to no pleasant billets, or even dug-outs or shelters, or even trenches, but just a ditch beside a road'.[193] However, officers could usually expect better accommodation. J.S. Knyvett, for example, slept in a farm, while his men were in dugouts in a field covered only by straw.[194] In later years, one battalion commander told his father how 'rest consists in living in dusty barns and disreputable houses'.[195]

It was difficult to improve accommodation as units were constantly on the move. A.P. Burke was forced to stay in a 'different billet every night'. On 21 November 1916, his unit was forced to 'kip down in an old pig sty with a well ventilated roof over you'. It was an imperfect reward for their hard work.[196] Many men complained that tented camps were 'filthy' or 'small and miserable'.[197] There was little impetus to clear out the mud or fix structural issues when stays were temporary. To counteract this, battalions began issuing tickets to confirm that camps, huts, and billets were spotless upon the unit's departure.

In many cases, it was impossible to improve the near-derelict billets found in many areas. It was hard to make a cow-byre, tool shed, hayloft, or hen house more homely. The beds – where there were beds – left a lot to be desired.

---

[189] P. Thompson, *The Edwardians: The Remaking of British Society* (London, 1975, 1992), pp. 11–12; Also, B.S. Rowntree, *Poverty: A Study of Town Life* (London, 1901), pp. 167–168.

[190] IWM Documents.16676: C. Dwyer, Diary 19 October 1914; Also IWM Documents.7490: L/Cpl. K.M. Gaunt, Letter 9 January 1915; IWM Documents.12027: S. Judd, Diary 12 and 16 November and 1, 9 and 28 December 1914; IWM Documents.18524: W. Tapp, Diary 1914, pp. 7–8.

[191] IWM Documents.11445: Brig. Gen. H.E. Trevor, Letter to his Mother 3 October 1914 and Postcard to Evelyn Parker 22 September 1914.

[192] Ibid. Letter to Mother 3 October 1914 and 13 November 1914.

[193] IWM Documents.10879: Lt. Col. C.S. Baines, Memoir of the First Battle of Ypres, 31 October 1914, p. 12.

[194] IWM Documents.12819: Maj. J.S. Knyvett, Journal 23 October 1914.

[195] IWM Documents.7233: Col. F. Hardman, Letter to Father 1 March 1918.

[196] IWM Documents.1665: A.P. Burke, Letter to Tot 21 November 1916.

[197] IWM Documents.16504: 2nd Lt. W.J. Lidsey, Diary 1 November 1916.

These usually included an itchy blanket on a 'bed with wire', a 'bed without wire', a 'bed with straw' or a 'bed without wire or straw'.[198] The conflict even intruded upon sleep as some men slept in sandbags for additional warmth.[199] Of course, vermin also plagued many of these locations.

Nissen huts had been introduced by 1916 in an attempt to improve the situation. These prefabricated half-cylindrical structures were encased in corrugated steel. They were an improvement, but some infantrymen felt that they were reserved for those with easier jobs, such as the cavalry, engineers, or the Army Service Corps.[200] Even when lucky enough to use these huts, soldiers still believed that they were lacking. *The Gloucester Gazette* published a satirical article describing a cat that had given birth to two kittens underneath a Nissen hut but 'decided that the hut did not provide sufficient security [and...] went out to find a "better 'ole"'.[201] Widespread 'scrounging' sometimes meant anything that could be used as firewood was removed, which did not help. Capt. A.J. Lord explained that 'the lining [of the hut] is only too frequently missing because of the selfishness of other troops who have used it as fuel'.[202] It was their sleeping quarters that ensured that 21 December 1916 became the 'worst day' J.M. Nichols' unit had encountered so far in the war.[203]

There was a hierarchy of discomfort: from trenches, through tents and huts, to billets.[204] It was impossible to escape the winter weather in the frontlines. Officers inhabited 'deep' and 'draughty' dugouts and the rank and file were forced into small 'cubby' or 'funkholes'.[205] Canvas offered some protection from the rain and snow, but camps were often erected on arable land that was prone to flooding and did little to protect men from the cold.[206] Even the more permanent structures gave cause for complaint. These buildings generally had uncomfortable floors, broken walls, and leaky roofs.[207] The satisfaction to be gained from the 'miserable dirty little huts' was their *comparative* comfort.[208] Unsurprisingly, then, men remembered civilian billets most warmly.

---

[198] 'Billets', *The Growler*, No. 9 (1 March 1916), p. 10.
[199] IWM Documents.1708: Lt. W.B. Medlicott, Diary 26 October 1916, p 18.
[200] 'Heart to Heart Talks: The Area Commandant – Illy and the Town Major – Igny', *The BEF Times*, Vol. 2, No. 6 (26 February 1918), p. 10.
[201] 'Of Pets – And a Cat', *The Fifth Glo'ster Gazette*, No. 22 (1 March 1918), p. 6.
[202] IWM Documents.17029: Capt. A.J. Lord, Letter to Father 29 December 1917.
[203] IWM Documents.15743: J.M. Nichols, Diary 21 December 1916.
[204] IWM Documents.1665: A.P. Burke Letters November 1916; IWM Documents.16504: W.J. Lidsey, Diary November 1916.
[205] IWM Documents.7035: Lt. J.H. Johnson, Diary 21 December.
[206] IWM Documents.22595: Capt. C.E.R. Sherrington, CES 1/2 – III: Memoir 1916; IWM Documents.14441: Lt. L.W. Cubbitt-Ireland, Letter 16 December 1916; IWM Documents.7650: Cpl. H. Harris, Memoir Late 1916.
[207] IWM Documents.7953: Pte. F.G. Senyard, Letter 26 December 1916; IWM Documents.12521: R.E.P Stevens, Diary 21 November.
[208] IWM Documents.15743: J.M. Nichols, Diary 21 December 1916.

Sickness

Fatigue and exposure sapped soldiers' strength, and there were higher sickness rates during winter. Frostbite, influenza, rheumatic fever, and respiratory diseases such as bronchitis were particularly common, as was pneumonia.[209] Some soldiers, desperate to keep warm, slept around coke braziers and succumbed to carbon monoxide poisoning. These mirrored the risks taken by the poorest of the urban working class during cold spells.[210] Less severe medical problems (such as dermatitis) added to men's discomfort.[211] Most famously, trench foot was an ailment linked to the season. Prolonged service in flooded trenches and long marches left men with hot and swollen feet that festered in cold mud. Ill-fitting boots did not help, nor did the regular frosts, thaws, and rain.[212] Sickness was also caused by 'chronic and acute nerve exhaustion'.[213] Physical stress added to this matrix.

The medical services became more adept at preventing and treating soldiers' illnesses as the war progressed. Frostbite, for example, affected 6,447 men (or 33.90 per 1,000) between August and December in 1914, and trench foot rates followed a similar pattern.[214] Both were less widespread (in relative terms) during 1916 and 1917/1918. The winter of 1914 put immense pressure on the medical apparatus of the BEF. Enteric fevers, such as typhoid, were at their highest rate per thousand in this first winter of the war. Yet many men faced these trials stoically; this was less true in later years. Nonetheless, winter illnesses were *less* prevalent. This was not necessarily due to any significant improvement in 'hygienic conditions'.[215] However, blankets and hot water bottles were more widely available. More significantly, increasing numbers of battle casualties had provoked a 'crisis expansion' in hospital capacity and the ability to treat men.[216] Every effort was made to ensure that hospital camps had high-quality buildings and were not overcrowded.[217] However, winter weather continued to cause medical complications and admissions, and evacuations were often higher between November and January (Table 2.2). In 1918, this peaked again during the early stages of the German offensive.

---

[209] Mitchell and Smith, *Medical Services*, pp. 99–100, 135.
[210] W.G. Macpherson, W.P. Herringham, T.R. Elliott, and A. Balfour, *History of the Great War Based on Official Documents: Medical Services Disease of the War*, Vol. II (London, 1923), p. 268.
[211] Ibid., p. 138.
[212] Mitchell and Smith, *Medical Services*, p. 90.
[213] Watson, *Enduring the Great War*, p. 40.
[214] Mitchell and Smith, *Medical Services*, p. 88.
[215] W.G. Macpherson, W.B. Leishman and S.L. Cummins (eds.), *Official History of the Great War Based on Official Documents: Medical Services Pathology* (London, 1923), p. 259.
[216] Macpherson et. al., *Medical Services*, p. 69.
[217] Ibid. p. 148.

Table 2.2 *Frostbite and trench foot admissions/evacuations in 1916*

	Frostbite and trench foot admissions	Frostbite and trench foot evacuations
1–28 Oct. 1916	854	691
29 Oct.–25 Nov. 1916	4,012	3,206
26 Nov.–30 Dec. 1916	9,370	8,806

Source: Mitchell and Smith, *Medical Services*, p. 89.

Table 2.3 *Frostbite and trench foot admissions/evacuations in 1917/1918*

	Frostbite and trench foot admissions	Frostbite and trench foot evacuations
6–27 Oct. 1917	2,982	2,765
28 Oct.–24 Nov. 1917	3,029	2,961
25 Nov.–29 Dec. 1917	2,982	2,697
30 Dec. 1917–26 Jan. 1918	5,151	4,186
27 Jan.–23 Feb. 1918	520	556
24 Feb.–30 Mar. 1918	225	202
31 Mar.–27 Apr. 1918	1,044	732

Source: Mitchell and Smith, *Medical Services*, p. 89.

There was opportunity in illness, and a fortunate few were evacuated home or to a base camp.[218] For most, though, sickness provided a temporary break from arduous military routines. Sick parades meant that they were assigned light duties. A.P. Burke used mild sickness to escape more difficult fatigues, which felt like a small victory.[219] An understanding junior officer might even turn a blind eye to feigned cases of illness (particularly if the man had served for a long time). Pte. P.N. Wright felt lucky to have a 'sympathetic' medical officer.[220] There was, however, a danger that a less sympathetic superior would see through this and report the man for punishment.[221] Any suspicion could

---

[218] IWM Documents.16676: C. Dwyer, Diary 21 November 1914.
[219] IWM Documents.1665: A.P. Burke, Letter to Reg 29 December 1916.
[220] RFM.ARC 2013.8.2: Pte. P.N. Wright, Diary 2–4 October 1917.
[221] Brophy and Partridge, *The Long Trail*, p. 180.

lead to poor reports about men's character.[222] Pte. C.E. Wild was sometimes lucky and received 'M & D', but was also punished 'for going sick' on other occasions, sometimes unfairly. On one occasion, he was reprimanded despite his foot needing lancing, which made his condition worse and eventually left him restricted to billets.[223]

Combat and Raiding

Offensives were generally paused during winter, but some military activities continued. 2nd Lt. W.J. Lidsey's battalion witnessed some heavy fighting at the beginning of November 1916 and captured several prisoners. Lidsey was relieved they would not be called upon again until spring.[224] Raiding was particularly resented during these months.[225] In early October 1916, A.P. Burke's unit witnessed a shambolic raid. The supporting artillery barrage fell short, flattened the frontlines, and prompted another unit to flee. Frustratingly, it left the Germans opposite more active than before. He assured his brother, however, that they were ready to repulse the enemy if need be.[226] Soldiers anxiously anticipated the enemy's response to raids since combat was singularly unwelcome in winter conditions.[227] Even the successful repulse of a German attack (usually a moment to celebrate) was simply an additional and unwanted trial.[228] Some men, on the other hand, found that an effective raid provided a brief escape from winter routines and even generated some agency. Training could also be a welcome diversion. Capt. Charles Carrington reported that 'we had a wonderful night operation last night, far more interesting than a real battle'. They 'raided an enemy post with as much realism and far more success than I have ever achieved at the front'.[229] The flexibility of these operations was sometimes welcomed. Admittedly, though, Carrington was writing in October 1918 and victory was already in sight. For most, violence made the already trying winter conditions worse.

****

Winter ate away at men's endurance. After the war, official historians accepted that 'there were limits to the powers of endurance of the human organism'. Combat was compounded by 'physical exhaustion', which induced 'a severe

---

[222] SOFO Box 23A Item 1: Capt. J.H. Early, Report for Sgt. Major Wootton 2 January 1917.
[223] MR 4/17/388/1: Pte. C.E. Wild, Diary 25 September 1917 and 18 March 1918.
[224] IWM Documents.16504: 2nd Lt. W.J. Lidsey, Diary 6 November 1916.
[225] Ashworth, *Trench Warfare*, pp. 91–92, 98, 179.
[226] IWM Documents.1665: A.P. Burke, Letter to Reg 12–15 October 1916.
[227] IWM Documents.7035: Lt. J.H. Johnson, Diary 15 and 25 December 1916.
[228] IWM Documents.17029: Capt. A.J. Lord, Letter to Father 8 February 1918.
[229] LIDDLE/WW1/GS/0273: Capt. C. Carrington, Letter 2 October 1918.

mental disability which rendered the individual affected temporarily, at any rate, incapable of further service'.[230] War neurosis or neurasthenia (as well as other 'nervous disorders') were relatively common during the war. In December 1914, one report indicated that between '7 to 10 per cent' of officers and '3 to 4 per cent' of other ranks admitted to Boulogne's hospitals were suffering from 'nervous or mental shock'.[231] Apparently, this became an even greater problem after 1917. The *Official Histories* estimated that there were only 80,000 (*reported*) cases on the Western Front, and many of these were recurring admissions. Yet, many men may have been suffering from nervous disorders that went unreported and unrecognised. Winter contributed to men's sense of chronic crisis and the regular use of words such as 'awful' and 'miserable' suggests winter sapped morale, at least in the short term. Psychological research indicates that 'bad' emotions form quickly and are more powerful than 'good'.[232] Winter was hated. Yet, soldiers were so focused on the problems of daily life that these trials often subsumed wider concerns.

Winter and Depression

It appears that many soldiers were susceptible to bouts of what might be described as depression. The very short days, heavily overcast skies, night work, and periods where rain restricted them to billets limited their exposure to light, which manages the body's functions.[233] A deficiency in Vitamin D, which is very common, impacts levels of melatonin (energy) and serotonin (influencing mood, appetite, and sleep).[234] This can cause irritability, feelings of despair and guilt, visions of worthlessness, low self-esteem, indecisiveness, stress, and anxiety.[235] Furthermore, there is a link between malnutrition and depression, and the paucity of men's supplies during winter could have compounded this problem.[236] What is more, exhaustion and chronic fatigue

---

[230] W.G. Macpherson, W.P. Herringham, T.R. Elliott and A. Balfour, *History of the Great War Based on Official Documents: Medical Services – Surgery of the War*, Vol. I (London, 1922), p. 1.

[231] Ibid., p. 2.

[232] R.F. Baumeister, E. Bratslavsky, C. Finkenauer and D. Kathleen, 'Bad Is Stronger than Good', *Review of General Psychology*, Vol. 5, No. 4 (December 2001), pp. 323–370.

[233] 'Seasonal Affective Disorder – Causes', www.nhs.uk/Conditions/Seasonal-affective-disorder/Pages/Causes.aspx, accessed 1 September 2020.

[234] T.A. Wehr and N.E. Rosenthal, 'Seasonality and Affective Illness', *American Journal of Psychiatry*, Vol. 146, No. 7 (July 1989), pp. 829–839.

[235] 'Symptoms of Seasonal Affective Disorder', www.nhs.uk/conditions/seasonal-affective-disorder/Pages/Symptoms.aspx, accessed 1 September 2020.

[236] C.S. Moliner, K. Norman, K.-H. Wagner, W. Hartig, H. Lochs and M. Pirlich, 'Malnutrition and Depression in the Institutionalised Elderly', *British Journal of Nutrition*, Vol. 102, No. 11 (December 2009), pp. 1663–1667.

can also induce similar symptoms to depression.[237] Depression and pessimism are unhappy bedfellows.[238] This could have impeded combatants' *ability* (rather than their willingness) to fight and remain disciplined.

Though the frontlines were 'miserable', many infantrymen in 1914 seem to have borne the strain suprisingly well.[239] Later in the war, exhaustion and depression appear more forcefully in soldiers' letters and diaries.[240] A.P. Burke exhibited many signs of emotional collapse in one letter to his brother on 15 December 1916. 'It's a bugger', he confessed. The weather had made his life one of 'hellish hardships'.[241] Other soldiers felt helpless and at the season's mercy. G.A. Stevens' letters became more negative as November 1916 dragged on; the weather was the focus of his despondency.[242] Lt. J.H. Johnson's diary entries exhibited low self-esteem. He described his 'mental numbness' and noted that he was 'bored, irritated and annoyed by people and things'. By 21 November, he had 'no interest – no keenness'. The next day he was occupied by 'Thoughts! Thoughts! Thoughts!' Members of his unit were also under great strain. A lance corporal intentionally shot his thumb off on 12 December.[243] When resilience failed or faltered, soldiers sometimes sought an 'immediate' solution to their suffering. The attitude of his comrades left Johnson wondering 'where is the Bairnsfather touch?'[244] The famous cartoonist (and veteran of the war) portrayed servicemen's suffering in a humorous manner. It became increasingly difficult for soldiers to paint their hardships so lightly. However, most men continued to endure hardships even if the suffering was widespread.

The winters of 1916 and 1917 left Charles Carrington tired and dejected. In 1916, he noted that he was 'very fed up', 'still fed up', and even began to contemplate the existence of ghosts (one of very few paranormal references found in his papers).[245] During the winter of 1917, he became self-critical. In October, he found that he was 'thoroughly ashamed of myself' and decided 'that I have come to the end of my tether'. After the new year, he sensed that

---

[237] A.L. Komaroff and D. Buchwald, 'Symptoms and Signs of Chronic Fatigue Syndrome', *Reviews of Infectious Diseases*, Vol. 13, No. Suppl. 1 (January 1991), pp. 8–11.

[238] A.K. MacLeod and E. Salaminiou, 'Reduced Positive Future-Thinking in Depression: Cognitive and Affective Factors', *Cognition and Emotion*, Vol. 15, No. 1 (2001), pp. 99–107.

[239] IWM Documents.17180: J. Shaddick, Memoir, p. 14.

[240] Macpherson et al., *Surgery of the War*, p. 2.

[241] IWM Documents.1665: A.P. Burke, Letter to Reg 15 December 1916.

[242] IWM Documents.12339: Brig. Gen. G.A. Stevens, Letters November 1916.

[243] IWM Documents.7035: Lt. J.H. Johnson, Diary 14, 15, 21 and 22 November and 12 December 1916.

[244] Ibid. Diary 11 December.

[245] LIDDLE/WW1/GS/0273: Capt. C. Carrington, Diary 27 December 1916, 18 and 19 January 1917.

'our nerves are all on edge' and was eventually posted to England.[246] Sydney Frankenburg was shocked and disheartened by the evidence of his men's trauma and exhaustion he found when censoring their letters.[247] Even G.A. Stevens, who was entering his fourth winter of the war, explained that he was 'getting awfully fed up'.[248] The snow fell heavily on H.T. Madders' battalion in January 1918, which coincided with one of his comrades shooting himself. Madders was unwilling to take such drastic action but acknowledged that he and his friends had all 'got the wind up'. He felt 'bilious'.[249] Tellingly, few of them had even served in the frontlines yet.

Men's depression dampened their motivation. They became wrapped up in their own feelings, thoughts, and problems. Depressed persons are more likely to be introvert and neurotic, and there is a direct relationship between the physical feeling of 'coldness' and impressions of social exclusion.[250] Ernest Marler was an example of this. During his first weeks in France, he had described recreational activities, other soldiers, and French civilians in positive terms. Yet, as the winter weather arrived, he became dejected and began rejecting social interaction.[251] This undoubtedly influenced infantrymen's attitudes and actions. In fact, depression amongst workers is a reliable indicator of deteriorating performance.[252] This possibly explains the correlation between winter and the BEF's worsening disciplinary record.[253] In individual cases, winter could cripple morale. Yet, many others deployed coping strategies, and the experience may have even engendered greater resilience.

Coping and Resilience

Men developed (or unconsciously mobilised) techniques to cope with winter's chronic crises. For instance, they grasped any evidence of the weather breaking.[254] Comparatively warm weather was celebrated, and days on which the temperature remained above freezing were welcomed. Sunny days helped 2nd

---

[246] Ibid. Diary 8 and 9 October and 30 December 1917.
[247] LIDDLE/WW1/GS/0583: 2nd Lt. Sydney Frankenburg, Letter 10 December 1917.
[248] IWM Documents.12339: Brig. Gen. G.A. Stevens, Letter to Mother 10 December 1917.
[249] IWM Documents.11289: H.T. Madders, Diary 25 and 27 January 1918.
[250] Chen-Bo Zhong and G.L. Leonardelli, 'Cold and Lonely: Does Social Exclusion Literally Feel Cold?', *Psychological Science*, Vol. 19 (September 2008), pp. 838–842.
[251] RFM.ARC.2012.958: E.T. Marler, Diary October–November 1916.
[252] R. Kessler, L.A. White, H. Birnbaum, Y. Qiu, Y. Kidolezi, D. Mallett and R. Swindle, 'Comparative and Interactive Effects of Depression Relative to Other Health Problems on Work Performance in the Workforce of a Large Employer', *Journal of Occupation and Environmental Medicine*, Vol. 50, No. 7 (July 2008), pp. 809–816.
[253] Bowman, *Irish Regiments in the Great War*, pp. 50–51.
[254] IWM Documents.12027: S. Judd, Diary 24–25 November; 26 and 29 December 1914; IWM Documents.12339: Brig. Gen. G.A. Stevens, Letter to his Mother 2 October 1917 and Easter Monday 1918.

Lt. W.J. Lidsey to remain positive. As the sun shone on the frontlines, he became derisive of the German bombardments and coped better with life in the trenches.[255] 'Fair' weather in December 1916 left 2nd Lt. Henrick Jones erroneously confident that winter would not be too severe.[256] On 2 October 1917, G.A. Stevens told his parents that 'we have been having a spell of really beautiful weather of late which makes such a difference to general comfort'.[257] Between January and March 1918, men noted any increase in temperature. A 'very warm day' often coincided with greater positivity.[258] On 19 January 1918, C.T. O'Neill reported that he was 'feeling much better in spirits, mainly owing to change in weather for better'.[259] During the spring offensives, L/Cpl. E. Lindsell found that better weather had 'made all the difference and its [sic] quite a treat to be without the incessant supply of mud'.[260] Even brief spells of better weather had rejuvenating effects.

Men's imaginations helped them to mitigate the effects of winter. They often diminished their discomfort by imagining the Germans' suffering. H.E. Trevor comforted himself on 'cold and damp nights' with thoughts 'that the Deutsche were much more miserable than us'.[261] S. Judd was similarly sustained by a belief that the enemy were starving. During the 1914 Christmas truce, the enemy's desire to exchange goods for bully beef appeared to confirm his suspicion.[262] Later in the war, G.A. Stevens admitted that 'the condition[s] for the men were awful but I hope Fritz was worse and I think he was'.[263] Sydney Frankenburg turned to fantasy. He would stare at the sky and imagine the pilots of German planes freezing as they 'ought to be'.[264] By focusing on the enemy's discomfort, soldiers downplayed their own trials. This mirrors modern studies that have built on Freud's concept of psychological projection – a cognitive defensive mechanism that allows humans to project negative emotions and traits onto others.[265]

---

[255] IWM Documents.16504: 2nd Lt. W.J. Lidsey, Diary 8 and 14 November 1916.
[256] IWM Documents.16345: 2nd Lt. D. Henrick Jones, Letter to Wife 25 December 1916.
[257] IWM Documents.12339: Brig. Gen. G.A. Stevens, Letter to Mother 2 October 1917.
[258] IWM Documents.11289: H.T. Madders, Diary 22 and 27 January 1918; IWM Documents.12105: Reverend M.A. Bere, Diary 8 January 1918; 2nd Lt. Sydney Frankenburg, Letter 26 January.
[259] SOFO Box 16 Item 30: C.T. O'Neill, Diary 19 January 1918.
[260] LIDDLE/WW1/GS/0144: A & C Black and Company, Letter from L/Cpl. E. Lindsell June 1918.
[261] IWM Documents.11445: Brig. Gen. H.E. Trevor, Letter to his Mother 3 October 1914.
[262] IWM Documents.12027: S. Judd, Diary 27 December 1914.
[263] IWM Documents.12339: Brig. Gen. G.A. Stevens, Letter 29 November 1916.
[264] LIDDLE/WW1/GS/0583: 2nd Lt. Sydney Frankenburg, Letter 10 December 1917.
[265] R.F. Baumeister, K. Dale and K. L. Sommer, 'Freudian Defense Mechanisms and Empirical Findings in Modern Social Psychology: Reaction formation, Projection, Displacement, Undoing, Isolation, Sublimation, and Denial', *Journal of Personality*, Vol. 66, No. 6 (December 1998), p. 1090.

Glimpses of the enemy helped in these circumstances. However, these were rare. In the winter of 1914, the armies were still quite active, and there were regular reconnaissance patrols as battalions extended their saps into No Man's Land. German flares and local attacks continued throughout the final month of the year.[266] The informal Christmas truces might have been 'friendly', but they also provided a clearer image of the enemy.[267] Bruce Bairnsfather remembered that:

> [A]fter months of vindictive sniping and shelling, this little episode came as an invigorating tonic, and a welcome relief to the daily monotony of antagonism. It did not lessen our ardour or determination; but just put a little human punctuation mark in our lives of cold and humid hate.[268]

In contrast, during the winters of 1916–1917 and 1917–1918 many unit diaries almost stopped referring to the Germans.[269] The cessation of military activities may have led infantrymen to dwell more obsessively on the weather. For some, the weather's impact was mitigated by military action, which offered a distraction.[270] Combat was more dangerous, but it was also an outlet and offered the semblance of agency, which contrasted starkly with the impotence and powerlessness men felt during winter.

Activities that disrupted winter routines bolstered men's morale. Christmas is the clearest example of this, despite the festive season being a time at which men felt their distance from home most forcefully.[271] Men in the frontlines were unlucky: 'we poor devils will most likely be starved to death, in the trenches keeping our eyes on Fritz to defend the old country'.[272] Yet, every unit enjoyed a holiday around Christmas (even if it was not on 25 December), which provided a moment of joy as they consolidated their more hopeful

---

[266] TNA WO 95/1565/1: War Diary 1st Bn. Devonshire Regiment and TNA WO 95/1484/1: 1st Bn. Royal Warwickshire Regiment October–December 1916. Also IWM Documents.18524: Pte. W. Tapp, Diary 22 November 1914.

[267] IWM Documents.17180: J. Shaddick, Memoir, p. 11; IWM Documents.12027: S. Judd, Diary 27 December 1914; IWM Documents.7715: T.A. Silver, Memoir 1914.

[268] B. Bairnsfather, *Bullets and Billets* (Project Gutenberg ebook, 2004), www.gutenberg.org/files/11232/11232-h/11232-h.htm, accessed 1 March 2021.

[269] TNA WO 95/2403/1: War Diary 11th Bn. Border Regiment, December; TNA WO 95/1348: War Diary 2nd Battalion Oxfordshire and Buckinghamshire Light Infantry, December; TNA WO 95/1857: War Diary 9th Bn. Royal Fusiliers, December.

[270] IWM Documents.11976: Lt. Col. A.H. Cope, Diary 29 March 1918; IWM Documents.12339: Brig. Gen. G.A. Stevens, Letter to his Mother Easter Monday 1918.

[271] IWM Documents.20770: A.L. Collis, Diary 25 December 1916; RFM.ARC.2012.958: E.T. Marler, Diary 25 December 1916.

[272] IWM Documents.1665: A.P. Burke, Letter to Tot 26 October 1916.

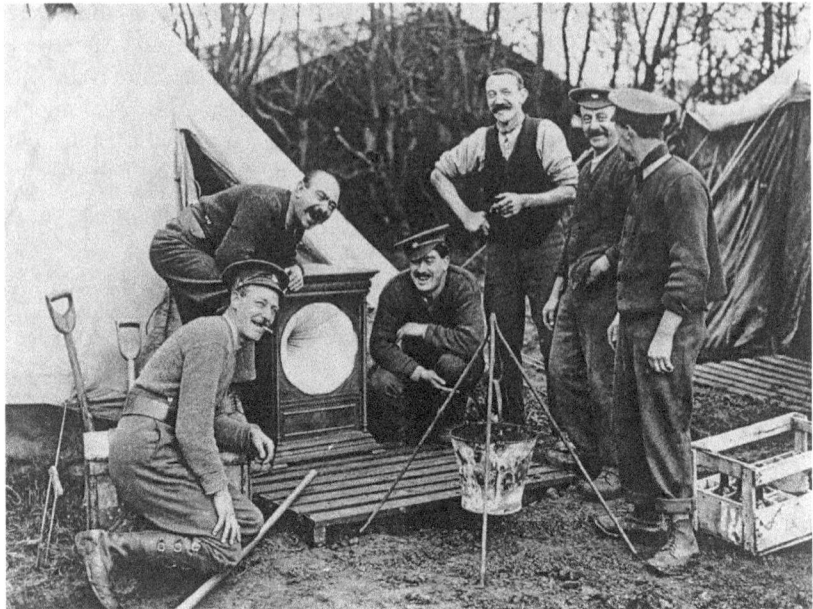

Figure 2.4 British soldiers with their Christmas gift of a gramophone, France, 1914–1918.

Source: Daily Herald Archive/National Science & Media Museum / SSPL via Getty Images.

thoughts.[273] It offered the semblance of normality.[274] A simple (but delicious) Christmas pudding ensured John Edwin Mawer had 'a very decent time'.[275] In the trenches, the unofficial truces of 1914 were welcomed partly because it felt strange to fight on a holiday.[276] In 1916, 2nd Lt. Henrick Jones felt closer to his wife on Christmas day: 'you must enjoy yourself. Forget all the lonely feelings and we'll be with each other all the time'.[277] Christmas dinner allowed officers to display care for their men; for the rank and file it was a pleasant break from usual rations and routines. For some, it may have been the most luxurious meal they had ever had.[278] Their detailed descriptions of the dinners

---

[273] IWM Documents.5092: Pte. W.M. Anderson, Letter to Wife 17 October 1916.
[274] IWM Documents.18455: Lt. Col. D.R. Turnbull, Letter to Mother and Father 15 December 1916; NAM 1990-12-95: Arthur Neilson, Letter to his Daughter 3 December [No Year]; SOFO Box 29 Item 4: Pte Percy Thompson, Letter to Adelaide [undated] from Rouen.
[275] SOFO Box 16 Item 35: Pte. J.E. Mawer, Letter to Wife [Doc. 29 c. Christmas 1914].
[276] IWM Documents.7490: L/Cpl. K.M. Gaunt, Letter (2) 25 December 1914.
[277] IWM Documents.16345: 2nd Lt. D. Henrick Jones, Letter to Wife 25 December 1916.
[278] IWM Documents.7953: Pte. F.G. Senyard, Letter to Wife 26 December 1916.

revealed their excitement and satisfaction.[279] Celebrations were often accompanied by concerts and sports, where men relaxed and drank to excess.[280] They forgot the war and even stopped describing the weather.[281] 2nd Lt. Sydney Frankenburg felt that a real sense of community was nurtured during this period. His men sang carols for their officers, who then invited them into their mess for a drink. The Sergeant's Mess hosted officers later in the day. It helped them to overcome some recent losses.[282] Christmas disrupted the pain of winter. Other smaller events (such as birthdays and football matches) also played such a role. Even if only occasional, they often provided just enough of a distraction to tide men over until spring.

****

Chronic crises could cripple men's morale if they were perceived as permanent states of being. Coping mechanisms, which often focused on a brighter future, were undermined by the perception of an everlasting present. At these moments, soldiers began to fear that they would never return home. Significantly, there was a correlation between peace talk in soldiers' letters and their fear of another winter in the trenches.[283] In 1917–1918, a dwindling faith in victorious peace coalesced with men's anticipation of another winter in Belgium and France. They became unable to frame this as their last winter at war. In August 1917, the III Army censor concluded that the 'minds of men are adversely affected far more by their continued absence from home and by the dread of winter than by the prospect of actual conflict with the enemy'. In fact, 'winter privations and ... lack of leave outnumbers references to the horror of fighting in the ratio of 5 to 1'.[284]

For many, winter symbolised failure to secure victory. Autumn was subsumed by the winter season, and the first signs of the weather worsening signalled another year of war. Once winter arrived, however, the weather became the focus of soldiers' discontent. The trials of daily life left them so exhausted that they could think of little else, drawing their attention away from the war's wider patterns.

The weather was so central to the experience of the war that one soldier argued that the veterans of 1914–1918 developed a heightened 'weather

---

[279] LIDDLE/WW1/GS/0144: A&C Black Publishers, Letter from E.P. Gilscott 28 December 1917; IWM Documents.5875: A. Beevers, Diary 1 January 1917.
[280] IWM Documents.14752: J. Grimston, Diary 25–26 December 1916.
[281] IWM Documents.16504: 2nd Lt. W.J. Lidsey, Diary 25 December 1916.
[282] LIDDLE/WW1/GS/0583: 2nd Lt. S. Frankenburg, Letter 27 December 1916.
[283] IWM Documents.4041: Capt. M. Hardie, 'Report on III Army Morale/Peace Sentiment August to September 1917'.
[284] Ibid. 'Report on III Army Morale, August 1917'.

memory'. Unlike civilians – to whom 'weather is of small concern' – soldiers became acutely aware of weather patterns. The author pointed to the heat that had plagued the retreat from Mons, the rain that fell incessantly during winter 1914–1915, the hard frosts of autumn 1915, the extreme heat of April 1916, the 'torrential rain ... after the taking of Beaumont Hamel', the 'thirsty days of frost' in early 1917, the 'snow showers' at Vimy and Arras, and the 'stormy weather of July 31st [1917] and the mud of Passchendaele'.[285] The most memorable conditions were often those associated with wintertime. These were more demoralising, especially when they undermined military campaigning.

The weather in 1917 and early 1918 was so bad that it appeared to have allied itself with the enemy.[286] Men remembered that they 'were beaten by the weather of that terrible winter'.[287] Maj. G.H. Greenwell believed it had been 'the worst experience of modern warfare I have yet struck'.[288] It created an epidemic of pessimism. So much so that as rain began to fall on 19 March 1918, J. Grimston wrote: 'Rain. Is it because the British intend another advance. It seems to usually rain whenever an advance is about to be attempted and consequently hamper our movements.'[289] Indeed, the weather, this time fog, helped to mask the German advance only two days later.[290] Yet, by allocating blame for military setbacks on the weather, men retained some confidence in their own martial abilities. Tellingly, August 1918 was a turning point in part because 'for the first time the "clerk of the weather" joined up on the British side and a wonderful spell was maintained almost unbroken until the final battle'.[291]

Soldiers' experience of weather influenced their perception of time. It encouraged men to imagine the future. Winter weather was an appropriate foil for depression, but spring and summer were catalysts for optimism and visions of peace. It seems likely that peace and spring became synonymous because of the cultural association of Easter and resurrection. A poem published in *The B.E.F. Times* lamented: 'Gone is the Summer, and ... the flies, / Gone the green hedges that gladdened our eyes'. Instead, the soldiers were faced by a 'landscape ... reeking with rain ... / Gone is all comfort – 'tis Winter again'.[292] It left men 'longing for the bright, warm spring day' when

---

[285] A Gunner Major, 'Weather Memory', *The Cologne Post*, No. 46 (23 May 1919), p .2.
[286] Lloyd, *Passchendaele*, esp. ch. 14.
[287] IWM Documents.1690: P.R. Hall, Memoir, p. 19.
[288] IWM Documents.11006: G.H. Greenwell, Letter 26 August 1917.
[289] IWM Documents.14752: J. Grimston, Diary 19 March 1918.
[290] Hart, *1918*, ch. 3. See also IWM Documents.20770: A.L. Collis, Diary 21 March 1918; SOFO Box 16 Item 29: Lt. J.E.H. Neville, Diary 21–22 March 1918; NAM 2006-04-25: Papers and maps sent to Sir John Fortescue by Lt Gen Sir Ivor Maxse in April and July 1918, Letter to Fortescue from Maxse 28 April 1918.
[291] A Gunner Major, 'Weather Memory', p. 2.
[292] 'To the P.B.I.: An Appreciation', *The B.E.F. Times*, Vol. 1, No. 1 (December 1916), p. 5.

'the rain is over and gone, the flowers appear on the earth, [and] the time of singing birds is come'.[293] Men were often sustained by these visions. As winter arrived in 1916, William Anderson consoled himself that spring would return and 'the sun will shine again'. He felt that this knowledge 'helps a lot'.[294] Pte. A. Conn and his comrades were elated when it did: 'the long winter months are over. Its [sic] good to sit on the fire step in the sun'.[295] The seasons fused themselves with men's faith, religious or otherwise.

Winter influenced soldiers' perception of violence. The war on the Western Front still loosely followed traditional 'campaigning seasons'. Battle raged from spring through summer but ebbed in the winter months. Yet, servicemen often described this period of least violence as the 'darkest' part of their war experience. Surviving a winter campaign was often the mark of a true veteran.[296] Those infantrymen that survived one winter were desperate to avoid another. Donald Hankey explained that 'personally I would far rather have another whack at the Hun than slide uncomfortably into a winter in the trenches. I think most people feel the same'.[297]

Some men actually enjoyed combat, but all soldiers felt that their war against winter was worse than the one raging against the enemy. Soldiers began nervously anticipating the change of weather in early summer. On 16 June 1916, Capt. Geoffrey Donaldson explained to his mother that 'I need hardly say everyone here dreads the idea of another winter campaign'.[298] In November, G.H. Greenwell was occupied by the 'terrible thought that winter is nearly upon us'. Battle might break the military deadlock *and* ensure that men avoided another winter in the trenches: '[o]nly one more month of rapidly fading summer and then the horrors of long black nights and wet days ... I only wish something decisive would happen'.[299] Many men painted military campaigning more positively than wintertime service. The year 1917 was horrible because there had not truly been a summer. The apparent failure of the Passchendaele campaign and the terrible weather left many some combatants contemplating the merits of a compromise peace.[300] There may have been an increased chance of violent death during the spring and summer, but

---

[293] IWM Documents.11173: Reverend E.N. Mellish, Writing in the March 1917 of *St Paul's, Deptford, Parish Church Magazine* describing Winter 1916; IWM Documents.12521: R.E.P. Stevens, Diary 14, 22 and 27 November and 3 December 1916.
[294] IWM Documents.5092: Pte. W.M. Anderson, Letter to Wife 6 December 1916.
[295] LIDDLE/WW1/GS/0347: Pte. A. Conn, Memoir, p. 41.
[296] SOFO Box 23A Item 1: Capt. J. Early, Diary 3 May 1915.
[297] D. Hankey, Letter to his Sister 18 September 1916 in D. Hankey, *A Student in Arms* (London, 1920), p. 349.
[298] IWM Documents.10933: Capt. G.B. Donaldson, Letter to his Mother 16 June 1916.
[299] IWM Documents.11006: G.H. Greenwell, Letters 1 September and 4 November 1916.
[300] IWM Documents.4041: Capt. M. Hardie, '3rd Section Report on Complaints, Moral etc. (1916)' and 'Report on III Army Morale/Peace Sentiment, August to October 1917'.

service during spells of good weather was infinitely preferable to the life of the infantrymen during winter.

The physical and psychological impact of winter dented men's resilience. Working-class infantrymen had feared winter all of their lives, but nothing could prepare them for winter at war.[301] It was an even starker lesson in the power of Mother Nature for wealthier soldiers and officers. Winter left the men immobile and impotent. They obsessed about the chronic crises and the season became a focus of their discontent. The temperature, the rain, the mud, the snow, the hard work, their lack of supplies, their inadequate billets, and sickness all fused to make the winter a period of perpetual crisis cycles. Nevertheless, the end of winter was met with joy, which might help to explain why the morale of the BEF had partially improved by spring 1918. Spring brought new hope. Nonetheless, morale and sensemaking rested on far more than the natural world, and the next chapter will analyse the cultural subtext of men's endurance and service: their perceptions of duty and obligation.

---

[301] For discussions of winter, the cold and the poor, see Pember Reeves, *Round about a Pound a Week* (London, 1913, 2008), p. 41.

PART II

Social Groups

3

Defining Duty
Obligation and the Cultural Foundations of Morale

Military service could be unpleasant, unnerving, and unwelcome. Yet, men's sense of obligation and duty regularly compelled them to endure. A.P. Burke returned reluctantly from leave in October 1916, horrified to find that winter had arrived in Belgium and France. Yet, in an impassioned letter home he still proclaimed: 'I knew I was doing my duty & considering I myself realize what that duty means, & at what risk we chaps out here do it.'[1] While he failed to expand upon what duty meant, Burke revealed its power as an implicit set of normative assumptions drawn from the soldiers' social setting, both civil and military. The army referred to 'duty' in the context of any number of practical activities. Yet, under closer scrutiny, narrow commonplace uses of the word – such a guard duty or latrine duty – give way to broader, deeper, and more complex meanings, involving codes of attitude and behaviour. After all, medals were awarded for 'devotion to duty'. This chapter will trace English infantrymen's' perceptions of duty and obligation by analysing the linkages between the military, crisis, duty, and morale.

Culture forms around a set of 'artificial instincts [... and] has its typical beliefs, norms and values, but these are in constant flux'. Cultures can 'transform' in response to environment, neighbouring cultures, and internal dynamics.[2] Duty existed as a set of often unspoken rules directing infantrymen's actions and perceptions. In 1911, the *Encyclopaedia Britannica* defined duty as an action 'which is regarded as morally incumbent', and existed 'apart from personal likes and dislikes or any external compulsion'. It argued that 'such action must be viewed in relation to a principle, which may be abstract in the highest sense', for example conscience, 'or based on local and personal relations'.[3] Duty was a product of diverse and abstract cultural and institutional foundations lying on bedrock of ideas. Culture plays a significant role in shared sensemaking, so revealing the cultural systems that influenced morale can be very fruitful. These were not only drawn from the civilian world. The

---

[1] IWM Documents.1665: A.P. Burke, Letter to Reg 12–15 October 1916. Underlined by author.
[2] Y.N. Harari, *Sapiens: A Brief History of Human kind*, trans. Y.N. Harari, J. Purcell and H. Watzman (London, 2011, 2014), p. 163.
[3] 'Duty', *Encyclopaedia Britannica*, Vol. 8 (London, 1911), p. 737.

military (through its powers of assimilation) also 'acculturated' recruits and provided frameworks for 'common ways of seeing the world'.[4] Ute Frevert has traced ideas such as honour, shame, and the impact of conscription on citizenship in Germany.[5] Importantly, she revealed the shifting *meaning* of these terms, discussing how they operated within a military that became a 'social event' in its own right.[6]

Perceptions of duty were an important feature of morale but have been understudied. There have been attempts to analyse the implicit moral universe of British society. However, much of this has focused on the high ideals and public-school ethos of the upper classes.[7] There is some disagreement on the extent to which this code diffused across society. Catriona Pennell suggests these ideals were, to some extent, universal. Ideas such as 'national honour, rule of law, justice, the rights of small nations, fair play, and anti-bullying' became explicit in public rhetoric and culture. Britons were expected to embrace appropriate attitudes: stoicism, selflessness, endurance, and equality. These were meant 'to make the soldiers' sacrifice abroad worthwhile'.[8] Other beliefs may have influenced Britons' sense of duty: from the feeling that the war was a defensive crusade and 'a moral duty', through to wartime 'reciprocal obligation and duty' as a feature of active citizenship. Some sense of duty pervaded Britain in 1914–1918, and people believed that the strains involved in performing one's duty should be borne equally.

Duty was relational and embedded in the individual's relationship with their social group or groups.[9] This could negatively impact morale. Wilhelm Deist has argued that there was a 'transformation of values and behaviour which ran counter to the hierarchical system' of the German military in 1914–1918.[10] In contrast, Gary Sheffield has contended that civilian attitudes in the British Expeditionary Force (BEF) provided a strong basis for officer–man harmony. These relations encompassed the duties of paternalism and deference.[11] Elsewhere, the ideology of sacrifice has been highlighted as a cross-class phenomenon throughout the war.[12]

---

[4] D. Kilcullen, 'Strategic Culture', in P.R. Mansoor and W. Murray (eds.), *The Culture of Military Organisations* (Cambridge, 2019), p. 34.

[5] U. Frevert, *Emotions in History – Lost and Found* (New York, 2011) and U. Frevert, *A Nation in Barracks: Modern Germany, Military Conscription and Civil Society*, trans. A. Boreham and D. Brückenhause (Oxford, 2004).

[6] Frevert, *A Nation in Barracks*, p. 6.

[7] P. Parker, *The Old Lie: The Great War and the Public-School Ethos* (London, 1987).

[8] Pennell, *A Kingdom United*, pp. 57–91.

[9] Gregory, *The Last Great War*, pp. 37, 71, 112–151, 187–212.

[10] W. Deist, 'The Military Collapse of the German Empire: The Reality of the Stab-in-the-Back Myth', trans. Feuchtwanger E.J., *War in History*, Vol. 3, No. 2 (1992), p. 191.

[11] Sheffield, *Leadership in the Trenches*, pp. 61–177.

[12] A. Watson and P. Porter, 'Bereaved and Aggrieved: Combat Motivation and the Ideology of Sacrifice in the First World War', *Institute of Historical Research*, Vol. 83, No. 219 (February 2010), pp. 146–164.

However, Edward Madigan has suggested that the 'conflict prompted a re-imagining of courage' by British combatants.[13]

The chasms that existed between social classes in early twentieth-century Britain (in terms of both lifestyle and perceptions) influenced soldiers' outlooks.[14] This was a central theme in Frederic Manning's semi-autobiographical novel *Her Privates We*. Manning, an Australian who served in the ranks of the British Army, developed a lasting impression of the mental universe of the Other Ranks (ORs). One particularly revealing episode found Mr Rhys, a platoon officer, lecturing his men:

> Only a very great man can talk on equal terms with those in the lower ranks of life [... Mr Rhys] would unpack a mind rich in a curious lumber of chivalrous commonplaces, and give an air in a curious unreality to values which for him, and for them all in varying measure, had the strength, if not altogether the substance, of fact. They [the rank and file] did not really pause to weigh the truth or falsity of his opinions, which were simply without meaning for them. They only reflected that gentlefolk lived in circumstances very different from their own, and could afford strange luxuries ... When he spoke to them of patriotism, sacrifice, and duty, he merely clouded their vision.[15]

All soldiers existed in the same institutional social setting with its own ethos, which exerted unique pressures.[16] Nevertheless, the expectations of the British military varied depending on rank. The virtues of officers such as Mr Rhys were 'luxuries' to working-class men in the ranks.[17] Cultural variations within seemingly coherent groups lead to different actions and outlooks.[18] Other Ranks and officers generally came from different social backgrounds and held different roles in the British Army. They interpreted their obligations in different ways. For both groups, however, their perceptions of duty helped them to understand and justify their sacrifices.

Ultimately, it was the military that defined duty and influenced soldiers' actions by creating several uniform duties and expectations that insisted servicemen remained obedient and cheerful. The civilian world also continued to exert pressure, and activities such as training were an opportunity for

---

[13] E. Madigan, '"Sticking to a Hateful Task": Resilience, Humour, and British Understandings of Combatant Courage, 1914-1918', *War in History*, Vol. 20, No. 1 (2013), pp. 76-98.

[14] P. Thompson, *The Edwardians: The Remaking of British Society* (London, 1975, 1992).

[15] F. Manning, *Her Privates We* (London, 1929, 1999), p. 149 [originally published as *The Middle Parts of Fortune*].

[16] Fox, *Learning to Fight*, esp. pp. 11-14 and 19-24.

[17] H. Cunningham, 'The Language of Patriotism, 1750-1914', *History Workshop Journal*, Vol. 12, No. 1 (October. 1981), pp. 25-26.

[18] F. Barth, *Ethnic Groups and Boundaries: The Social Organization of Culture Differences* (Long Grove, 1969, 1998).

education and self-improvement. Service records became evidence of men's good character, which would influence their futures. Soldiers also continued to maintain a strong sense of duty to their homelands.

The Language of Duty

The military exerted enormous pressure on its members. According to some scholars, organisational culture is more likely to influence soldiers' actions than ideology or policy. It creates an identity and set of attributes that differentiates servicemen from civilians and the combatants of other nations while providing a framework of expectations dictating how group members should act.[19] The British Army was no exception, and it sought to imbue men with its 'characteristic spirit'.[20] It seems that it was successful since most men accepted service as a duty.[21]

Amongst the plethora of military duties, there were common ideological threads that bound them together. *Infantry Training* (1905) accepted that 'the mental' faculties of recruits should be nurtured but focused on the practical aspects of instruction.[22] Duty became, at least institutionally, a psychological bond. In this context, it is no surprise that morale dropped its 'e' in publications of the era. In the same way that morale was not simply men's willingness to follow orders, duty was more than a set of activities; both became a network of interlocking characteristics.[23] In 1913, the Royal United Services Institution granted R.H. Beadon a prize for an essay on the development of 'moral qualities' in officers and men. He claimed moral education was key to victory.[24] The 'moral' tone of military training and education is evident in training manuals. *Infantry Training* (1914) was steeped in terms such as 'honour', 'self-restraint', 'courage', and the 'disgrace' of surrender.[25]

Alongside these characteristics, military training aimed to develop *esprit de corps*. The love of one's regiment was something that developed over time, but it was also taught and nurtured. Units organised lectures on regimental history while an array of books published for new recruits celebrated their units' past exploits.[26] The soldiers of 1914–1918 were told that they were contributing to

---

[19] P.R. Mansoor and W. Murray, 'Introduction', in Mansoor and Murray, *The Culture of Military Organisations*, pp. 1–16.
[20] Fox, *Learning to Fight*, p. 50.
[21] Watson, *Enduring the Great War*, pp. 44–56, 56–72.
[22] War Office, *Infantry Training* (London, 1905).
[23] Ussishkin, *Morale*, pp. 17–20.
[24] R.H. Beadon, 'Second Military Prize Essay, 1913', *Journal of the Royal United Services Institution*, Vol. 59 (1913), pp. 130–131.
[25] War Office, *Infantry Training (4 – Company Organisation)* (1914), p. 2.
[26] TNA WO 95/1348: War Diary 2nd Bn. Oxfordshire and Buckinghamshire LI. See also Ferryman, *Regimental War Tales* and Newbolt, *The Story of the Oxfordshire and Buckinghamshire Light Infantry*.

the regiment's heritage, and military communications made frequent reference to units' 'tradition' and 'honour'.[27]

Embarkation leaflets similarly emphasised duty's other more practical dimensions: 'It will be your duty not only to set an example of discipline and perfect steadiness under fire but also to maintain the most friendly relations with those whom you are helping in this struggle.'[28] The development of morals and morale continued on the Western Front. Training courses included sessions on marching discipline, which included advice on posture, how best to disperse after the halt had been ordered, and the rationing of one's water.[29] Trench warfare had not dampened the military's conviction that the 'moral factor' was pre-eminent. Trainers and training literature advised men not to become annoyed by orders and to learn to sing when on route marches. Moral education aimed to allow the British 'to lead' so that the Germans would 'follow'. Aggression – as well as courage, honour, and self-restraint – would translate into the constant 'harrying' of the opponent. 'This is', one lecturer argued, 'simply a question of human nature, and constitutes the moral factor'.[30] These more practical features of duty were intertwined with grander ideas of honour and nobility.[31]

Training helped to inculcate these ideas. In 1914, J.F.C. Fuller viewed training as the education of the soul and the mind. A soldier's key attributes were those of 'self-restraint, of self-sacrifice, of self-respect, of will, of courage, and of faith; of loyalty and devotion; of ability and endurance'.[32] Other publications also emphasised the importance of moulding the soldiers'

---

[27] TNA WO 95/2339: War Diary 16th Bn. Manchester Regiment, Appendix II: 16th Bn Manchester Regiment – The Commanding Officer's Address to Officers, NCOs, and men of the 19th Bn Regiment on 7.2.18; TNA WO 95/3056: War Diary 2/6th Bn. Royal Warwickshire Regiment, Appendix to War Dairy 172 Inf Bde. XVIII Corps No. G. a.155/5. 61st Division – Note from Lt. Gen. Ivor Maxse (CO XVIII Army Corps) 10 April 1918. Also 'What the Shropshire did on the Ypres-Langemarck Road', *The Dud*, Vol. 1, No. 2 (1 July 1917), p. 10; 'The Battle Honours of the Gloucestershire Regiment', *The Fifth Glo'ster Gazette*, No. 17 (1 February 1917), p. 5.

[28] NAM 1998-12-111-2: Lt. A.R. Bradbury, Printed Embarkation Leaflet.

[29] NAM 2005-09-57-10: Training literature 1916–1917, Notebook [1] March Discipline, p. 14.

[30] NAM 2005-09-57-10-5: Confidential: Trench Warfare, Lecture No. 1 Y.P.C. – 5,000 – 22/3/16. Also Lt. Col. J.E. Smart, [-8] Army Book 152: Correspondence Book. (Field Service) *Right Sub-Section Right Brigade Sector: Policy of Defence*.

[31] NAM 1998-12-111-14: Postcard: 'The King's Message to his Army, Buckingham Palace'. Signed George R.I.; NAM 1986-01-86: Three documents including Haig's 'Special Orders of the Day' (1918), Special Order of the Day by Field-Marshal Sir Douglas Haig K.T. G.C.B. G.C.V.O. K.C.I.E. Commander-in-Chief, British Armies in France. Gen. HQ 7 September 1918. Press A-9/18. 8601-86-2.

[32] Fuller, *Training Soldiers for War*, pp. 1–4.

minds.[33] It was believed that duty 'link[s] each man to his work' and to 'shirk a duty is dishonourable' while to neglect one was 'cowardly'. A 'duty cheerfully performed is a duty well performed' and 'a duty grudgingly performed is a duty scarcely accomplished'. This impulse was key to the 'spirit of self sacrifice for a [national and moral] cause which he instinctively feels is a just one'.[34] Duty was performative and related to men's patriotism. As Fuller argued, 'the first requirement of a sound army is a sound nation and a patriotic one, without which there can be no soundness at all'.[35] Soldiers' moral characteristics should mirror those of the British nation: 'bluff, forthright, and morally serious'.[36] After the war, Fuller continued to characterise morale as a 'mystical impulse which impels him to do certain things so that his race may continue and prosper'.[37] The conflation of race with morale and duty can be found elsewhere and suggests that both were associated with particular groups.[38] Military understandings of duty were steeped in moral attitudes and (upper-class) assumptions and reflect the 'ethos' of Britain's public schools.[39]

Officers' Social Contract

This was not a citizen army. Officers (and their men) pledged allegiance to the monarch, not to the state nor to Parliament. The officer corps was the guarantor of the ideals outlined above; it was expected to represent the best qualities of both Army and society. In 1914, the officer corps 'was still overwhelmingly Anglo-Saxon, Protestant, and upper class'.[40] Men born into Britain's elites were brought up to believe in the principles outlined by Fuller: self-sacrifice, social leadership, and paternalism. Education in one of Britain's recognised public schools developed these 'social and moral qualities'. In fact, Sandhurst, which was Britain's foremost military academy, could have been characterised as a finishing school.[41]

---

[33] Harper, *Notes on Infantry Tactics & Training*, p. 9.
[34] Ibid., p. 666.
[35] Fuller, *Training Soldiers for War*, pp. 19–20.
[36] Fox, *Learning to Fight*, p. 23.
[37] J.F.C. Fuller, 'Moral, Instruction, and Leadership', *Journal of the Royal United Services Institution*, Vol. 65 (1920), p. 656.
[38] IWM Documents.16345: 2nd Lt. D. Henrick Jones, 'Message: From Lieut.-General Sir Aylmer Hunter-Weston ... To All officers, N.C.O.'s and Men of VIII Army Corps', HQ VIII Corps 4 July 1916; NAM 1987-07-26: Papers of Lt. Gen. Sir Gerald Ellison, Special Order of the Day by Field Marshal Sir Douglas Haig K.T. G.C.B., G.C.V.O., K.C.I.E Commander-in-Chief, British Armies in France. D. Haig C-in-C, British Armies in France. GHQ 4 August 1918.
[39] Halstead, 'The First World War and Public School Ethos', pp. 209–229 and Parker, *The Old Lie*, pp. 163–256.
[40] Ibid., p. 27
[41] K. Simpson, 'The Officer', in I.F.W. Beckett and K. Simpson (eds.), *A Nation in Arms: A Social Study of the British Army in the First World War* (Manchester, 1985), pp. 64–66.

The amalgamation of class and rank was evident in *The King's Regulations*. If a man found 'himself unable to meet his [financial] engagements' he was not 'permitted to continue to hold His Majesty's Commission'.[42] The social composition of the officer corps may have diversified between 1914 and 1918, but each of the 229,316 men commissioned became a 'gentleman' even if only temporarily.[43]

As such, officers' moral and legal contracts did not change in tone during the war. There was a certain immeasurability to their duties. The King's Commission was given to all Regular, Territorial, and New Armies officers, and its wording remained the same. The officer's gazette was a personal agreement between the King and his 'trusty and well beloved' subject. King George V informed the officer that he had 'especial trust and confidence' in his 'loyalty, courage and good conduct'.[44] The script went on:

> You are therefore carefully and diligently to discharge your Duty as such ... and you are at all times to exercise and well discipline in Arms both the inferior Officers and Men serving under you and use your best endeavours to keep them in good Order and Discipline. And we do hereby command them to Obey you ... and you to observe and follow such Orders and Directions as from time to time you shall receive from Us or any superior Officer.[45]

The document reflected the continued power of *noblesse oblige*. Since the document was nominally prepared at the Court of St James, the weight of history and expectation would have been abundantly clear to those brought up to believe in the 'natural' social order and the primacy of the royal family.

The innumerable practical features of officers' duty were laid down in *The King's Regulations*. Paragraphs 99 through 108 explained the extent of a commanding officer's responsibilities. An officer was accountable for the health of *all* troops under his direct command; the upkeep of *all* weapons in his unit; its accounts, organisation, and discipline; any judicial decision making; its efficiency; and ensuring his subordinates understood and undertook all their duties.[46] Paragraphs 111 to 114 outlined regimental officers' duties. They were expected to acquaint themselves with the 'abilities and acquirements' of their subordinates. The officer, in short, should 'be perfectly acquainted with its [the unit's] interior management, economy, and

---

[42] Paragraph 447, *The King's Regulations and Orders for the Army* (London, 1912).
[43] Simpson, 'The Officer', p. 64.
[44] SOFO Box 29 Item 17: Frederick Symonds, Form T.1.A. King's Commission [2/Lt. Ralph Frederick Symonds 22 December 1914]; IWM Documents.13760: Maj. S.R. Hudson, King's Commission.
[45] Ibid.
[46] Paragraphs 99–108, *The King's Regulations*.

discipline'.[47] He was also accountable for the psychological welfare of his men: 'an officer of any rank will adopt towards his subordinates such methods of command and treatment as will not only ensure respect for authority, but also foster the feelings of self-respect and personal honour essential to military efficiency'.[48]

This fed into wartime publications, which described the morale and practical 'management' of soldiers and units, ranging from the 'supreme' management of the commanding officer to the more limited duties of subalterns.[49] Officers led by example. Their 'language and bearing as a gentleman' offered a model of obedience, punctuality, punctiliousness, and respect.[50] In fact, they were never 'off-duty'. One corps commander advised a graduating class of officer cadets that 'your chief duties [sic] is to be always thinking ... You must always be thinking'.

> You are responsible for the successful leading of your men in battle; you are responsible for their safety as far as such can be ensured in gaining success in battle; you are responsible for their health, for their comfort, for their good behaviour and discipline. Finally, and not least, you are responsible for maintaining the honour of England, for doing all you can to ensure the security of England, and of our women and our children after us.[51]

The army celebrated those who performed this idealised conception of duty.[52] Medals – such as the Military Cross or the Distinguished Service Order – were awarded for 'gallantry and devotion to duty'. These celebrated officers' capacity for command, leadership, organisation, and resourcefulness and the ways in which individuals won further 'honour' for their regiment. The reports that accompanied these decorations frequently foregrounded men's 'tireless energy', 'cheerful courage', 'daring', or 'coolness' in action. This all set 'a fine example to all ranks'.[53] One censorship officer internalised these attitudes. He claimed the 'story of the British infantry ... will be the new Bible'. The officer also lauded their perseverance, despite the absence of glory, and

---

[47] Ibid., Paragraphs 111–104.
[48] Ibid., Paragraph 435.
[49] Capt. B.R.N. Hood, *Duties for All Ranks* (London, c. 1916).
[50] Ibid.
[51] NAM 2005-09-57-12-26: Address by a Corps Commander to Young Officers on Leaving the Officers' School, Division Y.P.C. – 5,00 – 4/4/1916.
[52] MR 2/17/61: L/Cpl. Thomas Betteley, Commendation for Distinguished Conduct Medal: No. 40388; MR 2/17/67: Sgt. J. Palin, Certificate from General John Rawlinson, commander 4th Army, for his Military Medal 6 March 1919.
[53] See, for example, 'Honours and Awards', *The Snapper*, Vol. XI, No. 10 (1 October 1916), p. 175 and 'Honours and Awards', *The Snapper*, Vol. XIII, No. 4 (1 April 1918), p. 230.

concluded that men were 'just playing cricket for duty's sake, keeping fit to do their bit at the wicket, and bowl an over or two'.[54]

Officers' Perception of Duty

There was little glory in trench warfare. Nevertheless, in November 1914, the *Manchester Regiment Gazette* still reported their pride in the 'noble and glorious way' the second battalion had 'upheld and added to [their ...] great traditions' and 'laid down their lives for King and Country'.[55] Faced with the reality of the war, some officers became more sceptical in their diaries and letters. Looking back on the first months of the war, C.S. Baines related that 'to tell the truth, I had not found much pleasure in life ... and by the end of October I was really in need of a change of air'.[56] However, perceptions of duty continued to motivate these men. They remained focused on paternalism, 'self-sacrifice', and the greater good. Officers' responsibilities were so wide-reaching that they had little time to stop and think, and the pressure this caused left some men anxious.[57] Others were conscious that moral 'right' and personal comfort were often at odds, and continued to feel that 'we can't stop until we have whacked the beggars [the Germans]'.[58] The welfare of their men was of paramount concern, and officers wrote home asking their families to send supplies to make their wards (as they saw them) more comfortable.[59] The officers' duty of care translated into a deeper affinity with their men. H.E. Trevor developed a powerful relationship with his company. As their protector, the loss of his officers and non-commissioned officers (NCOs) upset him and he felt that he 'ought to have been killed'.[60] J.S. Knyvett recorded the name of every man killed in a skirmish or battle in his diary.[61] H.E. Trevor's references to his unit's 'wonderful manner' and resilience suggest that his duty towards these men was also driven by an emotional connection with them as individuals.[62]

In 1916, what chivalric ideals that had survived were eroded by the reality of the Somme campaign. On 2 July 1916, G.H. Greenwell still felt 'awfully glad

---

[54] IWM Documents.4041: Capt. M. Hardie, Anon. Letter 17 November 1915.
[55] *The Manchester Regiment Gazette* (November 1914), p. 412.
[56] IWM Documents.10879: Lt. Col. C.S. Baines, Memoir of the First Battle of Ypres, 31 October 1914, pp. 3-4.
[57] IWM Documents.11445: Brig. Gen. H.E. Trevor, Letter to Mother 4 October 1914.
[58] Ibid. Letter from Capt. L.F. Ashburner to Mrs Parker 14 October 1914.
[59] IWM Documents.9364: Lt. F.B. Anstruther, Letter to Mother 22 November 1914.
[60] IWM Documents.11445: Brig. Gen. H.E. Trevor, Letter to Evelyn Parker 26 September 1914. See also Sheffield, *Leadership in the Trenches*, esp. pp. 79-103.
[61] IWM Documents.12819: Major J.S. Knyvett, Diary 19 October 1914.
[62] IWM Documents.11445: Brig. Gen. H.E. Trevor, Letter to Mother 3 October 1914 and to Evelyn 6 October 1914.

that I have survived to see and take part in this show'. War was a 'tremendous experience'. By 6 July, however, the frontline had become a 'beastly place' and by November it was only his men that sustained him.[63] Maj. S.O.B. Richardson explained to his mother that 'when one sees war in its own setting and as it really is there are many sad things which one did not expect to see'.[64] Their innumerable duties did not prevent officers from feeling the strains of war; many became depressed and 'windy'. Donald Hankey found that the war had become 'too monotonous and irritating for words'.[65] Even those who missed the bloodiest battles were affected by the weather and boredom. Reginald Neville noted that 'we are so cheerful as we sit now, but God knows if we can keep it up'.[66]

Yet, these same men still felt motivated to endure further hardship. Neville believed that Germany needed to be defeated and was also driven by a passion for his regiment, both of which convinced him that 'I have got to go through it'.[67] S.O.B. Richardson was driven by his duty to those around him, feeling that it was 'wrong' to be in the comparative comfort of the reserve line while others fought and died.[68] This duty to their immediate social group played on their minds. In his diary, Lt. J.H. Johnson asked himself a rhetorical question: 'Am I always a victim of doing things for the sake of others' opinions and not what I really think?' His daily musings offer an insight into officers' sometimes paradoxical perceptions of duty. Johnson battled with knowledge that he was expected to fulfil a certain role, even considering a future in 'the non-combatant army'. Yet the belief that he must work for the benefit of others induced him to continue acting like a conscientious officer.[69]

The fighting in 1917 underlined and confirmed the horrors of modern war. Even the most conscientious officers returned from leave 'not quite' able to get 'used to it again'. F. Hardman confessed that he had 'not been so nervy since the end of my Gallipoli Campaign'.[70] Yet, he consoled himself that it was simply a case of 'getting over' the 'screams of desolation and blasted earth'. His men's suffering drove him to relegate his own challenges.[71] The care they had to show to their unit was both a strain and a diversion. Henry Lawson's 'wealthy' company commander spent generously on his men, giving them

---

[63] IWM Documents.11006: G.H. Greenwell, Letters 2 and 6 January and 4 November 1916.
[64] IWM Documents.8059: Maj. S.O.B. Richardson, Letter to Mother (No. 1) Late 1916.
[65] Keegan, *The Face of Battle*, p. 272; D. Hankey, Letter to Hilda 6 October 1916 in *A Student in Arms*, pp. 354–355.
[66] SOFO Box 16 3/4/N/2: Lt. Reginald N. Neville, Letters to Father 12, 16 and 24 December 1916.
[67] Ibid. Letter to Father 21 December 1916 and Letter to Sister 24 December 1916.
[68] IWM Documents.8059: Maj. S.O.B. Richardson, Letter to Mother (No. 2) Late 1916.
[69] IWM Documents.7035: Lt. J.H. Johnson, Diary 18 November and 24 November 1916.
[70] IWM Documents.7233: Col. F. Hardman, Letter to Parents 22 January. 4 and 8 February 1918.
[71] Ibid. 4 and 8 February 1918.

money, vegetables, and cigarettes as prizes in inter-company competitions'.[72] However, other long-serving junior officers found that they no longer believed in the sacrificial nature of their undertaking. In October 1917, Lawson complained that officers on his training course were discussing taking 'safe' jobs and their hope for a 'Blighty' wound – it was, he thought, evidence of 'bad moral'.[73] Sydney Frankenburg had twice refused 'easy jobs', feeling 'that I owed something to people at home also to myself'. However, in January 1918 he was willing to 'take the chance' on six months' training in England.[74] Nonetheless, the desire to be recognised for doing 'one's damnedest in utter danger and misery' remained significant.[75] Furthermore, officers remained role models and following a 'terrific' bombardment on 2 March Henry Lawson was much impressed by the 'patriotic and inspiring speeches' another officer had given on the way up the line.[76]

The German offensives of 1918 refocused many officers' perception of duty.[77] There was new purpose in their sacrifices. A.J. Lord found that there was 'nothing very wonderful' in war, but he believed 'it must be infinitely easier to die during tense moments of interest, excitement and duty well worth doing'.[78] Lt. J.E.H. Neville felt that the trials were neither heroic nor honourable, but were still necessary. It was 'grit' that 'pull[ed] you through'.[79] As later chapters will show, this acute military crisis did not necessarily translate into a crisis in morale as it encouraged many officers to recognise their duty. G.A. Stevens 'thought it my duty to get back after seeing the news in the papers and though I have had a rotten time am very glad I did come back'.[80] Illustratively, one officer of the Machine Gun Corps became detached from his unit and joined the 2nd Bn. Ox and Bucks on 23 March. He 'was in a pitiful state ... his hands bleeding, his jacket ripped from shoulder to wrist by shrapnel and puttees and breeches torn by wire ... he'd been blown up 3 times [... However,] he refused to move'. He 'swore that now he had struck the 52nd

---

[72] LIDDLE/WW1/GS/0933: H. Lawson, Letter to his Mother 19 and 27 February 1918.
[73] Ibid. Letter to Mother 16 September 1917.
[74] LIDDLE/WW1/GS/0583: 2nd Lt. Sydney Frankenburg, Letter to Charis Burnett 16 January 1918.
[75] IWM Documents.17029: Capt. A.J. Lord, Letter to Father 8 January 1918.
[76] LIDDLE/WW1/GS/0933: H. Lawson, Letter to Mother 3 March 1918.
[77] IWM Documents.11976: Lt. Col. A.H. Cope, Diary 21 March. A relevant thesis is that of C. Smith, *Awarded for Valour: A History of the Victoria Cross and the Evolution of British Heroism* (Basingstoke, 2008), pp. 110–64. VCs were increasingly awarded for the basic act of killing, rather for chivalry and self-sacrifice.
[78] IWM Documents.17029: Capt. A.J. Lord, Letter to Father 24 April 1918.
[79] SOFO Box 16 Item 29: Lt. J.E.H. Neville, Diary 21–26 March 1918. See also IWM Documents.7233: Col. F. Hardman, Letter to Parents 18 May and 14 June 1918.
[80] IWM Documents.12339: Brig. Gen. G.A. Stevens, Letter to Mother Easter Sunday 1918.

he would not [... retire] until he was killed'. The Ox and Bucks' officers were impressed to find that the man was 'still game' and 'plucky'.[81]

The noble ideals embedded in their commissions could seem irrelevant in a modern industrialised war. Maj. G.H. Greenwell felt that 'I shall never look on warfare either as fine or sporting again. It reduces men to shivering beasts'.[82] Yet, in moments of reflection, some soldiers returned to more romanticised definitions of duty. The classical ideals of honour and self-sacrifice, which had been central to so many of their educations, continued to exert a powerful influence. These were often intimately connected to their enduring duty to the dead. Lt. J.H. Johnson discovered that a friend had died and felt a sense of 'selfishness' at still being alive. He retreated into his imagination and spent 'the rest of the day with Greg' pondering '[t]he ancients'.[83] By considering the relationship between his present and antiquity, Johnson was placing his experiences in a wider historical context.

'Big words' such as honour and obligation could be used to legitimise experiences and sacrifices, at least retrospectively.[84] On learning that one of his men had been awarded the Victoria Cross posthumously, Lt. Col. Hardman mused 'the poor fellow is dead but he has won honour for his battalion'.[85] Honour was still a kind of currency for officers and for the regiment. Honorific ideas were invoked self-referentially in Charles Carrington's letters and diaries written when he was training men in England. This space (both temporal and geographical) afforded him the opportunity to reinterpret events in Belgium and France through the more traditional lens of duty. Despite months of mental turmoil at the front, he spent the majority of 1918 expressing his desire to be back in the thick of the fighting.[86] J.H. Johnson was immediately regretful when he left the front in February 1918. He claimed to have loved 'the glory of it' and would have 'stayed and see[n] it through'. Yet, only days previously the pressures of service had left him with 'no self-confidence'. When he returned to France in April 1918, he noted the 'horror of return to war'.[87] The use of 'traditional vocabulary' helped those processing grief after the war.[88] While officers were conscious of the frailty of high diction, they still resorted to such language when making sense of their trauma.

Duty motivated officers to endure. Ideas of honour and self-sacrifice found traction as they sought meaning amidst the horror, but duty most clearly

---

[81] SOFO Box 16 Item 29: Lt. J.E.H. Neville, Diary 23 March 1918.
[82] IWM Documents.11006: G.H. Greenwell, Diary 17 August 1916.
[83] IWM Documents.7035: Lt. J.H. Johnson, Diary 11 January 1918.
[84] S. Hynes, *The Soldiers' Tale: Bearing Witness to Modern War* (London, 1999), p. 57.
[85] IWM Documents.7233: Col. F. Hardman, Letter to Parents 15 February 1918.
[86] LIDDLE/WW1/GS/0273: Capt. C. Carrington, Letters to Mother 8 April and 7 July 1918.
[87] IWM Documents.7035: Lt. J.H. Johnson, Diary 16 and 21 February and 26 April 1918 and Letter from F.L. Clark 30 November 1917.
[88] Bourke, *Dismembering the Male*, p. 19; Winter, *Sites of Memory*, p. 2.

manifested itself in officers' devotion to their men and unit. The tone of the war poets – Sassoon, Graves, Owen, and others – reflects this. On returning to the Western Front in 1918, Siegfried Sassoon wrote, 'I am only here to look after some men.' Wilfred Owen similarly stated, 'I came out in order to help these boys – directly by leading them as well as an officer can.'[89] This could reflect the paternalism of the officer corps, but paternalism was less a moral impulse than a feature of men fulfilling an expected role and interpreting the world through the lens of officers' social contracts.[90]

Other Ranks' Social Contract

The military defined the duties of the rank and file very differently to those of officers. Each man's attestation form was a contract of service, which was more bureaucratic, clinical, and temporary than a commission. Servicemen were even expected to return 'all arms, clothing and appointments issued to you' when their service ended. Soldiers did not receive commissions.

It was only senior NCOs whose role was formalised in such a manner. Warrant Officers were granted a 'warrant' in which the Secretary of State for War appointed them with the 'authority' of the King and dictated the duration of their service. This suggestion that duty was finite was absent in the officers' commissions. Warrant officers were advised that he should 'carefully and diligently ... discharge [... his] Duty' by 'performing all manner of things' laid out in 'the Established Regulations of the Service'. They were to 'follow such Orders and Directions' as they might receive from any superior officer 'according to the Rules and Discipline of War'.[91]

Once men were promoted, their duties became more numerous, but they were still secular and finite and lacked the gold braid of ideas such as honour.[92] Where officers' roles were heavy with the weight of history, their men's relationship with the military was far more contractual. Though this was a contract with the King, not with the state. Servicemen took an oath of allegiance to the King and swore 'by Almighty God' that they would 'be faithful and bear true Allegiance' to him and his successors. They would 'as in duty bound, honestly and faithfully defend' the royal family in 'Person, Crown, and Dignity against all enemies'. However, even this oath included the caveat: 'according to the conditions of my service'.[93]

---

[89] S. Sassoon and W. Owen in S. Hynes, *A War Imagined: The First World War in English Culture* (London, 1992), p. 186.
[90] Sheffield, *Leadership in the Trenches*, pp. 79–102.
[91] SOFO Box 29 Item 16: C.S.M. A. Hearn, Warrant; MR 3/17/129: C.S.M. H. Merrick, Warrant.
[92] NAM 2004-05-27: L/Cpl. W. Burton, Notebook: 'Discipline' and 'Lecture: Duties in Barracks given by Reg. Sgt. Major Wombwell 1 August 1916'.
[93] TNA WO 363 and 364: Attestation Forms in Soldiers' Service Records.

Other Ranks' Perception of Duty

In 1914, regulars and reservists sometimes had contrasting perceptions of duty and war. The regulars were often entirely acculturated to the military. Soldiering was their profession, and many were driven by a desire to do a good job, which helped them to rationalise the conflict. Regular soldiers frequently described the war with a clinical eye, recording the violence and death in remarkably neutral terms. One soldier's battalion had suffered heavy casualties and by 11 November only 284 of the men who had disembarked in France in August remained uninjured. The deaths of close friends and old comrades were saddening, but his daily notations took the form of a learning log. They referred to the nuts-and-bolts of military life and the battles in which he had taken part.[94] On 11 December, he concluded that one skirmish had been 'the best fight we had all the time we were in the trenches'. Only when faced with overwhelming German firepower on 18 December did his professionalism falter.[95] Some men enjoyed the fighting and were sustained by the knowledge that their business was 'killing' and searched out opportunities to practice their trade.[96] After encountering Germans during a patrol, Sgt. Osborn wrote: 'shot one in doorway. One against wall, one in open, one against a door. Killed three and wounded one'.[97] The knowledge that he was duty-bound to kill the enemy made his interactions with enemy soldiers during the Christmas truce surreal.[98]

Other men were obsessed with the nature of the work and analysed the BEF's performance.[99] Some critiqued the quality of their enemy. One man was unconvinced by the German infantry, especially their rifle fire, but he was impressed by their artillery.[100] Some went so far as to characterise their experiences 'educational' and were surprised that 'it seems to have come quite naturally to us to sit in a small hole in the ground while German shells are bursting all around'.[101] Their professionalism meant that they felt immense

---

[94] IWM Documents.8631: Diary of an Unidentified Soldier in the Border Regiment, 22 and 28 October and 11 and 19 November 1914; IWM Documents.12027: S. Judd, Diary October–December 1914; IWM Documents.16676: C. Dwyer, Diary September–December 1914.
[95] IWM Documents.8631: Diary of an Unidentified Soldier in the Border Regiment, 11 and 18 December 1914.
[96] IWM Documents.18524: Pte. W. Tapp, Diary 24 and 26 November 1914.
[97] RFM.ARC.2012.264: Sgt. Osborn, Diary 14 September 1914.
[98] IWM Documents.7490: L/Cp. K.M. Gaunt, Letter 25 December 1914.
[99] IWM Documents.8674: Pocket Diary 1914, October–November 1914.
[100] IWM Documents.7371: Postcard Signed by 'The Mademoiselle from Armentieres', Extract from local paper.
[101] IWM Documents.14710: R.D. Sheffield, Letters to Father 9 November and 4 December 1914.

pride when senior officers' praised their 'good name' and told them they had 'made' new honour for the Regiment. 'Honour' was not a moral impulse but spoke to soldiers' martial qualities. Here, again, honour became currency (both individual and collective) and a synonym for success. An *esprit de corps* that formed around men's shared professional identity was essential in such circumstances.[102]

However, some men's sense of duty faltered, particularly in moments of acute crisis.[103] H.E. Trevor 'had a bone to pick with' a soldier in his unit who had 'put up a white handkerchief in one of the front trenches at Le Cateau'. This had precipitated another man's death as he tried to remove it. The man was 'said to have gone mad' and eventually had to be restrained by his comrades.[104] He had been overwhelmed by the reality of battle, but this does not appear to have been contagious. In other circumstances, men were liable to panic *en masse*. On 20 October, several sergeants in the 2nd Bn. Gordon Highlanders were so unnerved that they shouted for their men to retire, spurring a mass withdrawal amongst neighbouring units.[105] In such circumstances, it was important that officers took their duty to set an example to their men as seriously as they did. Soldiers' nervousness could coalesce with their limited training for the type of war that was being fought and sometimes led to them acting in undesirable ways. J.S. Knyvett described how, on first entering the firing line, soldiers often caught what he called 'the infection'. Thankfully, this generally just led to erratic rifle fire.[106]

These were momentary lapses in self-control rather than a product of faltering morale. Sgt. Osborn believed that most men's timidity was produced by shock rather than cowardice.[107] It was hard to prepare anyone for the reality of the Western Front. Nevertheless, military culture provided a framework that defined appropriate action, which helped soldiers overcome periods of acute crisis. W.J. Cheshire broke ranks during the retreat from Mons. Yet, he depicted this as evidence of initiative rather than an fatally fractured spirit. During their retirement on 2 September 1914 'a good lot of men fall out, I included myself, proper fed up with it'. They were not deserting, though, and continued to retire at their own pace. Cheshire failed to see this as problematic; it was logical in the circumstances. They attached themselves to the Lincoln Regiment and set off the next day 'to find our Regt'. On 5 September, they

---

[102] IWM Documents.8631: Diary of an Unidentified Soldier in the Border Regiment, 23 November and 25 December 1914; IWM Documents.16676: C. Dwyer, Diary 18 September and 24 October 1914.
[103] Watson, *Enduring the Great War*, p. 142.
[104] IWM Documents.11445: Brig. Gen. H.E. Trevor, Letter to Evelyn 6 October 1914.
[105] IWM Documents.8631: Diary of an Unidentified Soldier in the 2nd Bn. Border Regiment, 20 October 1914.
[106] IWM Documents.12819: Maj. J.S. Knyvett, Diary 10 October 1914.
[107] RFM.ARC.2012.264: Sgt. Osborn, Diary 4 November 1914.

heard the news that '5th Brigade are in action ... we hurry up'. The next day the British began 'pushing forward for the first time everybody is more happier [sic]'.[108] Others did the same, but despite their fatigue or pain eventually rejoined their units 'in dribs and drabs'.[109] Duty was infused with pragmatism as well as a desire to do a good job.[110]

However, new recruits and the men of the Special Reserve appear to have been less resilient. Some cared little about duty. T.A. Silver was sent to France with four months' training. Having only joined the army in June 1914, he did not view the world through the same lens as many of his professional peers. He was bitter about the conditions and his poor treatment at the hands of authority figures. Eventually catching frostbite, he was relieved to return to England.[111] Like many working-class men, Silver had joined the armed forces because he lacked other prospects. Unmoved by calls to patriotism, the war came as a shock. He failed to develop the knowledge and tools required to endure the war's chronic crises or respond effectively to acute crises.

Regulars frequently criticised reservists' indiscipline.[112] It appeared that they had a different world view. More civilian than soldier, many were less willing to endure the war's trials. Pte. Mawer was a reservist in the Ox and Bucks. He complained vocally about army life.[113] Summer training camps might have helped to maintain skills and knowledge, but they failed to restore the mentality of a regular infantryman or his perception of duty.

The influx of volunteers in 1916 changed the culture of the ranks. An article in *The Nation*, which discussed soldiers' newspapers, argued that 'there is always pathos in the face of death, no matter how stoical a cheerfulness may be assumed'.[114] Trench journals can be used to trace changes in the attitude and outlook of British servicemen. One Scottish battalion's journal asked the question: 'what is the matter with the British Army? Why are so many people hunting for soft jobs? In the earlier days ... everyone was content with the prospect of playing the part of soldier strictly.'[115] Men happily dodged erroneous duties and celebrated their success in doing so. Soldiers were said to have 'come the old soldier' if they had perfected duty dodging.[116]

An assumption existed that there was a limit to what a man should be subjected to. To some, war and the military remained incomprehensible.

---

[108] SOFO Box 16 Item 36: W.J. Cheshire, Diary 2–6 September 1914.
[109] IWM Documents.16676: C. Dwyer, Diary 4 October 1914.
[110] This reflects J. Baynes' findings in his study of the 2nd Scottish Rifles at Neuve Chapelle. See Baynes, *Morale*.
[111] IWM Documents.7715: T.A. Silver, Diary 1914.
[112] RFM.ARC.2012.264: Sgt. Osborn, Diary 14 August 1914.
[113] SOFO Box 16 Item 35: Pte. J.E. Mawer, Doc.25 Letter to Wife 30 November 1914.
[114] 'The Trench Journal', *The Nation*, Vol. 20, Issue 10 (9 December 1916).
[115] R. Birrell (ed.), *The Outpost*, Vol. IV, No. 1 (December 1916).
[116] Brophy and Partridge, *The Long Trail*, p. 86.

William Anderson wondered 'wherein lies [sic] the sense or even sanity in War at all'. He concluded that 'its [sic] part of the human burden'.[117] For several men, this was simply a more dangerous job. Considering his service, R.E.P. Stevens reflected in his diary that it 'means a little more work for some of us in our calling' when he 'heard [erroneous] news that Greece has declared war on England'.[118] Yet, instead of professional pride, this civilian force was driven by a more diverse range of impulses. Some found the work so tiring, difficult, and dangerous that it was impossible to frame their endeavours professionally. A friend of Charles Crump wrote to him explaining 'we are and have been terribly busy. You can guess that it is a complete and shocking change for ME to WORK (after some of the jobs I have had)'.[119] Men who came from civilian workplaces were also more willing to 'grouse' and complain about things perceived to be futile or unfair.[120] The tone of William Child's diary changed markedly particularly arduous fatigue duty on 5 December.[121] Men's dissatisfaction was sometimes expressed more explicitly, albeit generally in private. Around the same time, R.E.P Stevens noted bitterly in his diary: 'More foolish night operations. Not learned a scrap from any one of them yet – they are just an appetiser for the officers before their dinner I think.'[122]

Ideals such as honour and courage had limited traction amongst these men. Their songs reflected a more sombre attitude towards soldiering. The lyrics of 'I Don't Want to die', 'I Want to Go Home' and 'I Don't Want to Be a Soldier' revealed their dreams of escape. Desperate to survive, 'self-sacrifice' meant little to them. John Brophy and Eric Partridge, who served in the ranks, claimed that the lyrics of these songs 'ridicule[d] all heroics'. This was not a symptom of low morale but did reveal the lens through which the ranks interpreted their duty. These songs were also an important coping mechanism.[123] Letters, too, bemoaned 'the gloom and darkness of things', but this did not mean that the men were unconvinced by the justice of the British cause.[124] They were driven by a more parochial desire to do right by their comrades and family. At forty, F.S. Castle was much older than most of his unit. His officer had suggested that he make use of his medical experience and find a safer job with the battalion Medical Officer. However, in a letter to his niece,

---

[117] IWM Documents.5092: Pte. W.M. Anderson, Letter to his Wife 28 October 1916.
[118] IWM Documents.12521: R.E.P. Stevens, Diary 4 December 1916.
[119] IWM Documents.15069: C.P. Crump, Letter 11 September 1916.
[120] Ibid.
[121] SOFO Box 16 Item 42: F.W. Child, Diary 5 December 1916.
[122] IWM Documents.12521: R.E.P. Stevens, Diary 7 December 1916.
[123] Brophy and Partridge, *The Long Trail*, p. 17.
[124] IWM Documents.5092: Pte. W.M. Anderson, Letters to his Wife 1, 6, 11, 16 and 27 December 1916.

he explained that he 'would far sooner be [a] combatant' and 'he would do anything rather than be out of it and leave the boys'.[125]

Of course, duty had its limits. Shock and inadequate training continued to play an important role. Individuals still broke down. The 20th Bn. Manchester Regiment had an awful time in the frontlines during October 1916. A company clerk and eight men emerged from the trenches suffering from severe 'wind up' and 'Shell Shock'.[126] Some infantrymen's inability to cope with chronic crisis convinced them to take their fates into their own hands and a few resorted to self-inflicted wounds.[127] Many soldiers were willing to embrace even the slightest of wounds as a physical passport away from the trenches. Once injured, it had 'become customary' for combatants to remove their equipment. The implicit suggestion was that their duty was done.[128] Wound stripes on the soldiers' uniform became a physical manifestation of this.

Nevertheless, endurance and resilience were still the norm. One of G.A. Stevens' soldiers was sent to hospital with a bad case of boils on 28 October 1916. The doctor informed Stevens that 'he could have got to hospital any day the last week but stuck it out'.[129] This idea of 'sticking it out' had become common by 1916.[130] A.P. Burke believed that 'things must be borne'. Following a fierce skirmish in October, he simply concluded that they must 'endeavour to carry on until its [sic] all over'.[131] Similarly, William Anderson explained to his wife that he and his comrades were still willing 'to forfeit most', emphasising the need for patience.[132]

By late 1917, however, scepticism and the desire to escape were more widespread. The idea that service was a 'job' appears to have faded with compulsion. The BEF now included 'men of all opinions' – 'hard fighting patriots' served alongside 'ultra Socialists, pacificists and conscientious objectors'.[133] Unsurprisingly, then, there had been another shift in attitude. Capt. M. Hardie's survey of III Army morale in August 1917 argued that 'the old active enthusiasm [of 1916] is to some extent being replaced by passive

---

[125] IWM Documents.20755: F.S. Castle, Letter to Niece 23 September 1916.
[126] IWM Documents.1665: A.P. Burke, Letter to Reg 12–15 October 1916.
[127] IWM Documents.7035: Lt. J.H. Johnson, Diary 12 December 1916 – 'L/Cpl shoots his thumb off'.
[128] TNA WO 95/648: Headquarters II. Corps. Routine Orders: 17 October, 1916 – 281. General Routine Order 1358 para. 2 (A).
[129] IWM Documents.12339: Brig. Gen. G.A. Stevens, Letter to Mother 28 October 1916.
[130] IWM Documents.2554: W.J. Martin, Letter 7 December 1916.
[131] IWM Documents.1665: A.P. Burke, Letter to Reg 13 June and 12–15 October 1916.
[132] IWM Documents.5092: Pte. W.M. Anderson, Letters to Wife 14 October and 3 December 1916.
[133] Haig's Diary 25 February 1918. G. Sheffield and J. Bourne (eds.), *Douglas Haig: War Diaries and Letters, 1914–1918* (London, 2005), p. 383.

acceptance'.[134] At the same time, soldiers' perceptions of service began to reflect the ideas of 'economies of sacrifice' and 'workers' conditional sacrifice' that historian Adrian Gregory has suggested were prevelant on the Home Front.[135] Strikes were becoming more prevalent in Britain and it is unsurprising that a number of servicemen (who had returned home to work in industry) attended a meeting of the 'Home Counties and Training Reserve Branch of the Soldiers' and Workmen's Council'. Fearful that they might be called back to frontline service, they drafted a series of resolutions. The fourth of these asserted 'that wounded men now returned from the battle fronts be not sent out again until after an independent examination by a doctor'. They called on the government to protect those who 'are now being sent out for the 2nd, 3rd, and 4th time'. Such men had already 'done their bit'.[136]

Those on the frontlines fostered a similar perspective.[137] Servicemen returning to the Western Front would often find themselves in 'cushier' jobs on account of their previous service. Fourteen men in 11th Bn. Royal Fusiliers had 1914 Star ribbons pinned to their tunics in February 1918, and their survival was probably aided by their safer roles within the battalion. Pte. George Winnard returned to France after a long period recovering from enteric fever in England. An old comrade, now battalion quartermaster, 'said that I was finished going to the trenches' and would be 'store man'.[138] 'Soft jobs' (those that mostly restricted men to the rear zones) were welcomed in earlier years, but it was now widely accepted that old soldiers *deserved* safer positions.[139]

However, many were unable to escape frontline service, especially after March 1918. The stresses of the Ludendorff offensives incentivised many men to embrace any semi-legitimate strategy to escape combat. On 23 March, Pte. W.A. Hoyle recalled seeing two men and four stretcher-bearers accompany a single injured comrade (already carrying himself on crutches) to a first-aid post.[140] Hoyle himself 'stopped a Blighty one' three days later and made no effort to continue fighting. As he bandaged his wound, he got the 'wind up' and removed his equipment, leaving the line. He was unashamed of his actions and

---

[134] IWM Documents.4041: Capt. M. Hardie, 'Report on III Army Morale, August 1917'.
[135] Gregory, *The Last Great War*, pp. 112–151, 152–186.
[136] TNA WO 32/5455: Report from the meeting of the 'Home Counties and Training Reserve Branch of the Soldiers' and Workmen's Council, 18 July 1917' in 'Formation of Soldiers and Workmen Councils 1917'.
[137] NAM 1993-02-508: Letters sent to Bentley Bridgewater by his father in France, Letter 9 March 1918.
[138] IWM Documents.7807: Pte. G.G. Winnard, Memoir, pp. 87–88.
[139] NAM 1980-01-4: Field Message Book (Army Form 153), 21 (Service) Bn Manchester Regiment, Message 220 To Adjutant from O.C. B Coy 27/1/1918; IWM Documents.7953: Pte. F.G. Senyard, Letter to Wife 16 June 1918.
[140] IWM Documents.7312: H. Russell, Diary of Pte. W.A Hoyle, Diary 23 March 1918.

had been an active participant in the fighting beforehand.[141] It is difficult to disentangle this from basic survival instincts, but these incidents speak to other ranks' internalisation of a finite duty. Officers' very different code of conduct precluded taking these actions (or, at least, so freely admitting to it). Self-preservation was not inconsistent with duty. There was no irony in continuing to fight while watching jealously as a lightly wounded comrade made their way to an aid post.[142] Lt. Neville remembered seeing many 'wounded men crawling to safety' during the German offensives. One 'man whose ankle was smashed [...was] dragging his mutilated leg behind him' but managed a 'smile'. Neville believed this showed courage, but perhaps it was relief.

Other officers recalled seeing 'men being taken prisoner' who had 'made no effort to avoid' their capture.[143] Given the circumstances, the only other option was often fighting until they were killed. To many soldiers this was anathema; sacrifice need not be futile. R.C.A. Frost recounted how his unit (reduced to a wounded second lieutenant and fifteen men) had been surrounded with no hope of escape. A corporal had wanted to 'fight it out ... but we told him in no uncertain terms that he would be shot unless he surrendered'.[144] The confusion of the first few days of fighting meant that this was not an uncommon occurrence. Other men, too, made it very clear that surrender was their only remaining option.[145] Death and glory, or holding positions until the last man, did not necessarily speak to their perception of duty.

However, where retreat and continued resistance were possible, accounts highlight the remarkably ordered nature of the BEF's withdrawals.[146] It was a frustrating experience nonetheless. 2nd Lt. F.T.K. Woodworth's 'men [were] fed up' since 'we were losing men fast and weren't even striking back'.[147] Yet, once there was an opportunity to inflict casualties on the enemy his unit's mood improved. On 28 March he noted: 'Exciting, he [the enemy] turned and ran for cover. We raised a cheer, such as it was.'[148] Nevertheless, some men continued to seek out acceptable opportunities to escape danger. Illnesses, including toothache and influenza, were legitimate ways to escape the battle zone.[149] On 26 March, Pte. S.A. Clarke wrote that 'it's about time [we were relieved] as we have had six days of retiring and fighting a rear guard'. A few weeks later he was thankful that 'measles broke out so we had to stay in isolation.

---

[141] Ibid. Diary 26 March 1918.
[142] IWM Documents.16336: C.H. Isom, Diary 26 April 1918.
[143] IWM Documents.11976: Lt. Col. A.H. Cope, Diary 26 March 1918.
[144] IWM Documents.16824: R.C.A. Frost, Memoir, p. 2.
[145] LIDDLE/WW1/GS/0137: Pte. O. Billingham, Diary 25 March 1918.
[146] SOFO Box 16 Item 30: Lt. C.T. O'Neill, Diary 24–30 March 1918.
[147] MR 2/17/57: 2nd Lt. F.T.K. Woodworth, Diary 26 March 1918.
[148] Ibid. 28 March 1918.
[149] IWM Documents.11289: H.T. Madders, Diary 22 September 1918; IWM Documents.7953: Pte. F.G. Senyard, Letter to Wife 10 July 1918.

A good job too as we had done enough'.[150] Not everybody was so lucky, and some men found neither a legitimate route away from the firing line nor a 'safe' job in their battalion. M.F. Gower was aggrieved when a 'fine young' sergeant in his unit was killed: 'wounded stripes don't always count for duty done'.[151]

However, many continued to see purpose in fighting and some even enjoyed it. F. Hubard was proud that his division (unlike many others at the Battle of Cambrai) 'did not lose a yard of ground it took'. They had 'received congratulations from almost all the commanders including Sir Douglas Haig'. He went on: 'of course we suffered both in officers N.C.Os and men – that is inevitable'.[152] A.E. Heywood highlighted the 'tremendous odds' under which his unit had retired in March 1918.[153] Many fought on despite their wounds, and it was easier to find excitement in the semi-open character of the warfare after 21 March. Bonds created in platoons meant that men persevered so that they could support their comrades, and there were many examples of extreme bravery. For instance, in C Company 19th Bn. Royal Fusiliers a Lewis gunner's leg had been 'shattered' by enemy fire on 25 March. However, he continued firing 'his gun for half an hour ... to hold the enemy back'.[154] Others continued to describe the fighting in a very matter-of-fact manner. Fred Gelden wrote: 'Raid. 7 of us got detached. Rough time, nuff said.' Even limited successes could be a tonic, thoug. A month later he 'did a raid, out with L.G. Got two prisoners. Decent time'.[155] During March and April 1918, many officers were impressed by their men, who 'moved marvellously quickly ... in spite of their ... suffering'.[156]

Even in these circumstances, 'high diction' mattered little to the other ranks. Theirs was a more practical sense of obligation, often framed by perceptions of respectability. There is, however, a sense in which a particular perception of honour influenced these men. In 1914, this focused on their professional identity. The British Army's regimental system continued to nurture this throughout the war and the relationships and bonds formed within units continued to influence the rank and file. Later in the conflict, men's perception of duty was informed by the temporary nature of their military service; their obligations were *finite*. Nonetheless, perceptions of duty and duty fulfilment were still informed by the military as a social institution. It was only through

---

[150] SOFO Box 16 Item 28: Pte. S.A. Clarke, Diary 26 March and 14 April 1918.
[151] IWM Documents.255: M.F. Gower, Letter to Delia 12 May 1918.
[152] IWM Documents.202111: F. Hubard, Letter to Mr and Mrs Underhill 8 December 1917.
[153] IWM Documents.15040: A.E. Heywood, Diary 24 March 1918.
[154] IWM Documents.11976: Lt. Col. A.H. Cope, Diary 25 March 1918.
[155] RFM.ARC.3017: Fred Gelden, Diary 14, 26 May and 8 June 1918. Also IWM Documents.16336: C.H. Isom, Diary 24 and 25 March 1918; MR 4/17/388/1: Pte. C.E. Wild, Diary 25–27 March 1918.
[156] IWM Documents.17029: Capt. A.J. Lord, Letter to Father 1 April 1918; IWM Documents.8589: Capt. A.J.J.P. Agius, Extracts from a Letter from a Padre with the 21st Division Gunners, dated 30 March 1918.

interactions with the army itself that men were able to 'do' their duty. So, even as they sought escape routes, it was service rendered that mattered most. Arguably, this idea was embodied in the medals awarded to combatants and the chevrons and wound stripes sewn onto their uniforms.[157]

Obedience and Discipline

Military culture also provided, and articulated, a set of expectations that defined how servicemen should act. Most significantly, even if they internalised their duty in different ways, every man was aware that obedience was 'the primary duty of a soldier'. This message was repeated by superiors and was also repeated and reinforced in the Soldiers' Small Book and other pocket publications.[158]

'Obedience and respect' were 'the whole foundation of discipline'.[159] Commanders believed 'men must be made to understand why implicit obedience is demanded of them, and ... disaster must *always* follow indiscipline'.[160] Training manuals included guidance to help officers develop 'the ingrained habit of obedience which controls and directs the fighting spirit'.[161] In fact, J.F.C. Fuller argued this impulse had engendered the resilience that helped the BEF weather the campaign of 1914.[162] In battle – and during acute crisis – it was essential that men's 'self-control [was] reduced to habit'. Unconsciously, Fuller had underlined the potency of 'habituation', which is one of the key consequences of effective military training.[163]

Obedience was a salient feature of military life. Men's daily routines were directed by orders, while military doctrine was underwritten by obedience.[164] Training, which reinforced the need for obedience through drill, occupied between 10 and 21 per cent of units' time.[165] Tellingly, as they looked back on the war, obedience was often prominent in the memories and memoirs of

---

[157] MR 3/17/129: C.S.M. H. Merrick, Collection and Service Record: One Red Chevron, Three Blue Chevron, and One Wound Stripe.
[158] MR 3/17/96: Sgt. Maj. Herbert Chase, Soldier's 'Small Book'; MR 3/17/88: Michael Gleeson, Leather Pocket Book; MR 3/17/100: Pte. Thomas Mannion, Army Pay Book.
[159] Capt. B.R.N. Hood, *Duties for All Ranks* (London, c. 1916), p. 20.
[160] Beadon, 'Second Military Prize Essay, 1913', p. 144.
[161] TNA WO 40/1712: *Platoon Training (1918)*, p. 20; *Infantry Training* (London, 1905); Harper, *Notes on Infantry Training*, p. 22.
[162] Fuller, 'Moral, Instruction, and Leadership', p. 660.
[163] Strachan, 'Training, Morale and Modern War', pp. 211–227; Stouffer et al., *The American Soldier*, pp. 2, 220.
[164] SOFO Box 16 Item 36: W.J. Cheshire, Diary 16 September and 1 October 1914; RFM.ARC 2013.8.2: Pte. P.N. Wright, Notes/Diary 4 November 1916.
[165] IWM Documents.11006: G.H. Greenwell, 26 October 1917: Notes from a Platoon Officers and NCOs Conference. For statistics see Grayson, 'A Life in the Trenches?', p. 17.

veterans. W.G. Bentley remembered that 'discipline and implicit obedience were instilled in all soldiers'.[166] C.S. Baines recalled that even in the heat of battle 'it never entered my head that it was possible to retire without orders'.[167] Echoing this, in 1914 Arthur Guy Osborn argued that 'an Army Order is an Order, and has to be obeyed'.[168] Later, in 1917, Arthur Andrews also noted that 'orders are orders and must be obeyed'.[169] The salience of this idea was also reflected in a number of contemporary trench journals.[170]

Unsurprisingly, then, soldiers' obedience was also a theme in Frederic Manning's novel, which charted the latter stages of the Somme campaign. According to Manning, the rank and file were 'glad to have their action determined for them'. Orders were 'commonplace, mechanical, as though at some moment of ordinary routine', even if those orders obliged them to endanger their lives.[171] Men exercised a 'mechanical obedience' that was 'deliberate' and became 'so much a habit' that it even 'distracted their thoughts'.[172] Brophy and Partridge agreed that soldiers quickly 'grew used' to army rules and 'obeyed without thinking'.[173] This even influenced their pastimes. 'O'Grady', a game similar to 'Simon Says', was popular amongst soldiers at rest precisely because it played on their conditioning 'to an instantaneous and mindless response to drill orders' and this meant that 'to stop and think first was not so easy'.[174]

During the reverses in 1918, orders (real or fabricated) were used by officers to explain or justify their decisions during the chaotic retreat. J.E.H. Neville's short diary entries between 21 and 27 March refer to the orders his platoon received sixteen times. These always informed the course of action he chose. Significantly, too, an unwillingness to retreat without direction was sometimes seen as the key difference between good and bad battlefield performance during these pivotal months.[175]

---

[166] LIDDLE/WW1/GS/0125: W.G. Bentley, Memoir: The History of My 1914–1916 in the 19th Batt. Royal Fusiliers, p. 21.
[167] IWM Documents.10879: Lt. Col. C.S. Baines, Memoir of the First Battle of Ypres, 31 October 1914, p. 9.
[168] IWM Documents.315: Capt. A.G. Osborn, Diary 6 January 1915.
[169] IWM Documents.15946: A.W. Andrews, Diary 1917, pp. 112–113.
[170] 'Good Authority', *The Growler*, No. 2 (1 February 1915), p. 7; 'The Beauty of Obedience: A Story for Young and New Recruits', *The F.S.R: A Monthly Magazine* (1 October 1915), p. 4; Col. L.R.C. Boyle M.V.O., 'Discipline', *The Billet Doux*, No. 4 (17 December 1915), pp. 10–13; 'The Perfect Soldier', *The Sussex Patrol*, Vol. 1, No. 11 (April 1917), p. 1; 'Day of National Prayer: Appointed by the King', *The Snapper*, Vol. XII, No. 11 (November 1917), p. 1.
[171] Manning, *Her Privates We*, pp. 3, 7.
[172] Ibid., pp. 66, 148, 205.
[173] Brophy and Partridge, *The Long Trail*, p. 126.
[174] Ibid.
[175] SOFO Box 16 3/4/N/2: Lt. J.E.H. Neville, Diary 21–27 March 1918; IWM Documents.17029: Capt. A.J. Lord, Letter to Father 1 April 1918.

Such obedience was learned through training and discipline, which were inseparable in contemporary military discourse.[176] The military's coercive apparatus meant that obedience was often 'the least unattractive course' because of the frequently harsh penalties and social stigma that accompanied nonconfirmity.[177] Research suggests that, obedience is a human trait produced by particular social environments.[178] Stanley Milgram famously investigated obedience and the 'agentic state'. He concluded that people tend to see themselves as an 'instrument for carrying out another person's wishes' and can become no longer 'responsible for their actions'.[179] His trials suggested that humans frequently display unquestioning obedience.[180] While recent scholarship has questioned some of Milgram's findings (and methods), many studies have found even higher frequencies of absolute obedience.[181] It appears that the presence of authority figures and group pressure influence obedience and can even induce actors to follow orders that run counter to their own interests.[182]

Tellingly, there were relatively few incidences of major indiscipline and disobedience in the BEF. Douglas Haig proudly reported in March 1918 that there was a 'wonderful' absence of crime in his armies. Only one British soldier per thousand was in prison (compared to 9 Australians or 1.6 Canadians, New Zealand, and South Africans).[183] Haig pointed to the absence of capital punishment in Australian units as the key explanatory variable for their higher rates of incarceration. Important, too, was the decision to suspend penal sentences in February 1915, after which rates dropped from 5.1/1000 to 0.7/1000 within six months.[184] Imprisonment no longer offered an escape from frontline service. By September 1918, only 0.5 per cent of the British armed forces (31,405 individuals) had been tried for absence without leave or desertion. More strikingly, 'no more than forty-two men were charged with mutiny

---

[176] Watson, *Enduring the Great War*, p. 72.
[177] Ibid., p. 59.
[178] Winter, *The Experience of World War I*, p. 159; Sheffield, *Leadership in the Trenches*, pp. 72–73.
[179] S. Milgram, *Obedience to Authority* (London, 1974), p. xii.
[180] Ibid.
[181] See P.B. Smith, M.H. Bond and Ç. Kağitçibaşi, *Understanding Social Psychology Across Cultures* (London, 2006); W. Kilham and L. Mann, 'Level of Destructive Obedience as Function of Transmitter and Executant Roles in the Milgram Obedience Paradigm', *Journal of Personality and Social Psychology*, Vol. 29 (1974), pp. 696–702.
[182] B.J. Bushman, 'Perceived Symbols of Authority and their Influence on Compliance', *Journal of Applied Social Psychology*, Vol. 14 (1984), pp. 773–789; A.P. Brief, J.M. Dukerich and L.I. Doran, 'Resolving Ethical Dilemmas in Management: Experimental Investigations of Values, Accountability, and Choice', *Journal of Applied Social Psychology*, Vol. 21 (1991), pp. 380–396.
[183] Haig's Diary 3 March 1918. G. Sheffield and J. Bourne (eds.), *Douglas Haig: War Diaries and Letters* (London, 2005), p. 385.
[184] Ibid.

by the British Army on the Western Front'.[185] In fact, the significance of the 'mutiny' at Étaples in 1917 lies in its uniqueness, and some scholars argue that it might be better characterised as a strike against oppressive military trainers and military police.[186]

Other examples of disobedience occurred amidst acute crises, especially during battle. The relationship between training, habituation, and obedience was explored by organisational theorist Karl Weick in his work on 'cosmology episodes'. Generally speaking, 'people try to make things rationally accountable to themselves and others' and organisational structures influence the ways in which people perceive events (and crises). Individuals sometimes fail to recognise novelty and 'are susceptible to sudden losses of meaning' due to 'fundamental surprises'. At such moments 'people suddenly and deeply feel that the universe is no longer a rational, orderly system'.[187] Unhesitating obedience *and* inadequate training can leave people incapable of responding effectively in acute crises. In contrast, effective training (or relevant previous experience) can transform the 'contextual rationality' of a unit, helping its members to have similar reactions and trains of thought. For better or worse, training and innate obedience can distort frames of reference and create default settings and reactions.[188]

Poorly trained troops were sometimes overwhelmed, and command structures could break down when units experienced high casualties. Senior officers concluded that this had contributed to the British collapse during the German counterattack at Cambrai in December 1917.[189] Lt. Col. Arthur Stockdale Cope witnessed a similar thing during another enemy counterattack in May 1918: 'we tried to stop them ... but it was useless. They were nearly all boys of 18 and were quite done up.'[190] In such circumstances, servicemen experienced a 'sudden loss of meaning'. Acute crises could prove fatal if the military failed to inculcate the right 'ethos' and tactical awareness in its men. If this was done, however, then implicit obedience ensured that men responded correctly to the situation, followed orders, and avoided mass panic.

---

[185] Watson, *Enduring the Great War*, pp. 42–43.
[186] 'Perhaps the presence of both Scottish and Anzac ... soldiers gave the mutiny a cohesiveness which a riot could not have otherwise attained.' D. Gill and G. Dallas, 'Mutiny and Etaples Base in 1917', *Past & Present*, No. 69 (November 1975), p. 99.
[187] K.A. Weick, 'The Collapse of Sensemaking in Organizations: The Mann Gulch Disaster', *Administrative Science Quarterly*, Vol. 28, No. 4 (December 1993), pp. 628–652.
[188] Ibid., pp. 628–652.
[189] IWM Documents.3255: Gen. Sir Ivor Maxse, File 40: 'Lectures on the Lessons of the Battle of Cambrai, November 1917, and notes on the Court of Enquiry into the German Counter – Attack at Cambrai on 30 November 1917'.
[190] IWM Documents.11976: Lt. Col. A.H. Cope, Diary 29 May 1918.

It is important to note that even if moments of serious indiscipline were rare, this term covered a range of misdemeanours and many more 'subtle transgressions' took place.[191] The military's definition of poor discipline did not necessarily mirror soldiers' understanding of it. 'Minor offences' occurred regularly and often went unreported. Absence from parade, drinking, grousing, malingering, and insolence were all common.[192] In fact, soldiers actively celebrated scroungers.[193] However, the British Army has been characterised as uniquely severe in its punitive structures. Military law had been applied harshly in the regular army, and the BEF remained 'an environment of close supervision' throughout the war. Illustratively, the ratio of military policemen to soldiers increased from 1:3306 in 1914 to 1:292 by 1918.[194] Furthermore, the Corps of Military Police was supplemented by units of Regimental and Garrison Police. As such, these 'subtle transgressions' coexisted with this coercive and sometimes harsh disciplinary system, which suggests that' soldiers were still able to exercise agency and individuality. Significantly, it seems unlikely that this would have been possible without junior officers adopting a similarly flexible approach to discipline.

Cheeriness and Morale

These less obedient traits were fostered by other features of British military culture. Authority is frequently relational.[195] Englishmen's perception of obedience appears to have orientated around their relationship with their comrades, officers, unit, and the Army itself. Individual agency partly emerged in a relational space in which a soldier was expected to be cheerful.[196]

Laughter and humour are a natural reaction to trauma and can be found amongst the civilians and militaries of other belligerents in 1914–1918.[197] Humour played an important part in Britain's civilian culture, but cheeriness also lay at the heart of the military's social doctrine. Lord Moran, a medical officer during the war, believed that humour was 'a working philosophy that

---

[191] Rowe, *Morale and Discipline*, pp. 53–54.
[192] Manning, *Her Privates We*, pp. 142–150; Brophy and Partridge, *The Long Trail*, pp. 142–143.
[193] Gibson, *Behind the Front*, p. 193.
[194] Watson, *Enduring the Great War*, p. 59.
[195] Saint-Fuscien, *À vos ordres?*, pp. 17–19.
[196] TNA WO 231/404: 'Memorandum of Army Training, 1909'.
[197] V. Holman and D. Kelly, 'Introduction. War in the Twentieth Century: The Function of Humour in Cultural Representation', *Journal of European Studies*, Vol. 31, No. 23 (2001), pp. 247–263; J. Le Naour, 'Laughter and Tears in the Great War: The Need for Laughter/The Guilt of Humour', *Journal of European Studies*, Vol. 31, No. 123 (2001), pp. 265–275; Kessel, *The Politics of Humour*, pp. 82–107; J. Kazecki, *Laughter in the Trenches: Humour and Front Experience in German First World War Narratives* (Newcastle-upon-tyne, 2012).

carried us through the day'.¹⁹⁸ J.F.C. Fuller characterised it as an essential 'moral virtue' alongside patriotism and *esprit de corps*; he believed it was 'the oil of life'.¹⁹⁹ Cheeriness was expected of the infantry throughout the conflict and the pressure to remain 'cheery' was often projected in a top-down manner in the British Army. 'Dumb insolence' or 'allowing a derisive ... disbelieving ... amused ... or uninterested expression to appear on one's face' was considered a military misdemeanour. Cheeriness was also isolated as an indicator of high morale and a culture of willing obedience.²⁰⁰

Military publications reveal how men were expected to conform to this archetype. One of the primary goals of training was to 'help the soldier bear fatigue, privation, and danger cheerfully'.²⁰¹ Cheeriness was even celebrated before enlistment. One recruitment leaflet called on men 'to cheerfully don the King's uniform, and play a manly part by doing a man's work'.²⁰² Soldiers were made aware of how they should act, and the rank and file were expected to approach their service with a smile. The war changed little in this respect. A training pamphlet, published in the final year of the conflict, advised officers and senior NCOs that they should gain their men's 'confidence' and 'respect' by exhibiting their own 'obstinate good humour in the face of difficulties'.²⁰³ Their ability to do so reflected their skill as commanders. Men who followed orders 'with energy and with cheerfulness' and were 'smart, alert [... and] cheerful' in appearance provided important evidence of unit cohesion.²⁰⁴ 'The company or the battalion is the best looking-glass of its officers', in which 'you see the image of the officers – you see yourselves'.²⁰⁵ 'Slack-looking, miserable, dirty, slow, and almost sulky' men meant that 'you can tell at once that these are bad officers'.²⁰⁶ Internalising this, many officers insisted upon and tried very hard to foster a cheery attitude in their unit. Even during the German offensives in 1918, divisional leaders thanked soldiers for 'their cheerful endurance' before mentioning their 'gallant spirit'.²⁰⁷

Officers encouraged, enforced, and sometimes misrepresented (or misinterpreted) their men's cheery attitudes. Junior commanders such as Lt. J.H. Johnson

---

[198] Moran, *Anatomy of Courage*, p. 142.
[199] Fuller, 'Moral, Instruction, and Leadership', p. 666.
[200] Brophy and Partridge, *The Long Trail*, p. 95.
[201] *Infantry Training* (1914), p. 2. Cheerfully has been underlined by the author.
[202] LIDDLE/WW1/GS/0232: A.E. Burdfield, Recruitment Leaflet.
[203] *Platoon Training, (1918)*, p. 1.
[204] MR 3/13/2/35: *Duties of an Officer 42nd (East Lancashire) Division* (Aldershot, 1918), p. 4.
[205] Ibid., p. 6.
[206] Ibid.
[207] NAM 2006-04-25: Papers and maps sent to Sir John Fortescue by Lt Gen Sir Ivor Maxse, XVIII Corps No. G.a.155/4: 20th Division [1-3] and XVIII Corps No. G.a. 155/1: 30th Division [-1-4].

frequently commented on their men's cheeriness.[208] They became so concerned with cheeriness that it filtered into correspondence with their loved ones at home. 2nd Lt. D. Henrick Jones wrote to his wife on 21 March 1918 beseeching her to remain 'brave, and cheerful like you always are'. He consoled her that, despite the German offensive, 'we shall keep smiling and pluckily carry on always'.[209]

Even if it was a mask, men's apparently positive attitude could improve their comrades' moods. G.H. Greenwell used the 'quite cheery' attitude of 'four young fellows' in his unit to allay his parents' fears for his wellbeing.[210] The respect and compassion that junior officers felt for their men often stemmed from their cheeriness. G.A. Stevens wrote animatedly about his men's 'cheery' endurance, which was 'splendid' and showed that their 'spirit is beyond belief'.[211] Charles Carrington was even more effusive and proclaimed that 'I shall never think of the "Lower Classes" again in the way I used to after seeing them just as obscenely noisy and cheerful in a seven days bombardment as in a football match.'[212]

Humour was an important part of Edwardian society and popular culture, but it was also nurtured by the military.[213] The power of cheerfulness was evident in censorship reports, which suggest that its maintenance was something concerned commanders.[214] In January 1917, the III Army Censor recorded that 'with unfailing good humour he [Tommy] makes the best of conditions'.[215] His only report to find no evidence of cheerful endurance was his survey of soldiers' correspondence in October 1917. The men's inability to construe events with their usual light-heartedness was both a cause and a symptom of this dip in morale, and their inability to mobilise cheerfulness coincided with a dwindling belief that the war was winnable in late 1917.

---

[208] IWM Documents.7035: Lt. J.H. Johnson, Diary 26 April 1918; IWM Documents.11006: G.H. Greenwell, Letter 4 November 1916; LIDDLE/WW1/GS/0583: 2nd Lt. Sydney Frankenburg, Letter 12 December 1917 and 30 January 1918.
[209] IWM Documents.16345: 2nd Lt. D. Henrick Jones, Letter to his Wife 21 March 1918.
[210] IWM Documents.11006: Maj. G.H. Greenwell, Letter to his Father 4 November 1916.
[211] IWM Documents.12339: Brig. Gen. G.A. Stevens, Letter to Mother and Father 28 October 1916 and Letter to Mother 13 October 1917.
[212] LIDDLE/WW1/GS/0273: Capt. C. Carrington, Letter 25 October 1916 (No. 83).
[213] R. Alexander, 'British Comedy and Humour: Social and Cultural Background', *AAA: Arbeiten aus Anglistik und Amerikanistik*, Vol. 9, No. 1 (1984), pp. 63–83; K. Waddington, '"We Don't Want Any German Sausages Here!" Food, Fear, and the German Nation in Victorian and Edwardian Britain', *Journal of British Studies*, Vol. 52, No. 4 (2013), pp. 1017–1042. Ussishkin, *Morale*, pp. 3–4, 43.
[214] IWM Documents.4041: Capt. M. Hardie, '3rd Section Report on Complaints, Moral, Etc. (1916)'. Also TNA CAB 24/26/52: Note on the Morale of British Troops in France as disclosed by the Censorship, 13 September 1917; TNA CAB 24/36/44: W.R. Robertson, British Armies in France as Gathered from Censorship. Extract from C.I.G.S. 18 December 1917.
[215] IWM Documents.4041: Capt. M. Hardie, Report on III Army Morale, January 1917.

Cheeriness was replaced by a pattern of negativity and dangerously low morale.[216] This was a worrying trend. Humour helped to support morale by combatting negative thought patterns, allaying servicemen's fears for loved ones, and combatting the bitterness they felt towards superiors. So resilient was their cheerfulness that some at home were astounded by it.[217]

Of course, soldiers might have been hiding their true feelings behind the guise of cheeriness. Nonetheless, humour was a central feature of British military masculinity. Previously, historians have argued that combatants' emotions were characterised by stoicism, which focused on particular notions of character and force of will.[218] Cheeriness should be seen as a part of this matrix of stoicism. It was also a mechanism by which men made sense of their experiences.[219] During the next global conflict, humour became a defining feature of British responses to the Blitz, and in 1914–1918 it was a default setting for many troops in the British Army.[220]

This supported morale in a variety of ways. Humour was a reciprocal and relational process that bolstered *esprit de corps*. It helped soldiers to relax, combatted negativity, and drew individuals together. The social experience of 'cheeriness' strengthened the primary group. In fact, there is a positive relationship between success in crisis intervention and the quality of social support received.[221] Other men's capacity for humour was of enormous social and psychological benefit.[222] Modern studies demonstrate that this can alleviate anxiety.[223] Many servicemen celebrated the fact that 'everybody keeps cheery'.[224] It was an important theme in R.E.P. Stevens' diary. He regularly referred to his comrades' jokes and stories, explaining that his officer

---

[216] Ibid. Report on III Army Morale/Peace Sentiment, August–October 1917.
[217] IWM Documents.10814: Lt. F.A. Brettell, Letter from Peg 6 November 1916.
[218] J.A. Mangan, *Athleticism in the Victorian and Edwardian Public School* (Abingdon, 1989, 2000), p. 201; W. Westerman, *Gentleman: Australian Battalion Commanders in the Great War, 1914–1918* (Cambridge, 2017), p. 168.
[219] H. Ellis, 'Stoicism in Victorian Culture', in J. Sellars (ed.), *The Routledge Handbook of the Stoic Tradition* (Abingdon, 2016), pp. 325–326.
[220] E. Jones, R. Woolven, B. Durodié, and S. Wessely, 'Civilian Morale during the Second World War: Responses to Air Raids Re-Examined', *Social History of Medicine*, Vol. 17, No. 3 (2004), pp. 463–479; C. Peniston-Bird and P. Summerfield, '"Hey, You're Dead": The Multiple Uses of Humour in Representations of British National Defence in the Second World War', *Journal of European Studies*, Vol. 31, No. 3–4 (2001), pp. 413–435.
[221] D. Porritt, 'Social Support in Crisis: Quantity or Quality', *Social Science & Medicine. Part A: Medical Psychological and Medical Sociology*, Vol. 13 (1979), pp. 715–721.
[222] Watson, *Enduring the Great War*, p. 100.
[223] For humour and anxiety, see J. Bellert, 'Humour: A Therapeutic Approach in Oncology Nursing', *Cancer Nursing*, Vol. 12, No. 2 (April 1989) and N.A. Yovetich, J. Alexander Dale and M.A. Hudak, 'Benefits of Humor in Reduction of Threat-Induced Anxiety', *Psychological Reports*, Vol. 66 (1990), pp. 51–58.
[224] IWM Documents.20211: F. Hubard, Letter to Mr and Mrs Underhill 25 October 1916.

encouraged and nurtured this 'cheer'.[225] His comrades' interactions provided a 'splendid comic opera' and believed that 'if it were not for the quipps [sic] and jokes of the boys I think one would go mad'.[226] Capt. A.J. Lord found it difficult to maintain his cheerful demeanour under fire but argued that 'one is quite cheery again when circumstances alter or when the shelling ceases'.[227] Individuals share one another's emotions and the 'social role [of empathy] is to serve as the origin of the motivation for cooperative and prosocial behaviour, as well as help for effective social communication'.[228] Cheeriness helped to facilitate this.

It was his men's cheeriness that prompted Charles Carrington to write that 'there are no pessimists and cynics out there ... In the worst times there is such a cheery feeling about things and one laughs at hardships that would seem unbearable here'.[229] Stressful events can elicit responses such as this and often induce a pattern of mobilisation-minimisation. This is a 'physiological, cognitive and behaviour response' that helps to minimise or even to erase the impact of negative events.[230] Arguably, humour played a part in processes of mobilisation-minimisation amongst infantrymen during 1914-1918.[231] Though their cheeriness faltered on occasion, it helped to sustained them.

This culture of cheerfulness also offered the opportunity for veiled criticisms of military structures and authority. For instance, the songs that soldiers sang were often layered with a cynicism that would have been impossible to vocalise were it not framed as humour. This phenomenon might mirror the cultural shift towards irony described by Paul Fussell.[232] This was not purely a product of scepticism; irony played a constructive (and subversive) role by allowing servicemen to vent their emotions. The lyrics of songs such as 'We're Here Because' or 'They Were Only Playing Leap-Frog' were well known and sung 'with gusto'. The latter made fun of infantry tactics and highlighted the ineptitude of staff officers. One verse of 'We Haven't Seen the Sergeant' extended this criticism to unsympathetic (and unskilled) NCOs.[233] Songs such as these were popular in the theatre and music hall that proliferated behind the

---

[225] IWM Documents.12521: R.E.P. Stevens, Diary 21 November.
[226] IWM Documents.12521: R.E.P. Stevens, Diary 5 and 26 December 1916.
[227] IWM Documents.17029: Capt. A.J. Lord, Letter to his Father 13 September 1918.
[228] F. de Vignemont and T. Singer, 'The Empathic Brain: How, When and Why?' *Trends in Cognitive Sciences*, Vol. 10, No. 10 (October 2006), pp. 435–441.
[229] LIDDLE/WW1/GS/0273: Capt. C. Carrington, Letter 7 July 1918 (No. 141).
[230] S.E. Taylor, 'Asymmetrical Effects of Positive and Negative Events: The Mobilization-Minimization Hypothesis', *Psychological Bulleting*, Vol. 110, No. 1 (July, 1991), pp. 67–85.
[231] L.D. Henman, 'Humor as a Coping Mechanism: Lessons from POWs', *Humor: International Journal of Humor Research*, Vol. 14, No. 1 (2008), pp. 83–94; Madigan, 'Sticking to a Hateful Task', pp. 76–98.
[232] Fussell, *The Great War and Modern Memory*, pp. 7–18.
[233] Brophy and Partridge, *The Long Trail*, pp. 32, 35, 39, 40.

Figure 3.1 'The Jocks' (a Scottish entertainment troupe) waiting to give a show. Such groups were common to most divisions (and national groups). Undated photograph.

Source: George Rinhart/Corbis via Getty Images.

lines. Programmes for the shows indicate that satire was abundant in these productions. Officers and men would often share the stage. *The Crumps* (the theatre troupe of the 26th Bn. Royal Fusiliers) offered rank-and-file thespians the opportunity to play caricatures of their superiors. They actively mocked officer stereotypes and the greatest ridicule was reserved for the General Staff. Lt. D'Arcy and Capt. A. H. Reid joined the ORs on stage in one show and contributed to the denigration of General Commanding and his aide-de-camp, Lt. Albert Hall.[234] Men responded positively to the 'cheer' of these events, and many kept hold of programmes as souvenirs.[235] As well as a diversion and reminder of home, these events reveal that there was space – even amidst the otherwise coercive structures of the BEF – to voice individuality and critique one's superiors.

Cheeriness was a trait that was embraced by the British Army. Men were obliged to remain cheery, but this was also a mechanism for coping with the

---

[234] IWM Documents.4761: Cpl. R.G. Plint, Concert Party Programme; IWM Documents.7953: Pte. F.G. Senyard, Letter 16 June 1918.
[235] IWM Documents.7035: Lt. J.H. Johnson, Diary 8 December 1917.

war and military authority.[236] Albert Hirschman's discussion of cognitive dissonance in the workplace indicates that one way in which employees cope with unmatched expectations is by 'voicing' their discontent.[237] The army did not lend itself to free (especially critical) speech, but humour gave men some opportunity to vocalise grievances and became an essential outlet. Furthermore, it appears that when soldiers' cheeriness faltered the BEF's morale suffered.

Good Character and Respectability

Infantrymen were aware that their attitude and performance had a direct bearing on their futures. The military kept tabs on men's 'character' and, what constituted 'good character' was defined by the military: 'Resolution, Self-Confidence, [and] Self-Sacrifice'.[238]

Officers and the rank and file generally acted within the boundaries of militaristic respectability.[239] Respectability was an immensely powerful cultural force in Victorian and Edwardian Britain, and soldiers were aware that their wartime performance would influence their post-war social and economic standing.[240] Servicemen rarely acted in a manner that would see them stigmatised. Desertion, disobedience, and shirking were 'dishonourable' and punishable, but any misconduct might have left a stain on men's character and impacted their future prosperity by damaging their chance for gainful employment in the future.

Records of soldiers attitude and aptitude were fed back to them.[241] Capt. James Early forwarded the reports he received about his men's performance at various army, corps, and divisional schools. In one, L/Cpl. Burford was described as 'excellent', 'conscientious', and a 'thoroughly good instructor'. L/Cpl. Collier had been 'very good' at III Corps Stokes Mortar School. Sgt. Maj. Wootton did 'some very good work' and was a 'good N.C.O' but he 'unfortunately missed a lot of the course through illness'. Using language that

---

[236] For military cultures, see Hull, *Absolute Destruction*, pp. 2, 325.
[237] A. Hirschman, *Exit, Voice and Loyalty: Responses to Decline in Firms, Organizations, and States* (Cambridge, MA, 1970), pp. 1–21.
[238] NAM 2005-09-57-12-26: Address by a Corps Commander to Young Officers on Leaving the Officers' School, Division Y.P.C. – 5,00 – 4/4/1916.
[239] For 'respectability' in occupied France, see J. Connolly, 'Notable Protests: Respectable Resistance in Occupied Northern France, 1914–1918', *Historical Research*, Vol. 88, No. 243 (2015).
[240] F.M.L. Thompson, *The Rise of Respectable Society: A Social History of Victorian Britain, 1830–1890* (Cambridge, MA, 1988); C.W. Masters, *The Respectability of Late Victorian Workers: A Case Study of York, 1867–1914* (Newcastle upon Tyne, 2010); T.R.C. Gibson-Bryson, *The Moral Mapping of Victorian and Edwardian London: Charles Booth, Christian Charity, and the Poor-but-Respectable* (Montreal, 2016).
[241] 'The Law and Its Limbs', *The Gasper*, Vol. 21 (30 September 1916), p. 1.

Figure 3.2 A crowd of soldiers at a British Army training school on the Western Front c. 1916. There were plenty of opportunities for specialist training.

Source: Popperfoto via Getty Images/Getty Images.

fused race and class, he was described as 'a good type' and had 'taken good notes'.[242] Officers were assessed in a similar manner. Lt. Col. L.L.C. Reynolds' Army Book contained detailed notes about the officers in his battalion, which informed decisions about promotion or leave.[243] Elsewhere, 2nd Lt. F.T.K. Woodworth's company commander described his performance between 26 and 28 March 1918 in a report to his battalion's headquarters. He had exhibited 'great personal bravery and by his cheerfulness, and steadiness, set a fine example to his men'.[244]

These records mattered. Ex-servicemen could (and might have been expected to) provide character references to prospective employers. These reports accompanied their demobilisation certificate and outlined their service and the reasons for their discharge. Army Form Z.18 (a 'Certificate of Employment During the War') contained information about men's regimental employment, their previous trade or calling, courses they undertook, any qualifications they gained, and 'special remarks' about their contributions,

---

[242] SOFO Box 23A Item 1: Capt. J.H. Early, Reports for L/Cpl. Burford, L/Cpl Collier, Pte. Skinner and Sgt. Major Wootton.
[243] IWM 74/136/1: Lt. Col. L.L.C. Reynolds, Army Book.
[244] MR 2/17/57: 2nd Lt. F.T.K. Woodworth, Note to Adjutant C 127 from Capt. H.H. Nidd O/C B. Coy, 28 March 1918.

skills, and 'good work'. One man's form included a note that he had been 'very dependable in every way', while another serviceman's CO explained that he had been a 'good soldier' with 'an exemplary ... character'.[245]

These references suggest that some soldiers used the war as an opportunity for learning and training. Significantly, the army became increasingly specialised during the war, and men had the opportunity to finesse particular skills.[246] In 1914, aside from the medical officer, the 2nd Bn. Ox and Bucks LI contained only three specialist officers: a machine-gun officer, transport officer, and quartermaster. In contrast, by August 1918 the Headquarters Company consisted of the adjutant, the CO, a transport officer, a Lewis gun officer, a musketry officer, a gas officer, a camp commandant, a signals officer, an intelligence officer, a scouting officer, and a bombing officer.[247] Specialists learned new skills and were able to escape some of the infantryman's more trying duties. In fact, the adjutant of the 5th Bn. Ox and Bucks complained that there were so many specialists in the battalion that it left 'only 350–400 [men] available for working carrying parties'.[248] An infantryman could become a specialist in bombing, Lewis guns, heavy machine guns, carrier pigeons, signals, gas, and the use of respirators. Brigade or divisional specialist schools held training programmes, and the men then became instructors within their units. As well as improving one's day-to-day life, specialisation may have improved men's chances of survival since the core of a battalion left behind before an engagement or tour of the line was often primarily composed of specialists.[249]

In the war's later years, an infantryman was rarely *just* an infantryman, and men acquired new competencies. Ernest Grindley volunteered to be a signaller so that he could hone his knowledge of Morse code. However, he was upset to discover his job primarily involved improving the wire along the trench lines.[250] A.W.F. Fuller had no such regrets about becoming bombing officer and his regimental identity became intertwined with his professional pride. He enjoyed being a 'technical officer' and was proud when his CO purchased the battalion's bombers a special silver grenade button to wear on their uniforms.[251] The detailed journals and notebooks kept by soldiers like Fuller

---

[245] SOFO Box 23 Item 10 7/2/PL/4: Pte. Alfred Allen, Certificate of Employment; NAM 1990-01-58: Herbert Victor Aust, Army Form B. 2067.
[246] TNA WO 95/1900/4: War Diary, 5th Bn. Ox and Bucks LI.
[247] TNA WO 95/1348: War Diary, 2nd Bn. Ox and Bucks LI.
[248] TNA WO 95/1900/4: War Diary, 5th Bn. Ox and Bucks LI.
[249] Capt. J.E.H. Neville, *The War Letters of a Light Infantryman* (London, 1930), p. 35.
[250] IWM Documents.15268: E. Grindley, Memoir.
[251] NAM 1996-10-32, Papers of A.W.F. Fuller: Memorandum Army Form C.348 From AASS/AD1 36. T.R. Battn to Capt A.W.F Fuller [9610-32-2] and Newspaper Clipping from unknown source and date 'Modern War: Like Schoolboys Throwing Stones at One Another. A Terrible Romance' [9610-32-3].

when undertaking specialist training spoke to their engagement with their learning and, somewhat heartbreakingly, hint at how recently many of them had been in full-time education.[252] While in England, Lt. Frederic Brutton Anstruther Cardew explained to his mother that 'we do a lot of work and take a great many notes which require all the evening to copy out'.[253] W.M. Spencer Edge took pleasure in recording the details of visual training, including the nature of camouflage and distance estimation. His regular notations about pay suggest that he was a man who saw his service as transactional.[254] This was particularly true for younger men who still had their careers ahead of them. For this reason, Maj. G.H. Greenwell felt that his experiences during 1914–1918 had generally been positive. In 1929, he added a retrospective note in his wartime diary: '... to be perfectly fit, to live amongst pleasant companions, to have responsibility and a clearly defined job – these are great compensations when one is very young'.[255]

As men crafted narratives about their war experiences, they focused on the more constructive features of military service. For the younger men, especially those in their late teens and early twenties, it was an opportunity for *free* further education and training and a chance to improve their life chances. The certificates mentioned some pages back highlighted this, advising that 'The National Association for Employment of Ex-Soldiers exists for helping <u>men of good character to obtain employment</u>'. These records were 'based on continuous records of the holder's conduct and employment throughout his military career'. A.J. Allen's documents noted that he had 'served with the B.E.F. in France [and] proved himself an efficient soldier and carried out his duties to the satisfaction of his superiors. He is honest and reliable'.[256] Michael Gleeson (a regular who served throughout the war) described a 'steady and trustworthy Warrant Officer of very good character'.[257] William Morris left the military with two additional letters of recommendation from senior officers in his battalion. One of these 'recommend him in any capacity' and underlined his reliability, 'whole-hearted devotion to duty', and strong work ethic.[258] James Jayes' references were simpler: 'A sober honest and trustworthy man. He was wounded in action in 1916, and again in 1917, losing 4 fingers of his left

---

[252] Ibid. Notebook including Notes on Bomber Training [9610-32-1]. Also LIDDLE/WW1/GS/0582: 2nd Lt. R.V.D. Francis, Note Book esp. 'Notes – Sniping' and 'Notes – Gas Respirators'.
[253] IWM Documents.9364: Lt. F.B. Anstruther, Letter to Mother 6 February 1915.
[254] NAM 1979-07-178: Notebook of W.M. Spencer Edge.
[255] IWM Documents.11006: G.H. Greenwell, Diary, Front of Diary *c.* 1929.
[256] NAM 1990-01-58: Herbert Victor Aust, 'Character Reference'.
[257] MR 3/17/88: Michael Gleeson, 'Character Reference'.
[258] SOFO Box 23 Item 7: Pte. William Morris 201594, 'Letter of Recommendation from Lt. Colonel Ledward and Major W. Payne'.

hand.'[259] There was a contact address should prospective employers wish to delve deeper into a candidate's military past. As a consequence of this supervision, a lot of men were concerned with maintaining their 'good record'.[260] This was relevant during the war, too, since promotion was often performance related and sometimes offered an honourable route away from the trenches, especially for junior officers.[261] Indeed, officers also benefited from these references. Capt. Fullbrook-Leggatt left the military with a document that celebrated his 'aptitude for staff duties' and 'marked successes' commanding a company.[262] Men's War Badges provided physical evidence of men's 'Service Rendered' and provided evidence of duty done.[263]

Whilst large numbers of infantrymen never made it home, this did not diminish the power of good character. Huge emphasis was placed on 'character' in the letters from dead men's officers and comrades. Commanders often explained that their sacrifice had been a 'noble and brave act'.[264] Those from men's 'chums' were less idealistic and more frequently described their friendship with the deceased; outlined how they had died; and gave assurances that it had been quick, painless, or peaceful. They also consoled loved ones that the deceased had done his duty for King and Country and listed his other qualities.[265] Pte. J.H. Easton assured Mr and Mrs Thompson that their son had been a 'good straightforward and honest comrade'.[266] F.S. Castle's relatives were consoled that 'we who knew him felt the strength and beauty of his character'.[267] Letters were careful to explain that the dead man had a 'very nice grave' and had been buried 'quite decent'.[268] Such a concern with the quality of burials and coffins was also noted in soldiers' diaries.[269] At this time, the working classes spent a disproportionate portion of household earnings on burial insurance to avoid the shame of a parish burial, and the soldiers' desire to die respectably mirrored this trend.[270] Respectability was an idea bound up with and informed by class. Yet, even though it might have meant different things to officers and ORs, it played just as significant a role in influencing their perceptions of duty.

---

[259] MR 3/17/128: Pte J. Jayes, Army Form B. 2079 – Discharge Certificate and Character Reference.
[260] IWM Documents.7035: Lt. J.H. Johnson, Diary 28 January 1918.
[261] Ibid. 18 December 1916.
[262] SOFO Box 16 Item 12: Capt. L.E.W.O. Fullbrook-Leggatt, 'Army Book 439'.
[263] MR 3/17/96: Sgt. Maj. Herbert Chase, Army Memo No. B 337460 – War Badge.
[264] IWM Documents.21795: Mrs L.K. Briggs, Letter from Captain Walker 25 October 1917.
[265] MR 3/17/145: Pte. S. Smith, Letter to Mrs Smith.
[266] SOFO Box 29 Item 4 10/6/J/1: Pte. Percy Thompson, Letter Pte. J.H. Easton to Mr and Mrs Thompson.
[267] IWM Documents.20755: F.S. Castle, Letter from Private B Coy 26th Bn. Royal Fusiliers to Family.
[268] MR 3/17/145: Pte. S. Smith, Letter from Pte. E. Loose to Mrs Smith.
[269] MR 4/17/388/1: Pte. C.E. Wild Diary 3 May 1918.
[270] Pember Reeves, *Round about a Pound a Week*, pp. 59–60.

Defending the Homeland

Most infantrymen wanted to ensure that their military career would help them build a prosperous future at home (or at least would not hinder them doing so). More generally, though, many soldiers also felt it was their duty to protect their homeland and enlisted in their greatest numbers when Britain appeared to be facing an existential threat.[271] The sense that this was a defensive war underpinned servicemen's' perception of duty throughout the conflict. This was probably aided by the military's efforts to 'foster' patriotism through ideal 'mental, moral and physical qualities'.[272] However, the roots of this patriotism were already well established in the minds of the men studied here.

One censor, writing for *The Spectator* in 1917, underlined the importance of defensive patriotism. The author reported that war was mainly composed of 'monotony', 'toil', and immeasurable 'horrors'. Yet, despite this, the article advised readers that Tommy retained a sense of moral duty to his homeland. Seeing 'prosperous towns in ruins, old men and maidens lying cold in their own homes, the countryside devastated', the soldier had 'imagination enough to transplant the surroundings of Arras or Ypres to Kent and Cornwall ... It is borne upon him that he is fighting in very truth to guard his own home from the same destruction'. In such circumstances, the war became 'a personal matter'.[273] While this was pro-conscription propaganda, such ideas are found in the private notes of another censor. Capt. M. Hardie was moved by soldiers' explanations of how 'the England we so love dearer still' had seen 'the security and peace of the country' become 'in a sense a part' of them. These were the things for which they 'fought and died'.[274] Duty, *The Spectator* claimed, was born of the knowledge that 'he is fighting to save his own cottage from ruin, as surely as if he were standing at its threshold'.[275]

It was often during the periods of more mobile warfare that this 'defensive patriotism' was felt most strongly. During the retreat from Mons, Sgt. Osborn was horrified to witness impact of the war on civilians. He saw men, women, and children wounded by enemy weaponry and passed through villages ransacked by looters. It was 'very pitiful to see inhabitants leaving their homes'.[276] He was struck by the destruction and found that in many villages there was 'not a single house standing'. It was the sight of dead dogs, rabbits,

---

[271] Gregory, *The Last Great War*, pp. 32–33; Pennell, *A Kingdom United*, pp. 92–117.
[272] *Training and Manoeuvre Regulations* (London, 1913), p. 65.
[273] 'On Censoring Letters', *The Spectator* (14 July 1917), p. 33.
[274] IWM 84/45/1: Capt. M. Hardie, Notes from Censorship: 15 March 1916. IWM Documents.18524: Pte. W. Tapp, Diary 1914, p. 5; IWM Documents.1690: P.R. Hall, Memoir, p. 25.
[275] 'On Censoring Letters', *The Spectator* (14 July 1917), p. 33; Gibson, *Behind the Front*, p. 283.
[276] RFM.ARC.2012.264: Sgt. Osborn, Diary 22, 24 and 27 August and 16 September 1914.

and cattle alongside the discarded children's toys, family photographs, and old clothes that shocked W. Tapp the most. He only feel 'glad the enemy are not doing this in England'.[277] The memory of these things stayed with him and on meeting German soldiers in No Man's Land on 25 and 26 December he felt unable to shake their hands 'as I know I shouldn't if they were in our country, I have not forgotten Belgium'.[278] Pte. J.T. Greenwood's narrative of events after Mons was published in a local newspaper. In it he explained that 'it would make an Englishman weep if he saw this country the destruction they have created in the villages. You cannot describe it'.[279]

However, as the trench lines extended across the Western Front, the character of the war in Belgium and France meant such experiences were relatively rare after 1914 - at least until the Western Front became more mobile in 1918. Nonetheless, when men did encounter civilians, especially in the forward areas, they felt great sympathy for them. F. Hubard was touched by the heartfelt thanks of the people that they liberated from the German areas of occupation after their withdrawal to the Hindenburg Line in early 1917. He described them as 'prisoners' and was struck by the fact that most were 'young girls and women'. This, alongside the German's scorched earth policy, left him convinced that 'it is one of the most moving and saddest sights I have ever seen'.[280]

The sight of refugees uprooted from their homes became more common again during the German offensives the following spring. One soldier preferred this kind of fighting, but contrasted his 'wonderful' military experiences with the 'pathetic' sight of 'the civilians cleared out'.[281] A.J. Lord found the 'waste appalling' and was saddened by the sight of 'civilians scurrying away' and the destruction of 'neat' cottage gardens, scattered possessions, smouldering buildings, and dead livestock.[282] 'You should have seen us', wrote W. Vernon, 'the roads packed [...with] wounded walking for miles and miles'. Yet 'the worst of all was the civilians ... they had run for their lives ... it was heart-breaking to see them'.[283] Many saw the faces of their loved ones in those of the displaced. Perhaps because he had witnessed the plight of the displaced, P.R. Hall pleaded with his comrades to stand firm during a period of particularly intense fighting. He explained that 'we could

---

[277] IWM Documents.18524: Pte. W. Tapp, Diary 1914, p. 5.
[278] Ibid., p 10.
[279] IWM Documents.7371: Postcard Signed by 'The Mademoiselle from Armentieres', Extract from local paper.
[280] IWM Documents.20211: F. Hubard, Letter to Mr and Mrs Underhill 8 December 1917.
[281] IWM Documents.8589: Capt. A.J.J.P. Agius, Extracts from a letter received from France 28 March 1918 AJA 6.
[282] IWM Documents.17029: Capt. A.J. Lord, Letter to his Father 12 April 1918. Also C. Gibson, *Behind the Front*, pp. 5, 51, 361–362.
[283] IWM Documents.12771: W. Vernon, Letter to Miss L. Vernon 22 July 1918.

never forgive ourselves if we ran [and] the Germans got to the coast and our homes and families in England'.[284]

The predominantly static character of the war on the Western Front meant that men sometimes needed to be reminded that his was a defensive conflict. Three years on the offensive in a theatre of war increasingly devoid of civilians meant that this was sometimes easy to forget. However, the events after 21 March 1918 recast the BEF's (and Britain's) mission as one of defence, and men once again felt the pressure to protect their homeland.

****

The military influenced men's perceptions of duty. Whilst the experience of war undermined the power of some of the military's high diction, a sense of obligation remained pervasive. This supported morale by framing men's perceptions of the conflict and their role within it. It helped individuals to justify and endure the war's chronic crises and influenced their reactions to acute crises.

However, officers and men understood their duty in different ways. Janet Watson's discussion of 'war service' and 'war work' helps to explain this divergence in outlook and understanding. Officers felt intrinsically bound to their men and to the military and frequently framed 'ideas of service as a response to abstract notions of honour and glory, or to expectations about socially appropriate behaviour'.[285] Their men had a more varied and parochial perception of duty. It was 'work' and 'while generally articulating a clear patriotism, [they] saw their efforts on behalf of the war as work' or as 'a chance for better wages and working conditions'.[286] The professionalism of the regular soldiers of 1914 played an important role in framing their understanding of the war. Duty and honour were performance related. However, the reservists, volunteers, and conscripts who followed had a much more individualised perspective on duty. In 1916, the war was seen as an unpleasant necessity, but a job worth doing. However, in 1917 and 1918 war weariness had taken hold. The ORs felt that their duty was finite and often considered themselves (and their comrades) hard done by if they had already 'done their bit'.

Nevertheless, the military – and military service – remained the vehicle by which one did one's duty. As such, military culture influenced and limited men's choice parameters and perception of duty. Sociological studies indicate that 'paradoxical' situations can 'deframe' or invalidate previously held assumptions, prompting individuals to consider issues in new ways and

---

[284] IWM Documents.1690: P.R. Hall, Memoir, p. 25.
[285] J.S.K. Watson, *Fighting Different Wars: Experience, Memory, and the First World War in Britain* (Cambridge, 2004), pp. 8–9.
[286] Ibid.

enabling them 'to pursue new ways of understanding the environment'.[287] The British Army provided an interpretive framework that encouraged and coerced soldiers to act in a particular way, but also helped them to deflect chronic crisis and informed their reactions during moments of heightened acute crisis.

Michel Foucault's discussion of power and discipline helps to explain just how powerful this might have been. Discussing prisons, Foucault argued that an authority that *may* be monitoring convicts can induce individuals to regulate their own behaviour.[288] Consciously or not, the British Army might have done a similar thing as it first defined and then tracked men's character and actions. The threat of punishment was a potent reminder of the consequences of inappropriate behaviour. Yet, men's awareness that they were under surveillance (and that this record mattered for their futures) incentivised good behaviour and might arguably have been as potent a coercive tool as Field Punishment No. 1 since most men proved unwilling to jeopardise their futures.

Yet, military culture, particularly the focus on obedience and cheerfulness, played an important role in fostering resilience and helping men overcome and react to crisis. The emphasis on obedience, which was not unique to the BEF and its soldiers, encouraged individuals to habitually follow orders. In the heat of battle, this could prove to be the difference between life and death. Tellingly, nonconformity generally occurred in private, and outside moments of psychological shock or a breakdown of command these infantrymen tended to follow their superiors' directions. On the other hand, humour offered a legitimate opportunity for men to vent their frustrations, and this insistence on cheerfulness provided servicemen with an outlet and coping mechanism.

The culture of respectability was pervasive. Men's good character became a form of social currency, especially as they looked towards the future. During their time in khaki, their 'good character' was defined and monitored by their superiors. The created a powerful motivation to conform. Sociologist Erving Goffman's work helps to explain this. Goffman argued that 'when an individual appears in the presence of others, there will be usually some reason for him to mobilise his interests to activity so that it will convey an impression to others which it is in his interest to convey'.[289] Men conformed at least partly to maintain their good character.

Somewhat counterintuitively, conformity may have fostered some sense of agency amongst these soldiers. Goffman described human encounters as

---

[287] A. Westenholz, 'Paradoxical Thinking and Change in the Frames of Reference', *Organization Studies*, Vol. 14, No. 1 (January 1993), pp. 37–58.

[288] M. Foucault, *Discipline and Punishment: The Birth of the Prison*, trans. A. Sheridan (London, 1995), pp. 195–228.

[289] E. Goffman, *The Presentation of Self in Everyday Life* (London, 1959, 1990), pp. 15–16.

theatrical performances with a front stage, where one performs, and a backstage, where one can be oneself. An integral part of this metaphor was the role of props, costumes, and audiences.[290] Even though the officer corps changed demographically, military structures and the army's definition of duty changed little. There was also almost no opportunity to be 'backstage'. Men were constantly around their peers, if not their superiors. However, as the demographics of the rank and file changed so did the audience (and their interpretation of duty). Significantly, too, the army appears to have become more aware of the need to encourage its men, sometimes through civilian pastimes.[291] Nonetheless, its ethos remained more or less the same.[292] It provided consistent reminders of what constituted respectable action and, as a social institution, helped men make sense of the war.

Significantly, most servicemen believed that they were defending England, especially when German militancy appeared to rear its head. The next chapter will describe how infantrymen's memories of England and perceptions of their homeland informed their sensemaking and helped them to endure the Great War.

---

[290] Ibid., pp. 13–27.
[291] Mayhew, 'British Expeditionary Force Vegetable Shows', pp. 1355–1378.
[292] Fox, *Learning to Fight*, pp. 20–21.

4

Imagining Home
Englishness in the Trenches

Men's dislocation from home was amongst the war's worst chronic crises. It played constantly on soldiers' minds. One combatant, H.E. Cornwall, noted that '[h]ome ... pulls with intense power, and you will hear men ... say they can hardly stand it'. Yet, servicemen had to find ways to cope, and Cornwall reported that 'they have to "soldier" to stand it – by this I understand that if they have their fling occasionally, the tension is relieved'.[1] Where such a relief was unavailable, or seemed inappropriate, many men mobilised their memories and imagination.

In late 1916, military censor Capt. M Hardie found that 'mention of leave, past or future, occurs in almost every letter' sent home.[2] Hardie noted that 'nothing so cheers and heartens men as the prospect of leave ... It is the constant "lookforwardness [sic]" to eight or ten days in Blighty that, more than anything else, keeps them going'.[3] Home was 'the "crowning mercy" of their existence'.[4] Yet, while England might have only been a day's travel away from Belgium and France, their homeland felt very far away. Men longed to see their loved ones and complained vocally about perceived inequalities in the allocation of leave. Twelve months of uninterrupted service could feel like twelve years, especially when officers returned home more frequently.

However, their emotional connection with (and memories of) their homeland helped them to make sense of the war.[5] Hardie was struck by what he found in the letters that he censored and concluded that the 'security and peace of the country, his country, our country, are now in a real sense a part of him'.[6] He believed that it was ultimately the 'peace and beauty of our English country ... for which [... men] fought and died'.[7]

---

[1] IWM Documents.15139, H.E. Cornwall, unpublished autobiographical account, 30 July 1918, p. 23. I would like to thank Josh Bilton for bringing this quotation to my attention.
[2] IWM Documents.4041: Capt. M. Hardie, 3rd Section Report on Complaints, Moral, etc., Complaints, General, p. 3 and Report on III Army More, January 1917, p. 10.
[3] Ibid. Report on III Army More, January 1917, p. 10.
[4] Ibid.
[5] Ibid.
[6] Ibid. Notes 15 March 1916.
[7] Ibid.

Their visions of home also offered an imaginary space into which the men could escape. As H.T. Madders made his way up the line for the first time in spring 1918, he was shocked by the 'pandemonium' accompanying the German offensives. Deeply unhappy, he retreated into his imagination and focused on 'thoughts of Sunday night at home. Instead of the state, or the nation, it was to Herefordshire that Madders turned. He, and most of his comrades, embraced parochial scenes when envisioning their homelands. His memories of England were conjured by thoughts of the 'lilac trees' in his back garden or daydreams about his parents, comforting firesides, warm tea and teapots, delicious 'roast beef' on Sundays, his lovely local church, the market town of Ledbury, and the hedge-lined country roads meandering around the Malvern hills.[8]

Visions such as these provided a framework through which individuals understood their experiences.[9] Servicemen were constantly dreaming of home during moments of rest, boredom, and even trauma.[10] These connections with England were nurtured by correspondence from home and infantry regiments local ties and men's comrades, helping them to endure (and justify) their trials.[11] Like combatants across Europe, English infantrymen were driven by a 'duty to defend their home communities in time of national emergency'.[12] Yet, rather than necessarily being an expression of citizenship, this duty

---

[8] IWM Documents.11289: H.T. Madders, Diary 28 and 31 March and 3, 6, 7 and 8 and 17 April 1918.

[9] J. Bourke, 'Gender Roles in Killing Zones', in J. Winter (ed.), *The Cambridge History of the First World War, Volume 3: Civil Society* (Cambridge, 2014), p. 153; D. Englander, 'Soldiering and Identity: Reflections on the Great War', *War in History*, Vol. 1, No. 3 (November 1994), pp. 316–317; McCartney, *Citizen Soldiers*, pp. 7–8, 89–118; Bourke, *Dismembering the Male*, p. 152; Sheffield, *Leadership in the Trenches*, pp. 72, 151.

[10] This was also the case for French servicemen (and their families), see P. Brouland and G. Doizy, *La Grande Guerre des cartes postales* (Paris, 2013). POWs during the Second World War did a similar thing, see C. Makepeace, 'Living Beyond the Barbed Wire: The Familial Ties of British Prisoners of War Held in Europe during the Second World War', *Historical Research*, Vol. 86, No. 231 (February 2013), pp. 159–177.

[11] Roper, *Secret Battle*, pp. 10, 51, 169 and 'Nostalgia as an Emotional Experience in the Great War', *The Historical Journal*, Vol. 54, No. 2 (June 2011), pp. 433–434, 438.; Meyer, *Men of War*, p. 45; Hunter, 'More than an Archive of War', pp. 339–354; J. Kitchen, *The British Imperial Army in the Middle East: Morale and Identity in the Sinai and Palestine Campaigns* (London, 2014), ch. 4. For France, see C. Vidal-Naquet, *Couples dans la Grande Guerre: Le tragique et l'ordinaire du lien conjugal* (Lyon, 2014).

[12] Watson, *Enduring the Great War*, pp. 50, 62. This was not unique to British soldiers. For the French case, see J. Nicot, *Les poilus ont la parole: Lettres du front, 1917–1918* (Paris, 1998, 2003). For the German case, see G. Krumeich, 'Le soldat allemande sur la Somme', in J.-J. Becker and S. Audoin-Rouzeau (eds.), *Les sociétés européennes et la guerre de 1914–1918* (Nanterre, 1990), pp. 367–373.

stemmed from their relationship with what I have described elsewhere as the 'implicit nation'. This:

> focussed on emotive homelands composed of people and places, which related flexibly to the United Kingdom, the monarchy, and the empire. It did not necessarily embrace a national label. In fact, it was constructed internally and was evoked when individual combatants imagined their 'way of life'.[13]

Englishness did not take a single homogenous form nor, for that matter, did Britishness.[14] Both were fuelled by a loyalty to family, community, locality, socio-economic group, and then country.[15] As such, the infantrymen's feelings of Englishness took a variety of forms with local and regional ties (to places and people) frequently providing their strongest link to the homeland.[16]

As the preceding chapter revealed, men owed their ultimate allegiance to the King, not to the state, and it would be wrong to classify them as citizen soldiers.[17] The monarchy encouraged local (as well as national) allegiances.[18] What is more, there was generally an absence of political commentary in men's letters, diaries, and newspapers. While censorship clearly made such commentaries difficult, the men's world view tended not to orientate around politics. After all, many of them would have never voted because of age and income restrictions on suffrage.[19] It is true that servicemen were bitter about shirkers, journalists, and politicians on the Home Front, but their relationships with their homeland was the primary feature of their sensemaking.[20]

---

[13] Mayhew, 'English Patriotism and the Implicit Nation', p. 3.

[14] Ibid.

[15] D. Silbey, *The British Working Class and Enthusiasm for War, 1914–1916* (London, 2005). Also K. Grieves, 'The Propinquity of Place: Home, Landscape and Soldier Poets of the First World War', in J. Meyer (ed.), *British Popular Culture and the First World War*, esp. pp. 21–46.

[16] K.D.M. Snell has suggested that these had weakened before the First World War. See Snell, *Parish and Belonging*.

[17] H. Jones, *For King and Country: The British Monarchy and the First World War* (Cambridge, 2021), esp. chs. 1 and 2.

[18] Mayhew, 'English Patriotism and the Implicit Nation', p. 10. This is evidenced in one Scottish journal, 'Battalion Notes', *The Outpost*, No. 2 (November 1915), p. 110. Also, IWM Documents.11289: H.T. Madders, Diary 3 April 1918. The royal family has more frequently been seen as a vehicle for Britishness. D. Cannadine, 'The Context, Performance and Meaning of Ritual: The British Monarchy and the "Invention of Tradition", c. 1820–1977', in E. Hobsbawm and T. Ranger, eds., *The Invention of Tradition* (Cambridge, 1983), pp. 101–164; W.M. Kuhn, *Democratic Royalism: The Transformation of the British Monarchy, 1861–1914* (Basingstoke, 1996).

[19] N. Blewett, 'The Franchise in the United Kingdom, 1885–1918', *Past & Present*, No. 32 (December 1965), pp. 27–57.

[20] For the British case, Englander, 'Soldiering and Identity: Reflections on the Great War', pp. 313–315. For the French case, Audoin-Rouzeau, *Men at War 1914–1918*, pp. 92–154.

Of course, they felt a deep connection with their Scottish, Welsh, and Irish comrades (as well as servicemen from across the colonies and Dominions, though more often the white ones). Yet accent, culture, and dress reinforced differences between comrades fighting under Britain's flag. R.D. Sheffield was at pains to distinguish between the 'English' soldiers in his unit and the 'Welsh' infantrymen in a neighbouring corps.[21] Scottish units characterised themselves along national lines and celebrated their 'local' patriotisms.[22] Within English regiments, too, specific traits and idiosyncrasies were regularly highlighted as characteristics of particular counties, cities, and towns.[23] Broader understandings of their common Britishness tended to focus on shared language, interests, common ties, and a feeling of 'unity ... when that unity is threatened'.[24] At this time, Englishness (and Britishness) had a patchwork quality in which strong local identities fed into a more flexible and shared collective identity.[25] This did not diminish the power of national identity and, in fact, the flexibility of infantrymen's identities may have made them more more resilient. Despite the myriad faces of patriotism in the BEF, Capt. M. Hardie found 'a splendid unity of purpose' and a 'glowing sense of patriotism' in the letters he pored over.[26]

Soldiers' identities fed their sensemaking, but morale rested, at least in part, on their imaginative impulses. Imagination is a central (and possibly unique) facet of human cognition, which has underpinned our behaviour throughout history. Philosophers have long dwelt upon the nature of imagination, believing that it 'applies to things or people that are not now, or are not yet, or are not any more, or to a state of the world as it never could have been'.[27] Imagination creates fictions, but these are fictions that 'we could believe' real 'in a world that otherwise resembles our own'.[28] They encompass alternative realities in which past events turn out differently, or future events materialise, and can take the form of daydreams and fantasies.[29] Imagination is also the

---

For the influence of families and loved ones on men's morale, Watson, 'Morale', pp. 190–191. For the French case, M. Huss, *Histoires de famille, 1914/1918: Cartes postales et cultures de guerre* (Paris, 2000); M. Hanna, *Your Death Would Be Mine: Paul and Marie Pireaud in the Great War* (Cambridge, MA, 2006).

[21] IWM Documents.14710: R.D. Sheffield, Letter to Father 9 November 1914.
[22] IWM Documents.18524: Pte. W. Tapp, Diary 27 December 1914; IWM Documents.14752: J. Grimston, Diary 26 December 1916; IWM Documents.7312: H. Russell, Diary of Pte. W.A. Hoyle, 24 March 1918, pp. 17–18.
[23] 'What We Think of Ourselves', *The Fifth Glo'ster Gazette*, No. 23 (1 July 1918), p. 1.
[24] 'Esprit de Corps', *Chronicles of the White Horse*, No. 2 (1 April 1917), p. 4.
[25] Ibid. Mayhew, 'English Patriotism and the Implicit Nation'.
[26] IWM 84/45/1: Capt. M. Hardie, III Army Censorship Report 23 November 1916.
[27] D. Bromwich, *Moral Imagination* (Princeton, 2014), p. 3.
[28] Ibid.
[29] R.M.J. Byrne, *The Rational Imagination: How People Create Alternatives to Reality* (Cambridge, MA, 2005), p. 2.

product of lived, embodied, or 're-created experiences'.[30] It provides an 'image-based schematic' through which individuals order and make sense of events and becomes 'a faculty for fantasy and creativity'.[31] In fact, imagination is a rational and controllable mechanism that 'can help people make discoveries and deal with novelty'.[32] Identity and imagination interwove with morale, coalescing and providing a framework through which soldiers were able to maintain their proximity to home, justify their war experiences, and cope with the conflict's chronic crises.

****

J.G. Fuller argued that 'British and Dominion troops did not wear their patriotism on their sleeves', but this was not the case.[33] Men regularly articulated their attachment to England.[34] One man did acknowledge, however, that '[t]rue patriotism feels, but seldom reasons'.[35] These feelings were fed by an attachment to men's homelands, and patriotism was fed as much by individuals' memories of home as it was by popular culture and propaganda. Patriotism has been described 'devotion to a particular place and a particular way of life' or 'a natural ... expression of attachment to the land where we are born and raised, and of gratitude we owe it for the benefits of life on its soil, among its people and under its laws'.[36]

English infantrymen's patriotism drew its strength from their emotional relationships with local homelands.[37] These local identities were actively

---

[30] A.S. Brüggen, 'Imagination and Experience – A Commentary on Jérôme Dokic and Marherita Acangeli' in T. Metzinger and J.M Windt (eds.), *Open MIND*, Vol. 11 (Frankfurt am Main, 2014), pp. 1–10.

[31] M. Johnson, *The Body in the Mind: The Bodily Basis of Meaning, Imagination, and Reason* (Chicago, 1987, 1990), pp. xiv, xx and xxviii–xxix.

[32] Byrne, *The Rational Imagination*, pp. 3, 214–215.

[33] Fuller, *Troop Morale and Popular Culture*, p. 36. Lewis-Stempel, *Where the Poppies Blow*, ch. 1; Fletcher, *Life, Death and Growing Up*, p. 290.

[34] J. Stapleton, 'Citizenship versus Patriotism in Twentieth-Century England', *The Historical Journal*, Vol. 48, No. 1 (2005), p. 154.

[35] 'True Patriotism', *Signals*, No. 9 (10 March 1917), p. 9.

[36] G. Orwell, 'Notes on Nationalism', in S. Orwell and I. Angus (eds.), *The Collected Essays, Journalism and Letters of George Orwell* (London, 1968), p. 362. I. Primoratz and A. Pavković, 'Introduction', in I. Primoratz and A. Pavković (eds.), *Patriotism: Philosophical and Political Perspectives* (London, 2007), p. 1.

[37] Mayhew, 'English Patriotism and the Implicit Nation', pp. 27–30. For local identities in Britain, Hulme, 'A Nation of Town Criers', pp. 270–92; A. Bartie, L. Fleming, M. Freeman, T. Hulme, A. Hutton and P. Readman, 'Historical Pageants and the Medieval Past in Twentieth-Century England', *English Historical Review*, Vol. 133 (August 2018), pp. 866–902. For the power of the homeland, J. Horne, 'Patriotism and the Enemy: Political Identity as a Weapon', in Wouters and van Ypersele, *Nations, Identities and the First World War*, p. 17.

mobilised by politicians and military recruiters.[38] Unlike ideas of honour and self-sacrifice, they survived the war and helped to sustain men's confidence in the justice of their cause.[39] Nevertheless, as the years passed, a sense that there were 'two' Englands did emerge amongst some servicemen. The first, and most significant, crystalised around men's home and close community; the other, more embittering, England encompassed a wider and more impersonal socio-political entity. Perceptions of both Englands were fed by imagination. Men's impressions of the former were nurtured by close contact with family and friends, while the latter was coloured by stories and rumours gleaned from letters and newspapers.[40] Significantly, though, even as men lost confidence in the conduct of the war, the second of these Englands mattered less than the first, which was constructed around the landscapes of home, the men's families, and their community.

Perceptions of England in 1914

Regular soldiers rarely mentioned England. Long service meant that the army was their primary social framework. Reflecting on the campaign of 1914, one man explained that 'it did not come strange to me to be ... away from home as I have soldiered in several countries ... like all Tommies we soon made ourselves at home'.[41] For these men, then, *esprit de corps* was immensely significant.

For some soldiers the Home Front was a distant and even foreign place. Several infantrymen believed that those in England were unable to comprehend the war, generally misunderstanding, sometimes sensationalising, and frequently underestimating the seriousness of the war in Belgium and France. H.E. Trevor rarely described anything but France in his letters home, but when he did turn his attention to the homeland, he was derisive of the people there. Trevor was particularly unimpressed by the stories of German atrocities in the press, which he argued had been 'much exaggerated'. Nevertheless, he acknowledged the 'terrible' impact the war had wrought upon the locals; in fact, he asserted that 'I shall be much happier if it [the campaign] were in England so that people could realize what it was and take necessary action for

---

[38] IWM Art. IWM PST 5073: Posters, [No. 126] Is Your Home Here? Defend It!; Liddle WW1/GS/0505: Papers of Cpl. V. Edwards, 7th Bn. Royal Fusiliers' Recruitment Leaflet. For recruitment, Gregory, *The Last Great War*, esp. ch. 3; Pennell, *A Kingdom United*, esp. ch. 5; McCartney, *Citizen Soldiers*, p. 57; Connelly, *Steady the Buffs!*, p. 8.

[39] Wilcox, *Morale in the Italian Army*, pp. 140–142; Gregory, *The Last Great War*, pp. 12, 44–45, 49; Pennell, *A Kingdom United*, ch. 4.

[40] Esp. Hanna, *The Cambridge History of the First World War*, pp. 6–28; M. Pignot, 'Children', in Ibid., pp. 29–45; J. Winter, 'Families', in Ibid., pp. 46–68.

[41] NAM 1992-04-159: Anonymous Account of the Battle of Mons, pp. 2–3.

the future'.[42] More often than not, when he voiced an interest in England, it was because he craved information that might help him make sense of his war experiences. Several of his letters assessed the accuracy of *The Times*' war correspondent and in others he inquired if somebody at home had encountered a soldier from his regiment.[43]

Pte. J.E. Mawer held a similar belief and felt that those at home failed to register the seriousness of the war. On hearing that 'the Germans are giving you people in England the same as they have us out here', he explained it would wake the civilians up to events just across the Channel. 'I should think that will make fellows join the Army.'[44] Other men also recorded the news of German bombardments along the English coast but dismissed these as minor incidences when compared with their own recent experiences.[45] Otherwise, it appears that events on the Home Front were of little significance to many of the regulars.

Of course, this might be a false impression. At this stage of the war, there was limited time to maintain regular contact with home. Yet, Charles Dwyer's diary, which he kept throughout this period, also included very few references to England. He recorded the addresses of dead comrades, but the world outside of the Western Front only crept into his daily record when he encountered battalions with whom he had served in India. Years of overseas service had severed many of his links with England. His only 'conversation all about home' took place when he was briefly reunited with his brother (who was also serving in the armed forces). Thirteen years' service had made the military his primary social group and point of reference.[46]

However, home comforts certainly played on the minds of other men. Capt. Maurice Asprey kept up regular correspondence with his parents, often asking them to send toothbrushes, cigarettes, and clothing. His letters were generally addressed to his mother (who was also his source of Home Front gossip), but these requests were directed to his father.[47] The rank and file were less likely to ask their loved ones for luxuries, but they still requested items that were difficult to acquire in Belgium or France.[48] Family and friends provided a window onto the wider war. News from home was an opportunity to gain a better perspective on the now global conflict. This might be why the East

---

[42] IWM Documents.11445: Brig. Gen. H.E. Trevor, Letter to Mother 2 September 1914.
[43] Ibid. Letter to Evelyn 6 October 1914.
[44] SOFO Box 16 Item 35: Pte. J.E. Mawer, Undated Letter to Wife 1914, Doc. 27.
[45] IWM Documents.18524: Pte. W. Tapp, Diary 22 November 1914 [p. 10]; Sgt. Osborn, Diary 22 September 1914.
[46] IWM Documents.16676: C. Dwyer, Diary 1914 [27 September and 28 October 1914].
[47] NAM 2005-02-6: Capt. M. Asprey, Letter to Mother and/or Father 17 and 22 October; 15, 19, 25 and 29 November; 19 and 22 December 1914.
[48] IWM Documents.18524: Pte. W. Tapp, Diary 26 November 1914.

Yorkshire Regiment's monthly journal asked its readers in England to send serving soldiers 'newspapers and periodicals'. Whilst some servicemen were thirsty for information about the war and home, the editors acknowledged that most simply wanted things to smoke and eat, or items to make their lives a little more comfortable.[49]

Some servicemen maintained a keen interest in home and wished with all their hearts to return there as soon as possible. It might be that the war was easier on single men. It is clear that many married soldiers remained concerned for their families' welfare, devoting many of their thoughts to them.[50] This was a particular strain on reservists, many of whom had left well-established lives to return to the military. Christmas and New Year conjured thoughts of home with the greatest intensity.[51] Though J.E. Mawer felt embittered by much of the news from the Home Front, he also missed his family immensely. This homesickness fed a more general depression. He was obsessed with events in his hometown, Oxford, and devoured any information about what was taking place there – he constantly requested the latest issue of *The Oxford Times*. His family's welfare was of particular concern, especially the adequacy of the government money his wife was receiving in his absence. Depressingly, he found that he was also missing key moments in his young boy's life. The desire to remain a part of his domestic world could be painful, and any delay in his wife's letters left him anxious.[52]

Significantly, even if soldiers struggled to adjust to the demands of military service, they generally remained certain of their duty to their friends and family.[53] Illustratively, Trevor believed that it would be dishonourable to return to England before victory had been achieved.[54] Using similar language, Pte. Tapp was certain that his place was in France. In fact, the only reference to England in his diary came after the Christmas Truce when he encountered a German soldier who had worked in Manchester before the war.[55]

---

[49] *The Snapper*, IX.10 (1 October 1914), p. 160.
[50] LIDDLE/WW1/GS/0583: 2nd Lt. Sydney Frankenburg, Letter to Charles Burnett November 1914 and Letter 27 November 1914; IWM Documents.18524: Pte. W. Tapp, Diary 26 November and 22 December, pp. 6–10; IWM Documents.11445: Brig. Gen. H.E. Trevor, Letter from Capt. L.F. Ashburner to Mrs Parker 14 October 1914.
[51] IWM Misc 30 Item 550: Diary of Unidentified Border Regiment Soldier, 31 December 1914. Also AOC: Fred Dyke, Postcard to Bertie.
[52] SOFO Box 16 Item 35: Pte. J.E. Mawer, Letters 23 September, 1 and 19 October and Undated 1914, Doc.15.
[53] IWM Documents.11445: Brig. Gen. H.E. Trevor, Letter from Capt. A.F. Ashburner to Mrs Parker 14 October 1914; RFM.ARC.2012.264: Sgt. Osborn, Diary 28 August 1914.
[54] IWM Documents.11445: Brig. Gen. H.E. Trevor, Letter to Mother 3 October 1914.
[55] IWM Documents.18524: Pte. W. Tapp, Diary 25 December 1914, p. 11.

Perceptions of England in 1916

Unsurprisingly, the volunteers of 1916 maintained a much stronger interest in the world that they had only recently left behind. The higher levels of literacy in the New Armies also contributed to greater detail in their written record. Nevertheless, their links with home appear stronger than those of their professional forebears. England was their inspiration. William Anderson believed that he spoke for many when he exclaimed: '"God Bless Dear Old Blighty" and I think that it is most peoples [sic] sentiment too ... we are all interested in anything concerning home and getting there for good.'[56]

There was a greater interest in events beyond their family or community. Two years into a lengthy war soldiers were wondering if the Home Front really understood their plight and if they were actually doing their bit in the war effort. Pte. W.J. Martin devoured newspaper columns and became extremely concerned by reports of labour shortages.[57] R.E.P. Stevens did the same and recorded important Home Front events in his diary.[58] Lloyd George's premiership was met with excitement by many servicemen since it appeared to indicate that the war effort might finally shift into a higher gear, especially after Prime Minister Asquith's much-maligned 'Wait and See' policy.[59] Rumours about 'peace talks' had also reached the Western Front towards the end of the year. Spreading through the ranks, they were met with excitement by some.[60] Men gathered all the information they could to make sense of the war. Ultimately, this helped to build a picture of their return to 'dear homeland'.[61] Bitterness existed, but it was directed towards those that appeared to be undermining the war effort and delaying this return. Several infantrymen felt that some at home were not acknowledging soldiers' experiences, or their suffering, and that the contrasts between their lives were 'impregnable'.[62] In the soldiers' journal *The Gasper*, one author complained about munition workers' unmerited wages, while the editor called on

---

[56] IWM 96/24/1: Pte. W. Anderson, Letter to Wife 12 October and 20 November 1916.
[57] IWM Documents.2554: Pte. W.J. Martin, Letters to Wife 7 and Undated [No. 5] December 1916.
[58] IWM Documents.12521: R.E.P. Stevens, Diary 4 December 1916; IWM Documents.20933: Capt. R.E.M. Young, Letter to Constance 9 December 1916; IWM Documents.4041: Capt. M. Hardie, 'Report on III Army Morale, Jan. 1917'.
[59] IWM Documents.20933: Capt. R.E.M. Young, Letter to Constance 9 December 1916.
[60] IWM 96/24/1: Pte. W. Anderson, Letters 11 and 20 November, 3 and 27 December 1916; IWM Documents.7953: Pte. F.G. Senyard, Letter 14 December 1916.
[61] IWM 96/24/1: Pte. W. Anderson, Letter to Wife 11 November 1916.
[62] IWM Documents.1665: A.P. Burke, Letter to Reg 22 June 1916 and Letter to Tot 26 October 1916; RFM.ARC.2012.958: E.T. Marler, Diary 8 December 1916; IWM Documents.8059: Maj. S.O.B. Richardson, Letter Late 1916 [No. 2].

politicians to 'get on with the war'. Their harshest criticism was reserved for 'conscientious objectors' and the 'shirkers and blighters who discredit the fighters'.[63] Elsewhere, serving soldiers began differentiating between the conscript (a 'fetched slacker') and the still undrafted (a 'mass of lay-abouts').[64] It was because of groups such as this that Capt. R.E.M. Young remained sceptical about civilians' sacrifices and contemptuous of their contribution to the war.[65]

However, such complaints were relatively rare. References to conscientious objectors, 'conchies', or shirkers in British trench journals were limited (particularly when compared to those found in French trench journals).[66] Again, censorship restricted what soldiers were able to say, but some men *were* willing to voice concerns. It would appear that this silence reflects soldiers' parochial relationship with their homeland.

Unconcerned with the mechanisms of the state, and less interested in events on the wider Home Front, the majority of infantrymen (especially the rank and file) focused on the communities and landscapes of home. This might explain why, according to a book published by London postal censors after the war, soldiers' and their correspondents' 'attitude to life and to the Government is much juster [sic] than that of the article writers in the newspapers'.[67] These censors found that individuals were generally 'moved by those strong and simple emotions upon which family life and the broad truths of religion rest'.[68] Servicemen were desperate for news about their families or friends and craved the most mundane details about their lives. They did everything they could to preserve these relationships and they maintained an intimacy (and 'consctructed' their 'masculine identities') through their correspondence with

---

[63] 'Letter from "One of the First Half Million', 'Between and Betwixt' and 'Get on with the War', *The Gasper*, No. 21 (30 September 1916), pp. 2–4.
[64] 'The Brand of Cain', Ibid., p. 6.
[65] IWM Documents.20933: Capt. R.E.M. Young, Letter to Constance 9 December 1916.
[66] From a search of the ProQuest database of Trench Journals and Unit Magazines (British Library), including only 'Infantry' and 'Mixed' units serving in 'France', 'Belgium', and on the 'Western Front'. In publications released during the war 'Conchie' appeared only three times and 'Conscientious Objector' in 111 instances, while references to a 'Shirker' or 'Shirkers' occurred in only thirty-nine places. 'Striker' or 'Strikers' are referenced only thirty-six times. 'Politician' or 'Politicians' are discussed more frequently (228). Yet, the majority of these (179) come from one publication – *The Broad Arrow*, which was a 'high-brow' army and navy publication that was eventually incorporated into *The Army and Navy Gazette*. This compares to 6,024 references to 'Home' and 2,741 to 'England'. For the very different French case, see Audoin-Rouzeau's discussion of the 'hated' Home Front in French soldiers' newspapers, *Men at War*, esp. pp. 92, 111, 119.
[67] Postal Censor's Department, *The London Censorship, 1914–1919. By Members of the Staff Past and Present* (London, 1920), p. 9.
[68] Ibid.

loved ones.[69] Cecil White's thoughts regularly drifted back to his friends in Manchester. He was desperate to be reunited with them.[70] However limited, this contact with their community at home was often essential to soldiers' emotional survival.[71] The arrival of letters and parcels were amongst the most important events recorded in many diaries and delays in post created uneasiness that could only be alleviated when letters finally arrived.[72]

For many, if not most, military service was their most prolonged separation from home. Pte. William Anderson informed his wife that 'most chaps think more of home than ever before, but I don't think I was guilty of lack of appreciation before joining up'.[73] Distance had, it seems, nurtured an even deeper affection for England. 'One of the chaps said that we didn't know what fine wives we had before the war, but I told him I did.'[74] He himself lived 'in the one big hope that you and Tools [his daughter] are keeping well and comfortable and in no want of anything'.[75] Soldiers' newspapers echoed this sentiment with authors claiming to have developed a more sincere love for the landscapes of home.[76] Servicemen wanted to feel that were still a part of their community and often signed off their letters with an emotional request to be remembered 'to all at home'.[77]

The care that family and friends displayed towards soldiers through parcels and messages gave meaning to their experience and helped to sustain their sense of purpose.[78] F.S. Castle was 'deeply grateful' for his family's well wishes,

---

[69] Meyer, *Men of War*, p. 2. IWM Documents.16345: 2nd Lt. D. Henrick Jones, Letter to Wife 14 October 1916; IWM Documents.7953: Pte. F.G. Senyard, Letters to Wife 5 and 29 December 1916. See, also, Fox, '"I Have Never Felt More Utterly Yours"' pp. 1-26.

[70] RFM.ARC.3032: C. White, Diary 3 January 1917.

[71] Roper, *Secret Battle*, p. 51. Also IWM Documents.16345: 2nd Lt. D. Henrick Jones, Letter to Wife 25-26 December 1916.

[72] IWM Documents.20211: F. Hubard, Letter to Mr and Mrs Underhill 25 October 1916; LIDDLE/WW1/GS/0144: A&C Black Publishers, Letter from E.P. Gilscott 11 February 1917 – describing leave in late 1916. IWM Documents.15743: J.M. Nichols, Diary 18, 22, 23, 25, 26 December 1916; IWM Documents.5092: Pte. W.M. Anderson, Diary 9, 11, 12, 13, 14, 28 October and 2, 13, 16 November and 6, 14, 16 December 1916; IWM Documents.12521: R.E.P. Stevens, Diary 5 November and 1, 5, 6, 7, 28 December 1916; RFM.ARC.3032: L/Cpl. C. White, 3, 11, 16, 17 January and 12 February 1917; IWM Documents.1708: Lt. L.W.B. Medlicott, Diary 12 October 1916; IWM Documents.15743: J.M. Nichols, Diary 22-26 December 1916; IWM 96/24/1: Pte. W. Anderson, Letter 28 October 1916.

[73] IWM 96/24/1: Pte. W. Anderson, Letter to Wife 14 November 1916.

[74] Ibid. 16 December 1916.

[75] Ibid. 28 October 1916.

[76] Strozzi, 'Hullo England!', *The Gasper: The Unofficial Organ of the B.E.F.*, No. 20 (24 July 1916), p. 1.

[77] IWM Documents.16345: 2nd Lt. Henrick Jones, Letter to Wife 25-26 November 1916.

[78] IWM Documents.1665: A.P. Burke, Letter 12-15 October 1916; IWM 96/24/1: Pte. William Anderson, Letter 2 November 1916; IWM Documents.20755: F.S. Castle,

which made 'one feel one ought to do so much to be worthy of it all'. Castle implored them to continue writing since each letter provided a 'joy that is as fresh with the last letter as with the first'.[79] Parcels often contained traces of England and home. These could provide a material connection with the homeland. A few even included food, though the kippers, cakes, pork pies, sausages and mash, and fish and chips that some loved ones sent frequently arrived 'in an indescribable pulp'.[80] More long-lasting tokens of home included clippings of hair or photographic postcards of family and friends.[81] Soldiers also searched Belgium and France for reminders of home. In December, for instance, Pte. W.J. Martin was warmed by the familiar sight of London buses.[82] Officers and men from rural areas were able to find comfort in landscapes similar to those found in England.[83] The 'thick woods' around Reginald Neville's billet reminded him of Camberley in Surrey.[84] Capt. G.B. Donaldson's memory of home was aroused by the smell of a small red rose in a cottage garden.[85] For many, it was activities such as football or theatre that kindled the most vivid memories of home.[86] In other cases, the experience of attending a church service was another welcome reminder of the normal routines of life in England.[87]

However men's separation from England could sap their morale.[88] Ernest T. Marler was desperate to escape the Western Front and failed to mobilise the coping mechanisms that helped many of his comrades to remain resilient. Towards the end of the year, his diary included a series of increasingly desperate notations: 'how I want to be home', 'what a joy to be at home', 'how the comfort of home has been in my thoughts', and 'how I long to gaze

---

Letter to Ethel 29 September 1916; RFM.ARC.3032: L/Cpl. C. White, Diary 16 January 1917; IWM Documents.15773: N. Tattersall, Letter to Parents, also signed by brothers, 30 June 1916; IWM Documents.15433: S.B. Smith [Undated] Letter October 1916.

[79] IWM Documents.20755: F.S. Castle, Letter to Ethel 29 September 1916.

[80] IWM Documents.4041: Capt. M. Hardie, '3rd Section Report on Complaints, Moral, Etc.', p. 2.

[81] MR 3/17/145: Papers of S. Smith, Letter 29 October 1917 and Postcards: Photograph of Wife and Children and Photograph of Children [Ethel and Stephen Smith]; SOFO Box 15 Item 35: Pte. J.E. Mawer, Undated Letter [c. November 1914] to Wife [Doc. 24]. Also Mayhew, 'A War Imagined', pp. 9–12.

[82] IWM Documents.2554: W.J. Martin, Letter 25 December 1916.

[83] IWM Documents.12521: R.E.P. Stevens, Diary 2 and 13 November 1916.

[84] SOFO Box 16 3/4/N/2: Lt. Reginald N. Neville, Letter to Sister 16 December 1916.

[85] IWM Documents.10933: Capt. G.B. Donaldson, Letter to Mother 28 June 1916.

[86] IWM Documents.5092: Pte. W.M. Anderson, Letter 15 November 1916; IWM Documents.15743: Papers of J.M. Nichols, Diary 17, 18 and 19 December 1916.

[87] IWM Documents.12521: R.E.P. Stevens, Diary 12 November 1916; NAM 2003-10-8: Pte. Maurice Henry Polack, Letter to his Sister.

[88] IWM Documents.12521: R.E.P. Stevens, Diary 19 November and 1 December 1916; IWM Documents.2554: W.J. Martin, Letter 31 December 1916.

on the autumnal tints at home'.[89] Yet, the depths of Marler's despair was rare amongst the soldiers studied as part of this project. Nevertheless, even the most resilient men wanted 'to go home for good'.[90] Sgt. S. Gill's mood fluctuated with the letters he received, especially those describing his family's 'woes'.[91] Where friends and family were less diligent writers soldiers could be left depressed. Pte. William Anderson pitied comrades that received very little mail.[92] Even in these circumstances, though, memories of home still provided sustaining images of what individuals were fighting for. Most would have agreed with C.P. Crump, who noted in September that he 'hope[d] to be home soon [... but] Cheer Oh!'[93]

Perceptions of England in 1917 and 1918

It was around this time that censors began noticing that soldiers were becoming more willing to comment negatively on politics and events on the Home Front. It did not help that the press contained more reports of strikes and labour issues in England, descriptions of food queues, stories about domestic war weariness, and commentaries on international events such as the Stockholm Conference and German peace feelers. Only a year after celebrating David Lloyd George's ascent to power, many infantrymen now doubted his (or any) politicians' ability to orchestrate the war. It was, however, their continued absence from home (and the approach of winter) that appears to have been amongst the most significant factors in the malaise rapidly spreading through the ranks.[94]

To many soldiers, it appeared that the gulf between the fighting men and the Home Front had widened. Regimental chaplain E.N. Mellish described details of life at the front in letters published by his old parish magazine. In the Easter 1918 edition, he attempted to explain outlook of the servicemen in Belgium and France. He was at pains to tell the readers that they found it 'hard to hear that people at home are grumbling'.[95] Newspapers had long provided a window onto the Home Front, but journalists were becoming an object of bitterness. G.A. Stevens detested those 'writing rot' from their 'comfortable house ... where all war means ... is interesting reading in the daily papers'. In his view, they had

---

[89] RFM.ARC.2012.958: E.T. Marler, Diary 21–22 and 29 October and 6 November 1916.
[90] SOFO Box 16 Item 42: F.W. Child, Diary 29 November 1916.
[91] RFM.ARC.2495.5: Sgt. S. Gill, Diary 23 November 1916.
[92] IWM 96/24/1: Pte. William Anderson, Letter 16 December 1916.
[93] IWM Documents.15069: C.P. Crump, Letter 11 September 1916. IWM Documents.7953: Pte. F.G. Senyard, Letter 29 December 1916.
[94] IWM Documents.4041: Capt. M. Hardie, 'Report on III Army Morale, August 1917' and 'Report on III Army Morale/Peace Sentiment, August to October 1917'.
[95] IWM Documents.11173: Reverend E.N. Mellish, *St Paul's, Deptford, Parish Church Magazine*, Easter 1918.

neither the authority nor the right to speak of the war.[96] Lt. J.H. Johnson was likewise angry after 'reading newspapers with the usual ... result on account of food questions and the selfishness'.[97] How dare *they* be weary of the war. He resented the descriptions of 'profiteering', 'exemptions' and 'conchies'.[98] Capt. M. Hardie claimed that the rank and file were aggrieved by 'detailed reports, in a certain class of newspaper, of cases where soldiers' wives have committed misconduct'. Apparently, these affected 'the troops in a manner out of all proportion to the number of cases which are reported'.[99]

In some cases, however, the conditions on the Home Front could make men reflect on their own lot more positively. The inflated food prices and shortages caused by the German U-boat campaign led at least one infantrymen to reflect on 'the excellence of their living conditions in the B.E.F'.[100] C.W. Gray drew some solace when he read journalists that reflected his own world view. In fact, he actively collected articles condemning Lord Lansdowne's letter calling for a negotiated peace (this had been published in *The Telegraph* on 29 November 1917) because of the 'joy' it had given to pacifists.[101]

Some servicemen now nurtured a fierce anger towards politicians and civil society's elites. This might be expected of conscripts that had been compelled to serve. Yet, such an attitude was also prevalent amongst men with longer service records. In fact, earlier in the war officers writing in military journals were already sceptical about the government's ability to conduct the war.[102] This kind of rhetoric had now percolated throughout the British Expeditionary Force. In February 1918, C.T. O'Neill's brigadier had 'spoken strongly about politicians and young single men at home'.[103] Reginald Neville needed little encouragement to criticise Britain's political leaders. He was concerned about the chances of victory while 'blackguards' (such as Arthur Henderson, Ramsay MacDonald, and Winston Churchill) continued to influence events. He could not understand why they were 'tolerated' or had 'anything to do with the government'. Churchill had already 'played with sufficient men's lives'.[104] It is important to note, however, that most men's interest in politics and policy orientated around the war effort rather than the democratic process (or the injustices of conscription). Their criticism had little

---

[96] IWM Documents.12339: Brig. Gen. G.A. Stevens: Letter to Mother 27 January 1918.
[97] IWM Documents.7035: Lt. J.H. Johnson, Diary 30 January 1918.
[98] Lt. J.H. Johnson, Diary 28 December 1917. Also Capt. C. Carrington, Letter 22 June 1918.
[99] IWM Documents.4041: Capt. M. Hardie, 'Report on III Army Morale, August 1917', p. 3.
[100] Ibid.
[101] IWM Documents.11585: 2nd Lt. C.W. Gray, 'Politics and the Lansdowne Affair', Unknown Origin.
[102] 'Comments: The King in France', *The Broad Arrow: The Naval and Military Gazette*, xcv (5 November 1915), p. 505.
[103] SOFO Box 16 Item 30 3/4/J3/9: Lt. C.T. O'Neill, Diary 8 February 1918.
[104] SOFO Box 16 Item 3: Lt. Reginald N. Neville, Letter to Father 23 August 1917.

to do with active citizenship; they were venting their war-related frustrations. At least part of the dejection in the ranks of the British Army seems to have grown out of a belief that the war effort was being undermined by the Home Front.

A few men even began to question whether the Home Front was worth fighting for. Reverend M.A. Bere ended 1917 believing that 'I don't think we deserve to' win the war.[105] From his perspective, civilians were inherently self-interested. They had little or no empathy for the fighting men, and appeared to totally misunderstand soldiers plight.[106] After 1917's terrible fighting, news of the industrial strikes, workers' complaints (particularly about pay), or news regarding those in safe jobs were exceptionally embittering.[107] It is unclear how many serving infantrymen came from an industrial background or had sympathy for trade unionism. However, many skilled tradesmen were in reserved occupations or were posted to support arms and technical units. As such, they were probably less likely to end up in the infantry at this stage of the war.[108] This might be why frontline troops often viewed industrial workers with disdain. It was rare to find a message of support for strikes. For F. Hubard industrial workers' greater pay hard to fathom. Upon learning of a strike in Coventry during December 1917, he complained that it was 'absolutely wicked' that workers who ran 'NO risk [would ...] jeopardize the success of this war'.[109] Just a few months later, he hoped that the military crisis of spring 1918 would 'not go unheeded' and that the government would now 'rope in every young man they possibly can'. Hubard was so angry at the inequities of sacrifice that he became convinced that 'the whole of our manhood should have been enlisted at the standoff'.[110] Even as the tide turned in the summer of 1918 one officer still wondered whether some 'at home are not worth fighting for'.[111]

Despite this fissure widening, family, friends, and the landscapes of home remained most soldiers' primary points of reference. Most infantrymen focused on the implicit nation and continued to celebrate their visions of the

---

[105] IWM Documents.12105: Reverend M.A. Bere, Diary 7 December 1917, p. 134.
[106] IWM Documents.11173: Reverend E.N. Mellish, *St Paul's, Deptford, Parish Church Magazine*, Easter 1918; IWM Documents.7035: Lt. J.H. Johnson, Diary 6 January 1918.
[107] IWM Documents.12339: Brig. Gen. G.A. Stevens: Letter to Mother 27 January 1918; IWM Documents.17029: Capt. A. J. Lord, Letter to his Father, 26 April 1918; IWM Documents.7035: Lt. J.H. Johnson, Diary 1 January 1918; IWM Documents.11173: Reverend E.N. Mellish, *St Paul's, Deptford, Parish Church Magazine*, January 1918. See also 'Editorial', *The B.E.F. Times*, Vol. 1, No. 4 (1917), p. 1.
[108] Beckett, Bowman, and Connelly, *The British Army and the First World War*, p. 137.
[109] IWM Documents.20211: F. Hubard, Letter to Mr and Mrs Underhill 8 December 1917.
[110] Ibid. Letter to Mr and Mrs Underhill 8 April 1918. Also, IWM Documents.7233: Col. F. Hardman, Letter 3 April 1918.
[111] IWM Documents.7233: Col. F. Hardman, Letter to Frank 12 July 1918.

homeland.[112] This England remained a positive force.[113] Soldiers' families were central to their sensemaking (though the government feared what impact news of food shortages might have on serving soldiers) and their loved ones continued to be a source of energy.[114] Pte. W.G. Clayton's 1917 diary contained very few references to events in England or abroad, it was primarily a record of the letters he received from home.[115] Of course, postal delays still created unhappiness. Pte. C.E. Wild became depressed after receiving no letters for two weeks, but his mood improved markedly when he received a copy of the *Manchester Evening News*, where he read of a friend's marriage in the personal announcements.[116] H.T. Madders found that his mind always returned to his parents, the environs of Ledbury, and his partner, Olive. Every feature of 'good old sweet home' occupied his thoughts, especially during the fighting in spring 1918.[117] Pte. F.G. Senyard believed that news from home was 'extra welcome' at this time; visions of his family diluted the war's horrors. Even as he grappled with the sights and experiences of the German offensives, he felt that 'separation from home and all your people' was the 'worst part' of the Great War.[118]

Intensely nostalgic memories of home could undermine soldiers' fortitude, especially when it fed their desperate desires to return home. J. Grimston jealously recorded when friends returned to 'Blighty', either due to leave or fortuitous injury.[119] Furthermore, as the fighting became more intense – or the war dragged on ever longer – some men began to worry that they might never return home. This was difficult to fathom and actively undermined their resilience. At this time, 'Blighty' became a term that was increasingly used in reference to acceptable wounds and escape routes away from the Western Front.[120] Despite this, the term also stirred memories of family, community,

---

[112] IWM Documents.20211: F. Hubard, Letters to Mr and Mrs Underhill 8 December 1917 and 8 April 1918; LIDDLE/WW1/GS/0583: 2nd Lt. Sydney Frankenburg, Letter to Charis Burnett 16 January 1918; IWM Documents.7953: Pte. F.G. Senyard, Letter 16 June and 12 September 1918; MR 3/17/126: Pte. John Peat, Letter 11 October 1917.

[113] IWM Documents.11173: Reverend E.N. Mellish, *St Paul's, Deptford, Parish Church Magazine*, July 1918; LIDDLE/WW1/GS/0583: 2nd Lt. Sydney Frankenburg, Diary 7 February 1918.

[114] TNA MAF 60/243: 'The Effect of Food Queues at Home on the Men at the Front'; LIDDLE/WW1/GS/0144: A&C Black Publishers, Letter from E.P. Gilscott 20 May 1917. See also 'A B.E.F. Alphabet', *The Wipers Times*, Vol. 1, No. 4 (March 1917).

[115] MR 3/17/142: Pte. W.G. Clayton, Diary 1917.

[116] MR 4/17/388/1: Pte. C.E. Wild, Diary 10 and 14 March 1918.

[117] IWM Documents.11289: H.T. Madders, Diary April through July 1918.

[118] IWM Documents.7953: Pte. F.G. Senyard, Letter 22 May 1918.

[119] IWM Documents.14752: J. Grimston, Diary 24 March 1918.

[120] IWM Documents.11006: G.H. Greenwell, Letter 29 August 1918; MR3/17/118: Pte. William Adams, Diary 22 June 1918; IWM Documents.12105: Reverend M.A. Bere, Letter 24 October 1917. See, also, 'Personal: First Battalion Notes', *The Londoner*, Vol. 2,

and home. These in turn reminded men of their cause and nurtured a sense of purpose.[121]

****

Men's visions of their families, communities, and the landscapes of home were pictures of a world frozen in time, built around memories of England before war. The changing political scene mattered less than these subjective and intensely meaningful spaces. These generally young men were not citizen soldiers. Service in Britain's armed forces was not a vehicle for citizenship as it had become in continental Europe.[122] In fact, age, income, or political passivity meant that many servicemen had limited engagement with democratic politics. Soldiering was not approached with any sense that it entailed any reciprocal political rights. Indeed, the military (if not senior military figures) was self-consciously apolitical. Furthermore, even if servicemen had a pronounced sense of democratic citizenship, they were unable to exercise this in the British Army. As such, in 1917 several soldiers that had returned to industrial work (but remained in khaki) became embroiled in workplace unrest, but they found themselves unable to vocalise their grievances due to their continued attachment to the armed forces. Resultantly, their representatives complained that they had 'renounced most of their rights' upon enlistment.[123]

Thankfully, then, most soldiers' perceptions of England did not revolve around the state and citizenship. For the most part, they were 'structured around an implicit nation of meaningful, parochial, and frequently local spaces that were both rural and urban, natural and human'.[124] The historian Michael Roper has also previously suggested that 'most veterans probably imagined [England ... as] a short-hand for loved ones, bricks and mortar, a

---

No. 2 (1 September 1917), p. 49 and 'The Burning Question', *The B.E.F. Times*, Vol. 2, No. 3 (1 November 1917), p. 4.

[121] LIDDLE/WW1/GS/0144: A&C Black and Company, Letter from E.P. Gilscott 8 August 1917; IWM Documents.7953: Pte. F.G. Senyard, Letter to Wife 16 June 1918; LIDDLE/WW1/GS/0583: 2nd Lt. S. Frankenburg, Letter 7 February 1918.

[122] R. Brubaker, *Citizenship and Nationhood in France and Germany* (Cambridge, MA, 1992, 1994), pp. 104–105. Also Frevert, *A Nation in Barracks*; Mayhew, 'English Patriotism and the Implicit Nation', p. 8.

[123] TNA WO 32/18555: Members of Parliament on Active service: Expression of Political Views, 'Admissibility of MP's on Military Duties in Expressing Political Views in Press'; TNA WO 32/5455: Legal and Judicial: General (Cod 67(A)): Enforcement of King's Regulations Concerning Formation of Soldiers' and Sailors' Committees and Recall of Serving Soldiers Released for Munitions Work in Event of Strikes, 'Copies of Two Reports sent to Sir Reginald H. Brade at WO, "Soldiers Representatives."'

[124] Mayhew, 'English Patriotism and the Implicit Nation', pp. 3–4.

garden or a neighbourhood, perhaps a local landscape'.[125] Local civic and county connections remained significant throughout the war.[126] These were powerful bonds and Paul Readman has suggested that 'the locations of English identity were more various, more congenial to a range of ideological positions, and thus more effective as a vehicle of nationalist discourse, in all its complexity'.[127] A diverse group of soldiers could still be bound to the war effort (and one another) as these local patriotisms fed into broader shared identities.[128] This was underlined in commercial postcards produced during the war, which were kept by many soldiers, sometimes in their breast pocket. Some series showed a 'little grey home of the west', other collections depicted an idyllic 'village lane', while many celebrated industrial landscapes from across the country.

The soldiers' visions of home were informed by personal experience and popular culture. More often than not, they were constructed around positive (and sometimes fantastical) memories and driven by soldiers' innate imaginative impulses or fed by the correspondence they received. Indeed, the post that servicemen opened was generally a source of emotional nourishment. Censors' examinations of letters sent to the Western Front found 'little, if any trace' of defeatism and pessimism even when authorities feared that civilian morale was low.[129] Instead, letters were often filled to the brim with vibrant descriptions of the homeland. Through these – as well as books, newspapers, and postcards – men developed coherent and meaningful pictures of England. Their idea of home focused on landscapes, friends, and family. It was partly these visions that allowed soldiers to continue to feel connected to England and stimulated a sincere desire to protect the people, places, and spaces of home.

Local Homelands

Memories of the landscapes of home also helped servicemen to cope with the war. The British Army celebrated localism, especially in those regiments tied to a particular county or counties. British regiments 'reflected regional variety' and allegiances to particular people, places, and landscapes were actively encouraged.[130] The reader has already discovered how the 8th and 9th Bns. Devonshire Regiment adorned the graves of dead comrades with flowers from

---

[125] Roper, *Secret Battle*, p. 13.
[126] Connelly, *Steady the Buffs!*, esp. p. 224; McCartney, *Citizen Soldiers*, pp. 17–22.
[127] Readman, *Storied Ground*, p. 16.
[128] Ibid., pp. 88, 300–310. J. Rüger, 'Nation, Empire and Navy: Identity Politics in the United Kingdom, 1887–1914', *Past & Present*, No. 185 (2004), p. 163.
[129] TNA DEFE 1/131: War Office, *Report on Postal Censorship during the Great War (1914–1919)*, p. 196.
[130] Mayhew, 'English Patriotism and the Implicit Nation', pp. 9–10. A number of these examples can also be found in this article.

their home county. This impulse was not unique and other units drew heavily on specific landscapes and cityscapes while renaming and reimagining the Western Front.[131]

Regimental journals also painted very specific portraits of England. Very few of the journals published by the units focused upon in this monograph survive (if they ever existed). Nonetheless, other regiments' publications suggest that parochial visions of England were the norm. In the magazine of the 'The Buffs' (the Royal East Kent Regiment), Kent's wonderful 'richness' was celebrated. England's 'garden' tugged at the authors heartstrings: a landscape of hops, corn, and orchards (as well as fair maids) with a beauty that was unsurpassed.[132] In late 1916, *The Fifth Glo'ster Gazette* reviewed the recent anthology of soldier poet F.W. Harvey (who had served in the regiment but was now a POW). Harvey's verse contained an 'inarticulate longing for some little village garden in Gloucestershire or somewhere'. Thoughts of the Cotswolds and the Malvern Hills that stretching above the 'Severn plain' encouraged Harvey to 'hear the heart within me cry'.[133] It was not just Harvey who felt such a deep connection to his homeland. As it happens, the reviewer of Harvey's work believed that every serviceman longed 'for the wide prospects and spacious parks and mist-veiled heights' of his 'native island'.[134]

These imagined physical spaces held symbolic meanings. For *The Sussex Patrol*, the coastal landscapes of the south were a muse. The men of the regiment had guarded these gates of 'Old England ... in all her bloody wars'. Like the cliffs that rose from the sea, the soldiers of the Royal Sussex Regiment provided 'many, many watchers' for their homelands 'shores'. Their 'constant vigil' kept those at home 'safe'.[135] Elsewhere, other units also constructed their pictures of the homeland around the sights and sounds of their own counties.[136] In one regiment's journal, it was the rugged beauty of the West Country that resonated most forcefully. Dartmoor's ferns, foxgloves, and butterflies provided a welcome contrast to the destruction on the Western Front. This author longed to feel the 'soft springiness of the heather, to smell the bracken, and now and again to stretch out a hand to pick a whortleberry'. Such fantasies were soothing: 'the clouds drift over them [the moors], for I have turned my back on the sea and before me now are miles and miles of hills, apparently in utter

---

[131] Chasseaud, *Rats Alley*, pp. 22–23; Lt. C.E. Carrington, *The War Record of the 1/5th Battalion The Royal Warwickshire Regiment* (Birmingham, 1922), p. 16.

[132] Margaret A. Elmslie, 'Men of Kent', *War Dragon*, No. 4 (September 1916), p. 4.

[133] 'Review: F.W. Harvey, *A Gloucestershire Lad at Home and Abroad*, by Bishop Frodsham', *The Fifth Glo'ster Gazette*, No. 16 (December 1916), pp. 13–14.

[134] Ibid.

[135] E.M. 'Old England's Shores', *The Sussex Patrol*, Vol. 1, No. 7 (December 1916), p. 7.

[136] 'Signaller's Alphabet', *The Cherrybuff* (September 1917), pp. 17–18; The Editor, 'Editorial', *"Pellican Pie"*, No. 1 (December 1917), p. 20; R.W. Service, 'Going Home', *The Fifth Glo'ster Gazette*, No. 17 (February 1917), p. 10.

solitude'.[137] Solitude was a recurring theme in these kinds of articles, perhaps because it was so hard to find in the military.

Individual soldiers also articulated their local (or, at least, very specific) patriotisms.[138] Rural scenes were frequently muses, which mirrored the centrality of pastoral imagery in popular and political discourses at the time. Even men from urban areas drew on these frameworks.[139] The Edwardian penchant for day trips helped to expand horizons and popularise the countryside.[140] Sgt. Harry Hopwood received a postcard from a friend who had visited Whitsand Bay in Cornwall, which prompted him to 'remember going there from Penzance once with Sherring and having a bathe there'.[141] At this stage, around 92 per cent of the country remained rural and the 'pastoral England was very visible still'.[142] The world beyond the urban areas remained significant, particularly for those people who 'lived a life bounded by small-town horizons'.[143] Many people living in urban areas maintained features of rural life (for instance by keeping animals and allotments), and in many cases there was little more than a hedgerow between them and pastureland.[144] Popular culture also celebrated the countryside, which was a common theme in the work of many poets. For instance, A.E. Housman saw England's rural landscapes as a paradise, while Edward Thomas' pre-war poetry was inspired by Hampshire's rolling hills.[145] These themes permeated the latter's wartime works, too, in which the natural landscape became a foil for war's destruction.[146]

One article in *The Gasper*, a soldiers' newspaper published by a battalion of the Royal Fusiliers, asserted that England was 'a wonderful place'. 'How green the fields are and the trees [sic]. Everything is so clean and beautiful, so superlatively better than any other land you have ever seen.'[147] These kind

---

[137] 'A Breath of the Homeland', *The F.S.R.: A Monthly Magazine* (October 1915), p. 11. Also 'The Broken Mill', *The Dagger*, No. 1 (November 1918), p. 23.
[138] Lewis-Stempel, *Where the Poppies Blow*, ch. 1.
[139] P. Readman, *Land and Nation: Patriotism, National Identity, and the Politics of Land, 1880–1914* (Woodbridge, 2008).
[140] P. Johnson, 'Conspicuous Consumption and Working-Class Culture in Late-Victorian and Edwardian Britain', *Transactions of the Royal Historical Society*, Vol. 38 (December 1988), pp. 27–42; J. Hannavy, *The English Seaside in Victorian and Edwardian Times* (London, 2011).
[141] NAM 7403-29-486-144: Sgt. Harry Hopwood, Letter to Mother 3 November 1917.
[142] P.J. Waller, *Town, City and Nation: England 1850–1914* (Oxford, 1983, 1991), pp. 6–8; Thompson, *The Edwardians*, p. 17.
[143] Waller, *Town, City and Nation*, p. 8.
[144] Thompson, *The Edwardians*, p. 29.
[145] S.A.E. Housman, *A Shropshire Lad* (London, 1896, 1908); E. Eastaway [pseudonym of E. Thomas], *Six Poems* (Flansham, 1916).
[146] E. Thomas, *Last Poems* (London, 1918).
[147] Strozzi, 'Hullo England!', *The Gasper*, No. 20 (July 1916), p. 1.

of descriptions of the homeland provided a cathartic imaginative space. In their column space, authors described meandering train journeys through the English countryside. In one such article, a soldier watched as 'hills and valleys, streams and pools, fields and forests, flash by in one beautiful moving picture, and we are more than content. The dear, drowsy old towns we pass speak of nothing but peace, and the weight of war seems to shift from our shoulders for a while'.[148] An early issue of *The Bankers' Draft* (published by the 26th Bn. Royal Fusiliers) used historical and pastoral imagery in its description of 'Merrie England'. The homeland was made up of colours, scents, sights, and sounds that were rare in northern France and Flanders. There were placid lakes, blooming primroses, soothing birdsong, blossoming hedges, happy children, golden wheat fields, 'willow-shaded streams', colourful lilacs, and tall grasses. While it might have been an idealised picture of home, it was this world that men fought to preserve. These were visions of 'the finest land on earth'.[149]

Popular culture inflected soldiers' imagined England. For those with some education, especially officers, literary depictions of England were significant. Capt. G.B. Donaldson remained fascinated by the countryside and saw England as a composite of 'cottage gardens' and 'lanes and woodlands, or ... misty mountains and moors'.[150] Donaldson's England was a collage. On the other hand, Charles Carrington had a strong attachment to a specific archetype, probably nurtured during his childhood in New Zealand. He believed 'the South of England is the only place in the world for a white man to live in'.[151] In this way, landscape could become fused with ideas of race, respectability, and civility. Yet, Carrington was also drawn to Birmingham's urban sprawl. Some working-class men also felt a strong attachment to rural England. Pte. John Peat was from Manchester and kept a selection of postcards of England's southlands, including one showing Stonehenge in Wiltshire.[152] Such a captivation with the countryside also influenced men's choice of journal. Pte. C.L. Tully bought a diary that contained images and descriptions of the flora and fauna of the British Isles.[153] In these images, and in the soldiers' imaginations, England was a pure space, unadulterated by war, something to be protected at all costs.[154]

---

[148] Ibid.
[149] T.F.T. 'Oh for June in Merrie England!', *The Bankers' Draft*, Vol. 1, No. 2 (July 1916), p. 3. See also 'The Broken Mill', *The Dagger*, No. 1 (November 1918), p. 23.
[150] IWM Documents.10933: Capt. G.B. Donaldson, Letters to Mother 28 June and 9 July 1916. Also Dakers, *Forever England*, pp. 1–19. This reflects the variety of landscapes discussed by Paul Readman in *Storied Ground*.
[151] LIDDLE/WW1/GS/0273: Capt. C. Carrington, Letter to Mother 8 May 1918.
[152] MR 3/17/126: Pte. John Peat, Postcards of Stockton Church, Codford, Stonehenge, and Witley.
[153] LIDDLE/WW1/GS/1634: Pte. C.L. Tully, Diary.
[154] This reflects attitudes found in the pre-war preservationist movement. See J.K. Walton, 'The National Trust Centenary: Official and Unofficial Histories', *The Local Historian*,

However, for some men rural landscapes held little appeal. Henry Lawson, a platoon commander in 1918, regretted that besides two farmers and a gardener the rest of his unit were all 'town bred men' and 'not at all interested in the countryside'.[155] Many men thought exclusively of their urban homes. In their minds, England formed around the bustling streets and community in their hometown or city. The poor conditions found in some urban environments might have also left some soldiers more resilient to the conditions they encountered in Belgium and France. The lives of many of the urban working classes were plagued by 'ill health, insecurity, grinding poverty and resigned hopelessness'. Historian Adrian Gregory has argued that 'no view of the horrors of the First World War can be complete without a sense of the horrors of the pre-war peace'.[156] The rural poor (who were often appallingly paid farm labourers) lived in dwellings that were often equally dilapidated. Edwardian life was often dominated by uncertainty and destitution.[157] However, even those from small, cramped, and unhealthy homes often yearned to return to these places. In these (and other) cases visions of home were sanitised. Some men simply focused on the rooms of their house or the streets surrounding it.[158] R.E.P. Stevens, for instance, felt that England was the dining room fireside, 'the parish of Godly [and] every street' around his home, and the 'interiors of houses I was want [sic] to visit all at once'.[159]

Images of England were sometimes collectively constructed. Men of a similar backgrounds encouraged feelings of familiarity. The sound of a local accent could feed thoughts of home. L/Cpl. C. White, a Mancunian serving in the Royal Fusiliers, found that it was 'quite a treat to hear a North Country man' and that the 'badge of Manchester' was something 'pleasant to see nowadays'. According to Commonwealth War Graves Commission (CWGC) records, only twenty-five of the 731 Royal Fusiliers who died in late 1916 were from Manchester. As such, other Mancunians were a welcome 'reminder of home' for a man surrounded by people from elsewhere in the United Kingdom.[160] Accents (and attitudes or traits) could also emphasise difference.[161] A 'Scotch' accent was always noteworthy (especially for those

---

Vol. 26 (1996), pp. 80–88 and P.C. Gould, *Early Green Politics: Back to Nature, Back to Land, and Socialism in Britain 1880–1914* (Brighton, 1988).

[155] LIDDLE/WW1/GS/0933: H. Lawson, Letter to his Mother 7 March 1918.
[156] Gregory, *The Last Great War*, p. 278.
[157] Ibid.
[158] IWM 96/24/1: Pte. W. Anderson, Letter to Wife 14 November 1916.
[159] IWM Documents.12521: R.E.P Stevens, Diary 6 December 1916.
[160] RFM.ARC.3032: L/Cpl. C. White, Diary 4 January 1917.
[161] Connelly, *Steady the Buffs!*, p. 13. IWM Documents.12105: Reverend M.A. Bere, Letters esp. 29 June and 15 August 1916.

men who believed that 'Jocks' were particularly ruthless).[162] Yet, different experiences could still provide a 'common topic' for conversations and clarified images of home, emphasising how identities overlapped. Men were encouraged to see 'connections with lives they had left behind', and this helped them to develop relationships with their comrades.[163]

Friends and family were the human face of the homeland. Comrades with shared backgrounds provided soldiers with a social anchor.[164] Servicemen continued to seek out friends and family on the Western Front.[165] People from home offered an opportunity to discuss shared 'chums' and acquaintances, reminisce over old haunts, and consolidate images and memories of England.[166] Shared cultural norms and group membership are an important factor in increasing social attraction, which is a key ingredient in group cohesion.[167] The resilience of regional homogeneity in many county regiments helped this process.[168] It also offered a more open line of communication to England since friends sometimes helped one another to circumvent the Army's system of censorship by smuggling letters when returning to England on leave.[169] A.P. Burke used his connections within the 20th Bn. Manchester Regiment to send more frank and open letters to his family.[170] Officers regularly sought out friends from school and university and servicemen were often despondent if they were unable to find familiar faces in their camp or unit.[171]

There were other muses for men's visions of home. Newspapers, especially local newspapers, were a useful tool. Stories and reports fuelled soldiers

---

[162] IWM Documents.18524: Pte. W. Tapp, 27 December 1914; SOFO Box 16 Item 42: F.W. Child, Diary 21 November1916; SOFO Box 16 Item 30: Lt. C.T. O'Neill, Diary 15 February 1918; IWM Documents.12105: Reverend M.A. Bere, Letter 24 October 1917.

[163] Roper, 'Nostalgia as an Emotional Experience in the Great War', p. 439.

[164] SOFO Box 16 Item 35: Pte. J.E. Mawer, Letter 23 September 1914; SOFO Box 16 Item 29 3/4/J3/8: Lt. Reginald N. Neville, Letter to Sister 24 December 1916; NAM 7403-29-486-144: Sgt. Harry Hopwood, Letter to Mother 13 January 1918.

[165] SOFO Box 16 Item 31 3/4/J3/7: Pte. C. George, Diary 10 July and 13, 14, 16, 17, 28 October 1917; SOFO Box 16 Item 29 3/4/J3/8: Lt. Reginald N. Neville, Letter to Father 17 December 1917; IWM Documents.11289: H.T. Madders, Diary 1 June 1918; IWM Documents.7035: Lt. J.H. Johnson, Diary 11 October 1918; IWM 96/24/1: Pte. William Anderson, Letter 1 December 1916; IWM Documents.7953: Pte. F.G. Senyard, Letter 26 December 1916; RFM.ARC.2012.958: E.T. Marler, Diary 16 November 1916.

[166] LIDDLE/WW1/GS/0042: Pte. R. Argent, Letter from A.V. Peal to Mrs Argent.

[167] M.A. Hogg, 'Group Cohesiveness: A Critical Review and Some New Directions', *European Review of Social Psychology*, Vol. 4 (1993), pp. 85–111.

[168] See Appendix.

[169] *Report on Postal Censorship during the Great War*, p. 196.

[170] IWM Documents.1665: A.P. Burke, Letter to Reg 12–15 October 1916.

[171] LIDDLE/WW1/GS/0933: H. Lawson, Letter to Mother 12 September 1917; SOFO Box 16 Item 30: Lt. C.T. O'Neill, Diary 14 January 1918.

imaginations.[172] For three men – F.S. Castle, J. Grimston and C. White – particularly descriptive letters from their family played a similar role.[173] J.E. Mawer's England was composed of the colleges and streets of Oxford, his own house, alongside his family, friends, and wider community.[174] Officers, too, could have a parochial perception of the homeland. 2nd Lt. D. Henrick Jones often focused on his marital bedroom.[175] Capt. G.B. Donaldson thought about his university days in Cambridge at Queens' College.[176] For readers, literature was also a muse. Lt. J.H. Johnson immersed himself in Alec Waugh's *The Loom of Youth*. The novel drew on Waugh's school days in Sherborne, Dorset, and provided vivid descriptions of England's south-western coastlines. It may have taken Johnson back to his own childhood.[177] As the reader has seen, when picturing the homeland H.T. Madders thought only of the wooded Malvern Hills and the small villages and towns that populated them.[178] He imagined himself retracing the 'Worcester and Hereford roads' that criss-crossed this landscape.[179] Manchester was A.P. Burke's central focus including its industrial landscape and network of streets.[180]

The diffusion of regional identity within some units, and within brigades and divisions, helped to broaden soldiers' perspectives on England. According to historian Linda Colley, a similar thing process took place during the Revolutionary and Napoleonic wars as soldiers were deployed across the country and interacted with men of different backgrounds. These experiences, she argues, ensured that they developed a deeper-rooted sense of Britishness.[181] Some cultural diffusion took place within regiments. Men were struck (or sometimes frustrated) by interactions with new groups. Even in

---

[172] LIDDLE/WW1/GS/0583: 2nd Lt. S. Frankenburg, Letter to Charis Burnett Early November 1914; SOFO Box 23 Item 99: Sgt. J. Early, Journal 29 October 1915; IWM Documents.18455: Lt. Col. D.R. Turnbull, Letter to Mother and Father 15 December 1916; IWM Documents.15743: J.M. Nichols, Diary 25, 26 and 31 December 1916; IWM Documents.7035: Lt. J.H. Johnson, Diary 31 December 1916.
[173] IWM Documents.20755: F.S. Castle, Letter to Niece Ethel 29 September 1916; IWM Documents.14752: J. Grimston, Diary 12 November 1916; RFM.ARC.3032: L/Cpl. C. White, Diary 17 January 1917.
[174] SOFO Box 16 Item 35: Pte. J.E. Mawer, Doc. 14 Letter 23 September 1914, Doc.15 Letter Unknown Date 1914; Doc. 20 Letter to his Wife w/c 19 October; Doc. 27 Letter to Wife Undated [Mid-December 1914].
[175] IWM Documents.16345: 2nd Lt. D. Henrick Jones, Letter to Wife 25–26 December 1916.
[176] IWM Documents.10933: Capt. G.B. Donaldson, Letter to Mother 16 June 1916.
[177] IWM Documents.7035: Lt. J.H. Johnson, Diary 18 December 1917.
[178] IWM Documents.11289: H.T. Madders, Diary 1, 3 and 9 April 1918.
[179] Ibid. Diary 31 March 1918.
[180] IWM Documents.1665: A.P. Burke, Letters to Reg 21 November and 29 December 1916.
[181] L. Colley, *Britons: Forging the Nation 1707–1837* (New Haven, 2012), pp. 242–325; L. Colley, 'Whose Nation? Class and National Consciousness in Britain 1750–1830', *Past & Present*, No. 113 (1986), pp. 116–117.

relatively homogeneous units, they were forced to interact with people from other parts of England (and Britain).[182] A.T. Hollingsworth was a regular soldier from Wood Green, London, but served as a senior non-commissioned officer in the 2nd, 3rd, and 7th Bns. Border Regiment. This regiment became a melting pot of men from across England.[183] Lt. J.H. Johnson's was brought up in Brighton and Hove, but he also served in the Borders. Fascinated by these men, he recorded the quirks of their accents in his diary and became very fond of them.[184] Tom Eldridge was a sergeant in the Ox and Bucks but came from Fulham – a very different place to the towns and villages of the regiment's home counties.[185] Charles Dwyer was also from London but served in the Devonshire Regiment and adopted the coastal county as a surrogate home.[186]

Paul Readman has argued that the obsession with 'land and landscape' in early twentieth-century Britain 'represented a desire to come to terms with the rapid pace of social and economic change by maintaining a sense of continuity with the English past, so preserving a durable sense of national belonging'.[187] Yet, the form that this sense of national belonging took varied. Soldiers had very specific visions of England and home. Nonetheless, these fed broader understandings of Englishness and Britishness. There was a composite of multiple, overlapping, visions of England in the BEF. In 1918, one battalion of the Gloucestershire Regiment celebrated the other units in their brigade, which hailed from Worcestershire and Warwickshire. The men from these counties were considered to have specific traits and qualities, which were often tied to the counties' landscapes or urban areas.[188] Local and regional allegiances fuelled individuals' visions of their homeland, but also fed an appreciation of England (and Britain) as a whole.

Imagination and Morale

Michael Roper has argued that 'fantasies' about home were 'often expressed in the present or future tense, which suggests their significance in providing comfort'.[189] It would appear that soldiers' pictures of England were fed by memory but ultimately helped individuals to escape the present and (at their most powerful) project into the future. They were clarified during servicemen's

---

[182] 'Things We Want to Know', *The Fifth Glo'ster Gazette*, No. 14 (September 1916), p. 7.
[183] NAM 1990-06-389: C.S.M. Arthur Thomas Hollingsworth, Soldier's Pay Book.
[184] IWM Documents.7035: Lt. J.H. Johnson, Diary 26 November 1916 and 11 October 1918.
[185] NAM 7804-65: Sgt. Thomas Eldridge, Undated Letter to Children.
[186] IWM Documents.16676: C. Dwyer, Diary 1914, esp. 6 November 1914.
[187] Readman, *Land and Nation*, pp. 2–3.
[188] Mayhew, 'English Patriotism and the Implicit Nation', pp. 20–21.
[189] Roper, 'Nostalgia as an Emotional Experience', p. 440.

rare periods of leave. Ultimately, though, they were the product of imagination. They fused memories and fantasies, blurring conscious and unconscious thoughts to form very vivid daydreams. These were so common that they were referenced in popular culture. Wartime songs such as 'Keep the Home Fires Burning' consoled civilians that 'Though your lads are far away / They dream of home.' Other tunes played on similar themes. 'The Long, Long Trail' described soldiers journey back to 'the land of my dreams'.[190] The songs sung by men serving in Belgium and France frequently drew on strong and sustaining images of England.[191]

The power of imagination and dreams were common themes in soldiers' letters.[192] Of course, letters and parcels played a very significant role in helping them to enter their imagined worlds.[193] L/Cpl. C. White found that his 'thoughts are continually with them [his family] and all my desires for peace so that we may all return to our homes'. Reading their correspondence ensured that White and his comrades could continue to 'spend our days with those we love'.[194] He was clear about what benefits he derived from his daydreaming: 'I thought of what I used to be doing at this hour in past days and for a time the gloom and squalor of the filthy trench disappeared.'[195] C.T. O'Neill also did 'a lot of daydreaming'.[196] As did Pte. William Anderson. In one letter to his wife, he explained that:

> I often picture our house in my mind, and many a time I fancy my spirit (if this is not too fanciful) wanders through the rooms. In my mind I can see you ... during the evenings by the fire and I wonder when you go to bed and then fancy you ... lying down. You awake as usual. Its [sic] funny at times what you get thinking about.[197]

2nd Lt. D. Henrick Jones' dreams of his fiancée revealed the intimacy and desires of young lovers. He revelled in imagining:

> what we're going to do and all sorts of things. If you were only here or I were only there with you. I'd tell you things. Oh! Such things. I "pink" you'd have to hide your face on my shoulder during the telling; but I'd keep on kissing you all the same.[198]

---

[190] Brophy and Partridge, *The Long Trail*, p. 37.
[191] For a similar discussion of 'imaginative realms' and loved ones, see Roper, *Secret Battle*, pp. 68–72, and Makepeace, 'Living beyond the Barbed Wire', pp. 159–177.
[192] IWM Documents.10814: Lt. F.A. Brettell, Letter from Peggy 8 May 1916.
[193] NAM 7403-29-486-144: Sgt. Harry Hopwood, Letter to Mother 3 November 1917.
[194] RFM.ARC.3032: L/Cpl. C. White, Diary 12 February 1917.
[195] Ibid. Diary 19 February 1917.
[196] SOFO Box 16 Item 30: Lt. C.T. O'Neill, Diary 17 February and 18 March 1918.
[197] IWM Documents.5092: Pte. W.M. Anderson, Letter to Wife 14 November 1916.
[198] IWM Documents.16345: 2nd Lt. D. Henrick Jones, Letter to Fiancée 16 October 1916.

They were married towards the end of 1916. Possibly remembering their wedding night, in a letter written over Christmas he wrote that 'I can see that dear little room at the top of 29, and the most wonderful girl in the world snuggling down in the white bed.'[199] His (and other men's) dreams were an opportunity to explore his pent-up sexual desire.[200]

Soldiers' memories and imagination could provide provided a tonic in moments of extreme stress. Capt. L.F. Ashburner found that memories of fishing were particularly comforting during October 1914.[201] In December 1916, A.P. Burke was crouched in a dugout when a bombardment fell on his position. As the shells began to fall, he closed his eyes and could 'see' his whole family. '[A]lthough I was having a rotten time it was more than comforting to think you would all be so happy at home.'[202] Memories provided a kind of hallucination and brief but important glimpses of happiness.

Moments such as these were captured on commercial postcards, which frequently reproduced ideas found in soldiers' letters and diaries. Several series included cards depicting men daydreaming about home. Wives, mothers, and families appeared as apparitions while soldiers slept or stared wistfully into the distance. Conventional gender norms were often reproduced in these images. Women were depicted in locations such as parlours or kitchens, and the combatants were the breadwinners and heroes.[203] Scholars have argued that these postcards illustrated (and formed a part of) an imaginary universe that existed between soldiers and their loved ones, which helped them to maintain (and foster) relationships at a distance.[204] Other postcard series included images of all the features of England that men were fighting for. Beautiful natural landscapes, picturesque villages, impressive townscapes, plant and animal life, wives and sweethearts, and parents were all popular motifs.[205] Men retreated into these imaginary worlds.[206]

---

[199] Ibid. Letter to Wife 25–26 December 1916.

[200] Ibid. Letter to Wife 14 October 1916. Also N. Christie and M. Gauvreau, *Bodies, Love, and Faith in the First World War* (Cham, 2018), pp. 191–250 and Fox, '"I Have Never Felt More Utterly Yours"', pp. 4, 13, 24–25.

[201] IWM Documents.11445: Brig. Gen. H.E. Trevor, Letter from Capt. L.F. Ashburner to Mrs Parker. 14 October 1914.

[202] IWM Documents.1665: A.P. Burke, Letter to Tot 29 December 1916.

[203] Mayhew, 'A War Imagined', esp. pp. 320–321.

[204] Brouland and Doizy, *La Grande Guerre*, pp. 10–12, 38–46.

[205] T. Holt and V. Holt, *Till the Boys Come Home* (Barnsley, 1977, 2014) and P. Doyle, *British Postcards of the First World War* (London, 2011). Also Huss, *Histoires de famille, 1914/1918*; Vidal-Naquet, *Couples dans la Grande Guerre*; J. Le Naour, *La Grande Guerre à travers la Carte Postale Ancienne* (Paris, 2013).

[206] SOFO Box 16 Item 61: Collection of 15 Patriotic Cards 1914–1918 Vintage, Postcard: 'La Reve'; LIDDLE/WW1/GS/0746: H.O. Hendry, Postcard: 'I'm Thinking of You [No. 504]'.

Figure 4.1 Postcard: Take Me Back to Dear Old Blighty (2), Bamforth & Co. Ltd, Song Series No. 5006/2.

Source: Author's Own Collection.

Visions emerged most forcefully during moments of reflection and relaxation. Soldiers' newspapers highlighted the significance of these 'dreams of home'. An article in the *Cambridgeshire Territorial Gazette* described how, after returning from a tiring tour of duty, a Capt. Shore dragged himself 'mud-caked, hungry and tired' into an 'inviting armchair'. Taking the weight off his feet, he 'gazed into the glowing fire and was on the point of conjuring up visions of "leave" and London' until there was a knock at the door.[207] The *B.E.F. Times* published a poem that played on similar themes. 'Brazier Pictures' began: 'In my brazier as I gaze / Pictures come and pictures go, / Dimly seen across the haze- / Christmases we used to know.' This soldier's daydreams were 'burning clear' with 'visions of better days' that combated 'discomforts that are near'.[208] Another author described how the dawn light at 'stand-to' conjured visions of his 'dearest' in her 'silver shrouded dress'. '[T]he evening mists' could also paint a 'portrait'.[209] It was in similar circumstances that another man was able to envision 'green fields', 'peace', and drinking in his club.[210] Again, postcards played on these themes. For example, one card included the printed note 'night and a pause for a much-needed rest. Bringing sweet memories of all that's loved best'.[211] Some series reprinted soldiers' cartoons. On one such card a man was shown bathed in candlelight as he wrote a letter home. As he did so, the recipient appeared as a spectre in his mind's eye.[212]

Moments of rest allowed servicemen's minds to return 'back to home once more'.[213] Sleep and dreams (waking or otherwise) are important features of human cognition. Famously, Sigmund Freud believed that they were driven by wish fulfilment.[214] The soldiers' most sincere wish was to return home, and it was to their homes that they escaped to when their minds began to wander, or they fell asleep.[215] Shadows and firelight also had the capacity to turn tired soldiers' minds to the safety and warmth of England.[216] For these reasons, L/Cpl C. White found that 'letter writing is one of the greatest pleasures I have now'. As he scribed his messages home, he imagined 'pictures [of] those to whom one is writing' and 'it seems as though me [sic] is privileged to be in

---

[207] *Cambridgeshire Territorial Gazette*, No. 4 (October 1916), p. 88.
[208] 'Brazier Pictures', *The B.E.F. Times*, Vol. 1, No. 2 (1916), p. 3.
[209] 'The Sybarite's Soliloquy', Ibid., p. 8; 'To My Marraine', *The B.E.F. Times*, Vol. 1, No. 3, p. 2.
[210] 'Disturbing Influences', Ibid., p. 3.
[211] MR/2/17/65: John Douglas Powell, Postcard: 'Dreams of Home [No. 8]'.
[212] MR 3/17/126: Pte. John Peat, Postcard: 'Sketches of Tommy's Life. Out on Rest – No. 9'.
[213] IWM Documents.1665: A.P. Burke, Letter to Tot 26 October 1916.
[214] S. Freud, *The Interpretation of Dreams*, trans. A.A. Brill (New York, 1913), pp. 103–112.
[215] RFM.ARC.3032: L/Cpl. C. White, Diary 28 January 1917.
[216] IWM Documents.12521: R.E.P. Stevens, Diary 6 December 1916.

Figure 4.2 Postcard: Little Grey Home in the West (2), Bamforth & Co. Ltd, Song Series No. 4871/2.

Source: Author's Own Collection.

conversation with them'.[217] A similar thing could happen when the soldiers were reading. John Mawer's visions of home were given texture by his wife's descriptions of apparently mundane details of life at home such as when their neighbour had 'painted outside the house & the conservatory inside it does look a treat'.[218]

Objects (especially photographs of children, wives, girlfriends, or parents) were further tools soldiers could use to access their imaginative worlds.[219] These were cherished items.[220] Many men received (and requested) clippings of hair for similar reasons.[221] It might also explain why Pte. A. Joy kept a signature book during the war. In it he was able to read supportive messages from acquaintances and friends at home and from his time in Belgium and France.[222] Some speciality postcards were even scented with a loved one's perfume, allowing individuals to temporarily share a sensory space with the sender.[223] J.M. Humphries devoured books as he escaped his present and regularly acquired new reading material such as *Love and Mr Lewisham* by H.G. Wells. His parents also sent physical reminders of home in the form of Christmas and birthday presents, food, and small gifts such as cigarette cases.[224] Capt. Maurice Asprey was sent similar things, including waterproofs, extra clothing, toothbrushes, newspapers, razors, money, and tins of cigarettes.[225] Harry Hopwood's local Conservative Club mailed him a parcel, which included a Christmas card, tobacco, a pipe, and cigarettes.[226] Family members also sometimes enclosed small flowers in envelopes (and soldiers also sent these home). Reginald Neville, for example, was pleased to receive some English lavender from his father with whom he also played chess – each move being included in a

---

[217] RFM.ARC.3032: L/Cpl. C. White, Diary 7 January 1917.
[218] SOFO Box 16 Item 35: Pte. J.E. Mawer, Letter from Wife 8 October 1914; IWM Documents.10814: Lt. F.A. Brettell, Letter from Peg 27 December 1917.
[219] IWM Documents.15433: S.B. Smith, Letter 29 October 1917.
[220] MR 3/17/145: Pte. S. Smith, Postcards: Photograph of Wife and Children and Photograph of Children [Ethel and Stephen Smith]; SOFO Box 16 Item 35: Pte. J.E. Mawer, Undated Letter [c. November 1914] to Wife [Doc. 24].
[221] LIDDLE/WW1/GS/0699: J.L. Hampson, Clipping of Hair and Postcard: Photograph of Young Woman.
[222] NAM 1992-09-139: Pte. A. Joy, Autograph Book [9209-139-6] Notes from Mother, Maggie, Mrs Stagg, Emily and Reginald Birch.
[223] P. Tomczyszyn, 'A Material Link between War and Peace: First World War Silk Postcards', in N.J. Saunders (ed.), *Matters of Conflict: Material Culture, Memory and the First World War* (Oxford, 2004).
[224] NAM 1998-02-232: J.M. Humphries, Letter to 'Mater' Wednesday 13 September 1916, [-5] Letter to 'Mater' Undated [c. December 1916]; Letter to 'Mater' 13 October 1917.
[225] NAM 2005-02-6: Capt. M. Asprey, Letter to Mother and/or Father 17 and 22 October; 15, 19, 25 and 29 November; 19 and 22 December 1914.
[226] NAM 7403-29-486-144: Sgt. H. Hopwood, Letter 29 December 1914.

letter.[227] Something as simple as handwriting provided something familiar and allowed soldiers and civilians to feel some proximity to their family and friends.[228]

Activities in Belgium and France could also kindle memories of home. While watching football some men found themselves transported to a 'Saturday somewhere in England'.[229] Reginald Neville found that memories of Christmas at home were stirred by a familiar piece of gramophone music.[230] The festive period (and other holidays) was particularly potent fuel for men's imagination. In the days before Christmas 1916, R.E.P. Stevens recalled the holiday spirit and crowds of shoppers on the peaceful streets of his hometown.[231] On Christmas Eve 1914, Pte. W. Tapp remembered 'Xmas night ... four years ago when I stood under the Misteltoe [sic] with the girl I married later'.[232] More personal milestones and anniversaries were also of significance – the death of a parent, for example.[233] In some cases, religion also played an important role. Lt. W.B. Medlicott felt that prayer drew him to closer to those at home.[234]

These imaginary spaces were often inherently positive. Perhaps to protect themselves, many men shunned negative emotions. Even jealousy of love rivals rarely penetrated their daydreams. Nostalgia and associated psychological processes are frequently mobilised as defence mechanisms, which can distort authentic memories and imbue them with affirming ideas.[235] Michael Roper has suggested that nostalgia was a 'dominant emotion' during the First World War stemming from soldiers' 'wish to be home again'. It 'typically involves idealization, the imagining of a purer, simpler time and place'.[236] In this way, men's imagination became a cocoon and a place to escape.

Of course, combatants missed their loved ones but it was significant that their loved ones frequently acknowledged the sacrifices the soldiers were making.[237] Even as shirkers, strikers, or politicians on the Home Front became

---

[227] SOFO Box 16 3/4/N/2: Lt. Reginald N. Neville, Letters to Father 4 August and 4 October 1917. Vera Brittain also received violets from Roland Leighton, which he picked in Plug Street wood and sent home to her. See V. Brittain, *Testament of Youth* (London, 1933, 2004), p. 122. Also IWM Con Shelf: A.P. Burke, Letter to 'Tot' 1 June 1916.
[228] Vidal-Naquet, *Couples dans la Grande Guerre*; Roper, *Secret Battle*, pp. 93–101.
[229] IWM Documents.5092: Pte. W.M. Anderson, Letter 15 November 1916.
[230] Ibid. Letter to Sister 26 June 1917.
[231] IWM Documents.12521: R.E.P. Stevens, Diary 23 December 1916.
[232] IWM Documents.18524: Pte. W. Tapp, Diary 24/25 December 1914 [p 11].
[233] RFM.ARC.2012.958: E.T. Marler, Diary 27 and 31 October 1916.
[234] IWM Documents.1708: Lt. W.B. Medlicott, Letter 6 November 1916.
[235] C. Routledge, *Nostalgia: A Psychological Resource* (Abingdon, 2016).
[236] Roper, 'Nostalgia as an Emotional Experience', pp. 436–437.
[237] MR3/17/137: Pte. Norman Walker, Christmas Postcards 'Happy Christmas' with Floral Design and 'To Bring You Happiness'; SOFO Box 16 Item 7 3/4/C/3: Sgt. Sam Moulder, Letter to 'Tory, Ada and all'; SOFO Box 16 Item 35: Pte. J.E. Mawer, Letter

increasingly embittering, these relationships and positive visions of the homeland were far more resilient to change. Servicemen's more parochial visions of home were sustaining and provided the brightest of the 'many sweetnesses [sic] that make our life worth living'.[238] The soldiers' pleas to be 'remembered' suggests that they wanted to know (or at least to think) that they were the primary focus of their loved one's thoughts as well.[239]

The letters and cards they received certainly indicated that this was the case. One letter that was sent to Lt. L.W.C. Ireland read: 'I guess you remember me without a photo to see ... of course I am always with you in thoughts you see I love you better than anyone.'[240] Infantrymen's role as their family (and England's) protectors was generally implicit, but some men's families celebreated them as heroes.[241] Other men's families tried to nurture their confidence in the future. Harry Bridge, for instance, received a variety of postcards from close family. One signed by his niece was clearly chosen to reassure him and included the message: 'God be with you 'till we meet again' and assured the recipient that the sender 'daily pray[ed] that God will keep my hero in His care' and 'bring him safely back again'.[242] Another (this time from his sister) insisted that 'I'm thinking of You, dear, all the time'.[243] A final card, this time sent by his mother, promised that she was 'longing for Our Dear Absent Soldier'.[244]

Imagination was, and is, an important coping mechanism.[245] Their war experiences left many men feeling more drawn to their homeland, more in love with their families, and feeling more grateful towards those they left behind.[246] Imagining home helped them to escape their present and, at their most potent, these visions could transport infantrymen away from the trenches

---

23 September 1914 [Doc. 14]; SOFO Box 29 Item 1 (8) 10/7/C/1: [Anon.] 35 Postcards, Postcard to Ms A. Young 28 February 1917.

[238] Ibid.
[239] IWM Documents.12521: R.E.P. Stevens, Letter 9 November 1914; SOFO Box 16 Item 35: Pte. J.E. Mawer, Undated Letter c. September 1914 [Doc. 15]; SOFO Box 29 Item 4 10/6/J/1: Pte. Percy Thompson, Letter to his Sister (Adelaide) 29 September 1916; IWM Documents.8552: [Anon. Officer] 'Secret Code Used to Bypass the Censors', 'Remember me to Betty' and 'Remember me to Fred'.
[240] IWM Documents.14441: Lt. L.W. Cubbitt-Ireland, Letter from Beryl 6 December 1916; IWM Documents.10814: Lt. F.A. Brettell, Letter from Peg 25 October 1916.
[241] MR 12/17/65: J.D. Powell, Postcard 'A Message to My Hero'.
[242] MR 3/17/139: H. Bridge, Postcard from Niece.
[243] Ibid. Postcard from Sister.
[244] Ibid. Postcard from Mother.
[245] Roper, 'Nostalgia as an Emotional Experience', pp. 445–456.
[246] B. Aylor, 'Maintaining Long-Distance Relationships', in D.J. Canary and M. Dainton (eds.), *Maintaining Relationships through Communication: Relational, Contextual and Cultural Variations* (New York, 2003, 2014), pp. 130–132.

whilst simultaneously providing emotional sustenance.[247] Ultimately, these pictures of home also reminded soldiers of what they were fighting for.

****

Before they joined the colours, recruits were called on to 'play a manly part by doing a man's work in defence of all an Englishman holds dear – his King, Home, and Country'.[248] As they considered what this really meant, it was personalised and very subjective visions of home that proved paramount in their sensemaking. The men's imaginations helped them to feel closer to their family, friends, and community. As they briefly forgot their present, servicemen escaped into safer, more secure, idealised homelands. The meaningful narratives that soldiers crafted rested on their belief that they were defending these places. As historian Keith Grieves has argued, 'an intimate relationship arose between a precisely depicted still-tranquil "home" and ... patriotism'.[249]

Men's focus on community, family, and friends – as well as the landscapes of home – combatted the bitterness they felt towards politicians, profiteers, strikers, and slackers.[250] Of course, historians' over-reliance on men's correspondence might lead us 'to overstate the significance of home'. Yet the importance of this parochial England is confirmed by an array of other sources.[251] The strength of soldiers' patriotism was encouraged by their close emotional connection with their homeland.[252] Their visions of these people and places, which were often frozen in time, offered the opportunity for escape. In nurturing and cultivating these relationships, soldiers re-emphasised their role as England's protector.

As Michael Roper has suggested, 'memories and dreams such as these 'played a significant role as a coping mechanism, providing a sense of familiarity and release to men in disorientating, sometimes frightful and lonely situations'.[253] Amidst the destruction on the Western Front, soldiers' dreams of home allowed them to engage in a form of organic meditation. The chronic crises that were bred by their separation from home were averted (at least in part) by the strength and resilience of these connections with home. Importantly, these 'mind-pictures' rarely faltered, encouraging continued faith in the justice of Britain's cause, and nurturing hopeful perceptions of the future.[254]

---

[247] Watson, *Enduring the Great War*, p. 83.
[248] LIDDLE/WW1/GS/0232: A.E. Burdfield, 7th Bn. Royal Fusiliers Recruitment Leaflet.
[249] Grieves, 'The Propinquity of Place', p. 23.
[250] Watson, *Enduring the Great War*, pp. 190–191; Roper, *Secret Battle*, p. 13.
[251] Roper, 'Nostalgia as an Emotional Experience', p. 449.
[252] McCartney, *Citizen Soldiers*, pp. 7–8.
[253] Roper, 'Nostalgia as an Emotional Experience', p. 449.
[254] Ibid., p. 437.

PART III

Crisis and Morale

5

Hoping for Peace
Victory and the Future

Men were forever talking about peace. In the trench newspaper, *The Londoner*, a soldier, writing as much for himself as his peers, offered a welcome picture of what one could expect of the future:

> Peace had been declared, and I found myself walking down Piccadilly in a soft grey suit, and a nice clean linen collar which, by the way, was rubbing several blisters on my neck. Think what it is to be free and unrestrained by discipline. I know it requires a lot of imagination, but just shut your eyes and imagine for all you are worth.[1]

The war's length was the greatest of its chronic crises and underpinned many of the other traumas encountered in previous chapters. Yet, far from a symptom of their suffering, men were sustained by such visions. Another soldiers' journal, *The Gasper*, offered a similar glimpse into the future. This time it combined visions of peace and England in one 'beautiful moving picture' as a soldier sat staring out of the window of a train meandering through the English countryside after returning home victorious. The luxurious carriage was a welcome change from the cattle trucks in Belgium and France. So were the civilians waving and cheering him as he passed through 'real railway stations'.[2] Such scenes and visions also appeared regularly in men's diaries and letters.

Like their dreams of England, fantasies of peace offered a moment of escape and deflected the present. If home was constructed around memory and the past, and the war's chronic crises were a product of the present, then peace offered a window onto the future and a certainty that this future would eventually transpire. It gave men confidence that even if chronic crises seemed resistant to immediate change, they were by no means permanent.

However, combatants' very natural obsession with peace has often been associated with low levels of morale. This desire for war's end and servicemen's preoccupation with an uncertain future apparently sapped their endurance. If men's 'first concern was to survive', then this may have reminded them

---

[1] W.H.B. 'Appertaining to Instincts', *The Londoner*, Vol. 2, No. 5 (May 1918), p. 121.
[2] Strozzi, 'Hullo England!', *The Gasper*, Vol. 20 (July 1916), p. 1.

of their mortality.³ More dangerous still, Paul Fussell suggests that by the end of 1916 'the likelihood that peace (and therefore survival) would ever come was often in serious doubt'.⁴ If and when chronic crises threatened to become permanent states of being men's morale suffered. Others have also associated calls for peace with patterns of war weariness. Jean-Jacques Becker, for example, revealed that 1917 saw an increase in French citizens' 'desire for peace' as significant minorities began to support a compromise peace. Some even began calling for peace 'at any price'.⁵ Shock, too, could induce a temporary desire for 'an almost unconditional peace'.⁶ Yet, these visions of the future actually offered a tonic: a world in which the most overbearing features of military service had evaporated.

In the minds of most men, peace, their survival, and victory became synonymous. Even after the Somme campaign, 2nd Lt. D. Henrick Jones explained to his wife that 'everybody seems to think it can't last long now. Oh! I do hope so, dearest, don't you?'⁷ This was a recurring theme in the notes of censor Capt. M. Hardie. Earlier in the year, another man comforted a loved one: 'We must keep our hecker [sic] up, Kid, till old bill is smashed, and then for Blighty and home.'⁸ Hardie did not believe that the battles in Picardy during 1916 had dented this confidence, and most men continued to exhibit a 'splendid spirit'. One soldier exclaimed that 'they cannot make Tommy lose heart or spirits because we have got Old Fritz beat and he knows it well. So roll on the end'. Another man, more stoic than the last, noted that he and his chums had 'had enough' but 'we will have to keep pushing along until its all over'.⁹

Perceptions of peace provided visions of a future that allowed men to cope with their present.¹⁰ This became a 'subjective (and constructed) future space, in which the war has ended, and their worldly desires have been realised'.¹¹ The use of the future tense underpinned an optimism that was, for the most part, sustaining. Victorious peace was not framed in the conditional – it was 'when', not 'if', it would come. This was a very human response to trauma and the need to invest oneself in something better recurs across space and time.

---

³ Fuller, *Troop Morale*, p. 63.
⁴ Fussell, *The Great War*, p. 71.
⁵ J.J. Becker, *The Great War and the French People* (London, 1986), pp. 217–235.
⁶ McCartney, *Citizen Soldiers*, p. 214.
⁷ IWM Documents.16345: 2nd Lt. D. Henrick Jones, Letter to Wife 25 December 1916.
⁸ IWM Documents.4041: Capt. M. Hardie, Notes 14 March 1916.
⁹ Ibid. [All letters from November 1916] '3rd Section Report on Complaints, Moral, Etc', p. 6.
¹⁰ J. Horne, 'Entre expérience et mémoire. Les soldats français de la Grande Guerre', *Annales. Histoire, Sciences sociales*, Vol. 60 (2005), pp. 903–919.
¹¹ Mayhew, 'Hoping for Victorious Peace', p. 196.

The relationship between peace and victory was nurtured and amplified by the military. Mission success was peace achieved through the defeat of the enemy.[12] Of course, strategic priorities changed over the course of the war – but the army's primary function remained defeating the German armies in the field. Commanders made it clear that only victory could preserve the freedom of Belgium and save France.[13] Units, too, constantly framed military developments in terms of improvements in fighting efficiency that would secure a military victory.[14] Such a preoccupation with victory was common currency. All 'civil populations and combatant states expected and hoped for eventual victory'.[15]

Yet, as the war threatened to become endless, and chances of victory faded, chronic crises could become crippling. As it dragged on, 1917 proved to be increasingly difficult for all the combatant nations, and war weariness on the Home Front drove governments to attempt to remobilise their populations.[16] It was felt in the British military, too. The year started with little evidence 'of any wish in the Army for a premature peace'.[17] Yet, by August there was 'a feeling of uncertainty as to the progress of our arms to an ultimate victory' and an 'immense longing for a reasonable and honourable settlement that will bring the war to a close'.[18]

This chapter explains why men's hope for peace (and survival) remained interlinked with victory and how, in 1917 and 1918, the spirit of victory faded. It does so by focusing on hope. Soldiers' hopes for peace were a central feature of their morale and perceptions of crisis.[19] A confidence that victorious peace would arrive helped to offset the war's chronic crises. However, hope is referenced only in passing by historians.[20] Soldiers hoped for many things:

---

[12] TNA WO 256/27: Diary of Field Marshal Haig, 17 February 1918: 'I only had one object in view ... to beat the Germans'. D. French, *British Strategy and War Aims 1914-1916* (London, 1986); J. Black, *The Great War and the Making of the Modern World* (London, 2011), esp. p. 243.
[13] TNA WO 256/27: Diary of Field Marshal Haig, 1 January 1918.
[14] TNA WO 95/2339/1: War Diary 16th Bn. Manchester Regiment, 'Address by CO to the officers, NCOs and men of the 19th Battalion Manchester Regiment'.
[15] A.R. Seipp, *The Ordeal of Peace: Demobilization and the Urban Experience in Britain and Germany, 1917-1921* (Farnham, 2009), p. 3.
[16] Horne, 'Remobilising for "Total War"', in Horne, *State, Society and Mobilization*, pp. 195-211. This fed into education programmes in the BEF. See MacKenzie, 'Morale and the Cause', pp. 215-32. McCartney, *Citizen Soldiers*, p. 214.
[17] IWM Documents.4041: Capt. M. Hardie, 'Report on III Army More. January 1917', p. 6.
[18] Ibid. 'Report on III Army Morale. August 1917 – Peace', p. 3.
[19] IWM Documents.11445: Brig. Gen. H.E. Trevor, Postcard to Evelyn Parker 22 September 1914; IWM Documents.5092: Pte. W.M. Anderson, Letters to Wife 9, 17, 18, and October 1916; IWM Documents.7953: Pte. F.G. Senyard, Letters to Wife 5, 17, 26 December 1916, 18 September, 28 June and 10 July 1918.
[20] For an exception, see Mayhew, 'Hoping for Victorious Peace', pp. 194-219.

improved rations, the end of trench warfare, early peace, home, divine assistance, a 'Blighty' wound, and survival.[21] Alexander Watson has suggested that their 'disillusion with official war aims [... might have] prompted [... them] to hope for peace'.[22] This hope for peace was, however, a constant. It was the kind of peace they hoped for that mattered. The benefits of hope were demonstrated in one contemporary study of German soldiers' combat motivation, which found that 'general hope' was an effective coping strategy.[23] In fact, it has been suggested that the 'emphasis of morale' enables an individual 'to live and work hopefully and effectively'.[24] Nevertheless, without conceptualising hope, it is very difficult to understand its value to morale.

Many psychologists argue that hope is a cognitive function. As an objective and goal-orientated schematic, it is different from optimism and positivity.[25] Within such studies, 'hope is defined as goal-directed thinking in which people perceive that they can produce routes to desired goals (pathways thinking) and the requisite motivation to use those routes (agency thinking)'.[26] The time horizon for these goals can vary, and barriers might hinder them. Amidst the overlapping crises of war, there was little sense that peace would arrive immediately. As such, optimism and positivity – and their antitheses – were important engines for hope, which helped soldiers rationalise their present by focusing on future goals.[27] An optimistic explanatory style facilitates 'higher levels of motivation, achievement, and physical well-being and lower levels of depressive symptoms'.[28] Combatants often overestimated their chance of survival. In fact, Alexander Watson has already demonstrated that these 'positive illusions' – as well as 'optimistic reasoning' – were key psychological coping mechanisms.[29] Yet, their real importance rested on the way they nurtured soldiers' hopefulness; rather than sapping morale, men's obsession with peace helped them to endure so long as they remained confident that victory was the 'pathway' to peace.

---

[21] Watson, *Enduring the Great War*, pp. 40, 56, 95–97, 103–107. Also Boff, 'The Morale Maze: The German Army in Late 1918', *Journal of Strategic Studies*, Vol. 37, No. 6–7 (2014), p. 11; Watson, 'Morale', in Winter, *The Cambridge History of the First World War*, p. 187.

[22] Watson, *Enduring the Great War*, p. 75.

[23] Ibid., pp. 92, 162.

[24] R.A. Brotemarkle, 'Development of Military Morale in a Democracy', *Annals of the American Academy of Political and Social Science*, Vol. 216 (July, 1941), p. 79. Also Shephard, *A War of Nerves*, p. 41.

[25] Lopez, Snyder and Pedrotti, 'Hope: Many Definitions, Many Measures', in Lopez and Snyder, *Positive Psychological Assessment*, pp. 91–107.

[26] Ibid., p. 94.

[27] C.S. Carver and M. Scheier, 'Optimism', Ibid., p. 75.

[28] K. Reivich and J. Gillham, 'Learned Optimism: The Measurement of Explanatory Style', Ibid., p. 57.

[29] Watson, *Enduring the Great War*, p. 146.

Peace, then, was men's goal and sincerest desire. Military victory appeared to be the best possible guarantor of this outcome. As serving soldiers, their frames of reference encouraged them to see peace and victory as inseparable. Yet, as this chapter will reveal, there were other reasons why they viewed the world in this way. When confidence in this route to peace faltered, the men sensed a brewing crisis, and this threatened endurance and morale. In such moments, soldiers' faltering faith in any productive future pushed them to reassess the war.

****

Hoping for Peace in 1914

Whatever the year, peace quickly emerged as the central hope and goal of men fighting in France and Belgium.[30] The pressures of the present pushed them to use the future tense and fostered a sense that they were pursuing, as some described it, 'a common object'.[31] The term 'après la guerre' became popular and was 'a magical phrase used by soldiers ... longing for survival and for the return of peace'.[32] This was a symptom of the men's desire for a better future and, for much of the war, they remained confident that victory was the most likely guarantor of this. The ability to use the future tense with confidence played a subtle but profound role by inferring that their present trials were temporary and that they would survive. When this confidence faltered, however, morale suffered.

In 1914, the shocking reality of modern warfare left many yearning for peace. Yet they remained determined to see the war through to victory and were confident that this was imminent. Herbert Trevor, a subaltern at the time, felt disenchanted by the fighting during the retreat from Mons and at the Battle of Le Cateau. On 22 September, he expressed solidarity with the German prisoners he met and noted that it seemed 'everyone would like peace'.[33] The strains of this withdrawal were compounded by the unfulfilled expectations of many professional soldiers; war was neither romantic nor honourable. One officer recounted bitterly that he had sharpened his sword

---

[30] NAM 2005-02-6: Capt. M. Asprey, Letter Mother 27 September 1914; IWM Documents.12339: Brig. Gen. G.A. Stevens, Letter to Mother 11 November 1916; IWM Documents.7035: Lt. J.H. Johnson, Diary 28 and 31 December 1916; NAM 7403-29-486-144: Sgt. H. Hopwood, Letter 12 October 1917; IWM Documents.11289: H.T. Madders, Diary 14 October 1918.
[31] IWM Documents.8059: Maj. S.O.B. Richardson, Letter [No. 4] Late 1916.
[32] Brophy and Partridge, *The Long Trail*, p. 66.
[33] IWM Documents.11445: Brig. Gen. H.E. Trevor, HET/1 – Postcards to Evelyn Parker 2, 20 and 22 September 1914.

and symbolically dyed his white handkerchief red before his first battle.[34] Bruce Bairnsfather's cartoon *That Sword* echoed this sentiment.[35] This picture surely reflected his experience as an officer in the Royal Warwickshire Regiment at this time. The sword's only use was as a makeshift fork on which to toast bread over an open fire. Capt. L.F. Ashburner confessed that 'none of us like it'.[36] The emotional toll can be traced in regimental magazines. The *Manchester Regimental Gazette* pondered whether it should feel 'pride ... or sorrow at the large number of our comrades who have so heroically laid down their lives'.[37] The loss of so many friends and comrades was the conflict's most demoralising feature, particularly in units that had sometimes cultivated their *esprit de corps* over many years.[38] Nonetheless, the war could be normalised surprisingly quickly and one officer's diary simply became a series of notations that life was 'as usual'.[39]

There was some disagreement about the proximity of victorious peace. Capt. Maurice Asprey, for example, noted: 'Hope the war will stop for the winter or end by then.'[40] Yet, far from defeatist, he believed that the Germans needed to be vanquished. Somewhat puzzlingly, he told his father that 'some people out here seem to have a pretty hopeless outlook they seem to think that when we have squashed Germany we shall have trouble with Russia'.[41] Clearly, men's perception of the war's course was driven by inference and hearsay. Comrades in Asprey's unit had frank discussions that *assumed* their eventual victory. It was a case of *when* the Germans would capitulate, not *if*. Other men were less certain. H.E. Trevor admonished his mother for over-optimism, explaining that 'it's rubbish to say the Germans are done for. They fight devilish well and losses are nothing to them. What disheartens them much more is no food, wine or coffee or both'.[42] He felt, though, that 'the news seems better all round'.[43] Others clutched at any positive intelligence. One man's diary was a record of the rumours he heard. In August 1914 the news was 'not v. good'.[44] Yet, by 27 August, he noted that the '[n]ews seems rather

---

[34] IWM Documents.12819: Maj. J.S. Knyvett, Diary 6 October 1914.
[35] B. Bairnsfather, 'That Sword', *The Best of Fragments from France*, T. Holt and V. Holt (eds.) (Barnsley, 1978, 2014), p. 16.
[36] IWM Documents.11445: Brig. Gen. H.E. Trevor, HET/5 – Captain L.F. Ashburner to Mrs Parker, Letter 14 October 1914 and Letter to Mother 3 October 1914.
[37] *The Manchester Regiment Gazette*, Vol. 1, No. 7 (1 November 1914), p. 409.
[38] IWM Documents.11445: Brig. Gen. H.E. Trevor, Letter to Evelyn Parker 26 September 1914; IWM Documents.12819: Maj. J.S. Knyvett, Diary 19 October 1914.
[39] IWM Documents.8674: Pocket Diary 1914, October–December 1914.
[40] NAM 2005-02-6: Capt. Maurice Asprey, Letter to Mother 27 September and 5 November 1914.
[41] Ibid. Letter to Father 17 October 1914.
[42] IWM Documents.11445: Brig. Gen. H.E. Trevor, Letter to Mother 3 October 1914.
[43] NAM 2005-02-6: Capt. M. Asprey, Letter to Mother 28 December 1914.
[44] IWM Documents.8674: Pocket Diary 1914, 27 August 1914.

better, but v little'. In September, he was excited by stories that reached him of British victories. He noted that 'our people seem to be going ahead like anything' and later recorded a 'strong report that 8000 Germans have been taken'.[45] By October, the updates (like the frontlines) had become 'stationary'.[46] Nonetheless, the man kept his ear to the ground and on 26 November was delighted to learn of a 'Russian victory. Said to be 2 Army Corps surrendered'.[47] Men's frames of reference were limited by the information available to them, and their perception of the war was often driven by rumours. Yet, these tended to be welcomed as evidence that victory might be just over the horizon.

The rank-and-file soldiers yearned for peace. However, some focused on the mundane and more controllable aspects of their lives. Their desire for peace was a product of the environment in which they now lived. Combat left Sgt. C. Dwyer feeling 'queer'. He was sleep deprived and the ubiquitous destruction gave him the impression that 'nobody could live' under German artillery barrages.[48] Another man used similes to make sense of the scenes he witnessed. Battle was 'like being in a Blacksmith shop watching him swing a hammer on a red hot shoe and the sparks flying all round you ... were bullets ... As ... we lieyed [sic] there it was a pitiful sight to see and hear our Comrades dyeing [sic]'.[49] His unit suffered 148 casualties that day. These men were unprepared for the violence they encountered but, like their officers, downplayed Germany's military ascendancy through rumour and optimistic speculation. Sgt. Sam Moulder noted the inaccuracy of German weaponry and regularly recorded rumours of victories elsewhere along the front. In one letter, he recounted the tale of a French soldier shooting down a German plane with his rifle.[50] It showed that there was some power in the infantrymen's arsenal. Other soldiers normalised the combat that they had experienced.[51] It became so commonplace that W.J. Cheshire thought 11 September 1914 noteworthy because 'we have had no battle today'.[52] Despite the violence around him, John Mawer's most pressing concern was

---

[45] Ibid. 12 and 19 September 1914.
[46] Ibid. 25 October 1914.
[47] Ibid. 26 November 1914.
[48] Ibid. 8 November 1914
[49] IWM Documents.8631: Diary of an Unidentified Soldier in the 2nd Bn. Border Regiment, 18 December 1914.
[50] SOFO Box 16 Item 7 3/4/C/3: Sgt. Sam Moulder, Letter to 'May and All' 9 October 1914 and Letter to 'Tory, Ada and All' 9 October 1914.
[51] SOFO Box 16 Item 36: W.J. Cheshire, 2–5 September 1914; IWM Documents.16676: C. Dwyer, Diary 2 November 1914.
[52] Ibid. Diary 11 September 1914.

his poor pay and dwindling tobacco supply. He simply hoped 'to get back safe'.[53]

However, historian Alexander Watson has suggested that many soldiers 'failed to overcome the shock of battle'. Indeed, relative rates of desertion and surrender were higher in 1914 than at any other time in the war.[54] This, though, was evidence of men's failure to respond to the acute crisis of battle *not* of faltering morale in more general terms. Soldiers were unable to respond to events effectively, not unwilling to serve as soldiers. Reservists had been given little time to reintegrate into military life. The quality of servicemen's training informed how successfully they responded to the acute crises encountered during combat. The British Expeditionary Force (BEF) of 1914 was not prepared for the war it had to fight.[55]

What is more, the correlation between surrender rates and morale might not be all that revealing.[56] These were periods of mobile warfare where units became isolated, and command and control broke down. Interviews with POWs suggest that surrender was frequently a context-dependent act and the only option left to the men involved. Servicemen were sometimes injured or unable to escape the enemy. Many, perhaps with the benefit of hindsight, voiced disappointment at their capture. For example, Capt. R.T. Miller's ankle was wounded by machine-gun fire as he advanced in close support of the Suffolk Regiment at Le Cateau. Once they had retired, he was unable to escape.[57] Capt. J.H.W. Knight-Bruce was captured after being shot through the lungs during an assault. His company commander, whose knee had been shattered, was also taken. Knight-Bruce concluded bitterly: 'I think I may point out that the ruin of my career as a soldier is due entirely to ... [the] lack of ambulances.'[58] Other men were seized when their hospitals were overrun.[59] Hand-to-hand fighting gave men even less opportunity to retire safely. Pte. W.H. Meredith was shot through the shoulder at point-blank range and taken straight to a German Field Hospital.[60] Even uninjured men were often apprehended when exhausted and occupying an exposed position. For

---

[53] SOFO Box 16 Item 35: Pte. J.E. Mawer, Letters to Wife 23 September, 2 October, 19 October and 30 November 1914. Also SOFO Box 16 Item 36: W.J. Cheshire, Diary 11–13, 15, and 26–27 September and 2–4 October 1914.
[54] Watson, *Enduring the Great War*, pp. 141–146.
[55] Sheffield, *Forgotten Victory*, p. 117.
[56] Boff, 'The Morale Maze', pp. 869–871.
[57] TNA WO 161/95/93: POW Interviews, Capt. R.T. Miller: p 498; TNA WO 161/98/495: POW Interviews, 9647 Pte Albert George Hart: p. 317.
[58] TNA WO 161/95/42: POW Interviews, Capt. J.H.W. Knight-Bruce: p. 1.
[59] TNA WO 161/96/12: POW Interviews, Capt. Philip Godsal: p. 591.
[60] TNA WO 161/98/503: POW Interviews, 8493 Pte. W.H. Meredith: p. 341.

instance, Pte. James Robinson and twenty-six other men were mopped up one morning after taking cover in No Man's Land during the night.[61]

Men endured in part because they believed that victorious peace remained possible. Positive reasoning and rumour fuelled this misperception. One soldier's diary explained that the 'culling' of 60,000 Germans on 23 October had shortened the odds of victory to '4 to 1'.[62] The running odds indicate that there was an open debate about the likelihood of victory. After the Battle of the Aisne, W.J. Cheshire's section was convinced that 'the war will soon end'.[63] When R.D. Sheffield's battalion relieved another unit in the line on 9 November, they were met by men certain that 'this will be the last battle and if we win that the war will end before Christmas'.[64] Men sought out and celebrated evidence that they were on the 'pathway to peace'. Sgt. Osborn's diary chronicled small victories; each was represented a small step towards victorious peace.[65]

A similar confidence in victory was evident in some men's interactions with the enemy during the Christmas Truce.[66] The first question one man in the Border Regiment directed to his erstwhile foe was: 'when are you going to give in you are beat?'.[67] The truce along W. Tapp's stretch of the line lasted for several days. He was pleased that his officers 'took advantage' of the 'lull' to improve the position and lay new barbed wire.[68] He felt an affinity with the Scottish regiments who were apparently uninterested in any temporary armistice and considered the Germans 'ballad girls'.[69] Tapp found that 'I carnt [sic] understand the friendship between our fellows and Germans. It may be they are short of ammunition, if so, it is a clever trick of theirs ... they are Saxons though, and different to the Prussians and I think a little persuasion [sic] and they would all surrender'. He was certain that the best chance of victory lay in 'them advancing or us [doing the same]'.[70] Tapp concluded that 'I think they know that they are beaten'.[71] S. Judd would have agreed.

---

[61] TNA WO 161/99/87: POW Interviews, 1163 Pte. James Robinson: p. 1795.
[62] NAM 1997-02-11: Reminiscences of Unknown Guardsman 13 August to 3 November 1914, esp. 23 October 1914.
[63] Ibid. Diary 28 September 1914.
[64] IWM Documents.14710: R.D. Sheffield, Letter to Father 9 November 1914.
[65] RFM.ARC.2012.264: Sgt. Osborn, 1 and 10 September 1914.
[66] IWM Documents.7490: L/Cpl. K.M. Gaunt, Letter 25 December 1914; NAM 7403-29-486-144: Sgt. H. Hopwood, Letter 29 December 1914; IWM Documents.8631: Diary of an Unidentified 2nd Bn. Border Regiment Soldier, 25 December 1914.
[67] Ibid.
[68] IWM Documents.18524: Pte. W. Tapp, Diary 24–29 December 1914.
[69] Ibid. 27 December 1914.
[70] Ibid.
[71] Ibid. 24/25 December 1914.

He reacted with scorn when the Germans he encountered voiced their belief in imminent victory.[72]

Hoping for Peace in 1916

The Somme offensive failed to bring about the 'glorious victory' the troops were promised during its opening days.[73] 'War is hell', one soldier complained.[74] Any success was painful. On 7 July, A.P. Burke told his brother that '[W]e celebrated the glorious victory, but there was many a face missed ... keep smiling it will soon be over now.'[75] On 1 July, the men of 8th and 9th Bns. Devonshire Regiment had exalted in 'the welcome sight of Boche prisoners passing by looking mad with terror'.[76] Yet, over the next few days, 'the trenches had all been completely effaced'. Some men began to 'panic' while others became 'dejected'. Prolonged exposure to battle and shellfire was draining, and several soldiers were unable to cope. Some inflicted wounds upon themselves in a bid to escape, and many more got the 'wind-up'.[77] Charles Carrington was also 'getting very jumpy' towards the end of July. He explained that 'my martial instincts are now more than satisfied. I think what has done for them [his senses] is the smell of chalk dust impregnated with that of fortnight old corpses, gas-shells and high explosive fumes'.[78] Ernest Marler had not actually fought in the battles of 1916, but he arrived on the Western Front hankering for 'peace' and musing 'roll on when its [sic] over'.[79]

Outside of combat, very few men sensed that they had entered a period of 'crisis'. Apart from the German invasion of Romania, which created 'a general feeling of depression', there was a continued confidence in victory helped by the 'appointment of Lloyd George as Prime Minister'.[80] Captain M. Hardie noted that in the 'experience of those who have been censoring G.E. [green envelopes] for over a year proves emphatically that complaints in regard to food or any other subject show a remarkable decrease'.[81] The Battle of the Somme might have failed to bring victory, but many soldiers perceived it as a

---

[72] IWM Documents.12027: S. Judd, Diary 27 December 1914.
[73] IWM Documents.16345: 2nd Lt. D Henrick Jones, 'Message: From Lieut.-General Sir Aylmer Hunter-Weston ... To All officers, N.C.O'.s and Men of VIII Army Corps', HQ VIII Corps 4 July 1916.
[74] IWM Documents.4041: Capt. M. Hardie, Notes 2 July 1916.
[75] IWM Documents.1665: A.P. Burke, Letter to Reg 7 July 1916.
[76] IWM Documents.4772: Canon E.C. Crosse, Diary 1 July 1916.
[77] Ibid. Diary 2, 12, 14 and 16 July 1916.
[78] LIDDLE/WW1/GS/0273: Capt. C. Carrington, Letter to Mother 30 July 1916.
[79] RFM.ARC.2012.958: E.T. Marler, Diary 5 and 10 November 1916 and 1 January 1917.
[80] IWM Documents.4041: Capt. M. Hardie, 'Report on II Army Morale, January 1917', p. 1.
[81] Ibid. '3rd Section Report on Complaints, Moral, Etc. (1916)', p. 3.

great step towards peace.[82] Hardie sensed that there was a 'general acceptance of the idea that the War will not be over for another year'.[83] This was, however, underpinned by a 'confidence in the superiority over the enemy' in every sphere, which was 'everywhere noticeable'.[84] The persistent pounding of the enemy line in Picardy throughout the summer and autumn – with no major German counter-offensive – seems to have encouraged men to believe that they were in the ascendancy. Away from the lines, too, the censors pointed to the development of an effective programme of 'relaxation and sport of every kind, cinemas, follies, concerts, football, boxing'.[85] The semi-permanent camps in rear areas had also begun to cultivate allotments offering men further opportunities to relax.[86] These, historian John Fuller has argued, provided men with the opportunity to 'humanise' and 'adjust' to war.[87]

While forestalling crisis, such adjustments did not quench men's thirst for peace, which was now characterised by 'a dogged determination to see the thing through at any cost'.[88] Nevertheless, soldiers were still invested in the world *after* war. *The B.E.F. Times* played on this. In the 1 December edition, a poem claimed soldiers were 'always the same with your "apres la guerre"'.[89] On the last day of the year, Lt. J.H. Johnson scrawled passionately in his diary: 'will 1917 see peace?'.[90] More rhetorically, G.A. Stevens wondered 'what peace will be like when it comes along. I think one will have developed some strange habits. War is certainly a most ghastly, hideous, repulsive thing and the more one sees of it the more one hates it and its utterly remorseless cruelties'.[91] Pte. William Anderson asserted that 'we will still forfeit most'.[92] The war was the Allies' to win. Rumour continued to play a part in nurturing these positive feelings. N.R. Russell, for example, told his mother that he had 'heard a rumour about Austria telling Germany she wants to give up. I hope it is true. Germany will then get the whole energy of the Allies devoted to her'.[93] For

---

[82] Masefield, *The Old Front Line*, pp. 10, 17.
[83] IWM Documents.4041: Capt. M. Hardie, '3rd Section Report on Complaints, Moral, Etc. (1916)', p. 6.
[84] Ibid.
[85] Ibid., p. 5.
[86] Mayhew, 'British Expeditionary Force Vegetable Shows', pp. 1355–1378.
[87] Fuller, *Troop Morale and Popular Culture*, p. 175.
[88] IWM Documents.4041: Capt. M. Hardie, '3rd Section Report on Complaints, Moral, Etc. (1916)', p. 6.
[89] NAM 1959-03-34: Trench Newspapers, [5903-34 (1)] *The BEF Times*, Vol. 1, No. 2 (Monday, 25 December 1916).
[90] IWM Documents.7035: Lt. J.H. Johnson, Diary 31 December 1916.
[91] IWM Documents.12339: Brig. Gen. G.A. Stevens, Letter to Mother 11 November 1916.
[92] IWM Documents.5092: Pte. W.M. Anderson, Letter to Wife 14 October 1916. Also IWM Documents.4041: Capt. M. Hardie, '3rd Section Report on Complaints, Moral, Etc. (1916)', p. 6 and 'Report on III Army Morale, January 1917', p. 6.
[93] IWM Documents.9816: N.R. Russell, Letter to Mother 24 July 1916.

many, their obsession with peace had, like their visions of home, become a coping mechanism. Cecil White believed that it was 'the only thing worth carrying on for'.[94]

Men's sense of crisis was deflected, in part, by their continued belief in the proximity of victorious peace.[95] C.P. Crump received a letter from his friend, Donald Huntson, which concluded: 'P.S. The war will end at Xmas so hope to be home soon. Cheery OH!'[96] Another man expressed his earnest belief that 'it must end soon'.[97] 'Peace talk' was circulating constantly. Pte. F.G. Senyard informed his wife that 'the old dutch at the estaminet tonight said "Ze Kaiser allemagne make plenty peace want" so I supposes [sic] as far as I can see there is a chance of peace yet'.[98] Discussion of peace proposals in Home Front newspapers had caught the men's attention.[99] As late as October, William Anderson was still telling his wife: 'I haven't lost the idea that this business may well be over by Christmas.' He had heard 'an official war lecturer, Mr Lovell, in an address last Sat evening, [where he] made the very optimistic premise that it might take a week, or a month, or so, no one could prophecy [sic] but the finish might surprise most folk'.[100] A few days later, an apparently deflated Anderson admitted that 'mentioning the War is almost taboo and it's no use trying to discuss it, one way or the other, since we only know what we hear, and that's mostly rumour and we don't hear much'.[101]

Many soldiers' hope for victorious peace had been internalised, yet they remained certain it would eventually transpire.[102] News from elsewhere continued to play an important role (even if it was inaccurate). Reginald Neville was overjoyed by the news that the French had taken 9,000 prisoners and eighty-one guns at Verdun. Such a defeat must, he argued, have 'a great moral effect' on the enemy. The Germans would sue for peace by March.[103] A poem drafted by Pte. Percy Dalton in the back of his diary narrated the Battle of the Somme. Like many soldiers, he was imbued with a sense of forward moment: 'We pushed them back @ Every step / + put them to Disorder. / And we'll try our very Best if Poss to / Push them o'er the Border. / But while we try our very

---

[94] RFM.ARC.3032: L/Cpl. C. White, Diary 3, 8 and 16 January 1917.
[95] IWM Documents.20933: Capt. R.E.M. Young, Letter to Constance 9 December 1916; 'Tom', *The Gasper*, No. 21 (September 1916), p. 5; IWM Documents.12339: Brig. Gen. G.A. Stevens, Letter to Biddy 17 November 1916.
[96] IWM Documents.15069: C.P. Crump, Letter 11 September 1916.
[97] Ibid. Letter 16 September 1916.
[98] IWM Documents.7953: Pte. F.G. Senyard, Letter to Wife 14 December 1916.
[99] IWM Documents.4041: Capt. M. Hardie, 'Report on III Army Morale, January 1917' 1.
[100] IWM Documents.5092: Pte. W.M. Anderson, Letter to Wife 17 October 1916.
[101] Ibid. 24 October 1916.
[102] IWM Documents.10814: Lt. F.A. Brettell, Letter from Peg 30 November 1916;
[103] SOFO Box 16 Item 29 3/4/J3/8: Lt. Reginald N. Neville, Letter to Father 17 December 1916.

Best, to gain our / Great Ambition'.[104] One author in the *BEF Times* was more balanced but consoled himself and his readers that 'better days will come'.[105] Another man was concerned about the quality of those 'at the head of affairs' but concluded 'they say we are winning, and nothing else matters'.[106] Men were willing to endure the war, confident that victory and peace were on the horizon.[107]

Hoping for Peace in 1917 and 1918

Something changed in 1917. Soldiers became increasingly pessimistic about the possibility of victorious peace. Capt. M. Hardie, now producing censorship reports for the whole of III Army, reported that 'for the first time there is a frequent suggestion that the war cannot be won by military effort, but must end by political compromise'.[108] In August, he explained that 'it must be frankly admitted that the letters show an increasing amount of war-weariness' and a 'tinge of despondency that has never been apparent before'. This was made worse by 'a large amount of unsettled feeling about the continuation and conclusion of the war'. He believed that it was a 'mental' affliction and did not trouble discipline or bravery. In fact, it seems that it was a product of the environment, a perception of an everlasting present, rather than fighting. Any statistical analysis was limited, but Hardie believed that most complaints focused on absence from home and the physical conditions rather than the fighting.

Surprisingly, another report presented to the British War Cabinet found that only 0.61 per cent of 4,552 letters examined during September 1917 'contained any expression of complaint or war weariness'.[109] On the ground, however, the situation appeared very different to the censors in III Army. Capt. Hardie believed that the dejection of August had become more pervasive by October. Men's negativity was compounded by the year's terrible weather and a lack of success during the Passchendaele campaign. Pacifist sentiments broadcast through newspapers from the Home Front and rumours of

---

[104] NAM 2010-10-6: Pte. Percy Edward Dalton, [-1] Poem Undated Poem *c.* War Years [*c.* late 1916].
[105] NAM 1959-03-34 (1): 'Brazier Pictures', *The BEF Times*, Vol. 1, No. 2 (Monday 25 December 1916).
[106] IWM Documents.4041: Capt. M. Hardie, '3rd Section Report on Complaints, Moral, Etc'., p. 8.
[107] Ibid. 'Report on III Army Morale, January 1917'; LIDDLE/WW1/GS/0144: A&C Black and Company, Letter from Lance-Corporal E. Lindsell 6 December 1916.
[108] IWM Documents.4041: Capt. M. Hardie, 'Report on III Army Morale, August 1917', p. 1.
[109] TNA CAB 24/26/52: Note on the Morale of British Troops in France as disclosed by censorship, 13 September 1917.

proposed peace settlements were also feeding a fairly widespread desire for a negotiated peace.[110] There was an emerging consensus that military victory was unattainable, and soldiers appeared to be more willing to discuss peace as a political process.[111] Servicemen were now more ready to discuss politics in general where before they had been 'sublimely unconscious of political consideration'. Hardie also believed that the corporate and military identities of soldiers were giving way to individualism. Their temporal horizons had also changed. 'The war', Hardie explained, 'seems to have reached a state of stagnation' and soldiers felt 'that they are drifting into an endless destruction and sacrifice'.[112]

Hardie was careful to note that men were not calling for 'peace at any price'. They did, however, need to be 'shown a way out'. He believed that 'successful advances' were the best tonic and would reinforce 'the immense value' of victory.[113] Yet, the military operations of late 1917 were anything but successful; there was concern that neither the High Command nor the politicians in London were capable of breaking the 'apparent impasse'. The experience of Passchendaele's 'mechanical, impersonal slaughter' left Lt. J.H. Johnson thinking about the world 'after the war'.[114] Yet, this future seemed increasingly precarious and Johnson wondered whether 'the crisis and danger become greater if we are "winning the war"?'[115] Worse still was the news from elsewhere. Germany's successes in other theatres, the French mutinies, the Russian Revolution, and the Italian collapse at Caporetto all painted an increasingly bleak strategic picture.[116] Russia's defeat was particularly anxiety inducing. One man, writing in the *B.E.F. Times*, explained: 'We have heard so many tales from Hunland about what he's going to do to us now that he has fixed Russia.'[117] It seems that men's sense of crisis was informed by both the continued stalemate on the Western Front and the successes of the Central Powers in other arenas.

Many men's optimistic reasoning began to fail them; it became difficult to portray the war in a positive light. Even the British soldier's characteristic cheerfulness began to falter. In December, Lt. J.H. Johnson was dejected and felt that any vein of humour had disappeared within his

---

[110] IWM Documents.4041: Capt. M. Hardie, 'Report on III Army Morale/Peace Sentiment, August–October 1917', p. 1.
[111] Ibid., p. 2.
[112] Ibid.
[113] Ibid.
[114] IWM Documents.7035: Lt. J.H. Johnson, Diary 30 December 1917 and 6 January 1918.
[115] Ibid. Diary 14 December 1917. Also IWM Documents.11585: 2nd Lt. C.W. Gray, Clipping: 'Politics and Politicians: Lansdowne and After', *The Manchester Weekly Times* (15 December 1917) and Excerpt from Henry Petty-Fitzmaurice's, 5th Marquess of Lansdowne's open letter published in *The Telegraph*, 29 November 1917.
[116] D. Stevenson, *1917: War, Peace, and Revolution* (Oxford, 2017), pp. vi–vii.
[117] 'Editorial' *The B.E.F. Times*, Vol. 2, No. 5 (Tuesday, 22 January 1918), pp. 1–2.

unit.[118] Others became increasingly pessimistic about their chances of survival.[119] S.B. Smith told his wife that 'them that get through this war will be very lucky as it is getting worse every day'.[120] Echoing the censorship reports, he was unconvinced that 'thay [sic]', the High Command, were capable of ending the war.[121] C.T. O'Neill also dwelt on this. 'The more one thinks', he wrote in his diary, 'the more firmly is one convinced that the war cannot end by fighting alone which in this war is nothing less than whole murder'.[122]

This sentiment filtered into soldiers' newspapers, albeit more subtly. One article in the December issue of the Royal Warwickshire Regiment's magazine described a metaphorical football game. The author reported that the opposition, or the 'enemy', and the Warwickshires had found themselves 'unable to pass the halfway line'. The regiment had 'nobly upheld their record of this war [... but] a draw was the verdict'.[123] The editors also printed a satirical Battalion Order dated March 1919. Gone was any confidence that the next campaign would bring peace.[124] It was in this atmosphere that Bruce Bairnsfather produced his cartoon *A.D. Nineteen Fifty* depicting two grey-bearded veterans in a trench under an artillery barrage.[125]

2nd Lt. Sydney Frankenburg's devotion to duty was beginning to wane, and he began to give meaning to insignificant events. His perception of time slowed, and the war became a 'rotten' experience. As he wrote a letter on 9 January 1918, he became preoccupied with two bluebottle flies and narrated their deaths; they symbolised comrades and friends that had been 'smashed up' during the war.[126] Arthur Gregor Old's diary entries revealed similar disillusionment with military service.[127] In fact, pessimism had become so endemic in Pte. F.G. Senyard's unit that 'peace' became a synonym for something unbelievable.[128] Instead of embracing optimistic news, soldiers now responded derisively towards rumours of imminent victory, especially those originating in civilian circles.[129] S.B. Smith was unwilling to wait for an

---

[118] IWM Documents.7035: Lt. J.H. Johnson, Diary 11 December 1917.
[119] Gibson, *Behind the Front*, p. 349.
[120] IWM Documents.15433: S.B. Smith, Letter to his Wife 21 October 1917.
[121] Ibid. Letter 29 October 1917; IWM Documents.17029: Capt. A.J. Lord, Letter 29 December 1917.
[122] SOFO Box 16 Item 30 3/4/J3/9: Lt. C.T. O'Neill, Diary 16 February 1918.
[123] 'The Dear Old Regiment at Play: From Horton to Hartley – A Tale of Travel', *The Dear Old Regiment* (December 1, 1917), p. 3.
[124] Ibid., p. 11.
[125] B. Bairnsfather, 'A.D. Nineteen Fifty', *The Best of Fragments from France*, T. Holt and V. Holt (eds.) (Barnsley, 1978, 2014). Also, Fussell, *The Great War*, pp. 71–74.
[126] LIDDLE/WW1/GS/0583: 2nd Lt. Sydney Frankenburg, Letter 11 January 1918.
[127] LIDDLE/WW1/ADD/104: Pte. A.G. Old, Diary 1918.
[128] IWM Documents.7953: Pte. F.G. Senyard, Letter to Wife 18 September 1917.
[129] IWM Documents.11006: G.H. Greenwell, Diary 18 November 1917.

increasingly unlikely victory. He was not alone in expressing his hope that 'this war will soon come to an end'.[130]

Field Marshal Haig acknowledged that 1917 left the Army at a 'low ebb'.[131] The processes underpinning this will be explored further in the next chapter. However, High Command were so concerned that they began to study and combat the malaise. Understandably, this partly focused on improvements in fighting efficiency, which sought to improve soldiers' ability to respond to acute crises. Jan Smuts' enquiry into the events surrounding the enemy counterattack at Cambrai sought to understand the reverses there, while Brigadier Bonham-Carter introduced a centralised training programme to improve soldiers' military instruction. These changes were symptomatic of a transformation in institutional culture. Historian David Englander has argued that the BEF shifted its emphasis away from the 'domination' of its soldiers to their 'motivation'.[132] Pamphlets were produced, and lectures delivered to inform men about current affairs and the British cause, as well as telling them what they could expect from victorious peace. Such initiatives are more reminiscent of British military policy in the Second World War.[133] The desire to try and explain events such as the Russian Revolution and to demonstrate how the government would deliver a better post-war Britain is suggestive of an army responding to a collapse in motivation. 'The aim', historian Simon MacKenzie has claimed, 'was clearly to suggest there was something worth fighting for'.[134]

This need to 'remobilise' the British Army does not necessarily mean it had reached breaking point. In fact, other censorship reports presented to the War Cabinet were more optimistic. While such conclusions should be questioned, some were revealing. One, published in December, concluded 'war weariness there is, and an almost universal longing for peace but there is a strong current of feeling that only one kind of peace is possible and that the time is not yet come'.[135] Men were looking for the best route to peace, but a negotiated peace was not necessarily the answer. J.M. Humphries did not articulate what form peace would take, but still told his mother that 'everyone out here thinks the war will end this year'.[136]

---

[130] IWM Documents.15433: S.B. Smith, Letter 8–10 October 1917.
[131] 'Dispatch from Field-Marshal Sir Douglas Haig K.T., G.C.B., G.C.V.O., Commander-in-Chief, British Armies in France: Covering the period from 8th December to 30th April 1918' (London, 1918).
[132] Englander, 'Discipline and Morale in the British Army 1917–1918', p. 127.
[133] Fennell, *Fighting the People's War*, esp. pp. 215–255.
[134] MacKenzie, 'Morale and the Cause', p. 228.
[135] TNA CAB 24/36/44: W.R. Robertson, 'British Armies in France as Gathered from Censorship. Extract from C.I.G.S. 18 December 1917'.
[136] NAM 1998-02-232: J. M. Humphries, Letter to 'Mater' 13 October 1917 [No. 7].

Even men who had lost confidence in victorious peace remained stoic. P.R. Hall recounted that New Year found him and his comrades 'fed up with the ... helplessness of any future we could visualise'.[137] Yet, 'despite all this one could sense a sort of grim determination to carry on in spite of all'.[138] This was written retrospectively in the knowledge that the BEF would emerge victorious. Writing at the time, though, military chaplain Reverend E.N. Mellish described a similar attitude amongst the men in the 4th Bn. Royal Fusiliers.[139] G.A. Stevens was 'getting awfully fed up with this jolly old war it is a horrible strain and the more one gets potted at the more one hates it but I suppose it has to be gone through somehow'.[140]

By February, other soldiers had become more positive about the Allies' chances, perhaps buoyed by the knowledge that Americans were arriving in Belgium and France and more encouraging news from England. R.C.A. Frost's mother consoled him that 'nearly everyone here thinks the war will end soon but I believe they will keep it on just to let America have a go now she has got all the guns and things ... its [sic] got to be wait, wait, wait and all will be well'.[141] Time may have helped the men to partially recuperate from the disappointments of 1917. Furthermore, younger conscripts had begun to fill the ranks of the BEF and might have brought a more optimistic perception of the possibilities of victorious peace.[142]

Rumours of the imminent German offensives engendered no little nervousness, but also signalled a change in the pattern of the war. Some men believed that an enemy attack offered the British their best opportunity to deal a severe blow to the enemy.[143] The enemy's initiative had the potential to open a new pathway to peace. This might explain Pte. Hoyle's memories of the German shelling on 21 March. 'We were', he claimed, 'all in good spirits, and when a shell came particularly close, someone would shout "Where did that one go to Herbert" or some other popular catch word'.[144] It is hard to imagine Hoyle's unit would have been quite this blasé, given the intensity of the German bombardment on the first day of the offensives. Other men were less eager

---

[137] IWM Documents.1690: P.R. Hall, Memoir: p. 19.
[138] Ibid.
[139] IWM Documents.11173: Reverend E.N. Mellish, Letter in January edition of *St Paul's, Deptford, Parish Church Magazine*.
[140] IWM Documents.12339: Brig. Gen. G.A. Stevens, Letter to Mother 10 December 1917. No punctuation in the original.
[141] IWM Documents.16824: R.C.A. Frost, Letter from Mother 6 February 1917.
[142] LIDDLE/WW1/GS/0273: Capt. C. Carrington, Letter to Mother 22 June 1918; IWM Documents.11427: A. Thomas, Memoir: pp. 142–169; IWM Documents.17029: Capt. A.J. Lord, Letter to Father 22 February 1918.
[143] NAM 7403-29-486-144: Sgt. Harry Hopwood, Letter to Mother & All 3 March 1918; IWM Documents.20770: A.L. Collis, Diary 1 and 19 March 1918.
[144] IWM Documents.7312: H. Russell, Diary of W.A. Hoyle 21 March 1918.

to meet the enemy onslaught. Lt. J.H. Johnson attempted to assuage any of his wife's concerns as he waited to go up the line. However, his efforts were undermined by the shakiness in his hand. His uneven penmanship and incoherent syntax were unlike his previous letters.[145] Reverend E.N. Mellish described the month after 21 March as a 'colossal struggle'.[146]

Some soldiers recalled that their morale nearly reached 'breaking point' during the spring battles.[147] Yet, as the next chapter will argue, their response to acute crises in battle should be viewed through a different lens to their experiences of chronic crisis. Outside of the frontlines, many men failed to register the significance of events. C.T. O'Neill, for example, could hear the immense barrage but his battalion continued training and had a 'topping time' at talks, a football match, and a dinner with some 'Yanks' on 21 and 22 March.[148] Even when he saw 'visible signs' of the offensive and was forced to retire, he believed this was 'very ordered'. He concluded that the British soldiers were 'marvellous'.[149] Those occupying parts of the line as yet unaffected by the offensive had little sense of the unfolding acute military crisis. Another man was still able to write that: 'war is composed of boredom and fright. One in and the other out of the trenches and one's only thought is one's next meal'.[150]

Many servicemen (at least those who survived) saw the offensive as a turning point; battle offered a pathway to peace. The conflict entered a new phase, and static trench lines seemed like they might be something of the past. The panic that seems to have swept through High Command failed to register with soldiers on the ground, perhaps because they lacked the same strategic perspective or, possibly, because they were more attuned to the war's patterns. G.A. Stevens put the German successes down to luck and found the fighting 'intensely interesting'.[151] It offered opportunities that he thought had been lost in the mud of Passchendaele. Stevens, like many others, was convinced that 'our turn is coming and that we shall fairly "slip it across him"'.[152] He believed that 'these are wonderful times we are living in just now [,] every moment fraught with immense possibilities, but every day we can hold the Boche up

---

[145] IWM Documents.7035: Lt. J.H. Johnson, Letter to his Wife 21 March 1918.
[146] IWM Documents.11173: Reverend E.N. Mellish, *St Paul's, Deptford, Parish Church Magazine*, 18 April 1918.
[147] LIDDLE/WW1/GS/0313: Pte. C. Clark, Memoir: p. 31.
[148] SOFO Box 16 Item 30 3/4/J3/9: Lt. C.T. O'Neill, Diary 21–22 March 1918.
[149] Ibid. Diary 23–27 March 1918. Also, IWM Documents.11289: H.T. Madders, Diary 21–23 March 1918.
[150] IWM Documents.14517: Capt. P. Ingleson, Letter to Gwen *c.* April 1918.
[151] IWM Documents.12339: Brig. Gen. G.A. Stevens, Letter to his Mother Easter Sunday 1918.
[152] Ibid.

now is lessening his chances of victory'.[153] The semi-mobile warfare was 'far pleasanter' and enemy artillery played a more limited role.[154] Other men also found this kind of warfare a welcome change. It was more varied and preferable to tours of the trenches.[155] The visibility of the enemy, especially the sight of their massive losses during attacks, convinced Capt. A.J.J.P. Agius that 'better times are ahead'.[156] F. Hubard explained that 'everybody of importance out here does not take a gloomy view of it. In fact they seem to think that the Germans are overreaching themselves and will receive a pretty severe blow before long'.[157] Even new arrivals sensed this renewed optimism. H.T. Madders was nervous when he alighted in France with scores of other reinforcements on 27 March, but he still sent his diary home with a note stating he would be 'back in England for hop picking in September'.[158]

Capt. M. Hardie was correct that soldiers wanted 'to be shown a way out' of endless war.[159] For much of the conflict, servicemen remained confident victory was the pathway to peace.[160] In 1914 and 1916, men were fortified by a belief (though arguably a misplaced one) that the campaigns had improved their chances of winning the war. This made their suffering easier to bear. The cycles of the conflict became part of a longer, more lumbering, process towards victory and peace. The present and its overlapping chronic crises were beyond their capacity to change in the short term, but they were not a state of permanence. However, in 1917 men's confidence in the military pathway faltered. The war's stalemate took on an aura of permanence that pushed men to the edge. Yet, many others remained resilient. The German spring offensive renewed faith in the military pathway to peace. This acute crisis combated men's sense of chronic crisis as new patterns in the war offered reasons for optimism and soldiers frames of reference changed. Yet, why was their faith in victorious peace so resilient and how did hope for and visions of peace benefit morale?

---

[153] Ibid.
[154] Ibid. Letters to his Mother Easter Monday and 7 May 1918.
[155] SOFO Box 16 Item 30 3/4/J3/9: Lt. C.T. O'Neill, Diary 29 March 1918; Capt. A.J. Lord, Letter to Father 21 April 1918.
[156] IWM Documents.8589: Capt. A.J.J.P. Agius, 'Copy' – extract from a letter dated 29 March 1918.
[157] IWM Documents.20211: F. Hubard, Letter to Mr and Mrs Underhill 8 April 1918.
[158] IWM Documents.11289: H.T. Madders, Note: Diary 27 March 1918.
[159] IWM Documents.4041: Capt. M. Hardie, 'Report on III Army Morale, August–October 1917'.
[160] IWM Documents.7233: Col. F. Hardman, Letter to Parents February to March 1918; IWM Documents.11445: Brig. Gen. H.E. Trevor, HET/5 – Letter from Ashburner to Mrs Parker, Letter 14 October 1914.

Constructing a Future Space

Servicemen's hope helped them to craft meaningful narratives around their war experience and to endure chronic crises. Visions of peace were an escape mechanism and shaped how men made sense of their suffering. Peace was an abstraction and a construct fed, in part, by their memories, dreams, and fantasies of home.[161] It would be impossible to paint an average picture of peace. The power of hope rested on how it resonated with soldiers individually. There were, however, similar patterns in the way that soldiers constructed and invested themselves in this future space. Their hope for victorious peace helped to mitigate the trauma of war by expanding their temporal horizons. Peace provided an alternative world and a different reality where the war (and its accompanying chronic crises) had ended.

Men made very detailed plans for what they would do once peace returned and developed personal life goals.[162] Visions of peace usually involved a reunion and a return to a comfortable domestic space.[163] Married men, especially newlyweds such as 2nd Lt. D. Henrick Jones, were desperate to return to their wives.[164] Unmarried men in relationships saw future as a time for celebration with their partners. Capt. P. Ingleson's visions of his life with his girlfriend were 'inspiring', and he wanted to make sure that he was 'worthy' of her.[165] The future could inform actions in the present. Charles Carrington wanted to ensure that peace would bring cheer to his mother's life and was determined that his family would be 'flourishing'.[166] A.P. Burke wished only to return to Manchester so that he could converse face-to-face with his family members.[167] Some men fantasised about meeting friends.[168]

---

[161] IWM Documents.11173: Reverend E.N. Mellish, Letter in *St Paul's, Deptford, Parish Church Magazine*, July 1918.
[162] RFM.ARC.3032: L/Cpl. C. White, Diary 16 January 1917.
[163] SOFO Box 16 Item 35: Pte. J.E. Mawer, Doc. 25 Letter to Wife 30 November 1914 and Doc.29 Letter to Wife Undated [c. Christmas 1914]; IWM Documents.18524: Pte. W. Tapp, Diary 22 December 1914; IWM Documents.7953: Pte. F.G. Senyard, Letter to Wife 5 December 1916; IWM Documents.15069: C.P. Crump, Letter 11 September 1916; IWM Documents.11289: H.T. Madders, Diary 5 April 1918; IWM Documents.11068: 2nd Lt. H.M. Hughes, Letter to his Mother 3 January 1916; RFM.ARC.3032: L/Cpl. C. White, Diary 6 and 27 February 1917; NAM 1990-12-95: Arthur Neilson, Letter to his Daughter 3 December [No Year] [-4-1]; SOFO Box 29 Item 4: Pte. Percy Thompson, Letter to Adelaide [undated] from Rouen.
[164] IWM Documents.16345: 2nd Lt. D. Henrick Jones, Letters to Wife 14 October 1916 and 4 April 1918.
[165] IWM Documents.14517: Capt. P. Ingleson, Letter to Miss Fulton 2 January 1918.
[166] LIDDLE/WW1/GS/0273: Capt. Charles Carrington, Letter to Mother 19 October 1916 and 7 May 1918.
[167] IWM Documents.1665: A.P. Burke, Letter to Reg 22 June 1916.
[168] IWM Documents 1534: Capt. C.C. May, Letter from a member of his platoon (21090), c. July 1916.

2nd Lt. W.J. Lidsey looked forward to recouping cash from those he had lent money to.[169] F. Hubard was more concerned with repaying the kindnesses shown to his family by friends in his absence.[170] S.B. Smith, who came from farming stock, anticipated helping his wife bring in the barley.[171] Clearly, then, men's visions of the future could encompass all manner of things and extended to 'education, occupation, embracing an England not devastated by war, simply sitting at home, sleep, good meals, pastimes, . . . or grandiose ideas regarding the betterment of society'.[172]

The ability to construct peace around these personal (or sometimes not so personal) goals may well have helped to instil a depth of meaning that was sustaining. F. Hardman used his dreams of the 'dawn of peace' to combat the horror and suffering confronting him. By investing himself in future worlds he was reminded that 'I have something to live for beyond this world of carnage [and] bloodshed'.[173] Pte. William Anderson explained to his wife how his hopes for the future occupied his mind: 'men as a rule are more apt to look forward and my thoughts, while largely of how you are faring at the moment, are looking ahead full of hope to lighter days'.[174] '[T]he boys' around him talked of little else than what they would do after the war; he wanted to 'live a useful upright life' in which his wife and child would have 'no want of anything'.[175]

Humans seek meaning.[176] It is natural to create narratives that impose coherence and certainty on events that lack both. Maj. S.O.B. Richardson envisioned a future free of conflict. The 'chief justification [of the present conflict] lies in the fact that it will render future wars well-nigh impossible'.[177] Lt. Brettell and his sweetheart saw peace as an opportunity to profit from his service. In one letter, his partner, Peggy, described what their lives might look like: 'it simply seems to me that après la guerre everything will be glorious and perfect, and whatever happens now one must be content to exist till then. Here's to the end of the existence!' They decided that they would sell his paintings (he had been finessing his skills on deployment) and that these

---

[169] IWM Documents.16504: 2nd Lt. W.J. Lidsey, Diary 16 November 1916.
[170] IWM Documents.20211: F. Hubard, Letter to Mr and Mrs Underhill 25 October 1916.
[171] IWM Documents.15433: Pte. S.B. Smith, Letter to Wife 8–10 October 1917.
[172] Mayhew, 'Hoping for Victorious Peace', p. 201; Fletcher, *Life, Death and Growing Up*, p. 3.
[173] IWM Documents.7233: Col. F. Hardman, Letter to Parents 3 April 1918.
[174] IWM Documents.5092: Pte. W.M. Anderson, Letter to Wife 11 December 1916.
[175] Ibid. Letter to Wife 28 October 1916 and 10 December 1916.
[176] R.A. Emmons, 'Personal Goals, Life Meaning and Virtue: Wellsprings of a Positive Life', in C.L.M. Keyes and J. Haidt (eds.), *Flourishing: Positive Psychology and the Life Well Lived* (Washington, DC, 2003), p. 105.
[177] IWM Documents.8059: Maj. S.O.B. Richardson, Letter to Mother and Sister Late 1916 [No. 4].

would truthfully depict the difficulties of army life. They would make 'pots of money'.[178] C.T. O'Neill also hoped to 'make the best of things' once the war finished.[179] Pte. F.G. Senyard trusted that it would be 'glorious'.[180] Military service could not stop 2nd Lt. Henrick Jones courting his childhood sweetheart and their marriage left him proclaiming: 'what a wonderful future I've got to live for now'.[181] Hope drew men away from their present and helped them to see where the war might lead. This was particularly true of fathers who were desperate to see their children grow up and hoped to slot back into family life.[182] Having a goal, whatever that goal might be, allows people to 'construe their lives as meaningful or worthwhile'.[183] The diverse and multifaceted hopes men had for peace encouraged them to see beyond their suffering.

Sustaining Hope

Hope and the processes surrounding it are innate traits, but the resilience of men's hopes for victorious peace was not impervious to change. Cultural factors helped to sustain this cognitive process. Religion, or spiritual beliefs, fuelled and aided some men's hope and optimistic reasoning.[184] Adrian Gregory has suggested that there was widespread, albeit internalised, religiosity in Britain during this period.[185] Capt. M Hardie's censorship analysis led him to a similar conclusion: the 'Army is essentially religious', he wrote, 'not necessarily in outward expression, but in the widest sense of an inward faith and trust in Divine guidance'.[186] Another report found that twelve out of fifteen green envelopes had a 'definite expression of religious feeling'.[187]

It was beneficial, then, that optional Sunday church services (for Anglicans, Catholics, and non-conformists) remained a part of battalions' weekly

---

[178] IWM Documents.10814: Lt. F.A. Brettell, Letter from Peggy 30 November 1916 and 29 December 1917.
[179] SOFO Box 16 Item 30: Lt. C.T. O'Neill, Diary 26 January 1918.
[180] IWM Documents.7953: Pte. F.G. Senyard, Letter to Wife 18 September 1917.
[181] IWM Documents.16345: 2nd Lt. D. Henrick Jones, Letter to Wife 25 December 1916.
[182] NAM 1990-12-95: Arthur Neilson, Letter to Daughter [-1-1], Letter to Daughter 30 November [No Year] [2-1], Letter to Daughter 1 June [No Year] [-3-1] and Letter to Daughter 3 Dec [No Year] [-4-1]; SOFO Box 16 Item 35: Pte. J.E. Mawer, Undated Letter to Wife c. November 1914 [Doc.24]; MR 3/17/145: Pte S. Smith, Photograph Postcards of his Wife and Children; NAM 1993-02-508: Letters sent to Bentley Bridgewater by his Father in France, Letters 2 and 9 March and 2 May 1918.
[183] Emmons, 'Personal Goals', p. 105.
[184] Ziemann, *Violence and the German Soldier*, p. 36.
[185] Gregory, *The Last Great War*, pp. 152–186.
[186] IWM Documents.4041: Capt. M. Hardie, '3rd Section Report on Complaints, Moral, etc. (1916)', p. 9
[187] Ibid.

schedules. Clergy were a common sight in the frontlines and aid stations.[188] Religious service and prayer were a welcome break from the usual routines of army life. It played on some men's minds when they were unable to attend mass. One man, writing in the shadow of the Somme offensive, complained, 'Mummy ... Sundays don't exist out here'. Nevertheless, he felt that 'God seems very near at times. Often I think nothing exists but God'. He saw the Lord's proximity in a skylark whose song he heard coming from No Man's Land. 'He sang as the blessed angels sing.'[189] Others took solace from the fact that their trials were 'a small sacrifice in comparison with His life of sacrifice'.[190] Resilience born of faith was evident elsewhere. James Cooper's strong Church of England upbringing prompted him to pocket a service sheet when he embarked for the Western Front. It read, 'GOD is our Hope and Strength: a very present help in trouble. . . . Therefore will we not fear, though the earth be moved: and though the hills be carried into the midst of the sea'.[191] H.T. Madders copied a similar passage on to the final page of his diary.[192]

Men's families nurtured their faith at a distance, and this frequently revolved around God and the future.[193] Several postcards played explicitly on this theme.[194] Pte. H. Oldfield received two such cards at the end of 1917. The first, 'The Divine Comforter', showed Jesus holding the arm of an injured British soldier. It included an excerpt from the Book of 'Isaias [sic]: 'Fear not, for I am with thee; / turn not aside, for I am thy God'.[195] E. Grantham kept another simply entitled 'faith' in his wallet. This card exhorted its reader to have faith that a 'brighter' future would come.[196] Other soldiers' faith was more personal. 2nd Lieutenant D. Henrick Jones prayed to 'God every day' seeking assurances about the future.[197] Prayer helped to combat other anxieties. During a bombardment in 1914, one man described hearing men 'praying to God to look after there [sic] wife [sic] and children should an

---

[188] Madigan, *Faith under Fire*, pp. 139–148.
[189] IWM Documents.4041: Capt. M. Hardie, Notes 30 July 1916.
[190] Ibid. Notes 7 August 1916.
[191] MR 3/17/91: James Henry Cooper, Memorial Service Programme, St Mark's Parish Church, Dukinfield (4 August 1915).
[192] IWM Documents.11289: H.T. Madders, 'Believe in God' Note at End of 1917/18 Diary.
[193] NAM 1992-09-139: Pte. A. Joy, Autograph Book [9209-139-6] – Notes from Mother; IWM Documents.16824: R.C.A. Frost, Letter from Mother 3 January 1918.
[194] Mayhew, 'A War Imagined', p. 322; Davies, *A Supernatural War*, pp. 177–217.
[195] MR3/17/110: Pte H. Oldfield, Postcards 'The Divine Comforter' and 'The White Comforter'; MR 3/17/139: H. Bridge, Postcard from Niece.
[196] GWA (ww1lit.nsms.ox.ac.uk/ww1lit/items/show/5896, accessed 6 October 2016): Postcard Kept Throughout the War by Sapper E. Grantham.
[197] IWM Documents.16345: 2nd Lt. D. Henrick Jones, Letter to Wife 25/26 December 1916.

think [sic; anything] happen to them'.[198] Other men also put their faith in God to 'save us'.[199] God's benevolence would ensure soldiers' survival and Britain's victory.[200] Researchers have pointed to the role that religion played in social cohesion throughout human history.[201] Significantly, scholars have also highlighted the relationship between Christian 'utopia' and 'hope' with 'hope driving the utopian impulse, [and] utopianism inspiring hope'.[202]

Believing that forces outside their own comprehension controlled the world encouraged some men to toe the line. It also helped to nurture an unwavering faith in a brighter future, while prayer offered them the semblance of agency.[203] William Anderson assumed 'that there's a strong vein of religion down in most chaps, and it only wants tapping the right way'.[204] Anderson himself called on the 'Dove of Peace' to 'descend and make the World a brighter and happier place'.[205] Capt. A.J. Lord looked to the same symbol.[206] The material culture of the trenches mirrored this. Trench art saw bullets, shell casings, or even the remnants of zeppelins fashioned into crosses or other objects imbued with religious symbolism.[207] Reverend C.H. Bell believed that 'men certainly are a little more inclined to religion here than at home'.[208] Perhaps, then, war turned some towards God. However, this may also be read as the conclusion of a cleric reluctant to accept the secularism of the ranks.

---

[198] IWM Documents.8631: Diary of an Unidentified Soldier in the 2nd Bn. Border Regiment, 18 December 1914; MR 3/17/110: Pte. H. Oldfield, Letter from HSS Clarke 10 CCS BEF to Mrs Oldfield on 20 November 1917.

[199] IWM Documents.15433: Pte. S.B. Smith, Letter *c.* September 1916 and Letter 10 October 1916; IWM Documents.11289: H.T. Madders, Diary 7 April and 20 May 1918.

[200] IWM Documents.11289: H.T. Madders, Diary 20 April 1918; IWM Documents.1665: A.P. Burke, Letter to Reg 7 July 1916.

[201] A. Norenzayan and A.F. Sharif, 'The Origin and Evolution of Religious Prosociality', *Science*, Vol. 322, No. 5898 (2008), pp. 58–62; A. Norenzayan et al., 'The Cultural Evolution of Prosocial Religions', *Behavioural and Brain Sciences*, Vol. 39, No. 1 (2016), pp 1–65.

[202] D. Webb, "Christian Hope and the Politics of Utopia," *Utopian Studies*, 19, No. 1 (2008), p. 113.

[203] MR 3/17/110: Pte. H. Oldfield, Letter from HSS Clarke 10 CCS BEF to Mrs Oldfield on 20 November 1917; RFM.ARC.3032: L/Cpl. C. White, Diary 17 January and 18–19 February 1917; IWM 96/24/1: W.M. Anderson, Letter to Wife 21 December 1916; RFM.ARC.2012.958: E.T. Marler, Diary 22–23 October 1916.

[204] IWM Documents.5092: Pte. W.M. Anderson, Letter to Wife 5 November 1916.

[205] Ibid. Letter 21 December 1916.

[206] IWM Documents.17029: Capt. A.J. Lord, Letter 8 January 1918.

[207] See IWM EPH 10150: "Ring" or IWM EPH 1915: "Bullet Crucifix". The latter was produced on the Italian Front, but it is very likely that similar things were crafted in France and Belgium.

[208] IWM Documents.16060: Rev. C.H. Bell, Letter to Herbert 21 January 1918.

Certainly, some men failed to understand their compatriots' faith in God.[209] In fact, many soldiers rarely mentioned God or church services and when they did it was simply a part of common parlance: 'thank God', 'God help Fritz', 'By God', or 'God knows'.[210] Nonetheless, even a vague religiosity encouraged them to invest themselves in visions of peace.

However, hope was also supported by more practical considerations. Soldiers were receptive to and emphasised any sign of progress. The pursuit of a goal provided soldiers with a sense of forward momentum. Static warfare meant that an attritional tit-for-tat took place. A.P. Burke, for example, told his brother that his battalion had captured more than a thousand Germans early in the Somme battles.[211] W.J. Lidsey was similarly happy to hear that the battalion his unit relieved had captured 700 enemies, while suffering only 'very slight' casualties.[212] Activities could break the tedium and suggest progress. While many men feared raids, Fred Gelden had a 'decent time' when his party captured two prisoners in June 1918.[213]

War trophies and 'souvenirs' became evidence of military prowess.[214] There was even a black market for such objects.[215] Charles Dwyer acquired a German sign from his billet to keep as a memento.[216] Sgt. S. Gill obtained an eighteen-inch German shell casing and trench knife that he had taken from enemy trenches.[217] Other men even took postcards off the bodies of fallen enemy troops.[218] Several soldiers looked skyward and watched aerial dogfights, celebrating British victories and cheering as downed enemy planes careered towards the earth.[219] This explains one of Haig's 'lessons' of the Somme campaign, where the 'morale effect' of aerial superiority had been 'out of all proportion' to its material impact.[220]

---

[209] IWM Documents.7035: Lt. J.H. Johnson, Diary 21 November 1916.
[210] IWM Documents.8674: Pocket Diary 1914, 10 October 1914; NAM 1997-02-11: Reminiscences of Unknown Guardsman 13 August to 3 November 1914, 23 October 1914; IWM Documents 1534: Capt. C.C. May, Diary 1916: pp xix-xxi; IWM Documents.20211: F. Hubard, Letter to Mr and Mrs Underhill 8 December 1917; SOFO Box 16 Item 29: Lt. J.E.H. Neville, Diary 23 March 1918; LIDDLE/WW1/GS/0137: Pte. O.G. Billingham, Diary 25 March 1918.
[211] IWM Documents.1665: A.P. Burke, Letter to Reg 7 July 1916.
[212] IWM Documents.16504: 2nd Lt. W.J. Lidsey, Diary 3 and 6 November 1916.
[213] RFM.ARC.3017: Fred Gelden, Diary 8 June 1918.
[214] Advert: 'DO NOT READ THIS!!! Unless You Have a Girl at Home', *The B.E.F. Times*, Vol. 2, No. 5 (1917).
[215] RFM.ARC.2495: Sgt. S. Gill, Book 7, Diary 6 October 1916.
[216] IWM Documents.16676: C. Dwyer, Diary 11 September 1914.
[217] RFM.ARC.2495: Sgt. S. Gill, Book 8, Diary 8-9 December 1916.
[218] MR 3/17/126: Pte. John Peat, German Postcards; LIDLLE/WW1/GS/0758: Capt. E.L. Higgins, Postcards [Germans in Front of Train, Germans Next to Cross and German Officers in Bombed Church].
[219] IWM Documents.4041: Capt. M. Hardie, Notes 5 July 1916.
[220] TNA WO 256/14: Diary of Field Marshal Haig, 1 December 1916.

Infantrymen organised and mobilised the information available to them as they made sense of their surroundings and they desperately wanted evidence that they were treading the pathway to victorious peace. If there was some way to paint the war's progress positively, they did so.

Of course, much of the time there were few visible signals of success. In these circumstances, perceptions of victorious peace were often fed by rumour.[221] At least one trench newspaper poked fun at the proliferation of rumours.[222] In November 1914, H.E. Trevor received inaccurate reports that 'von Kluck's [First German] army is surrendering'.[223] S. Judd overheard an embellished narrative of the naval battle in the Falkland Islands. In this account, twenty-three German cruisers had been sunk, which compared favourably to the six British ships that had been lost.[224] Even the most implausible gossip encouraged discussions of victorious peace. Later, in 1916, William Anderson wrote home that 'if some of the rumours that are floating around have anything solid about them, I may God willing, be with you both soon. I trust that this is so'.[225] F.G. Senyard's thirst for news pushed him to request that his wife send him details of the rumours circulating in England.[226] Soldiers continued to lap up gossip until the moment of the Armistice.[227] On 11 November 1918, H.T. Madders wrote in his diary: 'the runner has gone to Coy orders and rumours are about, is it peace? It can't be, we've had some before; we hang on and duck as just before 11 o'clock old Jerry lets go his big stuff and makes the most of it; Then uncanny silence'.[228] Rumours have a social and communicative purpose and are used as a form of 'collective explanation'. They help to make sense of and give cohesion to events that are inexplicable or inherently chaotic.[229] In this instance, they helped to sustain men's hope for victorious peace.[230]

---

[221] IWM Documents.10933: Capt. G.B. Donaldson, Letter to his Mother 8 June 1916; IWM Documents.1665: A.P. Burke, Letter to Reg 12 November 1916; IWM Documents.5092: Pte. W.M. Anderson, Letter to his Wife 24 October 1916. Also Cook, *The Secret History of Soldiers*, pp. 143–162.

[222] 'If All the Rumours Came True', *The Bankers' Draft*, No. 1 and 2 Vol. 1. (June and July 1916).

[223] IWM Documents.11445: Brig. Gen. H.E. Trevor, Letter to Evelyn 6 October 1914.

[224] IWM Documents.12027: S. Judd, Diary 19 December 1914.

[225] IWM Documents.5092: Pte. W.M. Anderson, Letter to Wife 9 November 1916; LIDDLE/WW1/GS/1444: Pte. C.W. Sharp, Letter to Ethel 16 September 1916.

[226] IWM Documents.7953: Pte. F.G. Senyard, Letter to Wife 18 September 1917.

[227] IWM Documents.7035: Lt. J.H. Johnson, Diary 7 November 1918; IWM Documents.14752: J. Grimston, Diary 10 November 1918.

[228] IWM Documents.11289: H.T. Madders, Diary 11 November 1918.

[229] P. Bordia and N. DiFonzo, 'Problem Solving in Social Interactions on the Internet: Rumor As Social Cognition', *Social Psychology Quarterly*, Vol. 67, No. 1 (March 2004), pp. 33–49.

[230] For the operation of rumour, see G. Seal, *The Soldiers' Press: Trench Journals in the First World War* (Basingstoke, 2013), pp. 82–89.

The resilience of hope also lay in British perceptions of the enemy. The belief that this was a war of defence was far from empty rhetoric.[231] It reinforced the connection between victory and peace. British soldiers believed the German state was expansionist and generally accepted that peace needed to be fought for.[232] German military strategy reminded men of the threats facing the homeland, particularly during the offensives of 1914 and 1918.[233] During the Second World War, the experience of the Blitz nurtured a desire for revenge as well as stoicism and endurance.[234] In 1914, soldiers witnessed tragic scenes of civilian casualties and refugees forced out of their homes.[235] Charles Dwyer, amongst many others, believed that the German Army had acted 'disgracefully'.[236] In 1916, men were aware of enemy attempts to bleed France white at Verdun.[237] Finally, in 1918, the offensives rekindled soldiers' fears for home. The dislocation of the local populace hit servicemen forcefully.[238] Importantly, it also reminded them that they could lose the war and re-emphasised the Germans' role as 'the invader'.[239] In this way, acute crisis could act as a catalyst for morale. Victory became a necessary precursor to peace.

The German state was portrayed as a destructive enemy incapable of compromise. Such propaganda was internalised by soldiers. Postcards were a useful conduit for such messages. Infantrymen collected sets of cards depicting the destruction along the Western Front. These depicted the 'Hun's passion for destruction' and the 'devastation [caused] by the vampires'.[240] Sgt. S. Gill wrote angrily in his diary: 'damn those Prussians. Sodom and Jeremiah to

---

[231] T. Wilson, *The Myriad Faces of War: Britain and the First World War* (London, 1986, 2010), esp. ch. 77.
[232] IWM Documents.12771: W. Vernon, Letter to Miss L. Vernon 22 July 1918.
[233] Gibson, *Behind the Front*, pp. 383-384.
[234] D. Todman, *Britain's War: Into Battle, 1937-1941* (London, 2016, 2017), pp. 520-524.
[235] IWM Documents.12819: J.S. Knyvett, Diary 22 October 1914; RFM.ARC.2012.264: Sgt. Osborn, Diary 22, 24, and 27 August and 16 September 1914; IWM Documents.18524: Pte. W. Tapp, Diary 1914, p. 5; IWM Documents.7371: Postcard Signed by 'The Mademoiselle from Armentieres', Extract from local paper.
[236] IWM Documents.16676: C. Dwyer, Diary 10 September 1914.
[237] 'If All the Rumours Came True', *The Bankers' Draft*, Vol. 1 No. 2 (July 1916).
[238] IWM Documents.12339: Brig. Gen. G.A. Stevens, Letter to Mother 27 January 1918; IWM Documents.20761: H. Milner, Memoir, p. 32; IWM Documents.8589: Capt. Arthur J.J.P. Agius, Extracts from a letter received from France 28 March 1918; IWM Documents.17029: Capt. A.J. Lord, Letter to his Father 12 April 1918; IWM Documents.12771: W. Vernon, Letter to Miss L. Vernon 22 July 1918.
[239] IWM Documents.7233: Col. F. Hardman, Letter to Parents 4 April 1918.
[240] IWM Documents.7076: S.A. Newman, Postcards of Arras; IWM Documents.11289: H.T. Madders, Postcard Collection for Arthur; MR 3/17/145: Pte S. Smith, Postcards 3 (Albert) Somme and Guerre 1914-1916 No. 80 Albert (Somme).

the ... demonical ghoulish vampires'.[241] A.P Burke considered Germany to be an 'old Devil'.[242] Others were repulsed by stories of German mistreatment of Allied soldiers.[243] Charles Dwyer, for instance, was horrified by a tale about Northumberland Fusiliers who had been shot dead after they had surrendered in 1914.[244] Sometimes prejudices were confirmed by personal experiences in and out of battle. A couple of men obtained gruesome postcards from dead German soldiers. One series included photographs celebrating the British dead as evidence of success in battle. These appeared to offer evidence of the kind of foe they faced.[245] Servicemen often saw the Germans as the 'authors' of the war's evil and this engendered an 'intense determination to exact full retribution'.[246] It made peace at any price unquestionable.

There is, however, little to suggest that men fostered hatred for the enemy soldiers as individuals.[247] Some servicemen respected their enemy as clean fighters and appreciated it when local agreements allowed each side to bring in the wounded.[248] In the heat of battle, the death of comrades could create loathing for enemy combatants and in extreme cases individuals (and sometimes whole units) were driven by a 'blood lust'.[249] Usually a considerate and passive man, A.P. Burke confessed to his brother on 6 July 1916 that he and his comrades had 'begrudged' an order to take prisoners.[250]

[241] RFM.ARC.2495.5: Sgt. S. Gill, Diary 20 December 1916.
[242] Ibid. Letter to Reg 12–15 October 1916.
[243] IWM Documents.17029: Capt. A.J. Lord, Letter to Father 3 and 6 September 1918.
[244] IWM Documents.16676: C. Dwyer, Diary 21 September 1914.
[245] MR 2/17/53: Patrick Joseph Kennedy, German Postcards [Nos. 126, 138, 164, 282, 283, 284, 294 and 440]; IWM PC 1784: Maj. Frederick Hardman, Photographic Postcards of Various Dead British Soldiers; GWA (ww1lit.nsms.ox.ac.uk/ww1lit/items/show/6050, accessed 5 October 2016): German Postcard and Photograph Souvenired by George Powell. Mayhew, 'A War Imagined', pp. 24–27.
[246] IWM Documents.12339: Brig. Gen. G.A. Stevens, Letter to Mother 11 November 1916; 'Editorial', *The B.E.F. Times*, No. 3, Vol. 1 (1917) 1–2; 'Editorial', *The B.E.F. Times*, Vol. 2, No. 5 (1918) 1–2; IWM Documents.4041: Capt. M. Hardie, 'Report on III Army Morale, January 1917', p. 7.
[247] IWM Documents.11445: Brig. Gen. H.E. Trevor, Letter to Mother 2 September and 3 October 1914; IWM Documents.8631: Diary of an Unidentified Soldier in the Border Regiment, 11 December 1914; IWM Documents.12339: Brig. Gen. G.A. Stevens, Letter to Mother 2 November 1916; LIDDLE/WW1/GS/0313: Pte. C. Clark, Memoir, p. 14; IWM Documents.12105: Reverend M.A. Bere, Letter to Wife 17 September 1917; IWM Documents.11976: Lt. Col. A.H. Cope, Diary 28 March 1918; IWM Documents.14752: J. Grimston, Diary 29 March 1918; IWM Documents.17029: Capt. A.J. Lord, Letter to his Father 21 April and 25 August 1918.
[248] IWM Documents.4041: Capt. M. Hardie, Notes 19 July 1916.
[249] NAM 1982-12-70: Pte. A.E. Hutchinson, Journal: 'The True Story of My First Day of Captivity in the Hands of the Huns'.; IWM Documents.18524: Pte. W. Tapp, 24 and 26 November 1914; RFM.ARC.2012.264: Sgt. Osborn, Diary 22–23 and 25 August 1918.
[250] IWM Documents.1665: A.P. Burke, Letter to Reg 6 July 1916. For hatred of the enemy and prisoner killing, see Ferguson, *The Pity of War*, esp. pp. 357–58.

Yet, most men reserved their hatred for Germany's leaders. They were the propagators of 'kultur'.[251] Even as news of peace feelers filtered into the trenches, men tended to mistrust the 'terms outlined by the Allemands'.[252] Bruce Bairnsfather's illustration *The Tactless Teuton* reflected such ideas. In this image, a stick-thin German private from the 'Orphans' Battalion' was overlooked by an overbearing (and overweight) man of his own army's 'Gravediggers' Corps'. This was a state-run slaughter orchestrated by a devilish 'Hun'.[253] This 'powerful ideological' motivation was repeated by soldiers in their depictions of the enemy.[254] Many men used 'Hun' or 'Teuton' as a catchall term for the German troops.[255] This dehumanised the enemy and hinted at their perennial expansionism.[256] Responding to a letter from home (apparently about a colleague somewhere else on the Western Front), one man advised that '[I] heard all about the raid, it's a bad business and shows what a callous lot the Huns are ... They are only creating rage in the hearts of the chaps out here'.[257] A meaningful peace could only be produced by victory. Lt. Reginald Neville explained to his sister that:

> We want to exterminate, not so much the Germans as individuals for they are harmless enough, but their methods and principles; and worst of it is that there is only one way to do this and that is to kill the individuals. If only we could get hold of these abstract principles, turn them into concrete and then blow them off the face of the earth, our end would be attained.[258]

The Psychology of Hope

As earlier chapters have shown, morale was often supported by unconscious processes. Perhaps unsurprisingly, then, optimism was also a central component of men's hopefulness.[259] Alexander Watson's research indicates

---

[251] IWM Documents.10271: Pte. A.W. Lloyd, The U.P.S. Song Book Song: 'Marching Through Ashstead'.
[252] IWM Documents.4041: Capt. M. Hardie, 'Report on III Army Morale, January 1917', p. 7.
[253] Bairnsfather, *Best of Fragments from France*, p. 10.
[254] Gibson, *Behind the Front*, p. 12.
[255] IWM Documents.10933: Capt. G.B. Donaldson, Letter to Mother 2 July 1916; IWM Documents.9816: N.R. Russell, Letter to Mother 15 July 1916; IWM Documents.16504: 2nd Lt. W.J. Lidsey, Diary 2, 10, and 13-14 November 1916; IWM Documents.12339: Brig. Gen. G.A. Stevens, Letter to Father 12 February 1918.
[256] Jones, 'The Psychology of Killing', p. 244; M. Kestnbaum, 'The Sociology of War and the Military', *Annual Review of Sociology*, Vol. 35 (April 2009), pp. 242-243.
[257] LIDDLE/WW1/GS/0144: A&C Black Publishers, Letter from E. Lindsell 23 June 1917.
[258] SOFO Box 16 Item 3: Lt. Reginald N. Neville, Letter to Sister 2 August 1917.
[259] Watson, *Enduring the Great War*, pp. 92-93, 105-106, 234.

that 'psychological coping strategies were only coloured, not shaped by social influences'.[260] 'Human faith, hope and optimism', Watson argued, 'no less than cultural traits, discipline, primary groups and patriotism, explain why and how men were willing and able to fight in the horrendous conditions of the Western Front'.[261]

Innate cognitive mechanisms often helped soldiers make sense of the Great War. These coalesced with cultural, social, and environmental factors and fed soldiers' investment in a brighter future.[262] Imagination, as well as a human desire to craft narratives, allowed the men to build a picture of their future lives and played no small part in their ability to endure 1914–1918.[263] The power of hope was clearest when such processes failed, and soldiers became unable to envision this future, which was traumatic.[264] Visions of peace produced images of an alternative world.[265]

The Somme Times toyed with the idea that there was widespread overoptimism in the ranks of the British Army. One author mocked his peers:

1 - Do you suffer from cheerfulness?
2 - Do you wake up in a morning feeling that all is going well for the Allies?
3 - Do you sometimes think that the war will end within the next twelve months?
4 - Do you believe good news in preference to bad?
5 - Do you consider our leaders are competent to conduct the war to a successful issue?

The reader was consoled that 'we can cure you of this dread disease'.[266] All it took was a visit to the frontlines. Yet, optimism, and misplaced optimism, were a precondition for surviving the war's chronic crises.[267] Five months later, the same publication berated pessimists calling them 'strange elfish creature[s]'.[268] Soldiers sought to encourage and nurture optimism. Pte. Albert Joy's signature book contained a note from J. Baker, which advised 'Bert' to 'despond if you must. But never despair for remember that from our greatest failures arise our

---

[260] Ibid., p. 8.
[261] Ibid., p. 107.
[262] IWM Documents.7035: Lt. J.H. Johnson, Diary 18 August 1916; RFM.ARC 2013.8.2: Pte. P.N. Wright, Retrospective Diary, 10 November 1916.
[263] Watson, *Enduring the Great War*, p. 100 and S. Halifax, '"Over by Christmas": British Popular Opinion and the Short War in 1914', *First World War Studies*, Vol. 1, No. 2 (Oct. 2010), p. 106.
[264] SOFO Box 16 Item 29: Lt. J.E.H. Neville Diary 23 March 1918.
[265] LIDDLE/WW1/GS/0583: 2nd Lt. S. Frankenburg, Letter 1 December 1917.
[266] NAM 1959-03-34 (4): 'Are You a Victim of Optimism?', *The Somme Times*, Vol. 1, No. 1 (31 July 1916).
[267] Watson, *Enduring the Great War*, pp. 92–107.
[268] 'Editorial', *The BEF Times*, Vol. 1, No. 2 (Monday, 25 December 1916).

most Brilliant success'.²⁶⁹ Lt. Johnson's experiences convinced him that soldiers had a unique capacity to embrace both optimism and pessimism, while aligning perfectly with neither. The war was a paradox and engendered 'endurance, inventions, simplicity' and produced 'the one idea out here by us' – that a victorious peace would eventually transpire.²⁷⁰ Men were sometimes aware that their optimism was fatuous, but they remained resolutely forward-looking. It took a lot to turn a man into an arch-pessimist, but if hope faded this could become deeply corrosive.

However, for the most part, hope allowed men to break out of the temporal constraints of their present. They were able to plan and consolidate all that was good in their lives, which produced a conceptual pathway to peace. Their use of the future tense played an implicit role in diminishing their temporary misfortunes and assumed their survival. Pte. William Anderson offered a moving example of this when he sent his sketches of the frontlines home as 'a memory of very anxious times'.²⁷¹ Other men asked their families to keep postcards that they collected safely as personal mementoes. The letters A & C Black Publishers received from employees in khaki were obsessed with peace. They wrote regularly to discuss their jobs, to thank their employers for continuing to provide for their families, to enquire about the business, and to discuss their return to work after the war.²⁷²

This ability to imagine future episodes is an important part of human cognition.²⁷³ Cristina Atance and Daniela O'Neill describe this as 'episodic future thinking' and suggest it has a positive bearing on experience and behaviour.²⁷⁴ Importantly, writing about these goals improves subjective well-being. Historians have revealed the ways in which writing helped soldiers cope during wartime.²⁷⁵ More generally, writing about 'one's best possible self' can increase feelings of wellness. Tellingly, these benefits are felt more powerfully when future goals are deployed to combat shocking events.²⁷⁶ The very process of hoping, then, provided men with a protective psychological tool.

---

²⁶⁹ NAM 1992-09-139: Pte. A. Joy, Signature Book, esp. Message by J. Baker.
²⁷⁰ IWM Documents.7035: Lt. J.H. Johnson, Diary 30 December 1917 and 1 January 1918. Also, LIDDLE/WW1/GS/0273: Capt. C. Carrington, Letter to Mother 2 October 1918.
²⁷¹ IWM Documents.5092: Pte. W.M. Anderson, Letter to Wife 16 November 1916.
²⁷² LIDDLE/WW1/GS/0144: A&C Black and Company, Letters of E.P. Gilscott and L/Cpl. E. Lindsell.
²⁷³ K.K. Szpunar, J.M. Watson and K.B. McDermott, 'Neural Substrates of Envisioning the Future', *Proceedings of the National Academy of Sciences of the United States of America*, Vol. 104, No. 2 (July, 2006), pp. 642–647
²⁷⁴ C.M. Atance and D.K. O'Neill, 'Episodic Future Thinking', *Trends in Cognitive Sciences*, Vol. 5, No. 12 (December, 2001), pp. 533–539.
²⁷⁵ V. Wilcox, '"Weeping Tears of Blood": Exploring Italian Soldiers' Emotions in the First World War', *Modern Italy*, Vol. 17, No. 2 (2012), pp. 171–184.
²⁷⁶ L.A. King, 'The Health Benefits of Writing about Life Goals', *Personality and Social Psychology Bulletin*, Vol. 27, No. 7 (July 2001), pp. 798–807.

It was difficult for servicemen to imagine this as anything but the product of martial endeavour. Their frames of reference were moulded by their immediate social groups and structures. Training is, of course, a central feature of morale, and Hew Strachan sees the negation of the self as one of its outcomes.[277] This undoubtedly affected men's 'choice architecture'. This term was coined by behavioural economists Richard Thaler and Cass Sunstein and explains how consumer decision making is influenced by the information available to them and how these can be manipulated.[278]

Soldiers' world view was constrained in this manner, and this was revealed in their use of language. Within soldiers' letters and diaries, a number of 'voices' were operating. Michel Foucault's discussion of authorship helps to explain this; he argued that 'the author function operates so as to effect the dispersion of ... simultaneous selves'.[279] Identity is fluid and men pined for peace as civilians. Yet, their lexicon revealed their military identities. Their syntax was scattered with indications that they were at war, which represented the 'present' tense for them. Speakers look 'to establish or reinforce social identity or cohesiveness within a group' by using 'slang'.[280] As an earlier chapter demonstrated, the use of French became commonplace. Other slang, such as 'straffe' or 'straffing', 'wind-up', 'grousing', or 'napoo' quickly entered their vocabulary.[281] It even appeared in interactions with loved ones.[282] The war and their military experiences embedded themselves in soldiers' psyches and helps to explain why many were unable to contemplate peace through anything but military victory. As serving soldiers, the army offered *the* vehicle for change and some men articulated that peace would only be won in a 'great battle'.[283]

---

[277] H. Strachan, 'Training, Morale and Modern War', p. 216.
[278] R.H. Thaler and C.R. Sunstein, *Nudging: Improving Decisions about Health, Wealth, and Happiness* (London, 2009), esp. pp. 3–6, 10–13.
[279] M. Foucault, 'What Is an Author?' in M. Foucault, *Aesthetics, Methods and Epistemology* (ed. J.D. Faubion and trans. R. Hurley et al.) (New York, 1998), p. 216.
[280] C.C. Eble, *Slang & Sociability: In-Group Language among College Students* (Chapel Hill, 1996). Soldiers' slang has been explored elsewhere, see, for instance, Cook, *The Secret History of Soldiers*, pp. 90–117.
[281] IWM Documents.1665: A.P. Burke, Letter to Reg 12–15 October 1916; IWM 96/24/1: Pte. William Anderson, Letter to Wife 13 November 1916; IWM Documents.16345: 2nd Lt. D. Henrick Jones, Letter 25–26 December 1916; IWM Documents.7953: Pte. F.G. Senyard, Letter to Wife 26 December 1916 and 16 June 1918; RFM.ARC.2012.146.1: Albert Victor Arthur, Diary 24–30 September 1917; MR 3/17/126: Pte. John Peat, Letter 11 October 1917: IWM Documents.17029: Capt. A.J. Lord, Letter to Father 8 February 1918; IWM Documents.11289: H.T. Madders, Diary 17 March 1918; IWM Documents.16336: C.H. Isom, Diary 2 May 1918.
[282] IWM Documents.21795: Mrs L.K. Briggs, 41st Division Xmas Card 1916; IWM Documents.10814: Lt. F.A. Brettell, Letters from Peggy, esp. 8 May 1916.
[283] IWM Documents.7233: Col. F. Hardman, Letter 3 April 1918; IWM Documents.7035: Lt. J.H. Johnson, Diary 28 December 1917; IWM Documents.8674: Pocket Diary 1914, 7 September 1914.

Historians of the Home Front have argued that any 'short war illusion' disappeared quickly in 1914.[284] Yet, soldiers in France and Belgium continued to foster such ideas. In October 1914, L.F. Ashburner still ruminated 'I wonder if we shall be home by Xmas?'[285] Infantrymen continued to ask themselves such questions throughout the war.[286] Two years later, Pte. William Anderson confessed that 'I haven't lost the idea that this business may well be over by Christmas. Maybe my faith or hope is on the strong side'.[287] It was only in 1917–1918 that this optimistic forecasting faltered. Understandably, Christmas and New Year provided focal points for soldiers' aspirations for peace.[288] The festive holidays were *the* time for family and friends and, as such, December became a focal point. It reflected men's desperate desire to avoid winter in the trenches.[289] Yet, it also suggests that men viewed peace as a product of military campaigning since Christmas fell in the month after major campaigning usually ended. In early November 1914, R.D. Sheffield found that the men in his unit still 'all seem to say that they think this will be the last battle and if we win that the war will end before Christmas'.[290] In 1916, G.H. Greenwell asserted that 'everything sooner or later has an end' and trusted that a successful campaign would force a German collapse by Christmas.[291] Except in 1918, however, such hopes were never realised.[292]

Nevertheless, even false hope can be of benefit.[293] Hope is 'a positive motivational state that is based on an interactively derived *sense of success*',

---

[284] Pennell, *A Kingdom United*, p. 223.
[285] IWM Documents.11445: Brig. Gen. H.E. Trevor, HET/5, Letter from Capt. Ashburner to Mrs Parker 14 October 1914; IWM Documents.14710: R.D. Sheffield, Letter to Father 9 November 1914; SOFO Box 16 Item 35: Pte. J.E. Mawer, Letter to Wife 30 November 1914.
[286] IWM Documents.14710: R.D. Sheffield, Letter to Father 9 November 1914; IWM Documents.7953: Pte. F.G. Senyard, Diary 14 December 1916; RFM.ARC.2012.958: E.T. Marler, Diary 25 December 1916; LIDDLE/WW1/GS/0273: Capt. C. Carrington, Letter [No. 87] to Mother 29 December 1916; RFM.ARC.3032: L/Cpl. C. White, Diary 3 January 1917; IWM Documents.11173: Reverend E.N. Mellish, Letter in *St Paul's, Deptford, Parish Church Magazine*, January 1918.
[287] IWM Documents.5092: Pte. W.M. Anderson, Letter to Wife 17 October 1916; IWM Documents.15069: C.F. Crump, Letter 11 September 1916; RFM.ARC.2012.958: E. T. Marler, Diary 25 December 1916.
[288] This may have also been the product of religiosity, but there were few references connecting Easter and peace.
[289] IWM Documents.4041: Capt. M. Hardie, 'Report on III Army Morale, August–October 1917'.
[290] IWM Documents.14710: R.D. Sheffield, Letter to Father 9 November 1914.
[291] IWM Documents.11006: G.H. Greenwell, Letters 30 August and 4 November 1916.
[292] For the negative impact see E. Greenhalgh, '"Parade Ground Soldiers": French Army Assessments of the British on the Somme in 1916', *The Journal of Military History*, Vol. 63, No. 2 (April 1999), p. 302.
[293] Snyder et al., '"False" Hope', pp. 1003–1022.

which is fed by 'agency (goal-directed energy)' and 'pathways (planning to meet goals)'.[294] Rather than attainment being its only measure, hope is also 'influenced by a dispositional sense of abilities to produce pathways and agency across situations'.[295] As such, one can be motivated by perceived success. Infantrymen's morale was supported by the *feeling* of pursuing a legitimate course towards peace. What is more, high hopers have a slight propensity to interpret events with a 'positive self-referential bias'.[296] Men were sustained by the impression that they were winning and embraced *feelings* of success.[297] *Esprit de corps* (as well as friends and family at home) may have also cultivated high levels of hope since 'interpersonal relationships' support resilient hoping.[298] Such relationships existed. Charles Carrington saw 'friendships' as a key feature of his war experience. He feared the severance of these bonds, which remained a key theme in his post-war writings.[299] For a variety of reasons, men remained resiliently hopeful despite the persistent failure of victorious peace to materialise.

****

Combatants' capacity to endure war was bolstered if they perceived the conflict as productive, worthwhile, or just. Infantrymen's investment in their hopes for victorious peace allowed them to envisage pathways out of the present into a future devoid of war. Visions of their future lives helped them to justify their suffering. Combatants perceptions of peace imbued their war experience with greater meaning. As they sought to cope with the war's chronic crises, soldiers focused on and celebrated the proximity of peace. They often entered new campaigns in the belief that it would be *the* final victorious push towards peace. However, once their confidence in victorious peace collapsed, morale suffered immensely.

The war was the canvas for men's suffering *and* their best opportunity to return to their peaceful lives. As it dragged on, it became harder for

---

[294] C.R. Snyder, L. Irving and J.R. Anderson, 'Hope and Health: Measuring the Will and Ways', C.R. Snyder and D.R. Forsyth (eds.), *Handbook of Social and Clinical Psychology: The Health Perspective* (Elmsford, 1991), p. 287.

[295] Snyder et al., '"False" Hope', p. 1007.

[296] Ibid.

[297] IWM Documents.12027: S. Judd, Diary 27 December 1914; IWM Documents.1665: A.P. Burke, Letter to Reg 7 July 1916; IWM Documents.12339: Brig. Gen. G.A. Stevens, Letter to Mother Easter Monday 1918; LIDDLE/WW1/GS/0273: Capt. C. Carrington, Letter to Mother 28 March 1918 (No. 134).

[298] Snyder (et al.), '"False" Hope', p. 1016. Training manuals provide evidence that *esprit de corps* was seen as a key ingredient to 'moral'. See *Platoon Training (1918)*, p. 20. Also LIDDLE/WW1/GS/0451: L.M.E. Dent, Interview Transcript 1978.

[299] LIDDLE/WW1/GS/0273: Capt. C. Carrington, Letter to Mother 7 July 1918 and 13 October 1918.

servicemen to see peace as anything other than a product of the conflict and victory. As such, enduring chronic crises made sense. Such an outlook was supported by a variety of mechanisms. An internal faith as well as an inherent optimism, religious or otherwise, allowed soldiers to continue to believe in the likelihood of victory. Their contact and connection with their homelands also helped to preserve hope. Rumours, too, fed their belief that peace was near. Significantly, many servicemen, if not most, believed that the German state needed to be defeated before a lasting peace could be secured.

Yet, in autumn/winter 1917, confidence in victorious peace dwindled as men no longer believed battle would deliver peace. In such circumstances, chronic crises threatened morale to an extent otherwise rarely seen in earlier years of the war. However, it appears that the fighting after 21 March convinced many soldiers that the Germans would not accept a negotiated settlement and that defeat was a real possibility. What is more, the character of the warfare that accompanied these battles indicated the conflict had entered a new phase and offered new opportunities, especially for those who enjoyed fighting.

Human beings create narratives and naturally look to the future; we seek out evidence of forward momentum and try to impose meaning and purposefulness on our lives and actions. Infantrymen's visions of peace were invaluable to endurance, and most soldiers remained confident in their pathways thinking. The soldiers' military acculturation shaped their sensemaking and ensured that their perceptions were informed by the war and army. For much of the conflict, victory appeared to be the only route to peace. Yet, the chapter that follows will investigate why battle, and warfare more generally, no longer seemed to provide this pathway in late 1917 and early 1918.

6

Experiencing Crisis
Battle and Sensemaking c. July 1917–June 1918

Looking back on the war, Edmund Blunden recalled that 'the Passchendaele year ... was murder – not only to the troops but to their singing faiths and hopes'.[1] In 1917 and 1918, morale was suffering.[2] Senior politicians and soldiers feared that this had played a significant role in reverses during the German offensives in spring 1918. Policy makers were confronting *the* crisis of the war.[3] Unnerved by events in Belgium and France, the Canadian and New Zealand premiers arrived in London for the Council of Prime Ministers in June 1918 demanding answers from the Imperial War Cabinet. Jan Smuts – once an Afrikaner rebel but now a stalwart of the British Empire's war effort – responded honestly:

> [By] the end of 1917 ... the Army was really in a deplorable condition. Our men had been worn out by a summer and autumn of the most ceaseless, bloody, and muddy fighting in this whole War, and reached the end of that year tired, decimated in numbers, with their moral seriously impaired and the situation for us very [,] very serious indeed. The new drafts which had been hurried forward from time to time were imperfectly trained, and that made the position still more serious for the future. ... Our men, although in a tired, and, I think, disheartened condition, were set to dig trenches and to put up wire entanglements, and ... it was almost asking too much of human nature. We know, as a fact, that over certain parts of our line the defences were not in the best condition. The Officers in many cases had to make a choice either of training their men – because hundreds of thousands of their own recruits

---

[1] Edmund Blunden, 'Foreword', in B. Gardner (ed.), *Up the Line to Death* (York, 1964, 2007), p. vii.

[2] For a survey of this period, see Stevenson, *1917*, pp. 170–204 and *With Our Backs to the Wall*, pp. 30–111 and 244–310.

[3] There are several studies of this period but they tend to offer a broader or comparative perspective on the operational (or international) history. See, for instance, P. Dennis and J. Grey (eds.), *1917: Tactics, Training and Technology* (Cranberra, Australia, 2007). For a synthesis of some of the ideas found here, see A. Mayhew, 'Mud, Blood, and Not So Much Poppycock: "Myth" Formation and the British Army in Late 1917', *Bulletin of the Auckland Museum*, Vol. 21 (2020), pp. 39–44.

were in an untrained condition – or digging trenches. Some chose the alternative of digging trenches, others of training their men; in either case the men had been brought to a condition which was most deplorable. Then the German offensive started last March, and we know the results.[4]

Smuts correctly diagnosed the threats to morale as the war entered 1918 and the problems the British Expeditionary Force faced in training its men. However, he seems to have been unaware of one of the more surprising effects of the German spring offensives. This chapter will suggest that they transformed soldiers' sensemaking and *improved* their morale.

As Alexander Watson has argued, an 'analysis of morale ... is really a history of the peaks and troughs in their men's confidence to win the war and return home unscathed'.[5] Fatigue and pessimism were two of the war's most oppressive chronic crises. Training was also fundamental since it allowed infantrymen to respond intuitively to acute crises and provided a framework for understanding the world around them. Karl Weick, an organisational theorist whose work has already been mentioned, developed the concept of sensemaking to help explain 'how we structure the unknown so as to be able to act in it' and to develop 'a plausible understanding, a map, of a shifting world'.[6] 'Sensemaking', Weick and others have explained, 'involves the ongoing retrospective development of plausible images that rationalize what people are doing'.[7]

For much of the war, men's ability 'to rationalize' what they were doing helped to combat (and, perhaps, normalised) their suffering. However, in 1917 and 1918, infantrymen's conceptual frameworks were either refined or abandoned in response to a shifting reality. Hope dwindled as soldiers' 'desired goals', namely peace, no longer seemed attainable by military means.[8] Battle's fading fortunes lay at the heart of this process. As *the* pathway to victorious peace, once battle lost its meaning – as it did on the muddy fields of Passchendaele – men's morale suffered.

This chapter explores what underpinned men's changing perceptions of battle, their frames of reference, and their sensemaking between July 1917 and June 1918. To do so, it focuses on a variety of units' experiences during these

---

[4] TNA CAB 1/26/20: Report of the Committee of Prime Ministers. Preliminary Draft as a basis for consideration – Part I: Jan Smuts to Prime Ministers, p. 2.
[5] Watson, *Enduring the Great War*, p. 141.
[6] D. Ancona, 'Framing and Acting in the Unknown', in S. Snook, N. Noharia, and R. Khurana (eds.), *The Handbook for Teaching Leadership: Knowing, Doing, and Being* (Thousand Oaks CA, 2012), pp. 3–19.
[7] K.E. Weick and K.M. Sutcliffe, 'Organizing and the Process of Sensemaking', *Organization Science*, Vol. 16, No. 4 (July–August 2005), p. 409.
[8] Hope does not necessarily rest on an actor's ability to achieve their goals but draws on a *sense* that a goal is achievable. See E.M.W. Tong et al., 'Re-Examining Hope: The Roles of Agency and Pathways Thinking', *Cognition and Emotion*, Vol. 24, No. 7 (2010), p. 1213.

months: the fighting, the routines of military life, and their training.[9] Reconstructing the narrative of these twelve months (as it might have appeared to the men at the time) reveals how the reality of 1917 began to suggest that battle was futile, and its accompanying trials were no longer worthwhile. Optimism gave way to pessimism and dejection before, during the spring offensives, battle once again offered opportunities for peace and victory. The exhaustion and despondency that Smuts highlighted were initially only made worse by the changes that took place in the BEF during the winter of 1917–1918. The army's shift to a defensive policy created a lot of work for tired men, and perpetuated problems in a military that was already experiencing a manpower crisis. Worse still, it signalled that 1918 would not see victory. Units' training suffered as they invested their time in the reorganisation of the BEF.

So, as English infantrymen – and their comrades throughout the BEF – grappled with the war's chronic crises, they were left with inadequate skills to meet the acute crises in the defensive battles to come. However, somewhat paradoxically, the changes brought about by the fighting after March 1918 regalvanised soldiers and renewed their faith in battle as a pathway to victorious peace.[10] It may be the case, then, that the experience of acute crisis – and a renewed perception of agency – deflected the chronic crises that had caused men to suffer over the course of the winter.

****

The Prelude

Optimism and Early Operations

1917 did not begin so desperately. In fact, many British soldiers ended 1916 confident that the BEF was treading a path towards victory. On the Western Front, the early months of 1917 appeared to confirm this. First, operations on the Ancre and the Somme saw some minor victories. These had been, at least in the eyes of British soldiers, a prelude to the German withdrawals to the Hindenburg Line in February and March 1917. This line of fortified positions, which had been prepared during the 1916–1917 winter, allowed the German High Command to pursue a defensive policy in Belgium

---

[9] The analysis focuses on thirteen battalions, but not all of these kept thorough records so the reader will see that some of the statistics and tables are limited to those units that kept coherent records about, say, their drafts and casualties. A full list of these units can be found in the bibliography.

[10] Stevenson, *With Our Backs to the Wall*, pp. 267–268; Englander, 'Discipline and Morale', p. 141.

and France in 1917 from a position of strength.[11] Operation Alberich was a sound strategic move. Yet, to many in the BEF it appeared that the fighting had sapped their enemy's endurance. The Germans seemed to be on the back foot. Subsequent operations also pointed to positive changes, despite the crisis unfolding in the French Army as large numbers of troops engaged in collective ill-discipline. From the British perspective, though, the fighting at Arras (9 April–16 May), including Vimy Ridge, and then at Messines Ridge (7–14 June) indicated that battle could reap rewards.[12]

As soldiers crafted narratives, 1917's early months lay the foundations for a hopeful and victorious story in which soldiers were firmly on the pathway to peace. An important feature of sensemaking is that it is *retrospective* and that the information individuals process is often selective or confirms pre-existing ideas. Soldiers, seeking evidence that they were successfully navigating the war, used these months to substantiate such a perspective. Some of the clearest evidence of this can be found in battalion histories (even though they were written in the years after the war ended). Descriptions of the advance that took place as the Germans withdrew to the Hindenburg Line indicate that soldiers believed that these events validated the trials of 1916 and fed their optimism.

III Army censor, Capt. M. Hardie, was right to highlight the value of effective operations in the maintenance (or bolstering) of morale. Successful advances, however limited, were evidence that battle could bring about a victorious peace. Units involved in the Battle of Messines found this to be the case. Both the 8th Bn. Border Regiment and 10th Bn. Royal Warwickshire Regiment went into action on 7 June 1917 and achieved their objectives.[13] Not only did this increase the confidence of the survivors in their own abilities, the experience also suggested that they were in the ascendancy. The Warwickshires advanced through a copse occupied by the enemy and were only met by 'very short lived' resistance after which seventy Germans 'threw down their arms and came forward with their hands up (most of them in a state of abject terror)'. A Company captured another twenty officers (all of whom 'surrendered freely'), including the commander of the regiment facing them. Later in the afternoon, they also captured a battery of artillery and a

---

[11] J. Boff, *Haig's Enemy: Crown Prince Rupprecht and Germany's War on the Western Front* (Oxford, 2018), esp. pp. 148–150.

[12] It was not all positive. An unsuccessful attack at Bullecourt left Australian troops demoralised. The declining returns at the Battle of Arras led corps commanders to refuse an order for further assaults on 14 April. They dispatched a resolution calling for more preparation time directly to Douglas Haig (going over the head of their army commander, Edmund Allenby). See Beckett, Bowman, Connelly, *The British Army and the First World War*, pp. 307–318, esp. p. 318.

[13] TNA WO 95/2251/3: 8th Bn. Border Regiment, 7–10 June 1917; TNA WO 95/2085/3: 10th Bn. Royal Warwickshire Regiment, 7–10 June 1917.

further thirty prisoners on entering Oosttaverne. Their war diary proudly reported that the battalion's 'trophies' included four 4.2-inch howitzers and three machine guns.[14] Important, too, was the apparent fragility of captured enemy troops. According to Maj. C. Stone, author of the 22nd Bn. Royal Fusiliers' history, they encountered 'miserable creatures' during the fighting on the Ancre in early 1917.[15]

The sights men encountered during this period underlined the justice of their cause. As soldiers advanced in the wake of the enemy after the withdrawal to the Hindenburg Line, they were confronted by 'the wholesale massacre of the Germans of all objects both natural and artificial'. Buildings (from chateau to cottage), woods, factories, farmland, and even fishponds 'were victims of their madness'.[16] It was 'sheer wantonness' and the booby traps left by the retreating enemy appeared to confirm their devilishness.[17] Elsewhere, many of the men who entered the village of Pargny were confronted by their first sight of a permanent German cemetery, which was 'a hideous erection' that seemed to self-consciously represent 'the might of the fatherland'. It 'evidently displeased the British troops' and 'after a few days, the memory was found smashed to atoms'.[18]

Tellingly, battalion histories echoed the optimism that seemed to be sweeping through the army. Of course, the authors of these texts knew what was to come – first Third Ypres, then the German offensives, followed eventually by the advance to victory. Yet, their understanding of the broader historical narrative (and their desire to write objectively) did not entirely cloud the authors' memories of the positivity that seems to have characterised these early months of 1917. It appeared that 'the principle of manoeuvre had been restored', and this 'infused a sense of change and movement into the most static portions of the allied line'.[19]

Training played an important role in men's perception of victory and progress. Yet, during this critical period, the training they received was to an extent misdirected. Throughout these months, 'pamphlets proclaimed the creed of open warfare and bade perish the thought of gumboot or of trench' and changes in training reflected this.[20] In other words, expectations were set, which were later confounded. Units practised attacks behind ordered barrages, with patrols and scouts having free rein over the battle space. It was not that it

[14] TNA WO 95/2085/3: 10th Royal Warwickshire Regiment, 7 and 10 June 1917.
[15] Maj. C. Stone (ed.), *A History of the 22nd (Service) Battalion Royal Fusiliers (Kensingtons)* (London, 1923), p. 44.
[16] Rose, *2/4th Oxfordshire and Buckinghamshire Light Infantry*, p. 80.
[17] H.T. Chidgey, *Black Square Memories: An Account of the 2/8th Battalion the Royal Warwickshire Regiment, 1914–1918* (Oxford, 1924), p. 93.
[18] Ibid., pp. 92–93.
[19] Rose, *2/4th Oxfordshire and Buckinghamshire Light Infantry*, p. 81.
[20] Ibid., p. 48.

was fruitless: new platoon tactics helped to develop individual initiative and inculcate military discipline 'as a member of a herd'. There were also attempts to prepare men for the acute crises they might face on the battlefield. Soldiers were apparently cross-examined and 'asked what they would do in various emergencies'.[21] Nonetheless, all of this occurred in an environment that was preparing men for semi-open warfare and successful advances: things that became increasingly rare as the year went on.[22]

Regimental culture continued to be strong during this period. Some regular battalions, whose ranks had been thinned by nearly three years of war, maintained a relatively strong complement of regular infantrymen at their core. Before they were sent into the Passchendaele sector, the 2nd Bn. Ox and Bucks retained some four officers and eighty-eight other ranks who had embarked with the battalion on 13 August 1914. Of these, one officer and fifty-nine other ranks had served with the battalion continuously since then. It seems likely that these men occupied some of the 'cushier' roles, but it ensured that such units were able to maintain something of their pre-war culture and protected the battalion's collective memories of the conflict (and the regiment's deeper history).[23]

As spring turned to summer, many units began to hear the first rumours (or see the first evidence) of the great offensive to come. The 1/5th Bn. Royal Warwickshire Regiment were withdrawn from the line in Picardy to begin their training ahead of their transfer to the Ypres sector. Upon arriving in Flanders, it was hard not to be awed by the preparations for the victorious push. There were camps, bivouacs, horse lines, and dumps – all of which spoke to the immense strength of the BEF.[24] The full power of the British Army was about to be unleashed. Ominously, these scenes were accompanied by the first hints that the weather, 'pro-German as ever', would hinder forthcoming operations.[25]

Passchendaele

Pessimism, Futility, and Faltering Morale

In the years after the war, Third Ypres was remembered as a muddy, bloody, and seemingly futile tragedy fought over a wasteland of shell holes and saturated clay soils. The optimism nurtured by events in the earlier months

---

[21] Ibid., pp. 48–49. SS 143, *Instructions for the Training of Platoons for Offensive Action, 1917.*
[22] Rose, *2/4th Oxfordshire and Buckinghamshire Light Infantry*, p. 49.
[23] TNA WO 95/1348/5: 2nd Bn. Oxfordshire and Buckinghamshire LI, 'Additions to War Diary for August 1917'.
[24] Carrington, *The War Record of the 1/5th Battalion*, pp. 53–54.
[25] Ibid.

of 1917 was destroyed by the campaign. The lived experience of these months was compounded by events away from the Western Front, which conspired to destroy men's faith in victory. Delayed due to heavy rainfall, the battle commenced on 31 July. This first phase began with operations on Pilckelm Ridge and ended at the Battle of Langemarck on 16 August. General Gough's Fifth Army made only modest gains for very heavy losses. Poor weather plagued the fighting and made logistics – not to mention combat – a nightmare.

During the second phase of the battle, in September and early October, more limited 'bite-and-hold' tactics (pioneered in General Plumer's Second Army) offered some hope. These attacks on smaller fronts (and supported by a greater weight of artillery) were accompanied by better weather. The more limited objectives, as well as the focus on the consolidation of captured positions, reaped rewards at the battles of Menin Road Ridge, Polygon Wood, and Broodseinde. It seemed that progress had been made. Yet, the poor weather returned, and it was harder to hold onto the gains made at the Battle of Poelcappelle on 9 October. Thereafter, attempts to take the high ground during the two battles along Passchendaele ridge were a shambles.[26] This high ground (something of debatable tactical utility) was eventually captured, but the months symbolised the horror and futility of battle. The slim rewards did not merit the terror.

After Passchendaele, it was difficult to see battle as a pathway to peace. One battalion history noted that the battle was 'the most bloody and perhaps least profitable of the whole war'.[27] Warfare in the 'mud flats of Flanders' sapped morale and chipped away at endurance.[28] The 'whole battle-front had been transformed into a vast area of sticky mud and a continuous mass of shell-holes'.[29] At the worst of times, it was difficult to make any progress 'in the face of concentrated machine-gun fire and heavy artillery barrages' and German

---

[26] Despite the horrors of these months, historians have highlighted how the BEF's tactical and operational ability had improved and that the Germans nearly reached their breaking point. It was evident, too, that the BEF's men were able and willing to defeat the Germans in circumstances with a reasonable chance of success. Yet, it does not mean that the troops on the ground were aware of this at the times. See, esp., Sheffield, *Forgotten Victory*, pp. 180, 183–184; Lloyd, *Passchendaele*, pp. 1–7; Beckett, Bowman, and Connelly, *The British Army and the First World War*, pp. 337–338. Also N. Steel and P. Hart, *Passchendaele. The Sacrificial Ground* (London, 2000, 2001); P. Liddle (ed.), *Passchendaele in Perspective: The Third Battle of Ypres* (London, 1997); R. Prior and T. Wilson, *Passchendaele: The Untold Story* (New Haven and London, 1996, 2002).

[27] Rose, *2/4th Oxfordshire and Buckinghamshire Light Infantry*, pp. 114–115.

[28] *History of the 1/6th Royal Warwickshire Regiment* (Birmingham, 1922), p. 15.

[29] Chidgey, *Black Square Memories*, pp. 128–130.

pillboxes.³⁰ The experience of the 1/6th Bn. Royal Warwickshire was by no means unique. During an attack on 27 August, 'no ground could be gained but many fell where they stood, and, fallen, lay still'.³¹

Even in a war zone dominated by death, the Salient's horrors were especially unbearable. On 13 October 1917, following particularly heavy fighting near Poelcappelle, Gen. J.G. Matheson (commander of 4th Division) drafted a message for the troops under his command. 'Nobody', he explained, 'will ever forget the part taken by the 4th Division in the Great Battle Flanders'. He was 'proud' of his men, yet he acknowledged they had encountered 'the most trying conditions that any troops have had to endure'.³² Their Army commander agreed that their performance had been 'marvellous'. It seems unlikely that the infantrymen would have been quite so effusive about their experiences. In fact, beneath the veneer of positivity, senior officers also hinted at the reality of Passchendaele: 'successive fights ... in the worst weather conditions possible, which necessarily caused great exhaustion'. Matheson's message spoke to the unique horrors of the fighting around Ypres between July and November 1917, and men's faith in battle faltered (and sometimes died) there.

Events conspired to exhaust the men of the BEF and spread pessimism through its ranks. As the reader has seen, men's perception of the war was often built around partial pictures and was prone to symbolism. It was not only the difficulty of military operations that helped to colour their view of the war. It appeared to many that the weather itself had turned on the British. The rain and the mud appeared incessantly in soldiers' writings, war diaries, and recollections of the campaign. Modern warfare had not reduced the importance of climate in successful campaigning. This was especially true around Ypres, where dry weather compacted the topsoil creating 'favourable conditions for the attacker', but rain transformed it 'into a swam-like pulp' and put the defender in the ascendancy.³³ As the war dragged on, the BEF created its own Meteorological Section, and their climatological data for this period reveals how bad the conditions during the Third Ypres campaign were. Men felt that summer never arrived. A comparatively dry late winter and spring may have offered military planners (and the soldiers) false hope of a dry year. However, rainfall was especially heavy in July, August, and October, when data suggests it was at least twice as severe as the average year before 1914. During August there were only fourteen rainless days, which left no time for the

---

[30] Ibid.
[31] *History of the 1/6th Royal Warwickshire Regiment*, pp. 45–46.
[32] TNA WO 95/1484/5: 1st Bn. Royal Warwickshire Regiment, 'To All Ranks of the 4th Division' by Maj. Gen. J.G. Matheson, 13 October 1917'.
[33] Colonel Friderich Karl 'Fritz' von Lossberg in Lloyd, *Passchendaele*, p. 64.

ground to dry.³⁴ In September, the rain eased only to return with a vengeance the following month. The rainfall correlated strongly with some of the most difficult fighting and contributed to the dreadful conditions facing the men of the BEF. It symbolised the futility of further fighting. Indeed, the weather had a huge bearing on the success of British operations. It is no surprise that the period of successful 'bite-and-hold' operations under General Plumer (and the high point of the campaign at the Battle of Broodseinde) coincided with a period of relatively dry weather (see Tables 6.1 and 6.2).³⁵

The terrible summer of 1917 followed a particularly severe winter in 1916. The failure of better weather to arrive was a terrible blow, making an already horrible part of the line even worse. The 'low-lying, clayey soil, torn by shells and sodden with rain' became a 'succession of vast muddy pools'.³⁶ Shellfire had scarred the landscape removing points of familiarity and destroying the already badly damaged drainage systems.³⁷ One soldiers' newspaper described Zillebeke as a 'port'. Here 'the very sunlight was dimmed by the clouds of black smoke' mixed with the 'red mist of upflung brick dust' to engulf a 'strange vista of shattered walls, splintered trees, shell-pocked fields'.³⁸ The exposed positions around 'Wipers' (where trench breastworks were often above ground) made it a dangerous and sedentary location. An already high water table meant that rainfall in the summer months of 1917 left the boggy ground saturated. It was difficult to move up the line, let alone traverse No Man's Land and enemy positions.

Sacrifice is always relative, and losses are subjectively measured against tangible gains. Yet, palpable (or, at least, meaningful) successes were limited in the wastelands of 1917. The ground taken was often difficult to recognise as anything but more of Ypres' quagmire. At the same time, losses mounted. As friends and comrades were killed or disappeared, many units faced a crisis of identity. In the early months of the campaign, where any victory came at a high cost, this was of particular significance. The 16th Bn. Manchester Regiment attacked the enemy line between Clapham Junction and Surbiton Villas on 31 July alongside two of its sister battalions (the 17th and 18th Bns.). Having kept close behind their barrage, they reached their objectives but were then held up badly in the remains of Sanctuary Wood. Tellingly, the commanding officers' analysis of the attack barely registered this as a victory: units

---

[34] J. Hussey, 'The Monsoon in Flanders', *Journal of the Society for Army Historical Research*, Vol. 74, No. 300 (Winter 1996), p. 248.

[35] Lloyd, *Passchendaele*, pp. 218–219.

[36] Sir Douglas Haig in J.H. Boraston (ed.), *Sir Douglas Haig's Despatches* (1919) taken from Hussey, 'The Monsoon in Flanders', p. 246.

[37] Lloyd, *Passchendaele*, p. 105.

[38] 'The Port of Zillebeke: An Incident of the Third Battle of Ypres, August 1917', *The Dagger*, 1 November 1918, p. 31.

Table 6.1 *Monthly rainfall in Ypres (mm) 1916–1917 and 1917–1918*

	Jan	Feb	Mar	Apr	May	Jun	Jul	Aug	Sep	Oct	Nov	Dec	Total
1916	28	62	65	62	50	105	28	68	43	56	65	83	**715**
1917	74	13	49	49	25	72	82	127	40	107	43	19	**700**
1918	55	25	37	42	55	33	–	–	–	–	–	–	**247**

Source: National Meteorological Archive (NMA), Exeter, NMA MET/2/6/1/6/f: Rainfall investigation by E. Gold. Data not available for July–Dec 1918.

Table 6.2 Average monthly temperature (°C) in the British zone of operations 1915–1918

	Jan	Feb	Mar	Apr	May	Jun	Jul	Aug	Sep	Oct	Nov	Dec
1915	4.2	3.4	5.1	6.1	11.6	15.3	16.2	17.1	15.2	12.7	6.3	5.7
1916	6.5	5.1	4.2	6.6	11.9	13.5	15.3	17.1	14.9	12.1	5.8	3.5
1917	3.6	0.9	3.7	4.5	10.9	16.7	17	17	15.9	12.3	8.3	3.5
1918	2.7	5.3	5.3	7.1	11	14.6	15.7	17.1	15.2	11.4	9.6	

Source: NMA MET/2/6/1/6/f: Estimated earth temperatures at one foot in British army area 1915–1918, Meteorological Section Royal Engineers First Army, GHQ 12 December 1918. The data for November 1918 is limited to the first two weeks of the month.

had become badly mixed up, the pause at the Blue Line (the first objectives) had been too short, and communications had 'been very bad' with the 'small card maps' issued to men doing little but create 'ignorance of correct positions'.[39] This would be the last time the battalion was in the first wave of an attack at Passchendaele. Of the 347 casualties they suffered between July and November, 265 were incurred on this day alone.[40] This was a very heavy toll for the confused line of mud-encrusted trenches they had taken. Similarly, in August, during only one day of severe fighting around Inverness Copse, the 11th Bn. Royal Fusiliers suffered 339 other ranks and seventeen officer casualties. They had been flanked (which was easy in the confusion of the frontlines) and were subjected to intense rifle and machine-gun fire. Such losses could rip the heart out of any corporate entity in the pursuit of what often seemed like futile gains.[41]

The units that fought in the more successful 'bite-and-hold' battles and 'step-by-step' advances of September and early October may have had a different perspective.[42] Battalions trained on practice battle areas (probably now more accurate because of the better weather conditions) using new attacking formations (and mopping-up procedures). There were more successes at a reduced cost.[43] It is significant that censor Capt. M. Hardie suggested that 'peace talk' reduced during this time of more successful campaigning (and better weather).[44] It appeared this change in tactics could swing the initiative back to the BEF.[45] Where many battalions were withdrawn after a bloody but relatively brief period of combat, the 2/2nd Bn. London Regiment (Royal Fusiliers) were unlucky enough to attack enemy lines on several occasions during September. Nevertheless, they escaped relatively lightly, losing 120 men and seven officers over the course of the month.[46] Yet, as historians have noted, these 'minor victories only served to befog the situation' and encouraged 'bolder moves' that eventually brought greater bloodshed.[47] The casualties and losses incurred during

---

[39] TNA WO 95/2339/1: 16th Bn. Manchester Regiment, 'Summary of Impression of the Attack made upon immediate front'.
[40] Ibid., esp. 31 July 1917.
[41] TNA WO 95/2045/1: 11th Bn. Royal Fusiliers, 10 August 1917.
[42] Beckett, Bowman, and Connelly, *The British Army and the First World War*, pp. 333–335.
[43] TNA WO 95/2045/1: 11th Bn. Royal Fusiliers, 3–9 September 1917 and 'Training Programme 11th Bn. Royal Fusiliers: 9–15 September 1917'; TNA WO 95/3144/6: 2/5th Bn. Manchester Regiment, 'Short Summary of Events during Month – September 1917'.
[44] IWM Documents.4041: Capt. M. Hardie, 'Report on II Army Morale, August–October 1917'.
[45] Lloyd, *Passchendaele*, esp. pp. 187–189, 204. Also Sheffield, *Forgotten Victory*, p. 176; Steel and Hart, *Passchendaele*, p. 233. Robin Prior and Trevor Wilson are less convinced by such an analysis. See *Passchendaele*, p. 119.
[46] TNA WO 95/3001/4: 2/2nd Bn. London Regiment (RF), September 1917.
[47] Beckett, Bowman, and Connelly, *The British Army and the First World War*, p. 334.

October and November (alongside the horrors of those battles) left 'battle-hardened veterans ... wasted, and the morale of the survivors ... damaged'.[48]

Even those units that escaped the first waves of attacks did not leave Passchendaele unscathed, emotionally or physically. In support, life remained dangerous and unpleasant. On 4 October, for example, the 1st Bn. Royal Warwickshire reinforced the 2nd Bn. Seaforth Highlanders in trenches near 19 Metre Hill (close to Langemarck). Advancing in close support, they came under heavy machine-gun and sniper fire. As they took up positions on the reverse side of the high ground, it became clear that the next two days would be spent very uncomfortably as they consolidated and patrolled this desolate sector.[49] The weather, their duties, and a dangerous enemy left the whole battalion 'tired and fatigued', though the adjutant noted that all ranks had behaved 'gallantly under the most trying conditions'.[50]

For most, battle was a punctuation mark. Yet many unlucky battalions were posted to the Ypres front for prolonged periods and lived their day-to-day lives with the battle as a backdrop. Simply navigating the lines on working parties was an energy-draining and soul-destroying enterprise. The 5th Bn. Ox and Bucks' main experience of combat came while holding the line on the evening of 23/24 August. Their outposts were attacked by an enemy bombing party. All but one company was required to intervene, which was done successfully. During a month that mainly saw them consolidating exposed and hard-to-recognise positions, they suffered some 286 other ranks and nine officers wounded, killed, or missing.[51] Between July and November, they suffered a total of 528 casualties – a heavy rate of attrition in a unit that had few successes to celebrate.

The violence, the rain, and the mud contributed to the routine horrors of Passchendaele. These were wearying and terrifying in equal measure. Illustratively, on a tour of the line between 16 and 24 October, the battalion's war diary provided an example of the worst that Third Ypres had to offer. The companies trudged out of Ridge Wood at 11am on 16 October destined for a sector between Menin Road and Scherriabeek that appeared 'to be a pretty dirty one in both sense[s] of the word'. Possibly because of their experiences in August, the officers were uncertain about what they would encounter on this tour. They were meant to be going up to hold the line, but service at Passchendaele was characterised by uncertainty and 'one can never say for certain what will happen'. As they reached 'CLAPHAM JUNCTION', they were met by an intense artillery barrage. The men, burdened by packs and rations, were unable to respond quickly enough and forty soldiers were injured, including one company

---

[48] Ibid., pp. 337–338. The BEF's overall losses at Passchendaele were actually lower than they had been at the Somme.
[49] TNA WO 95/1484/5: 1st Bn. Royal Warwickshire Regiment, 4 October 1917.
[50] Ibid.
[51] TNA WO 951900/4: 5th Bn. Ox and Bucks LI, esp. 23/24 August 1917.

Figure 6.1 Allied troops and German prisoners at the Menin Road, near Ypres, Belgium, 30 October 1917.

Source: The Print Collector/Print Collector/Getty Images.

commander and his headquarters. Thankfully, their excellent guides navigated them away from danger. Other units were often not so lucky, either for want of guides or because of the darkness during night reliefs.[52]

The men of the 5th Bn. Ox and Bucks would have been relieved that this tour of the line did not involve any unexpected local offensives. Nevertheless, it was still deeply unpleasant. The enemy's artillery and snipers haunted them throughout the day and night. The dead and wounded were constant companions, and a seemingly unceasing stream of casualties passed through battalion HQ. This had been established in a secure pillbox (as had those of the companies in support). Frontline companies were not so lucky. The weather was a significant factor in the horrors facing these men. They were relieved when the day broke bright and sunny on 17 October. It was 'a pleasant change' and allowed the trenches to dry out a little, but it was clear that even 'a very little wet would make them almost untenable'. Unfortunately, the shelling was persistent and the next day the dreaded rain returned.[53]

[52] Ibid., 16 October 1917.
[53] Ibid., 17 October 1917.

Rear positions were often little better. The 1/5th Bn. Royal Warwickshire Regiment were posted to a reserve camp on their arrival in Flanders. The anglicised names of the locations surrounding their tents spoke to the nature of the sector; their position was in 'Slaughter Wood'. It was 'knee-deep with mud', and they spent much of the day waiting for orders 'under cascades of rain dripping from the oak trees'. As they moved further up the line, they found that rain and shellfire had turned the Steenbeek River into a 'slough of despond'. It was difficult to familiarise, let alone become attached to these landscapes. Some of the sights they encountered provided a visual metaphor for the campaign's futility. Supposedly war-winning materiel, in this case tanks, was found 'rusting in ... slime'.[54] The sights offered little to help men find meaning in battle. Tellingly, August 1917 was 'the worst month the battalion passed through'.[55] They had been ordered to complete 'a series of impossible tasks ordered under hopeless conditions' in which they conducted 'continual attacks by weak bodies against strong bodies of troops in concrete fortresses'. They could do little in such circumstances. Basic communication broke down, and the runners and signallers suffered particularly high casualties.[56]

Men's dwindling faith in battle and faltering morale can be traced in documents from the period. There are some clues in battalion war diaries, which indicate that officers were feeling the strain of service towards the end of 1917. Men began looking for 'soft jobs'. In several units, officers were sent to rest camps with greater regularity towards the end of the year.[57] Battalion commanders were also susceptible to the strains of the campaigning. As early as August 1917, Lt. Col. C.W.H. Birt (CO of 8th Bn. Border Regiment) began leaving his command for extended breaks, including 'rest at the sea side'.[58] Yet, these documents lack any commentary on such occasions. It is impossible to know exactly why these men were allowed to leave their units temporarily. However, it correlates with the signs of stress evident in the diaries and letters of junior officers.

It is very difficult to measure morale in any quantifiable way. As already explained, though, the few censorship reports that remain do indicate that something was afoot. It is no coincidence that the mutiny at Étaples occurred during this period. Elsewhere, too, it is possible to find subtle indicators of faltering morale in some (but certainly not all) units. The lack of consistency in what was and what was not recorded in battalion war diaries makes direct comparison very hard. However, problems seem to have been more common

---

[54] Carrington, *War Record*, p. 54.
[55] Ibid., pp. 56–57.
[56] Ibid.
[57] TNA WO 95/2085/3: 10th Bn. Royal Warwickshire Regiment, 22 October 1917.
[58] TNA WO 95/2251/3: 8th Bn. Border Regiment, 20 August 1917.

in battalions that spent prolonged periods in the Ypres sector during the latter part of 1917. Even regular battalions were not immune. The only desertions recorded in 1st Bn. Royal Warwickshire Regiment between July 1917 and June 1918 were in late October and early November, while another man was sent to prison for an unknown reason on 27 November.[59] The same regiment saw relatively high rates of sickness in autumn and winter. Between June and September 1917, no more than thirty-two men left the unit sick each month. However, after being deployed in a combat role in October, this rose to fifty-five and from January 1918 onwards sickness rates remained around at least fifty men per month. Unsurprisingly, this increased further after March, likely because of exposure (and later influenza) during the more mobile warfare in the spring and summer.[60] The sole recorded self-inflicted wound in 4th Bn. Royal Fusiliers came after the new year.[61] Earlier, on the afternoon of 13 September, the 5th Bn. Oxfordshire and Buckinghamshire Light Infantry (a New Army battalion) held its only court martial during the twelve-month period covered by this chapter. Less significantly, on 11 October 1917, the adjutant also reported that a lot of men had begun to fall out on their route marches. Yet, in such circumstances, exhaustion (rather than poor morale) seemed to be the greatest explanatory variable.[62]

Perhaps the clearest evidence of fragile morale can be found in the diary of 11th Bn. Royal Fusiliers. They had suffered badly at Passchendaele. Having fought there in August and October, the battalion lost some 682 casualties between July and November.[63] At Ypres, there had been a suspicion that 'stragglers' were escaping the battlefield by helping wounded friends back to aid posts. Resultantly, 'Stragglers Posts' were set up to 'take the numbers, names and units of all stragglers + send those who are fit back to their unit'. This battalion also saw a slew of courts of inquiry and court martials during October and November. There were several suspected cases of self-inflicted wounds, three of absence without leave, and at least two of desertion. In fact, on 21 November 1917, four separate men were charged with different offences. Pte. T. Gibbs was charged with desertion, Pte. T. Hagon with absence without leave, Pte. W. Wallace with disobedience, and Pte. C. Underwood with using insubordinate language. All were found guilty. The deserter, Gibbs, was sentenced to ten years of penal servitude (a punishment later confirmed by a Field General Court Martial). The other men all received Field Punishment

---

[59] TNA WO 95/1484/5: 1st Bn. Royal Warwickshire Regiment, 24 October, 8 and 27 November 1917.
[60] Ibid., June 1917 through June 1918.
[61] TNA WO 95/1431/3: 4th Bn. Royal Fusiliers, 26 January 1918.
[62] TNA WO 95/1900/4: 5th Bn. Oxfordshire and Buckinghamshire LI, 13 September and 11 October 1917.
[63] TNA WO 95/2045/1: 11th Bn. Royal Fusiliers, July–November 1917.

No. 1 (for sixty-three, twenty-eight, and fourteen days depending on the severity of their crime). Intriguingly, several officers were also reduced in rank during these months, though it remains unclear why.[64] Many soldiers (even in positions of power) appeared unsure that battle (at least 'set piece battles') offered a pathway to peace on the Western Front.[65]

Cambrai

The Final Straw?

As the BEF became stuck in the mud of Flanders, plans were developed for a surprise attack to the south.[66] Initially, it seemed to be an astonishing success and, famously, bells were rung across Britain to celebrate the victory on 20 November 1917. After the troops of Third Army emerged from their trenches, they advanced – alongside tanks – up to a depth of five miles. Significantly, the casualty bill was comparatively light, especially after the losses incurred around Ypres. Yet, the British advance slowed down quickly, and the offensive was eventually cancelled on 28 November when men were asked to dig in and prepare a new defensive line. German tactics now put great weight on the counterattack and a series of these had already helped to disrupt the BEF's advance. Then, on 30 November, and in the days following, a forceful enemy counterthrust retook much of the ground that had been won by the BEF to such great celebration. Success and victory were elusive, it seemed.

The Battle of Cambrai appeared to confirm the impression that battle had lost meaning. Importantly, it was also a warning that the BEF was ill-prepared to respond to an acute tactical crisis, but this went unheeded (or unacted upon). The reasons for the initial British successes and the causes of the successful German counterattack that followed have been discussed elsewhere. Surprise and the effective use of artillery and tanks were important ingredients in early British gains.

Yet, as the German counterattack unfolded on 30 November, battalion war diaries and battalion histories speak to a confusion that seems to have been endemic in the frontlines. Illustratively, the 22nd Bn. Royal Fusiliers were rushed into support of the 186th Brigade in Bourlon Wood after the initial enemy advances. They found themselves at a chalet in the woods near Anneux.

---

[64] Ibid., esp. 29–31 October, 6, 14, 21, and 28–30 November 1917.
[65] TNA WO 158/46: Reports by Lord French and Lt. Gen. Sir H. Wilson to War Cabinet. 29 October. O.A.D. 702 to CIGS, p. 1. Also TNA WO 158/25/362. 'Notes on the Economy of Manpower by Mechanical Means'. Copy. No. 10.
[66] B. Hammond, *Cambrai 1917: The Myth of the First Great Tank Battle* (London, 2009). It is important to note the tactical innovations that took place here (especially in combined arms) did eventually influence the more successful Allied offensives of 1918.

Unsure of what to do next, they sat breakfasting in 'scattered groups' alongside some dismounted cavalrymen, disabled tanks, and the dead. Suddenly a barrage came down creating 'a nightmare of bewilderment and ... discomfort, so that everyone was thankful to escape'.[67]

On 30 November, the battalions in reserve positions had been left in a state of readiness to move at two hours' notice for nearly forty-eight hours and must have been exhausted even before they were thrown into the heat of battle. Once they arrived in the frontlines, the situation was hardly any clearer. At 10am the 2nd Bn. Ox and Bucks began stocking their equipment that was surplus to fighting before making their way forward.[68] Upon arrival, they were ordered to counterattack in conjunction with the 24th Bn. Royal Fusiliers. Apparently, the forward brigades (16th and 99th) had been 'making a marvellous defence'. Nonetheless, it was evident to the men on the ground that considerable confusion and misunderstanding prevailed. This was not helped when company commanders were given map references for complicated trench systems in the dark. These were often composed of positions that were not easily defensible in the first place. After initial reverses, many of them 'consisted of an untraversed and painfully broad and shallow communication trench'. The withdrawals that then took place were equally demoralising. Units left booby traps and destroyed all that they left behind. Yet, manoeuvring dead pack horses to obstruct dugouts must not have been a pleasant experience, while relinquishing ground was undoubtedly demoralising.[69]

In a few units, however, close contact with the enemy engendered some sense of achievement. The opportunity to inflict heavy losses on the Germans helped to soften the blow caused by the loss of comrades and tactical reverses.[70] Nevertheless, the experience was hugely tiring, and (at least in the Ox and Bucks) the men needed nearly five days to recover. The 23rd Bn. Royal Fusiliers missed the initial blow on the British line on 30 November but arrived on 2 December and successfully counterattacked against the enemy before (to the men's 'great disappointment') retiring a few days later because of enemy successes elsewhere.[71] The soldiers of this battalion were similarly 'exhausted from the extremely heavy calls that had been made on them' but recovered after a few days' rest. Apparently, it was 'incredible ... how good their spirits were'.[72] Aware that 'they had killed large numbers of Germans', the unit were told they had 'successfully defeated a German attack which ...

---

[67] Stone, *A History of the 22nd*, p. 57.
[68] TNA WO 95/1348/5: 2nd Bn. Oxfordshire and Buckinghamshire LI, 30 November–1 December.
[69] Ibid., 5 December.
[70] Ibid., 6 December.
[71] F.W. Ward, *The 23rd (Service) Battalion Royal Fusiliers (First Sportsman's): A Record of its Services in the Great War, 1914-1919* (London, 1920), pp. 57-58.
[72] Ibid., pp. 5-6.

would have been a great disaster for the British'. Their unit history proudly reported that they had defeated six attacks on their line but regretted that their withdrawal had been necessary to escape the salient that had been created when the units on their flanks fell back.[73]

Nevertheless, it appears that such a sentiment was limited. The trauma of combat accompanied a feeling that these reverses revealed the enemy's ability to successfully push the BEF backwards. The confidence that had characterised the early months of 1917 had been replaced by a sense that the BEF had not quite got the hang of things. Battle, it seemed, offered little chance of bringing about peace. These events also reveal further layers in soldiers' sensemaking. The Cambrai Enquiry, undertaken at the behest of the British government, concluded that the German counterattack had achieved success for several reasons:

1. The outpost line had been taken by surprise.
2. Warnings from senior commanders had gone unheeded.
3. Aerial reconnaissance had been poor after 30 November.
4. Artillery had been lacking on the front of 55th Division.
5. The boundaries between different corps and divisions were inadequately understood.
6. Low-flying hostile aircraft had plagued the defenders.
7. There was a lack of defensive positions prepared in depth.
8. Soldiers had a weak understanding of the doctrine of defensive battles.
9. The propagation of rumour in the frontlines.[74]

This paints a picture of a complex of causation: an acute crisis perpetuated by a series of overlapping issues – some institutional, some psychological. The adjutant of the 2nd Ox and Bucks would have agreed with this. Despite believing his battalion had performed well, he pointed to the confusion once the lines became more fluid. Unit commanders entered the unknown and complicated trench systems without the opportunity for previous reconnaissance. He added that 'fiction sometimes becomes history' and that confusion had created rumours that became a part of official accounts.[75] Elsewhere, it was agreed that 'the gallantry of the young soldiers' had been 'conspicuous ... when all was going well with them, but the amount of discipline they had imbibed could not stand the ordeal of the heavy massed attacks on the 30th November'.[76]

---

[73] Ibid., p. 6.
[74] TNA WO 158/53: Cambrai Enquiry. File. No. 1, p. 7.
[75] TNA WO 95/1348/5: 2nd Bn. Oxfordshire and Buckinghamshire LI, 30 November 1917.
[76] TNA CAB 24/37/98: Secret G.T. 3198. War Cabinet, Cambrai Inquiry, Appendix B.i – Report by Third Army Commander.

537 LES RUINES DE LA GRANDE GUERRE. — Cambrai. — Patrouille « of the North Lancers dans la Ville. — Great War Ruins. — Cambrai. — Patrol of the North Lancers in the town. — LL.

Figure 6.2 Postcard of British troops patrolling the town of Cambrai after the fighting in November–December 1917.

Source: Photo12/Universal Images Group via Getty Images.

A variety of explanations were proffered for the reverses at Cambrai. Problems with (or an absence of) *esprit de corps* were pointed to, especially in the machine-gun batteries that reportedly failed to perform their duties effectively.[77] Importantly, 'lack of training and understanding on [the] part of subordinate and lower commanders regarding [the] application of defence in depth' had undermined defensive tactics and caused confusion.[78] It was, in this instance, their inability to respond to acute crises (rather than the corrosive impact of chronic crises) that played the most important part in military failure. This was in part a product of 'want of supervision on the part of higher commanders', which was 'essential to produce, enforce and maintain the doctrines which are to bear fruit when the test of battle ensues'.[79] It would, however, seem unfair to place blame solely at their door. They had only recently been tasked with training their men for battles of this character (and left with limited resources to do so by the government). What is more, the dissemination of doctrine takes time, which, at this stage of the war, was at a premium. Nevertheless, these warnings should certainly have given the High

[77] Haig's Diary, 19 December 1917. Sheffield and Bourne, *Douglas Haig: War Diaries and Letters*, p. 360.
[78] TNA WO 158/53: Cambrai Enquiry. File. No. 1, pp. 10–11.
[79] Ibid.

Command some food for thought and foreshadowed the events of a few months later. It appeared to many 'that the initiative has passed from the Allies to the enemy'.[80]

****

Winter 1917–1918

Exhaustion and Reorganisation

As winter's grip tightened over France and Flanders, the year's campaigning came to an ignominious end. The war entered its fifth year with little prospect of peace. The fighting at Ypres and Cambrai offered little hope of that. German successes in the East also promised that it would be a difficult year on the Western Front as enemy forces began arriving there. As such, it was decided that the British and French would shift to the defensive. This required an immense amount of work at a time where the Allies lacked time, manpower, and resources. Rightly or wrongly, the British government was holding back reserves of men and in January 1918 the BEF contained 100,000 fewer men than it had a year previously.[81] Worse still, the changes in tactical doctrine necessitated intensive construction work to the detriment of rest and training.

There was little time to build up the competencies required to respond to another acute crisis such as Cambrai. Winter was a busy time. There was also increasing scepticism about the ability of Allied leaders (political and military) to bring the war to a victorious conclusion. Reports in the home press appear to have continue to play a significant role in framing the war pessimistically. Not without reason, the 'L[loyd] G[eorge] Press' (as Haig called it) had 'commenced their attack' on the Field Marshal and others in the field. These papers also included news of strikes and food shortages at home. This worried Haig, who was more aware than ever that his army's morale was 'a very delicate plant'.[82]

As leave in the BEF was extended and more emphasis was put on recreation, further evidence emerged that morale was suffering. Day trips to Achiet le Grand and Amiens had been organised in February as an opportunity for rest and recuperation. Yet, the initiative lasted little more than four days. Men had been 'absenting themselves' while away and the 10th Bn. Royal Warwickshire Regiment cancelled all leave to Amiens on 21 February.[83] The

---

[80] TNA WO 158/20: General Staff Notes on Operations. No. 146.
[81] D.R. Woodward, 'Did Lloyd George Starve the British Army of Men Prior to the German Offensive of 21 March 1918?', *The Historical Journal*, Vol. 27, No. 1 (1984), pp. 241–252.
[82] Haig's Diary, 26 December 1917. Sheffield and Bourne, *Douglas Haig: War Diaries and Letters*, p. 362.
[83] TNA WO 95/2085/3: 10th Bn, Royal Warwickshire Regiment, 17 and 21 February 1918.

reasons for this were multilayered, but the experiences of winter played a significant part. Preparations for defence in depth (and the hard work accompanying this) coalesced with manpower shortages. An already tired and demoralised army became even more exhausted.

Military progress in 1917 had indicated that the war was far from being won and the changes that British soldiers witnessed over the winter provided a robust indication that battle was no longer a vehicle for peace. At Doullens in December 1917, Haig informed his army commanders that the BEF and her allies would be pursuing a defensive strategy in 1918.[84] The strategic situation left the British and French confronted by an uncomfortable reality. Lord French (the erstwhile commander of the BEF) and Sir Henry Wilson reported in October 1917 that '[i]t is not considered possible for the Allies under existing conditions to defeat the German arms to such an extent as would compel or induce the enemy to agree to our terms of peace'.[85] They (and others) advised that the best course of action was to wait for the United States to deploy large numbers of men, avoid offensive action in France and Flanders, focus on knocking one of Germany's weaker allies out of the war, and organise a Supreme War Council.[86]

Even in the higher echelons of the British Army, there was a sense that the war might have entered a state of stalemate. It is unsurprising that such perceptions filtered down the ranks. Despite German successes elsewhere in the world, however, there was little fear that Britain itself was threatened. In fact, it was generally 'assumed that the United Kingdom was safe from all serious invasion'.[87] Of course, the safety of France was less certain. Yet, even here, it was felt that France was safe so long as the Allies were able to maintain their numbers on the Western Front, bolster their supply of equipment, and develop a co-ordinated system of defence. Such deliberations would have influenced soldiers as they were echoed in newspapers, strategic communiqués, and directives and orders.[88] It helps to explain why soldiers began framing the war as a 'draw'.[89] Perhaps the most significant indicators – at least for the infantrymen – would have been the shift to the defensive. As units prepared for a campaign on the back foot, it would have been very hard to see any prospect of victorious peace.

---

[84] TNA WO 95/521/5: Operations Fifth Army, March 1918, p. 18.
[85] TNA WO 158/46: Reports by Lord French and Lt. Gen. Sir H. Wilson to War Cabinet on Present Situation and our Future Military Policy with Remarks – D.A.D. 702 to CIGS, p. 1.
[86] Ibid.
[87] TNA WO 158/57/29: Joint Note No. 12. Joint Note to the Supreme War Council by its Military Representatives. 1918 Campaign. Paragraph 3.
[88] Ibid. Paragraph 4.
[89] 'The Dear Old Regiment at Play: From Horton to Hartley – A Tale of Travel', *The Dear Old Regiment* (1 December 1917), p. 3.

Compounding this, it was agreed that the BEF would shoulder a greater burden for the defence of the Allied line. A few days before the new year, Fifth Army was notified that their responsibilities were about to increase substantially as they relieved the French Third Army between Urvilles and Barisis (south of the river Oise).[90] Stretched thin, the Fifth Army eventually held forty-two miles of front with eleven divisions in the line and only three divisions each of infantry and cavalry in reserve.[91] These soldiers arrived in unfamiliar land. The trenches had foreign names, and the villages bore little imprint of the British Army. In many places, the frontlines were in a very poor state of repair, leaving little time for these areas to be converted into zones that bore any resemblance to the doctrine of defence in depth. In other sectors, too, the new defensive works had to be constructed in the sections of the old Hindenburg Line. The landscape here also held few of the reference points found in older parts of the British line. The old enemy trench lines were built to face in a different direction, which created other challenges for the troops.

The men of the Fifth Army, on whom much of the German offensive would fall in March 1918, were most adversely affected. While every unit in the BEF faced a difficult winter, they found that the 'area taken over by the army was very inadequately organised for defence' and required a more thorough reorganisation. Every available man was employed constructing defences, and the lack of reserves meant that they 'had fewer opportunities for training than the rest of the B.E.F.'.[92] Consequently, there was little time to *learn* the new doctrine, let alone integrate new drafts.[93]

Wherever an infantryman found himself, the work was immense. The BEF's tactics required the construction of new trench lines and strong points. There were to be three 'belts' comprised of 'Forward', 'Battle', and 'Rear' zones 'organised in depth and designed for defence by fire'.[94] In the former, units were to be deployed in three lines, which were not contiguous and were instead composed of a series of strong points and redoubts. The 'garrisons' occupying each position would support one another but primarily fought as 'small detached groups' whose duty was to guard against surprise and destroy the cohesion of an enemy attack. The Battle Zone was where the 'main defensive battle' would take place. It was also 'organised in successive lines' with 'defended localities sited to take full advantage of the tactical advantages offered by the ground'. The bulk of the artillery was situated here, and it ranged in depth from one thousand to three thousand yards. In some

---

[90] TNA WO 158/51: Extension of Line held by British Army on Western Front. Correspondence re.
[91] TNA WO 95/521/5: Operations Fifth Army, March 1918, p. 8.
[92] Ibid., pp. 8–9.
[93] Ibid., p. 5.
[94] Ibid., p 18.

locations, it touched the forward zone while at others a 'No Man's Land' of between one and two thousand yards separated them. Lastly, the Rear Zone was organised in a similar manner to the Battle Zone with barbed wire being installed in specific localities that were prepared for defence.

Unfortunately, the weather – especially regular thaws – made this preparatory work hard. It 'was enough to dishearten anybody'.[95] Had they worked every hour of the day, it was probably an impossible task and large sections of the defences were left incomplete. Parts of the line were little more than a physical blueprint with waist-deep trenches in which it would be difficult to put up an effective defence.[96] On the eve of the German offensives, the Rear Zone had several important localities wired, but much of it consisted of trenches only a few inches deep. Even with all resources devoted to the preparation of the British line, the 'time and labour were insufficient'. Later, military leaders admitted that the demanding work schedule had diminished the efficiency of the BEF as the 'remodelling [of] the defensive system in accordance with the new doctrine of defence in depth' left little time for anything else – training or recreation.[97]

This was particularly significant given the heavy casualties suffered by many battalions during 1917. Table 6.3 shows the average casualties across twelve infantry battalions in the BEF. The typical size of a battalion was around one thousand men (including approximately thirty officers), though this figure was often much lower. Some had suffered worse than others. The 2nd Bn. Devonshire Regiment lost 531 men killed, wounded, or missing between July and December 1917, while the 2/2nd Bn. London Regiment lost 565 men, and the 11th Bn. Royal Fusiliers (who witnessed some of the clearest cases of ill-discipline) had the awful casualty bill of 611. There was an average wastage of 379. Of course, not every unit had been through the meat grinder at Passchendaele. The 2nd Bn. Ox and Bucks had avoided the worst fighting around Ypres. In 1917, they were engaged at Bapaume, Arras, Vimy, Scarpe, Arleux, and Cambrai – but they escaped the most intense battles below Passchendaele Ridge.[98] While other battalions suffered during August's bloody battles, they faced an 'extraordinarily quiet' enemy.[99] Unlike other units, during October and November they continued to benefit from some sophisticated recreation programmes.[100] Despite their presence at the Battle of

---

[95] TNA WO 95/1484/5: 1st Bn. Royal Warwickshire Regiment, Letter: 4th Division from Lt. Col., General Staff, to units 4th Division, 6 February 1918.
[96] Chidgey, *Black Square Memories*, p. 166.
[97] TNA WO 95/521/5: Operations Fifth Army, March 1918, p. 5.
[98] S. Harris, *History of the 43rd and 52nd (Oxfordshire and Buckinghamshire) Light Infantry in the Great War 1914–1918*, Vol. II (King's Lynn, 2012), pp. 418–527.
[99] TNA WO 95/1348/5: 2nd Bn. Ox and Bucks, 20 August 1917.
[100] Ibid., esp. 13, 17, and 23 October.

Table 6.3 *Average casualties (killed, wounded, gassed, and missing) in twelve battalions of the BEF, July–December 1917*

	OR wounded	OR killed	OR missing	Officers wounded	Officers killed	Officers missing	Total
Jul-17	31	6	4	2	0	0	43
Aug-17	87	10	8	2	1	1	109
Sep-17	52	12	3	2	1	0	70
Oct-17	64	12	19	2	1	0	98
Nov-17	20	5	1	1	0	0	27
Dec-17	28	7	1	2	0	0	38
Total	**280**	**49**	**35**	**11**	**3**	**1**	**379**

Cambrai, their casualties during the second half of 1917 were relatively low and they suffered no more than thirty-one in any single month between June 1917 and February 1918.[101] Perhaps it was because of such differences that some battalions entered the new year 'in fine fettle'. However, even if their morale had suffered less than others, they too would face 'a most disastrous blow' in March.[102]

Many battalions were populated by fresh drafts, but even veteran soldiers and commanders had little opportunity to learn new defensive methods (or, indeed, adapt to the changes in the structure of brigades and divisions). A swathe of new men (often conscripts) joined units over the winter and early spring. The 2nd Bn. Devonshire Regiment received drafts of around 390 men in September 1917, February 1918, and May 1918. It would be hard for the character of a unit not to change in such circumstances. A total of 428 new men arrived in the 2nd Bn. Ox and Bucks in February 1918, while the 10th Royal Warwickshire Regiment received 457 new members. Elsewhere, the 2/4th Bn. Ox and Bucks and 2/6th Bn. Manchester Regiment each had to integrate 300 rank and file. Yet, there appears to have been some attempt to reunite returning soldiers with their old battalions. Before February 1918, over 45 per cent of other rank drafts and 30 per cent of the officer drafts arriving in the 10th Bn. Royal Warwickshire Regiment were *re-joining* the unit – though it is questionable whether it was recognisable after losses in the intervening period (see Tables 6.4 and 6.5).[103]

---

[101] Ibid., June 1917–February 1918.
[102] Chidgey, *Black Square Memories*, p. 165.
[103] TNA WO 95/2085/3: 10th Bn. Royal Warwickshire Regiment, July 1917–January 1918. The proportion of returning officers in the 2nd Bn. Ox and Bucks (TNA WO 95/1348/5) was 35 per cent in the same period.

Table 6.4 *Average (mean) OR reinforcements across twelve battalions of the BEF, July 1917 through June 1918*

	Average OR reinforcements
Jul-17	62
Aug-17	142
Sep-17	105
Oct-17	60
Nov-17	18
Dec-17	21
Jan-18	75
Feb-18	230
Mar-18	104
Apr-18	248
May-18	101
Jun-18	150

Table 6.5 *Average (mean) officer reinforcements across twelve battalions of the BEF, July 1917 through June 1918*

	Average officer reinforcements
Jul-17	4
Aug-17	4
Sep-17	5
Oct-17	6
Nov-17	2
Dec-17	2
Jan-18	5
Feb-18	13
Mar-18	1
Apr-18	9
May-18	9
Jun-18	7

The reorganisation of the BEF compounded the negative indicators feeding soldiers' sensemaking. In the new year, one in four battalions ceased to exist and their men supplemented other units. This produced problems for command and control, but from the perspective of the infantrymen it was the impact on corporate identity that mattered most. This had been nurtured so carefully (and often at great cost). Even at this stage of the war, units worked hard to emphasise their *esprit de corps*. On leaving the 22nd Bn. Royal Fusiliers towards the end of 1917, Colonel Baker explained (in his parting speech to the regiment) that 'we owe [it] to our gallant comrades who gave their lives ... for their country [and...] for the glory of the Regiment' to add 'fresh laurels to our already glorious regiment'. It seems telling, though, that he had to remind the men that 'our job is to strafe Germans and not each other' since '[a]n unhappy man can't fight, and if a Regiment is full of imaginary grievances its fighting spirit disappears'.[104] When disbanded, a sense of 'doom' and 'feverish melancholy' fell over the officers of the battalion while other members of the Brigade (the 99th) expressed their 'deep regret' at their loss.[105]

Importantly, the men were allocated to 'sister' battalions (fifteen officers and 309 other ranks to the 23rd Bn. and a further fourteen commissioned and 274 non-commissioned men to the 24th Bn. Royal Fusiliers).[106] While they would 'never recapture the glories of old comradeship', they 'were received with the utmost consideration'.[107] Most men were sent to units in the same regiment, and they were often allowed to serve in the same companies once they arrived there. The use of the regimental system helped to maintain some sense of *esprit de corps*, making the process less painful than it might have been (see Table 6.6). Some were welcomed as 'part and parcel of us' and 'old friends'. They were 'all the same Regiment' after all.[108] The structure of soldiers' social groups was impacted less negatively than could have been the case. Nonetheless, such a significant policy change was not a positive indicator that the war was progressing towards victory.

---

[104] Stone, *A History of the 22nd*, pp. 54–55.
[105] Ibid., p. 60.
[106] Ibid., pp. 60–61.
[107] Ibid., p. 62.
[108] TNA WO 95/2339/1: 16th Bn. Manchester Regiment, Appendix II: The Commanding Officer's Address to 19th Bn. On 7.2.18.

Table 6.6 *Origin of drafts arriving during the reorganisation of the BEF in late January/early February 1917*

Receiving unit	OR	Officers	Draft origin(s)
2/2nd London Regiment (RF)	335	13	2/1st Bn. London Regiment (RF)
2/5th Bn. Manchester Regiment	184	10	2/8th Bn. Manchester Regiment
16th Bn. Manchester Regiment	280	13	19th Bn. Manchester Regiment
2nd Bn. Ox and Bucks LI	137	7	6th Bn. Ox and Bucks LI
2/4th Bn. Ox and Bucks LI	300	13	6th Bn. Ox and Bucks LI
5th Bn. Ox and Bucks LI	200	8	6th Bn. Ox and Bucks LI; Labour Company
4th Bn. Royal Fusiliers	232	15	1st Honourable Artillery Company; 5th Bn. Royal Fusiliers; 6th Bn. Royal Fusiliers; 8th Bn. Royal Fusiliers; 14th Bn. Royal Fusiliers; 20th Bn. Royal Fusiliers; 51st Training Reserve.
11th Bn. Royal Fusiliers	220	7	12th Bn. Royal Fusiliers
1st Bn. Royal Warwickshire Regiment	250	8	11th Bn. Royal Warwickshire Regiment
2/6th Royal Warwickshire Regiment	350	17	2/5th Royal Warwickshire Regiment
10th Bn. Royal Warwickshire Regiment	307	10	11th Bn. Royal Warwickshire Regiment

****

Winter Training

Failure to Prepare for Acute Crisis

> The failure of the BEF to introduce training programmes that prepared men for a defensive battle was the product of competing pressures. The manpower crisis, the logistical pressures associated with preparing the British defensive positions, not to mention the extension of the BEF's line, meant that there was little time to introduce new tactics.

Training failed to equip units with skills and knowledge needed to respond to the German offensives. If training in early 1917 had offered false hope, the programmes (where there was time for them) later in the year were bad omens and left men poorly prepared for future trials. Training is a central feature of morale. It helps men to learn their trade, creates new frames of reference that help them to make sense of war, and, significantly, provides them with the necessary skills and knowledge to respond to acute crises during battle. Reactions should be reduced to reflexes.

There are instances in which the record highlights how effective instruction helped men to survive. For example, earlier in 1917, the 2nd Bn. Ox and Bucks had relieved the 14th Bn. Royal Fusiliers in a very active sector and came under sustained gas bombardment. Their commanding officer believed that B Company would have suffered a casualty rate as high as 85 per cent had it not been for the quality of their gas drills before deployment. Where men did succumb to the gas, it was generally felt that 'had the men been better trained they would not have been effected'.[109] Despite evidence that deficiencies in training contributed to the disaster at Cambrai, the manpower and logistical demands of winter 1917–1918 left little time for the training of men in defensive tactics or the dissemination of new doctrine.

The training that men received did little to prepare them for the the battles to come. Where training occurred, it often provided infantrymen with the wrong tools (and continued to focus on the offensive). Alternatively, instruction in defensive tactics indicated that battle no longer offered a pathway to victory. For the most part, programmes reveal the inadequacy of training in the winter of 1917–1918. The four hours of classes put on for the men of 1st Bn. Royal Warwickshire Regiment each morning in December focused on physical training, bayonet fighting, section and platoon drill, and musketry. On some days, they practised open and trench warfare and continued to rehearse the various phases of attack rather than defence.[110] In the 11th Bn. Royal Fusiliers, the end of the year found the companies on ranges and taking part in shooting competitions. Elsewhere, a keynote lecture during January showed just how little impetus was put on educating men on the defensive (even as they were digging defensive lines). The areas of particular attention were:

(a) Training in discipline
(b) Training of section and platoon commanders, who must be forced to actually perform the executive
(c) Development of smartness and improvement in the turn out

---

[109] TNA WO 95/1348/5: 2nd Bn. Oxfordshire and Buckinghamshire LI, 12 June 1917.
[110] TNA WO 95/1484/5: 1st Bn. Royal Warwickshire Regiment, Appendix: Training Programme from 3rd to 8th December 1917.

(d) Obtaining men's closest attention, by enforcing stricter discipline, so as to prepare their minds to receive advanced instruction in the field
(e) Raising the morale of the troops by 'keen' games in the afternoons, amusements in the evening[111]

The desire to increase the morale of their men seems telling and speaks to the compound effects of the war's chronic crises. The focus on men's 'self-respect and pride' and on educating platoon commanders 'to take greater interest and pride in their platoons' suggests that some battalions were trying to rehabilitate their men.[112] It may be that the low levels of morale in the BEF (as well as the more practical concerns already discussed) diverted attention away from the practical preparation of men for battle.

Training generally played second fiddle to the other priorities. Even though the British Army had been promoting a 'general policy of training' since June 1917, any quality control procedures were difficult to implement and the time spent on training varied amongst units. Between July through November 1917, units devoted an average of 11.35 days to instruction.[113] In battalions preparing for battle, this rose as high as 16.40 days per month. Yet, during wintertime (December 1917 through March 1918), this decreased to 7.41 days. In several battalions, there were as few as five to six days each month devoted to training, which would have been little enough time to integrate new drafts, let alone to learn new tactical doctrine. Even in battalions that devoted more time to training, there was reduced capacity. The 11th Bn. Royal Fusiliers spent around thirteen days per month training (down from sixteen days in preceding months).[114] Other units' training regimes collapsed. The 16th Bn. Manchester Regiment's recorded training time reduced dramatically from 12.80 days per month in July–November to 3.75 days between December and March.[115] The 2/6th Bn. Royal Warwickshire Regiment's time descreased from some 14.20 days to only five.[116] Of thirteen battalions studied here, only one unit (the 8th Bn. Border Regiment) increased the time they devoted to training and only very marginally (8.60 days to 9.30).[117] Three others – the 1st Bn. Royal Warwickshire Regiment, 2nd Bn. Devonshire Regiment, and 4th Bn. Royal Fusiliers – managed to maintain their training days (a reduction of around one

---

[111] TNA WO 95/2045/1: 11th Bn. Royal Fusiliers, Appendix: Remarks – The Keynote of this Series of Training, January 1918, p. 126.
[112] Ibid.
[113] Average (mean) taken from an analysis of the daily routine of thirteen battalions in the BEF.
[114] TNA WO 95/2045/1: 11th Bn. Royal Fusiliers, December 1917–March 1918.
[115] TNA WO 95/2339/1: 16th Bn. Manchester Regiment, July 1917–March 1918.
[116] TNA WO 95/3056/2: 2/6th Bn. Royal Warwickshire Regiment, July 1917–March 1918.
[117] TNA WO 95/2251/3: 8th Bn. Border Regiment, July 1917–March 1918.

day).[118] It is striking that the latter were regular units. Other regular battalions also saw less of a stark change but still spent less time training.

What military instruction that took place appears to have prepared men for the wrong kind of warfare. Battalions continued to practice attacks in the final months of 1917: attacks at dawn, night concentration, and similar initiatives. In January 1918, the 8th Bn. Border Regiment continued rehearsing attacks on pillboxes amidst some 'wild' snowstorms.[119] Little of the training was concerned with defence in depth. On 18 January 1918, the 5th Infantry Brigade's exercises continued to focus on the offensive. The major lessons learned that day were to avoid consolidating positions on a forward slope and to ensure that flanks did not hang back during an advance. Where defence in depth was considered, it was in relation to consolidating gains made *during* an attack.[120]

In some cases, there was a shift to training that concentrated on the defence of outpost lines. Even where men did spend some time practising defensive tactics, it sometimes did little to increase their confidence and exposed troubling inefficiencies. Earlier, in November 1917, the 2nd Bn. Ox and Bucks had performed in a 'pitiable' manner during manoeuvres and displayed a 'lamentable ignorance of the subject of protection'. Ominously, A Company's outpost line had been surprised by the 'attacker' and a whole platoon was captured.[121] This was a battalion that had escaped relatively lightly (with regard to casualties) during 1917 and still entered 1918 struggling to adapt.

Nevertheless, it is possible that these lessons served the battalion well. During the spring offensives, their unit history reported that it was 'only the judgement and good learning of the captains [that] saved the companies'.[122] The problem was, though, that many other battalions were not learning these lessons. It is significant, then, that historians have often pointed to the improper understanding of defence in depth as the cause of the capitulations on 30 November 1917 and after 21 March 1918.[123] Deficiencies in training were exposed during the offensives. Defence on depth relied on several things: the initiative of local commanders who were often operating with little or no oversight *and* the ability of units to operate in conjunction with one another. The BEF was poorly prepared in both regards.

****

---

[118] TNA WO 95/1484/5: 1st Bn. Royal Warwickshire Regiment, July 1917–March 1918; WO 95/1712: 2nd Bn Devonshire Regiment, July 1917–March 1918; WO 95/1431/3: 4th Bn. Royal Fusiliers, July 1917–March 1918.

[119] TNA WO 95/2251/3: 8th Bn. Border Regiment, 7-9 January 1918.

[120] TNA WO 95/1348/5: 2nd Bn. Ox and Bucks, 18 January 1918.

[121] Ibid. 21–22 November 1917. Also 22 and 29 October 1917.

[122] Lt. Col. R.B. Crosse, *A Short History of the Oxfordshire and Buckinghamshire Light Infantry, 1741-1922* (Aldershot, 1925), p. 34.

[123] Samuels, *Command and Control*, pp. 214–221. For failures of High Command (especially Generals Gough and Byng) after 21 March, see Travers, *How the War was Won*, p. 90.

The German Offensives

Acute Crisis and Shifting Realities

It was clear that a German offensive was imminent. A sense of impending doom spread across the ranks of the BEF as spring approached. So, on the morning of the 21 March, when an immense German bombardment fell on the British line it was a shock, but not necessarily a surprise. German storm troopers burst through the fog and a period of crisis ensued. Operation Michael fell on the British Fifth and Third Armies and penetrated their lines to a depth of forty miles before it was called off on 5 April. The BEF lost over 170,000 men.[124] Next, between 9 and 29 April, the German offensives shifted to Flanders in the north. The British First Army met these attacks and they, too, were pushed back over nine miles with the BEF losing a further 80,000 men or more.[125] In both cases, however, the Germans failed to achieve their strategic objectives. From late April onwards, the enemy focused their attention on French positions along the Aisne (though these were also held by some tired British divisions) as they attempted to split the Allied line. By the summer it became increasingly clear that Germany's gamble had failed.

Historians have posited a variety of causes for the retreats along the British line: poor morale, the weather, sophisticated German tactics, and an array of other factors have been highlighted. In truth, it was a complex of causation made worse by the troops' poor training. Yet, despite the confusion and reverses, these events transformed soldiers' sensemaking. Even in retreat, the semi-open warfare suggested that battle held opportunities and renewed men's faith in the possibility (and necessity) of victorious peace.[126]

The German offensives did not come out of the blue. One battalion heard a rumour in early February that reconnaissance flights over the enemy lines had revealed 'a large number of new bridges over the St. Quentin canal opposite our Corps front'.[127] Rumours such as this fed soldiers' sensemaking. So, by the beginning of March, there was almost universal 'apprehension as to his [the enemy's] hostile intentions'. Early mornings were marked by daily artillery bombardments designed to break up German assembly positions. In this atmosphere of anxiety, units' understanding of the unfolding situation was

---

[124] J.E. Edmonds, *History of the Great War Based on Official Documents. Military Operations France and Belgium, 1918 March–April: Continuation of the German Offensives* (London, 1937), p. 490.
[125] Ibid., pp. 482–483.
[126] Lloyd, *The Western Front*, esp. chapter 20; Watson, *Enduring the Great War*, pp. 172–183; Hart, *1918*, esp. chapters 3–8; Middlebrook, *The Kaiser's Battle*; Macdonald, *To the Last Man*.
[127] Chidgey, *Black Square Memories*, pp. 168–169.

Figure 6.3 A Mark IV female tank passing through Péronne, 23 March 1918. An abandoned BEF canteen and smoke from burning stores can be seen in the background.

Source: 2nd Lt. T K Aitken/Imperial War Museums via Getty Images.

confused by changes in policy. In early March, some battalions reported a further shift in advice and tactics. In a few sectors, it was only at this stage that it was 'established [that the frontlines would be] in the nature of an outpost line', and it appeared to some as though 'clear arrangements [were being] made for withdrawal'.[128] Expectations of retreat were being set in the minds of the troops and, alongside this, some units were increasingly concerned that the British artillery could not be relied upon. The adjutant of the 2nd Bn. Ox and Bucks noted that they had been firing short so often that his commanding officer felt there had been 'a considerable decrease in the amount of support one might look for' from the Royal Artillery and trench mortars.[129]

One officer described the early days of the German offensives as ones of 'ignorance and blindness'.[130] Several factors conspired to produce chaos. The fog appears in many narratives. It covered the enemy advance, and many units were shocked by the rapidity with which German troops reached their

---

[128] TNA WO 95/1348/5: 2nd Bn. Oxfordshire and Buckinghamshire LI, 5–11 March 1918.
[129] Ibid.
[130] IWM Documents.17029: Capt. A.J. Lord, Letter to Father 1 April 1918; SOFO Box 16 Item 29: Lt. J.E.H. Neville, Diary 23 March 1918.

positions and fell back accordingly. As a battalion commander explained, 'the natural production of mist coincided with the launching of a great attack in which many men + munitions of war were mist, also many Huns were mist: The greatest chaos was produced in the mist'.[131] This was, though, also a product of poor preparation, and to some degree reflected soldiers' perceptions of their own role and duty. After all, limited withdrawals were an important part of flexible defence in depth but only when they occurred in conjunction with flanking units. Unfortunately, the lack of focused training (especially manoeuvres including multiple units) meant that this feature of the defensive strategy was improperly understood and created a chain reaction. Many units reported that their right or left flank had been left 'in the air'. German tactics were also successful. Many parts of the line had been 'driven right in'. Accordingly, in some sectors it appeared as though British divisions had simply melted away.[132]

Total sacrifice was not a part of the rank and file's perception of duty, so, when facing death, retreat or surrender were the rational choices. In many cases, withdrawals were also made necessary by the rapid enemy advance, which allowed machine guns to cut off defenders before they had an opportunity to respond.[133] Command and control were also lacking, with many commanding officers explaining that they were merely following orders when they retired. This, of course, is in part explained by a desire to absolve themselves of blame, but it also suggests that brigade and divisional commanders may have also only loosely understood the defensive tactics themselves.[134]

For the most part, however, the collapse of communications meant these were decisions taken by junior officers in the heat of the moment. As such, it is worth returning to the concept of cosmology episodes. The fighting after 21 March (and at Cambrai, albeit on a smaller scale) caused a 'sudden loss of meaning' created by a 'fundamental surprise'. Some soldiers feared that there was 'nothing' that could stop the German advance.[135] It was made worse by men's training, which left them with a set of default reactions that proved inadequate. The desire to retreat (or surrender) was, therefore, a response to acute crisis – and often an unconscious one. After 21 March, events were for the most part dictated by soldiers' (and the military's) ability to respond rather

---

[131] NAM 1992-04-57-16-5: Lt. Col. J.E. Smart, Field Message Book, Army Book 153.
[132] TNA WO 95/1484/5: 1st Bn. Royal Warwickshire Regiment, Narrative of Operations on 28th March 1918; TNA WO 95/2045/1: 11th Bn. Royal Fusiliers, 23 March 1918; TNA WO 95/3001/4: 2/2nd Bn. London Regiment, Message from BHQ Upstart to Brigade and Companies, 24 April 1918, To UPHILL S.186 8.35 a.m.
[133] TNA WO 95/2045/1: 11th Bn. Royal Fusiliers, 23 March 1918.
[134] TNA WO 95/2251/3: 8th Bn. Border Regiment, 21–22 and 26 March 1918.
[135] LIDDLE/WW1/GS/0137: Pte. O.G. Billingham, Diary 25 March 1918; IWM Documents.11976: Lt. Col. A.H. Cope, Diary 25, 27 and 29 March 1918; IWM Documents.11289: H.T. Madders, Diary 19 April and 29 May 1918.

than to endure. In many cases, withdrawal was probably a knee-jerk reaction. The foggy mornings played their part in helping to cover enemy movements, which caused some panic. Furthermore, as the frontlines became much more fluid, sunken roads and railway cuttings allowed the Germans to come up very close without revealing themselves. Enemy machine guns sometimes appeared suddenly and enfiladed British trenches causing 'very considerable trouble' and many casualties.[136]

Lt. Col. Arthur Stockdale Cope was disgusted when another battalion abandoned their rifles and stores before retreating.[137] Other diaries indicate that there was little choice but to retire, given the breakdown in command structures. Units relied on verbal orders and often responded to the local situation.[138] In some circumstances, withdrawal was unavoidable as panic spread in neighbouring battalions, or they withdrew without warning. There was widespread confusion, and this was evident in the driest of bureaucratic documents. One panicked message written by the BHQ of the 2/2nd Bn. London Regiment on 24 April revealed that the situation was often little better than 'obscure'.[139] More adequately trained and organised units (and defences) would have been better placed to respond proactively. At the very least, better knowledge of the defensive terrain (especially along the Fifth Army front) might have mitigated the impact of surprise.

Losses compounded the problems caused by inadequate training. The BEF was already hard-pressed before spring 1918. Enemy gas attacks sapped the strength of several battalions in the days before the offensive. Between 12 March and 21 March, 23rd Bn. Royal Fusiliers had lost eleven officers and 240 other ranks as gas casualties.[140] Units in the firing line witnessed heavy losses during the German offensives, which also points to deficiencies in training and gas drill within the battalion (see Tables 6.7 and 6.8). In March 1918, the 2/6th Bn. Royal Warwickshire Regiment suffered 457 other ranks casualties (wounded, killed, or missing) and lost sixteen officers, the 2/2nd Bn. London Regiment had a casualty bill of 650 men and twenty-one officers during the same month, and the 2nd Bn. Devonshire Regiment some

---

[136] TNA TNA WO 95/1348/5: 2nd Bn. Oxfordshire and Buckinghamshire LI, 23 March 1918. WO 161/100/400: POW Interviews, 245402 Sgt. Henry Ward; TNA WO 161/100/2336: POW Interviews, 75880 Pte. Edward Kierstenson; WO 161/100/1665-1666: POW Interviews, Ptes. 17025 W. Thomas and 12713 F. Spencer; TNA WO 161/100/1667-68: POW Interviews, Cpl. 20151 Ernest Jones 18/Field Ambulance R.A.M.C. and Pte. 20414 Frederick Leighton R.A.M.C.

[137] IWM Documents.11976: Lt. Col. A.H. Cope, Diary 24 March 1918.

[138] MR 2/17/57: 2nd Lt. F.T.K. Woodworth, Diary 26 March 1918; SOFO Box 16 Item 29: Lt. J.E.H. Neville, Diary 23 March 1918.

[139] TNA WO 95/3001/4: 2/2nd London Regt., April 1918 – Appendix I: Message to UPHILL S.186 8.35 a.m.

[140] Ward, *The 23rd (Service) Battalion Royal Fusiliers*, p. 61.

Table 6.7 Losses in five battalions in March 1918

Unit	OR wounded	OR killed	OR missing	Officer wounded	Officer killed	Officer missing	Total
Fifth Army							
2/4th Bn. Ox and Bucks LI	72	8	532	4	1	21	**638**
16th Bn. Manchester Regt.	8	0	593	6	1	18	**626**
Third Army							
2nd Bn. Ox and Bucks LI	179	29	45	4	4	2	**263**
4th Bn. Royal Fusiliers	142	26	25	10	3	0	**206**
1st Bn. Royal Warwickshire Regt.	64	7	0	3	2	0	**76**

Table 6.8 Losses in five battalions in April 1918

Unit	OR wounded	OR killed	OR missing	Officer wounded	Officer killed	Officer missing	Total
Fifth Army							
2/4th Ox and Bucks LI	127	23	11	7	2	0	**170**
16th Bn. Manchester Regt.	38	3	195	3	0	6	**245**
Third Army							
2nd Bn. Ox and Bucks LI	9	2	2	1	0	0	**14**
4th Bn. Royal Fusiliers	90	14	1	4	0	0	**109**
1st Bn. Royal Warwickshire Regt.	238	44	15	6	4	0	**307**

Table 6.9 *Officer casualties in the 8th Bn. Border Regiment, 21–22 March 1918.*
TNA WO 95/2251/3

Rank	Killed	Died of wounds	Wounded	Missing
Lt. Col.	0	0	0	0
Maj.	0	0	0	0
Capt.	1	0	1	1
Lt.	3	1	1	2
2nd Lt.	0	0	2	1

Table 6.10 *Officer casualties in the 8th Bn. Border Regiment, 10–19 April 1918.*
TNA WO 95/2251/3

Rank	Killed	Died of wounds	Wounded	Gassed	Wounded + missing	Unaccounted for
Lt. Col.	0	0	0	0	0	0
Maj.	0	0	1	0	0	0
Capt.	1	0	1	0	0	0
Lt.	1	0	0	0	0	1
2nd Lt.	1	0	3	0	1	6

304 rank and file alongside fourteen officers.[141] The number of soldiers reported missing speaks to endemic confusion, but losses were lower in units that had more time to react to events. However, even those units not in the frontlines lost heavily.[142] April saw other units suffer during the next phase of the offensive, and the 10th Bn. Royal Warwickshire Regiment lost close to 500 men.[143] Significantly, junior officers (who played an even more important role during the more open fighting) suffered particularly badly (see Tables 6.9, 6.10, and 6.11).

There was little respite as units were cycled in and out of the battles. Exhaustion and hunger became more pressing concerns for men on the ground than the strategic consequences of that day's action. Battalions were engaged in many more days of fighting than had previously been the norm. Between the emergence of static trench lines in 1914 and March 1918, it was

---

[141] TNA WO 95/3056/2: 2/6th Royal Warwickshire Regt, March 1918; TNA WO 95/3001/4: 2/2nd London Regt, March 1918; WO 95/1712: 2nd Bn. Devonshire Regt, March 1918.
[142] TNA WO 95/1348/5: 2nd Bn. Oxfordshire and Buckinghamshire LI, March 1918.
[143] TNA WO 95/2085/3: 10th Bn. Royal Warwickshire Regt, April 1918.

Table 6.11 *Casualties in the 8th Bn. Border Regiment, 27–31 May 1918. TNA WO 95/2251/3*

Rank	Killed	Wounded	Missing
Lt. Col.	0	0	0
Maj.	0	0	0
Capt.	0	0	1
Lt.	0	0	1
2nd Lt.	2	1	7
ORs	9	60	203

rare for units to face much more than two days of combat in any given month – after which they would move to quieter areas for recuperation. Yet, after March 1918, combat increased markedly. The twelve battalions studied here faced an average of 3.30 days of combat in March, a further two days in April, and then 0.90 in May.[144] The losses accompanying such intense fighting were traumatic. As well as mourning lost comrades, survivors found themselves shouldering an even greater burden. Companies and battalions were greatly reduced in strength, and there were desperate discussions in High Command and Whitehall about how to reorganise units.[145] By the end of April, the BEF had been forced to disband five divisions and four others were going to be reduced to cadre.[146] The loss of so many battalion and company leaders, experienced NCOs, and staff officers meant that there was a fear that the re-constitution of some divisions might prove impossible.[147]

It is unsurprising, then, that on the evening of 24 April, Haig was begging Ferdinand Foch (who was co-ordinating Allied forces by this stage) for reinforcements. The whole of III Corps was in the line except for one and a half British and two Australian brigades that had been held back for a counterattack on Villers Bretonneux. This corps (composed of the 8th, 18th, and 58th Divisions) had been fighting constantly since the opening of the enemy's most recent attack.[148] Many divisions existed in name only. At this and various other points brigades were formed into composite battalions. Where possible, however, the semblance of a battalion's integrity was maintained by grouping units as a single company (or companies) with their own

---

[144] These statistics were collated from across the twelve regiments studied elsewhere in this chapter.
[145] TNA WO 158/28/64: O.A.D. 822 Telegram 18 April 1918.
[146] TNA WO 158/28/81: O.A.D. 825/1 Haig to Foch 23 April 1918.
[147] TNA WO 1058/28/64: O.A.D. 822 Telegram 18 April 1918.
[148] TNA WO 158/28/110: O.A.D. 845 C-in-C British Armies to General-in-Chief Allied Forces 12 May 1918.

designation. The power of the regimental system was unshakeable and may have helped to protect some unit cohesion.[149]

Most divisions had 'suffered severely' and by May 'largely consist[ed] of young and inexperienced drafts'. Sixteen of the remaining forty-one British divisions had an average of 900 men per battalion with the remaining twenty-five having fewer than 900.[150] The German offensives had turned the whole of the British zone of operations into a 'battle front', and the BEF had a deficit of thirteen divisions. Casualties had led nine to be broken up, and another four were serving in French sectors.

These manpower problems meant that infantrymen were facing trials unlike anything since the earliest days of the war. The longer the offensives went on, the more tired the BEF's soldiers became. This and their exposure to the elements (not to mention the creeping spectre of influenza) does much to explain the much higher rates of sickness during this period.[151] Withdrawals often had to take place under the cover of darkness and thus interfered further with men's sleep. Exhausted and with bodies aching, they got what rest they could upon withdrawal from the line or while waiting for new orders.[152] The men's willingness to suffer this speaks volumes.

The already shaky system of defence collapsed as the BEF fell further and further back. Even battalions behind the lines were left unprepared for the rapidity of the German advance and lacked the tactical knowledge to respond effectively. The 23rd Bn. Royal Fusiliers were encamped near Équancourt when they saw the first indications of a breakthrough. Bullets began to fall in the camp like deadly metallic rain. The men were turned out and patrols sent forward to hold up the enemy advance. Yet, upon moving up the line, it transpired that the enemy had already established themselves there. They were able to beat back enemy attacks but, like many other battalions, found that their flanks were 'in the air' and had to retire.[153] In the days after, heavy German attacks forced the battalion into a rear-guard action and several night-time retirements towards the Ancre, eventually arriving on the old battlefields of 1916 around Beaumont Hamel. Along the way, it was clear to them, as it

---

[149] TNA WO 95/3144/6: 2/5th Bn. Manchester Regt., 26–31 March 1918; TNA WO 95/1348/5: 2nd Bn. Oxfordshire and Buckinghamshire LI, 1 April 1918; TNA WO 95/2251/3: 8th Bn. Border Regt., 16 April 1918; TNA WO 95/2085/3: 10th Bn. Royal Warwickshire Regt., 9 June 1918.

[150] TNA WO 158/28/110: O.A.D. 845 C-in-C British Armies to General-in-Chief Allied Forces 12 May 1918.

[151] TNA WO 95/1484/5: 1st Bn. Royal Warwickshire Regt, July 1917–June 1918. An average of 31.7 men went sick between July 1917 and February 1917, increasing to 86.5 between March and June 1918 (67 men in March; 96 in April; 108 in May; and 75 in June). More officers reported sick during this period, too.

[152] TNA WO 95/1348/5: 2nd Bn. Ox a, 29 March 1918; TNA WO 158/24: C-in-C British Armies and CIGS and Secretary of State, War Office – Correspondence and Signals, No. 333.

[153] Ward, *The 23rd (Service) Battalion Royal Fusiliers*, p. 58.

was to most British units, that they were inflicting very heavy casualties on their foes. Not only this, but as they fell further and further back, they began to traverse meaningful sights of collective memory: old battlefields, familiar trench networks and villages, and cemeteries filled with their dead forebears.

Despite the decline in morale before March 1918, there is little contemporary material that suggests that the reverses were primarily caused by a widespread unwillingness to fight or, by extension, poor morale. Douglas Haig – a commander not unknown for misplaced optimism – was unnerved by the speed of the British retreat and the possibility that the BEF might be cut off from the coast. So, on 11 April, fearing for the safety of Calais and Boulogne, he published his infamous Order of the Day. It read: 'Every position must be held to the last man: there must be no retirement. With our backs to the wall and believing in the justice of our cause each one of us must fight on to the end.' Yet, it appears that this may have come as a surprise to many of his subordinates. At the various HQs he visited during this time, he was met by a welcome confidence and energy. Where they were not caught by surprise, men had retreated while fighting. On 17 April, General Plumer, commander of the Second Army, reported that his 'troops have fought well and have held on to their positions and will, I am confident, continue to do so'.[154] Haig's diary referenced several now-lost censorship reports that painted a more positive picture than one might expect, given the circumstances. On 15 April, he noted that the 'Field Censor reports that judging from the letters written by the men, the moral of the troops is extremely good' and included two brief quotations: 'It can safely be said that it has never been higher' and 'As soon as the German offensive started, the tone of the letters improved; grousing ceased' to be 'replaced to a great extent by a confident tone'.[155] Censors were not blind to downturns in morale, as revealed in the reports from 1917.

Evidence elsewhere also suggests that far from being despondent, the survivors emerged from the fighting with a renewed sense of purpose. German interviews with captured British soldiers suggested that many continued to have confidence in Haig, Foch, and their own 'military prowess'. They were sure the BEF would emerge victorious in the end.[156] Despite the reverses, many men displayed a greater degree of optimism than some of their commanders could muster and seemed unaware of how serious the situation was.[157] It may be that their poor grasp of defensive tactics protected them

---

[154] TNA WO 158/28/63: Report Gen. Plumer, CO 2nd Army, 17 April 1918.
[155] Haig's Diary, 15 April 1918, Sheffield and Bourne, *Douglas Haig: War Diaries and Letters*, p. 404.
[156] Watson, *Enduring the Great War*, p. 182.
[157] IWM Documents.20770: A.L. Collis, Diary 21 March 1918; SOFO Box 16 Item 29: Lt. J.E.H. Neville, Diary 21 March 1918; LIDDLE/WW1/ADD/104: Pte. A.G. Old, Diary 29 March–25 April 1918.

from the true extent of the crisis. Yet, the fighting also offered them a welcome opportunity to strike back. Their enemy were visible and vulnerable to small arms fire and soldiers witnessed the casualties being inflicted first-hand. Furthermore, local counterattacks might have done little to delay the German offensive in the macro, but there were several limited but successful counterattacks that offered those involved an opportunity to gain credit for their regiment and to nurture some sense of agency.[158]

As in early 1917, it appeared that open warfare might have been restored. The focus on the tactical training of small units is likely to have underlined this (though war diaries suggest that much of this happened 'on the job').[159] Significantly, too, artillery's power was diluted by the flexibility of the fighting, which put a greater emphasis on the skills of the small unit.[160] The increasingly open character of the warfare signalled that a new reality had emerged.

The men perceived the offensives in a different way to their superiors. One article, found in the *Machine Gun Gazette*, described the enemy's gains in March as a 'pyrrhic march through the crater land of the Somme'. Battle was no longer a futile enterprise, and the author concluded that fighting had been a 'holocaust of human German sacrifice to the God of Battles for a temporary gain of devastated territory'.[161] This belief that the enemy's successes were only temporary can be found elsewhere. A poem, this time in the journal of the Royal Naval Division, was bitter that the Germans had pushed 'us where we were the year before'. Nevertheless, it concluded that their old billets, and '[t]he football pitch – *our* sacred reserve / Are Fritz's' but only 'for a week or two'.[162]

Such an impression would have been reinforced as men's sacrifices were acknowledged and celebrated by the Home Front. Haig's Special Orders of the Day highlighted the losses being inflicted on the enemy, and many also contained messages of goodwill from across the United Kingdom and British Empire.[163] In an army where good character and personal credit were central features of duty, this was significant. The continued bond

---

[158] TNA WO 95/1348/5: 2nd Bn. Oxfordshire and Buckinghamshire LI, 28 March 1918; IWM Documents.11976: Lt Col. A.H. Cope, Diary 22 March; NAM 1987-11-44: Arthur Hawtayne, 26 May–28 May 1918.
[159] Haig's Diary, 17 May 1918, Sheffield and Bourne, *Douglas Haig: War Diaries and Letters*, p. 411.
[160] Ibid. 11 June 1918, p. 420.
[161] Maj. A. Morris, 'Esprit de Corps – III. Von Ludendorff's Tribute to the MGC', *Machine Gun Corps Gazette*, Vol. 2 (1 April 1918).
[162] 'Some Reflections on the Evacuation', *The Mudhook*, Vol. 1 Issue 5 (1 May 1918).
[163] NAM 1987-07-26: Papers of Lt. General Sir Gerald Ellison, 870-34-248, Special Order of the Day by Field Marshal Sir Douglas Haig 23 March 1918.

Figure 6.4 New recruits at a British Army base camp at Étaples, 1918. Note how young many of the drafts were.

Source: 2nd Lt. D McLellan/Imperial War Museums via Getty Images.

between England (as well as Britain and the Empire) and soldiers was underlined. In some of these communiqués, the King spoke directly to his men.[164] On 25 March, he assured servicemen 'that the fortitude, courage, and self-sacrifice with which the troops ... are so heroically resisting greatly superior numbers is realised by me and my people'.[165] Similar messages arrived from the President of the United States, the Prime Minister of South Africa, the Governor General of New Zealand, and the Queen.[166] Telegrams were also received from local civic associations, religious organisations, and many other groups. Men in the Devonshire Regiment

---

[164] For the powerful influence of the monarch in the armed forces, see Jones, *For King and Country*, esp. ch. 2.
[165] NAM 1987-07-26: Papers of Lt. General Sir Gerald Ellison, Ibid. 8704-35-249, Special Order of the Day by Field Marshal Sir Douglas Haig 25 March 1918.
[166] Ibid. 8704-35-249 through 254.

would have been pleased to hear that the mayor and 'Council of the Borough of Plymouth' conveyed 'their admiration of the splendid fighting qualities shown by all ranks'. The Town Council of Middleton in Lancashire similarly expressed their 'unbounded admiration and its due appreciation of the splendid work done by our gallant soldiers in opposing the terrific onslaught of the German offensive' and pledged 'to do everything that lies in its power to back up and support the Army and Navy'.[167] Instead of news of strikers and peace proclamations, this demonstrated to the men that their service was being acknowledged and that they were heroes; their sacrifice was meaningful.

This was probably of greatest value to the swathes of young conscripts now being called (or compelled) to join the colours. Earlier, Tables 6.4 and 6.5 revealed that between April and June those units that were not disbanded received large drafts of new men. By this stage, many of these servicemen were very young (see Tables 6.12, 6.13, and 6.14 – the modal ages being the most significant). The age at which soldiers could be sent overseas had been reduced to eighteen and a half. Even the 8th Bn. Border Regiment, which had a relatively high modal age, reported that its drafts were 'young boys mostly'.[168] Even if they were conscripts, and even if their training had been lacking, they were now playing their part in combatting one of the great crises of the war. As young men, with their careers and futures ahead of them, the social credit this might bring could have been even more significant.

Importantly, they arrived at the time where trench warfare was no longer in the ascendancy and brought with them the higher risk taking often associated with people in lower age groups. Sometimes referred to as 'young male syndrome', men in their teens and twenties (especially if unmarried or unemployed) are more likely to participate in high-risk behaviours.[169] These young men were often unencumbered with memories of 1917, their war was one of movement, initiative, and change. Several war diaries reported positively on the drafts arriving in the late spring.[170] Haig's diaries also suggest that these new soldiers were performing well and that, by the latter part of May, it was the dearth of experienced battalion and company commanders that was now the 'main difficulty'.[171]

---

[167] Ibid. 8704-35-254: Special Order of the Day by Field Marshal Sir Douglas Haig 11 April 1918.
[168] TNA WO 95/2251/3: 8th Bn. Border Regiment, 18 April 1918.
[169] M. Wilson and M. Daly, 'Competitiveness, Risk Taking, and Violence: The Young Male Syndrome', *Ethology and Sociobiology*, Vol. 6, No. 2 (1985), pp. 59–73.
[170] Haig's Diaries, 8 May 1918, Sheffield and Bourne, *Douglas Haig: War Diaries and Letters*, p. 411.
[171] Ibid. 20 May, p. 414.

Table 6.12 Mean ages of soldiers who died on the Western Front[1]

	Border Regt.	Devonshire Regt.	Manchester Regt.	Ox and Bucks LI	Royal Fusiliers	Warwickshire Regt.
1914: Mean Age	26.97	26.79	28.82	25.67	26.84	28.14
1916: Mean Age	26.16	26.9	27.58	26.17	26.27	25.39
1917/18: Mean Age	25.76	26.13	24.05	25.06	26.71	25.86

Source: This data has been extracted from the Commonwealth War Grave Commission's (CWGC) list of dead, www.cwgc.org/find-war-dead.aspx and have been filtered by regiment and dates (1 October–31 December 1914, 1 October–31 December 1916 and 1 October 1917–31 January 1918). This excludes units serving away from the Western Front, but includes men who died in the United Kingdom but were members of battalions that were serving in Belgium and France.

Table 6.13 *Modal age(s) of soldiers who died on the Western Front*

	Border Regt.	Devonshire Regt.	Manchester Regt.	Ox and Bucks LI	Royal Fusiliers	Warwickshire Regt.
1914: Modal Age	28	22	30	19 + 31	30	23
1916: Modal Age	21	21 + 27	21	24	21	20
1917/18: Modal Age	24	19	20	20 + 21	19	20

Source: see Table 6.12.

Table 6.14 *Median age of soldiers who died on the Western Front*

	Border Regt.	Devonshire Regt.	Manchester Regt.	Ox and Bucks LI	Royal Fusiliers	Warwickshire Regt.
1914: Median Age	27	26	28	26	27	29
1916: Median Age	25	26	24	25	25	24
1917/18: Median Age	25	25	24	23	25	24

Source: see Table 6.12.

In the 40th Division, and probably elsewhere, these drafts were supplemented by 'B Class' men. Many were 'old veterans' rather than new conscripts. Some might have returned having recuperated from injuries incurred during 1917, but others may have escaped the worst of 1917's fighting. They arrived back to a very different Western Front. It was unstable and appeared to promise new opportunities even as the BEF remained on the defensive. Several senior officers were gratified to have these old soldiers holding support lines and quiet sectors (though the need for men was so pressing that any reinforcements were welcome). While men's sacrifice may have been perceived as 'finite', these servicemen were apparently willing to put themselves in danger once again.[172] Demographically, the BEF's frontline infantry in late spring and early summer was almost a new force and was fighting a different kind of war. Even though some were veterans, many of the younger drafts would only ever know this more mobile form of warfare. While the fighting would have been no less horrific, for those inclined to relish battle there was more enjoyment to be derived in open warfare. There was once again some purpose in the sacrifices being demanded of them. Battle appeared to be a more likely avenue to peace.

****

It is essential to study morale across time. It was rarely in stasis, more often in flux, with the factors influencing men's sensemaking changing regularly with the patterns of the war. In 1917, the evidence men had of the war's progress painted a dark picture. While battle has been at the heart of this chapter, this was also a time at which war weariness and shortages were spreading on the Home Front while the enemy were in the ascendancy away from Belgium and France.[173] It was, though, the fighting at Third Ypres and the events that followed which indicated that battle was a less and less likely avenue to peace (and survival). However, somewhat paradoxically, the experience of retreat (namely inflicting casualties and witnessing semi-open warfare) helped to change men's sensemaking. Demographic alterations also flooded the army with young men whose youth was dominated by war and who had not had to experience the fighting in 1917. Horrible though it was, 21 March and the enemy offensives afterwards also re-emphasised the enemy's expansionist nature so that even old soldiers would have seen new meaning (and opportunity) in battle. For those men who enjoyed fighting, or derived excitement from it, there was also greater agency in this type of warfare.[174] This marked a

---

[172] Ibid. 24 June, p. 422.
[173] Gregory, *The Last Great War*, esp. p. 213; Stevenson, *1917*, esp. Part II.
[174] Bourke, *Intimate History of Killing*, esp. ch. 1; Gray, *The Warriors*, esp. ch. 2.

palpable change in the character of the war in Belgium and France and acute crisis may have helped to offset the impact of chronic crisis: victory was more likely and more necessary than it had been for a long time.

It is, then, important to distinguish between the chronic crises underpinning men's dwindling faith in battle and the acute crises that emerged after 21 March. They may have overlapped, but they were also distinct and had different causes and consequences. It was about *coping* with the former and *responding* to the latter. Soldiers' perceptions of battle and the war more generally should be seen as different, though related, features of their sensemaking.

After Cambrai, senior commanders quickly came to question whether the 'break on our front was due to the fighting value of the troops' or because 'the task assigned to them [...was] greater than they could reasonably be expected to carry out'.[175] Similar questions were being asked after March 1918. This analysis would suggest that reverses were primarily caused by the latter: the men of the BEF had not been adequately prepared to fight the defensive battle expected of them. In such circumstances, it is not surprising that they were liable to panic and retreat. It was a close-run thing, but the men fighting were rarely so fearful as their commanders that this was the first stage of Germany's march to victory. Less concerned with the strategic picture, perhaps they were also protected by their loose understanding of the BEF's defensive doctrine.

Reality shifts and frames of reference change. Battle, men's survival, and the possibility of peace were inextricably linked. Significantly though, their faltering faith in battle only ever revealed itself in relatively subtle ways. Nonetheless, it does help to explain why hope seemed to be faltering. A starker example of what could happen when battle lost its meaning occurred during the 'strikes' in the French Army. These took place in April–May 1917 (only a few months before the beginning of Third Ypres). The heavy losses incurred during the Nivelle offensives left servicemen complaining about poorly thought-through tactics and futile sacrifices.[176] In contrast, the German High Command's decision to shift to an offensive strategy on the Western Front in 1918 was in part a consequence of just how demoralising the costly defensive battles around Ypres had been for their troops. This process was more drawn-out in the BEF. As it was, the early signs in 1917 were that battle could offer a pathway to peace. This pathway then seemed to have been blocked by the fighting at Passchendaele and Cambrai as initiative shifted to the enemy; before,

---

[175] TNA WO 158/24/333. Point 6.
[176] L.V. Smith, 'War and "Politics": The French Army Mutinies of 1917', *War in History*, Vol. 2, No. 2 (1995), pp. 180–201 and *Between Mutiny and Obedience*, pp. 175–214.

finally, being cleared by the German offensives in the spring. Sensemaking helps 'meanings to materialize' and is 'an issue of language, talk, and communication' in which '[s]ituations, organizations, and environments are talked into existence'.[177] As infantrymen, and the military, sought to make sense of the reverses, they crafted new narratives in which battle had a purpose once more.

---

[177] Weick and Sutcliffe, 'Organizing and the Process of Sensemaking', p. 409.

Conclusion

This book has explored 'the subjective interpretive models of soldiers' and traced how English infantrymen made sense of their war experiences.[1] Their morale, as well as their perception of crisis, was conditioned by their environment, social groups, and internal psychological mechanisms. These overlapped and informed how soldiers navigated the world. The subtext of this analysis has been the interrelationship of crisis and morale. Combatants frequently failed to register acute military crises in the ways that historians (or their generals) might have expected. However, their lives were plagued by constant chronic crises, and most men developed mechanisms to endure and overcome these. In 1917 and 1918, however, the compound effects of increasingly corrosive chronic crises threatened to undermine men's morale. When the German offensives broke on the British Expeditionary Force (BEF) in March 1918, its men were tired and weary, but these reverses are more easily explained by their lack of training, which left them unable to respond effectively to this acute tactical crisis. Strangely, though, these events also changed men's sensemaking and helped them to see a new pathway to victorious peace.

To understand how men endured the war, the preceding chapters have revealed a variety of mechanisms that helped them to deflect and overcome chronic crises. In the first chapter, the reader discovered the ways in which men became attached to the Western Front. Next, they saw how winter and exhaustion were generally met with resilience and that the experience of colder weather transformed soldiers' perspectives on the conflict during spring and summer. Ultimately, the more active campaigning seasons was often preferable to the stasis of winter. The third chapter revealed how military service could also be a chronic crisis but highlighted how men's sense of duty and obligation was a sustaining force in their morale. Again, their ability to construe service as personally significant (and constructive) helped them to make sense of military life. Following this, the fourth chapter explained how men's dislocation from home was also capable of sapping men's resilience. Yet, soldiers' imaginative impulses and strong memories of the people and

---

[1] Ziemann, *War Experiences in Rural Germany*, p. 11.

landscapes of their homeland offered both a justification of their suffering and a coping mechanism. Soldiers love of their homelands made the war's length – the focus of the fifth chapter – a very pressing issue and significant chronic crisis. However morale suffered most when their confidence in victorious peace (and, therefore, survival) began to wane. A loss of hope was a very dangerous thing. In the final chapter, the reader has seen how this was related to men's perception of battle and why in 1917 men's confidence in battle's capacity to engineer victory collapsed on the battlefields around Ypres.

Yet, the withdrawals that took place after 21 March 1918 were not caused primarily by this downturn in morale. Of course, the effects of the war's chronic crises could make infantrymen less effective, especially if they failed to see the sacrifices that were being demanded of them as justifiable or worthwhile. Nevertheless the reverses during the German spring offensives were primarily caused by the BEF's failure to prepare its men to respond to the acute crises that occurred during these defensive battles. In this way, morale was a balancing act: men needed to be helped to endure the chronic crises of war and to be provided with the necessary skills to be able (and willing) to react effectively in moments of acute crisis. In some ways, this mirrors the distinction between morale and military effectiveness. The former tends to orientate around a soldier's *willingness* to follow a particular course of action, but the latter is more concerned with their *ability* to do so.[2]

Ultimately, servicemen's willingness to endure chronic crises and respond to acute situations was underpinned by their central, unshakeable, goal: victorious peace. Their morale was sustained by a belief in the necessity and possibility of military victory. Morale (and endurance) was buttressed by a variety of other mechanisms, too, especially soldiers' personal and collective attachment to and investment in the Western Front, their strong and sustaining relationship with specific English homelands, and their powerful sense of duty. As such, Eric Leed was wrong to suggest that the war stripped away combatants' pre-war identities.[3] Soldiers continued to draw heavily on these.[4] After all, in crafting narratives about their experiences, their pasts and futures played a fundamental role. Nonetheless, the military did constrain sensemaking, as did Belgium and France. Men's emotional survival also rested on the power and resilience of the psychological processes explored throughout this book. These unseen forces were fundamental, and given that some 43 per cent of our daily

---

[2] P. Tuunainen, *Finnish Military Effectiveness in the Winter War, 1939–1940* (London, 2016), p. 26; A.R. Millett, W. Murray and K.H. Watman, 'The Effectiveness of Military Organizations', *International Security*, Vol. 11, No. 1 (Summer 1986), pp. 37–71.
[3] Leed, *No Man's Land*, pp. 210–213; Smith, *Between Mutiny and Obedience*, p. 245.
[4] Meyer, *Men of War*, esp. pp. 14–46; Roper, *The Secret Battle*, esp. pp. 47–84.

actions are unconscious, historians should always investigate combatants' involuntary responses to conflict.[5]

****

Soldiers' perception of crisis was an important feature of their morale. Humans can experience both chronic crises, which are ongoing but bearable through adaptation, and acute crises, which are immediate and require action if they are not to become overwhelming. Morale can be sapped by both and has the capacity to undermine responses to the latter. Yet, if chronic crises (and the present) threatened to become everlasting, an acute crisis (such as the combat after 21 March 1918) could speed up time, change men's sensemaking, and improve morale.

Outside of moments of acute crisis, however, morale rested on soldiers' ability to overcome and adapt to the war's chronic crises. The coping strategies deployed informed sensemaking and helped infantrymen to survive. As a group, they demonstrated a remarkable immunity to the acute crises described by historians, perhaps because they occurred on political and strategic levels that existed beyond their frames of references. Like most humans, these men were able to mould themselves to their environment. Ross Wilson and Alexander Watson have shown how vital processes of familiarisation, normalisation, and habituation were to morale.[6] This book has reaffirmed the essential role these and other psychological processes played. It is true that soldiers felt the pressures of service deeply: the destruction in the war zone, the bleakness of winter, the omnipresence of death, the discomfort of daily life, and their separation from home all occupied their minds. Yet, they adapted, and it is possible that these 'chronic' crises occupied their attention and clouded their wider perspective. These struggles plagued day-to-day life and absorbed soldiers' time and energies, leaving little time to consider the wider war.

These chronic crises could be normalised and sometimes became routine. This was a conscious and unconscious process, which was evident in soldiers' use of language, imagery, and dark humour. Many men focused on the positive and constructive aspects of their existence, and their visions of home and hopes for victorious peace reflected this. These dreams equipped them with mechanisms to endure the war by supplying a picture of the homeland

---

[5] D.T. Neal, W. Wood, M. Wu and D. Kurlander, 'The Pull of the Past: When do Habits Persist Despite Conflict with Motives?', *Personality and Social Psychology Bulletin*, Vol. 37, No. 11 (2011), p. 1428; W. Wood, J.M. Quinn, and D.A. Kashy, 'Habits in Everyday Life: Thought, Emotion, and Action', *Journal of Personality and Social Psychology*, Vol. 83, No. 5 (2002), pp. 1281–1297.

[6] Wilson, *Landscapes of the Western Front*, pp. 102–105; Watson, *Enduring the Great War*, pp. 57, 87.

and brighter future that they fought for. It was only once these visions began to falter that chronic crisis began to chip away at men's endurance.

Ultimately, men's morale rested on their ability to develop meaningful and affirming narratives about their war experience and their perception of time. John Horne has argued that:

> contemporaries were acutely aware that they were living through a moment of epochal change. By the measure of historical time, no event since the French Revolution and the Napoleonic Wars had, for Europeans at least, assumed such epic proportions and seemed so certain to change the destinies of countries, empires, and regimes.[7]

What was true of countries was also true of individuals. Individuals' 'subjective [or personal] time' contrasted with understandings of 'standard time'. The former 'was elastic, stretching from an eternal present of waiting to the compressed instant of an air raid or attack'. The use of the 'past tense . . . sharpened memories', while the 'future [was] so uncertain that . . . it dissolved into multiple uses of the conditional tense'.[8] The present was overbearing; it was a part of the matrix of chronic crises and helped to distort soldiers' sensemaking, especially in 1917 and 1918, but the present was made more bearable by soldiers' certainty in the future. References backwards and forwards in time made the present meaningful and transient. It was when the future did become conditional, as happened after Third Ypres, and the present threatened to become eternal that men's sensemaking collapsed as their narratives about the war changed.

English soldiers merged past and future as they made sense of their world and crafted meaningful narratives. Their presents could only be survived insofar as they were perceived as fleeting. A sense of forward momentum was essential to morale, as was a preoccupation with the future. These soldiers employed an unconditional future tense that assumed their survival. The personal opportunities offered in the future helped to justify suffering in the present. Yet, these future spaces were constructed around memories of the past and visions of the homeland. In this way, the war was a bridge between past and future.

Men's perceptions of time influenced their perceptions of crisis and conflict. However, all these things were constrained by their frames of reference, which were themselves informed by their environment and social groups. The narratives soldiers created about their service responded to both. The environment was a physical and a metaphysical space. A source of many of their 'chronic' crises, it was also a canvas onto which they projected their emotions, and from which they could draw sustenance. Soldiers became attached to the Western Front: normalising the sites they encountered, investing meaning in

---

[7] J. Horne, 'Foreword', in Halewood, Luptak and Smyth, *War Time*, p. vii.
[8] Ibid.

the physical world, and layering the landscape with memories, which helped them to overcome the conflict's other-worldliness. Soldiers' psychologies filtered what they saw and how they interpreted experiences. Sensations, sights, and sounds were internalised and re-projected as something comprehensible. This was an important feature of their psychological resilience.

Other innate coping mechanisms helped them to deflect chronic crises (and to overcome acute ones, too). English infantrymen exhibited many of the ingredients of resilience highlighted in modern studies.[9] They mobilised many 'individual-level factors'. There was evidence of positive coping (whereby soldiers managed their circumstances); spiritual coping (men embracing faith-based beliefs and support); positive affect (in which servicemen deployed positive emotions); positive thinking (combatant's innate enthusiasm, reframing of situations, and hope); realism (particularly when individuals perceived agency); and behavioural control (ranging from instances of self-regulation, through self-management, to self-enchantment). Unit-level factors included a positive command climate (pride in their unit, support from comrades and officers, and effective leadership); teamwork (co-ordination and flexibility within soldiers' social group); and cohesion (combined actions in training or sports, bonding with others, and commitment to them). Lastly, community-level factors such as men's sense of belonging (their integration within a unit and friendship with other soldiers); their feeling of cohesion (bonds with community, or communities, and sharing values with others); and their sense of connectedness with people or places. This was supported by the men's preoccupation with the future, generally positive reasoning, tendency towards psychological projection, and their imagination.

Such conclusions support the general findings of the *Annales* school, which stresses 'the *longue durée* (long run) of resilience and social cohesion beneath the *événements* (particular events) of cultural fragmentation that so traumatised ... elites'.[10] They also speak to histories of what are described as 'war culture(s)'.[11] This concept describes the 'broad-based system through which belligerent populations made sense of the war and persuaded

---

[9] L.S. Meredith et al. 'Promoting Psychological Resilience in the U.S. Military', *Rand Health Quarterly*, Vol. 1, No. 2 (Summer 2011), p. 2.

[10] Smith, *Between Mutiny and Obedience*, pp. 255–256. Also L. Hunt, 'French History in the Last Twenty Years: The Rise and Fall of the *Annales* Paradigm', *Journal of Contemporary History*, Vol. 21 (1986), pp. 209–224.

[11] Audoin-Rouzeau and Becker, *14–18*, pp. 102–3, 147, 166. The concept has been rebuffed by the Collectif de Recherche International et de Débat sur la Guerre de 1914–1918. Their perspective and ideas can be explored at www.crid1418.org (accessed 11 January 2022) or at F. Buton, A. Loez, N. Mariot and P. Olivera, '1914–1918: Understanding the Controversy', *Books and Ideas* (11 June 2009).

themselves to continue fighting it'.[12] Scholars have shown that this rested on actors' consent. Individuals internalised their country's cause and embraced the demonisation of their enemy. For this reason, these ideas have become associated with the theory that the Great War 'brutalised' European society. Yet, as this book has shown, sensemaking was multifaceted and highly heterogeneous. In this case, there is little evidence that English soldiers gloried in violence. Of course, the darker side of men's character may have been omitted from letters, but it is also rare to find such sentiments in men's private diaries or the newspapers published by soldiers.

This might have been a product of the space they inhabited and the enemy they confronted. Vejas Gabriel Liulevicius has argued that German soldiers on the Eastern Front exhibited a hatred of their Slavic enemy. Perceptions of 'races and spaces' were embedded in the 'ethnic' programme of the German authorities in the *Ober Ost*.[13] In contrast, R.L. Nelson found that 'hatred of the enemy is almost completely absent from [German] soldier newspapers'. 'Soldiers' consent', he concluded, 'can be achieved through the perception of a legitimate cause ... Hatred of the enemy is not necessary and should be dropped from the "war culture" argument'.[14] English soldiers despised the Wilhelmine state and believed its defeat was a necessary ingredient of any lasting peace, but they did not hate the enemy as individuals. Despite this, like the men sitting across No Man's Land, most of them 'accepted the orders and "mission" they were given, believed that what they were doing was right and deeply hoped and believed that they should and would win'.[15]

****

Yet, in some cases, men failed to adapt and cope with the chronic crises that they encountered in military service. These could become overwhelming, or sap morale to dangerous levels, though this was generally a temporary state of being. Depressed French soldiers described having *le cafard* – the cockroach, or the blues.[16] In the BEF, servicemen embraced a different phrase, which was borrowed from the professional army's slang. When they felt fearful or pessimistic, they explained that they had the 'wind up'.[17] In these moments,

---

[12] J.M. Winter and A. Prost, *The Great War in History: Debates and Controversies, 1914 to the Present* (Cambridge, 2005), p. 159.

[13] Liulevicius, *War Land on the Eastern Front*, pp. 114, 219–220.

[14] R.L. Nelson, *German Soldier Newspapers of the First World War* (Cambridge, 2010), p. 242.

[15] Ibid.

[16] C. Rearick, *The French in Love and War: Popular Culture in the Era of the World Wars* (New Haven and London, 1997), p. 15; Hanna, 'A Republic of Letters', pp. 1350–1352.

[17] 'On Getting the "Wind Up"', *The Outpost*, Vol. IV, No. 5 (1 March 1917), p. 158; 'Wind Up', *The Cyclometer*, Vol. 1, No. 1 (1 November 1917), p. 9.

they could be more anxious or nervous and were more vulnerable to fluctuations in morale. Nonetheless, comrades helped one another through such situations and individuals tended to insist that this feeling would pass.[18] Yet, shell shock and breakdown did occur. Every man had his limit, and prolonged exposure to combat, shellfire, or the elements could eventually undermine resilience.

One of the men encountered in this book failed to adapt. Ernest Marler found the war's chronic crises overwhelming, though he was an exception. His age may have made it harder for him to adapt. At thirty-seven, he was significantly older than many men in the Royal Fusiliers and was less able to adjust to military service. Born in Norfolk to a publican, he moved to London later in his life. At the beginning of the war, he had been a butler for a family of stockbrokers living on Hanover Square. He had been accustomed to a life of authority and cleanliness but arrived in a mud-caked France as a lowly private. It became a living nightmare. His diary entries revealed his torment:

> 4/10/16: 'Drizzling rain more or less all day. Barlin [Pas-de-Calais] a horribly dirty place ... A puddle of mud'.
>
> 6/10/16: 'Morning parcel from home, torch, canvas shoes, apples etc. ... Headquarters staff billets. Stables; Barns; Fowl houses and old buildings, some absolutely unfit for human beings to occupy'.
>
> 24/10/16: '... No work all day its gets on one's nerves, when one thinks of the work one might be doing at home ...'
>
> 29/10/16: 'Cold, wet and windy. The same routine ... How wretched I feel ... How the comfort of home has been in my thoughts. The life out here is hell no comfort of cleanliness, fire, food[,] or anything else, one simply exists. Hard biscuits and cheese for dinner, having to work on a Sunday is galling. May God soon send peace'.
>
> 3/11/16: 'Weather fine. Awful puddle under foot. The food seems like poison to me. Continual pain in stomach all the week ... Vile smell from farmyard, bad enough to cause fever ... How I wish it would all end, long for the comfort of home, ... life is hell. A horrible goat here, which stinks the whole place'.
>
> 14/11/16: 'Afternoon went and saw where they were burying the dead. Long trenches about 200 yds, 4 ft deep, poor fellows simply sewn in a blanket ... How awful. That there should be such a terrible thing as war'.

---

[18] IWM Documents.10933: Capt. G.B. Donaldson, Letter to Mother 6 June 1916; IWM Documents.1665: A.P. Burke, Letter to Reg 12–15 October 1916; IWM Documents.17029: Capt. A.J. Lord, Letter to Father 8 February 1918; LIDDLE/WW1/GS/0137: Pte. O.G. Billingham, Diary 8 March 1918.

13/12/16: 'Wicked billet no fire – no comfort. If one washes their clothes no means of drying. Billet a rotten loft, dark, stinks. Enormous amount of waste in the army. New under clothes, thrown away. Food, ammunition etc'.

1/1/17: 'New Years [sic] Day. May God send peace in 1917'.[19]

The chronic crises plaguing him were all too recognisable to his comrades. They, too, complained about the weather, their billets, the food, the death, and the remoteness of peace. Yet, unlike other servicemen, Marler was unable to rationalise his suffering. His comments about 'the work one might be doing at home' suggest that he failed to register military service as an obligation. France and Belgium were a distressing contrast to the 'comfort of home', and it was difficult to habituate himself to war. Feeling little sense of forward momentum, the apparent permanency of his present weighed heavily on his mind. The innate mechanisms that helped other men to craft meaningful and sustaining narratives had little power.

****

The effects of chronic crises shed light on the (admittedly limited) incidences of larger-scale insubordination, 'collective disobedience', or mutiny involving British soldiers. These often occurred when soldiers were 'liable to react to what they perceived as unfair treatment by their military superiors by going on strike or voicing discontent.[20] Several minor incidences occurred within Territorial units in England during 1914 and 1915. According to reports, the complaints stemmed from the application of 'regular army discipline' in units that were unused to it.[21] Social norms influence the way that groups navigate and interpret the world. It is striking that such complaints rarely led to similar incidences once Territorial battalions arrived on the Western Front. Yet, these may have had more to do with leadership. An enquiry into 'discontent' within the 1/4th Bn. Norfolk Regiment concluded that this stemmed from concerns about their colonel's ability. The men believed in the cause and felt a strong sense of obligation but wanted to ensure they would be led into battle by a competent commander.[22]

The events at Étaples during September 1917 were much more troubling. It is significant that *the* major 'mutiny' in the BEF occurred during a period in

---

[19] RFM.ARC.2012.958: E.T. Marler, Diary 4, 6, 24, and 29 October 1916; 3 and 14 November 1916; 13 December 1916; and 1 January 1917.
[20] Sheffield, *Leadership in the Trenches*, p. 151.
[21] Ibid., pp. 151–152.
[22] TNA WO 32/18563: 'Discontent among Battalion [1/4th Norfolk Regiment] owing to Colonel Harvey's unsympathetic consideration for officers and men under his command'. Also WO 32/1858: 'Report on Officers of 201st Brigade and 202nd Brigade'.

which morale was fragile.²³ The arrest of a New Zealander, followed by the shooting of a member of the Gordon Highlanders, led to several days' unrest. Nonetheless, the few historians that have studied these events in detail suggest that they emerged from local complaints about poor food, inadequate conditions and facilities, boredom, brutal training, inappropriate disciplinary systems, disrespectful NCOs and officers, and an absence of *esprit de corps*.²⁴ There was 'little ... evidence of mutineers expressing resentment of regimental officers' or of calls for peace at any price. Australians seem to have been the most active participants in this 'strike' and English soldiers' involvement was relatively limited. A variety of chronic crises underpinned these events as did the fact that military authorities appeared to be contributing to (rather than alleviating) the problems facing servicemen.

When the war ended, disobedience became more widespread. A series of 'demobilisation disturbances' took place after the Armistice – though, these 'were [also] transitory'.²⁵ The cessation of hostilities left servicemen 'more inclined than ever to contrast their lot with that of the men employed in England'.²⁶ Their demands were often very specific. Soldiers in Le Havre called for shorter working hours, more holidays, and an increased bread ration. Elsewhere, in Dannes (a village in Pas-de-Calais) men were embittered by 'the substitution of time work for task work', which could be more demanding.²⁷ Further north, in Calais, the local 'Area Soldiers and Sailors Association' protested the unjust incarceration of another New Zealander.²⁸ At Dunkirk, a group of servicemen demanded a definite date for demobilisation. They were concerned that the men who had already returned home would have readier access to the new jobs and better pay that peace would bring. Gary Sheffield believed that 'the breakdown of discipline in the army after the Armistice owed much to a widespread feeling among the troops that they had enlisted to a do a job, the task was completed – Germany was defeated – and their part of the contract was fulfilled'.²⁹

Many men perceived their duty as finite. Their rationalisation of their service revolved around the war, victorious peace, as well as good character and respectability. These central frames of reference were evident during these

---

[23] The 'Singapore Mutiny' was the largest of the conflict and involved 400 men of the British Indian Army. I.F.W. Beckett, 'The Singapore Mutiny of February 1915', *Journal of the Society of Army Historical Research*, Vol. 62 (1984), pp. 132–153.
[24] Sheffield, *Leadership in the Trenches*, p. 152; Gill and Dallas, 'Mutiny at Etaples Base in 1917', pp. 88–112.
[25] G. Sheffield, *A Short History of the First World War* (London, 2014), pp. 178–179.
[26] G. Dallas and D. Gill, *The Unknown Army: Mutinies in the British in World War I* (London, 1985), pp. 89–90.
[27] Ibid.
[28] Ibid. pp. 90–98.
[29] Sheffield, *A Short History*, pp. 178–179.

'disturbances'. The power of men's hopes for victorious peace explains why these episodes occurred *after* 11 November 1918. The central justification for their suffering had evaporated with the Armistice. Furthermore, having invested so much time in creating a future space during their service, once hostilities ceased, they were desperate to start their new lives. Tellingly, though, these events tended not to involve the infantry. The key protagonists were members of the Army Service Corps and Royal Engineers, which suggests that another study might find that a different social world and culture existed in these auxiliary units.[30] It is possible that men serving in these units were more likely to have a background in industry and trade unionism. Revealingly, it was the 105th Infantry Brigade that was ordered to 'assist in quelling' the riots taking place in Calais.[31]

****

The war, men's environment, and their social groups shaped sensemaking, framed experiences, and informed understandings of military service. The power and strength of English infantrymen's belief in the peace-victory dynamic was fundamental to the narratives they constructed about their wartime experience. Yet, how did this differ from the hope nexus in other armies? Were there any differences between these Englishmen and servicemen serving in the same environment for a similar timeframe?

The BEF did not face a collapse in morale comparable in magnitude to those afflicting their allies in the French Army or their enemies in the Imperial German Army. Amongst a host of variables, including the higher quality of British soldiers' food and their sophisticated systems of rotation, was the nature of their contract with the British Army. Unlike German or French combatants, soldiers in the BEF were subjects rather than citizens. Because of age and institutional culture, these infantrymen had a less developed sense of citizenship or reciprocal rights and were generally less inclined (or able) to voice the kinds of concerns and discontent one finds elsewhere. Nevertheless, their relationship with the homeland (parochial though it might have been) was still significant. The lack of major upheaval on the Home Front helped to sustain men's morale and their belief in victorious peace.

Furthermore, soldiers' apparent inability to perceive acute tactical crises helped to preserve the dynamic between victory and peace. Their preoccupation with the chronic crises of day-to-day life protected them from acute crises. From their perspective, 1917's disappointments and the retreats after March 1918 were narratives dominated by the pressures of daily existence and could even be put down to the weather. The character of warfare on the

---

[30] Mayhew, 'British Expeditionary Force Vegetable Shows', esp. pp. 1372–1377.
[31] Dallas and Gill, *Unknown Army*, p. 99.

Western Front (and the limited perspective of individual soldiers) meant that small incremental gains, or limited opportunities to exercise agency, were often more significant than the strategic reality. Yet, the feeling that the war had entered a period of perpetual stalemate was detrimental to morale, and the painful and limited advances along the Passchendaele front, as well as the disaster at Cambrai, seemed to indicate that victorious peace was a very distant prospect. This was made worse by events elsewhere – particularly Russia's revolution and military collapse. Yet, while the chronic crises of 1917 threatened morale, when the BEF met the acute crises of spring 1918 it did not disintegrate and (even as it was found wanting) the BEF survived and adapted. The increasingly young soldiers filling its ranks responded to the German offensives with a renewed sense of purpose and faith in victorious peace.

In contrast, several historians have argued that the German Army collapsed in autumn 1918 as soldiers' hopes for victorious peace were left in tatters by deteriorating conditions in Germany, Allied material superiority, and the failure of the spring offensives. By this stage, German soldiers 'lost all hope that further fighting would serve their main aim, to secure peace and go home'.[32] A belief in and commitment to victory were essential ingredients in morale. It helped combatants see worth in their military service. Yet, according to some scholars, in many German units there was 'a mass refusal to fight' as 'individuals ... acted on their own initiative to seek their way back to the safety of home'.[33] Historian Benjamin Ziemann believes two factors undermined German soldiers' endurance: 'first, their living conditions deteriorated substantially during the war. Second ... open advocacy of annexationist views repudiated the myth of a defensive war'.[34] This was compounded by a declining allegiance to the monarchical system.[35] According to others, this revealed itself as an 'ordered surrender' caused by 'exhaustion and disillusionment'.[36]

In this case, chronic crises depleted the morale of the German Army to an extent that it undermined their response to acute military crises during the Allied counterthrusts in 1918. Despite the strain of 1917, English infantrymen generally remained certain of their cause and much better provided for. The entry of the United States into the war offered renewed hope despite the setbacks on the Eastern Front. It made sense to fight the defensive battles of 1918. The German collapse also owed much to soldiers' relationship with the

---

[32] B. Ulrich and B. Ziemann (eds.), *German Soldiers in the Great War: Letters and Eyewitness Accounts*, trans. C. Brocks (Barnsley, 2010).
[33] Ziemann, *Violence and the German Soldier*, p. 136.
[34] Ziemann, *War Experiences*, p. 271; Nelson, *German Soldier Newspapers*, pp. 5, 10, 240.
[35] Ibid. Also S. Stephenson, *The Final Battle: Soldiers of the Western Front in the German Revolution of 1918* (Cambridge, 2009).
[36] Watson, *Enduring the Great War*, pp. 215–231.

state. Conscription and citizenship were interwoven, and (like the French) many Germans' 'sacrifices' and 'entitlements' were implicitly tied to their allegiance to the nation.[37] Political reform was the topic of lively debate amongst the soldiers of Imperial Germany who concentrated 'on the perceived injustice both at the front and on the home front', which 'paved the way' for revolution'.[38]

The French Army did not experience a collapse comparable in scale. Yet, the relationship between peace and victory (and the coalescence of chronic and acute crisis) was evident during the Nivelle offensive.[39] A sequence of futile attacks left units uncertain that *this* battle could bring about peace. *Poilus* were willing to voice and act upon their apprehensions. Historian L.V. Smith believes the French mutinies of 1917 emerged from the interaction of military service and republican citizenship.[40] The relationship between citizen soldiers and their commanders was built upon 'the official French ideology of popular sovereignty'. Soldiers obeyed 'a source of authority originating, ultimately, in themselves and their compatriots'.[41] As such, 'for French soldiers, the issue revolved around whether and under what circumstances they considered the levels of offensive violence expected of them relevant to the goal they shared with their commanders of winning the war'.[42] The authority for directing the 'pathway' to victorious peace was partially invested in the men themselves. Furthermore, the politicisation of military service can also explain the more negative relationship between *poilus* and the 'hated home front'.[43] Their engagement with the political sphere might have made French soldiers more vocally critical of the war's orchestration. Nonetheless, They retained a love for their country and a belief in their cause.[44] Unlike many German combatants in 1918, French servicemen 'did not reject military service outright. Rather, their mutiny was a way to renegotiate their terms of service, which they understood as a duty of every male citizen'.[45] Of course, even a mutiny built around negotiation risked catastrophe.

English soldiers' choice architecture may have been constrained by their very different relationship with politics and military service. These were subject soldiers who owed their allegiance to the King. Their membership of

---

[37] Ulrich and Ziemann, *German Soldiers*, p. 11. Also R. Brubaker, *Citizenship and Nationhood in France and Germany* (Cambridge, MA, 1992, 1994), pp. 14, 104.
[38] Ulrich and Ziemann, *German Soldiers*, p. 11.
[39] Smith, 'War and "Politics"' pp. 180–201.
[40] Smith, *Between Mutiny and Obedience*, p. 10.
[41] Ibid., pp. 8, 16.
[42] Ibid., p. 17.
[43] Audoin-Rouzeau, *Men at War*, pp. 92, 111, 119.
[44] Ziemann, *Violence and the German Soldier*, p. 152.
[45] Ibid.

the armed forces had less to do with active citizenship than patriotic impulses and their relationship with the implicit nation.[46] Historically, the British Army had existed on the periphery of political life and until the Great War national conscription had never been imposed. In fact, there was a long-held suspicion of standing armies in the United Kingdom.[47]

The men of 1914–1918 entered a military that did not model itself on democratic society. More politically motivated 'soldiers and workmen's councils' on the Home Front complained about this in 1917. As revealed in the fourth chapter, one group of servicemen who had returned to work in industry believed that 'the Army Acts and the King's Regulations were drawn up to deal with a completely different army from that which we have now. In the old voluntary force, the men composing it voluntarily renounced most of their rights as citizens'.[48] Another group articulated something similar:

> We have no vote, no status, and only the right of an individual appeal, no matter what the injustice. We plead as beggars for what our comrades can demand as citizens. We ask to be citizens with the privileges as well as the responsibilities.[49]

It is telling that similar concerns were not voiced (at least publicly) on the Western Front. Mass military service and conscription were novelties in Britain, which was arguably not even a full democracy in 1914. It might be, then, that English soldiers' political passivity played an important role in their willingness to endure (or, at least, to toe the line). The age of many of the English infantrymen studied here means that they would have never voted in national elections. Historian Helen McCartney accepts this but argues that there was still 'consultation and bargaining' drawing on 'the conventions of pre-war society'.[50] This may well be true, but it took place within units and did not offer the same opportunity to question the legitimacy of orders *en masse*. English infantrymen were less inclined to question the higher conduct of the war or lacked the vocabulary to do so. Once in khaki, citizenship, sovereignty, and suffrage mattered less than home, survival, and respectability, and perhaps this parochial patriotism was more resilient to change.[51]

---

[46] Smith, *Between Mutiny and Obedience*, pp. 10, 248.

[47] J.W.M. Hichberger, *Images of the Army: The Military in British Art, 1815–1914* (Manchester, 1988), pp. 38, 124; G. Harries-Jenkins, *The Army in Victorian Society* (Abingdon, 1977, 2007), p. 10.

[48] TNA WO 32/5455: 'Copies of Two Reports sent to Sir Reginald H. Brade at WO, Soldiers Representatives'.

[49] Ibid. Report from the Meeting of the 'Home Counties and Training Reserve Branch of the Soldiers' and Workmen's Council, 18 July 1917.

[50] McCartney, *Citizen Soldiers*, p. 122.

[51] Nelson, *German Soldier Newspapers*, p. 241; Ziemann, *Violence and the German Soldier*, p. 38.

English infantrymen's attachment to the homeland mattered most to their morale.[52] This focused on family, friends, community, and locality; visions of home helped them to justify their suffering and helped them to cope with the war's chronic crises. England was imagined as a social and physical space composed of people(s), place(s), and landscape(s). Both Britain and the Empire were filtered through men's very personal feelings of Englishness, which was their primary identity but overlapped with those of their comrades. Drawing on past, present, and future, these visions of home were a central feature of the narratives men wove about the war. Men joined the army to protect their homeland and continued to fight for this implicit nation as they endured the trials of the trenches in Belgium and France.[53]

****

L.V. Smith's concluding remarks about the French military experience of the Great War speak just as well to the ways in which English infantrymen navigated and made sense of their world:

> I find the axiom of a human spirit broken or maimed by World War I highly problematic outside intellectual or artistic circles. My conclusions certainly suggest that the human capacity to adapt and endure is stronger than an impulse towards spiritual entropy in the face of calamity.[54]

Soldiers' sensemaking and morale rested upon many innate and often unconscious coping mechanisms and ultimately rested on the remarkable resilience of humankind. Combatants' psychological apparatus provided a shield and an engine for their sensemaking. It helped them to find agency and create meaningful narratives about their wartime experiences; their often instinctive reactions to the conflict allowed them to adjust to and make sense of the Great War. Ultimately, their visions of the future and desire to protect England convinced them of the justice of their cause, which also helped them to deflect the present. These are mere windows into a vast universe, but to understand endurance and morale historians must delve deeper into the minds of historical actors. It is only then that the power of the human spirit will be revealed in its full colour.

---

[52] Mayhew, 'English Patriotism and the Implicit Nation', pp. 6, 32.
[53] C. Messenger, *Call to Arms: The British Army 1914-1918* (London, 2005), p. 96; Beckett, Bowman and Connelly, *The British Army*, pp. 9-12; Gregory, *The Last Great War*, pp. 32, 75.
[54] Smith, *Mutiny and Obedience*, p. 247.

Appendix

Demographics of Six English Regiments in the BEF

Table A.1 *Home addresses of Border Regiment soldiers, 1914–1918*[1]

	Cumberland	Westmoreland	Northern England[2]	London	Rest of England	Great Britain	Ireland
Oct.–Dec. 1914[3]	10.71%	0.00%	32.86%	27.86%	24.29%	4.28%	0.00%
Oct.–Dec. 1916[4]	32.04%	9.09%	29.44%	3.46%	21.21%	4.33%	0.43%
Oct. 1917–Jan. 1918[5]	26.67%	7.54%	40.29%	5.51%	12.75%	6.66%	0.58%

[1] The statistics that follow have been converted from the Commonwealth War Grave Commission's (CWGC) list of dead, www.cwgc.org/find-war-dead.aspx and have been filtered by unit and dates (1 October–31 December 1914, 1 October–31 December 1916 and 1 October 1917–31 January 1918). This excludes units serving away from the Western Front, but includes men who died in the United Kingdom but were members of battalions that were serving in Belgium and France. They only reflect those casualties whose home or family address was included in the CWGC records. It should also be remembered that many men who no longer lived in a county or region might have been recent migrants away from it. These statistics are based on their address in 1914. In these tables Great Britain means the rest of Great Britain and refers only to Scotland and Wales. On the rare occasion that an individual had an international address this has been removed from the data set.

[2] This is not to suggest that 'Northern England' is a homogeneous area. It is used as a broad category and refers to the historic counties of Cheshire, Cumberland, County Durham, Lancashire, Lincolnshire, Northumberland, and Westmoreland.

[3] Taken from an available sample of 140 Border Regiment soldiers.

[4] Taken from an available sample of 231 Border Regiment soldiers.

[5] Taken from an available sample of 345 Border Regiment soldiers.

Table A.2 Home addresses of Devonshire Regiment soldiers, 1914–1918

	Devonshire	West Country	London	Rest of England	Great Britain	Ireland
Oct.–Dec. 1914[1]	63.64%	9.09%	11.52%	9.69%	5.45%	0.61%
Oct.–Dec. 1916[2]	56.10%	17.07%	6.10%	17.07%	3.66%	0.00%
Oct. 1917–Jan. 1918[3]	41.80%	17.55%	7.40%	30.02%	2.54%	0.69%

[1] Taken from an available sample of 165 Devonshire Regiment soldiers.
[2] Taken from an available sample of eighty-two Devonshire Regiment soldiers.
[3] Taken from an available sample of 433 Devonshire Regiment soldiers.

Table A.3 *Home addresses of Manchester Regiment soldiers, 1914–1918*

	Manchester	Lancashire	Northern England	London	Rest of England	Great Britain	Ireland
Oct.–Dec. 1914[1]	36.84%	20.40%	9.21%	10.53%	11.18%	7.89%	3.95%
Oct.–Dec. 1916[2]	42.76%	29.33%	9.89%	2.12%	12.72%	2.47%	0.71%
Oct. 1917–Jan. 1918[3]	42.66%	24.09%	17.74%	1.29%	9.75%	4.00%	0.47%

[1] Taken from an available sample of 152 Manchester Regiment soldiers.
[2] Taken from an available sample of 283 Manchester Regiment soldiers.
[3] Taken from an available sample of 851 Manchester Regiment soldiers.

Table A.4 *Home addresses of Oxfordshire and Buckinghamshire Light Infantry soldiers, 1914–1918*

	Oxfordshire	Buckinghamshire	South East	London	Rest of England	Great Britain	Ireland
Oct.–Dec. 1914[1]	28.73%	19.54%	25.29%	3.45%	20.69%	2.30%	0.00%
Oct.–Dec. 1916[2]	20.71%	17.14%	14.29%	7.14%	36.43%	4.29%	0.00%
Oct. 1917–Jan. 1918[3]	21.90%	13.33%	11.43%	7.62%	41.91%	3.81%	0.00%

[1] Taken from an available sample of eighty-seven Ox and Bucks Light Infantry soldiers.
[2] Taken from an available sample of 140 Ox and Bucks Light Infantry soldiers.
[3] Taken from an available sample of 105 Ox and Bucks Light Infantry soldiers.

Table A.5 *Home addresses of Royal Fusiliers soldiers, 1914–1918*

	Inner London	Outer London[1]	Rest of England	Great Britain	Ireland
Oct.–Dec. 1914[2]	64.74%	9.62%	21.15%	1.93%	2.56%
Oct.–Dec. 1916[3]	26.83%	8.21%	59.10%	3.28%	1.23%
Oct. 1917–Jan. 1918[4]	27.95%	7.99%	59.20%	3.99%	0.87%

[1] 'Outer London' refers to settlements in counties such as Kent or Middlesex that were part of London's 'environs'.
[2] Taken from an available sample of 156 Royal Fusiliers soldiers.
[3] Taken from an available sample of 731 Royal Fusiliers soldiers.
[4] Taken from an available sample of 576 Royal Fusiliers soldiers.

Table A.6 *Home addresses of Royal Warwickshire Regiment soldiers, 1914–1918*

	Birmingham	Warwickshire	West Midlands	London	Rest of England	Great Britain	Ireland
Oct.–Dec. 1914[1]	43.48%	24.64%	3.86%	5.80%	18.84%	1.93%	1.45%
Oct.–Dec. 1916[2]	33.83%	16.73%	9.67%	2.60%	32.71%	2.97%	1.49%
Oct. 1917–Jan. 1918[3]	28.18%	16.82%	6.82%	5.91%	38.33%	2.88%	1.06%

[1] Taken from an available sample of 207 Royal Warwickshire Regiment soldiers.
[2] Taken from an available sample of 269 Royal Warwickshire Regiment soldiers.
[3] Taken from an available sample of 660 Royal Warwickshire Regiment soldiers.

Table A.7 *Size of settlement: Homes of soldiers who died between October and December 1914*

	Settlement < 10,000 inhabitants[1]	Settlement > 10,000 inhabitants
The Border Regiment	9.22%	90.78%
The Devonshire Regiment	29.52%	70.48%
The Manchester Regiment	15.38%	84.62%
The Ox and Bucks Light Infantry	45.98%	54.02%
The Royal Fusiliers	11.54%	88.46%
The Royal Warwickshire Regiment	13.58%	86.42%

[1] Numbers were taken from the CWGC records using the same dates as Tables A.1–A.6. The settlements' population data has been taken from the 1911 Census (available at www.visionofbritain.org.uk/, accessed 29 July 2016).

Table A.8 *Size of settlement: Homes of soldiers who died between October and December 1916*

	Settlement < 10,000 inhabitants	Settlement > 10,000 inhabitants
The Border Regiment	36.22%	63.68%
The Devonshire Regiment	41.96%	58.04%
The Manchester Regiment	16.78%	83.22%
The Ox and Bucks Light Infantry	38.79%	61.21%
The Royal Fusiliers	24.46%	75.54%
The Royal Warwickshire Regiment	28.00%	72.00%

Table A.9 *Size of settlement: Homes of soldiers who died between October 1917 and January 1918*

	Settlement < 10,000 inhabitants	Settlement > 10,000 inhabitants
The Border Regiment	30.86%	69.14%
The Devonshire Regiment	43.60%	56.40%
The Manchester Regiment	12.14%	87.86%
The Ox and Bucks Light Infantry	25.22%	74.78%
The Royal Fusiliers	28.41%	71.59%
The Royal Warwickshire Regiment	23.10%	76.90%

English battalions contained predominantly English soldiers and retained a strong regional cohort throughout the war.[1] Given that the counties of Cumberland and Westmoreland were relatively sparsely populated and rural, it is no surprise that the Border Regiment contained more Londoners than locals in 1914. In fact, voluntarism and then conscription led to an increase in the number of local men filling the regiment's ranks. The proportion of men from the north of England remained high, and the amount of soldiers from elsewhere in England declined.

Devon lacked the sprawling conurbations found elsewhere in the country. Yet, in 1914 the Devonshire Regiment had a strong contingent of local men. Even in late 1917 and early 1918, nearly half of the regiment's servicemen were from Devon, with another 18 per cent coming from the West Country.

The Manchester Regiment recruited from a large industrial city. In 1914, nearly 40 per cent of the regulars and reservists were from Manchester and another 20 per cent came from elsewhere in Lancashire. The surge of voluntarism after 1914 swelled the Mancunian and Lancastrian component. The regiment's four 'City' battalions fused regional and socio-economic identity as they formed around professions and skills. Conscription – and the arrival of Territorials – ensured that the units of the Manchester Regiment in Belgium and France retained a large core of men from Manchester and Lancashire. Over the same period, the number of men from other parts of England and the British Isles steadily declined.

The Oxfordshire and Buckinghamshire Light Infantry recruited from two counties with relatively small populations that lacked large cities. There were a limited number of units raised under the regiment's flag. The Ox and Bucks saw a moderate decline in the numbers of men from its home counties, while the percentage of soldiers from London and other parts of England increased. Despite this, over 45 per cent of servicemen in late 1917 and early 1918 were still hailed from the South East.

The Royal Fusiliers, who were based in London, were the British Army's largest regiment. In 1914, nearly 75 per cent of the Royal Fusiliers' men hailed from London. By late 1916, however, over 60 per cent of its servicemen were from outside of the capital. The regiment contained several units with no affiliation to London, which were instead built around social and professional groups. Amongst the New Army battalions, the 10th Bn. Royal Fusiliers were informally known as the 'Stockbrokers' Battalion', the 18th through 21st Bns. were 'Public Schools' units, while the 26th Bn. became the 'Bankers' Battalion'.

---

[1] T. Bowman and M. Connelly, *The Edwardian Army: Recruiting, Training, and Deploying the British Army, 1902–1914* (Oxford, 2012). For the resilience of regionalism in English regiments during the war, see Connelly, *Steady the Buffs!* p. 233 or McCartney, *Citizen Soldiers*, pp. 62–66.

Only the 22nd Bn. (Kensington) and 32nd Bn. (East Ham) were a product of London's voluntary effort.

The Royal Warwickshire Regiment recruited heavily from the industrialised areas around Birmingham, as well as rural parts of Warwickshire. The Royal Warwickshire's proportion of locals declined as the war progressed. Yet, men from the county and the West Midlands still accounted for over 50 per cent of the regiment in late 1917 and early 1918, and this proportion would probably have been much higher in the City and 'Pals' units (the 14th, 15th and 16th Bns.).

These infantrymen outside of the capital. from urban backgrounds.[2] In 1914, approximately 80 per cent of Britain lived in towns or cities of over 10,000 inhabitants.[3] However, the Oxfordshire and Buckinghamshire Light Infantry and Devonshire Regiment had sizable groups of men from rural areas or small market towns. By late 1916, there were more men from such backgrounds. Indeed, soldiers from rural or semi-rural areas were statistically overrepresented in all units bar the Manchester Regiment, which saw little change. Nonetheless, most men came from England's middling through to very large urban zones.

The BEF's soldiers were younger by the end of the war (see p. 276-278).[4] Significantly, age and morale are interrelated. The German military derived two benefits from their organisation of units by age: 'it raised the physical standard of combat divisions' and their psychological resilience since older troops were less able to bear the strains of frontline service and grumbled more openly.[5] Men were apparently more willing to follow their social and generational superiors. Illustratively, in 1914, only 34 per cent of the Liverpool Scottish's officers were under twenty-four, which appeared to improve their efficiency.[6]

Younger men bore the brunt of the frontlines' dangers. Eighty per cent of Britain's war-dead were under thirty and 40 per cent were younger than twenty-four.[7] By 1918, the largest demographic groups in many units were men of only nineteen or twenty years old. As a result, the BEF was increasingly an army of single (or, at least, unmarried) men. The average age of marriage had been steadily rising in the United Kingdom before 1914 and men tended to remain unmarried until the age of twenty-five, and many waited until they

---

[2] J. Winter, 'Families', in J. Winter (ed.), *The Cambridge History of the First World War. Vol. III: Civil Society* (Cambridge, 2014).

[3] Waller, *Town, City and Nation*, pp. 2-6.

[4] See p. 186. Also F.J. Hodges, *Men of 18 in 1918* (Ilfracombe, 1988); Ziemann, *Violence and the German Soldier*, p. 22.

[5] Watson, *Enduring the Great War*, pp. 158-160; Ziemann, *Violence and the German Soldier*, p. 22.

[6] McCartney, *Citizen Soldiers*, p. 139.

[7] Winter, *The Great War and the British People*, p. 267.

were twenty-seven or older.[8] Tellingly, in the BEF, servicemen over twenty-five were often considered to have entered 'old age'.[9] Donald Hankey believed that anyone over twenty-three was an 'old man'.[10] Significantly, even after the 1884 Representation of the People Act, the franchise was restricted to men over the age of twenty-one and this was only if they paid rent or owned land worth at least £10. Given that there had not been an election since 1910, younger servicemen would have had relatively limited engagement with national politics, and many would have never voted in a general election even if they were eligble to.

[8] E. Garrett et al., *Changing Family Size in England and Wales: Place, Class and Demography, 1891–1911* (Cambridge, 2001, 2004), pp. 230–232. Also J. Harris, *Private Lives, Public Spirit: Britain 1870–1914* (London, 1993, 1994).
[9] Lyricus, 'What Lloyd George Told Me! John Dull in Blighty', *The Lead Swinger* (Feb. 1918), p. 393.
[10] Hankey, *Student in Arms*, p. 106.

BIBLIOGRAPHY

Archival Material

The British Library, London

First World War, Misc. Leaflets, Programmes   BL Tab.11748.aa.4.1-122
Sketches of V.G. Bell [OR]   BL RP9518

Military and Trench Journals (via ProQuest)

24th Battalion Journal
The Army and Navy Gazette
The Bankers' Draft: Magazine of the 26th Battn. (Bankers') Royal Fusiliers
The B.E.F. Times
The Billet Doux
The Broad Arrow: The Naval and Military Gazette
Cambridgeshire Territorial Gazette
The Castronical: The Official Organ of the 6th London Rifles
The Cherrybuff: The Magazine of a Battalion of the Cheshire Regiment
Chronicles of the White Horse: Queen's Own Royal West Kent Regiment
The Cologne Post: A Daily Newspaper Published by the Army of the Rhine
The Cyclometer
The Dagger or *"London in the Line"*
The Dear Old Regiment
The Dud
The Fifth Glo'ster Gazette: A Chronicle, Serious and Humorous, of the Battalion while Serving with the British Expeditionary Force
The F.S.R: A Monthly Magazine
The Gasper: The Unofficial Organ of the 18th, 19th, 20th and 21st Royal Fusiliers
The Gasper: The Unofficial Organ of the BEF
The Growler: The Organ of the 16th Service Bat. Northumberland Fusiliers, Alnwick
The Hanger Herald
Highland Light Infantry Chronicle
Journal of the Royal United Services Institution
The Lead Swinger: The Bivouac Journal of the 1/3 West Riding Field Ambulance
The Londoner: The Journal 1/25th Battalion, The London Regiment

Machine Gun Corps Gazette
The Manchester Regiment Gazette
The Mudhook
The Mudlark or the *Bedfordshire Gazette*
The Outpost
"Pellican Pie": *The Official Organ of a West Riding Division*
The Red Feather
Signals
The Snapper: The Monthly Journal of the East Yorkshire Regt. (The Duke of York's Own)
The Somme Times: with which are incorporated *The Wipers Times, The "New Church" Times & The Kemmel Times*
Sports and Spuds
The Spud
The Sussex Patrol: Incorporating the Sussex Signal
The Talavera Magazine
The Wipers Times: A Facsimile Reprint of the Trench Magazine
War Dragon: Regimental Magazine of "The Buffs" (East Kent Regiment)

Newspapers (via ProQuest)

The Nation
The Spectator
The Times

Commonwealth War Graves Commission Archive, Maidenhead

Acquisition of Land – France – DGRE Files	CWGC/1/1/1/WG 549.1
Memorial Crosses and Unit Memorials – General File	CWGC/1/1/10/C/WG 1406:
Memorial Crosses and Unit Memorials	CWGC/1/1/10/C/WG1406.1 PT.1
Memorial Crosses and Unit Memorials	CWGC/1/1/10/C/WG 1406.2
Narrative Letters and Reports	CWGC/1/1/1/MU 1 Catalogue 1 Box 2029
Early Letters about Graves	CWGC/1/1/1/MU 3 Catalogue No. 3 Box 2029
A.W. Hill's Reports on Horticulture	CWGC/1/1/1/SDC 72
Ypres – General File	CWGC/1/1/9/B/WG 360 PT.1:

Imperial War Museum, London

Documents

Agius, Capt. A.J.J.P.	IWM Documents.8589
Anderson, Pte. W.M.	IWM Documents.5092

BIBLIOGRAPHY

Andrews, A.W. [OR] — IWM Documents.15946
Baker, H.E., [OR] — IWM Documents.20329
Baines, Lt. Col. C.S. — IWM Documents.10879
Bate, Canon H.R. [Officer] — IWM Documents.10782
Beevers, A., [OR] — IWM Documents.5875
Bell, Reverend C.H. [CoE Battalion Chaplain] — IWM Documents.16060
Bere, Reverend M.A. [CoE Battalion Chaplain] — IWM Documents.12105
Brettell, Lt. F.A. — IWM Documents.10814
Briggs, Mrs L.K. — IWM Documents.21795
Burke, A.P. [OR] — IWM Documents.1665
Cardew, Lt. F.B.A. — IWM Documents.9364
Castle, F.S. [OR] — IWM Documents.20755
Collis, A.L. [OR] — IWM Documents.20770
Cornwall, A.E. [OR] — IWM Documents.15139
Crosse, Canon E.C. [CoE Battalion Chaplain] — IWM Documents.4772
Crump, C.P. [OR] — IWM Documents.15069
Cubbitt-Ireland, Lt. L.W. — IWM Documents.14441
Donaldson, Capt. G.B. — IWM Documents.10933
Dwyer, C. [OR] — IWM Documents.16676
Ferrie, Capt. W.S. — IWM Documents.12643
Frost, R.C.A. [OR] — IWM Documents.16824
Gaunt, L/Cpl. / 2nd Lt. K.M. — IWM Documents.7490
Gower, M.F. [OR] — IWM Documents.255
Gray. 2nd Lt. C.W. — IWM Documents.11585
Greenwell, Capt. / Maj. G.H. — IWM Documents.11006
Grimston, J. [OR] — IWM Documents.14752
Grindley, E. [OR] — IWM Documents.15268
Hall, P.R. [OR] — IWM Documents.1690
Hardie, Capt. M. [Censor] — IWM Documents.4041
Hardman, Col. F. — IWM Documents.7233
Harris, Cpl. H. — IWM Documents.7650
Henrick Jones, 2nd Lt. D. — IWM Documents.16345
Heywood, A.E. [OR] — IWM Documents.15040
Hubard, F. [OR] — IWM Documents.20211
Hudson, Maj. S.R. — IWM Documents.13760
Hughes, 2nd Lt. H.M. — IWM Documents.11068
Ingleson, Capt. P. — IWM Documents.14517
Isom, C.H., [OR] — IWM Documents.16336
Johnson, Lt. J.H. — IWM Documents.7035
Judd, S., [OR] — IWM Documents.12027
Knyvett, Maj. J.S. — IWM Documents.12819
Lidsey, 2nd Lt. W.J. — IWM Documents.16504
Lloyd, Pte. A.W. — IWM Documents.10271

Lord, Capt. A.J.	IWM Documents.17029
Lycette, Capt. E.	IWM Documents.16020
Madders, H.T. [OR]	IWM Documents.11289
Martin, W.J. [OR]	IWM Documents.2554
Maxse, Gen. Sir Ivor [Director of Training]	IWM Documents.3255
May, Capt. C.C.	IWM Documents 1534
Medlicott, Lt. W.B.	IWM Documents.1708
Mellish, Reverend E.N. [CoE Battalion Chaplain]	IWM Documents.11173
Milner, H. [OR]	IWM Documents.20761
Newman, S.A. [OR]	IWM Documents.7076
Nichols, J.M. [OR]	IWM Documents.15743
Osborn, Capt. A.G.	IWM Documents.315
Plint, Cpl. R.G.	IWM Documents.4761
Richardson, Maj. S.O.B.	IWM Documents.8059
Russell, H. [OR]	IWM Documents.7312
Russell, N.R. [OR]	IWM Documents.9816
Senyard, Pte. F.G.	IWM Documents.7953
Shaddick, J. [OR]	IWM Documents.17180
Sheffield, R.D. [OR at the Time]	IWM Documents.14710
Sherrington, Capt. C.E.R.	IWM Documents.22595
Silver, T.A. [OR]	IWM Documents.7715
Skelton, Sgt. G.	IWM Documents.13966
Smith, S.B. [OR]	IWM Documents.15433
Spencer, Lt. Col. A.V.	IWM Documents.1422
Stevens, Brig. Gen. G.A. [Regimental Officer at the Time]	IWM Documents.12339
Stevens, R.E.P. [OR]	IWM Documents.12521
Cope, Lt Col. A.H.	IWM Documents.11976
Summers, Sgt. W.	IWM Documents13260
Tapp, Pte. W.	IWM Documents.18524
Tattersall, N. [OR]	IWM Documents.15773
Thomas, A. [OR]	IWM Documents.11427
Tofts, Maj. Gen. V.G. [Regimental Officer at the Time]	IWM Documents.14169
Tower, Lt. Col. K.F.B.	IWM Documents.11442
Trevor, Brig. Gen. H.E. [Regimental Officer at the Time]	IWM Documents.11445
Turnbull, Lt. Col. D.R.	IWM Documents.18455
Vernon, W. [OR]	IWM Documents.12771
Westropp, Col. L.H.M.	IWM Documents.7453
Wilson, L. [OR]	IWM Documents.2619
Worrall, F. [OR]	IWM Documents.14707

Winnard, Pte. G.G.   IWM Documents.7807
Wyatt, Lt. Col. J.D.   IWM Documents.4160
Young, Capt. R.E.M.   IWM Documents.20933
[Anon. OR] Postcard Signed by 'The Mademoiselle from Armentieres.'   IWM Documents.7371
[Anon. Officer] 'Secret Code Used to Bypass the Censors'   IWM Documents.8552
Diary of an Unidentified [OR] Soldier of the 2nd Bn. Border Regiment   IWM Documents.8631
Pocket Diary 1914 [OR]   IWM Documents.8674

Images

Photographs of Maj. Frederick Hardman   IWM PC 1784

Objects

"Ring"   IWM EPH 10150
"Bullet Crucifix"   IWM EPH 1915

Sound

Quinnell, C., [OR]   IWM Sound 554

Keep Museum, Dorchester

Blunt, Pte. J.   TKM Item 98/99/2/1
Brockwood, H.C. [OR]   TKM Item 95/160/24-26
Bull, T.C. [OR]   TKM Item 03/446/1-3
Fellows-Prynne, Capt. A.I.   TKM Item 00/230/6-12
Peyps, Col. C. (Misc. Letter)   TKM Item 97/117/14/1
Peyps, Col. C. (Letters to Parents)   TKM Item 97/413/1
Richards, C.J. [Officer]   TKM Item 90/50/2
Shears, Pte. G.L.   TKM Item 98/85/24
Walker's University Expert Manuscript Book – "Refresher" Bombing Course. Nov. 6th 1916.   TKM Item 230/5/2000

Liddle Collection, University of Leeds

Argent, Pte. R.   LIDDLE/WW1/GS/0042
Ashmole, Capt. B.   LIDDLE/WW1/GS/1847
Bailey, Capt. H.R.   LIDDLE/WW1/ADD/069
Bates, S.H. [OR]   LIDDLE/WW1/GS/0099
Bentley, W.G. [OR]   LIDDLE/WW1/GS/0125

Billingham, Pte. O.G.   LIDDLE/WW1/GS/0137
A&C Black and Company [ORs]   LIDDLE/WW1/GS/0144
Broad, R.D. [OR]   LIDDLE/WW1/GS/1847
Brooks, 2nd Lt. H.J.   LIDDLE/WW1/GS/0204
Bryan, J.L. [Officer]   LIDDLE/WW1/GS/0218
Bryson, Capt. G.L.U.   LIDDLE/WW1/GS/0222
Burdfield, A.E. [OR]   LIDDLE/WW1/GS/0232
Burrows, M.K. [Officer]   LIDDLE/WW1/GS/0246
Cannon, Pte. E.A.   LIDDLE/WW1/GS/0266
Carrington, Capt. C.   LIDDLE/WW1/GS/0273
Chapman, 2nd Lt. G.   LIDDLE/WW1/GS/0292
Clark, Pte. C.   LIDDLE/WW1/GS/0313
Conn, Pte. A.   LIDDLE/WW1/GS/0347
Crook, 2nd Lt. W.G.   LIDDLE/WW1/GS/0398
Cumberlege, 2nd Lt. G.F.J.   LIDDLE/WW1/GS/0505
Dent, L.M.E., [Officer]   LIDDLE/WW1/GS/0451
Edwards, Cpl. V.   LIDDLE/WW1/GS/0505
Field, A.J. [Officer]   LIDDLE/WW1/GS/0553
Frankenburg, 2nd Lt. S.   LIDDLE/WW1/GS/0583
Fraser, Sgt. A.T.   LIDDLE/WW/GS/02585
Fulton, A. [Officer]   LIDDLE/WW1/GS/0596
Gresham, T.B. [OR / Officer]   LIDDLE/WW1/GS/0662
Greenslade, C. [Officer]   LIDDLE/WW1/GS/0663
Greenwell, G.H. [Officer]   LIDDLE/WW1/GS/0664
McIver Grierson, K. [OR / Officer]   LIDDLE/WW1/GS/0670
Hampson, J.L. [OR]   LIDDLE/WW1/GS/0699
Harris, Cpl. D.   LIDDLE/WW1/GS/0715
Harrop, Pte. W.   LIDDLE/WW1/GS/0716
Harvey, Pte. R.A.   LIDDLE/WW1/GS/0723
Hay, D.F. [OR]   LIDDLE/WW1/GS/0728
Hendry, H.O. [OR]   LIDDLE/WW1/GS/0746
Heywood, 2nd Lt. H.C.L.   LIDDLE/WW1/GS/0752
Heywood, Sgt. J.A.   LIDDLE/WW1/ADD/015
Higgins, Capt. E.L.   LIDLLE/WW1/GS/0758
Hobbs, Pte. H.H.   LIDDLE/WW1/GS/0774
Hold, Pte. J.C.   LIDDLE/WW1/GS/0781
Horan, 2nd Lt. P.   LIDDLE/WW1/GS/0797
Houghton, Capt. J.R.   LIDDLE/WW1/GS/0805
Hunter-Blair, 2nd Lt. Sir J.   LIDDLE/WW1/GS/0820
Hunter, 2nd Lt. L.W.   LIDDLE/WW1/GS/0822
Innes, Pte. H.S.   LIDDLE/WW1/GS/0833
Isherwood, Capt. J.   LIDDLE/WW1/GS/0837

Lawson, H. [Officer]   LIDDLE/WW1/GS/0933
Leatherland, Pte. C.E.   LIDDLE/WW1/GS/0939
Lewisohn, Pte. J.   LIDDLE/WW1/GS/0952
MacDonald, W.S. [Officer]   LIDDLE/WW1/GS/1008
McDonald, 2nd Lt. J.R.   LIDDLE/WW1/GS/1005
Middleditch, 2nd Lt. A.W.   LIDDLE/WW1/GS/1096
Le May, D.G. [OR / Officer]   LIDDLE/WW1/GS/0946
Old, Pte. A.G.   LIDDLE/WW1/ADD/104
Sharp, Pte. C.W.   LIDDLE/WW1/GS/1444
Slater, Pte. J.E.   LIDDLE/WW1/GS/1484
Tully, Pte. C.L.   LIDDLE/WW1/GS/1634
Walley, Reverend S.C. [CoE Battalion Chaplain]   LIDDLE/WW1/GS/1680
Wilson, H. [OR]   LIDDLE/WW1/GS/1763
Woodworth, 2nd Lt. F.T.K.   LIDDLE/WW1/GS/1785

Liddell Hart Centre for Military Archives, King's College London
Robertson 2/2/1-111
Robertson 7/1/1

Manchester Regiment Archive, Ashton-Under-Lyne

Adams, Pte. W.   MR 3/17/118
Bedford, Pte. F.H.   MR 3/17/98/1
Betteley, L/Cpl. Thomas   MR 2/17/61
Bridge, Pte. H.   MR 3/17/139
Chase, Sgt. Maj. Herbert   MR 3/17/96
Clayton, Pte. W.G.   MR 3/17/142
Cleasby, Pte. Edgar   MR 3/17/124
Cooper, James Henry [OR]   MR 3/17/91
Doherty, Sgt. W.R.   MR 3/17/107
Dorling, Lt. Col. F.H.   MR 1/17/34
Gleeson, RSM Michael   MR 3/17/88
Irwin, Pte. G.   MR 3/17/115
James, Sgt, C.   MR 3/17/90
Jayes, Pte. J.   MR 3/17/128
Kennedy, Patrick Joseph [OR]   MR 2/17/53
Mannion, Pte. Thomas   MR 3/17/100
Merrick, CSM Harry   MR 3/17/129
Mutters, Sgt. Maj. C.W.   MR 3/17/112
Oldfield, Pte. H.   MR 3/17/110
Palin, Sgt. J.   MR 2/17/67
Peat, Pte. John   MR 3/17/126

Powell, Pte. John Douglas   MR/2/17/65
Smith, Pte. S.   MR 3/17/145
Walker, Pte. Norman   MR 3/17/137
Wild, Pte. C.E.   MR 4/17/388/1
Woodworth, 2nd Lt. Frederick Thomas Kearsley   MR 2/17/57
Duties of an Officer, 42nd (East Lancashire) Division   MR 3/13/2/35

National Archives, Kew

War Cabinet & Cabinet   CAB 24
Report on Postal Censorship during the Great War (1914–1919)   DEFE 1/131
Ministry of Food and Board of Trade Food Departments, 1916–1936   MAF 60/243
War Office and Successors   WO 32
First World War and Army of Occupation War Diaries   WO 95
Trench Maps   WO 153
Military Headquarters: Correspondence and Papers, First World War   WO 158
Committee on the Treatment of British Prisoners of War Interviews and Reports.   WO 161/95–100
Trench Maps   WO 207
Wt. W. 15534-9497. Spl. 4000. 2/17. F. & Q. (H.C.) Ltd. P. 17: Notes on the Area of the Ablainzeveille, Achiet-le-Grand, Achiet-le-Petit, Bihucourt, Bucquoy, Gomiecourt and Logeast Wood: Prepared by General Staff, Fifth Army   WO 223
'Memorandum of Army Training, 1909'   WO 231/404
Field Marshal D. Haig's Diary   WO 256
Attestation Forms in Soldiers' Service Records   WO 363 and 364

National Army Museum, London

Asprey, Capt. M.   NAM 2005-02-6
Aust, Herbert Victor [OR]   NAM 1990-01-58
Bradbury, Lt. Arthur Royce   NAM 1998-12-111-2
Burton, L/Cpl. W.   NAM 2004-05-27
Dalton, Pte. Percy Edward   NAM 2010-10-6
Eldridge, Sgt. Thomas   NAM 1978-04-65
Ellison, Lt. Gen. Sir Gerald   NAM 1987-07-26
Fitzgerald, 2nd Lt. R.A.   NAM 1979-07-136

BIBLIOGRAPHY 317

Fuller, A.W.F. [Officer] — NAM 1996-10-32
Hawtayne, Arthur [Officer] — NAM 1987-11-44
Hollingsworth, C.S.M. Arthur Thomas — NAM 1990-06-389
Hopwood, Sgt. H. — NAM 7403-29-486-144
Humphries, J.M. [OR / Officer] — NAM 1998-02-232
Hutchinson, Pte. A.E. — NAM 1982-12-70
Joy, Pte. A. — NAM 1992-09-139
Mahany, F.G.E. [OR] — NAM 2001-06-113
Neilson, Arthur [OR] — NAM 1990-12-95
Platt, Pte. Sidney and Platt, Pte. Vincent — NAM 1999-09-74
Polack, Pte. Maurice Henry — NAM 2003-10-8
Smart, Lt. Col. J.E. — NAM 1992-04-57-16-5
Selley, Sgt. Henry — NAM 2000-09-153-51
Symonds, Pte. A. J. — NAM 1998-08-31
Toft, Pte. H. — NAM 1960-11-40
Trench Newspapers — NAM 1959-03-34
A detailed account of the battle of Arras from 2nd Lieut. R.A. FITZGERALD to his Father — NAM 1979-07-136
Field Message Book (Army Form 153), 21 (Service) Bn Manchester Regiment — NAM 1980-01-4
Three documents including Haig's 'Special Orders of the Day' — NAM 1986-01-86
Anonymous account of Battle of Mons — NAM 1992-04-159
Letters sent to Bentley Bridgewater by his father in France — NAM 1993-02-508
Reminiscences of Unknown Guardsman 13 August to 3 November 1914 — NAM 1997-02-11
The Soldier's Word + Phrase Book French and German: Compiled by a Committee of Well-Known Teachers from Actual Experience of Soldiers' Needs (London: George G. Harrap & Company [Undated]) — NAM 1998-10-306
Anonymous: Postcard: 'The King's Message to his Army, Buckingham Palace. Signed George R.I.' — NAM 1998-12-111-14
Notes on the Area of Ablainzevile, France, from General Staff, 5th Army — NAM 2000-10-304
Training literature 1916–1917 — NAM 2005-09-57-10
Address by a Corps Commander to Young Officers on Leaving the Officers' School — NAM 2005-09-57-12-26

Papers and maps sent to Sir John Fortescue by   NAM 2006-04-25
Lt Gen Sir Ivor Maxse

National Meteorological Archive, Exeter

Bulletin International du Bureau Métérologique de France LVe Année 1914 2e Semestre	NMA 82 (43)
Rainfall Investigation by E. Gold / Gradient Wind Over Flanders	NMA 100 16
Estimated Earth Temperatures at One Foot in British Army Area 1915–1918, Meteorological Section Royal Engineers First Army, GHQ 12 December 1918', World War I – Analysis of Weather in Battlefield Area Compiled by R.G.K. Lampfert	NMA MET/2/6/1/6/f

Royal Fusiliers Museum, London

Arthur, Albert Victor [OR]	RFM.ARC.2012.146.1
Gelden, Fred [OR]	RFM.ARC.3017
Gill, Sgt. S.	RFM.ARC.2495.5
Marler, E.T. [OR]	RFM.ARC.2012.958
Osborn, Sgt.	RFM.ARC.2012.264
White, L/Cpl. C.	RFM.ARC.3032
Wright, Pte. P.N.	RFM.ARC 2013.8.2
Miscellaneous Documents (Standing Orders and Cards)	RFM.ARC.2013.9

Soldiers of Oxfordshire Museum, Woodstock

Allen, Pte. Alfred	SOFO Box 23 Item 10
Cheshire, Pte. W.J.	SOFO Box 16 Item 36
Child, F.W. [OR]	SOFO Box 16 Item 42
Clarke, Pte. S.A.	SOFO Box 16 Item 28
Early, Capt. J.H.	SOFO Box 23A Item 1
Early, Sgt. J.	SOFO Box 23 Item 99
Fullbrook-Leggatt, Capt. L.W.E.O.	SOFO Box 16 Item 12
George, Pte. C.	SOFO Box 16 Item 31
Hearn, C.S.M. A.	SOFO Box 29 Item 19
Jackson, Reverend K.C. [CoE Battalion Chaplain]	SOFO Box 23A Box 2E
Mawer, Pte. J.E.	SOFO Box 16 Item 35
Morris, Pte. William	SOFO Box 23 Item 7
Moulder, Sgt. Sam	SOFO Box 16 Item 7
Neville, Lt. J.E.H.	SOFO Box 16 Item 29
Neville, Lt. Reginald N.	SOFO Box 16 Item 3

O'Neill, Lt. C.T.   SOFO Box 16 Item 30
Symonds, Frederick   SOFO Box 29 Item 17
Thompson, Pte. Percy   SOFO Box 29 Item 4
[Anon.] 35 Postcards   SOFO Box 29 Item 1
Collection of 15 Patriotic Cards 1914–1918 Vintage   SOFO Box 16 Item 61

Tate Archive, London

Nash, P. [Officer]   TGA 8313

Wellcome Library, London

'Extracts from the proceedings of a court of   RAMC 446/18
enquiry re failure on the part of the 11th Border
Regiment, 97th Infantry Brigade, to carry out an attack'

Online Archival Material

Europeana

Griffiths, D.I., www.europeana1914-1918.eu/en/contributions/20788#prettyPhoto, accessed 15 November 2016

Great War Archive

Grantham, E., http://ww1lit.nsms.ox.ac.uk/ww1lit/gwa/document/9212, accessed 13 December 2023

Commonwealth War Graves Commission

Statistics in the Appendix are taken from from the Commonwealth War Grave Commission's (CWGC) list of dead, www.cwgc.org/find-war-dead.aspx

Operation War Diary

A crowdsourcing partnership between The National Archives, The Imperial War Museum, and Zooniverse that 'tags' war diaries for their information. See www.operationwardiary.org/, accessed 24 May 2018

Private Archival Material

Author's Own Collection

Anonymous Postcard Collection
Dyke, Fred
[No Surname], John
Smith, Miss. H., Brothers of

Published Primary Material

Anon., *A Pilgrim's Guide to the Ypres Salient* (London, 1920)
Bairnsfather, B., *The Best of Fragments from France*, T. Holt and V. Holt (eds.) (Barnsley, 1978, 2014)
Brittain, V., *Testament of Youth* (London, 1933, 2004)
Brophy, J., and Partridge E., *The Long Trail: Soldiers' Songs and Slang 1914-18* (Aylesbury, 1965, 1969)
Brotemarkle, R.A., 'Development of Military Morale in a Democracy', *Annals of the American Academy of Political and Social Science*, vol. 216, no. 1 (July 1941)
Carrington, Lt. C.E., *The War Record of the 1/5th Battalion The Royal Warwickshire Regiment* (Birmingham, 1922)
Chidgey, H.T., *Black Square Memories: An Account of the 2/8th Battalion the Royal Warwickshire Regiment, 1914-1918* (Oxford, 1924)
Crosse, Lt. Col. R.B., *A Short History of the Oxfordshire and Buckinghamshire Light Infantry, 1741-1922* (Aldershot, 1925)
Coop, J.O., *A Short Guide to the Battlefields* (Liverpool, 1920)
Eastaway, E. [pseudonym of E. Thomas], *Six Poems* (Flansham, 1916)
Edmonds, J.E., *History of the Great War Based on Official Documents. Military Operations. France and Belgium 1914. Mons, The Retreat to the Seine, the Marne and the Aisne August-October 1914* (London, 1925)
  History of the Great War Based on Official Documents. Military Operations France and Belgium, 1918 March-April: Continuation of the German Offensives (London, 1937)
Encyclopaedia Britannica, vol. 8 (London, 1911)
Ferryman, A.F.M., *Regimental War Tales, 1741-1914: Told for the Soldiers of the Oxfordshire and Buckinghamshire Light Infantry: The Old 43rd and 52nd* (Oxford, 1915)
Fortescue, J.W., *The British Soldier's Guide to Northern France and Flanders* (London, Undated)
Fuller, J.F.C., *Training Soldiers for War* (London, 1914)
  'Moral, Instruction, and Leadership', *Journal of the Royal United Services Institution*, vol. 65 (1920)
Gardner, B. (ed.), *Up the Line to Death* (York, 1964, 2007)
Gurfein, M.I., and Janowitz, M., 'Trends in Wehrmacht Morale', *The Public Opinion Quarterly*, vol. 10, no. 1 (Spring, 1946)
Hankey, D., *A Student in Arms* (London, 1920)
Harper, Lt. Gen. Sir. G.M., *Notes on Infantry Tactics & Training* (London, 1919)
  History of the 1/6th Royal Warwickshire Regiment (Birmingham, 1922)
HM Stationery Office, *Statistics of the Military Effort of the British Empire* (London, 1922)
Hood, Capt. B.R.N., *Duties for All Ranks* (London, c. 1916)
Housman, S.A.E., *A Shropshire Lad* (London, 1896, 1908)
Levi, P., *If this is a Man: The Truce*, trans. Woolf, S. (London, 1987)

Lowe, Lt. Col. T.A., *The Western Battlefields: A Guide to the British Line* (London, 1920)

Macpherson, W.G., Herringham, W.P., Elliott, T.R., and Balfour, A. (eds.), *History of the Great War Based on Official Documents: Medical Services – Surgery of the War*, vol. I (London, 1922)

History of the Great War Based on Official Documents: Medical Services – Disease of the War, vol. II (London, 1923)

Macpherson, W.G., Leishman, W.B., and Cummins, S.L. (eds.), *Official History of the Great War Based on Official Documents: Medical Services: Pathology* (London, 1923)

Manning, F., *Her Privates We* (London, 1999)

Marshall, S.L.A., *Men Against Fire: The Problem of Battle Command in Future War* (New York, 1966)

Masefield, J., *The Old Front Line* (New York, 1918)

McAdie, A., 'Has the War Affected the Weather?', *The Atlantic* (1916), www.theatlantic.com/magazine/archive/2014/08/has-the-war-affected-the-weather/373427/, accessed 24 August 2017

Michelin's Illustrated Guides to the Battlefields (1914–1918), *Amiens: Before and during the War* (Michelin & Cie, 1919)

Ypres and The Battles of Ypres (Clermont-Ferrand, 1919)

Mitchell, Maj. T.J., and Smith, G.M., *History of the Great War Based on Official Documents: Medical Services, Casualties and Medical Statistics of the Great War* (London, 1931)

Neville, J.E.H., *The War Letters of a Light Infantryman* (London, 1930)

Newbolt, Sir. H., *The Story of the Oxfordshire and Buckinghamshire Light Infantry: The Old 43rd and 52nd* (London, 1915)

Pember Reeves, M., *Round About a Pound a Week* (London, 1913, 2008)

Postal Censor's Department, *The London Censorship, 1914–1919: By Members of the Staff Past and Present* (London, 1920)

Rose, G.K., *The Story of the 2/4th Oxfordshire and Buckinghamshire Light Infantry* (Oxford, 1920)

Rowntree, B.S., *Poverty: A Study of Town Life* (London, 1901)

Sassoon, S., *The War Poems of Siegfried Sassoon* (London, 1919)

Shils, E.A., and Janowitz, M., 'Cohesion and Disintegration in the Wehrmacht in World War II', *Public Opinion Quarterly*, vol. 12, no. 2 (1948)

Stone, Maj. C. (ed.), *A History of the 22nd (Service) Battalion Royal Fusiliers (Kensingtons)* (London, 1923)

Stouffer, S.A., Suchman, E.A., DeVinney, L.C., Star, S.A., and Williams Jr, R.M., *The American Soldier: Adjustment during Army Life: Volume 1* (New York, 1949)

Thomas, E., *Last Poems* (London, 1918)

The King's Regulations and Orders for the Army (London, 1912)

Training and Manoeuvre Regulations (London, 1913)

U.S. Department of Agriculture, Weather Bureau: C.F. Martin, 'Notes on the Climate of France and Belgium, by Preston C. Day (October 1917)',

Climatological Data: Oklahoma, Volumes 23–28 (National Oceanic and Atmospheric, Environmental Data and Information Service, National Climatic Center (USA), 1914–1919)

War Office, *Infantry Training* (London, 1905)

Infantry Training (4 – Company Organisation) (1914)

SS 143, *Instructions for the Training of Platoons for Offensive Action*, 1917

40/1712, *Platoon Training* (1918)

Training and Manoeuvre Regulations (1913)

SS 143, *The Training and Employment of Platoons*, 1918

Ward, F.W., *The 23rd (Service) Battalion Royal Fusiliers (First Sportsman's): A Record of its Services in the Great War, 1914–1919* (London, 1920)

West, A.G., *The Diaries of a Dead Officer: Being the Posthumous Papers of A.G. West*, ed. C.J.M. West (London, 1918)

Williamson, H., *The Wet Flanders Plain* (Norwich, 1929, 1987)

Wheeler, Lt. Col. C. (ed.), *Memorial Record of the Seventh (Service) Battalion The Oxfordshire and Buckinghamshire Light Infantry* (Oxford, 1921)

Online Published Primary Material

Bairnsfather, B., *Bullets and Billets* (Project Gutenberg EBook, 2004), www.gutenberg.org/files/11232/11232-h/11232-h.htm, accessed 24 August 2015

Published Secondary Material

Aaronson, L.S. et al., 'Defining and Measuring Fatigue', *Journal of Nursing Scholarship*, vol. 31, no. 1 (March 1999)

Alexander, R., 'British Comedy and Humour: Social and Cultural Background', *AAA: Arbeiten aus Anglistik und Amerikanistik*, vol. 9, no. 1 (1984)

Allport, A., *Browned Off and Bloody-Minded: The British Soldier Goes to War* (New Haven, 2015)

Ancona, D., 'Framing and Acting in the Unknown', in S. Snook, N. Nohaira, and R. Khurana (eds.), *The Handbook for Teaching Leadership: Knowing, Doing, and Being* (Thousand Oaks, 2012)

Anderson, B., *Imagined Communities: Reflections on the Origins and Spread of Nationalism* (London, 1986, 2006)

Ashworth, T., *Trench Warfare, 1914–1918: The Live and Let Live System* (London, 1980, 2000)

Atance, C.M., and O'Neill, D.K., 'Episodic Future Thinking', *Trends in Cognitive Sciences*, vol. 5, no. 12 (December 2001)

Audoin-Rouzeau, S., 'Combat and Tactics', in J. Winter (ed.), *The Cambridge History of the First World War Volume II: The State* (Cambridge, 2014)

Men at War 1914–1918: National Sentiment and Trench Journalism in France during the First World War, trans. H. McPhail (Oxford, 1992, 1995)

Audoin-Rouzeau, S., and Becker, A., *14–18: Understanding the Great War*, trans. C. Temerson (New York, 2002)
Aylor, B., 'Maintaining Long-Distance Relationships', in D.J. Canary and M. Dainton (eds.), *Maintaining Relationships through Communication: Relational, Contextual and Cultural Variations* (New York, 2003, 2014)
Bamberg, M., and Andrews, M., *Consider Counter-Narratives: Narrating, Resisting, Making Sense* (Amsterdam, 2004)
Bamji, A., 'Facial Surgery: The Patient's Experience', in H. Cecil and P. Liddle (eds.), *Facing Armageddon: The First World War Experienced* (London, 1996, 2003)
Barth, F., *Ethnic Groups and Boundaries: The Social Organization of Culture Differences* (Long Grove, 1969, 1998)
Bartie, A., Fleming, L., Freeman, M., Hulme, T., Hutton, A., and Readman, P., 'Historical Pageants and the Medieval Past in Twentieth-Century England', *English Historical Review*, vol. 133, no. 563 (August 2018)
Bartov, O., *Hitler's Army: Soldiers, Nazis, and War in the Third Reich* (Oxford, 1992)
Baumeister, R.F., Bratslavsky, E., Finkenauer, C., and Kathleen, D., 'Bad Is Stronger Than Good', *Review of General Psychology*, vol. 5, no. 4 (December 2001)
Baumeister, R.F., Dale, K., and Sommer, K.L., 'Freudian Defense Mechanisms and Empirical Findings in Modern Social Psychology: Reaction Formation, Projection, Displacement, Undoing, Isolation, Sublimation, and Denial', *Journal of Personality*, vol. 66, no. 6 (December 1998)
Baynes, J., *Morale: A Study of Men and Courage: The Second Scottish Rifles at the Battle of Neuve Chapelle 1915* (London, 1987)
Beattie, O., and Geiger, J., *Frozen in Time: The Fate of the Franklin Expedition* (London, 1987, 2004)
Beaupré, N., 'La guerre comme expérience du temps et le temps comme expérience de guerre: hypothèses pour une histoire du rapport au temps des soldats français de la grande guerre', *Vingtième Siècle: Revue d'histoire*, no. 117 (2013)
Becker, A., 'Le front militaire et les occupations de la Grande Guerre comme laboratoires de destruction de la nature et de la culture', in P. Bonin and T. Pozzo (eds.), *Nature ou Culture: Les colloques de l'institut universitaire de France* (Saint-Étienne, 2015)
Becker, J.J., *The Great War and the French People* (London, 1986)
Beckett, I.F.W., 'The Nation in Arms, 1914–18', in I.F.W. Beckett and K. Simpson (eds.), *A Nation in Arms: A Social Study of the British Army in the First World War* (Manchester, 1985)
— 'The Singapore Mutiny of February 1915', *Journal of the Society of Army Historical Research*, vol. 62, no. 251 (1984)
Beckett, I.F.W., Bowman, T., and Connelly, M., *The British Army and the First World War* (Cambridge, 2017)
Beckett, I.F.W., and Simpson, K. (eds.), *A Nation in Arms* (Barnsley, 1985, 2014)

Bellert, J., 'Humour: A Therapeutic Approach in Oncology Nursing', *Cancer Nursing*, vol. 12, no. 2 (April 1989)

Bet-El, I.R., *Conscripts: Forgotten Men of the Great War* (Stroud, 2009)

Black, J., *The Great War and the Making of the Modern World* (London, 2011)

Blewett, N., 'The Franchise in the United Kingdom, 1885-1918', *Past & Present*, no. 32 (December 1965), pp. 27-57

Boff, J., *Haig's Enemy: Crown Prince Rupprecht and Germany's War on the Western Front* (Oxford, 2018)

'The Morale Maze: The German Army in Late 1918', *Journal of Strategic Studies*, vol. 37, no. 6-7 (2014)

Winning and Losing on the Western Front: The British Third Army and the Defeat of Germany in 1918 (Cambridge, 2012)

Borgas, J.P., Vincze O., and László, J., 'Social Cognition and Communication: Background, Theories and Research', in J.P. Borgas, O. Vincze and J. László (eds.) *Social Cognition and Communication* (New York, 2014)

Bordia, P., and DiFonzo, N., 'Problem Solving in Social Interactions on the Internet: Rumor As Social Cognition', *Social Psychology Quarterly*, vol. 67, no. 1 (March 2004)

Bourke, J., *An Intimate History of Killing: Face-to-Face Killing in Twentieth Century Warfare* (London, 1999)

Dismembering the Male: Men's Bodies, Britain and the Great War (London, 1996)

Fear: A Cultural History (London, 2005)

'Gender Roles in Killing Zones', in J. Winter (ed.), *The Cambridge History of the First World War Volume 3: Civil Society* (Cambridge, 2014)

Bourne, J., 'The British Working Man in Arms', in H. Cecil and P. Liddle (eds.), *Facing Armageddon: The First World War Experienced* (London, 1996, 2003)

Bowlby, J., *Attachment and Loss: Vol: 1 Attachment* (New York, 1973)

'The Nature of the Child's Tie to His Mother', *International Journal of Psycho-Analysis*, vol. 39 (1958)

Bowman, T., *The Irish Regiments in the Great War: Discipline and Morale* (Manchester, 2004)

Bowman, T., and Connelly, M., *The Edwardian Army: Recruiting, Training, and Deploying the British Army, 1902-1914* (Oxford, 2012)

Braudel, F., *The Mediterranean and the Mediterranean World in the Age of Philip II Vol: I-II*, trans. S. Reynolds (London, [1949] 1972-73, 1995)

Brief, A.P., Dukerich, J.M., and Doran, L.I., 'Resolving Ethical Dilemmas in Management: Experimental Investigations of Values, Accountability, and Choice', *Journal of Applied Social Psychology*, vol. 21 (1991)

Brimblecombe, P., *The Big Smoke: A History of Air Pollution in London Since Medieval Times* (Cambridge, 1987)

Bromwich, D., *Moral Imagination* (Princeton and Woodstock, 2014)

Brouland, P., and Doizy, G., *La Grande Guerre des cartes postales* (Paris, 2013)

Brubaker, R., *Citizenship and Nationhood in France and Germany* (Cambridge, 1992, 1994)
Brüggen, A.S., 'Imagination and Experience', in *Open MIND* (Frankfurt, 2014)
Bullock, A., and Stallybrass, O. (eds.), *The Fontana Dictionary of Modern Thought* (Bungay, 1977)
Bura, P., 'Étude anthropologique de la sépulture multiple', *Sucellus*, vol. 54 (2003)
Bushman, B.J., 'Perceived Symbols of Authority and their Influence on Compliance', *Journal of Applied Social Psychology*, vol. 14 (1984)
Byrne, R.M.J., *The Rational Imagination: How People Create Alternatives to Reality* (Cambridge, 2005)
Cannadine, D., 'The Context, Performance and Meaning of Ritual: The British Monarchy and the "Invention of Tradition", c. 1820–1977', in E. Hobsbawm and T. Ranger, eds., *The Invention of Tradition* (Cambridge, 1983), pp. 101–164
  Victorious Century: The United Kingdom, 1806–1906 (London, 2017)
Carver, C.S., and Scheier, M., 'Optimism', in S.J. Lopez and C.R. Snyder (eds.), *Positive Psychological Assessment: A Handbook of Models and Measures* (London, 2003)
Chandler, D., and Beckett, I., *The Oxford Illustrated History of the British Army* (Oxford, 1994)
Chasseaud, P., *Rats Alley: Trench Names of the Western Front, 1914–1918* (Stroud, 2006)
Chatterjee, S., 'Children's Friendship with Place: A Conceptual Inquiry', *Children, Youth and Environments*, vol. 15 (2005)
Cherry, B., *They Didn't Want to Die Virgins: Sex and Morale in the British Army on the Western Front* (Wolverhampton, 2016)
Christie, N., and Gauvreau, M., *Bodies, Love, and Faith in the First World War* (Cham, 2018)
Colley, L., *Britons: Forging the Nation 1707–1837* (New Haven, 2012)
  'Whose Nation? Class and National Consciousness in Britain 1750–1830', *Past & Present*, vol. 113, no. 1 (1986)
Colls, R., *Identity of England* (Oxford, 2002)
Connelly, M., *Steady the Buffs! A Regiment, a Region, and the Great War* (Oxford, 2006)
  'The Ypres League and the Commemoration of the Ypres Salient, 1914–1940', *War in History*, vol 16, no. 1 (2009)
Connelly, M., and Goebel, S., *Ypres* (Oxford, 2018)
Connolly, J.E., 'Notable Protests: Respectable Resistance in Occupied Northern France, 1914–1918', *Historical Research*, vol. 88, no. 243 (2015)
  The Experience of Occupation in the Nord, 1914–1918 (Manchester, 2018)
Conway, G., 'Presidential Address: Geographical Crises of the Twenty-First Century', *The Geographical Journal*, vol. 175, no. 3 (September 2009), p. 221
Cook, T., *The Secret History of Soldiers: How Canadians Survived the Great War* (London, 2018)
Cornish, P., and Saunders, N., *Bodies in Conflict: Corporeality, Materiality, and Transformation* (London, 2009)

Modern Conflict and the Senses: Killer Instincts? (London, 2016)

Cornwall, M., 'Morale and Patriotism in the Austro-Hungarian Army, 1914–1918', in J. Horne (ed.), *State, Society and Mobilization in Europe during the First World War* (Cambridge, 1997)

The Last Years of Austria-Hungary: Essays in Political and Military History (Exeter, 1990)

The Undermining of Austria-Hungary: The Battle for Hearts and Minds (Basingstoke, 2000)

Corrigan, G., *Mud, Blood and Poppycock: Britain and the First World War* (London, 2003, 2004)

Cowman, K., 'Touring Behind the Lines: British Soldiers in French Towns and Cities during the Great War', *Urban History*, vol. 41, no. 1 (February 2014)

Croy, I., Maboshe, W., and Hummel, T., 'Habituation Effects of Pleasant and Unpleasant Odors', *International Journal of Psychophysiology*, vol. 88, no. 1 (April 2013)

Cunningham, H., 'The Language of Patriotism, 1750–1914', *History Workshop Journal*, vol. 12, no. 1 (October 1981)

Curran, J., '"Bonjoor Paree!" The First AIF in Paris, 1916–1918', *Journal of Australian Studies*, vol. 23, no. 60 (1999)

Danchin, E., 'Destruction du patrimoine et figure du soldat allemand dans les cartes postales de la Grande Guerre', *Amnis*, vol. 10 (2011)

Le temps des ruines 1914–1921 (Rennes, 2015)

Dakers, C., *Forever England: The Countryside at War, 1914–1918* (London, 2015)

Deist, W., 'The Military Collapse of the German Empire: The Reality of the Stab-in-the-Back Myth', trans. E.J., Feuchtwanger, *War in History*, vol. 3, no. 2 (1992)

Dennis, P., and Grey, J. (eds.), *1917: Tactics, Training and Technology* (Canberra, Australia, 2007)

Dainton, M., and Aylor, B., 'Patterns of Communication Use in the Maintenance of Long-Distance Relationships', *Communication Research Reports*, vol. 19, no. 2 (2002)

Daly, S., Salvante, M., and Wilcox, V. (eds.), *Landscapes of the First World War* (Cham, 2018)

Das, S., *India, Empire and First World War Culture: Writings, Images and Songs* (Cambridge, 2018)

Touch and Intimacy in First World War Literature (Cambridge, 2005)

Davies, O., *A Supernatural War: Magic, Divination, and Faith during the First World War* (Oxford, 2019)

Desfossés, P.Y., Jacques, A., and Prilaux, G., 'Arras "Actiparc" les oubliés du "Point du Jour"', *Sucellus*, vol. 54 (2003)

De Vignemont, F., and Singer, T., 'The Empathic Brain: How, When and Why?', *Trends in Cognitive Sciences*, vol. 10, no. 10 (October 2006)

Dixon, N., *On the Psychology of Military Incompetence* (London, 1976, 1994)

Dowdall, A., 'Civilians in the Combat Zone: Allied and German Evacuation Policies at the Western Front, 1914–1918', *First World War Studies*, vol. 6, no. 3 (2015)

Doyle, P., *British Postcards of the First World War* (London, 2011)
Duffett, R., *The Stomach for Fighting: Food and the Soldiers of the Great War* (Manchester, 2012)
Eble, C.C., *Slang & Sociability: In-Group Language among College Students* (Chapel Hill, 1996)
Edensor, T., 'Sensing the Ruin', *The Senses and Society*, vol. 2, no. 2 (2007)
Ellis, H., 'Stoicism in Victorian Culture', in J. Sellars (ed.), *The Routledge Handbook of the Stoic Tradition* (Abingdon, 2016)
Emmons, R.A., 'Personal Goals, Life Meaning and Virtue: Wellsprings of a Positive Life', in C.L.M. Keyes and J. Haidt (eds.), *Flourishing: Positive Psychology and the Life Well Lived* (Washington, 2003)
Englander, D., 'Discipline and Morale in the British Army, 1917–1918', in J. Horne (ed.), *State, Society and Mobilization in Europe during the First World War* (Cambridge, 1997)
  'Soldiering and Identity: Reflections on the Great War', *War in History*, vol. 1, no. 3 (November 1994)
Fennell, J., *Combat and Morale in the North African Campaign* (Cambridge, 2011)
  Fighting the People's War: The British and Commonwealth Armies and the Second World War (Cambridge, 2019)
  'In Search of the "X" Factor: Morale and the Study of Strategy', *Journal of Strategic Studies*, vol. 37, no. 6-7 (2014)
  'Soldiers and Social Change: The Forces Vote in the Second World War and New Zealand's Great Experiment in Social Change', *The English Historical Review*, vol. 132, no. 554 (2017)
Ferguson, N., *The Pity of War: Explaining World War I* (London, 1998)
Fletcher, A., *Life, Death and Growing Up on the Western Front* (Cambridge, 2013)
Foucault, M., *Aesthetics, Methods and Epistemology*, ed. J.D. Faubion and trans. R. Hurley et al. (New York, 1998)
  Discipline and Punishment: The Birth of the Prison, trans. A. Sheridan (London, 1995)
Fox, A., '"I Have Never Felt More Utterly Yours": Presence, Intimacy, and Long-Distance Marriages in the First World War', *Journal of British Studies*, vol. 61, no. 3 (July 2022)
  Learning to Fight: Military Innovation and Change in the British Army, 1914–1918 (Cambridge, 2018)
French, D., *British Strategy and War Aims 1914–1916* (London, 1986)
  Military Identities: The Regimental System, the British Army and the British People (Oxford, 2005)
Freud, S., *The Interpretation of Dreams*, trans. A.A. Brill (New York, 1913)
  New Introductory Lectures on Psycho-Analysis, trans. W.J.H. Sprott (New York, 1933)
Frevert, U., *A Nation in Barracks: Modern Germany, Military Conscription and Civil Society*, trans. A. Boreham and D. Brückenhause (Oxford, 2004)
  Emotions in History – Lost and Found (New York, 2011)

Fry, D.P., *The Human Potential for Peace: An Anthropological Challenge to Assumptions about War and Violence* (Oxford, 2005)
Fuller, J.G., *Troop Morale and Popular Culture in the British and Dominion Armies, 1914-1918* (Oxford, 1991)
Fussell, P., *The Great War and Modern Memory* (Oxford, 1975, 2000)
Gadamer, H.G., *Truth and Method* (London, 1975)
Garrett, E., Reid, A., Schürer, K., and Szreter, S., *Changing Family Size in England and Wales: Place, Class and Demography, 1891-1911* (Cambridge, 2001, 2004)
Gerry, C.J., 'Review: Crisis and the Everyday in *Postsocialist Moscow* by Shevchenko, Olga', *The Slavonic and East European Review*, vol. 89, no. 1 (2011), p. 184
Gerwarth, R., *The Vanquished: Why the First World War Failed to End, 1917-1923* (London, 2016)
Gerwarth, R., and Horne, J., 'Vectors of Violence: Paramilitarism in Europe after the Great War, 1917-1923', *The Journal of Modern History*, vol. 83, no. 3 (September 2011)
Gibson, C., *Behind the Front: British Soldiers and French Civilians 1914-1918* (Cambridge, 2014)
  'Sex and Soldiering in France and Flanders: The British Expeditionary Force along the Western Front, 1914-1919', *International History Review*, vol. 23 (2001)
Gibson-Bryson, T.R.C., *The Moral Mapping of Victorian and Edwardian London: Charles Booth, Christian Charity, and the Poor-but-Respectable* (Montreal, 2016)
Gigerenzer, G., and Goldstein, D.G., 'Reasoning the Fast and Frugal War: Models of Bounded Rationality', *Psychological Review*, vol. 103, no. 4. (1996)
Gilbert, A., *Challenge of Battle: The Real Story of the British Army in 1914* (Oxford, 2014)
Gill, D., and Dallas, G., 'Mutiny and Etaples Base in 1917', *Past & Present*, no. 69 (November 1975)
  The Unknown Army: Mutinies in the British in World War I (London, 1985)
Glenn Gray, J., *The Warriors: Reflections on Men in Battle* (New York, 1959, 1970)
Goebel, S., *The Great War and Medieval Memory: War, Remembrance and Medievalism in Britain and Germany, 1914-1940* (Cambridge, 2007)
Goffman, E., *The Presentation of Self in Everyday Life* (London, 1959, 1990)
Golman, R., Hagmann, D., and Loewenstein, G., 'Information Avoidance', *Journal of Economic Literature*, vol. 55, no. 1 (March 2017)
Gough, P., *A Terrible Beauty: British Artists in the First World War* (Bristol, 2010)
Gould, P.C., *Early Green Politics: Back to Nature, Back to Land, and Socialism in Britain 1880-1914* (Brighton, 1988)
Grayson, R., 'A Life in the Trenches? The Use of *Operation War Diary* and Crowdsourcing Methods to Provide an Understanding of the British Army's Day-to-Day Life on the Western Front', *British Journal for Military History*, vol. 2, no. 2 (2016)

Belfast Boys: How Unionists and Nationalists Fought and Died Together in the First World War (London, 2009)

Grayzel, S., 'Mothers, Marraines, and Prostitutes: Morale and Morality in First World War France', *International History Review*, vol. 19 (1997)

'"The Outward Sign and Visible Sign of Her Patriotism": Women, Uniforms, and National Service during the First World War', *Twentieth Century British History*, vol. 8, no. 2 (1997)

Green, A., *Writing the Great War: Sir James Edmonds and the Official Histories 1915-1948* (London, 2003)

Greenhalgh, E., '"Parade Ground Soldiers": French Army Assessments of the British on the Somme in 1916', *The Journal of Military History*, vol. 63, no. 2 (April 1999)

Gregory, A., *The Last Great War: British Society and the First World War* (Cambridge, 2008)

Grieves, K.,'The Propinquity of Place: Home, Landscape and Soldier Poets of the First World War', in J. Meyer (ed.), *British Popular Culture and the First World War*

Griffith, P., 'The Extent of Tactical Reform in the British Army', in P. Griffith (ed.), *British Fighting Methods in the Great War* (London, 1996)

Guoqi, X., *Strangers on the Western Front: Chinese Workers in the Great War* (London, 2011)

Hage, G., 'A Not so Multi-Sited Ethnography of a Not So Imagined Community', *Anthropological Theory*, vol 5, no. 4 (2005)

Halifax, S., '"Over by Christmas": British Popular Opinion and the Short War in 1914', *First World War Studies*, vol. 1, no. 2 (October 2010)

Hall S. (ed.), *Representation: Cultural Representations and Signifying Practices* (London, 1997, 2003)

Halstead, T., 'The First World War and Public School Ethos: The Case of Uppingham School', *War & Society*, vol. 34, no 3 (2015)

Hammond, B., *Cambrai 1917: The Myth of the First Great Tank Battle* (London, 2009)

Hanna, E., '"Say it with Music": Combat, Courage and Identity in the Songs of the RFC/RAF, 1914-1918', *British Journal for Military History*, vol. 4, no. 2 (2018)

Sounds of War: Music and the British Armed Forces during the Great War (Cambridge, 2020)

Hanna, M., 'A Republic of Letters: The Epistolary Tradition in France during World War I', *American Historical Review*, vol. 108, no. 5 (2003)

'The Couple', in J. Winter (ed.), *The Cambridge History of the First World War: Vol. III: Civil Society* (Cambridge, 2014)

Your Death Would Be Mine: Paul and Marie Pireaud in the Great War (Cambridge, 2006)

Hannavy, J., *The English Seaside in Victorian and Edwardian Times* (London, 2011)

Harari, Y.N., *Sapiens: A Brief History of Human kind*, trans. Y.N. Harari, J. Purcell, and H. Watzman (London, 2011, 2014)
Harraway, D., *Simians, Cyborgs, and Women: The Reinvention of Nature* (London, 1991)
Harries-Jenkins, G., *The Army in Victorian Society* (Abingdon, 1977, 2007)
Harris, J., *Private Lives, Public Spirit: Britain 1870-1914* (London, 1993, 1994)
Hart, B.H.L., *New Methods in Infantry Training* (Cambridge, 1918), p. 3
Hart, P., *1918: A Very British Victory* (London, 2008, 2009)
Hashemnezhad, H., Heidari, A.A., and Hoseini, P.M., '"Sense of Place" and "Place Attachment": A Comparative Study', *International Journal of Architecture and Urban Development*, vol. 3, no. 1 (2013)
Henman, L.D., 'Humor as a Coping Mechanism: Lessons from POWs', *Humor: International Journal of Humor Research*, vol. 14, no. 1 (2008)
Hichberger, J.W.M., *Images of the Army: The Military in British Art, 1815-1914* (Manchester, 1988)
Hiebert, P.G., *Transforming Worldviews: An Anthropological Understanding of How People Change* (Grand Rapids, 2008)
Hirsch, E., and O'Hanlon, M.O. (eds.), *The Anthropology of Landscape: Perspective on Space and Place* (Oxford, 1995)
Hirschman, A., *Exit, Voice and Loyalty: Responses to Decline in Firms, Organizations, and States* (Cambridge, 1970)
Hobsbawm, E., *Nations and Nationalism since 1780* (Cambridge, 1990)
Hodges, F.J., *Men of 18 in 1918* (Ilfracombe, 1988)
Hodgkinson, P., *Glum Heroes: Hardship, Fear and Death – Resilience and Coping in the British Army on the Western Front, 1914-1919* (Exeter, 2016)
Hoffenberg, P.H., 'Landscape, Memory and the Australian War Experience, 1915-18', *Journal of Contemporary History*, vol. 36, no. 1 (January 2001)
Hogg, M.A., 'Group Cohesiveness: A Critical Review and Some New Directions', *European Review of Social Psychology*, vol. 4 (1993)
Holman, V., and Kelly, D., 'Introduction. War in the Twentieth Century: The Function of Humour in Cultural Representation', *Journal of European Studies*, vol. 31, no. 23 (2001)
Holmes, R., *The Western Front* (London, 1999)
Holt, P., and Stone, G., 'Needs, Coping Strategies and Coping Outcomes Associated with Long-Distance Relationships', *Journal of College Student Development*, vol. 29 (1988)
Holt, T., and Holt, V., *Till the Boys Come Home* (Barnsley, 1977, 2014)
Hough, M., Ballinger, S., and Katwala, S., *A Centenary Shared: Tracking Public Attitudes to the First World War, 2013-16* (London, 2016)
Herwig, H., *The First World War: Germany and Austria-Hungary, 1914-1918* (New York, 1997)
Horne, J., 'Entre expérience et mémoire. Les soldats français de la Grande Guerre', *Annales Histoire, Sciences Sociales*, vol. 60 (2005)
—— 'Foreword', in A. Luptak, H. Smyth, and L. Halewood (eds.), *War Time: First World War Perspectives on Temporality* (Abingdon, 2018)

'Patriotism and the Enemy: Political Identity as a Weapon', in. N. Wouters and L. van Ypersele (eds.), *Nations, Identities and the First World War: Shifting Loyalties to the Fatherland* (London, 2018)

(ed.) *State, Society and Mobilization in Europe during the First World War* (Cambridge, 1997)

'The End of a Paradigm? The Cultural History of the Great War', *Past & Present*, vol. 242, no. 1 (February 2019)

Houlihan, P.J., *Clergy in the Trenches: Catholic Military Chaplains of Germany and Austria Hungary* (Chicago, 2011)

Hull, I.V., *Absolute Destruction: Military Culture and the Practices of War in Imperial Germany* (Cornell, 2005)

Hulme, T., '"A Nation of Town Criers": Civic Publicity and Historical Pageantry in Inter-War Britain', *Urban History*, vol. 44, no. 2 (May 2017)

Hunt, L., 'French History in the Last Twenty Years: The Rise and Fall of the *Annales* Paradigm', *Journal of Contemporary History*, vol. 21 (1986)

Hunter, K., 'More than an Archive of War: Intimacy and Manliness in the Letters of a Great War Soldier to the Woman He Loved, 1915–1919', *Gender & History*, vol. 25, no. 2 (August 2013)

Huss, M.M., *Histoires de famille, 1914/1918: cartes postales et cultures de guerre* (Paris, 2000)

Hussey, J., 'The Monsoon in Flanders', *Journal of the Society for Army Historical Research*, vol. 74, no. 300 (Winter 1996)

Hynes, S., *A War Imagined: The First World War in English Culture* (London, 1992)

The Soldiers' Tale: Bearing Witness to Modern War (London, 1999)

Inglis, K.S., *Sacred Places: War Memorials in the Australian Landscape* (Melbourne, 1998, 2008)

Jahr, C., *Gewöhnliche Soldaten: Desertion und Deserteure im deutschen und britischen Heer 1914–1918* (Göttingen, 1998)

Johnson, M., *The Body in the Mind: The Bodily Basis of Meaning, Imagination, and Reason* (Chicago, 1987, 1990)

Johnson, P., 'Conspicuous Consumption and Working-Class Culture in late-Victorian and Edwardian Britain', *Transactions of the Royal Historical Society*, vol. 38 (December 1988)

Jones, E., 'The Psychology of Killing: The Combat Experience of British Soldiers during the First World War', *Journal of Contemporary History*, vol. 41, no. 2 (2006)

'War Neuroses', *Journal of the History of Medicine and Allied Sciences*, vol. 67, no. 3 (2012)

Jones, E., and Wessely, S., *Shell Shock to PTSD: Military Psychiatry from 1900 to the Gulf War* (Hove, 2005)

Jones, E., Woolven, R., Durodié, B., and Wessely, S., 'Civilian Morale during the Second World War: Responses to Air Raids Re-Examined', *Social History of Medicine*, vol. 17, no. 3 (2004)

Jones, H., *For King and Country: The British Monarchy and the First World War* (Cambridge, 2021)

'The Nature of Kingship in First World War Britain', in M. Glencross, J. Rowbotham, and M.D. Kandiah (eds.), *The Windsor Dynasty 1910 to the Present: Long to Reign Over Us?* (London, 2016)

Kahneman, D., 'A Perspective on Judgement and Choice', *The American Psychologist*, vol. 59, no. 9 (2003)

'Maps of Bounded Rationality: Psychology for Behavioral Economics', *The American Economic Review*, vol. 93, no. 5 (December 2003)

Thinking, Fast and Slow (London, 2012)

Kay, J., '"No Time for Recreations till the Vote is Won"? Suffrage Activists and Leisure in Edwardian Britain', *Women's History Review*, vol. 16, no. 4 (2007)

Kazecki, J., *Laughter in the Trenches: Humour and Front Experience in German First World War Narratives* (Newcastle-upon-tyne, 2012)

Keegan, J., *The Face of Battle: A Study of Agincourt, Waterloo and the Somme* (Harmondsworth, 1983)

The First World War (London, 1998, 1999)

Keller, T., *Apostles of the Alps: Mountaineering and Nation Building in Germany and Austria* (Chapel Hill, 2016)

'Mobilizing Nature for the First World War: An Introduction', in R.P. Tucker, T. Keller, J.R. McNeill and M. Schmid (eds.) Environmental Histories of the First World War (Cambridge, 2018)

'The Mountains Roar: The Alps during the Great War', *Environmental History*, vol. 14, no. 2 (2009)

Kelly, V., *Soap and Water: Cleanliness, Dirt and the Working Classes in Victorian and Edwardian Britain* (London, 2010)

Kessel, M., 'Talking War, Debating Unity: Order, Conflict, and Exclusion in "German Humour" in the First World War', in M. Kessel and P. Merziger (eds.), *The Politics of Humour: Laughter, Inclusion, and Exclusion in the Twentieth Century* (London, 2012)

Kessler, R., White, L.A., Birnbaum, H., Qiu, Y., Kidolezi, Y., Mallett, D., and Swindle, R., 'Comparative and Interactive Effects of Depression Relative to Other Health Problems on Work Performance in the Workforce of a Large Employer', *Journal of Occupation and Environmental Medicine*, vol. 50, no. 7 (July 2008)

Kestnbaum, M., 'The Sociology of War and the Military', *Annual Review of Sociology*, vol. 35 (April 2009)

Kilcullen, D., 'Strategic Culture', in P.R. Mansoor and W. Murray (eds.), *The Culture of Military Organisations* (Cambridge, 2019)

Kilham, W., and Mann, L., 'Level of Destructive Obedience as Function of Transmitter and Executant Roles in the Milgram Obedience Paradigm', *Journal of Personality and Social Psychology*, vol. 29 (1974)

King, L.A., 'The Health Benefits of Writing about Life Goals', *Personality and Social Psychology Bulletin*, vol. 27, no. 7 (July 2001)

Kitchen, J., *The British Imperial Army in the Middle East: Morale and Identity in the Sinai and Palestine Campaigns* (London, 2014)

Komaroff, A.L., and Buchwald, D., 'Symptoms and Signs of Chronic Fatigue Syndrome', *Reviews of Infectious Diseases*, vol. 13, no. suppl. 1 (January, 1991)

Koselleck, R., *Futures Past: On the Semantics of Historical Time*, trans. K. Tribe (New York, [1979] 2004)

Koss, M.P., Figueredo, A.J., Bell, I., Tharan, M., and Tromp, S., 'Traumatic Memory Characteristics: A Cross-Validated Mediational Model of Response to Rape among Employed Women', *Journal of Abnormal Psychology*, vol. 105, no. 3 (1996)

Kramer, A., *Dynamic of Destruction: Culture and Mass Killing in the First World War* (Oxford, 2007)
  'Recent Historiography of the First World War – Part I', *Journal of Modern European History*, vol. 12 (2014)
  'Recent Historiography of the First World War – Part II', *Journal of Modern European History*, vol. 12 (2014)

Kramer, L., *Nationalism in Europe and America: Politics, Cultures, and Identities since 1775* (Chapel Hill, 2011)

Krumeich, G., 'Le soldat allemande sur la Somme', in J.-J. Becker and S. Audoin-Rouzeau (eds.), *Les sociétés européennes et la guerre de 1914-1918* (Nanterre, 1990)

Kuhn, W.M., *Democratic Royalism: The Transformation of the British Monarchy, 1861-1914* (Basingstoke, 1996)

Kyle, G.T., Mowen, A.J., and Tarrant, M., 'Linking Place Preferences with Place Meaning: An Examination of the Relationship between Place Motivation and Place Attachment', *Journal of Environmental Psychology*, vol. 24 (2004)

Larsdotter, K., 'Culture and Military Intervention', in J. Angstrom and I. Duyvesteyn (eds.) *Understanding Victory and Defeat in Contemporary War* (Abingdon, 2007)

Latour, B., 'The Powers of Association', in J. Law (ed.), *Power, Action and Belief: A New Sociology of Knowledge?* (London, 1987)

László, J., *The Science of Stories: An Introduction to Narrative Psychology* (Abingdon, 2008)

Leed, E.J., *No Man's Land: Combat and Identity in World War I* (Cambridge, 1979, 1981)

Leese, P., *Shell Shock: Traumatic Neurosis and the British Soldiers of the First World War* (Basingstoke, 2002)

Le Naour, J., 'Laughter and Tears in the Great War: The Need for Laughter/The Guilt of Humour', *Journal of European Studies*, vol. 31, no. 123 (2001)
  La Grande Guerre à travers la Carte Postale Ancienne (Paris, 2013)

Lewis-Stempel, J., *Six Weeks: The Short and Gallant Life of the British Officer in the First World War* (London, 2010)
  Where the Poppies Blow: The British Soldier, Nature, the Great War (London, 2016)

Liddle, P., *The Soldier's War 1914-18* (London, 1988)

Passchendaele in Perspective: The Third Battle of Ypres (London, 1997)

Linden, S., *The Called it Shell Shock: Combat Stress in the First World War* (Exeter, 2016)

Liulevicius, V.G., *War Land on the Eastern Front: Culture, National Identity, and German Occupation in World War I* (Cambridge, 2009)

Lloyd, N., *Passchendaele: A New History* (London, 2017)

The Western Front: A History of the First World War (London, 2021)

Locher, F., and Quenet, G., 'Environmental History: The Origins, Stakes, and Perspectives of a New Site for Research', trans. W. Bishop, *Revue d'histoire moderne et contemporaine*, vol. 56–4, no. 4 (2009)

Longworth, P., *The Unending Vigil: The History of the Commonwealth War Graves Commission* (Barnsley, 1967, 2003)

Lopez, S.J., Snyder, C.R., and Pedrotti, J.T., 'Hope: Many Definitions, Many Measures', in S.J. Lopez and C.R. Snyder (eds.), *Positive Psychological Assessment: A Handbook of Models and Measures* (London, 2003)

Low, S.M., Cross-Cultural Place Attachment: A Preliminary Typology', in Y. Yoshitake, R.B. Bechtel, T. Takahashi, and M. Asai (eds.), *Current Issues in Environment-Behavior Research* (Tokyo, 1990)

'Symbolic Ties that Bind', in I. Altman and S.M. Low (eds.), *Place Attachment* (New York, 1992)

Luptak, A., Smyth, H., and Halewood, L. (eds.), *War Time: First World War Perspectives on Temporality* (Abingdon, 2018)

Macdonald, L., *To the Last Man: Spring 1918* (London, 1998)

MacKenzie, H.M., *The Empire of Nature: Hunting, Conservation and British Imperialism* (Manchester, 1988)

MacKenzie, S.P., 'Morale and the Cause: The Campaign to Shape the Outlook of Soldiers in the British Expeditionary Force, 1914–1918', *Canadian Journal of History/Annales Canadiennes d'Histoire*, vol. 25, no. 2 (August 1990)

MacLeod, A.K., and Salaminiou, E., 'Reduced Positive Future-Thinking in Depression: Cognitive and Affective Factors', *Cognition and Emotion*, vol. 15, no. 1 (2001)

Madigan, E., *Faith Under Fire: Anglican Army Chaplains and the Great War* (Basingstoke, 2011)

'"Sticking to a Hateful Task": Resilience, Humour, and British Understandings of Combatant Courage, 1914–1918', *War in History*, vol. 20, no. 1 (2013)

Maguire, A., *Contact Zones of the First World War: Cultural Encounters across the British Empire* (Cambridge, 2021)

Makepeace, C., 'Living Beyond the Barbed Wire: The Familial Ties of British Prisoners of War held in Europe during the Second World War', *Historical Research*, vol. 86, no. 231 (February 2013)

'Male Heterosexuality and Prostitution during the Great War: British Soldiers' Encounters with *Maisons Tolérées*', *Cultural and Social History*, vol. 9, no. 1 (2012)

Malvern, S., 'War Tourisms: "Englishness", Art and the First World War', *Oxford Art Journal*, vol. 24, no. 1 (2001)

Mandler, P., 'Against "Englishness": English Culture and the Limits to Rural Nostalgia, 1850–1940', *Transactions of the Royal Historical Society*, vol. 7, no. 1 (December 1997)

Mangan, J.A., *Athleticism in the Victorian and Edwardian Public School* (Abingdon, 1989, 2000)

Mansoor P.R., and Murray W. (eds.), *The Culture of Military Organisations* (Cambridge, 2019)

Marcora, S.M., Staiano, W., and Manning, V., 'Mental Fatigue Impairs Physical Performance in Humans', *Journal of Applied Physiology*, vol. 106, no. 3 (January 2009)

Marwick, A., *The Deluge: British Society and the First World War* (London, 1989)

War and Social Change in the Twentieth Century (London, 1974)

Masefield, J., *The Old Frontline* (New York, 1918)

Masters, C.W., *The Respectability of Late Victorian Workers: A Case Study of York, 1867–1914* (Newcastle upon Tyne, 2010)

Mayhew, A., 'A War Imagined: Postcards and the Maintenance of Long-Distance Relationships during the Great War', *War in History*, vol. 28, no. 2 (April 2021)

'British Expeditionary Force Vegetable Shows, Allotment Culture, and Life Behind the Lines during the Great War', *Historical Journal*, vol. 64, no. 5 (December 2021)

'English Patriotism and the Implicit Nation: Homelands and Soldiers' National Identity during the Great War', *English Historical Review*, Forthcoming

'Hoping for Victorious Peace: Morale and the Future on the Western Front', in A. Luptak, H. Smyth and L. Halewood (eds.), *War Time: First World War Perspectives on Temporality* (Abingdon, 2018)

'Mud, Blood, and Not So Much Poppycock: "Myth" Formation and the British Army in Late 1917', *Bulletin of the Auckland Museum*, vol. 21 (2020)

Mazumdar, S., and Mazumdar, S., 'Religion and Place Attachment: A Study of Sacred Place', *Journal of Environmental Psychology*, vol. 24, no. 3 (2004)

McCartney, H., *Citizen Soldiers: The Liverpool Territorials in the First World War* (Cambridge, 2011)

McGarry, R., Walklate, S., and Mythen, G., 'A Sociological Analysis of Military Resilience: Opening Up the Debate', *Armed Forces & Society*, vol. 41, no. 2 (2015)

Meinig, D.W. (ed.), *The Interpretation of Ordinary Landscapes* (Oxford, 1979)

Meredith, L.S., 'Promoting Psychological Resilience in the U.S. Military', *Rand Health Quarterly*, vol. 1, no. 2 (Summer 2011)

Messenger, C., *Call to Arms: The British Army 1914–1918* (London, 2005)

Meyer, J., *Men of War: Masculinity and the First World War in Britain* (Basingstoke, 2009)

Michelson, W., *Man and his Urban Environment: A Sociological Approach, with Revisions* (Reading, 1976)

Middlebrook, M., *The Kaiser's Battle* (Barnsley, 1978, 2009)

Milgram, S., *Obedience to Authority* (London, 1974)

Millett, A.R., Murray, W., and Watman, K.H., 'The Effectiveness of Military Organizations', *International Security*, vol. 11, no. 1 (Summer 1986)

Moliner, C.S., Norman, K., Wagner, K-H., Hartig, W., Lochs, H., and Pirlich, M., 'Malnutrition and Depression in the Institutionalised Elderly', *British Journal of Nutrition*, vol. 102, no. 11 (December 2009)

Monger, D., *Patriotism and Propaganda in First World War Britain: The National War Aims Committee and Civilian Morale* (Liverpool, 2012)

Moran, Lord, *The Anatomy of Courage: The Classic WW1 Study of the Psychological Effects of War* (London, 1945, 2007)

Mosse, G.L., *Fallen Soldiers: Reshaping the Memory of the World Wars* (Oxford, 1990)

Nash, L., 'Furthering the Environmental Turn', *The Journal of American History*, vol. 100, no. 1 (June 2013)

Nash, R., *Wilderness and the American Mind* (New Haven, 1967, 1982)

Neal, D.T., Wood, W., Wu, M., and Kurlander, D., 'The Pull of the Past: When do Habits Persist Despite Conflict with Motives?', *Personality and Social Psychology Bulletin*, vol. 37, no. 11 (2011)

Neitzel, S., and Welzer, H., *On Fighting, Killing and Dying: The Secret Second World War Tapes of German POWs* (New York, 2012)

Nelson, R.L., *German Soldier Newspapers of the First World War* (Cambridge, 2010)

Newcombe, N.S., Uttal, D.H., and Sauter, M., 'Spatial Development', in P.D. Zelazo (ed.), *The Oxford Handbook of Development Psychology: Volume I Body and Mind* (Oxford, 2013)

Nicot, J., *Les poilus ont la parole: Lettres du front, 1917–1918* (Paris, 1998, 2003)

Nindl, B.C. et al., 'Perspectives on Resilience for Military Readiness and Preparedness: Report of an International Military Physiology Roundtable', *Journal of Science and Medicine in Sport*, vol. 21, no. 11 (November 2018), pp. 1116–1124

Nora, P. (ed.), *Realms of Memory: The Construction of the French Past: Vol. 1: Conflicts and Divisions*, trans. A. Goldhammer (New York, 1996)

O'Keefe, M., 'Chronic Crises in the Arc of Insecurity: A Case Study of Karamoja', *Third World Quarterly*, vol. 31, no. 8 (2010), p. 1271

Olusoga, D., *The World's War: Forgotten Soldiers of Empire* (London, 2014)

Oram, G., 'Pious Perjury: Discipline and Morale in the British Force in Italy, 1917–1918', *War in History*, vol. 9, no. 4 (2002)

Orwell, G., 'Notes on Nationalism', in Orwell, S., and Angus, I. (eds.), *The Collected Essays, Journalism and Letters of George Orwell* (London, 1968)

Osgood, R., and Brown, M., *Digging up Plugstreet: The Archaeology of a Great War Battlefield* (Sparkford, 2009)

Ottewill, D., *The Edwardian Garden* (New Haven, Conn, 1989)
Parker, P., *The Old Lie: The Great War and the Public-School Ethos* (London, 1987)
Pearson, C., *Mobilizing Nature: The Environmental History of War and Militarization in Modern France* (Manchester, 2012)
Pellegrino, R., Sinding, C., de Wijk, R.A., and Hummel, T., 'Habituation and Adaptation to Odors in Humans', *Physiology and Behaviour*, vol. 177 (August 2017)
Peniston-Bird, C., and Summerfield, P., '"Hey, You're Dead": The Multiple Uses of Humour in Representations of British National Defence in the Second World War', *Journal of European Studies*, vol. 31, no. 3-4 (2001)
Pennell, C., *A Kingdom United: Popular Responses to the Outbreak of the First World War in Britain and Ireland* (Oxford, 2012)
Philpott, W., *Bloody Victory: The Sacrifice on the Somme* (London, 2010)
Pignot, M., 'Children', in J. Winter (ed.), *The Cambridge History of the First World War: Vol. III: Civil Society* (Cambridge, 2014)
Porritt, D., 'Social Support in Crisis: Quantity or Quality', *Social Science & Medicine: Part A: Medical Psychological and Medical Sociology*, vol. 13 (1979)
Primoratz, I., and Pavković, A., *Patriotism: Philosophical and Political Perspectives* (London, 2007)
Prior, R., and Wilson, T., *Passchendaele: The Untold Story* (New Haven and London, 1996, 2002)
Porter, B., *The Absent-Minded Imperialists: Empire, Society, and Culture in Britain* (Oxford, 2004)
Rankin, C.H., et al., 'Habituation Revisited: An Updated and Revised Description of Behavioural Habituation', *Neurobiology of Learning and Memory*, vol. 92, no. 2 (2009)
Reader, W.J., *'At Duty's Call': A Study in Obsolete Patriotism* (Manchester, 1988)
Readman, P., *Land and Nation: Patriotism, National Identity, and the Politics of Land, 1880–1914* (Woodbridge, 2008)
    Storied Ground: Landscapes and the Shaping of English National Identity (Cambridge, 2018)
    '"The Cliffs are not Cliffs": The Cliffs of Dover and National Identities in Britain, c.1750–c.1950', *History: The Journal of the Historical Association*, vol. 99, no. 335 (April 2014)
    'The Place of the Past in English Culture c. 1890–1914', *Past & Present*, vol. 186, no. 1 (February 2005)
Rearick, C., *The French in Love and War: Popular Culture in the Era of the World Wars* (New Haven and London, 1997)
Reid, F., *Broken Men: Shell Shock, Treatment and Recovery in Britain, 1914–1930* (London, 2011)
Reivich, K., and Gillham, J., 'Learned Optimism: The Measurement of Explanatory Style', in S.J. Lopez and C.R. Snyder (eds.), *Positive Psychological Assessment: A Handbook of Models and Measures* (London, 2003)

Ricoeur, P., *Time and Narrative: Volume 3* (Chicago, Il., 1988)
Richardson, F.M., *Fighting Spirit: A Study of Psychological Factors in War* (New York 1978)
Robert, K., 'Gender, Class, and Patriotism: Women's Paramilitary Units in First World War Britain', *The International History Review*, vol. 19, no. 1 (1997)
Roper, M., *The Secret Battle: Emotional Survival in the Great War* (Manchester, 2009)
—— 'Nostalgia as an Emotional Experience in the Great War', *The Historical Journal*, vol. 54, no. 2 (June 2011)
Rosburg, T., and Sörös, P., 'The Response Decrease of Auditory Evoked Potentials by Repeated Stimulation – Is There Evidence for an Interplay between Habituation and Sensitization?', *Clinical Neurophysiology*, vol. 127, no. 1 (January 2016)
Routledge, C., *Nostalgia: A Psychological Resource* (Abingdon, 2016)
Rowe, L., *Morale and Discipline in the Royal Navy during the First World War* (Cambridge, 2018)
Rüger, J., 'Nation, Empire and Navy: Identity Politics in the United Kingdom, 1887–1914', *Past & Present*, vol. 185 (2004)
Ruickbie, L., *Angels in the Trenches: Spiritualism, Superstition and the Supernatural during the First World War* (London, 2018)
Sachs, J.D., 'Resolving the Debt Crisis of Low-Income Countries', *Brookings Papers on Economic Activity*, vol. 2002, no. 1 (2002), pp. 257–286
Saint-Fuscien, E., *À vos orders? La relation d'autorité dans l'armée française de la Grande Guerre* (Paris, 2011)
Samuels, M., *Command or Control? Command, Training and Tactics in the British and German Armies, 1888–1918* (London, 1995, 2003)
Sanborn, J.A., *Drafting the Russian Nation: Military Conscription, Total War and Mass Politics 1905–1925* (DeKalb, 2002)
—— *Imperial Apocalypse: The Great War and the Destruction of the Russian Empire* (Oxford, 2014)
Saunders, N.J., 'Material Culture and Conflict', in N.J. Saunders (ed.), *Material Culture, Memory and the First World War* (Abingdon, 2004)
Scalise Sugiyama, M., 'Food, Foragers, and Folklore: The Role of Narrative in Human Subsistence', *Evolution and Human Psychology*, vol. 21 (2001)
Scannell, L., and Gifford, R., 'Defining Place Attachment: A Tripartite Organizing Framework', *Journal of Environmental Psychology*, vol. 30 (2010)
Seal, G., *The Soldiers' Press: Trench Journals in the First World War* (Basingstoke, 2013)
Searle, G.R., *A New England? Peace and War, 1886–1918* (Oxford, 2004)
Seipp, A.R., *The Ordeal of Peace: Demobilization and the Urban Experience in Britain and Germany, 1917–1921* (Farnham, 2009)
Sheffield, G., *A Short History of the First World War* (London, 2014)
—— *Command and Morale: The British Army on the Western Front 1914–1918* (Barnsley, 2014)
—— *Forgotten Victory: The First World War: Myths and Realities* (London, 2002)

Leadership in the Trenches: Officer–Man Relations, Morale and Discipline in the British Army in the Era of the First World War (Basingstoke, 2000)

Sheffield, G., and Bourne, J. (eds.), *Douglas Haig: War Diaries and Letters, 1914–1918* (London, 2005)

Sheffield, G., and Todman, D., 'Command and Control in the British Army on the Western Front', in Sheffield, G., and Todman, D. (eds.), *Command and Control on the Western Front: The British Army's Experience 1914–18* (Chalford, 2007)

Shephard, B., *A War of Nerves: Solders and Psychiatrists, 1914–1994* (London, 2002)

Silbey, D., *The British Working Class and Enthusiasm for War, 1914–1916* (London, 2005)

Silk, N., '"Some Corner of a Foreign Field That Is Forever England": The Western Front as the British Soldiers' Sacred Land', in A. Beyerchen and E. Sencer (eds.), *Expeditionary Forces in the First World War* (London, 2019), pp. 289–311

Simkins, P., 'Everyman at War: Recent Interpretations of the Front Line Experience', in B. Bond (ed.), *The First World War and British Military History* (Oxford, 1991)

Kitchener's Army: The Raising of the New Armies (Barnsley, 1988, 2007)

Simpson, K., 'The Officer', in I.F.W. Beckett and K. Simpson (eds.), *A Nation in Arms: A Social Study of the British Army in the First World War* (Manchester, 1985)

Smith, C., *Awarded for Valour: A History of the Victoria Cross and the Evolution of British Heroism* (Basingstoke, 2008)

Smith, L.V., *Between Mutiny and Obedience: The Case of the French Fifth Infantry Division during World War I* (Princeton, 1994)

'Mutiny', in J. Winter (ed.), *The Cambridge History of the First World War Volume II: The State* (Cambridge, 2014)

Smith, P.B., Bond, M.H., and Kağıtçıbaşı, Ç., *Understanding Social Psychology Across Cultures* (London, 2006)

Snell, K.D.M., *Parish and Belonging: Community, Identity and Welfare in England and Wales, 1750–1950* (Cambridge, 2006)

Snyder, C.R., Irving, L., and Anderson, J.R., 'Hope and Health: Measuring the Will and Ways', C.R. Snyder and D.R. Forsyth (eds.), *Handbook of Social and Clinical Psychology: The Health Perspective* (Elmsford, 1991)

Snyder, C.R., Rand, K.L., King, E.A., Feldman, D.B., and Woodward, J.T., '"False" Hope', *Journal of Clinical Psychology*, vol. 58, no. 9 (2002)

Spiers, E., 'The Scottish Soldier at War', in H. Cecil and P. Liddle (eds.), *Facing Armageddon: The First World War Experienced* (London, 1996, 2003)

Stapleton, J., 'Citizenship Versus Patriotism in Twentieth-Century England', *The Historical Journal*, vol. 48, no. 1 (2005)

Steel, N., and Hart, P., *Passchendaele: The Sacrificial Ground* (London, 2000, 2001)

Stephenson, S., *The Final Battle: Soldiers of the Western Front in the German Revolution of 1918* (Cambridge, 2009)

Stevenson, D., *1914–1918: The History of the First World War* (London, 2004), p. 182
With Our Backs to the Wall: Victory and Defeat in 1918 (London, 2014)
1917: War, Peace, and Revolution (Oxford, 2017)
Stock, P. (ed.), *The Uses of Space in Early Modern History* (Basingstoke, 2015)
Stout, J.P., *Coming Out of War: Poetry, Grieving, and the Culture of the World Wars* (Tuscaloosa, 2005, 2016)
Strachan, H., 'Training, Morale and Modern War', *Journal of Contemporary History*, vol. 41, no. 2 (2006)
Strack F., and Deutsch, R., 'Reflective and Impulsive Determinants of Social Behaviour', *Personality and Social Psychology Review*, vol. 8, no. 3 (2004)
Strange, J-M., *Death, Grief and Poverty in Britain, 1870–1914* (Cambridge, 2005)
'"She Cried a Very Little": Death, Grief and Mourning in Working-Class Culture, c. 1880–1914', *Social History*, vol. 27, no. 2 (2002)
Summers, J., *Remembered: The History of the Commonwealth War Graves Commission* (London, 2007)
Sutter, P., 'The World with Us: The State of American Environmental History', *Journal of American History*, vol. 100, no. 1 (June 2013)
Szpunar, K.K., Watson, J.M., and McDermott, K.B., 'Neural Substrates of Envisioning the Future', *Proceedings of the National Academy of Sciences of the United States of America*, vol. 104, no. 2 (July 2006)
Taylor, A.J.P., *The First World War: An Illustrated History* (London, 1963, 1969)
Taylor, S.E., 'Asymmetrical Effects of Positive and Negative Events: The Mobilization-Minimization Hypothesis', *Psychological Bulleting*, vol. 110, no. 1 (July 1991)
Thaler, R.H., and Sunstein, C.R., *Nudging: Improving Decisions About Health, Wealth, and Happiness* (London, 2009)
Tholas-Disset, C., and Ritzenhoff, K.A., *Humor, Entertainment, and Popular Culture during World War I* (New York, 2015)
Thompson, F.M.L., *The Rise of Respectable Society: A Social History of Victorian Britain, 1830–1900* (Cambridge, 1988)
Thompson, P., *The Edwardians: The Remaking of British Society* (London, 1975, 1992)
Tilley, C., *A Phenomenology of Landscape: Paths, Places and Monuments* (Oxford, 1994)
Todman, D., *Britain's War: Into Battle, 1937–1941* (London, 2016, 2017)
The Great War: Myth and Memory (London, 2005)
Tomczyszyn, P., 'A Material Link Between War and Peace: First World War Silk Postcards', in N.J. Saunders (ed.), *Matters of Conflict: Material Culture, Memory and the First World War* (Oxford, 2004)
Tong, E.M.W., et al., 'Re-Examining Hope: The Roles of Agency and Pathways Thinking', *Cognition and Emotion*, vol. 24, no. 7 (2010)
Torre, A., 'A "Spatial Turn" in History? Landscapes, Visions, Resources', *Annales Histoire, Sciences Sociales*, vol. 63, no. 5 (2008)
Tosh, J., *A Man's Place: Masculinity and the Middle-Class Home in Victorian England* (Bath, 1999)

Travers, T., *The Killing Ground: The British Army, the Western Front & the Emergence of Modern War* (Barnsley, 2009)

Tuan, Y., *Topophilia: A Study of Environmental Perception, Attitudes, and Values* (Engle-wood Cliffs, NJ, 1974)

Tucker, R.P., Keller, T., McNeill, J.R., and Schmid, M. (eds.), *Environmental Histories of the First World War* (Cambridge, 2018)

Tuunainen, P., *Finnish Military Effectiveness in the Winter War, 1939–1940* (London, 2016)

Twigger-Ross, C.L., and Uzzell, D.L., 'Place and Identity Processes', *Journal of Environmental Psychology*, vol. 16 (1996)

Ueköter, F., 'Memories in Mud: The Environmental Legacy of the Great War', in R.P. Tucker, T. Keller, J.R. McNeill, and M. Schmid (eds.), *Environmental Histories of the First World War* (Cambridge, 2018)

Ulrich, B., and Ziemann, B. (eds.), *German Soldiers in the Great War: Letters and Eyewitness Accounts*, trans. C. Brocks (Barnsley, 2010)

Ussishkin, D., *Morale: A Modern British History* (Oxford, 2017)

Van Creveld, M., *Fighting Power: German and US Army Performance: 1939–1945* (London, 1983)

Van Emden, R., and Humphries, S., *All Quiet on the Home Front: An Oral History of Life in Britain during the First World War* (Barnsley, 2003, 2017)

Vidal-Naquet, C., *Couples dans la Grande Guerre: Le Tragique et l'ordinaire du lien conjugal* (Lyon, 2014)

Waddington, K., '"We Don't Want Any German Sausages Here!" Food, Fear, and the German Nation in Victorian and Edwardian Britain', *Journal of British Studies*, vol. 52, no. 4 (2013)

Walker, J., *Words and the First World War: Language, Memory and Vocabulary* (London, 2017)

Waller, P.J., *Town, City and Nation: England 1850–1914* (Oxford, 1983, 1991)

Walton, J.K., 'The National Trust Centenary: Official and Unofficial Histories', *The Local Historian*, vol. 26 (1996)

Ward, C., *Living on the Western Front: Annals and Stories, 1914–1919* (London, 2013)

Ward, P., '"Women of Britain Say Go": Women's Patriotism in the First World War', *Twentieth Century British History*, vol. 12, no. 1 (2001)

Watson, A., 'Culture and Combat in the Western World, 1900–1945', *The Historical Journal*, vol. 51, no. 2 (June 2008)

Enduring the Great War: Combat, Morale and Collapse in the German and British Armies (Cambridge, 2008)

'Fighting for Another Fatherland: The Polish Minority in the German Army, 1914–1918', *English Historical Review*, vol. 125, no. 522 (October 2011)

'Morale', in J. Winter (ed.), *The Cambridge History of the First World War Volume II: The State* (Cambridge, 2014)

Watson, A., and Porter, P., 'Bereaved and Aggrieved: Combat Motivation and the Ideology of Sacrifice in the First World War', *Institute of Historical Research*, vol. 83, no. 219 (February 2010)

Watson, J.S.K., *Fighting Different Wars: Experience, Memory and the First World War* (Cambridge, 2004)

Walvin, J., 'Dust to Dust: Celebrations of Death in Victorian England', *Historical Reflections/ Réflexions Historiques*, vol. 9, no. 3 (Fall 1982)

Wearn, J.A., Philip Budden, A., Veniard, S.C., and Richardson, D., 'The Flora of the Somme Battlefield: A Botanical Perspective on a Post-Conflict Landscape', *First World War Studies*, vol. 8, no. 1 (2017)

Webb, D., 'Christian Hope and the Politics of Utopia', *Utopian Studies*, vol. 19, no. 1 (2008)

Wehr, T.A., and Rosenthal, N.E., 'Seasonality and Affective Illness', *American Journal of Psychiatry*, vol 146, no. 7 (July 1989)

Weick, K.E., 'The Collapse of Sensemaking in Organizations: The Mann Gulch Disaster', *Administrative Science Quarterly*, vol. 28, no. 4 (December 1993)

Weick, K.E., and Sutcliffe, K.M., 'Organizing and the Process of Sensemaking', *Organization Science*, vol. 16, no. 4 (July–August 2005)

Wessely, S., 'Twentieth-Century Theories of Combat Motivation and Breakdown', *Journal of Contemporary History*, vol. 41, no. 2 (April 2006)

West, A.G., *The Diary of a Dead Officer*, pp. 79–81

Westerman, W., *Gentleman: Australian Battalion Commanders in the Great War, 1914–1918* (Cambridge, 2017)

Westenholz, A., 'Paradoxical Thinking and Change in the Frames of Reference', *Organization Studies*, vol. 14, no. 1 (January 1993)

White, H., *Metahistory: The Historical Imagination in Nineteenth Century Europe* (Baltimore, 1973)

'The Value of Narrativity in the Representation of Reality', in W.J.T. Mitchell (ed.), *On Narrative* (Chicago, Il., 1981)

White, R., 'The Nationalization of Nature', *Journal of American History*, vol. 86, no. 3 (December 1999)

Wilcox, V., 'Morale and Battlefield Performance at Caporetto, 1917', *Journal of Strategic Studies*, vol. 37, no. 6–7 (2014)

Morale and the Italian Army during the First World War (Cambridge, 2016)

'Training, Morale and Battlefield Performance in the Italian Army, 1914–1917', in J. Krause (ed.), *The Greater War: Other Combatants and Other Fronts, 1914–1918* (Basingstoke, 2014)

'"Weeping Tears of Blood": Exploring Italian Soldiers' Emotions in the First World War', *Modern Italy*, vol. 17, no. 2 (2012)

Wilson, R. '"Tommifying" the Western Front, 1914–1918', *Journal of Historical Geography*, vol. 37, no. 3 (2011)

Wilson, R.J., *Landscapes of the Western Front: Materiality during the Great War* (London, 2012)

'Strange Hells: A New Approach to the Western Front', *Historical Research*, vol. 81, no. 211 (2008)

Winter, D., *Death's Men: Soldiers of the Great War* (London, 1978)

Winter, J., 'British National Identity and the First World War', in S. Green and C. Whiting (eds.), *The Boundaries of the State in Modern Britain* (Cambridge, 1996)
'Families', in J. Winter (ed.), *The Cambridge History of the First World War: Vols. I–III* (Cambridge, 2014)
'Popular Culture in Wartime Britain', in A. Roshwald and R. Stites (eds.), *European Culture in the Great War; The Arts, Entertainment and Propaganda, 1914–1918* (Cambridge, 1999)
Sites of Memory Sites of Mourning: The Great War in European Cultural History (Cambridge, 1995, 2003)
(ed.) *The Cambridge History of the First World War: Vols. I–III* (Cambridge, 2014)
The Experience of World War I (London, 1988, 2000)
The Great War and the British People (Basingstoke, 2003)
Winter, J., and Prost, A., *The Great War in History: Debates and Controversies, 1914 to the Present* (Cambridge, 2005)
Wood, C.E., *Mud: A Military History* (Washington, 2006, 2007)
Wood, W., Quinn, J.M., and Kashy, D.A., 'Habits in Everyday Life: Thought, Emotion, and Action', *Journal of Personality and Social Psychology*, vol. 83, no. 5 (2002)
Woodfin, E., *Camp and Combat on the Sinai and Palestine Front* (London, 2012)
Woodward, D.R., 'Did Lloyd George Starve the British Army of Men Prior to the German Offensive of 21 March 1918?', *The Historical Journal*, vol. 27, no. 1 (1984)
Wouters N., and van Ypersele L. (eds.), *Nations, Identities and the First World War: Shifting Loyalties to the Fatherland* (London, 2018)
Wright, T.A., and Cropanzano, R., 'Emotional Exhaustion as Predictor of Job Performance and Voluntary Turnover', *Journal of Applied Psychology*, vol. 83, no. 3 (June 1998)
Yovetich, N.A., Alexander Dale, J., and Hudak, M.A., 'Benefits of Humor in Reduction of Threat-Induced Anxiety', *Psychological Reports*, vol. 66 (1990)
Zhong, Gheng-Bo., and Leonardelli, G.L., 'Cold and Lonely: Does Social Exclusion Literally Feel Cold?', *Psychological Science*, vol. 19 (September 2008)
Ziemann, B., *Violence and the German Soldier in the Great War: Killing, Dying, Surviving*, trans. A. Evans (London, 2017)
War Experiences in Rural Germany (Oxford, 2011)
Zohar, D., 'Predicting Burnout with a Hassle-Based Measure of Role Demands', *Journal of Organizational Behaviour*, vol. 18, no. 2 (1997)
Zuckoff, M., *Frozen in Time: An Epic Story of Survival and a Modern Quest for Lost Heroes of World War II* (London, 2013)

Unpublished Secondary Material

Lauwers, D., 'Le Saillant d'Ypres entre reconstruction et construction d'un lieu de mémoire: un long processus de négociations mémorielles de 1914 à nos jours', unpublished Ph.D. thesis, European University Institute (2014)

Internet Resources

Baker, C., The Long, Long Trail: Researching Soldiers of the British Army during the Great War of 1914–1919, www.longlongtrail.co.uk, accessed 28 March 2022

Buton, F., Loez, A., Mariot, N., and Olivera, P., '1914–1918: Understanding the Controversy', *Books and Ideas* (11 June 2009), www.booksandideas.net/1914-1918-Understanding-the.html, accessed 1 June 2018

Frederickson, B.L., 'Why Choose Hope?', *Psychology Today* (23 March 2009), www.psychologytoday.com/blog/positivity/200903/why-choose-hope, accessed 19 May 2016

Leonard, M., 'A Senseless War', *World War I Centenary: Continuations and Beginnings*, ww1centenary.oucs.ox.ac.uk/body-and-mind/a-senseless-war/, accessed 19 June 2016

'Seasonal Affective Disorder – Causes', www.nhs.uk/Conditions/Seasonal-affective-disorder/Pages/Causes.aspx, accessed 14 August 2015

'Symptoms of Seasonal Affective Disorder', www.nhs.uk/conditions/seasonal-affective-disorder/Pages/Symptoms.aspx, accessed 14 August 2015

Talks and Lectures

Horne, J., 'Inventing the "Front": Cognition and Reality in the Great War', Lecture at King's College London, 1 November 2016

INDEX

absence without leave, 142, 150, 247, 252–253
age of soldiers, 14, 213, 275–276, 303–306
Agius, Arthur, Capt., 85, 156, 215
Allen, A.J., 153
Anderson, William, Pte.
  on duty, 136
  home, thoughts of, 168, 170, 172, 185
  on incomprehensibility of war, 135
  on peace, 18, 207, 220, 222, 229
  on post-war life, 217, 227
  on weather conditions, 84, 115
Andrews, Arthur, 141
Anglicisation of place names, 8, 37, 41–42, 61–62
Anstruther, Frederic B., Lt., 41, 153
après la guerre phrase, 201, 207, 217
artworks. *See* drawings and paintings
Ashburner, A.F., Capt., 127, 186, 202, 229
Ashworth, Tony, 8, 12
Asprey, Maurice, Capt., 46, 166, 190, 202
Atance, Cristina, 227
attachment theory, 37–38, 77–79
Audoin-Rouzeau, Stéphane, 8, 286–287

Baines, C.S., Lt. Col., 102, 127, 141
Bairnsfather, Bruce, 89, 108, 111, 202, 211, 225
Baker, H.E., 91
Bate, H.R., Canon, 80
Baynes, John, 9, 24
Beadon, R.H., 122
Becker, Jean-Jacques, 198, 286–287

'Before You Come Up' phrase, 53–54
Bell, C.H., Reverend, 220–221
Bell, V.G., 53, 69
Bentley, W.G., 141
Bere, M.A., Reverend, 94, 95–96, 174
billets, 38, 41–42, 67, 82, 101–104
Billingham, O., Pte., 101
Birt, C.W.H., Lt. Col., 246
'Blighty' term, 175–176
Blunden, Edmund, 232
Boff, Jonathan, 27
Bonham-Carter, Charles, Brig., 212
Border Regiment. *See* regimental culture
  in 1914 campaigns, 83, 89, 205
  age of soldiers, 275
  home locations of soldiers, 30, 184, 305
  in Messines, Battle of (1917), 235
  in Somme Campaign (1916), 69
  in winter 1917–1918, 261
bounded rationality theory, 21
Bowman, Timothy, 1
Brettell, F.A., Lt., 217–218
Bridge, Harry, 192
Bridgewater, infantryman (father of Bentley), xxi–xxii
British Army culture. *See* duty, sense of
culture concept, xxiii–xxiv, 119
  duty of cheeriness, 1–2, 124, 126–127, 144–150
  esprit de corps, 9–12, 25, 29–31, 122–124, 133
  good character and respectability, 150–154, 158–159

British Army culture. (cont.)
  obedience and discipline, 12, 140–145, 150, 158, 289–290
  regimental culture. *See* regimental culture
  sociological analysis, 157–159
  training imbuing. *See* training, military
British identity, 28–29, 163, 176
  Englishness preferred. *See* Englishness, sense of
Bromwich, David, 163
Brophy, John, 96, 135, 141, 145, 201
brutalisation, 15–16, 287
Bullock, Alan, 20
burials, 71, 72–73, 177–178
Burke, A.P.
  censorship circumvention by, 182
  on duty, 119, 136
  on enemy soldiers, 224
  on exhaustion, 102, 105, 108
  on food shortages, 111
  home, thoughts of, 180, 216
  in October 1916, 106
  on peace, 206
  on sounds of comrades, 59
  on weather conditions and mud, 83, 87, 90, 94
Burns, E.L.M., Lt. Gen., 89

Cambrai, Battle of (1917)
  account of, 248–249
  causes of British collapse, 143, 250, 251–252, 260, 280
  destruction at, 52
  responses to, 139, 212, 249–250
Cannon, E.A., Pte., 56
Cardwell, Edward, 10, 29–30
Carrington, Charles, Capt.
  on cheerfulness, 146, 148
  on duty, 130
  on friendship, 230
  home, thoughts of, 180, 216
  mental turbulence (1916), 51, 108–109, 206
  on training, 106
cartoons, 89, 108, 202, 211, 225

Castle, F.S., 135–136, 170–171, 183
casualties
  generally. *See* death; injuries
  of German spring offensives (1918), 266–270
  of Passchendaele, Battle of (Third Ypres, 1917), 255–256
Chapman, Guy, 2nd Lt., 55, 68, 83
character references for employers, 151–154
Chasseaud, Peter, 62
cheeriness as duty, 1–2, 124, 126–127, 144–150
Cheshire, W.J., 83, 93, 133–134, 203, 205
Child, Frederick William, 40–41, 84, 90, 135
Childers, Hugh, 29–30
Christmas generally, 100, 111–113, 191, 229
Christmas truces (1914)
  emotional responses to, 89–90, 111–112, 132, 155–156
  enemy encounters, 90, 110, 167–168, 205
  silence of, 58
Churchill, Winston, 173
civilian culture (1914–18), 12–13, 120, 181
  of civilian life, 12–13
civilians, soldiers' relations with, 13, 36–37, 46, 47, 67, 155–157, 223
Clark, F.L., 48
Clarke, S.A., Pte., 138–139
Clayton, W.G., Pte., 175
clergy, military, 14, 219
cold weather, 82–85, 93–96
Colley, Linda, 183
Collis, A.L., 58
combat narratives, xxvii
Conn, A., Pte., 115
Connelly, Mark, 31
conscientious objectors, views of, 169
Cooper, James, 219
coping mechanisms
  fantasy. *See* fantasy
  gardening, 6–9, 37, 43, 73–74, 207
  generally, xxvi, 22, 282–283, 286

INDEX

home, thoughts of. *See* Englishness, sense of; homeland imaginings
humour and satire. *See* humour and satire
leave, prospect of, 160
letters. *See* letters to and from home
narratives. *See* narratives
peace, hopes for. *See* peace, hopes for
recreation and sport. *See* recreation and sport
religious faith and observance, 14, 71, 115, 171, 191, 218–221
singing. *See* songs
for winter weather, 109–113
cosmology episodes (loss of meaning), 143–144, 265–266
crises
  of 1914, xxv, 23–25, *See* Le Cateau, Battle of (1914); Mons, retreat from (1914)
  'crisis' concept, 21–22
  German and French soldiers' morale in, 109, 235, 280, 291–293
  German spring offensives. *See* German spring offensives (1918)
  historiographical analysis, 22–27
  and hopes for peace. *See* peace, hopes for
  Somme Campaign. *See* Somme Campaign (1916)
  whether perceived as such by soldiers, xxv–xxvi, 23, 206–207, 214–215, 284–285
  winter 1917–1918. *See* winter 1917–1918
Crosse, E.C., Canon, 90, 206
Crosse, R.B., Lt. Col., 262
Crump, C.P., 172, 208
culture. *See* duty, sense of; Englishness, sense of
  of British Army. *See* British Army culture
  civilian culture (1914–1918), 12–13, 120, 181
  concept, xxiii–xxiv, 119

Dagger, The (soldiers' newspaper), 31, 35–36
Dallas, Gloden, 290
D'Arcy, Lt., 149
Das, Santanu, 8
daydreams. *See* fantasy
death
  awareness of, 8, 48, 55–56, 64, 69–71
  by drowning, 90, 91
  duty to the dead, sense of, 130, 154
  eulogies, 154
  gravestones and monuments, 68–69, 71–79
  interment ceremonies, 71, 72–73, 177–178
  supernatural visions, 51–52, 108
decorations, 126, 130, 140
'defence in depth' strategy (1917–1918), xxi, 26–27, 101, 234, 254–255, 262
defensive patriotism. *See* duty, sense of; Englishness, sense of
  civilian encounters triggering, 155–157, 223
  Home Front, whether 'deserving' of, 174, 193
  homeland imaginings triggering, 27–28, 159, 161–162, 174, 193, 223, 295
  victorious peace goal, xxii, 18, 173, 199, 210, 223, 228–229, 283
Deist, Wilhelm, 120
demobilisation disturbances, 290–291
depression, 107–109, 167–168, 171–172, 287–289
desertion, 142, 150, 247
destruction, scenes of, 48–49, 52–53, 62–63, 65–66, 67, 236
Devonshire Regiment. *See* regimental culture
  German spring offensives (1918), casualty figures, 266–269
  home locations of soldiers, 30, 184, 274–275, 305, 306
  in Passchendaele, Battle of (Third Ypres, 1917), 91, 255
  in Somme Campaign (1916), 73, 206
  in winter 1917–1918, 256, 261–262
  interment ceremonies, 73, 177–178

diaries, xxviii, 227–229
discipline and obedience, 12, 140–145, 150, 158, 289–290
Donaldson, Geoffrey B., Capt., 115, 171, 180, 183
drawings and paintings
  cartoons, 89, 108, 202, 211, 225
  Over the Top (Nash painting), 94–95
  scenes of destruction, 52–53
  trench art, 220
drowning in mud, 90, 91
dual-process theory, 17
duty, sense of. *See* British Army culture
  as subject, not citizen, soldiers, 29, 291, 293–294
  cheeriness as duty, 1–2, 124, 126–127, 144–150
  duty concept, 119–122, 157–158
  duty to the dead, 130, 154
  embarkation leaflets imbuing, xxiii, 123
  finite nature of, 131, 138, 139, 157, 279, 290–291
  good character and respectability, 150–154, 158–159
  obedience and discipline, 12, 140–145, 150, 158, 289–290
  patriotic duty. *See* defensive patriotism; local patriotism
  rank and social class affecting, 121, 124, 157
    officers' perception of duty, 127–131
    officers' social contract, 124–127
    other ranks' perception of duty, 132–140
    other ranks' social contract, 131–132
  training imbuing, 122–124, 140
Dwyer, Charles
  on arrival in France, 40, 46
  commemoration of the dead by, 71, 166, 184
  on enemy conduct, 223, 224
  on war experience, 203
  on weather conditions, 82–83, 86, 102, 166, 184

Early, James, Capt., 150–151
Edensor, Tim, 16
Edmonds, James, 23–24, 26
Eldridge, Thomas, Sgt., 80, 184
embarkation leaflets, xxiii, 123
Empire Day, 29
endurance. *See* resilience
enemy. *See* German soldiers
Englander, David, 27, 212
Englishness, sense of
  Anglicisation of place names, 8, 37, 41–42, 61–62
  British Army's encouragement of, 177–179
  Britishness distinguished, 28–29, 163, 176
  compatriotism fostered by, 181–184
  contact with home. *See* letters to and from home
  defensive patriotism. *See* defensive patriotism
  franglais slang, 63–64, 228
  generally, xxix, 27–29
  historical contextualisation of Great War, 76–77
  Home Front, views on, 165–166, 168–169, 172–174, 193
  homeland imaginings. *See* homeland imaginings
  homesickness, 167–168, 171–172
  local patriotism. *See* local patriotism
environment and morale
  Anglicisation of place names, 8, 37, 41–42, 61–62
  destruction, scenes of, 48–49, 52–53, 62–63, 65–66, 67, 236
  exhaustion, environment causing. *See* exhaustion
  fearful environments, 51–52
  gardening by soldiers, 6–9, 37, 43, 73–74, 207
  habituation to environments. *See* habituation
  introduction to study, 5–9
  memorial narratives and souvenirs, 65–68
  'mindscapes' concept, 15, 77
  mud, 8, 40, 80, 89–93, 240–243

place attachment theory, 37–38, 77–79
sounds of war, 57–61
stench of trenches, 55–57
weather conditions. *See* weather conditions
escapism. *See* fantasy
esprit de corps, 9–12, 25, 29–31, 122–124, 133
Étaples 'Bull Ring' training base, xxv, 43–44, 143, 246, 289–290
exhaustion
  combat fatigue, 26, 69
  depression due to, 107–108
  'shell shock' due to, 69, 81, 106–107
  sickness due to, 104, 247, 271
  sleeping quarters, 82, 101–104
  weather conditions causing, 81, 85, 94, 96–101

familiarisation. *See* habituation
fantasy. *See* narratives; sensemaking
  alternative maps of landscapes, 8, 35–36, 37
  enemy's discomfort imagined, 110–111
  fictional narratives, xxi–xxii
  homeland imaginings. *See* homeland imaginings
  sensemaking through, 163–164
  supernatural visions, 51–52, 108
  victorious homecomings imagined, 197, 216–217
fatigue. *See* exhaustion
fear
  in combat, 133–134, 143, 214
  fearful sounds and silences, 57
  supernatural visions, 51–52, 108
  'wind-up' phenomenon, 19, 109, 287–288
Fearns, Bert, Pte., 56
Fennell, Jonathan, 3–5
Ferguson, Niall, 1
Ferrie, W.S., Capt., 67
fictional narratives, xxi–xxii
Foch, Ferdinand, 270
fog, xxv, 26–27, 84, 94, 114, 264–265
food shortages, 98, 99, 107, 111

Fortescue, J.W., 76–77
Foucault, Michel, 158, 228
frames of reference theory, 20–21, 82, 285
franglais slang, 63–64, 228
Frankenburg, Sydney, Lt.
  on Christmas celebrations, 113
  declining morale (1917–1918), 109, 129, 211
  on weather conditions and mud, 84–85, 91, 95, 110
French soldiers' morale, 235, 280, 291, 293
French, John, Lord, 253
Freud, Sigmund, 110–111, 188
Frevert, Ute, 120
frost and snow, 82–85, 93–96
Frost, R.C.A., 138, 213
frostbite, 104
Fry, Douglas, 16
Fullbrook-Leggatt, L.E.W.O., Capt., 154
Fuller, A.W.F., 152–153
Fuller, J.F.C., 2–11, 123–124, 140, 145
Fuller, John G., 13, 164, 207
funerals, 71, 72–73, 177–178
Fussell, Paul, 25, 148, 198

gardening by soldiers, 6–9, 37, 43, 73–74, 207
Gaunt, K.M., L/Cpl., 58, 83
Gelden, Fred, 139
George V, 125, 162, 176, 274
German soldiers
  Christmas truces (1914), encounters with, 90, 110, 167–168, 205
  discomfort imagined, 110–111
  hostility towards, 155–156, 223–225, 236, 287
  morale levels of, 2, 109, 280, 291, 292–293
German spring offensives (1918)
  account of, 263–264, 271–272
  British casualties, 266–270
  causes of British retreats, 264–266, 283
  exhaustion and supply shortages, 101, 269
  officers' responses to, 129–130

German spring offensives (1918) (cont.)
　peace, renewed hopes for, 213–215, 231
　reinforcements and army reorganisation, 270–271, 275–276, 278–279
　surrender and escape strategies, 137–138, 265–266
　weather conditions, 85, 88–89, 93, 96, 114, 264–265
　whether crisis of morale, xxv, 26–27, 129, 157, 234, 272–275, 279–280
Gerry, Christopher J., 22
Gibbs, T., Pte., 247–248
Gibson, Craig, 13
Gifford, Robert, 77, 79
Gill, Douglas, 290
Gill, Sydney, Sgt., 63, 87, 172, 223–224
Gleeson, Michael, 153
Goffman, Erving, 158–159
good character and respectability, 150–154, 158–159
Gower, M.F., 42, 139
Grantham, E., Sapper, 219
gravestones and monuments, 68–69, 71–79
Gray, C.W., 2nd Lt., 173
Greenwell, G.H., Maj.
　on cheerfulness, 146
　on peace, 229
　on war experience, 62, 127–128, 130, 153
　on weather conditions and mud, 90, 91, 114, 115
Greenwood, J.T., Pte., 156
Gregory, Adrian, 14, 30, 137, 181, 218
Grieves, Keith, 193
Griffith, Paddy, 24
Griffiths, David Isaac, 51
Grimston, J., 46, 52, 88, 96, 114, 175, 183
Grindley, Ernest, 152

habituation. *See* resilience
　breakdown of. *See* 'shell shock'
　concept, 18–20
　to death of comrades. *See* death

　generally, 6, 35–38, 53, 64, 284–285
　on journeys to Western Front, 40–48
　obedience and discipline, 12, 140–145, 150, 158, 289–290
　slang terms, 63–64, 228
　to sounds of war, 57–61
　to stench of trenches, 56–57
　training for, 18, 43–44, 140–141
　to violence, 15–16, 287
　working-class poverty contributing to, 12–13, 181
Haig, Douglas, Field Marshal
　in 1917, 139, 212, 252
　in 1918, 270, 272, 273
　on army discipline, 142
　on weather conditions, 82
Haldane, Richard, 10
Hall, P.R., 43, 87, 91, 156–157, 212–213
Hall, Stuart, xxiii–xxiv
Hampson, J.L., 67
Hankey, Donald, 115, 128, 307
Hanna, Emma, 59
Hardie, M., Capt. (military censor)
　on cheerfulness and absence of complaints, 100, 126–127, 146, 206–207
　concerns for morale (1917), 136–137, 146, 172, 209–210, 215
　on morale generally, 6, 235
　on patriotism expressed in letters, 155, 160–161, 163
　on religious faith, 218
Hardman, F., Col.
　on duty, 128, 130
　on exhaustion, 101, 102
　on Home Front, 174
　on post-war life, 217
　on weather conditions, 85, 87
Hart, Peter, 26–27
Harvey, F.W., 178
Haywood, A.E., 46
Hendry, H.O., 63
Henrick Jones, D., Lt.
　on cheerfulness, 146
　home, thoughts of, 112, 183, 185–186, 216, 218
　religious faith, 219

INDEX

Rouen, plan to visit, 62
  on weather conditions, 110
Her Privates We (Manning), 121, 141
Heywood, A.E., 71, 139
Hirschman, Albert, 150
historical contextualisation of Great War, 76–77
Hodgkinson, Peter, 12–13
Hollingsworth, A.T., 184
Home Front, views on, 165–166, 168–169, 172–174, 193
homeland imaginings. *See* Englishness, sense of; fantasy
  defensive patriotism triggered by, 27–28, 159, 161–162, 174, 193, 295
  homesickness, 167–168, 171–172
  morale benefits, 160–161, 163–164, 174–176, 177, 184–186, 188–193
  newspapers and popular culture triggering, 179–181, 185, 188
  postcards triggering, 177, 179, 186, 188
  triggers in foreign settings, 171, 191
  victorious homecomings imagined, 197, 216–217
honour, sense of. *See* duty, sense of
Hood, B.R.N., Capt., 126
hope theory, xxiv, 17–18, 199–201, 229–230
  hopes for peace. *See* peace, hopes for
Hopwood, Harry, Sgt., 67, 179, 190
Horne, John, 285
hospital care, 104
Houlihan, Patrick, 14
Housman, A.E., 179
Hoyle, W.A., Pte., 137–138, 213
Hubard, F., 139, 156, 174, 215
Hudson, S.R., 47
Hull, Isabel V., 9
humour and satire
  cartoons, 89, 108, 202, 211, 225
  morale benefits, 147–150, 158
  in songs and theatre shows, 13, 148–149
  in trench journals, 13, 35–36, 56–57, 211, 222, 226

Humphries, J.M., 53, 190, 212–213
Hutchinson, A.E., Pte., 89

ill health. *See* sickness
imagination. *See* fantasy
industrial action (1917), 174, 176
Ingleson, P., Capt., 93, 214, 216
injuries. *See* sickness
  'Blighty ones', 137–138, 175
  return to service after, 137, 278–279
  self-inflicted, 22, 24, 108, 136, 206, 247
  surrender decisions due to, 204–205
Insom, C.H., 68
interment ceremonies, 71, 72–73, 177–178
Ireland, L.W.C., Lt., 90–91, 192

Janowitz, Morris, 9
Jayes, James, 153–154
Johnson, L.H., Lt.
  anxiety and depression of, 108, 214
  on duty, 128, 130, 145–146
  on food shortages, 100
  on Home Front newspaper articles, 173
  home, thoughts of, 183, 184
  on peace, 207, 210, 227
  on scenes of destruction, 50, 51
  on weather conditions and mud, 93, 95
Johnson, Mark, 164
journals, soldiers'. *See* trench journals
journeys to Western Front, 40–48
Joy, A. Pte., 68, 190, 226–227
Judd, S., 83, 86, 89, 93–94, 110, 205–206, 222

Kahneman, Daniel, 21
Kaiserschlacht. *See* German spring offensives (1918)
Keegan, John, 11, 14, 25, 26
Keller, Tait, 36, 39
King's Regulations, The, 125
Kirkwood, G.N., Lt., 69
Knight-Bruce, J.H.W., Capt., 204
Knyvett, J.S., Maj., 58, 88, 102, 127, 133
Koselleck, Reinhart, 22

352   INDEX

Lansdowne letter affair, 173
Lawson, Henry, 47, 128–129, 181
Le Cateau, Battle of (1914), 24, 133, 201, 204
Leed, Eric, 11, 283
leisure. *See* recreation and sport
letters to and from home. *See* postcards
   academic value, xxviii, 193
   Bridgewater's letters to young son, xxi–xxii
   censor's reports on. *See* Hardie, M., Capt. (military censor)
   censorship circumvention, 182
   homesickness induced by, 167, 171–172
   morale benefits, 13–14, 169–170, 175, 188–193, 227–229
   parcels of home comforts, 99, 166–167, 170–171, 190–191
   views expressed in. *See under* sender's name
Levi, Primo, 81
Lidsey, W.J., 2nd Lt.
   on billets, 44, 102
   on exhaustion, 99
   in November 1916, 106
   on weather conditions and mud, 84, 87, 90, 94, 109–110
Lindsell, E., L/Cpl., 110
Liulevicius. V.G., 15, 287
Lloyd George, David, 168, 172, 206
local patriotism. *See* duty, sense of; Englishness, sense of
   Englishness over Britishness, 28, 162–163, 176–177
   regimental culture fostering, 10, 29–31, 122–123, 177–179, 184
Locher, Fabien, 5
Loom of Youth, The (Waugh), 183
Lord, A.J., Capt.
   on cheerfulness, 139, 148
   on civilian casualties, 156
   on duty, 129
   on Nissen huts, 103
   religious faith, 220
   on weather conditions, 85, 95, 100
Lowe, T.A., Lt. Col., 46, 68

Ludendorff offensives. *See* German spring offensives (1918)

Macdonald, Lyn, 26
MacKenzie, Simon, 212
Madders, H.T.
   home, thoughts of, 161, 175, 183, 188, 215
   Le Havre, impressions of, 42
   religious faith, 219
   on rumours of peace, 222
   on smell and sounds of trenches, 55, 57
   on weather conditions and mud, 88, 91–93, 96, 109
Madigan, Edward, 14, 121
Malvern, Sue, 29
Manchester Regiment. *See* regimental culture
   in 1914 campaigns, 127, 202
   in German spring offensives (1918), 93
   home locations of soldiers, 30, 305–306
   memorials to the dead, 74–75
   in Messines, Battle of (1917), 70
   in Passchendaele, Battle of (Third Ypres, 1917), 240–243
   in Somme Campaign (1916), 136
   in winter 1917–1918, 256, 261
manliness (stoicism), 12–13, 120, 145, 147
Manning, Frederic, 121, 141
marches, 44–45, 82, 94, 123
Marler, Ernest T., 91, 109, 171–172, 206, 288–289
Marshall, S.L.A., 2, 10
Martin, W.J., Pte., xxiii, 168, 171
Marwick, Arthur, 15
Masefield, John, 53
Matheson, J.G., Gen., 239
Mawer, John Edwin, Pte.
   Christmas celebrations, 111–112
   complaints, 83, 134, 203–204
   home, thoughts of, 166, 183, 190
Mayhew, Alex, 162
McCartney, Helen, 31, 294
medals, 126, 130, 140
medical care, 104

INDEX

Medlicott, W.B., Lt., 49, 191
Meinig, D.W., 77
Mellish, E.N., Reverend, 84, 99, 100, 172, 213, 214
memorials, 64–69, 71–79
Meredith, Lisa S., 18
Meredith, W.H., Pte., 204
Middlebrook, Martin, 26
Milgram, Stanley, 142
military culture. *See* British Army culture
military discipline, 12, 140–145, 150, 158, 289–290
military training. *See* training, military
Miller, R.T., Capt., 204
Milner, H., 100–101
Mons, retreat from (1914), xxv, 24–25, 82, 114, 133–134, 155–156, 201
monuments and gravestones, 68–69, 71–79
morale. *See* resilience
  coping mechanisms for. *See* coping mechanisms
  crises of. *See* crises
  environment and. *See* environment and morale
  exhaustion sapping. *See* exhaustion
  hope fostering. *See* peace, hopes for
  patriotism fostering. *See* defensive patriotism; local patriotism
  as process, xxiii–xxiv, xxvi, 3–5
  psychological approaches, 14–18, 20–21, 225–226
  resilience, relationship with, xxiii–xxiv, xxvi, 17–18
  scholarly definitions, 1, 3
  Second World War studies on, 2–3, 10, 20
  social groups and. *See* duty, sense of; Englishness, sense of
Moran, Charles Wilson, 1st Baron, 144–145
Morris, William, 153
mortality. *See* death
Mosse, George, 36
Moulder, Sam, Sgt., 203
mud, 8, 40, 80, 89–93, 240–243
musical reviews, 13, 43, 148–149

narratives. *See* fantasy
  battalion histories, 236
  of combat, xxvii
  fictional, xxi–xxii
  frames of reference theory, 20–21, 82, 285
  memorial narratives, 65–67, 68
  of post-war life, 216–218, 227–228, 285
  sensemaking role. *See* sensemaking
Nash, John, 94–95
Nash, Linda, 6
Nash, Paul, 51, 53
Neitzel, Sönke, 20–21
Nelson, R.L., 287
Neuve Chapelle, Battle of (1915), 9, 24
Neville, J.E.H., Lt., 89, 129–130, 138, 141–142
Neville, Reginald, 70, 128, 171, 173, 190–191, 225
newspapers
  Home Front journalism, views on, 172–173
  homeland imaginings triggered by, 182–183
  soldiers'. *See* trench journals
Nichols, J.M., 94, 103
Nissen huts, 103
No Man's Land, 51, 55–56, 111
Nora, Pierre, 65
nostalgia. *See* homeland imaginings

obedience and discipline, 12, 140–145, 150, 158, 289–290
officers and other ranks, sense of duty compared. *See under* duty, sense of
O'Grady (game), 141
Old, Arthur Gregor, 211
Oldfield, H., Pte, 219
O'Neill, C.T.
  on cheerfulness, 214
  on Home Front, 173
  home, thoughts of, 185, 218
  on peace, 211
  on weather conditions, 85, 87–88, 110
O'Neill, Daniela, 227
optimism. *See* peace, hopes for
Osborn, A.G., Capt., 141

Osborn, Sgt., 132, 155, 205
Over the Top (Nash painting), 94–95
Owen, Wilfred, 131
Oxfordshire and Buckinghamshire Light Infantry. *See* regimental culture
  in 1914 campaigns, 45
  in 1917 campaigns, 244, 245–246, 247, 249, 250, 255–256, 260
  in German spring offensives (1918), 129–130, 264
  history of, 29–30, 237
  home locations of soldiers, 30, 184, 305, 306
  memorials to the dead, 75
  specialist soldiers in, 152
  in winter 1917–1918, 256, 262

paintings. *See* drawings and paintings
pals' units, 30
paranormal visions, 51–52, 108
Partridge, Eric, 96, 135, 141, 145, 201
Passchendaele, Battle of (Third Ypres, 1917)
  account of, 237–246
  British casualties, 255–256
  destruction, scenes of, 50–79
  mud, 91, 240–243
  officers' responses to, 128–129, 239
  weather conditions, 87, 94, 115, 239–240, 245–246
  whether crisis of morale, xxi, 26, 246–248, 279
patriotism. *See* defensive patriotism; local patriotism
peace, hopes for
  in 1914, 201–206
  in 1916, 168, 198, 206–209
  in 1917 (spring–summer), 234–236
  in 1917–1918 (autumn–winter), 113, 197–198, 199, 209–213, 231
  in 1918 (spring), 213–215
  homecoming fantasies, 197, 216–217
  hope theory, xxiv, 17–18, 199–201, 229–230
  morale benefits, 17–18, 198–201, 215–216, 225–230

  post-war life, narratives of, 215–218, 227–228, 285
  resilience of hope, 218–225, 230–231
  victorious peace goal, xxii, 18, 173, 199, 210, 223, 228–229, 283
  weather conditions affecting, 113, 114
Peat, John, Pte., 180
Philpott, William, 25–26
Picardy region, 39, 46, 49–79
place attachment theory, 37–38, 77–79
Plint, R.G., Cpl., 86
Plumer, Herbert, Gen., 272
politics, soldiers' engagement with, 168–169, 172–174, 176, 209–210, 294–295
Poperinghe ('Pop'), 47, 67
Porter, Bernard, 29
postcards. *See* letters to and from home
  of French and Belgian locations, 46, 63, 65–66
  homeland scenes, 177, 179, 186, 188
  morale benefits. *See under* homeland imaginings
  photographs of comrades, 67
  with religious themes, 186, 219
  of scenes of destruction, 223–224
  scented, 190
post-traumatic stress disorder. *See* 'shell shock'
prayer, 219–221
primary group theory, 9

Quenet, Grégory, 5
Quinnell, Charles, 57, 71

rain, 85–89, 93–94, 114, 239–240
  mud, 8, 40, 80, 89–93, 240–243
Readman, Paul, 177, 184
recreation and sport
  morale benefits, 59, 113, 148–149, 171, 191, 207
  theatre shows, 13, 43, 148–149
  weather conditions preventing, 87, 94, 109
recruitment for British Army, 31, 275–276
regimental culture. *See* British Army culture

army reorganisations (1917–1918), impact on, 258, 270–271
  in early 1917, 237
  local patriotism fostered by, 10, 29–31, 122–123, 177–179, 184
  regiments focused on, 30, 303–305, *See* Border Regiment; Devonshire Regiment; Manchester Regiment; Oxfordshire and Buckinghamshire Light Infantry; Royal Fusiliers; Royal Warwickshire Regiment
Reid, A.H., Capt., 149
religious faith and observance, 14, 71, 115, 171, 191, 218–221
resilience. *See* morale
  civilian culture contributing to, 12–13
  concept, 18
  coping mechanisms for. *See* coping mechanisms
  crises of. *See* crises
  exhaustion sapping. *See* exhaustion
  factors promoting, 18
  habituation contributing to. *See* habituation
  of hope, 218–225, 230–231
  manliness (stoicism), 12–13, 120, 145, 147
  morale, relationship with, xxiii–xxiv, xxvi, 17–18
  respectability and good character, 150–154, 158–159
Reynolds, L.L.C., Lt. Col., 151
Richardson, S.O.B, Maj., 128, 217
Rivers, W.H.R., 8
Robertson, William, 98
Robinson, James, Pte., 204–205
Roper, Michael, xxviii, 14, 176–177, 184, 191, 193
Rose, G.K., Capt., 52–53
route marches, 44–45, 82, 94, 123
Royal Fusiliers. *See* regimental culture
  in 1914 campaigns, 44–45
  in 1917 campaigns, 243–244, 247–250, 255, 258
  age of soldiers, 288

  home locations of soldiers, 30, 306
  in German spring offensives (1918), 101, 137, 139, 266, 271
  in Somme Campaign (1916), 51
  theatre troupe and trench journals, 149, 179–180
  in winter 1917–1918, 213, 258, 260–261
Royal Warwickshire Regiment. *See* regimental culture
  in German spring offensives (1918), 247, 266–269
  home locations of soldiers, 30, 306
  in Messines, Battle of (1917), 235–236
  in Passchendaele, Battle of (Third Ypres, 1917), 239, 244, 246
  trench journals, 211
  in winter 1917–1918, 247, 252–253, 256, 260, 261
rumours of peace, 222–223
Russell, N.R., 207

Sachs, Jeffrey D., 21–22
Sanborn, Joshua, 13
Sandhurst military college, 124–125
Sassoon, Siegfried, 51, 131
satire. *See* humour and satire
Scalise Sugiyama, Michelle, xxii–xxiii
Scannell, Leila, 77, 79
Second World War studies, 2–3, 10, 20
Seipp, Adam R., 199
self-inflicted wounds, 22, 24, 108, 136, 206, 247
Selly, Henry, Sgt., 63
sensemaking. *See* fantasy; narratives
  cosmology episodes (loss of meaning), 143, 265–266
  mechanisms of, xxiv, 16–17, 163–164, 235, 283–287, 295
  purpose of, xxii–xxiii, xxv–xxvi, 231, 233, 280
Senyard, F.G., Pte., 49, 100, 175, 211, 218, 222
Shaddick, J., 89, 98–99
Sheffield, Gary, 12, 24, 25, 120, 290
Sheffield, R.D., 41, 163, 205, 229

'shell shock' ('war neurosis'; PTSD)
  contributory factors, 25, 69, 81, 106–107, 288
  prevalence, 19–20, 23–24, 69, 107
  smell as trigger, 56
Shils, Edward A., 9
'shirkers', views of, 169
sickness. *See* exhaustion; injuries
  depression, 107–109, 167–168, 171–172, 287–289
  exhaustion causing, 104, 247, 271
  feigned or welcome, 105–106, 138–139
  weather conditions causing, 86, 104
silence, 58
Silver, T.A., 83, 134
Simkins, Peter, 12
Singer, Tania, 148
Skelton, G., Sgt., 83
slang terms, 63–64, 228
sleeping quarters, 82, 101–104
smell of trenches, 55–57
Smith, Leonard V., 13, 295
Smith, S., Pte., 65–66
Smith, S.B., 211–212
Smuts, Jan, 212, 232–233
snow and frost, 82–85, 93–96
social groups and morale. *See* duty, sense of; Englishness, sense of
Somme Campaign (1916)
  British line in, 39
  mud, 90–91
  officers' responses to, 127–128
  peace, hopes for, 168, 198, 206–209, 234–235
  Picardy region, destruction of, 46, 49–79
  weather conditions, 83–84, 86–87, 94
  whether crisis of morale, xxv, 25–26
songs
  Christmas carols, 113
  humorous and satirical, 13, 148–149
  marching songs, 44, 59
  morale benefits, 59, 60–61
  nostalgic, 185
  sombre, 135
sounds of war, 57–61
souvenirs and memorial narratives, 64–68
specialist skills training, 152–153

Spencer Edge, W.M., 153
sport. *See* recreation and sport
spring offensives (1918). *See* German spring offensives (1918)
stage shows, 13, 43, 148–149
Stallybrass, Oliver, 20
stench of trenches, 55–57
Stevens, G.A., Brig. Gen.
  on Amiens, 66–67
  on cheerfulness, 146
  on duty, 129, 136
  on enemy discomfort, 110
  on Home Front newspaper articles, 172–173
  on peace, 207, 213, 214–215
  on St. Quentin line, 51
  on weather conditions and mud, 83–84, 85, 90, 108, 110
Stevens, R.E.P.
  on cheerfulness, 147–148
  on duty, 135
  France, impressions of, 42
  on Home Front, 168
  home, thoughts of, 181, 191
  on training, 43
  on weather conditions, 84, 86–87, 91, 94, 100
Stevenson, David, 27, 39
Stockdale Cope, Arthur, Lt. Col., 85, 101, 139, 143, 266
stoicism (manliness), 12–13, 120, 145, 147
Stone, C., Maj., 236, 249
Stouffer, Samuel, 2–3, 10
Strachan, Hew, 11, 228
strikes (1917), 174, 176
Sunstein, Cass, 228
supernatural visions, 51–52, 108
supply shortages, 98, 99, 107, 111
surrender, decisions to, 138, 204–205
Sutcliffe, Kathleen M., 280

Tapp. W., Pte.
  on Germans and Christmas truce (1914), 58, 89–90, 155–156, 167–168, 205
  home, thoughts of, 191

INDEX

on weather conditions and mud, 86, 89–90, 93
territorial army divisions, 30
terror. *See* fear
Thaler, Richard, 228
theatre shows, 13, 43, 148–149
Third Ypres. *See* Passchendaele, Battle of (Third Ypres, 1917)
Thomas, Edward, 179
Thompson, Percy, Pte., 94
tiredness. *See* exhaustion
Todman, Dan, 8, 24
Toft, V.G., Maj. Gen., 91
Tower, K.F.B., Lt. Col., 86
training, military
  for acute crisis response, 22, 140–141, 204, 236–237, 251
  British Army training manuals, 1–2, 122–123, 145
  deficiencies (1917–1918), 232–233, 236–237, 251, 259–262, 265
  for *esprit de corps*, 10–11, 25, 122–124
  Étaples base mutiny (September 1917), xxv, 43–44, 143, 246, 289–290
  for habituation, 18, 43–44, 140–141
  specialist skills training, 152–153
  training camps, 43–44
  in winter, 106
travel to Western Front, 40–48
Travers, Tim, 25
trench art, 220
trench foot, 104
trench journals
  cynicism in, 134–138, 169
  examples, 31, 297–300
  of German soldiers, 287
  homeland imaginings in, 179–180, 188, 197
  humour and satire in, 13, 35–36, 56–57, 211, 222, 226
Trevor, Herbert E., Brig. Gen.
  as commander, 127, 133
  on duty, 167
  Home Front, disconnection from, 165–166
  on peace, 201, 202, 222

on weather conditions, 83, 86, 102, 110
Tuan, Yi-Fu, 64
Tully, C.L., Pte., 180

Ussishkin, Daniel, 1

Vernon, W., 45, 63, 156
victory, hopes for. *See* peace, hopes for
Vignemont, Frederique de, 148
violence, habituation to, 15–16, 287
volunteers, 25–26, 134–138, 157

Ward, Chris, 37
Ward, F.W., 249–250
Warwickshires. *See* Royal Warwickshire Regiment
Watson, Alexander
  on crises of morale, 24, 26, 200, 204, 292
  on morale, xxvi, 3, 17, 27, 225–226, 233, 284
  on resilience, 8, 15–16, 70–71
Watson, James, 157
Waugh, Alec, 183
weather conditions. *See* environment and morale
  cold, snow and frost, 82–85, 93–96
  coping mechanisms for, 109–113
  depression and nervous disorders due to, 106–109
  exhaustion due to, 81, 85, 94, 96–101
  fog, xxv, 26–27, 84, 94, 114, 264–265
  rain, 85–89, 93–94, 114, 239–240
  mud, 8, 40, 80, 89–93, 240–243
  sickness due to, 86, 104
  in Somme Campaign (1916), 83–84, 86–87, 94
  weather-proof clothing, shortages of, 98, 99
  in winter 1917–1918, xxi, xxv, 26–27, 84–85, 87–89, 94–96, 114, 291
  winter weather generally, 7–8, 80–82, 113–116
Weick, Karl, 143, 233, 280
Welzer, Harold, 20–21

West, A.G., 55
Western Front
  British line, changes over time, 38–40
  destruction, scenes of, 48–49, 52–53, 62–63, 65–66, 67, 236
  environment of. *See* environment and morale; weather conditions
  habituation to. *See* habituation
  journeys to, 40–48
White, Cecil, L/Cpl.
  home, thoughts of, 170, 181, 183, 185, 188–190, 207–208
  on Somme destruction, 52
  on training camp, 44
Wilcox, Vanda, xxix, 1, 3, 54, 60
Wild, C.E., Pte., 85, 88–89, 93, 106, 175
Williamson, Henry, 68
Wilson, Ross, xxvii, 7, 37, 77, 284
Wilson, Sir Henry, 253
'wind-up' phenomenon, 19, 109, 287–288
Winnard, George, Pte., 137
winter 1917–18
  activities during, 98, 111, 252, 254–255
  battle casualties, 255–256
  British line in, 39
  Cambrai, Battle of. *See* Cambrai, Battle of (1917)
  'defence in depth' strategy, xxi, 26–27, 101, 234, 254–255, 262
  Étaples base mutiny (September 1917), xxv, 43–44, 143, 246, 289–290
  exhaustion and supply shortages, 100–101, 252–253
  Home Front, cynicism towards, 172–174
  mud, 91–93, 240–243
  Passchendaele, Battle of. *See* Passchendaele, Battle of (Third Ypres, 1917)
  peace, diminishing hopes for, 113, 197–198, 199, 209–213, 231
  reinforcements and army reorganisation, 256, 258
  sickness and medical care, 104
  training, deficiencies of, 232–233, 236–237, 251, 259–262, 265
  weather conditions, xxi, xxv, 26–27, 84–85, 87–89, 94–96, 114, 291
  whether crisis of morale, 26–27, 113, 146–147, 232–234, 246–248, 252–254, 279
winter activities, 98, 106, 111
winter weather. *See* weather conditions
Winter, Denis, 11–12
Winter, Jay, 12, 28
women. *See* homeland imaginings
  defensiveness towards, 155–157, 186
  feminisation of weapons, 59–60
  soldiers' relationships with, 13, 42
  wives, girlfriends and mothers, 170, 173, 185–186, 216
Wood, C.E., 90
Woodfin, Edward, 7
Woodworth, F.T.K., 2nd Lt., 138, 151
World War II studies, 2–3, 10, 20
wounds. *See* injuries
Wright, P.N., Pte., 105

young age of soldiers, 14, 213, 275–276, 303–306
Young, R.E.M., Capt., 84, 100, 169
Ypres
  destruction of city, 48–49
  district of, 39, 40, 46, 47, 56
  as monument, 75
  Third Ypres. *See* Passchendaele, Battle of (Third Ypres, 1917)

Ziemann, Benjamin, 16, 292

For EU product safety concerns, contact us at Calle de José Abascal, 56–1°, 28003 Madrid, Spain or eugpsr@cambridge.org.